# LEARNING
## Microsoft® Office
## Word 2003

### Suzanne Weixel

**Vice President and Publisher:** Natalie E. Anderson
**Executive Acquisitions Editor:** Jodi McPherson
**Executive Editor:** Jennifer Frew
**Manufacturing Buyer:** Natacha St. Hill Moore
**Technical Editors:** Joyce Nielsen and James Reidel
**Cover Designer:** Amy Capuano
**Composition:** Shu Chen and Elviro Padro
**Associate Director, Multimedia Production:** Karen Goldsmith
**Manager, Print Production:** Christy Mahon
**Printer/Binder:** Quebecor World Book Services/Dubuque
**Cover Printer:** Phoenix Color Corporation

Credits and acknowledgements borrowed from other sources and reproduced, with permission, in this textbook are as follows:

Microsoft, Windows, PowerPoint, Outlook, FrontPage, Visual Basic, MSN, The Microsoft Network, and/or other Microsoft products referenced herein are either trademarks or registered trademarks of Microsoft Corporation in the U.S.A. and other countries. This book is not sponsored or endorsed by or affiliated with Microsoft Corporation.

10 9 8 7 6 5 4 3
ISBN 0-13-189324-6

# Contents

# Contents

# Contents

# Introduction

## How We've Organized the Book

Each lesson in **Learning Microsoft® Office Word 2003** is made up of several lessons. Lessons are comprised of short exercises designed for using Word 2003 in real-life business settings. Every application exercise (except for the Critical Thinking exercises) is made up of seven key elements:

- **On the Job**. Each exercise starts with a brief description of how you would use the features of that exercise in the workplace.

- **Exercise Scenario**. The Word tools are then put into context by setting a scenario.

- **Terms**. Key terms are included and defined at the start of each exercise, so you can quickly refer back to them. The terms are then bolded in the text.

- **Notes**. Concise notes describe and outline the computer concepts.

- **Procedures**. Hands-on mouse and keyboard procedures teach all necessary skills.

- **Application Exercise**. Step-by-step instructions put your skills to work.

- **On Your Own**. Each exercise concludes with a critical thinking activity that you can work through on your own. You are challenged to come up with data and then additionally challenged to use the data in a presentation. The *On Your Own* sections can be used as additional reinforcement, for practice, or to test skill proficiency.

- In addition, each lesson ends with **Critical Thinking Exercises**. As with the *On Your Owns*, you need to rely on your own skills to complete the task.

## Working with Data and Solution Files

As you work through the exercises in this book, you'll be creating, opening, and saving files. You should keep the following instructions in mind:

- Many exercises instruct you to open a file from the CD-ROM that comes with this book. The data files are used so that you can focus on the skills being introduced—not on creating lengthy documents. The files are located in the **Datafiles** folder on the CD-ROM.

- The Directory of Data Files on CD-ROM lists the data files you can use to complete each exercise.

- Unless the book instructs otherwise, use the default settings when creating a document. If someone has changed the default software settings for the computer you're using, your exercise files may not look the same as those shown in this book. In addition, the appearance of your files may look different if the system is set to a screen resolution other than 800 x 600.

# To Access the Files Included with This Book ☉

1. Insert the *Learning Microsoft Office Word 2003* CD in the CD-ROM drive.

2. Navigate to your CD-ROM drive; right-click [ ⊞ start ] and choose Explore from the shortcut menu.

3. Navigate to your CD-ROM drive.

4. Right-click the **datafiles** folder.

5. Navigate to the location where you wish to place the folder.

6. Right-click and choose Paste from the Shortcut menu.

# Support Material

A complete instructor support package is available with all the tools teachers need:

- **Annotated Teacher's Guide** includes entire student book with teacher notes, course curriculum guide, and lesson plans. Solution files included on CD-ROM.
  (ISBN: 0-13-189329-7)

- **Test Booklet with TestGen CD-ROM** includes application pretests, posttests, and final exam. Includes customizable test bank on CD-ROM.
  (ISBN: 0-13-189331-9)

- **Solutions Manual** includes printouts of exercise solutions with solution file CD-ROM.
  (ISBN: 0-13-189330-0)

- **Solution Files** on CD-ROM.
  (ISBN: 0-13-147439-1)

- **Visual Aids**, 25-slide PowerPoint presentation correlated to the book.
  (ISBN: 0-13-127063-X)

# Microsoft® Office Specialist Information

## What does this logo mean?

It means this courseware has been approved by the Microsoft® Office Specialist Program to be among the finest available for learning Microsoft Office Word 2003. It also means that upon completion of this courseware, you may be prepared to take an exam for Microsoft Office Specialist qualification.

## What is a Microsoft Office Specialist?

A Microsoft Office Specialist is an individual who has passed exams for certifying his or her skills in one or more of the Microsoft Office desktop applications such as Microsoft Office Word, Microsoft Office Excel, Microsoft Office PowerPoint, Microsoft Office Outlook, or Microsoft Office Access. The Microsoft Office Specialist Program typically offers certification exams at the "Specialist" and "Expert" skill levels. The Microsoft Office Specialist Program is the only program approved by Microsoft for testing proficiency in Microsoft Office desktop applications. This testing program can be a valuable asset in any job search or career advancement.

### More Information:

- To learn more about becoming a Microsoft Office Specialist, visit www.microsoft.com/officespecialist

- To learn about other Microsoft Specialist approved courseware from Pearson Education visit www.phschool.com.

*The availability of Microsoft Office Specialist certification exams varies by application, application version, and language. Visit www.microsoft.com/officespecialist for exam availability.

Microsoft, the Microsoft Office Logo, Word, and Outlook are trademarks or registered trademarks of Microsoft Corporation in the United States and/or other countries, and the Microsoft Office Specialist Logo is used under license from owner.

# Microsoft Office Specialist Index

Microsoft Office Specialist is a certification program to help users prove their ability to use Microsoft Office desktop application programs. Microsoft Office Specialist offers two levels of Word 2003 certification: Specialist and Expert. All of the Word 2003 objectives are covered in this book.

| Specialist | Skill Sets and Skills Being Measured | Exercise |
|---|---|---|
| **WW03S-1** | **Creating Content** | |
| WW03S-1-1 | Insert and edit text, symbols and special characters | 6, 11, 16, 17, 22 |
| WW03S-1-2 | Insert frequently used and pre-defined text | 9, 12, 74 |
| WW03S-1-3 | Navigate to specific content | 53, 54 |
| WW03S-1-4 | Insert, position and size graphics | 78, 79, 81 |
| WW03S-1-5 | Create and modify diagrams and charts | 91 |
| WW03S-1-6 | Locate, select and insert supporting information | 60 |
| **WW03S-2** | **Organizing Content** | |
| WW03S-2-1 | Insert and modify tables | 33, 38, 39, 40, 41, 42, 43 |
| WW03S-2-2 | Create bulleted lists, and numbered lists and outlines | 23, 50 |
| WW03S-2-3 | Insert and modify hyperlinks | 30 |
| **WW03S-3** | **Formatting Content** | |
| WW03S-3-1 | Format text | 10, 20, 21, 23, 24, 37 |
| WW03S-3-2 | Format paragraphs | 13, 26, 27, 72 |
| WW03S-3-3 | Apply and format columns | 38 |
| WW03S-3-4 | Insert and modify content in headers and footers | 52 |
| WW03S-3-5 | Modify document layout and page setup | 27, 51 |
| **WW03S-4** | **Collaborating** | |
| WW03S-4-1 | Circulate documents for review | 67, 100 |
| WW03S-4-2 | Compare and merge document versions | 65 |
| WW03S-4-3 | Insert, view and edit comments | 65 |
| WW03S-4-4 | Track, accept and reject proposed changes | 65 |
| **WW03S-5** | **Formatting and Managing Documents** | |
| WW03S-5-1 | Create new documents using templates | 73 |
| WW03S-5-2 | Review and modify document properties | 51 |
| WW03S-5-3 | Organize documents using file folders | 6, |
| WW03S-5-4 | Save documents in appropriate formats for different uses | 32, 61 |
| WW03S-5-5 | Print documents, envelopes and labels | 7, 13, 34, 54, 68, 101 |
| WW03S-5-6 | Preview documents and Web pages | 7, 34, 54, 61 |
| WW03S-5-7 | Change and organize document views and windows | 3, 8, 33, 50, 54, 61, 87, 88 |

| Expert | Skill Sets and Skills Being Measured | Exercise |
|---|---|---|
| **WW03E-1** | **Formatting Content** | |
| WW03E-1-1 | Create custom styles for text, tables and lists | 23, 24, 37 |
| WW03E-1-2 | Control pagination | 51 |
| WW03E-1-3 | Format, position and resize graphics using advanced layout features | 78, 79, 81, 85 |
| WW03E-1-4 | Insert and modify objects | 74, 78, 90, 91, 94 |
| WW03E-1-5 | Create and modify diagrams and charts using data from other sources | 88, 89, 90, 91 |
| **WW03E-2** | **Organizing Content** | |
| WW03E-2-1 | Sort content in lists and tables | 23 |
| WW03E-2-2 | Perform calculations in tables | 42 |
| WW03E-2-3 | Modify table formats | 38, 39, 40, 41, 42 |
| WW03E-2-4 | Summarize document content using automated tools | 11, 53 |
| WW03E-2-5 | Use automated tools for document navigation | 53 |
| WW03E-2-6 | Merge letters with other data sources | 45, 46 |
| WW03E-2-7 | Merge labels with other data sources | 47 |
| WW03E-2-8 | Structure documents using XML | 92 |
| **WW03E-3** | **Formatting Documents** | |
| WW03E-3-1 | Create and modify forms | 76 |
| WW03E-3-2 | Create and modify document background | 62, 85 |
| WW03E-3-3 | Create and modify document indexes and tables | 56, 57 |
| WW03E-3-4 | Insert and modify endnotes, footnotes, captions, and cross-references | 29, 56 |
| WW03E-3-5 | Create and manage master documents and subdocuments | 55 |
| **WW03E-4** | **Collaborating** | |
| WW03E-4-1 | Modify track changes options | 65 |
| WW03E-4-2 | Publish and edit Web documents in Word | 61, 63 |
| WW03E-4-3 | Manage document versions | 66 |
| WW03E-4-4 | Protect and restrict forms and documents | 66, 76 |
| WW03E-4-5 | Attach digital signatures to documents | 66 |
| WW03E-4-6 | Customize document properties | 35 |
| **WW03E-5** | **Customizing Word** | |
| WW03E-5-1 | Create, edit, and run macros | 75 |
| WW03E-5-2 | Customize menus and toolbars | 22 |
| WW03E-5-3 | Modify Word default settings | 73 |

# Directory of Data Files on CD-ROM

| Exercise # | File Name | Page # |
|---|---|---|
| 85 | 85JOBFAIR, SOAR.wmf | 453 |
| 86 | COW1.wmf | 457 |
| 87 | 87MEMO, 87DATA.xls, 87PRES.ppt | 463 |
| 88 | 88DELIVERY, 88COSTS.xls | 466 |
| 89 | 89COSTMEMO, 89Q1.xls | 471 |
| 90 | 90RETREAT, 90BUDGET.xls | 476 |
| 91 | 91CHARTS, 91SURVEY.xls | 484 |
| 92 | 92CONFIRM | 493 |
| 93 | 93STUDENTS.mdb | 497 |
| 94 | 94COVER, 94BSDPRES.ppt | 502 |
| 95 | 95MONTREAL.ppt, 95FINANCE.xls, 95MEMBERS.mdb | 506, 507 |
| 96 | 96HSOATRIP, 96LODGING.xls, 96EXCHANGE.mht | 512 |
| 97 | 97HSOATRIP2, CITY1.wmf, GARDEN1.jpg, 97LODGING2.xls | 515 |
| 98 | 98BLOOMSDATA.mdb | 518 |
| 99 | 99CAMERAS, Compare.htm | 520 |
| 100 | 100TOUROUT | 524 |
| 101 | GARDEN2.jpg, SUNFLOWER1.jpg, CONFERENCE1.wmf, 101TOUR.mht | 529, 530 |
| 102 | NONE | 533 |
| 103 | 103INVEST, 103STOCKS.xls | 534 |
| 104 | 104HIRES.mdb, 104LSIHIRES, 104COURSES.xls | 537 |
| 105 | 105DAIRYDATA.mdb, COW1.wmf, 105SIDEB, DELIVERY.wmf, PEN.wmf | 539, 540 |
| 106 | NONE | 543 |

# Lesson 1

## Word 2003 Basics

### Exercise 1
- Evaluate Word Processing Software
- About Microsoft® Word 2003
- Conventions Used in This book
- Use the Mouse
- Use the Keyboard
- Start Word 2003
- The Word Window
- Exit Word

### Exercise 2
- Execute Commands
- Use Menus
- Use Toolbars
- Use Dialog Box Options
- Use Shortcut Menus
- Use Task Panes

### Exercise 3
- Use Window Controls
- Use Zoom
- Scroll a Window

### Exercise 4
- Display the Help Task Pane
- Search for Help
- Use the Help Table of Contents
- Control the Help window
- Get Help Online
- Recover a File
- Computer Ethics

### Exercise 5
- Critical Thinking

# Exercise 1

Skills Covered:

◆ **Evaluate Word Processing Software** ◆ **About Microsoft® Office Word 2003** ◆ **Conventions Used in This book** ◆ **Use the Mouse** ◆ **Use the keyboard** ◆ **Start Word 2003** ◆ **The Word Window** ◆ **Exit Word**

## On the Job

Microsoft Office Word 2003 is a word-processing application you can use to prepare many different types of documents. Word 2003 makes it easy to create simple documents such as letters and memos, as well as more complex documents such as newsletters and brochures. You can use Word 2003 with only a keyboard, or with a combination of the mouse and the keyboard.

You've just been hired as the assistant to the president of Long Shot, Inc., a manufacturing company that produces golf equipment, apparel, and accessories. She has asked you to become familiar with Microsoft Office Word 2003, since the company uses it throughout its business operations. In this exercise, you'll practice using the mouse and the keyboard to start and exit Word 2003, and you will review the screen elements of the Word window so you can use these skills on the job.

## Terms

**Word processing** The act of creating text-based documents.

**Compatibility** The ability to work with another program or hardware device.

**Format** Arrange and enhance a document to improve its appearance.

**Internet** A global network of computers.

**Conventions** Consistent organization and use of language that make it easy to understand the material in this book.

**Font size** The size of the characters typed in a document. Font size is measured in points, with approximately 72 points in a vertical inch.

**Mouse** An input device that allows you to interact with a program running on your computer

**Mouse pointer** A marker on your computer screen that shows you where the next mouse action will occur. The mouse pointer changes shapes depending on the current action.

**Toolbar button** Buttons listed on a toolbar that are used to select features and commands.

**Insertion point** The flashing vertical line that indicates where text will be inserted in a document on-screen.

**Scroll wheel** A wheel on some mouse devices used to navigate through a document on-screen.

**I-beam** A mouse pointer shape resembling the uppercase letter I.

**Hyperlink** Text or graphics in a document set up to provide a direct connection with a destination location or document. When you click a hyperlink, the destination is displayed.

**Mouse pad**  A smooth, cushioned surface on which you slide a mouse.

**Keyboard shortcuts**  Key combinations used to execute a command without using the mouse.

**Current document**  The document currently open and in use. Actions and commands will affect the current document.

**Menu**  A list of commands.

**Web browser**  A program used to locate and display information stored on the Internet or World Wide Web.

**E-mail program**  A program used to create, manage, send, and receive e-mail messages.

**Window**  The area on-screen where an application is displayed.

**Default**  A standard setting or mode of operation.

**Elements**  Menus, icons, and other items that are part of Word's on-screen interface.

**Scroll**  To page through a document in order to view some part of its contents that is not currently displayed.

**Zoom**  To increase (zoom in) or decrease (zoom out) the displayed size of the document on-screen.

# Notes

## Evaluate Word Processing Software

- There are many **word processing** programs available for use on desktop and networked personal computers.
- They range from basic text editing programs, such as Microsoft WordPad, to full-featured programs, such as Microsoft Office Word 2003.
- Text editing programs have minimal features for entering and editing text, while full-featured programs include sophisticated tools for formatting, desktop publishing, and sometimes even graphics manipulation.
- When evaluating software packages, consider the following:
  - Tasks you need to accomplish
  - Cost
  - Ease-of-use
  - **Compatibility** with other programs you already own
  - Compatibility with your hardware system
- You can research software using the Internet, consulting a magazine or buyer's guide, or by visiting a retailer to talk to a salesperson.
- Some software manufacturers provide trial versions of a program that you can test for a limited number of days.
- Most stores will not let you return software once you open the package. Take the time to make sure you are purchasing the software that best meets your needs.

## About Microsoft® Office Word 2003

- Microsoft Office Word 2003 is designed to make it easy for you to create, edit, **format**, and distribute word processing documents.
- With Word 2003 you can easily include text and graphics in documents.
- You can transfer data between documents and between different applications running under the Windows operating environment.
- You can even collaborate with others to create and edit documents.
- Word 2003 also provides tools for accessing the **Internet** and for creating documents for distribution on the Internet.
- If you have used previous versions of Microsoft Word, you will notice many similarities as well as many new features and enhancements.
- If you are using Word 2003 as part of the Microsoft Office 2003 Suite of applications, you will find it easy to transfer your knowledge of Word 2003 to any of the other Office programs.

## Conventions Used in This Book

- **Conventions** are used throughout this book to make it simple for you to understand the concepts and the skills required to use Word 2003 effectively.
  - Definitions of new words are provided in the Terms sections.
  - Concepts are introduced in the Notes sections.
  - Actions are listed in the Procedures sections.

- Exercise Directions provide step-by-step instructions for applying the new skills.
- Illustrations are included to provide visual support for the text.

■ Documents used to illustrate exercises are created using a 12-point **font size**, unless otherwise noted.

  ✓ *If the default font size on your computer system is 10 points, your instructor may ask you to change it so your completed documents match the solution files provided with this book. Changing fonts and font sizes are covered in Lesson 2, Exercise 10.*

■ This book assumes you have installed all of the features covered. If necessary, run Word 2003 Setup again to install additional options.

## Use the Mouse

■ Use your **mouse** to point to and select commands and features of Word 2003.

■ Traditional mouse devices work by sliding a tracking ball on your desk.

■ Newer devices might work using light or a wireless connection.

■ When you move the mouse on your desk, the **mouse pointer** moves on-screen. For example, when you move the mouse to the left, the mouse pointer moves to the left.

■ When you click a mouse button, Word 2003 executes a command. For example, when you move the mouse pointer to the Print **toolbar button** and then click, the program prints the current document or file.

■ Clicking a mouse button can also be used to move the **insertion point** to a new location.

■ A mouse may have one, two, or three buttons. Unless otherwise noted, references in this book are to the use of the left mouse button.

■ Your mouse might have a **scroll wheel**. Use the scroll wheel to move through the file open on your screen.

■ The mouse pointer changes shape depending on the program in use, the object being pointed to, and the action being performed. Common mouse pointer shapes include an arrow used for selecting, an **I-beam**, which indicates location on-screen, and a hand with a pointing finger, which indicates a **hyperlink**.

■ You should use a mouse on a **mouse pad** that is designed specifically to make it easy to slide the mouse.

  ✓ *You can move the mouse without moving the mouse pointer by picking it up. This is useful if you move the mouse too close to the edge of the mouse pad or desk.*

## Use the Keyboard

■ Use your keyboard to type characters, including letters, numbers, and symbols. The keyboard can also be used to access Word commands and features.

■ In addition to the regular text and number keys, computer keyboards have special keys used for **keyboard shortcuts** or for executing special commands.

- Function keys (F1-F12) typically appear in a row above the numbers at the top of the keyboard. They can be used as shortcut keys to perform certain tasks.

- Modifier keys (Shift, Alt, Ctrl) are used in combination with other keys or mouse actions to select certain commands or perform actions. In this book, key combinations are shown as the modifier key followed by a plus sign, followed by another key or mouse action. For example, Ctrl+S is the key combination for saving the **current document**.

- The Numeric keys include the keypad to the right of the main group of keyboard keys on an enhanced keyboard.

- On laptop and notebook computers the numeric keys are integrated into the keyboard.

- When the Num Lock (number lock) feature is on, the keypad can be used to enter numbers. When the feature is off, the keys can be used to move the insertion point in the open document.

- The Escape key (Esc) is used to cancel a command.

- Use the Enter key to execute a command or to start a new paragraph when typing text.

- Directional keys, such as the up, down, left, and right arrows, and the Page Up and Page Down keys, are used to move the insertion point.

- Editing keys (Insert, Delete, and Backspace) are used to insert or delete text.

- The Windows key (sometimes called the Winkey) is used alone to open the Windows Start **menu**, or in combination with other keys to execute certain Windows commands.

- The Application key is used alone to open a shortcut menu of commands or in combination with other keys to exercise certain application-specific commands.

- Some keyboards also have keys for launching a **Web browser**, opening an **e-mail program,** or controlling media functions such as sound.

## Start Word 2003

- To use Word 2003 you must first start it so it is running on your computer.
- Use Windows to start Word:

  - Select Microsoft Office Word 2003 from the Microsoft Office folder accessed from the All Programs menu.

  - Use the New Office Document command on the All Programs menu.

  - If Word has been pinned to the Windows Start menu, or if it has been used recently, you may select it directly from the Start menu.

  - There may be a Word shortcut icon on the Windows desktop or on the Windows Taskbar that you can use to start Word.

## The Word Window

- When Word is running, it is displayed in a **window** on your screen.
- The **default** Word window displays **elements** for creating, editing, formatting, and distributing a document.
- The figure on the following page identifies the default elements of the Word window. The numbers denoting each element correspond to the numbers next to the descriptions.

  ✓ *There are many ways to customize the appearance of Word. If your Word window does not look exactly the same as the one shown in this book, it may have been customized. You learn more about customizing Word in other exercises.*

### Title bar (1)

- Displays the name of the program and the name of the current document.

### Menu bar (2)

- Displays the names of the main menus. Select a menu name to drop down a list of commands or options.

### Standard toolbar (3)

- Displays buttons for accessing common features and commands such as saving, opening, and printing a file.

  ✓ *Toolbar buttons change depending on the most recent selections. To see additional buttons, click Toolbar Options.*

### Formatting toolbar (4)

- Displays buttons for accessing common formatting features and commands such as centering text.

  ✓ *By default, the Standard and Formatting toolbars are displayed on the same line. In Exercise 2 you learn how to move a toolbar.*

### Rulers (5)

- Horizontal ruler measures width of the document page and displays information such as left and right margins, tabs stops, and indents.

- Vertical ruler measures height of the document page and displays the top and bottom margins.

  ✓ *Vertical ruler is only displayed in Print Layout view and Print Preview.*

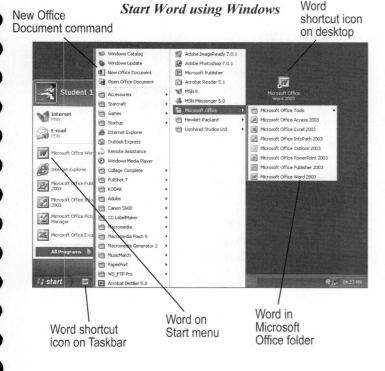

***Start Word using Windows***

New Office Document command

Word shortcut icon on desktop

Word shortcut icon on Taskbar

Word on Start menu

Word in Microsoft Office folder

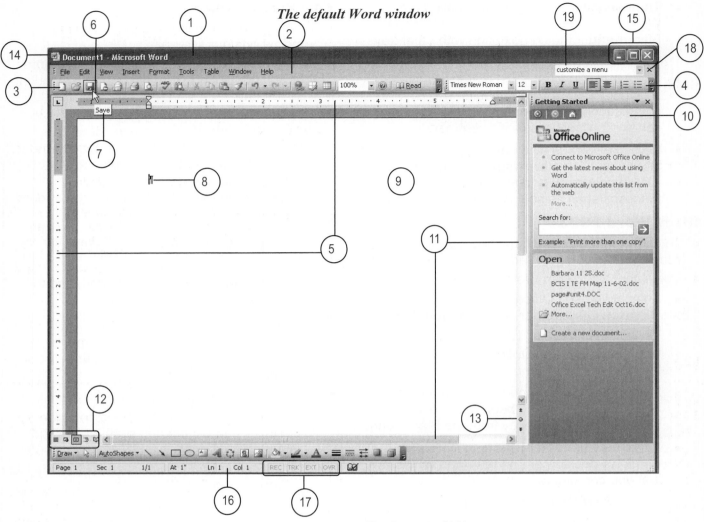

*The default Word window*

## Mouse pointer (6)

- Marks the location of the mouse on-screen.
  - ✓ *The appearance of the mouse pointer changes depending on the program being used and the current action.*

## ScreenTip (7)

- Displays the name of the element on which the mouse pointer is resting.

## Insertion point (8)

- A blinking vertical line displayed to the right of the space where characters are inserted in a document.

## Document window (9)

- The area in which you type document text.

## Task pane (10)

- An area on the right side of the program window that can be used to access some common features, such as creating new documents, searching for files, and inserting clip art.

## Scroll bars (11)

- Used with a mouse to shift the on-screen display up and down or left and right.

## View buttons (12)

- Used to change to one of five available document views. These options are also available on the View menu.

## Select Browse Object (13)

- Used to shift the on-screen display according to a selected object, such as by page, by picture, or by heading.

### Program Control icon (14)

- Used to display a menu of commands for controlling the size and position of the Word program window.

### Control buttons (15)

- Used to control the size and position of the current window. Or to close the current window.

### Status bar (16)

- Displays document information, such as which page is displayed, where the insertion point is located, and which mode buttons are active.

### Mode buttons (17)

- Used to change the way Word operates to make creating and editing documents easier.

   ✓ *Active mode buttons appear bold.*

### Close Window button (18)

- Used to close the document window.

### Type a question for help box (19)

- A box at the right end of the menu bar that is used to access Word's Help program.

   ✓ *You learn about getting help in Exercise 4.*

### Exit Word

- When you are done using Word, you exit the Word program.
- When you exit, the program window and all open documents close.
- If you try to exit Word without saving your documents, Word prompts you to do so.
- If you exit Word without closing your saved documents, Word closes them automatically.
- To exit Word, click the Close button at the right end of the Title bar, or select the Exit command from the File menu.

# Procedures

### Conventions Used in This Book

Throughout this book, procedures for completing a task are documented as follows:

- **Keyboard shortcut** keys (if available) are listed next to the task heading.
- Mouse actions are numbered on the left.
- Keystrokes are listed on the right.

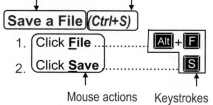

### Use the Mouse

#### Move the mouse pointer:

- **Right**     Move mouse to right.
- **Left**      Move mouse to left.
- **Up**        Move mouse away from you.
- **Down**      Move mouse toward you.

#### Mouse actions:

- **Point to**      Move mouse pointer to touch specified element.
- **Click**         Point to element then press and release left mouse button.
- **Right-click**   Point to element then press and release right mouse button.
- **Double-click**  Point to element then press and release left mouse button twice in rapid succession.
- **Drag**          Point to element, hold down left mouse button, and then move mouse pointer to new location.

   ✓ *Element, or icon representing element, moves with mouse pointer.*

- **Drop**          Drag element to new location, and then release mouse button.

#### Mouse Wheel Actions:

- **Scroll**   Rotate center wheel backward to scroll down or forward to scroll up.
- **Pan**      Press center wheel and drag up or down.
- **Zoom**     Hold down Ctrl and rotate center wheel.

### Use the Keyboard

- Press specified key on the keyboard.

#### For key combinations:

1. Press and hold modifier key(s) ................ Ctrl, Alt, Shift
2. Press combination key.

   ✓ *Remember, key combinations are written with a plus sign between each key. For example, Ctrl+Esc means to press and hold Ctrl, while you press and release Esc.*

3. Release both keys.

## Start Word

1. Click **Start** button  .................
2. Click **All Programs**............ [P]
3. Click the **Microsoft Office** folder icon.
4. Click **Microsoft Office Word 2003**.

OR

1. Click **Start** button .................
2. Click **All Programs**............ [P]
3. Click **New Office Document** .
4. Click **General** tab.

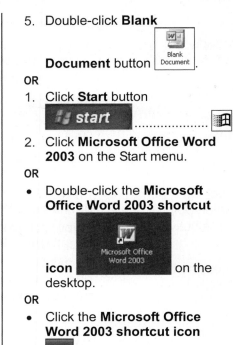

5. Double-click **Blank Document** button .

OR

1. Click **Start** button .................
2. Click **Microsoft Office Word 2003** on the Start menu.

OR

- Double-click the **Microsoft Office Word 2003 shortcut icon** on the desktop.

OR

- Click the **Microsoft Office Word 2003 shortcut icon** on the Taskbar.

## Exit Word *(Alt + F4)*

- Click **Close** button [X].

OR

1. Click **File** .................... [Alt]+[F]
2. Click **Exit**........................... [X]
3. Click **Yes** to save open documents................ [Y]
   OR
   Click **No** to close without saving .................... [N]

# Exercise Directions

1. Start your computer.
2. Move the mouse pointer around the Windows desktop.
3. Point to the Start button.
   ✓ *A ScreenTip is displayed.*
4. Point to the Recycle Bin icon.
5. Click any icon on the desktop.
   ✓ *The icon is selected.*
6. Right-click the Recycle Bin icon.
   ✓ *A menu is displayed.*
7. Press Esc to cancel the menu.
8. Use the All Programs menu to start Microsoft Office Word 2003.
   a. Click the Start button.
   b. Click All Programs on the Start menu.
   c. Click Microsoft Office on the All Programs menu.
   d. Click Microsoft Office Word 2003 on the Microsoft Office menu.

9. Point to each button on the Standard and Formatting toolbars to see the ScreenTips.
10. Move the mouse pointer over the document window.
    ✓ *It changes from an arrow to an I-beam.*
11. Press [Alt]+[F].
    ✓ *The File menu opens. At first only recently used commands are displayed, but if you leave the menu open for a few seconds, the entire menu is displayed, as shown in Illustration A. You learn about using menus in Exercise 2.*
12. Press Esc.
    ✓ *The File menu closes.*
13. Exit Word.
    - Click the Close button.
      ✓ *Click No if a box is displayed asking if you want to save the changes.*

*Illustration A*

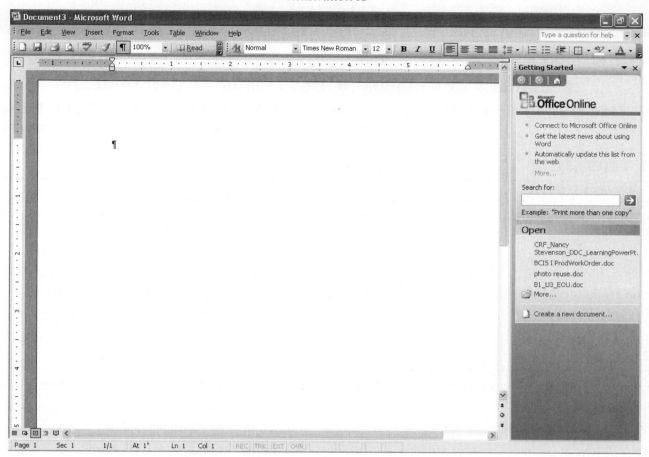

# On Your Own

## Part I

1. Working alone or in a group, make a list of tasks you use a word processing software package to accomplish. For example, the list might include typing and printing letters and envelopes, creating a newsletter, and preparing reports for distribution.

2. Research at least three word processing packages. You can locate information on the Internet, in a magazine or by calling or visiting a retail store.

3. Compile the following information about each package:

   - Does it offer the features you need to accomplish the tasks listed in step 1?

   - What is the price?

   - What are the system requirements?

   - Is it compatible with other programs?

4. Using the information you compiled, make a decision about which software package you think would be the best one to purchase.

5. Prepare an oral report to present your recommendation to your class. Include information from your research to support your decision.

## Part 2

1. Practice starting and exiting Word using the mouse.

2. Practice moving the mouse around the Word window to identify different elements.

3. Point to the View buttons.

4. Point to the Close button.

5. Point to the Mode buttons.

6. Practice starting and exiting Word using the keyboard.

# Exercise 2

◆ **Execute Commands** ◆ **Use Menus** ◆ **Use Toolbars**
◆ **Use Dialog Box Options** ◆ **Use Shortcut Menus** ◆ **Use Task Panes**

## On the Job

To accomplish a task in Word, you must execute a command. You select the commands using menus, toolbars, and dialog boxes. Once you learn to use these tools, you will be able to access the features you need to create documents with Word.

To get up to speed using Word 2003, you want to spend more time exploring the menus, toolbars, and dialog boxes. In this exercise, you will practice using toolbars, selecting menu commands, and choosing options in dialog boxes.

## Terms

**Command** Input that tells the computer which task to execute.

**Menu** A list of commands.

**Toolbar** A row of buttons used to execute commands. Each button displays an icon (picture) representing its command.

**Dialog box** A window in which you select options that affect the way Word executes a command.

**Task pane** An area on the right side of an Microsoft Office 2003 program window in which you can access commands and options for certain program features.

**Icon** A picture used to identify an element on screen, such as a toolbar button.

**Toggle** A command that can be switched off or on.

**Ellipsis** A symbol comprised of three periods (…) that indicates more will follow.

**Submenu** A secondary or subordinate menu that is displayed when you select a command on another menu.

**Hotkey** The underlined letter in a command name.

**ScreenTip** A box containing information that is displayed when you rest your mouse pointer on certain screen elements.

**Shortcut menu** A menu of context-appropriate commands that appears when pointing at an item and then right-clicking the mouse. Also called a *context menu*.

## Notes

### Execute Commands

■ To accomplish a task in Microsoft Office Word, you execute **commands**. For example, *Save* is the command for saving a document.

■ Commands are accessible in four ways:
  • **Menus**
  • **Toolbars**
  • **Dialog boxes**
  • **Task panes**

■ You use the mouse and/or the keyboard to select and execute commands.

*Menu bar*

*The Standard toolbar*

Handle    Dimmed buttons    Toggled button    Toolbar Options button

## Use Menus

■ Word groups commands into nine menus, which are listed on the menu bar.

■ When you select—or open—a menu, a list of commands you use most often drops down into the window.

■ You can expand the menu to see all commands in that group.

• The menu automatically expands when left open for a few seconds.

• You can click the arrow at the bottom of the menu to expand it.

■ Commands that are not available appear dimmed on the expanded menu.

■ Command names are listed on the left side of a drop-down menu.

■ If a toolbar button is available for a menu command, the button **icon** is displayed to the left of the command name.

■ Some commands are **toggles** that can be either active or inactive. A check mark or bullet to the left of a toggle command means the command is already active.

Icon

Command name

*Tools menu*

Arrowhead

Submenu

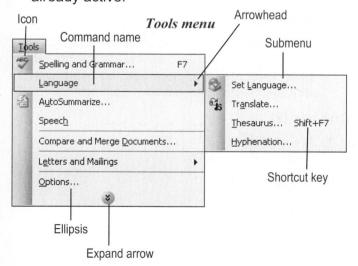

Ellipsis

Expand arrow

Shortcut key

■ Shortcut keys and other symbols are listed on the right side of the menu:

• an **ellipsis** (…) indicates that the command opens a dialog box.

• an arrowhead indicates that the command opens a **submenu**.

■ Each menu and command has an underlined letter called a **hotkey**. Hotkeys are used to select commands with the keyboard.

## Use Toolbars

■ Word comes with more than twenty toolbars which provide quick access to common commands.

■ By default, only the Standard and the Formatting toolbars are displayed.

■ You can display or hide toolbars as needed.

■ When you point to a toolbar button with the mouse, the button is highlighted and a **ScreenTip** displays the name of the button.

■ Some buttons are toggles; they have a dark outline and a colored background when they are active, or "on."

■ Buttons representing commands that are not currently available are dimmed.

■ Using the toolbar handle, you can drag a toolbar to any side of the Word window, move it above, below, or beside other toolbars, or float it over the document window area.

■ All toolbars have a *Toolbar Options* button you can use to select options for displaying buttons.

■ If there are buttons available that do not fit on the toolbar, the Toolbar Options button will have a right-pointing double-arrow on it ▓. Click it to select other buttons.

## Use Dialog Box Options

- Word displays a dialog box when you must provide additional information before executing a command. For example, in the Print dialog box, you can specify which pages to print.

- You enter information in a dialog box using a variety of elements.

- To move from one element to another you press the Tab key or use a hotkey combination.
  - ✓ *If you do not see hotkeys in a dialog box, press the Alt key to display them.*

- Use the numbers to locate the corresponding element in the figures below.

*Font dialog box*

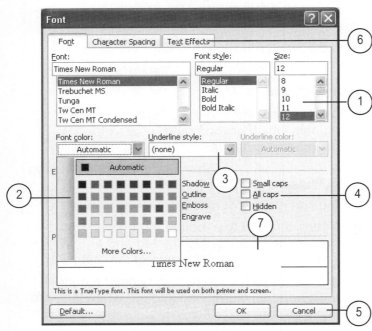

*Print dialog box*

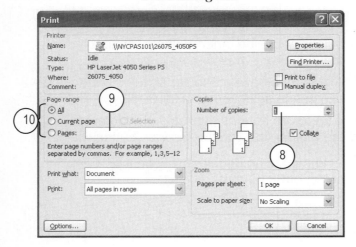

### List box (1)
- A list of items from which selections can be made. If more items are available than can fit in the space, a scroll bar is displayed.

### Palette (2)
- A display, such as colors or shapes, from which you can select an option.
  - ✓ *Some menu commands (such as Background on the Format menu) and some toolbar buttons (such as Font Color on the Formatting toolbar) also open palettes.*

### Drop-down list box (3)
- A combination of text box and list box; type your selection in the box or click the drop-down arrow to display and select from the list.

### Check box (4)
- A square that you click to select or deselect an option. A check mark in the box indicates that the option is selected.

### Command button (5)
- A button used to execute a command. An ellipsis on a command button means that clicking the button opens another dialog box.

### Tabs (6)
- Markers across the top of the dialog box that display additional pages of options within the dialog box.

### Preview area (7)
- An area where you can preview the results of your selections before executing the commands.

### Increment box (8)
- A space where you type a value, such as inches. Increment arrows beside the box are used to increase or decrease the value with a mouse. Sometimes called a spin box.

### Text box (9)
- A space where you type variable information, such as a file name.

### Option buttons (10)
- A series of circles; only one of which can be selected at a time.

## Use Shortcut Menus

- **Shortcut menus** are useful for quickly accessing commands pertaining to the current task.

- Shortcut menus are sometimes referred to as *context menus*.

- Commands on shortcut menus vary depending on the action being performed.

## Use Task Panes

- Word 2003 has **task panes** that you can use to access certain program features.

- For example, you can use the **New Document task pane** to create new files, or open existing files.

- Other features that can be accessed from a task pane include the Microsoft Office Clipboard, Help, Mail Merge, and Search.

- Task panes have some elements in common with dialog boxes. For example, some have text boxes in which you type text as well as drop-down list boxes, check boxes, and option buttons.

- The task pane elements vary depending on the specific task pane that is displayed.

- Like toolbars, the task pane can be moved to a different location on the screen. It can also be resized to make it larger or smaller.

- You can leave the task pane open while you work, or you can open it only when you need it.

*The Clip Art task pane*

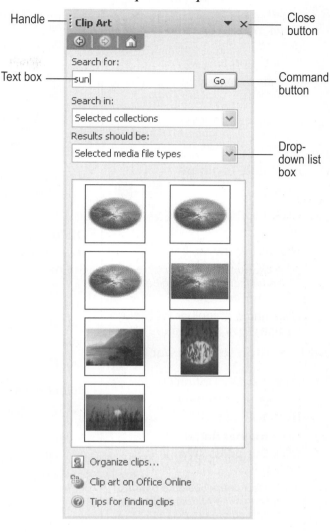

Handle — Clip Art — Close button
Text box — sun — Command button
— Drop-down list box

# Procedures

**Open a Menu with the Mouse**

- Click the menu name.

**Open a Menu with the Keyboard**

1. Press and hold .................... `Alt`
2. Press hotkey in menu name.
   OR
   a. Press **left** or **right arrow** key to select menu name .............. `→`, `←`
   b. Press **Enter**.

**Expand a Menu**

- Click **expand arrows** at menu bottom `⊻`.
   OR
- Open menu and wait a few seconds.

**Select a Menu Command**

1. Click menu name... `Alt`+*hotkey*
2. Click the desired command ........................ *hotkey*
   OR
   a. Press **up** or **down arrow** to highlight command .. `↑`, `↓`

   b. Press **Enter** ................ `Enter`

   ✓ *If a submenu is displayed, select the command from the submenu.*

**Close a Menu without Making a Selection**

- Click the menu name again.

   ✓ *If the menu expands instead of closing, click it again.*

   OR
- Click in the document window.
   OR
- Press **Esc** .......................... `Esc`

## Select a Command from a Toolbar

1. Move mouse pointer to rest on desired toolbar button.
2. Click button.
   - ✓ If the button you want is not displayed, click the **Toolbar Options** `⋮` to display additional buttons, and then click the button.

## Display/Hide Toolbars

1. Click **V**iew ................... `Alt` + `V`
2. Click **T**oolbars .................... `T`

   OR

   Right-click any toolbar.
   - ✓ A checkmark beside a toolbar name indicates the toolbar is already displayed.
3. Click name of toolbar to display or hide.

## Add a Button to a Toolbar

1. Click **Toolbar Options** button `⋮`.
2. Click **A**dd or Remove Buttons ............................. `A`
3. Click **toolbar name**.
4. Click **button** you want to add or remove.
   - ✓ A check mark beside a button indicates the button is already displayed on the toolbar.

## Show Standard and Formatting Toolbar Buttons on Two Rows

1. Click **Toolbar Options** button `⋮`.
2. Click **Sh**ow Buttons on Two Rows ..................... `H`
   - ✓ Repeat to show buttons on one row.

## Move a Toolbar

1. Move the mouse pointer so it touches a toolbar handle.
   - ✓ The mouse pointer changes from an arrow to a cross with 4 arrows ✛.
2. Drag the toolbar to a new location.

## Use a Dialog Box

1. Select a command followed by an ellipsis (…).
2. Make selections or type text entries in dialog box.
3. Click **OK** command button.............................. `Enter`
   - ✓ Sometimes command button displays Close or Yes in place of OK.

   OR

   Click **Cancel** to close dialog box without making changes ............................. `Esc`

## Dialog Box Options

**Move from one option to the next:**

- Click desired option.

  OR

- Press **Tab** key ...................... `Tab`

  OR

- Press ..................... `Alt` +hotkey

**Select from a list box:**

- Click desired item ..... `↓`, `Enter`

**Select from a drop-down list box:**

1. Click **drop-down arrow**.................... `Alt` +hotkey
2. Click desired item ..... `↓`, `Enter`

**Select/deselect check box:**

- Click check box...... `Alt` +hotkey
  - ✓ A check mark indicates a box is selected. Repeat action to remove check mark and deselect the box.

**Display tabbed pages:**

- Click desired tab .... `Alt` +hotkey
  - ✓ If no hotkey is displayed, press Ctrl+Tab.

**Use a text box:**

1. Click in text box ..... `Alt` +hotkey
2. Type data.

**Use an increment box:**

1. Click in increment box ........ `Alt` +hotkey
2. Type value.

   OR

Click **increment arrows** to change value.

**Select option button:**

- Click option button ..................... `Alt` +hotkey
  - ✓ A dot indicates option is selected. Select alternative option button to change setting.

**Select palette option:**

1. Click **palette drop-down arrow** .. `Alt` +hotkey
   - ✓ Some palettes are always open. If the palette is open, skip to step 2.
2. Click desired option ................. `↓`, `→`, `Enter`

## Use Shortcut Menus

1. Right-click element on-screen ................. `Shift` + `F10`

   OR

   Press **Application key** on keyboard ..................... `▤`
2. Click command...............hotkey
   - ✓ If no hotkeys are available, use arrow keys to select command, then press Enter.

## Open the Task Pane (*Ctrl+F1*)

1. Click **V**iew .................. `Alt` + `V`
2. Click **Task Pane** .................. `K`
   - ✓ A check mark indicates the task pane is currently displayed.

## Select a Different Task Pane

1. Click the **Other Task Panes** drop-down arrow `▼` on the task pane title bar.
2. Click desired task pane.

   OR

- Click the **Back** arrow `◀` on the task pane title bar to display the previously open task pane

   OR

- Click the **Forward** arrow

  to display the task pane that had been opened before you moved back.

  OR

- Click the **Home** button to display the Getting Started task pane

### Scroll the Task Pane Display

- Click **Scroll arrow** at bottom of task pane

  to scroll down.

  OR

- Click **Scroll arrow** at top of task pane

  to scroll up.

  ✓ *If the scroll arrows are not displayed, all available information is displayed.*

### Move the Task Pane

1. Move the mouse pointer so it touches the task pane handle.

   ✓ *The mouse pointer changes from an arrow to a cross with 4 arrows* ✥.

2. Drag the task pane to a new location.

### Resize the Task Pane

1. Move the mouse pointer so it touches a task pane border.

   ✓ *The mouse pointer changes to a double-headed arrow* ↔.

2. Drag the border to change the size of the task pane.

### Hide the Task Pane

1. Click **View** ................... Alt + V

2. Click **Task Pane** ................. K

   OR

- Click **Close** button ✕ on task pane title bar.

# Exercise Directions

## Use Menus

1. Start Word.

2. Open the File menu using the mouse.
   - Click the word File on the menu bar.

3. Let the menu expand to show all commands.

4. Note the commands on the File menu.

5. Close the menu.
   - Click the word File on the menu bar, or press Esc.

6. Open the View menu using the keyboard.
   - Press Alt + V.

7. Select the Toolbars commands.
   - Click the word Toolbars, or press the T key.

8. Look at the submenu of available toolbars.

   ✓ *Notice the checkmarks next to the toolbars that are currently displayed.*

9. Close the menu.
   - Click the word View on the menu bar, or press Esc twice.

## Use a Dialog Box

1. Open the Format menu.

2. Select the Font command.
   - Press the F key, or click the command name.

3. Select Bold in the Font style list box.

4. Select the Superscript check box.

5. Select the Text Effects tab to show another page of options.

6. Select the Font tab.

7. Open the Font Color palette.
   - Click the drop-down arrow, or press Alt + C.

8. Select the color red.

9. Open the Underline style drop-down list.
   - Click the drop-down arrow, or press Alt + U.

10. Cancel the dialog box without making any of the selected changes.
    - Click the Cancel command button, or press Esc.

## Use Task Panes

1. Display the task pane if it is not already displayed.

2. Change to the Clip Art task pane.

3. Type **sun** in the Search for text box.

4. Click the Go button.

   ✓ *Available clip art items related to stars are displayed. You learn how to use clip art in Exercise 80.*

5. Change to the New Document task pane.

6. Go back to the Clip Art task pane.

7. Change to the Getting Started task pane.

8. Close the task pane.

## Use Toolbar Buttons and Shortcut Menus

1. Click the Bold button on the Formatting toolbar.
   - If the Bold button is not displayed, use the Toolbar Options button to locate it and select it.
   - ✓ *Bold is a toggle; it remains on (pressed in) until you turn it off.*

2. Click the Bold button again.

3. Right-click anywhere in the document window to open a shortcut menu of common commands.

4. Select the Paragraph command from the shortcut menu to open the Paragraph dialog box.
   - Click the command.

5. Note that the Paragraph dialog box includes increment boxes, drop-down lists, and a preview area, as shown in Illustration A.

6. Cancel the dialog box without making any changes.
   - Click the Cancel command button or press Esc.

7. Exit Word.
   - ✓ *If Word prompts you to save changes, select No.*

### Illustration A

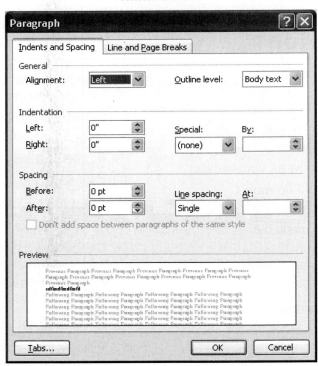

## On Your Own

1. Start Word and explore the nine menus.

2. Look to see which commands are on each menu.

3. Notice which commands open dialog boxes, which open submenus, and which have corresponding toolbar buttons.

4. Select a command that opens a dialog box. For example, try opening the Options dialog box from the Tools menu.

5. If the dialog box has multiple pages, check out each page. Note the different options available on each page.

6. Use the Toolbar Options button on the Standard and/or Formatting toolbars to see what other buttons are available.

7. Try moving the toolbars to other locations on the screen.

8. Move them back.

9. Exit Word without saving any changes.

# Exercise 3

## On the Job

Controlling the way Word 2003 documents are displayed on your computer is a vital part of using the program successfully. For example, you can control the size and position of the program window on-screen, and you can control the size of a document that is displayed.

As you spend more time working with Word 2003, you'll find that there are many tools that help you do your job more efficiently. In this exercise, you will learn how to maximize, minimize, and restore the Word window on your screen, and you will experiment with the zoom level. You'll also practice scrolling through a document.

## Terms

**Minimize** Hide a window so it only appears as a button on the Windows taskbar.

**Taskbar button** A button on the taskbar that represents an open program, file, or group of files.

**Maximize** Enlarge a window so it fills the entire screen.

**Restore Down** Return a window to its previous size and position on the screen.

**Zoom in** Increase the size of the document as it is displayed on-screen. This does not affect the actual size of the printed document.

**Zoom out** Decrease the size of the document as it is displayed on-screen. This does not affect the actual size of the printed document.

**Scroll** Shift the displayed area of the document up, down, left, or right.

## Notes

### Use Window Controls

■ By default, when you start Word 2003 the Word program window opens with a new blank document displayed in Print Layout view.

> ✓ *You learn more about views in Exercise 8.*

■ You can control the size and position of the Word window.

- You can **minimize** the window to a **taskbar button**.

- You can **maximize** the window to fill the screen.

- You can **restore down** a window that has been maximized to its previous size and/or position.

  > ✓ *The Restore Down button is only available if a window has been maximized.*

■ There are three ways to control the Word window:

- With the Control buttons located on the right end of the title bar.

Maximize   Minimize   Restore

- With the Program Control icon drop-down menu.

*Program Control drop-down menu*

- With the taskbar button shortcut menu.

*Taskbar button shortcut menu*

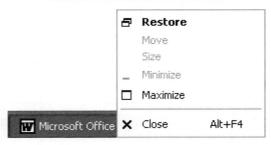

## Use Zoom

- You can adjust the zoom magnification setting to increase or decrease the size Word uses to display a document on-screen.

- Set the zoom using the Zoom drop-down list box on the Standard toolbar, or the Zoom dialog box.

*Zoom dialog box*

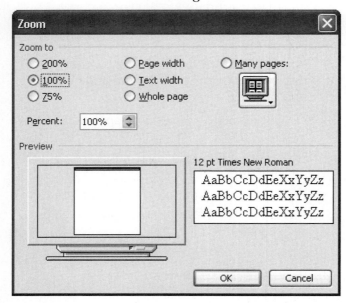

- **Zooming in** makes the document appear larger on-screen. This is useful for getting a close look at text or data.

*Zoom in to display the document in a large size*

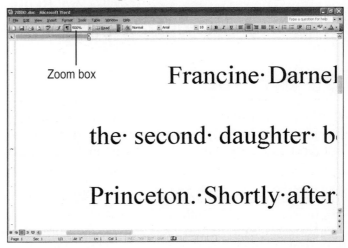

✓ *When you zoom in, only a small portion of the file will be visible on-screen at a time.*

- **Zooming out** makes the document appear smaller on-screen. This is useful for getting an overall look at the document page.

*Zoom out to get an overall view of one or more pages*

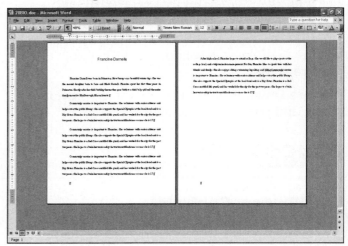

- You can set the zoom magnification as a percentage of a document's actual size. For example, if you set the zoom to 50%, Word displays the document half as large as the actual printed document. If you set the zoom to 200%, Word displays the document twice as large as the actual printed document.

- You can also select from four preset sizes:
  - Page Width. Word automatically sizes the document so that the width of the page matches the width of the screen. You see the left and right margins of the page.
  - Text Width. Word automatically sizes the document so that the width of the text on the page matches the width of the screen. The left and right margins may be hidden.
  - Whole Page. Word automatically sizes the document so that one page is visible on the screen.
  - Many Pages. Word automatically sizes the document so that the number of pages you select can all be seen on the screen. This option is available in the Zoom dialog box.
  - Two Pages. Word automatically sizes the document so that two whole pages are visible on the screen. This option is available from the drop-down menu.
    - ✓ Some options may not be available, depending on the current view. Options that are not available will be dimmed.

## Scroll a Window

- When there is more text in a document or dialog box than can be displayed on-screen at one time, you must **scroll** to see the hidden parts.
- You can scroll up, down, left, or right.

- You can scroll using the directional keys on the keyboard, or using scroll bars in the Word window or in a dialog box.
  - ✓ *Some mouse devices have scroll wheels that are used to scroll.*

*Tools for scrolling in a document*

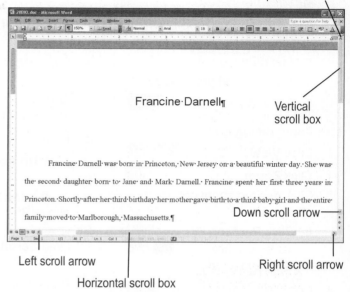

- The size of the scroll boxes change to represent the percentage of the file visible on the screen.
- For example, in a very long document, the scroll boxes will be small, indicating that a small percentage of the document is visible. In a short document, the scroll boxes will be large, indicating that a large percentage of the document is visible.

# Procedures

| **Control Windows** | **Maximize a window:** | **Restore a window:** |
|---|---|---|
| **Minimize a window:** | • Click the **Maximize** button ▢. | • Click the **Restore Down** button ▢. |
| • Click the **Minimize** button ▬. | **OR** | **OR** |
| **OR** | 1. Click the **Program Control** icon ▣. | 1. Click the **Program Control** icon ▣. |
| 1. Click the **Program Control** icon ▣. | 2. Click **Ma̲ximize**...............X | 2. Click **R̲estore**.................R |
| 2. Click **Mi̲nimize**.................N | **OR** | **OR** |
| **OR** | 1. Right-click the taskbar button. | 1. Right-click the taskbar button. |
| 1. Right-click the taskbar button. | 2. Click **Ma̲ximize**...............X | 2. Click **R̲estore**.................R |
| 2. Click **Mi̲nimize**.................N | | |

## Adjust Zoom

### Use zoom drop-down list:

1. Click **Zoom** drop-down arrow `88%` on Standard toolbar.
2. Click desired percentage.
   OR
   Click preset option.
   OR
   a. Click in **Zoom** drop-down list box `88%` on Standard toolbar.
   b. Type desired percentage.
   c. Press **Enter** .............. `Enter`

### Use Zoom dialog box:

1. Click **View** .................. `Alt`+`V`
2. Click **Zoom** ....................... `Z`
3. Click desired zoom option.
   OR
   a. Click **Percent** increment box ........ `Alt`+`E`
   b. Type percentage.
4. Click **OK** ........................... `Enter`

## Scroll

### Scroll down:

- Click **Down scroll arrow** `▼` ................. `↓`
  OR
- Click in **Vertical Scroll Bar** below Scroll box.
  OR
- Drag **Scroll Box** down.
  OR
- Press **Page Down** ............. `Page Down`
  OR
- Spin scroll wheel on mouse toward your palm.

### Scroll up:

- Click **Up scroll arrow** `▲` .... `↑`
  OR
- Click in **Vertical Scroll Bar** above Scroll Box.
  OR
- Drag **Scroll Box** up.
  OR
- Press **Page Up** .................. `Page Up`
  OR
- Spin scroll wheel on mouse away from your palm.

### Scroll left:

- Click **Left Scroll Arrow** `◄` ................. `←`
  OR
- Click in **Horizontal Scroll Bar** to left of Scroll Box.
  OR
- Drag **Scroll Box** left.

### Scroll right:

- Click **Right Scroll Arrow** `►` ................. `→`
  OR
- Click in **Horizontal Scroll Bar** to right of Scroll Box.
  OR
- Drag **Scroll Box** right.

# Exercise Directions

1. Start Word.
2. Minimize the Word window.
3. Maximize the Word window.
4. Restore the Word window.
5. Click in the document window and type your name.

   ✓ *Do not worry about making errors while you type. This is just a practice exercise, and you will not save the document. You learn more about typing and correcting errors in Exercise 6.*

   ✓ *As you type characters that Word uses to identify special information may appear on your screen. Ignore these characters for now. You learn more about them in future exercises.*

6. Press Enter.
7. Type the first line of your address.
8. Press Enter.
9. Type the next line of your address.
10. Press Enter.
11. If necessary, type the next line of your address.
12. Set the Zoom to 25%.
13. Set the Zoom to 500%. It should look similar to the document shown in Illustration A.
14. Scroll down to the bottom of the document.
15. Scroll up to the top of the document.
16. Scroll to the right margin.
17. Scroll to the left margin.
18. Set the Zoom to Page Width.
19. Exit Word.

   ✓ *When Word prompts you to save the changes, select No.*

*Illustration A*

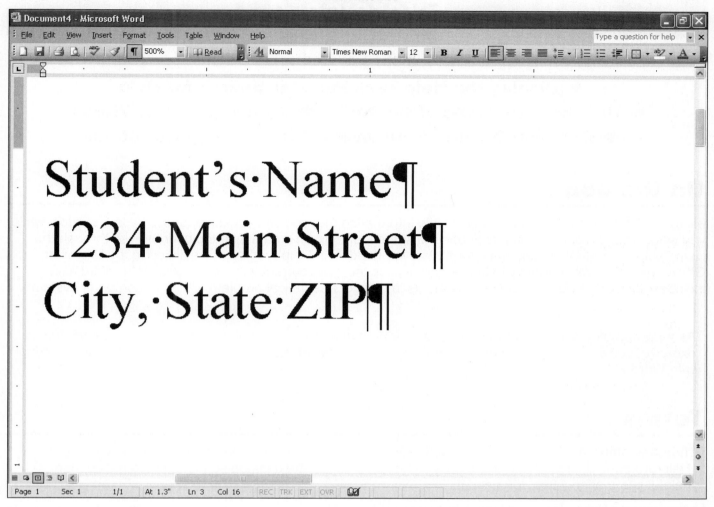

## On Your Own

1. Start Word.

2. Practice maximizing, minimizing, and restoring the Word window, using all three available methods.

3. Type some text in the Word document window.

   ✓ *Click the mouse pointer anywhere in the document window and start typing. You learn more about typing in a Word document in Exercise 6.*

4. Try different zoom magnifications to see how the display is affected.

5. Set the zoom very high so you have to scroll down to see the end of the document.

6. When you are finished, leave the Word window maximized and the zoom set to page width.

7. Exit Word without saving the document.

# Exercise 4

## Skills Covered:

◆ **Display the Help Task Pane** ◆ **Search for Help**
◆ **Use the Help Table of Contents** ◆ **Control the Help Window**
◆ **Get Help Online** ◆ **Recover a File** ◆ **Computer Ethics**

## On the Job

Microsoft Office Word 2003 comes with Help information that you can access and display in a window while you work. You can use the Help task pane to search for help on a particular topic, or browse through the Help Table of Contents to find the information you need. The Help programs are linked to the Microsoft Office Web site making it easy to locate and access the most current information available. Word also includes safety features to recover documents in case of a technical problem with your computer system.

As a new employee at Long Shot, Inc., it's important to learn how to solve problems on your own. In this exercise, you will learn how to use the Help system to answer the questions you may have while working with Word 2003.

## Terms

**Office Assistant** A feature of the Microsoft Office Help program, designed to make it easy to locate helpful information when you need it.

**Hyperlinks or links** Text or graphics in a document set up to provide a direct connection with an Internet destination location or document. When you click a hyperlink, the destination is displayed.

**Tile** Position more than one window side by side on the desktop so that they do not overlap.

**Internet** A worldwide network of computers.

**World Wide Web** A system for finding information on the Internet through the use of linked documents.

## Notes

### Display the Help Task Pane

■ Use the Help task pane to search for help topics, access the Help Table of Contents, or link to additional resources on the Microsoft Office Web site.

■ You can open the Help task pane using one of the following methods:

- Select the Microsoft Office Word Help command from the Help menu.

- Press the F1 key.

- Select the Task Pane command from the View menu, and then select the Help task pane.

  ✓ *For information on using the task pane, refer to Exercise 2.*

- Type a question in the Type a question for help box on the menu bar.

- Type a question in the **Office Assistant** bubble.

■ If you are connected to the Internet, by default the Help task pane provides links to the Microsoft.com Web site. If you are not connected, the links may still be displayed, but the online content will not be available.

■ No matter which methods you use, a list of related topics is displayed in the Search Results task pane.

■ Click a topic to display the Help information.

*Help Task pane*

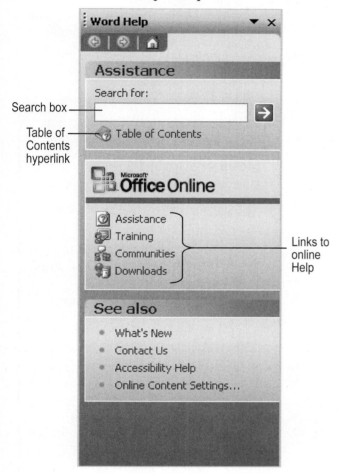

*Help search results*

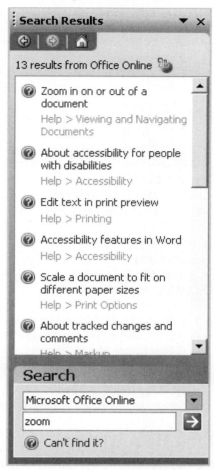

## Search for Help

■ You can search for a Help topic using three methods:

   • Open the Help task pane and use the Search feature.

   • Use the Type a question for help box on the Word window menu bar.

   • Use the Office Assistant.

      ✓ *The Office Assistant may not be installed on your computer. If you want to use it you must install it by running the Microsoft Office 2003 Setup program.*

## Use the Help Table of Contents

■ Browse through the Help Table of Contents to find the information you need.

■ Each topic in the table of contents appears with a small book icon.

   • Open the book to display its subtopics.

   • Close the book to hide its subtopics.

■ Click a Help icon to display the help information.

*Select a topic from the Table of Contents*

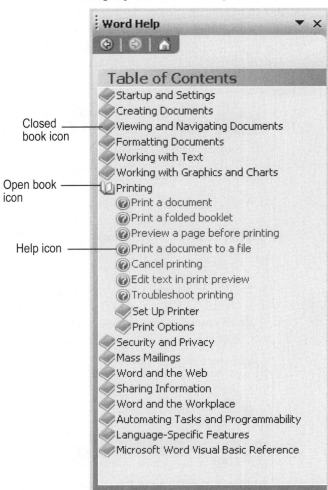

Closed book icon

Open book icon

Help icon

## Control the Help Window

- Help information opens in its own window along the right side of your screen.

- Use **hyperlinks** in the Help window to display additional information, such as step-by-step instructions or a definition of a term.

- Hyperlinks are formatted in blue; when the mouse pointer touches a hyperlink, an underline is displayed and the mouse pointer changes to a hand with a pointing finger.

- If there is a right-pointing arrowhead next to the text, it means you can expand the text to show additional information not currently displayed. A down-pointing arrowhead means you can collapse the displayed information.

- You can also use the Show All or Hide All link to display or hide all of the additional information for the current pane.

- Use Help toolbar buttons to **tile** the Help window with the program window, scroll back and forward through previously displayed Help topics, or to print the current topic.

  ✓ *If you are connected to the Internet, most Help windows include a question asking if you found the information helpful. Click the Yes or No button to send your response to Microsoft.*

*Information in the Help Pane*

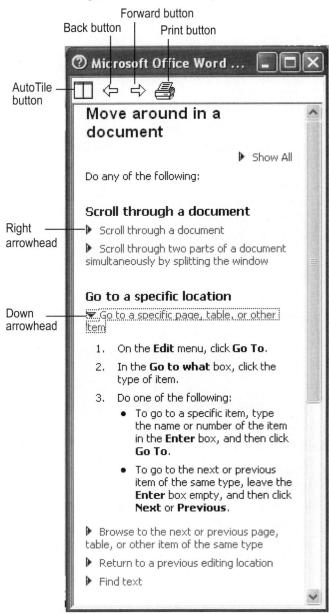

Back button

Forward button

Print button

AutoTile button

Right arrowhead

Down arrowhead

## Get Help Online

- If you are connected to the **Internet**, Help automatically includes information from the Microsoft.com Web site in all searches.

- You can also use the links in the Help task pane to access up-to-date information and support for Word and all the Microsoft Office 2003 programs.

## Recover a File

- In the event of a system failure Word will attempt to save your most recent changes.

- If any damage was done to the file data during the crash, the program will attempt to repair it.

- When you open the program again, the Document Recovery task pane will be displayed, listing original files, recovered files (if any), and repaired files (if any).

- Click the drop-down arrow beside a file name to display a list of options for opening the file, saving it with a new name, deleting it, or showing repairs.

- In addition, in the event of a program crash Word displays a dialog box asking if you want to send a report to Microsoft. If you agree to send a report, your computer will log on to the Internet and transmit the information.

## Computer Ethics

- In general, the ethics for computer use should follow the same basic code as ethics for all business and personal conduct.

- Most companies and organizations establish corporate computer application policies or rules.

- These policies address the legal and social aspects of computer use and are designed to protect privacy while respecting personal and corporate values.

- Some topics typically covered by corporate computer application policies include the type of language allowed in documents and messages, permissions for accessing files and data, and even the types of programs that may be used.

# Procedures

### Display Help Task Pane (*F1*)

- Click **Microsoft Office Word Help** button 🔘 on Standard toolbar.

OR

1. Click **Help** .................... Alt + H
2. Click **Microsoft Office Word Help** .......................... H

OR

1. Click **View** .................... Alt + V
2. Click **Task Pane** .................. K

   ✓ *A check mark indicates the task pane is currently displayed.*

3. Click the **Other Task Panes** drop-down arrow on the task pane Title bar ▾.
4. Click **Help**.

### Search for Help

1. Display Help task pane.
2. Click in **Search for** text box.
3. Type keyword, topic, or question.

4. Click **Start Searching** button ➡ .......................... 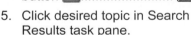 Enter
5. Click desired topic in Search Results task pane.

### Control Help Window

- Click **Print** button 🖶 to print current help information.

- Click **Back** button ⬅ to display previous Help window.

- Click **Forward** button ➡ to return to the next Help window.

- Click **AutoTile** button ⬚ to tile Help window and program window.

- Click **Untile** button ⬚ to position the Help window in front of the program window.

### Use Help Table of Contents

1. Display Help task pane.
2. Click **Table of Contents** hyperlink.

3. Click **Closed Book icon** to display subtopics.
4. Click **Help** icon to display help information.

### Close Help Window

- Click Help window's **Close** button ✖ ......... Alt + F4

### Get Help Online

1. Display Help task pane.
2. Click link to desired online Help source.

OR

1. Click **Help** .................. Alt + H
2. Click **Microsoft Office Online** ...................... M
3. Follow steps to **connect** to Internet.
4. Click **hyperlinks** to display related topics.
5. Follow steps to **disconnect** from Internet.

✓ *To connect to the Internet you must have a computer with a modem or other Internet connection and an account with an Internet Service Provider.*

## Use Type a Question for Help Box

1. Click in **Type a question for help** box.
2. Type question.
3. Press **Enter**.................... `Enter`
4. Click desired topic in Search Results task pane.

## Use Office Assistant

1. Click **Help** .................. `Alt`+`H`
2. Click **Show the Office Assistant**............................ `O`

   ✓ *If the Office Assistant Help bubble is not displayed, click the Office Assistant.*

3. Type question in text box.

   ✓ *Replace existing text if necessary.*

4. Click **Search** .................... `Enter`

   ✓ *If the Office Assistant is covering information you want to see on-screen, drag it out of the way.*

5. Click desired topic in Search Results task pane.

## Hide Office Assistant

1. Right-click **Office Assistant**.
2. Click **Hide**............................ `H`

OR

1. Click **Help**.................. `Alt`+`H`
2. Click **Hide the Office Assistant** .......................... `O`

## Change Office Assistant animation:

1. Right-click **Office Assistant**.
2. Click **Choose Assistant** ............. `C`
3. Click **Next**.................... `Alt`+`N`
4. Repeat step 3 until desired animation is displayed.
5. Click **OK** ................. `Tab`, `Enter`

   ✓ *If selected animation has not been installed, install it, or select a different animation.*

## Change Office Assistant options:

1. Right-click **Office Assistant**.
2. Click **Options** ..................... `O`
3. Select or deselect options as desired.
4. Click **OK** ......................... `Enter`

## Turn off Office assistant:

1. Right-click **Office Assistant**.
2. Click **Options** .................... `O`
3. Click the **Use the Office Assistant** check box ... `Alt`+`U` to deselect it.
4. Click **OK** ........................... `Enter`

## Recover a File

   ✓ *If Word was able to recover or repair a file, it will display the Document Recovery pane automatically when you restart.*

1. Click drop-down arrow beside desired file in Document Recovery pane.

   ✓ *You can review each file to see which one you want to keep.*

2. Click desired option to open, save, or delete file.

   ✓ *Steps for saving files are covered in Exercise 6.*

   ✓ *If you save a repaired file, the program will prompt you to review the repairs before continuing.*

# Exercise Directions

1. Start Word, if necessary.
2. Display the Help task pane (if it is not already displayed).
3. Search for help topics about changing the Zoom magnification.

   a. Type **Zoom** in the Search for text box.

   b. Click the Start searching button.

4. Read the available topics.
5. Select the topic: *Zoom in on or out of a document*.
6. Read the Help topic.
7. Close the Help window
8. Display the Help task pane again.
9. Display the Table of Contents.
10. Open the topic: *Printing*.
11. If you are not working with an open connection to the Internet, the available topics may be different. If *Printing* is not listed, open the topic *Printing and Viewing Documents*.
12. Select *Print a document*.
13. Again, if you are not working online, the available topics may be different. If necessary, open the topic: *Printing Documents,* and then select *Print a Document*.
14. Tile the Help window with the program window.
15. Expand the additional text for *Preview a Document*. Your screen should look similar to Illustration A.
16. Read the Help information.

17. Close the Help pane.
    - Click the **Close** button in the upper-right corner or press Alt + F4.
18. Use the Type a question for help box to locate information about displaying toolbars.
19. If you have a connection to the Internet, display the Help task pane and click the link for Assistance on Office online.

20. Explore the available information.
21. Disconnect from the Internet.
22. Close the Help Task Pane.
23. Exit Word.

*Illustration A*

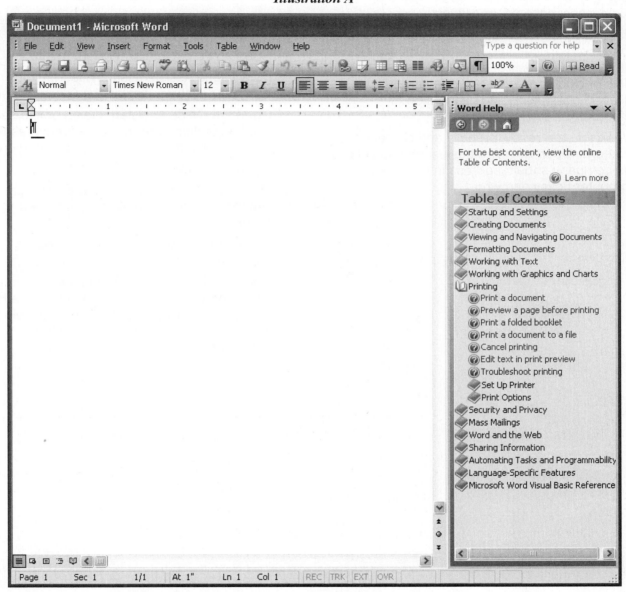

# On Your Own

## Part 1

1. Working alone or in a group, make a list of the types of issues you think should be covered by a corporate computer policy. If possible, research the topic using the Internet or the library, or by reading policies compiled by businesses, schools, or organizations.

2. Make another list of the ways you think computer applications can affect privacy, ethics and values. For example, the list might include personal use of a computer at work, plagiarism, and distribution of offensive material.

3. When you are ready, prepare and present a brief oral report detailing the issues you believe the company should address in its corporate computer policy and why.

## Part 2

1. Start Word and display the Help task pane.
2. Search for help topics related to menus.
3. Open any topic that sounds interesting.
4. Go back to the Help task pane.
5. Open the Table of Contents and explore the topics.
6. Open any topic that sounds interesting.
7. If the Office Assistant is installed on your computer system, display the Office Assistant.
8. Open the Office Assistant dialog box to see what animations are available for use as the Office Assistant.
9. If you find one you like, select it.
10. Open the Office Assistant dialog box again to see the options available for controlling the Office Assistant.
11. Close the dialog box without making any changes.
12. Continue to explore the help topics as long as you want. When you are done, close the Help window, the Office Assistant and the Help task pane and exit Word. Do not save the document.

# Exercise 5

The Marketing Director at Long Shot, Inc. has asked you to write a letter to a client. In this exercise, you will use the basic skills you have learned in this lesson to start Word, use the keyboard and the mouse, execute commands, zoom in the Word window, and use the Help program.

## Exercise Directions

1. Start Word, if necessary.
2. Minimize the Word window.
3. Maximize the Word window.
4. Set the zoom to 200%.
5. Type **Dear Mrs. Jones**,
6. Press Enter.
7. In the Type a question for help box, type **How do I use toolbars?** and then press Enter.
8. Look over the available topics.
9. Select the topic *Move a toolbar*.
10. Read the topic.
11. In the Word window, move the Formatting toolbar to the line below the Standard toolbar.
12. Display the Help task pane.
13. Display the Help Table of Contents.
14. Open the topic *Startup and Settings*.
15. Click *Getting Help*.
16. Select *About getting help while you work*.
17. Expand the text under the topic Type a question for help box. The Help window should look similar to the one in Illustration A.
18. Close the Help window and the task pane.
19. Set the zoom to Page Width.
20. Exit Word. Do not save any changes when prompted.

*Illustration A*

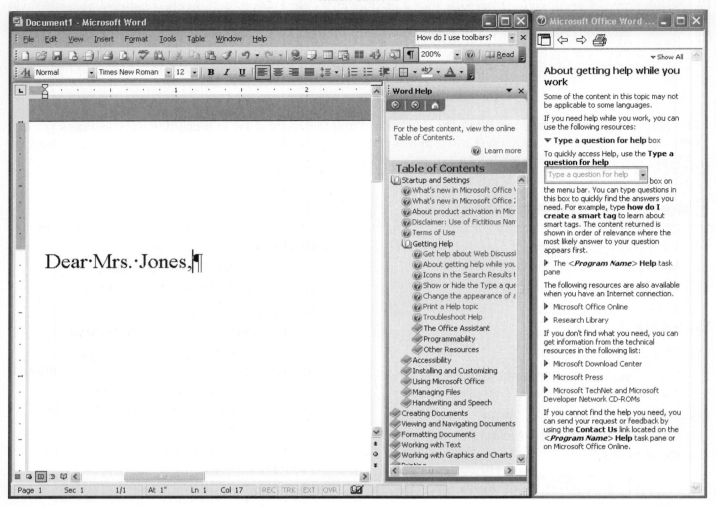

# Lesson 2

## Create, Save, and Print Documents

**Exercise 6**

- ◆ Create a New Document
- ◆ Type in a Document
- ◆ Use Click and Type
- ◆ Correct Errors
- ◆ Use Undo, Redo, and Repeat
- ◆ Save a New Document
- ◆ Create and Name Folders
- ◆ Close a Document

**Exercise 7**

- ◆ Types of Business Documents
- ◆ About Press Releases
- ◆ Preview a Document
- ◆ Print

**Exercise 8**

- ◆ Insertion Point Movements
- ◆ Change the View
- ◆ Full Screen View
- ◆ Show/Hide marks
- ◆ Rulers

**Exercise 9**

- ◆ About Memos
- ◆ Use AutoCorrect
- ◆ Select Text in a Document
- ◆ Replace Selected Text
- ◆ Align Text Horizontally
- ◆ Save Changes

**Exercise 10**

- ◆ Select a Font
- ◆ Change Font Size
- ◆ Apply Font Styles

**Exercise 11**

- ◆ Correct Spelling as You Type
- ◆ Correct Grammar as You Type
- ◆ Check Spelling
- ◆ Check Grammar
- ◆ Set Spelling and Grammar Options
- ◆ Use the Thesaurus

**Exercise 12**

- ◆ Format a Full-Block Business Letter
- ◆ Insert the Date and Time
- ◆ Use Shrink to Fit

**Exercise 13**

- ◆ Set Tabs
- ◆ Format a Modified-block Business Letter
- ◆ Create Envelopes
- ◆ Create Labels

**Exercise 14**

- ◆ Critical Thinking

# Exercise 6

### Skills Covered:

◆ **Create a New Document** ◆ **Type in a Document**
◆ **Use Click and Type** ◆ **Correct Errors** ◆ **Use Undo, Redo, and Repeat**
◆ **Save a New Document** ◆ **Create and Name Folders**
◆ **Close a Document**

## On the Job

You use Word to create text-based documents such as letters, memos, reports, flyers, and newsletters. Now that you know how to get started with Word, the next step is learning how to create, save, and close documents.

You are the owner of Liberty Blooms, a plant and flower shop in Philadelphia, Pennsylvania. You want to type up descriptions of the most popular items to give to customers, starting with roses. In this exercise, you will start Word, create and save a document, and then exit Word.

## Terms

**Word wrap** A feature that causes text to move automatically from the end of one line to the beginning of the next line.

**Paragraph mark (¶)** A nonprinting character inserted in a Word document to indicate where a paragraph ends.

**Horizontal alignment** The position of text on a line in relation to the left and right margins.

**Undo** The command for reversing a previous action.

**Redo** The command for reversing the Undo command.

**Save** Store a file on a disk.

**File type** The format in which a file is saved. Some common file types include graphics files, text files, and word processing files.

**Folder** Location on a disk where Word and other Windows applications store files.

## Notes

### Create a New Document

- Word starts with a new blank document open.
- By default the new document is named *Document1* until you save it and give it a new name.
- Create additional new documents without closing and restarting Word, by using either of the following methods:

- The New Document task pane
- The New Blank Document button 🗋 on the Standard toolbar.

- Each new document is named using consecutive numbers, so the second document is *Document2*, the third is *Document3*, and so on until you exit Word.

## Type in a Document

■ By default, the insertion point is positioned at the beginning (left end) of the first line of a new document.

■ Simply begin typing to insert new text.

■ Characters you type are inserted to the left of the insertion point.

■ **Word wrap** automatically wraps text at the end of a line to the beginning of the next line.

■ When you press Enter, Word inserts a **paragraph mark** and starts a new paragraph.

■ After you type enough text to fill a page, Word automatically starts a new page.

   ✓ *Note that Word includes many features designed to make your work easier, such as a spelling checker. These features are often displayed automatically on-screen as colored underlines or buttons. Simply ignore these features for now; you learn to use them later in this book.*

## Use Click and Type

■ Use the Click and Type feature to position the insertion point anywhere in a blank document to begin typing.

   ✓ *Click and Type cannot be used in Normal view or Outline view. Changing the view is covered in Exercise 8.*

■ When Click and Type is active, the mouse pointer changes to indicate the **horizontal alignment** of the new text.

   ✓ *You learn more about horizontal alignment in Exercise 9.*

*Alignment of text*

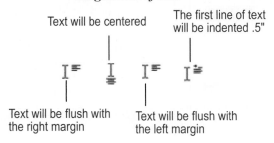

Text will be centered

The first line of text will be indented .5"

Text will be flush with the right margin

Text will be flush with the left margin

## Correct Errors

■ Delete characters to the left of the insertion point by pressing the Backspace key.

■ Delete characters to the right of the insertion point by pressing the Delete key.

■ Cancel commands before you execute them by pressing the Escape key or clicking a Cancel button if available.

## Use Undo, Redo, and Repeat

■ Use the **Undo** command to reverse a single action made in error, such as deleting the wrong character.

■ The Undo command also lets you change your mind about an entire series of actions used to edit or format a document.

■ Use the **Redo** command to reinstate any actions that you reversed using the Undo command.

■ If the Undo command and the Undo button are dimmed, there are no actions that can be undone.

■ If the Redo button is dimmed, there are no actions that can be redone.

■ Sometimes, the Repeat command is available from the Edit menu in place of Redo. Use Repeat to repeat the most recent action.

## Save a New Document

■ To have a file available for future use, you must **save** it on a removable disk, on an internal fixed disk, or on a network drive.

■ When you save a new document, use the Save As dialog box to give it a name and select the location where you want it stored.

*Save As dialog box*

Save in drop-down list

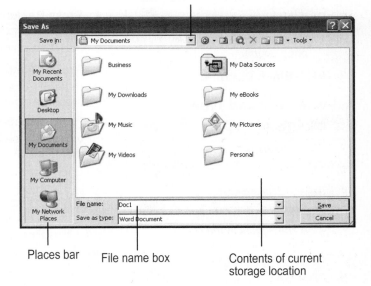

Places bar

File name box

Contents of current storage location

- Word automatically adds a period and a three-character file extension to the end of the file name to identify the **file type**. By default, the file extension is *.doc*, which identifies a Word document file.

  ✓ *Usually, the file extension is hidden, but Windows can be set to display extensions in the title bar.*

- To select a storage location, specify the disk and/or **folder** where you want to save the file.

- Disks are usually named with letters. Floppy disk drives are usually drives A: and B:. A hard drive is usually drive C:

- Additional storage locations are labeled consecutively. For example, a CD-RW drive may be D, and so on.

  ✓ *The drive letter may be followed by a plain English name.*

## Create and Name Folders

- Word saves files in the My Documents folder by default, but your computer may be set to save files in another folder.

- You can create a new folder when you save a document.

- You may want to create folders for different projects, personal documents, budgets, and so on.

- When you create a new folder it is named New Folder by default, but you can name and rename folders at any time.

## Close a Document

- A document remains open on-screen until you close it.

- Close a document when you are finished working with it.

- If you try to close a document without saving it, Word prompts you to save it.

- You can close a document without saving it if you do not want to keep it for future use or if you are not happy with changes you have made.

# Procedures

### Create a New Document
*(Ctrl+N)*

- Click **New Blank Document** button 🗋 on the Standard toolbar.

OR

1. Click **File** ..................... `Alt`+`F`

2. Click **New** ........................... `N`

   ✓ *The New Document task pane opens.*

3. Click **Blank Document** 🗋.

### Activate Click and Type

1. Click **Tools** ................. `Alt`+`T`

2. Click **Options** ..................... `O`

3. Click **Edit** tab .............. `Ctrl`+`Tab`

4. Select **Enable click and type** check box ............ `C`

   ✓ *A checkmark in the check box indicates the option is already active.*

5. Click **OK** ........................... `Enter`

### Use Click and Type

1. Move mouse pointer where you want to position insertion point.

2. Double-click.

3. Type new text.

### Correct Errors

- Press **Backspace** key to delete character to *left* of insertion point ............ `Backspace`

- Press **Delete** key .............. `Del` to delete character to *right* of insertion point.

- Press **Escape** key .............. `Esc` to cancel command or close dialog box.

- Click **Cancel** button `Cancel` to close dialog box.

### Undo the Previous Action
*(Ctrl+Z)*

- Click **Undo** button 🔄.

OR

a. Click **Edit** ................... `Alt`+`E`

b. Click **Undo** .......................... `U`

### Undo a Series of Actions
*(Ctrl+Z)*

- Click **Undo** button 🔄 repeatedly.

OR

a. Click **Undo** drop-down arrow 🔄▾.

   ✓ *The most recent action is listed at the top of the Undo drop-down list.*

b. Click last action in the series to undo all previous actions.

### Redo the Previous Action
*(Ctrl+Y)*

- Click **Redo** button 🔄.

OR

a. Click **Edit** ................... `Alt`+`E`

b. Click **Redo** .......................... `R`

## Redo a Series of Actions
*(Ctrl+Y)*

- Click **Redo** button ↻.repeatedly.

OR

a. Click **Redo** drop-down arrow ↻ ▾.

b. Click the last action in the series to redo all previous actions.

## Repeat the Previous Action
*(Ctrl+Y or F4)*

1. Click **Edit** ...................... Alt + E

2. Click **Repeat** ........................ R

## Save a New Document
*(Ctrl+S)*

1. Click **Save** button 💾.

   OR

   a. Click **File** ................ Alt + F

   b. Click **Save** ...................... S

   OR

   - Click **Save As** ................ A

2. Click **Save in** drop-down arrow ......... Alt + I

3. Select storage drive and folder.

   ✓ *Alternatively, click location in Places bar.*

4. Select **File name** text box .................. Alt + N

5. Type file name.

   ✓ *You may have to delete text already entered in the box.*

6. Click **Save** .................. Alt + S

## To create a new folder for storing a file:

1. Click **File** ...................... Alt + F

2. Click **Save As** ...................... A

3. Click **Create New Folder** button 🗀.

4. Type new folder name.

5. Click **OK** .......................... Enter

   ✓ *The new folder automatically becomes the current folder.*

## To rename a folder:

1. Click **File** .................. Alt + F

2. Click **Save As** .................. A

3. Select folder to rename.

4. Click **Tools** button Tools ▾ ............. Alt + L

5. Click **Rename** .................. M

6. Type new folder name.

7. Press **Enter** ...................... Enter

## Close a Document *(Ctrl+W)*

1. Click **Close Window** button ✖.

   OR

   a. Click **File** ............... Alt + F

   b. Click **Close** ................... C

2. Click **Yes** to save document .......................... Y

   OR

   Click **No** to close without saving .................... N

# Exercise Directions

✓ *Note that the Word documents in the illustrations use a 12-point Times New Roman font unless otherwise noted.*

1. Start Word, if necessary.

2. Type your name on the first line of the document.

3. If you make a typing error, press Backspace to delete it, and then type the correct text.

   ✓ *Word marks suspected spelling errors with a red wavy underline and suspected grammatical errors with a green wavy underline. If you see these lines in the document, proofread for errors. You learn about checking spelling and grammar in Exercise 11.*

4. Close the document without saving it.

5. Create a new document.

6. Save the document with the name **ROSES**.

   a. Click File.

   b. Click Save As.

   c. Select storage location from Save in list.

✓ *Your instructor will tell you where to save the documents you create for use with this book. If necessary, create a new folder.*

   d. Type file name in the File name box.

   e. Click Save.

7. Use Click and Type to position the insertion point in the center of the first line of the document.

   ✓ *If necessary, activate the Click and Type feature. If after activating the feature it still does not work, you may not have the document displayed in Print Layout view. In that case, type the document even with the left margin. Changing views is covered in Exercise 8.*

   a. Move the mouse pointer across the first line of the document until it changes to include lines of centered text.

   b. Double-click.

8. Type the title as shown in Illustration A.

9. Use Click and Type to leave a blank line and position the insertion point at the left side of the document.

a. Move the mouse pointer down and to the left until it changes to include lines of left-aligned text.

b. Double-click.

10. Type the first full paragraph shown in Illustration A.

✓ *Remember that you do not have to press Enter at the end of each line. Word wrap automatically moves the text to the next line as necessary.*

11. Press Enter twice to start a new paragraph and insert a blank line between paragraphs.

12. Undo the previous action.

13. Redo the previous action.

14. Type the second paragraph shown in Illustration A.

15. Close the document.

16. When Word prompts you to save the changes, click Yes.

17. Exit Word.

*Illustration A*

Roses: Symbol of Love

For thousands of years roses have captivated people with their color, fragrance, and beauty. Red roses were grown in ancient times in countries as wide spread as Egypt and China. Now, roses are cultivated around the world in many styles and colors, including yellow, peach, white, and, of course, red.

With proper care your cut roses should last a week or more. Start with a clean vase filled about two-thirds with water. Use cool water if you want to delay the rose from opening and use warm water to make the rose bloom sooner. Cut each stem about 1 inch from the bottom on an angle and immerse in the water immediately. Remove all of the leaves that fall below the water lines. Keep the flowers out of direct sunlight and change the water daily.

# On Your Own

1. For this exercise, work in pairs. Interview your partner to learn as much as you can about each other. For example, share information such as where you live, where you go to school or work, the names of your family members and pets, and things you like to do. Take notes so you will remember the details.

2. When the interview is complete, create a new document in Word.

3. Save the document as **OWD06**.

4. Type a heading, centered at the top of the document and then type a brief biography about your partner, using at least two paragraphs.

5. Correct errors as necessary.

6. Close the document, saving all changes, and exit Word when you are finished.

# Exercise 7

## Skills Covered:
◆ **Types of Business Documents** ◆ **About Press Releases**
◆ **Preview a Document** ◆ **Print**

## On the Job

Unless a document is designed to be read while displayed on-screen, you must print it in order to distribute it. For example, you must print a letter in order to deliver it by mail. Preview a document before you print it to make sure the document is correct and looks good on the page. You save time and paper by correcting errors and adjusting layout before you print.

As a marketing assistant at Blue Sky Dairy Co., a manufacturer of ice cream and other specialty dairy products, you are responsible for generating press releases. In this exercise, you will create a new document and type a press release announcing a new product. When you have completed the document, you will preview it, and then print it.

## Terms

**Business Document** A professional document used to communicate information within a company, or between one company and another.

**Personal Business Document** A document used to communicate information between an individual and a company.

**Print** Create a hard copy of a document file on paper.

**Hard copy** A version of a document printed on paper.

## Notes

### Types of Business Documents

- Some common **business documents** used by most companies include letters, memos, fax covers, invoices, purchase orders, press releases, agendas, reports, and newsletters.

- Certain businesses—or departments within a larger company—have specialized documents. For example, a law office or legal department produces legal documents such as wills, contracts, and bills of sale.

- In addition, individuals create **personal business documents** such as letters, research papers, and resumes.

- Most business documents have a standard format, which means each type of document includes similar parts. For example, an agenda should always include the following:
  - The meeting start and end time and location
  - The topics to be covered
  - The duration each topic will be discussed
  - The main speakers for each topic
- Throughout this book you learn how to set up and create many types of business documents.

## About Press Releases

- Use a press release to announce information about your company to media outlets, such as newspapers, radio stations, television stations, and magazines.
- For example, you can issue a press release about new products, trends, developments, and even to provide tips or hints.
- The media outlet may provide you with publicity by reporting the information.
- A press release should be no more than one page in length. It should provide the basic facts, details that define why the content is newsworthy, and who to contact for more information.
- The basic parts of a press release include the following:
  - Contact information
  - Headline
  - Location
  - Lead paragraph
  - Additional information and details

## Preview a Document

- Use Print Preview to display a document as it will look when printed.
- By default, Word displays one full page of a document at a time in Print Preview.

- You can change the Zoom setting in Print Preview to zoom in or out on the document.

*Print Preview screen*

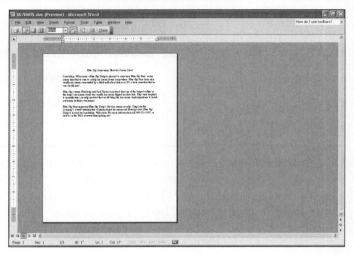

## Print

- **Printing** creates a **hard copy** version of a document.
- Your computer must be connected to a printer in order to print.
- You can quickly print a single copy of the current document using the default print settings from the Standard toolbar, or you can use the Print dialog box to select Print options.

*Print dialog box*

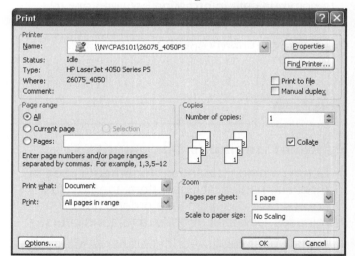

# Procedures

### Preview Document

1. Click **Print Preview**
   button 🔍.
   OR
   a. Click **F**ile................ Alt + F
   b. Click **Print Pre**v**iew** ........ V
2. Press **Page Down** to see
   next page.
3. Press **Page Up** to see
   previous page.
   ✓ *Use Zoom to increase or
     decrease the magnification
     on screen.*
4. Click **Close** button Close
   to close Print
   Preview....................... Alt + C

### Print *(Ctrl+P)*

- Click **Print** button 🖨.
OR
1. Click **F**ile ................... Alt + F
2. Click **Print** ......................... P
3. Click **OK** .......................... Enter

### Print Multiple Copies

1. Click **F**ile................... Alt + F
2. Click **P**rint.......................... P
3. Click **Number**
   **of** **c**opies ................... Alt + C
4. Type **number**.
5. Click **OK**........................... Enter

# Exercise Directions

1. Start Word, if necessary.
2. Create a new document and save it as **BARS**.
3. Type the document shown in Illustration A.
   a. Use Click and Type to center line as indicated.
   b. Use Click and Type to start paragraphs flush
      left as indicated.
   c. Press the Enter key twice between each
      paragraph to leave a blank line.
4. If you make typing errors, use Backspace or
   Delete to erase them.

5. Display the document in Print Preview.
6. Increase the zoom to 100%. The document
   should look similar to the one shown in
   Illustration A.
7. Decrease the zoom to Whole Page.
8. Close Print Preview.
9. Print one copy of the document.
10. Close the document, saving all changes.
11. Exit Word.

Blue Sky announces New Ice Cream Treat

Cambridge, Wisconsin – Blue Sky Dairy is pleased to announce Blue Sky Bars, an ice cream treat that is sure to satisfy ice cream lovers everywhere. Blue Sky Bars have rich vanilla ice cream surrounded by a thick milk chocolate coat. It's a taste sensation that no one should miss.

Blue Sky owners, Kimberly and Jack Thomson, noticed that one of the biggest sellers at the dairy's ice cream stand was vanilla ice cream dipped in chocolate. They were inspired to manufacture a novelty product that would bring the ice cream stand experience to retail customers in their own homes.

Blue Sky Bars represent Blue Sky Dairy's first ice cream novelty. They join the company's award-winning line of prepackaged ice cream and frozen yogurt. Blue Sky Dairy is located in Cambridge, Wisconsin. For more information call 608-555-2697, or visit us on the Web at www.blueskydairy.net.

# On Your Own

1. Create a new document.
2. Save the file as **OWD07**.
3. Type a press release announcing that you are taking a course to learn how to use Microsoft Office Word 2003.
4. Using Click and Type, center a headline at the top of the document.
5. Using Click and Type, move the pointer back to the flush left and type the city and state where you live, followed by the first paragraph of the press release.
6. Type at least three paragraphs but no more than one page. Include information such as your instructor's name, the textbook you are using, and when the course will be completed. You can also include information about the different types of documents you would like to create using Word. You can include the purpose of each type of document, the contents of each type of document, and whether or not you would need to print each type of document.
7. Preview the document to see how it will look when printed.
8. Print one copy of the document.
9. Ask someone in your class to read the document.
10. Close the document when you are finished, saving all changes, and exit Word.

# Exercise 8

## Skills Covered:

◆ **Insertion Point Movements** ◆ **Change the View**
◆ **Full Screen View** ◆ **Show/Hide Marks** ◆ **Rulers**

## On the Job

Mastering insertion point movements in Word is necessary to enter and edit text anywhere in a document. Changing the view allows you to see your document in different ways in order to select the view most suitable for the current task. You can also display and hide different screen elements to ensure you have the tools you need when you need them.

As the owner of Liberty Blooms, a plant and flower shop in Philadelphia, Pennsylvania, you want to post your freshness guarantee in the store so all customers can see it. In this exercise, you will create a document about the policy that you can print and hang in the store.

## Terms

**Insertion point** The flashing vertical line that indicates where the next action will occur.

**Web page** A document stored on the World Wide Web.

**Nonprinting characters** Characters, such as paragraph marks and tab symbols, that are not printed in a document but that can be displayed on-screen.

## Notes

### Insertion Point Movements

- The **insertion point** indicates where text will be inserted or deleted.

- You can move the insertion point anywhere in the existing text with keystrokes or mouse clicks.

- If Click and Type feature is enabled, you can move the insertion point anywhere in a blank document as well.

- Scrolling to shift the document view does not move the insertion point.

### Change the View

- There are five views plus Print Preview that you can use to display documents in Word.

  ✓ *Print Preview is covered in Exercise 7.*

  ◆ Normal view is used for most typing, editing, and formatting. Some features,

such as headers and footers, cannot be displayed in Normal view.

  ◆ Print Layout view displays a document on-screen the way it will look when it is printed.

  ✓ *By default, white space between pages is shown in gray in Print Layout view. You can hide the white space if you want.*

  ◆ Web Layout view wraps text to fit the window, the way it would on a **Web page** document.

  ◆ Outline view is used to create and edit outlines.

  ✓ *You learn more about Outline view in Exercise 50.*

  ◆ Reading Layout view adjusts the display of text to make it easier to read documents on the screen.

  ✓ *You learn more about Reading Layout view in Exercise 54.*

- By default, Word starts with documents displayed in Print Layout view.

- You can change the view at any time using commands on the View menu or the View buttons.
- The View buttons are located on the bottom left of the Word window.

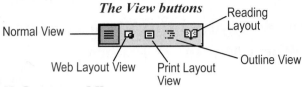

*The View buttons*

Normal View

Reading Layout

Web Layout View

Print Layout View

Outline View

## Full Screen View

- In any view, including Print Preview, use Full Screen view to display a document without the title bar, menu bar, toolbars, ruler, scroll bars, status bar, or taskbar.
- Full Screen view lets you see more of your document on-screen at one time.

*Full Screen view*

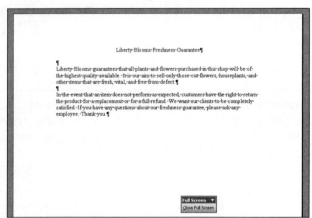

## Show/Hide Marks

- When typing, you insert **nonprinting characters** like spaces, tabs, and paragraph marks, along with printing characters like letters and numbers.
- Displaying nonprinting characters on-screen is helpful because you see where each paragraph ends and if there are extra spaces or unwanted tab characters.
- On-screen, the most common nonprinting characters are displayed as follows:
  - Space: dot (•)
  - Paragraph: paragraph symbol (¶)
  - Tab: right arrow (→)
- Other nonprinting characters include optional hyphens and line breaks.

## Rulers

- The horizontal ruler measures the width of the document page. It displays information such as margins, tabs stops, and indents.
- The vertical ruler measures the height of the document page.
- The vertical ruler can only be displayed in Print Layout view and Print Preview.

# Procedures

**Insertion Point Movements**

**With the mouse:**

- Click mouse pointer in text where you want to position insertion point.

- ✓ *If the Click and Type feature is enabled, double-click anywhere in a blank document in Print Layout view to position insertion point.*

**With the Keyboard:**

| To Move | Press |
| --- | --- |
| • One character left | ← |
| • One character right | → |
| • One line up | ↑ |

- One line down .......................↓
- Previous word ..............Ctrl+←
- Next word ...................Ctrl+→
- Up one paragraph........Ctrl+↑
- Down one paragraph ...Ctrl+↓
- Top of screen .....Alt+Ctrl+Page Up
- Bottom of screen ..............Alt+Ctrl+Page Down
- Beginning of document................Ctrl+Home
- One screen down ...............Page Down
- One screen up ....................Page Up

- One page down .........Ctrl+Page Down
- One page up ............Ctrl+Page Up
- End of document........Ctrl+End
- Beginning of line ..............Home
- End of line .........................End

**Change View**

- Click desired view button:
  - **Normal** ☰
  - **Web Layout** ☐
  - **Print Layout** ☐
  - **Outline** ☰
  - **Reading Layout** ☐

OR

1. Click **View** .................... `Alt`+`V`
2. Click **Normal** ...................... `N`

   OR

   Click **Web Layout** ............... `W`

   OR

   Click **Print Layout** .............. `P`

   OR

   Click **Outline** ...................... `O`

   OR

   Click **Reading Layout** ......... `R`

   ✓ *Also, to switch to Reading Layout mode you may click the Read button* `📖 Read` *on the Standard toolbar.*

### Full Screen View

1. Click **View** .................... `Alt`+`V`
2. Click **Full Screen** ................ `U`

**To display screen elements again:**

• Press **Esc** .......................... `Esc`

OR

Click **Close Full Screen** button `Close Full Screen` ....... `Alt`+`C`

### Hide Space Between Pages in Print Layout View

• Click on gray area between pages.

   ✓ *When positioned correctly, mouse pointer shows arrows pointing up and down toward each other and ScreenTip displays Hide White Space.*

OR

1. Click **Tools** .................. `Alt`+`T`
2. Click **Options** ...................... `O`
3. Click **View** tab ............ `Ctrl`+`Tab`
4. Deselect **White space between pages (Print view only)** .......................... `Alt`+`)`
   in Print and Web layout options section.

   ✓ *A check mark in the box indicates the option is selected.*

5. Click **OK** .......................... `Enter`

### Show Space Between Pages in Print Layout View

• Click on black line between pages.

   ✓ *When positioned correctly, mouse pointer shows arrows pointing up and down away from each other and ScreenTip displays Show White Space.*

OR

1. Click **Tools** .................. `Alt`+`T`
2. Click **Options** ...................... `O`
3. Click **View** tab ............ `Ctrl`+`Tab`
4. Select **White space between pages (Print view only)** .......................... `Alt`+`)`
   in Print and Web layout options section.

   ✓ *A check mark in the box indicates the option is selected.*

5. Click **OK** .......................... `Enter`

### Full Screen View

1. Click **View** .................. `Alt`+`V`
2. Click **Full Screen** ............... `U`

**To display screen elements again:**

• Press **Esc** .......................... `Esc`

OR

• Click **Close Full Screen** ...................... `Alt`+`C`

### Show or Hide Marks
*(Ctrl + Shift +8)*

• Click **Show/Hide ¶** button `¶` on the Standard toolbar.

OR

1. Click **Tools** .................. `Alt`+`T`
2. Click **Options** ...................... `O`
3. Click **View** tab ............ `Ctrl`+`Tab`
4. Select **All** check box ... `Alt`+`L`
   in Formatting marks section.

   ✓ *A check mark in the box indicates the option is already selected.*

5. Click **OK** .......................... `Enter`

### Show or Hide Ruler

1. Click **View** .................. `Alt`+`V`
   ✓ *Check mark next to ruler indicates ruler is displayed.*
2. Click **Ruler** ........................ `L`

# Exercise Directions

1. Start Word, if necessary, and create a new document.

2. Save the new document with the name **GUARANTEE**.

3. Display nonprinting characters.

4. Use Click and Type to position the insertion point in the center of the first line and type the heading, as shown in Illustration A.

5. Use Click and Type to position the insertion point flush left, two lines down, then type the first paragraph shown in Illustration A.

• Notice the paragraph marks that are inserted automatically in the document.

6. Press Enter twice to start a new paragraph and insert a blank line.

7. Type the second paragraph shown in Illustration A.

8. Move the insertion point to the beginning of the word **Freshness** in the heading.

9. Press the Delete key ten times to delete the word **Freshness** and the space following it.

10. Use the Undo command to restore the word **Freshness**.

11. Change to Web Layout view.

12. Change to Normal view.

13. Change to Print Layout view.

14. Hide the rulers.

15. Show the rulers.

16. Use Print Preview to preview the document.

17. Print one copy of the document.

18. Close the document, saving all changes.

19. Exit Word.

*Illustration A*

Liberty·Blooms·Freshness·Guarantee¶

¶

Liberty·Blooms·guarantees·that·all·plants·and·flowers·purchased·in·this·shop·will·be·of·the·highest·quality·available.·It·is·our·aim·to·sell·only·those·cut·flowers,·houseplants,·and·other·items·that·are·fresh,·vital,·and·free·from·defect.¶

¶

In·the·event·that·an·item·does·not·perform·as·expected,·customers·have·the·right·to·return·the·product·for·a·replacement·or·for·a·full·refund.·We·want·our·clients·to·be·completely·satisfied.·If·you·have·any·questions·about·our·freshness·guarantee,·please·ask·any·employee.·Thank·you.¶

# On Your Own

1. A mission statement is used to define the purpose and goals of a business or organization. It may be as brief as a sentence or two, or as long as a few paragraphs. Try to find a mission statement for one or two companies or organizations. You may be able to find them on the Internet or in a publication such as an annual report. Your school may even have a mission statement.

2. Think about your purpose and goals for a specific aspect of your life. For example, it might be for the year, for this or another class, or for an organization to which you belong. Consider what you hope to achieve, what you would like to learn, as well as how you want to interact with other people.

3. When you are ready, create a new document in Word.

4. Save the document as **OWD08**.

5. Type your own mission statement in the blank document. Include a centered title and at least two paragraphs. If you make any errors, move the insertion point to the correct location and fix the mistake.

6. Print the document.

7. Ask someone in your class to read the statement and to provide written and oral feedback.

8. Close the document, saving all changes, and exit Word when you are finished.

# Exercise 9

**Skills Covered:**

◆ **About Memos** ◆ **Use AutoCorrect** ◆ **Select Text in a Document**
◆ **Replace Selected Text** ◆ **Align Text Horizontally** ◆ **Save Changes**

## On the Job

As you type a document, Word's AutoCorrect feature automatically corrects common spelling errors before you even know you've made them. You must select text in a document in order to edit it or format it. Save changes to a document to keep it up-to-date and accurate and to insure that you don't lose work in the event of a power failure or computer problem. Set horizontal alignment to improve the appearance of a document and make it easier to read.

You work in the personnel department at Long Shot, Inc., a manufacturer of golf equipment. In this exercise, the personnel director has asked you to type a memo to employees about new security policies. In this exercise, you create and type the memo document.

## Terms

**AutoCorrect** A Word feature that automatically corrects common spelling and typing errors as you type.

**Caps Lock** Keyboard key used to **toggle** uppercase letters with lowercase letters.

**Toggle** A command that turns a particular mode on and off. Also, to switch back and forth between two modes.

**Select** Mark text for editing.

**Contiguous** Next to or adjacent.

**Noncontiguous** Not next to or adjacent.

**Highlight** To display text in different colors than the surrounding text.

**Horizontal alignment** The position of text in relation to the left and right page margins.

**Flush** Lined up evenly along an edge.

**Selection bar** A narrow strip along the left margin of a page. When the mouse pointer is in the selection area, it changes to an arrow pointing up and to the right.

## Notes

### About Memos

- A memo, or memoranda, is a business document commonly used for communication within a company.

- Unlike a letter, a memo is not usually addressed to a particular individual and does not include a formal closing.

  ✓ *You learn about business letters in Exercises 12 and 13.*

- Usually, a memo includes the company name, the word Memo, the headings To:, From:, Date:, and Subject, and the memo text.

- Whenever you see the words **Today's date** as part of an exercise, insert the current date.

- One blank line is used to separate parts of a memo.

- The writer may include his or her name, title, and/or signature at the end of the memo text.

- If someone other than the writer types the memo, the reference initials should be entered below the memo text. Reference initials are the initials of the person who wrote the memo in uppercase, followed by a slash, followed by the initials of the person who typed the memo in lowercase.

  ✓ *Whenever you see "yo" as part of the reference initials in an exercise, type your own initials.*

- If there is an attachment or an enclosure, the word Attachment or Enclosure should be entered below the text (or the typist's initials).

- Some variations on the standard memo format include typing headings in all uppercase letters, typing the subject text in all uppercase letters, and leaving additional spacing between memo parts. Also, the word memo may be omitted.

## Use AutoCorrect

*AutoCorrect dialog box*

- **AutoCorrect** automatically replaces spelling or common typing errors with the correct text as soon as you press the spacebar or type a punctuation mark such as a period.

- Word comes with a built-in list of AutoCorrect entries including common typos like *adn* for *and* and *teh* for *the*.

- AutoCorrect can also replace regular characters with symbols, such as the combination of the letters *T* and *M* enclosed in parentheses (TM) with the trademark symbol, ™. It also inserts accent marks in words such as café, cliché, crème, and déjà vu.

- AutoCorrect also corrects capitalization errors as follows:

  - TWo INitial CApital letters are replaced with one initial capital letter.
  - The first letter in a sentence is automatically capitalized.
  - The days of the week are automatically capitalized.
  - Accidental use of the cAPS LOCK feature is corrected if the **Caps Lock** key is set to ON.

- You can add words to the AutoCorrect list. For example if you commonly misspell someone's name, you can add it to the list.

- You can also set Word to use the spelling checker dictionary to determine if a word is misspelled and to correct it automatically.

  ✓ *You learn how to use Word's spelling checker in Exercise 11.*

- If AutoCorrect changes text that was not incorrect, you can use Undo or the AutoCorrect Options button to reverse the change.

- If you find AutoCorrect distracting, you can disable it.

## Select Text in a Document

- **Select** text already entered in a document in order to edit it or format it.

- You can select any amount of **contiguous** or **noncontiguous** text.

- You can also select non-text characters such as symbols, nonprinting characters such as paragraph marks, and graphics such as pictures.

- Selected text appears **highlighted** on-screen. For example, standard black characters on a white background is highlighted as white characters on a black background.

*Selected text in a document*

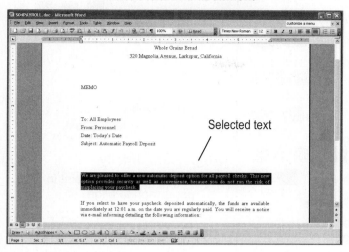

**Right.** Text is flush with right margin. The left margin is uneven.

- **Center.** Text is centered between margins.

- **Justify.** Text is spaced so both left and right margins are even.

■ You can use different alignments in a document.

*Text aligned in a document*

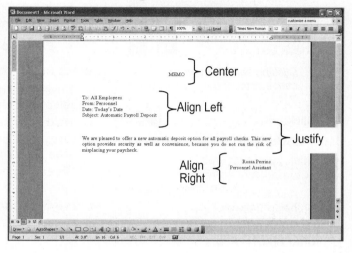

## Replace Selected Text

■ Replace selected text simply by typing new text.

■ Delete selected text by pressing the Delete key or the Backspace key.

✓ *If you accidentally replace selected text, use the Undo command to undo the action.*

## Align Text Horizontally

■ **Horizontal alignment** adjusts the position of paragraphs in relation to the left and right margins of a page.

✓ *You have already used Click and Type to align text horizontally in a document.*

■ There are four horizontal alignments:

- **Left.** Text is **flush**—or even—with left margin. The right margin is uneven (or ragged). Left is the default horizontal alignment.

## Save Changes

■ To keep revisions permanently, you must save the document.

■ Saving frequently ensures that no work will be lost if there is a power outage or you experience computer problems.

✓ *The Document Recovery feature also helps insure that you won't lose your work in case of a failure. Refer to Exercise 4 for more information.*

■ Saving replaces the previously saved version of the document with new changes.

# Procedures

**Use AutoCorrect**

**Add words to the AutoCorrect list:**

1. Click **Tools** .................. `Alt`+`T`
2. Click **AutoCorrect Options** ............................. `A`
3. Click in **Replace** text box ........................ `Alt`+`R`
4. Type misspelled word to add.
5. Click in **With** text box... `Alt`+`W`
6. Type correct word.

7. Click **Add** button

   Add ................. `Alt`+`A`
8. Click **OK** .......................... `Enter`

**Set AutoCorrect Options:**

1. Click **Tools** .................. `Alt`+`T`
2. Click **AutoCorrect Options** ............................. `A`
3. Select or deselect check boxes as desired:
   - **Sh**ow AutoCorrect Options buttons.... `Alt`+`H`

- **C**orrect TWo INitial CApitals................. `Alt`+`O`
- **Capitalize first letter of sentences** ........ `Alt`+`S`
- **Capitalize first letter of table cells**.......... `Alt`+`C`
- **Capitalize names of days**.................. `Alt`+`N`
- **Correct accidental usage of cAPS LOCK key** ............. `Alt`+`L`

- **Automatically use suggestions from the spelling checker**... `Alt`+`G`
4. Click **OK**.................... `Enter`

## Disable AutoCorrect:

1. Click **Tools**.................. `Alt`+`T`
2. Click **AutoCorrect Options** ............................ `A`
3. Clear **Replace text as you type** check box.................... `Alt`+`T`
   - ✓ *Clicking should remove check mark; if not, click check box again.*
4. Click **OK**........................... `Enter`

## Use AutoCorrect Options button:

1. Click word that was automatically corrected.
   - ✓ *A small blue box is displayed below the word.*
2. Rest mouse pointer on **blue box** ▭.
   - ✓ *The AutoCorrect Options button is displayed.*
3. Click **AutoCorrect Options** button `⚡▾`.
4. Select one of the following:
   - **Change Back** ................ `H`
     to reverse the change.
   - **Stop Automatically Correcting**...................... `A`
     to remove the word from the AutoCorrect list.
   - **Control AutoCorrect Options** ......................... `C`
     to open the AutoCorrect dialog box.

## Select Using the Keyboard

1. Position insertion point at the location where you want to start selecting.
2. Use following key combinations:
   - One character right....................... `Shift`+`→`
   - One character left.......................... `Shift`+`←`

- One line up ............ `Shift`+`↑`
- One line down........ `Shift`+`↓`
- To end of line ....... `Shift`+`End`
- To beginning of line ............... `Shift`+`Home`
- To end of document..... `Shift`+`Ctrl`+`End`
- To beginning of document .. `Shift`+`Ctrl`+`Home`
- Entire document ..... `Ctrl`+`A`

## Select using the Mouse

1. Position insertion point to the left of first character to select.
2. Hold down left mouse button.
3. Drag to where you want to stop selecting.
4. Release mouse button.

## Mouse Selection Shortcuts

### One word:
- Double-click word.

### One sentence:
1. Press and hold **Ctrl**............. `Ctrl`
2. Click in sentence.

### One line:
- Click in **selection bar** to the left of the line.
  - ✓ *In the selection bar, the mouse pointer changes to an arrow pointing up and to the right* ⬀.

### One paragraph:
- Double-click in selection bar to the left of the paragraph you want to select.

### Document:
- Triple-click in selection bar.

### Select noncontiguous blocks:
1. Select first block.
2. Press and hold **Ctrl**............. `Ctrl`
3. Select additional block(s).

## Cancel a Selection

- Click anywhere in document.
OR

- Press any arrow key ........ `←`, `→`, `↓`, `↑`

## Replace Selected Text

1. Select text to replace.
2. Type new text.
   OR
   Press **Delete** .................... `Del`
   to delete selected text.

## Align Horizontally

1. Position insertion point in paragraph to align.
   OR
   Select paragraphs to align.
   OR
   Position insertion point where you intend to type text.
2. Click alignment button:
   - **Center** ▤.............. `Ctrl`+`E`
   - **Right** ▤ ................ `Ctrl`+`R`
   - **Justify** ▤ .............. `Ctrl`+`J`
   - **Left** ▤ .................. `Ctrl`+`L`
OR
1. Click **Format**.............. `Alt`+`O`
2. Click **Paragraph** ................. `P`
3. Click **Alignment** drop-down arrow.......... `Alt`+`G`
4. Click desired alignment option.......................... `↓`, `↑`
   - **Left**
   - **Centered**
   - **Right**
   - **Justified**
5. Click **OK** ......................... `Enter`

## Save Changes
*(Ctrl+S)*

- Click **Save** button 🖫 on Standard toolbar
OR
1. Click **File**..................... `Alt`+`F`
2. Click **Save** .......................... `S`

# Exercise Directions

1. Start Word, if necessary.

2. Create a new document and save it as **SECURITY**.

3. Display nonprinting characters, if necessary.

4. Open the AutoCorrect dialog box.

   a. Add the misspelled name **Itaca** to the AutoCorrect list; Replace it with the correctly spelled **Ithaca**.

   b. Add the misspelled word **personell** to the AutoCorrect list; Replace it with the correctly spelled **personnel**.

   c. Add the misspelled word **Securaty** to the AutoCorrect list; Replace it with the correctly spelled **Security**.

   d. Be sure the *Replace text as you type* check box is selected, then close the dialog box.

5. Type the document shown in Illustration A.

   - Type the actual date in place of the text **Today's date**.

   - Type the circled errors exactly as shown in the illustration.

     ✓ *Notice that Word automatically corrects the errors.*

   - Press Enter twice to start new paragraphs and leave blank lines as marked on Illustration A.

6. Save the changes to the document.

7. Horizontally align the text in the document as marked on Illustration A.

   a. Select the lines marked for centering.

   b. Center the selected text.

   c. Select the paragraphs marked for justification.

   d. Justify the selected paragraphs.

   e. Select the lines marked for right alignment.

   f. Right align the selected text.

8. Select the text **Personnel Director** on the **From:** line near the top of the document and replace it with the name **George Younger**.

9. Display the document in Print Preview. It should look similar to Illustration B.

10. Close Print Preview.

11. Save the changes to the document.

12. Print the document.

13. Close the document, saving all changes.

14. Exit Word.

Long Shot, Inc.
234 Simsbury Drive, Itaca, New York 14850 } *Center*

MEMO

To: All Employees
From: Personell Director
Date: Today's date
Subject: Securaty Policy

As most of you are aware, Long Shot, Inc. has been working to develop a comprehensive security policy for all sites and facilities. Our goal is to insure teh safety of our employees and our products while respecting each individual's right to privacy. THe new policy has been finalized and Stage One is set to go into effect on monday, which is the first of next month.

Although many of the changes take place behind the scenes, a few will impact you directly. Following is a list of security measures of which you should be aware: } *Justify*

ID tags worn at all times
No entrance through bakc doors
GUards may check bags
Cameras installed int he common areas } *Center*

We ask for your cooperation in making sure the implementation of this phase of the project goes smoothly. Please have patience as we all become used to the new procedures.

If you have any questions, or would like to read the complete Securaty Policy document, please contact me. } *Justify*

George Younger
Personell Director } *Right align*

GY/yo

*Illustration B*

Long Shot, Inc.
234 Simsbury Drive, Ithaca, New York 14850


MEMO


To: All Employees
From: George Younger
Date: Today's date
Subject: Security Policy


As most of you are aware, Long Shot, Inc. has been working to develop a comprehensive security policy for all sites and facilities. Our goal is to insure the safety of our employees and our products while respecting each individual's right to privacy. The new policy has been finalized and Stage One is set to go into effect on Monday, which is the first of next month.

Although many of the changes take place behind the scenes, a few will impact you directly. Following is a list of security measures of which you should be aware:

ID tags worn at all times
No entrance through back doors
Guards may check bags
Cameras installed in the common areas

We ask for your cooperation in making sure the implementation of this phase of the project goes smoothly. Please have patience as we all become used to the new procedures.

If you have any questions, or would like to read the complete Security Policy document, please contact me.


George Younger
Personnel Director

GY/yo

# On Your Own

1. Create a new document in Word.

2. Save the file as **OWD09**.

3. Add a common misspelling of your name to the AutoCorrect list. You can add your first name, your last name, or both.

4. Add other words that you commonly misspell.

5. Type a memo to your instructor introducing yourself. Use correct formatting for a memo.
   - Type the word Memo or Memorandum at the top of the page.
   - Include the To, From, Date, and Subject lines.
   - Leave appropriate spacing between sections and paragraphs.

6. In the body of the memo, include your name and things you think are your strengths and your weaknesses. Try deliberately misspelling words to see if AutoCorrect fixes them.

7. Save the changes.

8. Change the horizontal alignment of some of the text in the memo. For example, center the word MEMO on the page.

9. Save the changes.

10. Print the document.

11. Ask someone in your class to read the document and offer suggestions.

12. Incorporate the suggestions into the document and save the changes.

13. Close the document, saving all changes, and exit Word.

# Exercise **10**

**Skills Covered:**

◆ **Select a Font**

◆ **Change Font Size** ◆ **Apply Font Styles**

## On the Job

Use fonts, font sizes, and font styles to dress up the appearance of a document. Fonts are a basic means of applying formatting to text and characters. They can set a mood, command attention, and convey a message.

The store hours at Liberty Blooms are changing. In this exercise, you will write a memo to employees telling them about the change. You will use fonts, font sizes, and font styles to affect the appearance of the document and to emphasize certain words.

## Terms

**Font** A complete set of characters in a specific face, style, and size.

**Font face** The character design of a font set.

**Serif** A font face that has curved or extended edges.

**Sans Serif** A font face that has straight edges.

**Script** A font face that looks like handwriting.

**Decorative** A font face that has embellishments.

**Current font** The font applied to the characters where the insertion point is currently located.

**Font size** The height of an uppercase letter in a font set.

**Font style** The slant and weight of characters in a font set.

## Notes

### Select a Font

- A **font** is a set of characters that all have the same design.

- Each font set includes upper- and lowercase letters, numbers, and punctuation marks.

- There are four basic categories of **font faces**:
  - **Serif** fonts are easy to read and are often used for document text.

    A Serif Font

- **Sans serif** fonts are often used for headings.

    A Sans Serif Font

- **Script** fonts are often used to simulate handwriting on invitations or announcements.

    *A Script Font*

- **Decorative** fonts have embellishments such as curlicues, double lines, or even graphics designed to dress up, enhance the characters, or convey a particular mood or feeling.

# A Decorative Font

✓ *There are also symbol fonts, which are collections of symbols and icons that you can insert into a document just like text characters. You learn about symbols in Exercise 22.*

- The default Word font for new blank documents is Times New Roman, a serif font.
- It is possible to change the default font.
- The **current font** name is displayed in the Font box on the Formatting toolbar.
- Select a font from the Font drop-down list, or in the Font dialog box.
- The font list is always alphabetical; however, recently used fonts are listed at the top of the drop-down list.

**The Font box and drop-down list**

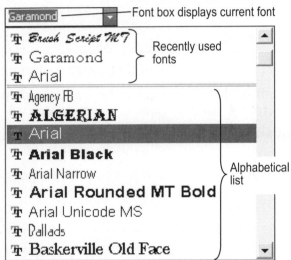

- Both Word and Windows come with built-in fonts; you can install additional fonts.
- Fonts can be selected before or after you enter text in a document.
- You can set the tone of a document by putting thought into the fonts you select.
- Keep in mind, however, that more than two or three font faces makes a document look disjointed and unprofessional.

## Change Font Size

- **Font size** is measured in points. There are approximately 72 points in an inch.
- The default Word font size is 12 points.

- The current font size is displayed in the Font Size box on the Formatting toolbar.
- Select a font size from the Font Size drop-down list, or in the Font dialog box.
- Alternatively, type a font size into the Font Size box, and then press Enter to make the change. You can even type half sizes, such as 10.5, 12.5, and so on.

**Font Size box and drop-down list**

## Apply Font Styles

- The most common **font styles** are bold and italic.
- When no style is applied to a font, it is called regular.
- Combine font styles to achieve different effects, such as ***bold italic***.
- Apply font styles using toolbar buttons, or by selecting the styles in the Font dialog box.

**The Font dialog box**

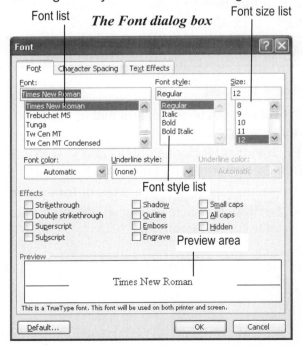

# Procedures

### Select a Font

1. Select text.
   OR
   Position insertion point where new text will be typed.
2. Click **Font** drop-down arrow on Formatting toolbar.
3. Click font name ......... ↓, Enter

OR

1. Select text.
   OR
   Position insertion point where new text will be typed.
2. Click **Format** ............... Alt+O
3. Click **Font** ......................... F
4. Click font name in **Font** list ............. Alt+F, ↓
5. Click **OK** .......................... Enter

### Change Font Size

1. Select text.
   OR
   Position insertion point where new text will be typed.
2. Click **Font Size** box on Formatting toolbar.
3. Type new font size.

OR

a. Click **Font Size** drop-down arrow on Formatting toolbar.
b. Click font size ...... ↓, Enter

OR

1. Select text.
   OR
   Position insertion point where new text will be typed.
2. Click **Format**............... Alt+O
3. Click **Font** ......................... F
4. Click font size in **Size** list ............... Alt+S, ↓
5. Click **OK** .......................... Enter

### Apply Font Styles

1. Select text.
   OR
   Position insertion point where new text will be typed.
2. Click font style button:
   - **Bold** **B** ................ Ctrl+B
   - **Italic** *I* ................ Ctrl+I
   
   ✓ *To remove font styles repeat steps 1 and 2.*

OR

1. Select text.
   OR
   Position insertion point where new text will be typed.
2. Click **Format** ............... Alt+O
3. Click **Font**......................... F
4. Click font style in **Font style** list ....... Alt+Y, ↓
   
   ✓ *To remove font styles click Regular.*
5. Click **OK** .......................... Enter

### Change the Default Font

1. Click **Format** ............... Alt+O
2. Click **Font**......................... F
3. Select font formatting options as desired.
4. Click **Default** ............... Alt+D
5. Click **Yes** ........................... Y
   to change the default font for the current document template.
   OR
   Click **No**.............................. N
   to leave the default font unchanged.

# Exercise Directions

1. Start Word, if necessary.
2. Create a new document and save it as **HOURS**.
3. Type the memo shown in Illustration A.
   - You may select the font formatting before you type the document, or type the document using the default font, and then apply the font formatting as marked on the illustration.
   
   ✓ *Notice as you type the days of the week that Word displays a ScreenTip. This is part of a feature called AutoText, which is similar to AutoCorrect. You can ignore the ScreenTip and continue typing, or you can press Enter to insert the text shown in the ScreenTip. You learn more about using AutoText in Exercise 74.*

4. Use the default font except where marked on the illustration.
   
   ✓ *If the specified font is not available on your computer, select a different, comparable font.*

5. Use the default font size except where marked on the illustration.
6. Apply the specified font styles as marked.
7. Preview the document. It should look similar to Illustration A.
8. Print the document.
9. Close the document, saving all changes.

# Liberty Blooms Flower Shop —— *Curlz MT (decorative), 28 points, bold*

## MEMO —— *Arial (sans serif), 20 points, bold*

*Insert your own name*

To: All Employees
From: Student's Name
Date: June 1
Subject: Summer Hours

*Garamond (serif), 14 points, regular*

*Bold italics*

*Garamond (serif), 14 points, regular, justified*

It's time again to switch to our summer hours schedule! Starting next week we will be open an extra two hours on *Fridays, Saturdays,* and *Sundays.* Please let me know as soon as possible if you have conflicts, or if you want to add hours so I can put the schedule together. Thanks for your cooperation.

## New Store Hours —— *Arial (serif), 18 points, bold, centered*

*Bold*

**Monday through Thursday:**
9:00 a.m. until 7:00 p.m.

**Fridays and Saturdays:**
9:00 a.m. until 9:00 p.m.

*Arial (serif), 14 points, centered*

**Sundays:**
12:00 p.m. until 9:00 p.m.

# On Your Own

1. Create a new document in Word.

2. Save the file as **OWD10**.

3. Write a note to a friend suggesting plans for the weekend. You might include possible movies to see or rent, a day at the mall, or anything else you like to do together.

4. Use different fonts, font sizes, and font styles in your note.

5. Preview the note, and then print it.

6. Ask a classmate to review the document and offer comments and suggestions.

7. Incorporate the suggestions into the document.

8. Close the document, saving all changes, and exit Word.

# Exercise 11

## Skills Covered:

◆ **Correct Spelling as You Type** ◆ **Correct Grammar as You Type**
◆ **Check Spelling** ◆ **Check Grammar**
◆ **Set Spelling and Grammar Options** ◆ **Use the Thesaurus**

## On the Job

A professional document should be free of spelling and grammatical errors. Word can check the spelling and grammar in a document and recommend corrections.

A press release is an efficient way to notify the public about the change in hours at Liberty Blooms. In this exercise, you will type the press release, and then improve it by correcting the spelling and grammar.

## Terms

**Smart tag** A feature designed to let you perform actions within one program that you would normally have to open another program to accomplish. For example, you can add a person's name and address to an Outlook contact list using a smart tag in Word.

**Thesaurus** A listing of words with synonyms and antonyms.

**Synonyms** Words with the same meaning.

**Antonyms** Words with opposite meanings.

## Notes

### Correct Spelling as You Type

- By default, Word checks spelling as you type and marks presumed misspelled words with a red, wavy underline.

  > This is an example of a missspelled word.

- Any word not in the Word main dictionary is marked as misspelled, including proper names, words with unique spellings, and many technical terms. Word also marks double occurrences of words.

- You can ignore the wavy lines and keep typing, correct the spelling, or add the marked word to the dictionary.

- If the wavy underlines distract you from your work, you can turn off the Check spelling as you type feature.

  ✓ *Word uses a few other underlines to mark text on-screen. For example, blue wavy underlines indicate inconsistent formatting and purple dotted lines indicate **smart tags**. You learn about checking for inconsistent formatting in Exercise 24. You learn about smart tags in Exercise 92.*

### Correct Grammar as You Type

- Word can also check grammar as you type, identifying presumed errors such as punctuation, matching case or tense, sentence fragments, and run-on sentences.

- Word marks grammatical errors with a green, wavy underline.

> This is an example of a grammatical errors.

- As with the Spelling Checker, you can ignore the green wavy lines and keep typing, or correct the error.
- If the wavy underlines distract you from your work, you can turn off the Check grammar as you type feature.

## Check Spelling

- You can check the spelling in an entire document or in part of a document.
- To check the spelling in part of a document, you must first select the section you want checked.
- The Spelling Checker identifies any word not in the Word dictionary as misspelled, including proper names, words with unique spellings, and technical terms.
- When Word identifies a misspelled word, you can correct the spelling, ignore the spelling, or add the word to the dictionary.

*Correct spelling with Spelling Checker*

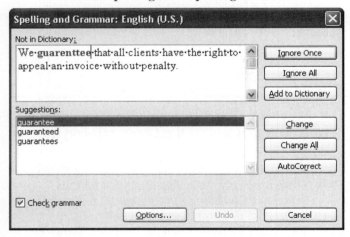

## Check Grammar

- By default, Word checks the grammar in a document at the same time that it checks the spelling.
- When Word identifies a grammatical mistake, you can accept the suggestion or ignore it.

*Correct grammar with Grammar Checker*

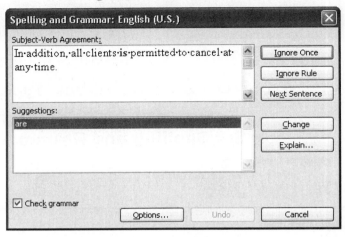

## Set Spelling and Grammar Options

- Use the Spelling & Grammar tab in the Options dialog box to customize the way Word checks your spelling and grammar.

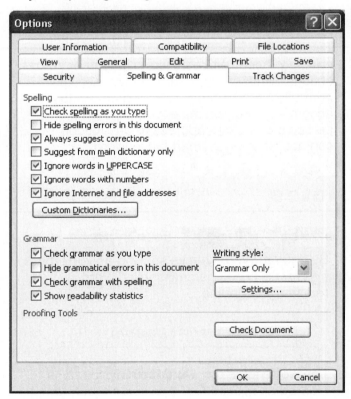

- Spelling options include checking words that are in all uppercase, checking Internet addresses, and using only the main dictionary.
- You can also change the default dictionary to a custom dictionary.
  - ✓ *You can create custom dictionaries, or import from another source.*

- Grammar options include showing readability statistics, checking style as well as grammar, and selecting the specific grammar and style usage items you want flagged.

- Readability statistics include the number of words, characters, paragraphs, and sentences, the average number of sentences per paragraph, words per sentence, and characters per word, and an evaluation of the readability based on the Flesch standardized scale.

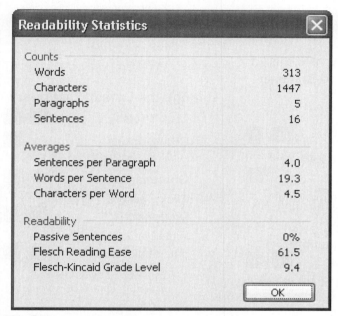

- By default, Word searches an English thesaurus, but you can select to search all available reference books, or a thesaurus in a different language.
  - ✓ *The available options depend on whether you are working online or offline.*

- A thesaurus can improve your writing by helping you eliminate repetitive use of common words and to choose more descriptive words.

*Thesaurus results in the task pane*

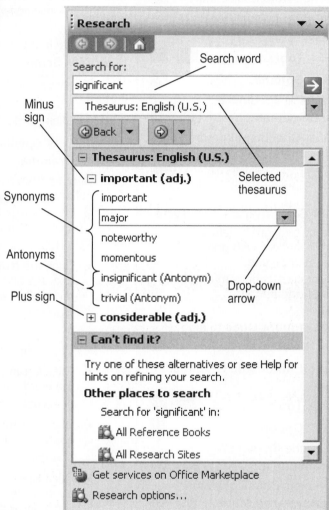

## Use the Thesaurus

- Use the **thesaurus** to locate **synonyms**, definitions, and **antonyms** for words typed in a document.

- The results of the search are displayed in the Research task pane.

- Click a plus sign to expand the list to show additional words.

- Click a minus sign to collapse the list to hide some words.

- Use the available drop-down list to insert a word from the results list at the current insertion point location, copy it at a different location, or look it up in the thesaurus.

# Procedures

## Correct Spelling as You Type

1. Right-click red, wavy underline.
2. Click correctly spelled word on shortcut menu.
   OR
   - Click **Ignore All**.............. `I`
   - Click **Add to Dictionary** to add word to dictionary.... `A`

## To turn off Automatic Spelling Checker:

1. Click **Tools**.................. `Alt`+`T`
2. Click **Options**...................... `O`
3. Click the **Spelling & Grammar** tab ............. `Ctrl`+`Tab`
4. Clear **Check spelling as you type** check box .......... `Alt`+`P`
5. Click **OK**.......................... `Enter`

## Correct Grammar as You Type

1. Right-click grammatical error marked with green, wavy underline.
2. Click correct grammar option on shortcut menu.
   OR
   Click **Ignore Once** to hide the underline ....................... `I`

## To turn off Automatic Grammar Checker:

1. Click **Tools**.................. `Alt`+`T`
2. Click **Options**...................... `O`
3. Click the **Spelling & Grammar** tab ............. `Ctrl`+`Tab`
4. Deselect **Check grammar as you type** check box .... `Alt`+`G`
5. Click **OK**.......................... `Enter`

## Select Grammar Style

1. Click **Tools**.................. `Alt`+`T`
2. Click **Options**...................... `O`
3. Click the **Spelling & Grammar** tab ............. `Ctrl`+`Tab`
4. Click **Writing style** drop-down arrow ......... `Alt`+`W`
5. Click desired style .................. `↓`, `↑`, `Enter`
6. Click **OK** .......................... `Enter`

## Check Spelling (F7)

1. Position insertion point where you want to start checking.
   ✓ *Word checks document from the insertion point forward.*
   OR
   Select text you want to check.
2. Click **Spelling and Grammar** button `ABC✓`.
   OR
   a. Click **Tools** ............. `Alt`+`T`
   b. Click **Spelling and Grammar** ...................... `S`
3. Choose from the following options:
   - Click correctly spelled word in **Suggestions list**. ...................... `Alt`+`N`
   - Click the **Not in Dictionary:** text box and edit the misspelled word manually ............... `Alt`+`:`, type changes
   - Click **Change** ......... `Alt`+`C`
   - Click **Change All** to change the word everywhere in document............... `Alt`+`L`
   - Click **Ignore Once** to continue without changing word ........ `Alt`+`I`
   - Click **Ignore All** to continue without changing word and without highlighting it anywhere else in document .... `Alt`+`G`
   - Click **Add to Dictionary** add word to dictionary ............ `Alt`+`A`
   - Click **AutoCorrect** to add the word to the AutoCorrect list ...... `Alt`+`R`
   - Click **Undo** to reverse the last change ............. `Alt`+`U`

4. Repeat step 3 options for every misspelled word.
5. Click **OK** when Word completes check. ............ `Enter`
   ✓ *Word may prompt you to check the formatting in your document. Click Yes to check the formatting, or No to close the prompt without checking the formatting. For more information on checking formatting, refer to Exercise 24.*

## Change the Default Dictionary

1. Click **Tools**.................. `Alt`+`T`
2. Click **Options**...................... `O`
3. Click the **Spelling & Grammar** tab ............. `Ctrl`+`Tab`
4. Click **Custom Dictionaries**................ `Alt`+`D`
5. Highlight desired default dictionary .......... `↓`, `↑`
   ✓ *Check box beside desired dictionary should be selected.*
6. Click **Change Default** ........................ `Alt`+`C`
7. Click **OK** .......................... `Enter`

## Set Word to Check Grammar with Spelling

1. Click **Tools**.................. `Alt`+`T`
2. Click **Options**...................... `O`
3. Click the **Spelling & Grammar** tab ............. `Ctrl`+`Tab`
4. Click **Check grammar with spelling** check box ..... `Alt`+`H`
5. Click **OK**.......................... `Enter`

## Check Grammar (F7)

1. Position insertion point where you want to start checking.
   OR
   Select text you want to check.
2. Click **Spelling and Grammar** button `ABC✓`.
   OR

a. Click **Tools** ............. `Alt`+`T`

b. Click **Spelling & Grammar** ....................... `S`

3. Choose from the following options:

- Click the correct grammar in **Suggestio̱ns** list ..... `Alt`+`N`
- Edit the error manually in the available box.
    - ✓ *The name of the box will vary depending on the type of error.*
- Click **Change** .......... `Alt`+`C`
- Click **Ignore Once** to continue without changing text .......... `Alt`+`I`
- Click **Ignore Rule** to continue without changing text and without highlighting error if it occurs anywhere else in document .... `Alt`+`G`
- Click **Next Sentence** to skip highlighted error and continue checking document ............... `Alt`+`X`
- Click **Explain** to display information about grammatical error ... `Alt`+`E`
- Click **Undo** to reverse the last change ............ `Alt`+`U`

4. Repeat step 3 for every grammatical error.

5. Click **OK** when Word completes check ............. `Enter`

## Set Word to Show Readability Statistics

1. Click **Tools** ................. `Alt`+`T`
2. Click **Options** ..................... `O`
3. Click the **Spelling & Grammar** tab ............ `Ctrl`+`Tab`
4. Click **Show readability statistics** check box.... `Alt`+`R`
5. Click **OK** .......................... `Enter`

## Search the Thesaurus *(Shift+F7)*

1. Click on the word you want to look up.
    - ✓ *The insertion point must be positioned within the word.*
2. Click **Tools** ................. `Alt`+`T`
3. Click **Language** ................. `L`
4. Click **Thesaurus** ................ `T`

OR

1. Display the Research task pane.
2. Enter desired word in Search for box.
3. Click **Show results from:** drop-down arrow.
4. Select desired thesaurus.
5. Click **Start searching** button `→` ....................... `Enter`

## Insert a synonym:

1. Position the insertion point where you want to insert the word.

    OR

    Select the word to replace.
2. Move the mouse pointer to touch the synonym in the Results list.
    - ✓ *A drop-down arrow is displayed.*
3. Click the drop-down arrow to the right of the synonym.
4. Click **Insert** ......................... `I`

## Look up a synonym:

1. Click the word in the Results list.

    OR

    Move the mouse pointer to touch the word in the Results list.
    - ✓ *A drop-down arrow is displayed.*
2. Click the drop-down arrow to the right of the word.
3. Click **Look Up** ..................... `L`

## Copy a synonym:

1. Move the mouse pointer to touch the word in the Results list.
    - ✓ *A drop-down arrow is displayed.*
2. Click the drop-down arrow to the right of the word.
3. Click **Copy** .......................... `C`
4. Right-click in the document where you want to insert the copied word.
5. Click **Paste** ......................... `P` on the shortcut menu.

## Locate a synonym as you type:

1. Right-click on the word you want to look up.
2. Click **Synonyms** on shortcut menu ............... `Y`
3. Click desired **synonym** on submenu ........... `↓`, `↑`, `Enter`

    OR

    Click **Thesaurus** ................ `T` to open the Research task pane.

# Exercise Directions

1. Start Word, if necessary.

2. Create a new document.

3. Save the file as **PRESS**.

4. Display paragraph marks.

5. On the Spelling & Grammar tab of the Options dialog box make sure all options are selected except the following:
   - Hide spelling errors in this document.
   - Hide grammatical errors in this document.

6. Begin at the top of the screen and type the paragraphs shown in Illustration A, including all the circled errors.

   ✓ *Use the default font settings except where noted.*

7. As you type, correct the spelling of the word **Anounces**.

8. As you type, do not correct the spelling of the word **Chesttnut**.

9. As you type, correct the grammar in the last sentence of the first paragraph.

10. Complete typing the text as shown, without correcting any more errors.

11. When you have finished typing, check the spelling and grammar starting at the beginning of the document.
    a. Correct the spelling of all occurrences of the word **Chestnut**.
    b. Ignore all occurrences of the proper name **Dadarian**.
    c. Correct the grammar of the word **Its** in the second paragraph.
    d. Change the double comma after the word **flowers** in the last paragraph to a single comma.

12. Note the percentage of passive sentences in the Readability Statistics dialog box.

13. Delete the text **,when the new hours were announced** from the first sentence of the second paragraph.

14. Run the Spelling checker again.

15. Note the percentage of passive sentences in the Readability Statistics dialog box.

16. Use the Thesaurus to locate synonyms for the word **expanded** in the first sentence.

17. Insert the word **extended** as a replacement.

18. Display the document in Print Preview.

19. Print the document.

20. Close the document, saving all changes.

21. Exit Word.

*4x*

*Illustration A*

**FOR IMMEDIATE RELEASE** — *Bold*

*4X*

*Arial, 16 points, centered*

*Bold italics*

## Liberty Blooms Anounces Summer Hours

*Philadelphia, PA* – Anticipating longer days and more foot traffic, Liberty Blooms, an independently-owned flower shop on Chesttnut Street, has expanded its hours for the summer months. The longer hours will allowing the shop to service more customers.

"Its been a long winter," remarked Kristin Dadarian, a store employee, when the new hours were announced. "People are ready to stay out later and buy more flowers and plants." Ms. Dadarian said she believes the new hours will appeal to tourists as well as to the long-time clients who live or work in the area.

Liberty Blooms has been in business for eight years. It offers cut flowers,, houseplants, floral arrangements for all occasions, and gift items with a floral theme. It is located at 345 Chesttnut Street in Philadelphia. For more information, call 215-555-2837.

# On Your Own

1. Create a new document.

2. Save the document as **OWD11**.

3. Make sure that the spelling and grammar checking options are set to display errors.

4. Type a press release announcing something that is happening in your life. For example, you might announce a birthday or other milestone, a new job, the results of a recent game, or an upcoming event such as a concert.

5. Use different fonts, font sizes, font styles, and alignments.

6. Include the important parts of a press release, such as the location and contact information.

7. Type at least three paragraphs.

8. When you are finished, check and correct the spelling and grammar.

9. Use the Thesaurus to improve the wording of your document.

10. Save your changes.

11. Print the document.

12. Share the document with a classmate and ask for comments and suggestions.

13. Incorporate the suggestions into the document.

14. Save your changes, close the document, and exit Word when you are finished.

# Exercise 12

◆ **Format a Full-block Business Letter** ◆ **Insert the Date and Time**
◆ **Use Shrink to Fit**

## On the Job

As a representative of your employer, you write business letters to communicate with other businesses, such as clients or suppliers, or to communicate with individuals, such as prospective employees. For example, you might write a business letter to request a job quote from a supplier, or to inquire about a loan from a bank. You write personal business letters to a business on behalf of an individual. For example, you might write a personal business letter to your insurance company to ask about a claim that needs to be paid, or to a prospective employer asking about job opportunities.

You are the Assistant to Jason Hadid, Marketing Director of Long Shot, Inc., a company that designs and manufactures golf equipment. In this exercise, you will create a full-block business letter on behalf of Mr. Hadid, confirming an appointment with Hugh McLaughlin, the Manager of a golf resort in Myrtle Beach, South Carolina.

## Terms

**Business letter** A letter from one business to another business or individual.

**Personal business letter** A letter from an individual to a business.

**Full block** A style of letter in which all lines start flush with the left margin.

**Modified block** A style of letter in which some lines start at the center of the page.

**Salutation** The line at the start of a letter including the greeting and the recipient's name, such as *Dear Mr. Doe*.

**Letterhead stationery** Stationery that already has a company's or individual's name and address printed on it.

**Computer's clock** The clock/calendar built into your computer's main processor to keep track of the current date and time.

## Notes

### Format a Full-block Business Letter

- A letter written to or from any type of business is considered a **business letter**.
- A business letter written on behalf of an individual is considered a **personal business letter**.

- There are two common styles used for either type of business letter:
  - In a **full-block** business letter, all lines start flush with the left margin.
  - In a **modified-block** business letter, certain lines start at the center of the page.
  - ✓ *Formatting a modified-block business letter is covered in Exercise 13.*

*A Full-block Business Letter*

Today's date ——— *Date*

CERTIFIED MAIL ——— *Mail service notation*

Mr. Hugh McLaughlin
Manager
Hideaway Golf Club and Resort } *Inside address*
2242 Ocean Boulevard
Myrtle Beach, SC 29577

Dear Mr. McLaughlin, ——— *Salutation*

Subject: Appointment Confirmation ——— *Subject notation*

This letter is to confirm our appointment scheduled for 9:00 a.m. next Monday at my office. I
am looking forward to meeting with you to discuss the possibility of Long Shot, Inc.
sponsoring a tournament at Hideaway Golf Club and Resort.

As we discussed on the telephone, Long Shot, Inc. is eager to find an appropriate host site for
the Long Shot Championship. The Myrtle Beach location combined with the fact that you } *Body*
have so many amenities on-site makes the Hideaway an ideal choice. We are confident that
we will be able to work out the details and make this a successful venture.

Enclosed please find a brochure highlighting some of our newest products. Feel free to
contact me or my assistant is you have any questions.

Sincerely, ——— *Closing*

Jason Hadid ——— *Signature*
Marketing Director ——— *Title*
Long Shot, Inc.
234 Simsbury Drive } *Return address*
Ithaca, NY 14850

JH/yo ——— *Reference initials*

Enclosure ——— *Enclosure notation*

Copy to: M. Whitman ——— *Copy notation*

- The parts of a business letter are the same regardless of the style.
- Vertical spacing is achieved by inserting blank lines between letter parts.
- Refer to the illustration on the previous page to identify the parts of a business letter.
  - Date. The date the letter is written.
  - Inside address. Indicates to whom the letter is being sent.
  - **Salutation.** The greeting.
  - Body. The text that comprises the letter.
  - Closing. The closing sentiment, such as Sincerely, or Best regards.
  - Signature line. The typed name of the letter writer.
  - Title line. The job title of the letter writer.
  - Return address. Indicates from whom the letter is being sent.
    - ✓ *Omit the return address if the letter is printed on **letterhead stationery**.*
  - Reference initials, which are the initials of the person who wrote the letter, followed by a slash, followed by the initials of the person who typed the letter.
    - ✓ *Whenever you see "yo" as part of the reference initials in an exercise, type your own initials.*
  - Special notations are included when appropriate:
    - Mail service notation indicates a special delivery method. It is typed in all capital letters, two lines below the date. Typical mail service notations include *CERTIFIED MAIL, REGISTERED MAIL,* or *BY HAND.*
    - Subject notation identifies or summarizes the letter topic. The word *Subject* may be typed in all capital letters or with just an initial capital. It is placed two lines below the salutation.
      - ✓ *The word* Re *(meaning* with regard to*) is sometimes used in place of the word* Subject.
    - Enclosure or attachment notation indicates whether there are other items in the envelope. It is typed two lines below the reference initials in any of the following styles: *ENC., Enc., Encl., Enclosure, Attachment.*

  - ✓ *If there are multiple items, the number may be typed in parentheses following the notation.*
  - Copy notation indicates if any other people are receiving copies of the same letter. It is typed two lines below either the enclosure notation, or reference initials, whichever is last. It may be typed as Copy to:, cc:, pc: (photocopy), or bc: (blind copy) with the name(s) of the recipient(s) listed after the colon.
    - ✓ *When a blind copy is sent, the copy notation is placed on the copy only; the original does not include a copy notation*

## Insert the Date and Time

- Use the Date and Time feature to insert the current date and/or time automatically in a document.
- The inserted date and time are based on your **computer's clock**. A variety of date and time formats are available.

*Date and Time dialog box*

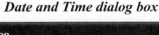

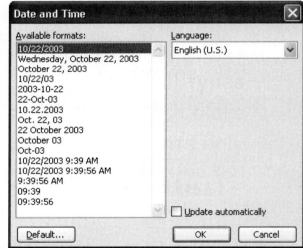

- You can set Word to update the date or time automatically whenever you open or print the document.

## Use Shrink to Fit

- Shrink to Fit automatically reduces the font size and spacing in a document just enough to fit the document on one less page.
- Use Shrink to Fit if the last page of a document contains only a small amount of text.
- The Shrink to Fit feature can only be accessed from the Print Preview toolbar.

# Procedures

### Format a Full-block Business Letter

1. Start 2" from the top of the page .................. `Enter` **5x**

   ✓ *By default, Word leaves a 1" margin between the top of the page and the first line of text. Press Enter five times to move the insertion point down another 1", resulting in 2" of space. If you are using a larger font size, if there is a printed letterhead, or if the margins are different, you may have to adjust the spacing. Use the vertical ruler for reference.*

2. Insert the date.

3. Leave one blank line and type the mail service notation ........................ `Enter` **2x**

4. Leave three blank lines and type the inside address ........................ `Enter` **4x**

5. Leave a blank line and type the salutation .............. `Enter` **2x**

6. Leave one blank line and type the subject notation ..... `Enter` **2x**

7. Leave a blank line and type the letter body ..... `Enter` **2x**

8. Leave a blank line and type the closing .......... `Enter` **2x**

9. Leave three blank lines and type the signature line ............. `Enter` **4x**

10. Press **Enter** ..................... `Enter`

11. Type the title line ............. `Enter`

12. Press **Enter** ..................... `Enter`

13. Type the return address information.

    ✓ *If you are using letterhead stationery, skip step 13.*

14. Leave a blank line and type the reference initials. .. `Enter` **2x**

15. Leave a blank line and type the enclosure notation ...... `Enter` **2x**

16. Leave a blank line and type the copy notation .............. `Enter` **2x**

### Insert Date and/or Time

1. Position the insertion point.

2. Click **Insert** .................. `Alt`+`I`

3. Click **Date and Time** ........... `T`

4. Click the desired format.

5. Do one of the following:
   - Select **Update automatically** check box ............... `Alt`+`U` to automatically update the date and/or time when you save or print.

   OR

   - Deselect **Update automatically** check box ............... `Alt`+`U` to keep date and/or time from updating.

     ✓ *A check mark in the box indicates the option is selected.*

6. Click **OK** .......................... `Enter`

### Use Shrink to Fit

1. Click **Print Preview** button.

   OR

   a. Click **File** ............... `Alt`+`F`

   b. Click **Print Preview** ....... `V`

2. Click **Shrink to Fit** button.

3. Click **Close** button  .............. `Alt`+`C`

# Exercise Directions

1. Start Word, if necessary.

2. Create a new document and save it as **CONFIRM**.

3. Type the letter shown in Illustration A.
   - Use the default font and font size (12-point Times New Roman).

     ✓ *Word may display ScreenTips as you type certain parts of the letter (for example, Subject). Simply ignore them and continue typing.*

   - Press the Enter key to leave blank lines between parts of the letter as shown.
   - Insert the current date using the MONTH DAY, YEAR format found third from the top in the Date and Time dialog box.
   - Set the date so that it does not update automatically.

4. Check the spelling and grammar in the document.
   - Accept Word's suggestions to correct errors as necessary.
   - Ignore all proper names.

5. Display the document in Print Preview.

6. If necessary, use the Shrink to Fit option to ensure that the letter fits on a single page.

7. Print one copy of the document.

8. Close the document, saving all changes.

9. Exit Word.

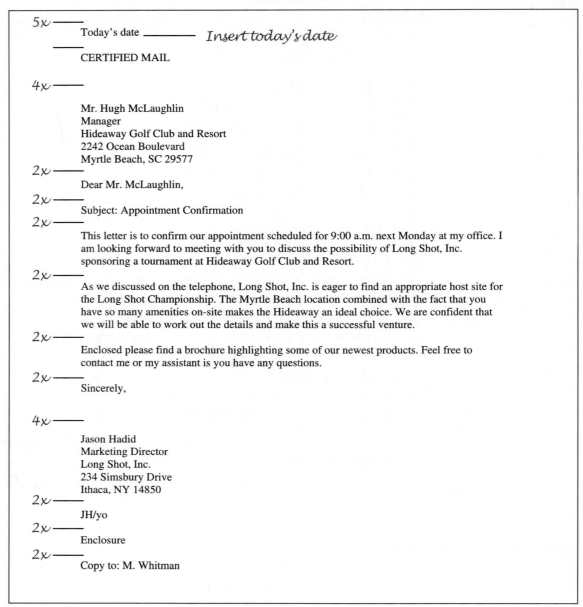

5x Today's date ——— *Insert today's date*

CERTIFIED MAIL

4x

Mr. Hugh McLaughlin
Manager
Hideaway Golf Club and Resort
2242 Ocean Boulevard
Myrtle Beach, SC 29577

2x Dear Mr. McLaughlin,

2x Subject: Appointment Confirmation

2x This letter is to confirm our appointment scheduled for 9:00 a.m. next Monday at my office. I am looking forward to meeting with you to discuss the possibility of Long Shot, Inc. sponsoring a tournament at Hideaway Golf Club and Resort.

2x As we discussed on the telephone, Long Shot, Inc. is eager to find an appropriate host site for the Long Shot Championship. The Myrtle Beach location combined with the fact that you have so many amenities on-site makes the Hideaway an ideal choice. We are confident that we will be able to work out the details and make this a successful venture.

2x Enclosed please find a brochure highlighting some of our newest products. Feel free to contact me or my assistant is you have any questions.

2x Sincerely,

4x

Jason Hadid
Marketing Director
Long Shot, Inc.
234 Simsbury Drive
Ithaca, NY 14850

2x JH/yo

2x Enclosure

2x Copy to: M. Whitman

# On Your Own

1. Create a new document in Word.
2. Save the document as **OWD12**.
3. Representing your school or organization, draft a full-block business letter to a local newspaper asking them to include information about upcoming events in a schedule or calendar listing. School events might include a football game, club activities, field trips, band and choir concerts, or vacation days.
4. In the letter, indicate that you have attached the necessary information and that you are sending a copy to your instructor.
5. Check the spelling in the document and correct errors as necessary.
6. Print the document.
7. Ask a classmate to read the letter and offer comments and suggestions.
8. Incorporate the suggestions into the document.
9. Save your changes, close the document, and exit Word when you are finished.

# Exercise 13

## On the Job

You use tabs to align text in a document, such as the date in a modified-block business letter. Handwriting on an envelope looks unprofessional. With Word you can set up and print envelopes to match your letters. You can also create and print mailing labels or return address labels.

You are interested in obtaining a position as a golf clothing designer. In this exercise, you will create a personal business letter asking about job opportunities at Long Shot, Inc. You will also create an envelope to accompany the document. Finally, you will create return address labels and save them in a separate document.

## Terms

**Tab** A location (or measurement) you use to align text.

**Tab leader** A repeated character, such as a dot or underline, that fills the space between tab stops.

**Delivery address** The recipient's address printed on the outside of an envelope.

**Return address** The letter-writer's address, typically appearing at the very top of the letter as well as in the upper-left corner of an envelope.

## Notes

### Set Tabs

- **Tabs** are used to indent a single line of text.
- Press the Tab key to advance the insertion point to the next set tab stop.
- There are five types of tab stops:
  - Left ⌊L⌋: Text starts flush left with the tab stop.
  - Right ⌊⌐⌋: Text ends flush right with the tab stop.
  - Center ⌊⊥⌋: Text is centered on the tab stop.
  - Decimal ⌊⊥⌋: Decimal points are aligned with the tab stop.
  - Bar ⌊│⌋: A horizontal bar is displayed at the tab stop position. Text starts 1/10" to the right of the bar.

- By default, left tab stops are set every ½" on the horizontal ruler.
- You can set any type of tab stop at any point along the ruler.
- Use the Tabs dialog box to set precise tab stops.
- Select a **tab leader** in the Tabs dialog box to fill the space between tab stops with a character such as a dot or an underline.
- Set tabs before you type new text for the current existing paragraph or for selected multiple paragraphs.
- Once you set tabs the formatting is carried forward each time you press the Enter key to start a new paragraph.

*Tabs dialog box*

*Tabs dialog box*

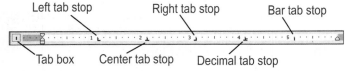

*Tab stops on the horizontal ruler*

Left tab stop    Right tab stop    Bar tab stop

Tab box    Center tab stop    Decimal tab stop

## Format a Modified-block Business Letter

- The parts of a modified-block style letter are the same as those of a full-block style letter.
  - ✓ *Refer to Exercise 12 for a list of the parts of a business letter.*
- However, in a modified-block style letter the return address, date, closing, signature, and title lines begin at the center point of the page.
- A left tab stop set at the center point of the page enables you to position the insertion point quickly where you need it.
  - ✓ *Using a center tab stop or centered alignment centers the text; you must use a left tab stop in order to position the text to start at the center point of the page.*
- When you create a modified-block business letter that is not printed on letterhead stationery, type the return address above the date.

## Create Envelopes

- Word has a feature that automatically sets up an envelope for printing.
- By default, Word creates standard size 10 envelopes ($4\frac{1}{8}$" by $9\frac{1}{2}$").
- If a letter document is open on-screen, Word picks up the inside address for the envelope's **delivery address**.
  - ✓ *You can also select text in the document to use as the delivery address.*
- You can print the envelope directly or add it to the beginning of the open document and save it.

*The Envelopes page of the Envelopes and Labels dialog box*

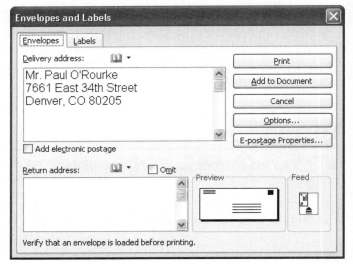

## Create Labels

- Use the Label feature to create mailing labels, **return address** labels, file folder labels, or diskette labels.
- The Label feature automatically sets up a document to print on predefined label types.
- You select the manufacturer and label type loaded in the printer.
- By default, Word creates a full page of labels using the inside address from the current document, or the selected address.
- You can change the default to create labels using the return address or to create a single label.

# Procedures

## Set Tabs

### To set a left tab stop:

1. Position insertion point in paragraph to format.
   OR
   Select paragraphs to format.
2. Click ruler where you want to set tab stop.

### To set a different type of tab stop:

1. Position insertion point in paragraph to format
   OR
   Select paragraphs to format
2. Click the **Tab** box.
   - ✓ *Each time you click, the tab icon changes. Stop when tab style you want is displayed.*
3. Click ruler where you want to insert new tab stop.

### To set a precise tab stop:

1. Position insertion point in paragraph to format.
   OR
   Select paragraphs to format.
2. Click **F**ormat ............... Alt +O
3. Click **T**abs ........................... T
4. Select type of tab:
   - **L**eft ......................... Alt +L
   - **C**enter .................... Alt +C
   - **R**ight ...................... Alt +R
   - **D**ecimal ................. Alt +D
   - **B**ar ......................... Alt +B
5. Click in the **Tab** stop position box ....... Alt +T
6. Type precise position.
7. Select leader, if desired:
   - **1** None .................. Alt +1
   - **2** ......................... Alt +2
   - **3** ------- ................ Alt +3
   - **4** _____ ................. Alt +4
8. Click **OK** ........................... Enter

## To clear tab stops:

1. Position insertion point in paragraph to format.
   OR
   Select paragraphs to format.
2. Drag tab stop marker off ruler.
   OR
1. Click **F**ormat ............... Alt +O
2. Click **T**abs ........................... T
3. Click **Clear A**ll ............. Alt +A
   OR
   a. Select tab stop(s) to clear.
   b. Click **Cl**ear ............. Alt +E
4. Click **OK** ......................... Enter

## Format a Modified-block Business Letter

1. Start 2" from top of page ...................... Enter **5x**
   - ✓ *Press Enter five times to leave 2" of space.*
2. Set left tab stop at 3".
3. Press **Tab** ........................... Tab
4. Insert date.
5. Leave three blank lines and type inside address .... Enter **4x**
6. Leave a blank line and type the salutation ...... Enter **2x**
7. Leave a blank line and type the letter body..... Enter **2x**
8. Leave a blank line ....... Enter **2x**
9. Press **Tab** ........................... Tab
   - ✓ *This moves the insertion point to the tab stop you set in step 2.*
10. Type the closing.
11. Leave three blank lines .................. Enter **4x**
12. Press **Tab** ........................... Tab
13. Type signature line.
14. Move to next line and press **Tab**.......... Enter , Tab
15. Type title line.
16. Leave a blank line and type reference initials . Enter **2x**

## Create an Envelope

1. Click **T**ools.................. Alt +T
2. Click **L**etters and Mailings ...................... E
3. Click **E**nvelopes and Labels............................... E
4. Click **E**nvelopes tab ... Alt +E
5. Type **D**elivery address ...................... Alt +D
   - ✓ *If inside address is already entered, skip step 6.*
6. Type **R**eturn address... Alt +R
   OR
   Select **O**mit check box..................... Alt +M
   - ✓ *If Omit check box is selected, you cannot type in Return address text box.*
7. Click **P**rint button
    ... Alt +P
   - ✓ *You are prompted to save the new return address as the default. Click No to leave the address as is.*
   OR
   Select **A**dd to Document .................. Alt +A

## Create a Single Label

1. Click **T**ools.................. Alt +T
2. Click **L**etters and Mailings............................. E
3. Click **E**nvelopes and Labels............................... E
4. Click **L**abels tab .......... Alt +L
5. Click **Si**ngle label option button .............. Alt +N
6. Click **O**ptions..................... O
7. Select label type from **Label p**roducts list .............. Alt +P
8. Select label product number from **Product number** list ................. Alt +U
   - ✓ *Make sure correct printer and tray information is selected.*

9. Click **OK**...........................`Enter`

10. Type label text.
   - ✓ *If inside address is already entered, skip step 10*

11. Make sure labels are loaded in printer.

12. Click **Print** button

   [ Print ] ... `Alt`+`P`

### Create Return Address Labels

1. Click **Tools**..................`Alt`+`T`

2. Click **Letters and Mailings**...........................`E`

3. Click **Envelopes and Labels**...............................`E`

4. Click **Labels** tab ..........`Alt`+`L`

5. Select **Use return address** check box......`Alt`+`R`

6. Click **Options** .............`Alt`+`O`

7. Select label type from **Label products** list......`Alt`+`P`

8. Select product number from **Product number** list ...`Alt`+`U`
   - ✓ *Make sure the correct printer and tray information is selected.*

9. Click **OK** ..........................`Enter`
   - ✓ *Make sure labels are loaded in printer.*

10. Click **Print** button

   [ Print ] ... `Alt`+`P`

   **OR**

   a. Click **New Document** ............`Alt`+`D`

   b. If prompted to save the return address, click **No** ..`N`

   c. Click **Save** button 💾 to open the Save As dialog box to save label document.

# Exercise Directions

1. Start Word, if necessary.

2. Create a new document and save it as **NEWJOB**.

3. Type the letter shown in Illustration A.
   - ✓ *You may type the name and address of the letter writer as shown in the illustration, or use your own name and address.*
   - Use the default font and font size (12-point Times New Roman).
     - ✓ *If Word displays ScreenTips, ignore them and continue typing.*
   - Press the Enter key to leave blank lines between parts of the letter as shown.
   - Align the return address, date, closing, and signature with a left tab stop set at 3" on the horizontal ruler.
   - Insert the current date using the MONTH DAY, YEAR format found third from the top in the Date and Time dialog box.
   - Set the date so that it does not update automatically.

4. Check the spelling and grammar in the document, and correct errors as necessary.

5. Create an envelope for the letter.
   a. Use the inside address for the account executive at Long Shot, Inc.
   b. Enter the return address as it appears in the document you typed—either use your own address or the one shown in the illustration.

6. Add the envelope to the document.
   - When prompted to save the new return address as the default, choose No.

7. Display the document in Print Preview.

8. Print the document.

9. Create a full page of return address labels using the return address as it appears in the document. Select an appropriate label, such as Avery Standard # 3261R—Return Address
   - ✓ *Do not save the return address as the default.*

10. Save the labels in a new document with the name **LABELS**.

11. Preview the new label document. It should look similar to the one in Illustration B depending on the Product # selected.

12. Print the **LABELS** document.
   - ✓ *You can print the labels on standard letter-sized paper if you do not have labels available.*

13. Close the label document, saving all changes.

14. Close the letter document, saving all changes.

15. Exit Word.

*Illustration A*

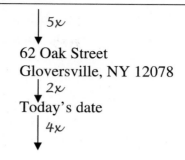

↓ *5x*

62 Oak Street
Gloversville, NY 12078

↓ *2x*

Today's date

↓ *4x*

Mr. George Younger
Personnel Director
Long Shot, Inc.
234 Simsbury Drive
Ithaca, NY 14850

↓ *2x*

Dear Mr. Younger:

↓ *2x*

Subject: Employment opportunities

↓ *2x*

I am writing to inquire about job opportunities at Long Shot, Inc. I have recently graduated from the State University of New York at Oswego with a degree in textile design, and I am eager to enter the exciting field of sports apparel.

↓ *2x*

My qualifications for a job at Long Shot include the above mentioned degree as well as practical experience in the industry. I spent the second semester of my junior year as an intern at a clothing manufacturing company in New York City, and I design and produce garments for myself and my friends. I also love to golf.

↓ *2x*

Please take the time to review the attached resume, or pass it on to someone else at Long Shot who may be interested in hiring someone with my qualifications. I look forward to hearing from you.

↓ *2x*

Sincerely,

↓ *4x*

Drew Pierce

↓ *2x*

Attachment

| | | |
|---|---|---|
| Drew Pierce<br>62 Oak Street<br>Gloversville, NY 12078 | Drew Pierce<br>62 Oak Street<br>Gloversville, NY 12078 | Drew Pierce<br>62 Oak Street<br>Gloversville, NY 12078 |
| Drew Pierce<br>62 Oak Street<br>Gloversville, NY 12078 | Drew Pierce<br>62 Oak Street<br>Gloversville, NY 12078 | Drew Pierce<br>62 Oak Street<br>Gloversville, NY 12078 |
| Drew Pierce<br>62 Oak Street<br>Gloversville, NY 12078 | Drew Pierce<br>62 Oak Street<br>Gloversville, NY 12078 | Drew Pierce<br>62 Oak Street<br>Gloversville, NY 12078 |
| Drew Pierce<br>62 Oak Street<br>Gloversville, NY 12078 | Drew Pierce<br>62 Oak Street<br>Gloversville, NY 12078 | Drew Pierce<br>62 Oak Street<br>Gloversville, NY 12078 |
| Drew Pierce<br>62 Oak Street<br>Gloversville, NY 12078 | Drew Pierce<br>62 Oak Street<br>Gloversville, NY 12078 | Drew Pierce<br>62 Oak Street<br>Gloversville, NY 12078 |
| Drew Pierce<br>62 Oak Street<br>Gloversville, NY 12078 | Drew Pierce<br>62 Oak Street<br>Gloversville, NY 12078 | Drew Pierce<br>62 Oak Street<br>Gloversville, NY 12078 |
| Drew Pierce<br>62 Oak Street<br>Gloversville, NY 12078 | Drew Pierce<br>62 Oak Street<br>Gloversville, NY 12078 | Drew Pierce<br>62 Oak Street<br>Gloversville, NY 12078 |
| Drew Pierce<br>62 Oak Street<br>Gloversville, NY 12078 | Drew Pierce<br>62 Oak Street<br>Gloversville, NY 12078 | Drew Pierce<br>62 Oak Street<br>Gloversville, NY 12078 |
| Drew Pierce<br>62 Oak Street<br>Gloversville, NY 12078 | Drew Pierce<br>62 Oak Street<br>Gloversville, NY 12078 | Drew Pierce<br>62 Oak Street<br>Gloversville, NY 12078 |
| Drew Pierce<br>62 Oak Street<br>Gloversville, NY 12078 | Drew Pierce<br>62 Oak Street<br>Gloversville, NY 12078 | Drew Pierce<br>62 Oak Street<br>Gloversville, NY 12078 |

# On Your Own

1. Create a new document in Word.

2. Save the document as **OWD13-1**.

3. Draft a personal letter to a company with whom you do business. You may want to ask for a credit on returned merchandise, or solicit donations for a charity of organization. For example, you may want to ask for donations for an auction or raffle to raise money for a school club or sports team.

4. Create an envelope for your letter, and add it to the document.

5. Check the spelling and grammar in the document and correct errors as necessary.

6. Save your changes and then print the document.

7. Ask a classmate to read the letter and offer comments and suggestions.

8. Incorporate the suggestions into the document.

9. Create your own mailing labels using the return address from your letter. Save the mailing labels document as **OWD13-2**.

10. Save the changes, close the document, and exit Word when you are finished.

# Exercise 14

## ◆ Critical Thinking

You are the owner of Liberty Blooms, a flower shop in Philadelphia, Pennsylvania. In this exercise, you will write a letter to a local community center asking if they will publicize some of the activities going on at your shop. You will create an envelope to accompany the letter and a page of return address labels that the community center can use to send you the requested information. Finally, you will create a flyer about Liberty Blooms that she can hang up in the center. You will use alignments and font formatting to make the flyer visually exciting.

## Exercise Directions

### Type a Business Letter

1. Start Word, if necessary.
2. Create a new document and save it as **IDEA**.
3. Display nonprinting characters.
4. Make sure AutoCorrect is on.
5. Type the letter in Illustration A exactly as shown, including all circled errors.
6. Insert the date in the Month Date, Year format so that it does not update automatically.
7. Correct spelling and grammatical errors.
   - Ignore all proper names.
   - Correct all other spelling and grammatical errors that AutoCorrect did not automatically change.
8. Use the Thesaurus to find an appropriate replacement for the word **wide** in the second paragraph.
9. Save the changes you have made to the document.
10. Display the document in Print Preview.
11. Shrink the document to fit on one page.
12. Display the document in Full Screen view.
13. Return the document to Normal view.

### Create an Envelope and Label

1. Create an envelope for the letter using the inside address and return address from the letter.
2. Add the envelope to the document.
3. Print the document.

4. Create a full page of mailing labels using the return address in the document:

   **Your Name**
   **Liberty Blooms Flower Shop**
   **345 Chestnut Street**
   **Philadelphia, PA 19106**

5. Save the label document with the name **RETURN**
6. Display the **RETURN** document in Print Preview, and then print it.
   - ✓ *If you do not have labels available, print it on regular paper.*
7. Close all open documents, saving all changes.

### Create a Flyer

1. Create a new document and save it as **FLYER**.
2. Display nonprinting characters.
3. Type and format the document shown in Illustration B, using the specified alignments, font formatting, and tabs.
   - ✓ *Use the Comic Sans MS font unless otherwise noted. If the font is not available on your system, select a different font.*
4. Check the spelling and grammar in the document.
5. Correct all errors, but leave capitalization as shown in the illustration.
6. Display the document in Print Preview.
7. If the document is longer than one page, shrink it to fit on one page.
8. Print the document.
9. Close the document, saving all changes.

*Illustration A*

Today's date


Ms. Jocelyn Rodriquez
Activities Directory
Chestnut Street Comunity Center
578 Chestnut Street
Philadelphia, PA 19106

Dear Ms. Rodriquez:

I am the owner of the Liberty Blooms Flower Shop, located at 345 Chestnut Street. I was at the business buraeu meeting last week where you spoke about ways that the retail shops in the area can reach out to the residents of the comunity.

Liberty Blooms has been in business for eight years. In addition to selling a wide variety of plants, cut flowers, and gift items, I offers free classes and seminars on horticultural topics ranging from flower arrangement to bonsai maintenance. DUe to the small size of my shop, class size is usually limited to ten people. However, if you is willing, I could offer some classes at the comunity center where I could accommodate a larger group.

I have attached a flyers describing some of the events I have planned for the near future. Please feel free to hang the flyer at the comunity center or distirbute it to your patrons. I have also enclosed return address labels that you can use to send me information about the comunity center.

I would like very much to meet with you. Please contact me as soon as possible.

Sincerely,



Your Name
Liberty Blooms Flower Shop
345 Chestnut Street
Philadelphia, PA 19106

Attachment
Enclosure

*Centered* {

# Liberty Blooms — 36 points

## Flowers, Plants, and More — 18 points

*3x*

*20 points, justified* {

Liberty    Blooms    offers    (cut    flowers,) (houseplants,    floral    arrangements) for    all occasions, (gift items) with a (floral theme.) — *Bold*

*2x*

Liberty Blooms also conducts (free) classes and seminars on a wide range of topics.

*3x*

*16 points, centered, italics* }

*Class size is limited, so please register in advance. For more information stop by the shop, give us a call, or look us up on-line at www.libertyblooms.net.*

*2x*

Schedule of Upcoming Events:

*Left tab at 1"; Right tab at 5.5" with a dot leader* {

All About Roses ....................................... April 7
Water Gardens........................................ April 14
Dried Flowers ........................................ April 21
Indoor Herb Gardens .........................April 28

} *16 points*

*3x*

*24 points, bold* — **Liberty Blooms** — *Right-aligned*

*16 points* { 345 Chestnut Street
Philadelphia, PA 19106
Phone: (215) 555-2837

78

# Lesson 3

## Open and Edit Documents

# Exercise 15

◆ **Open a Saved Document** ◆ **Open a Recently Used Document**
◆ **Save a Document with a New Name**

## On the Job

When you are ready to revise and improve a document that you've already created and saved, open it again in Word. When you save changes, Word updates the document stored on the disk. Use the Save As command when you want to leave the original document unchanged and save a copy of the document with a new name or in a new location. For example, you can save a letter with a new name and then change the inside address to send it to someone else.

The letter you sent to the Personnel Director at Long Shot, Inc. asking about employment opportunities resulted in a job interview. You want to write another letter thanking the interviewer for his time. Since you are writing to the same person at the same address, you can save time by revising the existing letter. In this exercise, you will open the existing letter document and save it with a new name. You will then revise the document and save the changes. Finally, you will print the document.

## Terms

**Revise** Edit, change, or update a document.

## Notes

### Open a Saved Document

- To **revise** a Word document that has been saved and closed, open it again in Word.
- Use the Open dialog box to locate files that you want to open.

*Open dialog box*

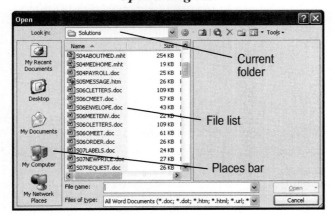

### Open a Recently Used Document

- The four most recently used Word documents are listed at the bottom of the File menu and in the Open section on the Getting Started task pane.
  - ✓ *The listed file names may also include the complete path to the file, which means the folder and/or disk where the file is stored. Since you can have a file with the same name stored in different locations, be sure you select the one you really want to open.*

*Open recently used documents from the File menu*

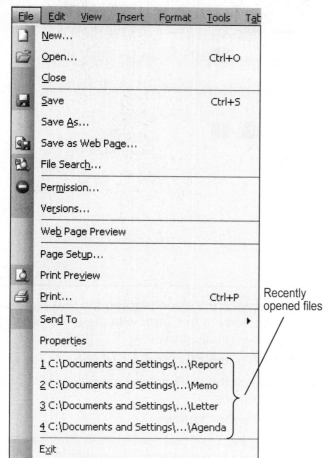

Recently opened files

*Open recently used documents from the Getting Started task pane*

Recently opened files

■ You can also display a list of shortcuts to recently used files and folders in the Open dialog box.

  ✓ *Recently used documents of all types may be listed on the My Recent Documents menu in Windows. Open the Start menu, click My Recent Documents, then click the document you want to open.*

## Save a Document with a New Name

■ The Save As command lets you save a copy of a document in a different location or with a different file name.

■ Use the Save As command to leave the original document unchanged while you edit the new copy.

# Procedures

### Open a Saved Document
*(Ctrl+O)*

1. Click **Open** button 📂.
   OR
   a. Click **File** ............... `Alt`+`F`
   b. Click **Open** ..................... `O`
2. Click **Look in** drop-down arrow ........................... `Alt`+`I`

3. Select drive or folder.
   ✓ *If necessary double-click folder name.*
   OR
   Click folder in Places Bar to open it.
4. Double-click document name.
   OR
   a. Click document name.
   b. Click **Open** ................... `O`

### Open a Recently Saved Document

1. Click **File** ................... `Alt`+`F`
2. Click document name at bottom of menu.
   OR
1. Click **View** .................. `Alt`+`V`
2. Click **Task Pane** ................. `K`
   ✓ *If the Getting Started task pane is not displayed, select it from the Other Task Panes drop-down list.*

3. Click document name.

OR

1. Click **Open** button 📂.

   OR

   a. Click **F**ile ............... `Alt`+`F`

   b. Click **O**pen ..................... `O`

2. Click My Recent Documents button in Places bar.

3. Double-click document name.

   OR

   a. Click document name.

   b. Click **O**pen ..................... `O`

### Save a Document with a New Name

1. Click **F**ile ..................... `Alt`+`F`

2. Click Save **A**s ..................... `A`

3. Type new file name.

4. Select new drive and/or folder.

5. Click **S**ave button

   [Save] ............. `Alt`+`S`

## Exercise Directions

1. Start Word, if necessary.

2. Open ⌨NEWJOB or open 💿15NEWJOB.

   ✓ If necessary ask your instructor where this file is located.

3. Save the document as **THANKS**.

4. Revise the document according to the following steps, to create the document shown in the Illustration.

   ✓ For a refresher on selecting and replacing text, refer to Exercise 9.

5. Leave the envelope at the top of the document unchanged.

6. Replace the date in the letter with the current date.

7. Replace the Subject notation text with the text shown in Illustration A.

8. Replace the three paragraphs that comprise the body of the letter with the three paragraphs shown in Illustration A.

9. Delete the Attachment notation.

10. Check the spelling and grammar, correcting all errors.

11. Save the changes.

12. Display the document in Print Preview. It should look similar to Illustration A.

13. Print the document.

14. Close the document, saving all changes.

15. Exit Word.

## On Your Own

1. Open ⌨OWD12, the letter you created in the On Your Own section of Exercise 12, or open 💿15EVENTS.

2. Save the document as **OWD15**.

3. Edit the letter so that you can send it to a different newspaper. For example, replace the date with the current date and replace the name and address of the recipient.

4. Check the spelling and grammar in the document.

5. Print the document.

6. Ask a classmate to review the letter and make suggestions and comments.

7. If necessary, incorporate the suggestions into the letter.

8. Save your changes, close the document, and exit Word when you are finished.

*Illustration A*

62 Oak Street
Gloversville, NY 12078

Today's date

Mr. George Younger
Personnel Director
Long Shot, Inc.
234 Simsbury Drive
Ithaca, NY 14850

Dear Mr. Younger:

Subject: Interview follow-up

Thank you very much for taking the time to meet with me this morning to discuss job opportunities at Long Shot, Inc. I enjoyed the tour of the offices and design facilities and I appreciated the chance to meet some of the employees.

Since our meeting, I am more certain than ever that I would be a valuable asset to Long Shot. I believe that my qualifications make me uniquely suited for the position of assistant designer, which is currently available. I am sure that I would fit in very well with the current design team, and that I would be able to meet all challenges and responsibilities.

Again, thank you for meeting with me. I look forward to hearing from you about the possibility of my employment.

Sincerely,

Drew Pierce

# Exercise 16

## Skills Covered:

◆ **Use Proofreaders' Marks** ◆ **Insert Text**
◆ **Use Overtype Mode** ◆ **Use Uppercase Mode** ◆ **Change Case**

## On the Job

Making changes to existing documents is a key benefit of using Word 2003. Some of the most important revisions can be made using simple features. For example, you can insert new text to add to a document, you can type over existing text to change a document, and you can change the case of text in order to improve a document.

Some employees of Liberty Blooms are confused about the new hours. You have decided to modify the original memo to help make the information easier to understand. In this exercise, you will open the memo document and save it with a new name. You will then revise the document and save the changes. Finally, you will print the document so you can distribute it.

## Terms

**Proofreaders' marks** Symbols written on a printed document by a copyeditor or proofreader to indicate where revisions are required.

**Insert mode** The method of operation used for inserting new text within existing text in a document. Insert mode is the default.

**Overtype mode** The method of operation used to replace existing text in a document with new text.

**Case** The specific use of upper- or lowercase letters.

## Notes

### Use Proofreaders' Marks

■ Often you may need to revise a Word document based on a marked-up printed copy of the document. **Proofreaders' marks** on printed documents are written symbols that indicate where to make revisions.

■ Following is a list of common proofreaders' marks:

• ᜱᜱᜱᜱᜱ indicates text to be bold.

• ∧ indicates where new text should be inserted.

• ___𝒴 indicates text to be deleted.

• ¶ indicates where a new paragraph should be inserted.

• ≡ indicates that a letter that should be capitalized.

• _____ or ⟨ital⟩ indicates text to be italicized.

• ⟨highlight⟩ indicates text to highlight.

• ] [ indicates text to center.

✓ *There are many other common proofreading symbols. You can find a list in reference books such as* Webster's Collegiate Dictionary, *or* The Chicago Manual of Style.

## Insert Text

- By default, you type new text in a document in **Insert mode**. Existing text moves to the right as you type to make room for new text.
- You can insert text anywhere in a document.
- You can also insert nonprinting characters, such as paragraph marks to start a new paragraph, tabs, and spaces.

## Use Overtype Mode

- To replace text as you type, use **Overtype mode**.
- In Overtype mode, existing characters do not shift right to make room for new characters. Instead, new characters replace existing characters as you type, deleting existing characters.
- When Overtype mode is active, the OVR indicator on the Status bar is displayed in bold: OVR. When Overtype mode is off, the OVR indicator is dimmed, and the default Insert mode is active.
- Overtype mode is useful when you have to replace an entire block of text.
- However, most editing should be done in Insert mode so you do not accidentally type over text that you need.

## Use Uppercase Mode

- Use Uppercase mode to type all capital letters without pressing the Shift key.
- Uppercase mode affects only letter characters.
- When Uppercase mode is on, the Caps Lock indicator on your keyboard is lit.

## Change Case

- You can automatically change the **case** of text in a document.
- There are five case options:
  - Sentence case: First character in sentence is uppercase.
  - lowercase: All characters are lowercase.
  - UPPERCASE: All characters are uppercase.
  - Title Case: First character in each word is uppercase.
  - tOGGLE cASE: Case is reversed for all characters.

*Change Case dialog box*

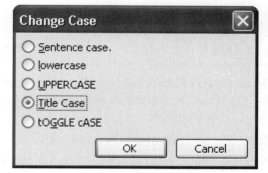

# Procedures

## Insert Text

1. Position insertion point to right of character where you want to insert new text.
2. Type new text.

## Use Overtype Mode

1. Position insertion point to left of first character you want to replace.
2. Press **Insert** key ................ Ins

   OR

- Double-click **OVR** indicator OVR on status bar.

  ✓ *OVR indicator appears in bold when active.*

3. Type new text.

**Turn off Overtype mode:**

- Press **Insert** key ....... Ins

  OR

- Double-click **OVR** indicator OVR again.

  ✓ *OVR indicator appears dimmed when inactive.*

## Use Uppercase Mode

1. Press **Caps Lock** key .......
2. Type text.

**To turn off Uppercase mode:**

- Press **Caps Lock** key .......

## Change Case

1. Select text.

   OR

   Position insertion point where new text will begin.

2. Click **Format** ............. `Alt`+`O`

3. Click **Change Case** ............ `E`

4. Click the case you want:

   - **Sentence case** .............. `S`

   - **lowercase** ..................... `L`

   - **UPPERCASE** ................. `U`

   - **Title Case** ..................... `T`

   - **tOGGLE cASE** .............. `G`

5. Click **OK** ........................... `Enter`

   ✓ *You can also select text and then press **Shift+F3** to toggle through sentence case, lowercase, and uppercase. Release the keys when the desired case is in effect.*

# Exercise Directions

1. Start Word, if necessary.

2. Open ⌨**HOURS** or open ⊙**16HOURS**.

   ✓ *If necessary, ask your instructor where this file is located.*

3. Save the document as **NEWHOURS**.

4. Make the revisions as marked in Illustration A.

   - Insert new text and paragraphs as marked.

   - Use Overtype mode to replace text as necessary.

   - Change case as marked.

   - Apply font formatting as marked.

5. Check the spelling and grammar and make necessary corrections.

6. Display the document in Print Preview.

7. Print the document.

8. Close the document, saving all changes.

# On Your Own

1. Open **OWD14**, the document you created in the On Your Own section of Exercise 14, or open ⊙**16FUNDS**.

2. Save the document as **OWD16**.

3. Print the document, and then have a classmate read it and use proofreaders' marks to suggest insertions, deletions, case changes, and formatting changes.

4. Make the revisions.

5. Save your changes, close the document, and exit Word when you are finished.

*Illustration A*

# Liberty Blooms Flower Shop

## MEMO

To: All Employees
From: Student's Name
Date: June ~~8~~ 4
Subject: Summer Hours

*Bold and Italics*

*I hope this memo will clarify the summer schedule.*
~~It's time again to switch to our summer hours schedule!~~ Starting ~~next week we will be~~ open an extra two hours on ***Fridays***, ***Saturdays***, and ***Sundays***. Please
let me know as soon as possible if you have conflicts, or if you want to add
hours so I can put the schedule together. Thanks for your cooperation.

(FRIDAY) the shop will stay

*Bold*

*There Is No Obligation For Any Of You To Work Additional Hours Unless You Want To.*

## New Store Hours

### Monday through Thursday:
9:00 a.m. until 7:00 p.m.

### Fridays and Saturdays:
9:00 a.m. until 9:00 p.m.

*Ital*

### Sundays:
12:00 p.m. until 9:00 p.m.

# Exercise 17

## Skills Covered:

◆ **Move Text** ◆ **Cut and Paste Text**
◆ **Use the Clipboard** ◆ **Use Drag-and-Drop Editing**
◆ **Select Paste Formatting Options** ◆ **Move a Paragraph**

## On the Job

Move text to rearrange a document quickly without retyping existing information. You can move any amount of text, from a single character to an entire document.

StyleEyes, a national chain of eyewear stores, has hired you to manage a new franchise in Cleveland, Ohio. To help you announce the grand opening, the corporate marketing department sent you a press release that was used by a franchise in a different location. In this exercise, you will open the existing document, reorganize the information, and edit and format the text to suit your needs.

## Terms

**Cut** To delete a selection from its original location and move it to the Clipboard.

**Paste** To insert a selection from the Clipboard into a document.

**Clipboard** A temporary storage area that can hold up to 24 selections at a time.

**Drag-and-drop editing** The action of using a mouse to drag a selection from its original location and drop it in a new location.

## Notes

### Move Text

- While editing, you may decide you need to move text that is already typed in a document to a new location.
- Word's move commands can save you from deleting and retyping text.
- Be sure to consider nonprinting characters when you select text to move:
  - Select the space following a word or sentence to move along with text.
  - Select the paragraph mark following a paragraph or line to move paragraph formatting with text.
  - Use Undo to reverse a move that you made unintentionally.

### Cut and Paste Text

- Use the **Cut** and **Paste** commands to move text in a document.
- The Cut command deletes selected text from its original location and moves it to the **Clipboard**.
- The Paste command copies the selection from the Clipboard to the insertion point location.
- Up to 24 selections can remain in the Clipboard at one time.
- You can access the Cut and Paste commands from the Edit menu, from the Standard toolbar, from a shortcut menu, or with keyboard shortcuts.

## Use the Clipboard

- Use the Clipboard task pane to access selections for pasting.

- The last 24 items cut or copied are displayed in the Clipboard.

- You can paste or delete one or all of the items.

- You can turn the following Clipboard options off or on:

  - Show Office Clipboard Automatically. Sets the Clipboard task pane to open automatically when you cut or copy a selection.

  - Show Office Clipboard When Ctrl+C Pressed Twice. Sets Word to display the Clipboard task pane when you press and hold the Ctrl key and then press C on the keyboard twice.

  - Collect Without Showing Office Clipboard. Sets the Clipboard task pane so it does not open automatically when you cut or copy data.

  - Show Office Clipboard Icon on Taskbar. Displays a Clipboard icon at the right end of the Taskbar if there are selections on the Clipboard. Double-click the icon to open the task pane.

  - Show Status Near Taskbar When Copying. Displays a ScreenTip with the number of items on the Clipboard when you cut or copy a selection.

## Use Drag-and-Drop Editing

- Use **drag-and-drop editing** to move text with the mouse.

- Drag-and-drop editing is convenient when you can see the text to move and the new location on the screen at the same time.

### Select Paste Formatting Options

- When you paste text into a new location Word automatically displays the Paste Options button.

  Click the Paste Options button to display a list of options for formatting the text in the new location.

*The Paste Options button*

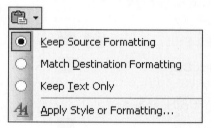

## Move a Paragraph

- You can quickly move an entire paragraph up or down in a document.

*Clipboard Task Pane*

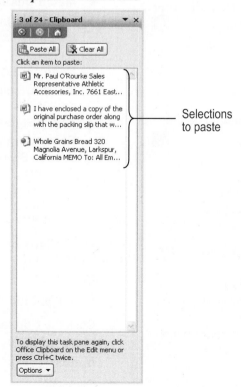

Selections to paste

# Procedures

## Move Text

1. Select text to move.
2. Press **F2** key ...................... `F2`
3. Position insertion point at new location.
4. Press **Enter** ...................... `Enter`

## Use Cut and Paste to Move Text *(Ctrl+X, Cltr+V)*

1. Select text to move.
2. Click **Cut** button ✂.
   OR
   a. Click **E**dit ............... `Alt`+`E`
   b. Click **Cu**t ........................ `T`
   OR
   a. Right-click selection.
   b. Click **Cu**t ........................ `T`
3. Position insertion point in new location.
4. Click **Paste** button 📋.
   OR
   a. Click **E**dit ............... `Alt`+`E`
   b. Click **P**aste ..................... `P`
   OR
   a. Right-click new location.
   b. Click **P**aste ..................... `P`

## Display the Clipboard Task Pane

1. Press and hold **Ctrl** ........... `Ctrl`
2. Press **C** ............................. `C`
3. Press **C** ............................. `C`
   OR
1. Click **E**dit ........................... `E`
2. Click **Office Clip**board ...... `B`
   OR
1. Click **V**iew .................. `Alt`+`V`
2. Click Tas**k** Pane ................. `K`
3. Click **Other Task Panes** drop-down arrow.
4. Click **Clipboard**.

## Paste an Item from the Clipboard

1. Display Clipboard task pane.
2. Position insertion point in new location.
3. Click item to paste.
   OR
   Click **Paste All** button
   📋 `Paste All` to paste all selections from the Clipboard.

## Set Clipboard Options

1. Display Clipboard task pane.
2. Click **Options** drop-down button `Options ▼`.
3. Select desired option:
   - **Show Office Clipboard Automatically** ............... `A`
   - **Show Office Clipboard When Ctrl+C Pressed Twice** ...................... `P`
   - **C**ollect Without Showing Office Clipboard ............ `C`
   - **Show Office Clipboard Icon on Taskbar** ............ `T`
   - **Show Status Near Taskbar When Copying** .............. `S`
   ✓ *A check mark indicates the option is selected.*

## Delete Selections from the Clipboard

1. Right-click selection to delete.
2. Click **Delete** ........................ `D`
   on shortcut menu
   OR
   Click **Clear All** button
   ✗ `Clear All` to delete all selections from the Clipboard.

## Use Drag-and-Drop Editing to Move Text

1. Select text to move.
2. Move mouse pointer anywhere over selected text.
3. Press and hold left mouse button.
4. Drag mouse to position mouse pointer/insertion point at new location.

✓ *As you drag, the mouse pointer changes to a box with a dotted shadow attached to an arrow* ⬚.

5. Release mouse button to move selection.

## Move a Paragraph

1. Position insertion point anywhere within paragraph to move.
   OR
   Select the paragraphs to move.
2. Press ................. `Alt`+`Shift`+`↑`
   OR
   Press ................. `Alt`+`Shift`+`↓`
3. Repeat step 2 until paragraph is in desired location.

## Select Paste Formatting Options

1. Paste text at new location.
2. Click **Paste Options** button 📋.
3. Select one of the following:
   - **Keep Source Formatting** ...................... `K`
     to maintain formatting from original location.
   - **Match Destination Formatting** ...................... `D`
     to apply existing formatting to new text.
   - **Keep Text Only** .............. `T`
     to remove all applied formatting.
   - **Apply Styles or Formatting** ...................... `A`
     to open Styles and Formatting task pane.
   ✓ *The Styles and Formatting task pane is covered in Exercise 24.*

## If Paste Options button is not displayed:

1. Click **Tools** ................. `Alt`+`T`
2. Click **Options** ...................... `O`
3. Click the **Edit** tab ........ `Ctrl`+`Tab`
4. Select **Show Paste Options buttons** check box ...... `Alt`+`O`
5. Click **OK** ........................ `Enter`

# Exercise Directions

1. Start Word, if necessary.

2. Open 🖝 **17STYLE**.

3. Save the file as **STYLE**

4. Replace the text **Your Name** with your own name.

5. Follow the steps below to rearrange the text in the document to create the document shown in Illustration A.

   a. Move the two lines with the contact information to the first line of the document.

   b. Move the last line in the document (**FOR IMMEDIATE RELEASE**) to the first line of the document.

   c. Insert 1" of blank space (three blank 14 point lines or four blank 12 point lines) between the new first line and the contact information.

   d. Insert four blank 12 point lines between the contact phone number and the headline.

   e. Move the middle paragraph to the end of the document.

   f. Move the last sentence in the first paragraph so it becomes the first sentence in the second paragraph.

6. Check the spelling and grammar in the document and make all necessary corrections.

7. Display the document in Print Preview. It should look similar to Illustration A. Insert or delete blank lines and spaces as necessary.

8. Print the document.

9. Close the document, saving all changes.

# On Your Own

A resume is a document that you send to potential employers to give the employer a general idea of the candidate's qualifications. Although there are different styles of resumes, they all usually include a list of schools a person attended as well as a list of jobs he or she has had. Some include other information such as hobbies, certifications, and awards.

1. Think about how you would create a resume for yourself.

2. Look up information about how to format a resume. You might find the information in a career guidance center, in the library, or on the Internet.

3. Once you have selected a format, gather the information you would like to include on the resume. For example, you should include the schools you have attended, as well as any volunteer or paid work experience. Be sure to include the dates and locations.

4. You can also include clubs, teams and organizations to which you belong, awards that you have won, certifications that you have received, and any other interests that you have.

5. When you have all of the information you need, create a new document in Word.

6. Save the file as **OWD17**.

7. Based on the format you selected, enter the text to create the resume.

8. Save the changes as you work.

9. Apply font formatting and effects to enhance the appearance of the text.

10. Use tabs to align the text so it looks good and is easy to read.

11. Rearrange text and paragraphs so that the information in is the correct order, and so that it looks good on the page. For example, switch the position of the Education section with the Work Experience section to decide which should come first. Make sure the information is listed in reverse chronological order (most recent first).

12. When you have completed the document, check the spelling and grammar.

13. Print the document.

14. Ask a classmate to review the document and make comments and suggestions.

15. Incorporate the suggestions into the document.

16. Close the document, saving all changes, and exit Word.

**FOR IMMEDIATE RELEASE**

Contact:          Your Name
                  216-555-1228

## StyleEyes Franchise Opens in Cleveland

*Cleveland, Ohio* – A branch of the StyleEyes national chain of eyewear stores has recently opened in downtown Cleveland. StyleEyes is well known for its vast selection of eyeglass frames, accessories, and eye care products as well as its competitive pricing. It offers eye exams, contact lens fitting, and laser surgery evaluations and referrals.

The new store is an independent franchise owned by Lamont Franklin. Mr. Franklin also owns a StyleEyes franchise in Columbus. "I am excited about the opportunity to introduce Cleveland to the wonderful shopping experience to be found at StyleEyes," said Mr. Franklin. Mr. Franklin, who plans to split his time evenly between his two stores, has hired a full-time manager for the new Cleveland location.

StyleEyes is located at 754 Erieside Avenue, across from the Rock and Roll Hall of Fame. For directions, store hours, and other information, call 216-555-1228.

# Exercise 18

◆ **Use Copy and Paste**
◆ **Copy Text with Drag-and-Drop**

## On the Job

Copy text from one location to another to speed up your work and avoid repetitive typing. You can copy any amount of text, from a single character to an entire document.

The owner of the StyleEyes franchise sent you a file to use as an advertising flyer for the grand opening. You think you can improve the flyer by making editing and formatting changes. In this exercise, you will open the flyer and revise it using some of the editing and formatting techniques you have learned so far in this book.

## Terms

**Copy**  To create a duplicate of a selection and place it on the Clipboard.

## Notes

### Use Copy and Paste

- Use the Copy and Paste feature to copy existing text from one location in a document and paste it to another location.

- The **Copy** command stores a duplicate of selected text on the Clipboard, leaving the original selection unchanged.

- The Paste command pastes the selection from the Clipboard to the insertion point location.

- You can access the Copy and Paste commands from the Edit menu, the Standard toolbar, or from a shortcut menu.

- Use the Clipboard task pane to choose which selection to paste into the document.

  ✓ *The same Clipboard used for moving is used for copying. For more information, refer to Exercise 17.*

- Use the Paste Options button to control formatting when copying text just as you use it when moving text.

  ✓ *For more information about the Paste Options button, refer to Exercise 17.*

### Copy Text with Drag-and-Drop

- Use drag-and-drop editing to copy text with the mouse.

- The drag-and-drop feature is convenient when you can see the text to copy and the new location on the screen at the same time.

# Procedures

## Use Copy and Paste
*(Ctrl+C, Ctrl+V)*

1. Select the text to copy.
2. Click **Copy** button 📋.
   OR
   a. Click **Edit** ............... `Alt`+`E`
   b. Click **Copy** ..................... `C`
   OR
   a. Right-click selection.
   b. Click **Copy** ..................... `C`
3. Position insertion point in new location.
4. Click **Paste** button 📋.
   OR
   a. Click **Edit** ............... `Alt`+`E`
   b. Click **Paste** ................... `P`
   OR
   a. Right-click new location.
   b. Click **Paste** ................... `P`

   ✓ *To paste the text more than once, repeat steps 3 and 4.*

## Display the Clipboard Task Pane

1. Press and hold **Ctrl** ............. `Ctrl`
2. Press **C** ............................... `C`
3. Press **C** ............................... `C`
   OR
1. Click **Edit** ......................... `E`
2. Click **Office Clipboard** ....... `B`
   OR
1. Click **View** .................. `Alt`+`V`
2. Click **Task Pane** ................. `K`
3. Click **Other Task Panes** drop-down arrow.
4. Click **Clipboard**.

## Paste an Item from the Clipboard

1. Display Clipboard task pane.
2. Position insertion point at new location.
3. Click item to paste.
   OR
   Click **Paste All** button
   📋 Paste All to paste all selections from the Clipboard.

## Set Clipboard Options

1. Display Clipboard task pane.
2. Click **Options** drop-down button `Options ▼`.
3. Select desired option:
   - **Show Office Clipboard Automatically** ................ `A`
   - **Show Office Clipboard When Ctrl+C Pressed Twice** ............................... `P`
   - **Collect Without Showing Office Clipboard** ............ `C`
   - **Show Office Clipboard Icon on Taskbar** ............ `T`
   - **Show Status Near Taskbar When Copying** .............. `S`

   ✓ *A check mark indicates the option is selected.*

## Delete Selections from the Clipboard

1. Right-click selection to delete.
2. Click **Delete** .......................... `D`
   on shortcut menu
   OR
   Click **Clear All** button
   📋 Clear All to delete all selections from the Clipboard.

## Use Drag-and-Drop to Copy Text

1. Select text to copy.
2. Move mouse pointer anywhere over selected text.
3. Press and hold left mouse button.
4. Press and hold the **Ctrl** key ...................................... `Ctrl`
5. Drag mouse to position mouse pointer/insertion point at new location.
   ✓ *As you drag, the mouse pointer changes to a box with a dotted shadow and a plus sign attached to an arrow.*
6. Release mouse button to copy selection.
7. Release the **Ctrl** key ........... `Ctrl`

# Exercise Directions

1. Start Word, if necessary.

2. Open 📀 **18STYLEAD**.

3. Save the file as **STYLEAD**.

4. Use the following steps to revise the document to create the document shown in Illustration A.

   a. Copy the store name, **StyleEyes**, and the paragraph mark following it from the first line of the document to the Clipboard.

   b. Select the word **it** at the beginning of the fourth line of text, and then paste the selection from the Clipboard to replace it.

   c. Select the word **It** at the beginning of the fifth line of text and, again, paste the selection from the Clipboard to replace it.

   d. Position the insertion point at the beginning of the line **store to see what all the excitement is about.**

   e. Paste the selection from the Clipboard.

   f. Position the insertion point at the beginning of the last line in the document and paste the selection one more time.

   g. Select the address information on the third line of the document and copy it to the Clipboard.

   h. Position the insertion point at the beginning of the last line in the document and paste the address information.

      ✓ If necessary, insert a paragraph mark to separate the address from the text in parentheses.

5. Check the spelling and grammar in the document.

6. Display the document in Print Preview. It should look similar to the one in Illustration A.

   ✓ If necessary, use Shrink to Fit to fit the document on a single page.

7. Print the document.

8. Close the document, saving all changes.

9. Exit Word

# StyleEyes
## has come to Cleveland!

Conveniently located at 754 Erieside Avenue,

# StyleEyes
## has something for everyone.

# StyleEyes

is one of the nation's premier eyewear stores. Products include frames from all the leading designers, accessories, and eye care essentials. The store offers eye exams with certified optometrists and ophthalmologists as well as contact lens fitting, laser surgery evaluations and referrals.

## Stop by the newest
# StyleEyes
## store to see what all the excitement is about!

# StyleEyes
## 754 Erieside Avenue
### (Across from the Rock and Roll Hall of Fame)

# On Your Own

1. Open ⌨**OWD06**, the file you created in the On Your Own section of Exercise 6, or open 💿**18PORTRAIT.**

2. Save the file as **OWD18.** This is a description of yourself or someone in your class.

3. At the end of the document, start a new paragraph and type a sentence or two explaining that you are going to list the most important characteristics of the person.

4. Copy at least three descriptive characteristics from the description and paste them at the end of the document to create a list.

5. Display the document in Print Preview. Make editing or formatting changes as necessary.

6. Print the document.

7. Ask a classmate to read the document and offer comments or suggestions.

8. If necessary, incorporate the comments into the document.

9. Close the document, saving all changes.

# Exercise 19

Liberty Blooms is having a sale. In this exercise, you will use the skills you have learned to create a flyer advertising the sale. You will start by opening an existing document that you can modify to create the flyer. You will save the document with a new name. You will insert and replace text. You will use different cases in the document, and you will copy and move text to improve the flyer. Finally, you will print the flyer.

## Exercise Directions

1. Start Word, if necessary.
2. Open the document ⊙**19SALE**.
3. Save the document as **SALE**.
4. Make the insertions and deletions marked on Illustration A.
5. Change case as marked on Illustration A.
6. Copy and move text as marked on Illustration A.
7. Adjust spacing by inserting or deleting blank lines and spaces as necessary.
8. Check the spelling and grammar in the document.
9. Correct all errors, but leave capitalization as shown in the illustration.
10. Display the document in Print Preview. It should look similar to Illustration B.
11. Print the document.
12. Close the document, saving all changes.
13. Exit Word.

*Illustration A*

16 points, centered

20 points, centered, bold, italics

*Announcing the* ANNUAL SUMMER CLEARANCE SALE

# Liberty Blooms

Flowers, plants, and more

Title case

Copy first two lines and paste above last paragraph

Liberty Blooms offers cut flowers, houseplants, floral arrangements for all occasions, gift items with a floral theme. Take advantage of special savings on everything in the store, including the following items:

$24.99

| Topiaries | $9.95 and up |
| Bonsai trees | $34.99 and up |
| Hanging planters | $10.00 and up |
| Dried floral arrangements | $7.50 and up |

Title case

Set left tab at 1"; set decimal tab with dot leader at 4.5"

345 Chestnut Street
Philadelphia, PA 19106
Phone: (215) 555-2837

Move up to follow first two lines

**Liberty Blooms conducts free classes and seminars on a wide range of topics, such as roses, herbs, and water gardens. For a complete schedule give us a call, or look us up on-line at www.libertyblooms.net.**

*Ital*

# Liberty Blooms

## Flowers, Plants, And More

345 Chestnut Street
Philadelphia, PA 19106
Phone: (215) 555-2837

Announcing the

## *ANNUAL SUMMER CLEARANCE SALE*

Take advantage of special savings on everything in the store, including the following items:

Topiaries ......................................$9.95 and up
Bonsai Trees............................. $24.99 and up
Hanging Planters .......................$10.00 and up
Dried Floral Arrangements .......$7.50 and up

# Liberty Blooms

## Flowers, Plants, And More

***Liberty Blooms conducts free classes and seminars on a wide range of topics. For a complete schedule give us a call, or look us up on-line at www.libertyblooms.net.***

# Lesson 4

## Text Formatting

**Exercise 20**
- ◆ Apply Font effects
- ◆ Apply Text effects
- ◆ Apply Underlines
- ◆ Apply Font Color

**Exercise 21**
- ◆ Highlight Text
- ◆ Copy Formatting
- ◆ Adjust Character Spacing

**Exercise 22**
- ◆ Insert Symbols and Special Characters
- ◆ Customize Toolbars and Menus

**Exercise 23**
- ◆ Bulleted Lists
- ◆ Numbered Lists
- ◆ Sort

**Exercise 24**
- ◆ Apply Styles
- ◆ Create a Style
- ◆ Modify a Style
- ◆ Reapply Direct Formatting
- ◆ Check Formatting
- ◆ Clear Formatting

**Exercise 25**
- ◆ Critical Thinking

# Exercise 20

## Skills Covered:

◆ **Apply Font Effects** ◆ **Apply Text Effects**
◆ **Apply Underlines** ◆ **Apply Font Color**

## On the Job

You can enhance text using font effects, text effects, underlines, and colors. These techniques are useful for printed documents or documents you intend to post on the World Wide Web. Some of these formatting features, such as text effects, color, shadow, and fancy underline styles, are useful for creating exciting documents in which the text jumps out to capture a reader's attention. Alternatively, some formatting features are useful for adding subtle description to text, such as a single underline or superscript.

Blue Sky Dairy is sponsoring a contest to name a new ice cream flavor. You have been asked to design a document advertising the contest. If the company approves of the document, it will be made available at retail stores and posted as a Web page on the company Web site. In this exercise, you will create the document using font effects, text effects, and color.

## Terms

**Font effects** Formatting features used to enhance or emphasize text.

**Text effects** Effects used to animate text on-screen.

## Notes

### Apply Font Effects

■ Word includes numerous **font effects** for enhancing and emphasizing text, including the ones available in the Font dialog box:

- ~~Strikethrough~~
- ~~Double strikethrough~~
- Superscript
- Subscript
- Shadow
- Outline
- Emboss
- Engrave
- Small Caps
- ALL CAPS

✓ Hidden is also an option in the Effects area of the font dialog box. Hidden text is not displayed on-screen or printed unless you select to display it.

*Font dialog box—Font tab*

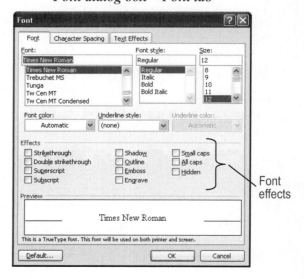

102

## Apply Text Effects

- Word has six **text effects** you can apply to text for viewing on-screen.
- Text effects are animations used in documents that will be viewed on-screen. They cannot be printed.
- Select text effects in the Font dialog box.

*Font dialog box—Text Effects tab*

## Apply Underlines

- There are 17 types of underlines available in Word, including the following:
  - <u>Single</u> (underlines all characters, including nonprinting characters, such as spaces and tabs)
  - <u>Words</u> <u>only</u>
  - <u>Double</u>
  - <u>Dotted</u>
  - <u>Thick</u>
  - <u>Dash</u>
  - <u>Dot dash</u>
  - <u>dot dot dash</u>
  - <u>Wave</u>
- Select an underline in the Font dialog box.

## Apply Font Color

- Use color to enhance text in documents that will be viewed on-screen or printed on a color printer.
- You select a font color using the Font Color button **A** on the Formatting toolbar, or from the Color palette in the Font dialog box.
- You can change the color of an underline independently from the color of the font.

# Procedures

### Apply Font Effects

1. Select text.
   OR
   Position insertion point where new text will be typed.
2. Click **F**or**m**at...............**Alt**+**O**
3. Click **F**ont ...........................**F**
4. Select check box for desired effect(s).
   - ✓ Clear checkmark to remove effect.
5. Click **OK**...........................**Enter**
   - ✓ Select text and press Ctrl+Spacebar to remove all character formatting.

### Apply Text Effects

1. Select text.
   OR
   Position insertion point where new text will be typed.
2. Click **F**or**m**at ...............**Alt**+**O**
3. Click **F**ont...........................**F**
4. Click **T**ext **E**ffects
   page tab .......................**Alt**+**X**
5. Click desired
   **Animation**......**Alt**+**A**, **↑**/**↓**
   - ✓ View a sample of the effect in the Preview area.
6. Click **OK** ...........................**Enter**

### Apply Underlines *(Ctrl+U)*

1. Select text.
   OR
   Position insertion point where new text will be typed.
2. Click **U**nderline button **U**.
   - ✓ Repeat steps to remove underline.

OR

1. Select text.
   OR
   Position insertion point where new text will be typed.
2. Click **F**or**m**at ...............**Alt**+**O**
3. Click **F**ont ...........................**F**

4. Click **Underline style** drop-down arrow ......... `Alt`+`U`

5. Click desired underline type.

   ✓ *Click (none) to remove underline*

6. Click **OK** ........................... `Enter`

## Apply Font Color

1. Select text.

   OR

   Position insertion point where new text will be typed.

2. Click **Format** ............... `Alt`+`O`

3. Click **Font** .......................... `F`

4. Click **Font color** drop-down arrow ......... `Alt`+`C`

5. Click desired color ..................... `↑`/`↓`, `Enter`

   ✓ *Click Automatic to select default color.*

6. Click **OK** ........................... `Enter`

   OR

1. Select text.

   OR

   Position insertion point where new text will be typed.

2. Click **Font Color** button 🅰 on Formatting toolbar to apply color displayed on button.

   OR

   a. Click **Font Color** drop-down arrow 🅰▾ on Formatting toolbar.

   b. Click desired color.

## Apply Color to Underlines

1. Select underlined text.

   OR

   Position insertion point where new underlined text will be typed.

2. Click **Format** ............... `Alt`+`O`

3. Click **Font** ......................... `F`

4. Click **Underline color** drop-down arrow ......... `Alt`+`I`

5. Click desired color .................. `↑`/`↓`, `Enter`

   ✓ *Click Automatic to select default color.*

6. Click **OK** .......................... `Enter`

# Exercise Directions

1. Start Word, if necessary.

2. Open 💿 **20CONTEST**.

3. Save the document as **CONTEST**.

4. Apply the formatting shown in the illustration.

   a. Change all text to Comic Sans MS or a similar sans serif font.

   b. Apply font sizes as marked.

   c. Apply font styles as marked.

   d. Set horizontal alignments as marked.

   e. Apply font and text effects as marked.

   f. Change font color as marked.

   g. Apply underlines and underline colors as marked.

5. Check the spelling and grammar and correct errors as necessary.

6. Display the document in Print Preview. It should look similar to the illustration.

   ✓ *The animated effects do not appear in Print Preview or in a printed document.*

   ✓ *If the document is longer or shorter than the one shown, check to see if you inadvertently formatted the blank lines between paragraphs. In the illustration, all blank lines have the default 12-pt. Times New Roman formatting.*

7. Save the changes.

8. Print the document.

9. Close the document, saving all changes.

10. Exit Word.

# On Your Own

1. Create a new document in Word.

2. Save the document as **OWD20**.

3. Use the formatting techniques you have learned so far to design an invitation to an event such as a birthday party, graduation, or meeting.

4. Use font formatting, font effects, and text effects, including different colors and underline styles.

5. Preview the document and, when you are satisfied, print it.

6. Ask a classmate to review the document and make comments or suggestions.

7. Incorporate the suggestions into the document, if necessary.

8. Save your changes, close the document, and exit Word.

*Illustration A*

IMAGINE...

*24 points, shadow, outline, all caps, blue, centered*

*20 points, small caps, black, justified*

CHOCOLATE AND BUTTERSCOTCH CHIPS BLENDING WITH SILKY THREADS OF RICH CHOCOLATE FUDGE AND SWEET STRAWBERRY SYRUP, ALL FLOATING DELICIOUSLY IN A SEA OF VANILLA ICE CREAM.

*48 points, shadow, outline, all caps, blue, centered*

IS YOUR MOUTH WATERING YET?

*18 points, all caps, red, centered, with sparkle text effect*

BLUE SKY DAIRY

Proudly Invites

*Blue double underline*

Everyone and Anyone

*18 points, bold, red, centered*

to

NAME THAT FLAVOR

*Sparkle text effect*

Deadline for submissions
Winner will be announced

*Blue font and single underline*

March 1
June 1

*14 points, blue, left tab at 4"*

The Grand Prize is a year's supply of Blue Sky Dairy Ice Cream. Other prizes include gift certificates, hats, t-shirts, and more.

*14 points, black, flush left*

Entry blanks are available wherever Blue Sky Dairy products are sold, or write your idea on an index card, along with your name, address, and phone number and send it to:

*18 points, engrave, small caps, blue, centered*

BLUE SKY DAIRY FLAVOR CONTEST

Highway 73
Cambridge, Wisconsin 53523

*14 points, blue, left tab at 1.75"*

# Exercise 21

## Skills Covered:

◆ **Highlight Text** ◆ **Copy Formatting** ◆ **Adjust Character Spacing**

## On the Job

You can highlight text to change the color around the text without changing the font color. Highlighting is useful for calling attention to text and for making text stand out on the page. Use the Format Painter to quickly copy formatting from one location to another. The Format Painter saves you time and makes it easy to duplicate formatting throughout a document.

As a marketing assistant at Blue Sky Dairy, the owners have asked you to review the contest flyer and make suggestions for improvements. They have asked you to highlight formatting you don't think is effective, and change formatting you think could be improved. In this exercise, you will open the flyer document and modify it using the Format Painter, character spacing, and the highlighter.

## Terms

**Highlight formatting** Change the color around text in a document.

**Kerning** Spacing between pairs of characters.

**Baseline** The bottom of a line of text.

## Notes

### Highlight Text

- **Highlight formatting** places a color background on text.

- You can highlight text as a decorative or visual effect, but Word's Highlighter feature is commonly used like a highlighter pen on paper to mark text that requires attention.

- Yellow is the default highlight color, but you can select from a palette of highlight colors, including green and pink.

- Highlighting prints in color on a color printer and in gray on a black and white printer.

*Palette of highlight colors*

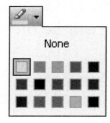

### Copy Formatting

- Use the Format Painter to copy formatting from existing formatted text to existing unformatted text.

- You can copy character formatting, such as fonts and font effects as well as paragraph formatting, such as horizontal alignments.

  ✓ *The Format Painter will not copy case changes.*

## Adjust Character Spacing

- In Word, the amount of space between characters is determined by the current font set.

- When certain characters that are wider than other characters in a font set are next to each other, they may appear to run together.

- Set the **kerning** to automatically adjust the space between certain pairs of characters.

- You can also adjust spacing between characters by changing the scale, the spacing, or the position.

- Set the scale to adjust the amount of space between all selected characters based on a percentage. For example, set the character spacing scale to 200% to double the amount of space.

- Set the spacing to expand or condense the spacing between all selected characters by a specific number of points.

- Set the position to raise or lower characters relative to the text **baseline** by a specific number of points.

- Use character spacing to control the amount of text that fits on a line or on a page as well as to improve the readability of the text.

*Character Spacing tab of the Font dialog box*

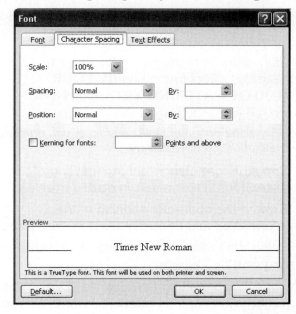

# Procedures

### Apply Highlights

**Highlight existing text:**

1. Select text.

2. Click **Highlight** button .

   ✓ *Repeat steps to remove highlight.*

OR

1. Click **Highlight** button .

   ✓ *Mouse pointer changes to look like an I-beam with a highlighter pen attached to it* .

2. Drag across text to highlight.

3. Click **Highlight** button again to turn off Highlight feature.

**Change highlight color:**

1. Click **Highlight** button drop-down arrow .

2. Click new color.

   ✓ *Click None to select the automatic background color.*

### Copy Formatting

**Copy formatting once:**

1. Position insertion point in formatted text.

2. Click **Format Painter** button .

   ✓ *The mouse pointer looks like an I-beam with a paintbrush.*

3. Select text to format.

**Copy character formatting to a single word:**

1. Position insertion point in formatted text.

2. Click **Format Painter** button .

   ✓ *The mouse pointer looks like an I-beam with a paintbrush.*

3. Click word to format.

### Copy paragraph formatting to an entire paragraph:

1. Position insertion point in formatted text.

2. Click **Format Painter** button .

   ✓ *The mouse pointer looks like an I-beam with a paintbrush.*

3. Click paragraph to format.

**Copy formatting repeatedly:**

1. Position insertion point in formatted text.

2. Double-click **Format Painter** button .

3. Select text to format.

4. Repeat step 3 until all text is formatted.

5. Click **Format Painter** button to turn off Format Painter.

# Exercise Directions

1. Start Word, if necessary.

2. Open 🖳CONTEST or open 💿21CONTEST.

3. Save the document as **REVCONTEST**.

4. Use yellow to highlight the two lines that have text effect formatting (**IS YOUR MOUTH WATERING YET?** and **NAME THAT FLAVOR**).

   ✓ *Since the document will be printed, you don't think text effects are necessary.*

5. Copy the formatting from the first line of text (**IMAGINE...**) to the text **Proudly Invites**.

6. Expand the character spacing of the reformatted text **Proudly Invites** by 2 points.

7. Raise the position of the words **Everyone** and **Anyone** by 2 points.

8. Copy the formatting from the text **Everyone** (or **Anyone**) to the underlined words **Grand Prize** and **Blue Sky Dairy Ice Cream** in the second to last paragraph and to the text **Blue Sky Dairy** in the first sentence of the last paragraph.

9. Select the text **Blue Sky Dairy Flavor Contest** near the end of the document (third line from the end) and expand the character spacing to 1.5 pts.

10. Use pink to highlight the word **IMAGINE...** at the beginning of the document.

11. Copy the formatting from the last line of text (the address) to the paragraph at the beginning of the document describing the new flavor.

12. Type an ellipsis (three dots) at the beginning of the paragraph, then highlight the three dots in pink.

13. Check the spelling and grammar.

14. Preview the document. It should look similar to the one in Illustration A.

15. Print the document.

16. Close the document, saving all changes.

17. Exit Word

# On Your Own

1. Open 🖳OWD20, the document you created in the On Your Own section of Exercise 20, or open 💿21INVITE.

2. Save the document as **OWD21**.

3. Use highlights to either indicate parts of the invitation you think could be improved or as a formatting technique to enhance the appearance of the document.

4. Use the Format Painter to copy formatting from one part of the document to another.

5. Adjust the character spacing of some of the text in order to make it easier to read, or to control the amount of text on a line.

6. Check the spelling and grammar in the document.

7. Preview the document and then print it.

8. Ask a classmate to review the document and make comments and suggestions.

9. Incorporate the suggestions into the document.

10. Save your changes, close the document, and exit Word.

*Illustration A*

# IMAGINE...

...chocolate and butterscotch chips blending with silky threads of rich chocolate fudge and sweet strawberry syrup, all floating deliciously in a sea of vanilla ice cream.

## IS YOUR MOUTH WATERING YET?

# BLUE SKY DAIRY
## PROUDLY INVITES

**Everyone** and **Anyone**

to

## NAME THAT FLAVOR

Deadline for submissions                    March 1
Winner will be announced                    June 1

The **Grand Prize** is a year's supply of **Blue Sky Dairy Ice Cream**. Other prizes include gift certificates, hats, t-shirts, and more.

Entry blanks are available wherever **Blue Sky Dairy** products are sold, or write your idea on an index card, along with your name, address, and phone number and send it to:

### BLUE SKY DAIRY FLAVOR CONTEST
Highway 73
Cambridge, Wisconsin 53523

# Exercise 22

## Skills Covered:

◆ **Insert Symbols and Special Characters**
◆ **Customize Toolbars**

## On the Job

Use symbols to supplement the standard characters available on the keyboard and to add visual interest to documents. For example, you can insert shapes such as hearts and stars into documents as borders or separators. You can also insert special characters such as paragraph marks and hyphens. Word's toolbars provide quick access to commonly used features. If the default buttons don't include the features you need, you can easily customize any toolbar. You can even create a new toolbar all your own.

The owner of Liberty Blooms has asked you to enhance the sale flyer you created in an earlier exercise. In this exercise, you will open the existing flyer, create a custom toolbar, apply font effects, underlines and color, and insert symbols.

## Terms

**Symbol** A character that is part of a font set but that is not included on the keyboard, including foreign alphabet characters and icons.

**Special characters** Additional characters that are not included on the keyboard, such as paragraph marks, ellipsis, or em dashes (—).

## Notes

### Insert Symbols and Special Characters

- **Symbols** are characters that cannot be typed from the keyboard, such as hearts, stars, and other shapes as well as foreign alphabet characters.

- Several symbol fonts come with Microsoft Office 2003 and others are available through vendors and shareware.

- Many regular character fonts also include some symbol characters.

- To insert a symbol, you select a font in the Symbol dialog box, and then select the desired symbol.

- You can also select from a list of recently used symbols.

- Most symbols have a character code that is displayed in the Character code box in the Symbol dialog box. If you happen to know a symbol's character code, you can type it in the box to select the desired symbol.

- Some symbols have shortcut keys you can use to insert the symbol into a document.

- When you insert symbols, the default font formatting is applied to the character. You can change the font size, style, and effects just as you can for regular text characters.

*Symbol dialog box—Symbols tab*

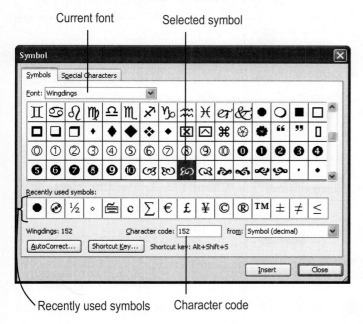

## Customize Toolbars and Menus

- By default, Word's toolbars include buttons for accessing the most commonly used tasks.

- Use the Customize dialog box to customize toolbars to display buttons for accessing the tasks that you perform most frequently and to remove buttons you do not use.

- For example, by default, the Formatting toolbar includes buttons for applying bold, italic, and continuous underline effects. However, if you frequently apply the small caps effect, or the double underline effect, you can add those buttons to the Formatting toolbar.

- You can also create a new toolbar; the new toolbar is added to the list of toolbars displayed from the View, Toolbars command so that you can display it or hide it like other toolbars.

*Customize dialog box—Commands tab*

- The Symbol dialog box also includes a list of **special characters** that you can insert in a document.

- For example, you can insert a paragraph mark character, or an ellipsis.

*Symbol dialog box—Special Characters tab*

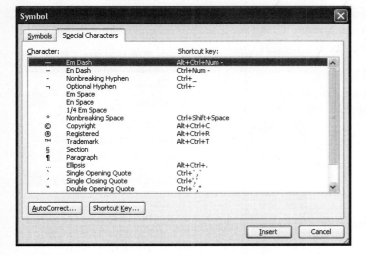

- Menus can also be customized. Full menus can be set to display and you can set the size of the menu icons.

# Procedures

## Insert Symbols

1. Position insertion point where you want to insert a symbol.
2. Click **Insert** ................. `Alt`+`I`
3. Click **Symbol**. .................... `S`
4. Click **Font** drop-down arrow ........ `Alt`+`F`
5. Select any symbol font............... `↓`, `Enter`

   ✓ *You can scroll through the font list, or start typing the name of the desired font in the Font box. Word will jump through the alphabetical list to get the character(s) you type.*

6. Click desired symbol .... `Tab`, `→`
7. Click **Insert** ................. `Alt`+`I`

   ✓ *Repeat the steps to insert additional symbols without closing the Symbol dialog box.*

8. Click **Close** ...................... `Enter`

## Insert Special Characters

1. Position insertion point where you want to insert a special character.
2. Click **Insert** ................. `Alt`+`I`
3. Click **Symbol**. .................... `S`
4. Click **Special Characters** tab .......... `Alt`+`P`
5. Click desired character ....... `↓`
6. Click **Insert** ................. `Alt`+`I`

   ✓ *Repeat the steps to insert additional characters without closing the Symbol dialog box.*

7. Click **Close** ...................... `Esc`

## Customize Toolbars

### Add a toolbar button:

1. Display the toolbar to which you want to add a button.
2. Click **Tools**.................. `Alt`+`T`

   OR

   Right-click any toolbar.

   OR

   a. Click **View**.............. `Alt`+`V`

---

   b. Click **Toolbars** .............. `T`

   OR

   a. Click **Toolbar Options** button `▾` on any toolbar.

   b. Select **Add or Remove Buttons**......................... `A`

3. Click **Customize**................. `C`

   ✓ *If necessary drag the Customize dialog box to move it away from the toolbar.*

4. Click the **Commands** tab .......... `Alt`+`C`
5. In the **Categories** list box, select the category that contains the desired button............. `Alt`+`G`, `↓`, `↑`
6. In the **Commands** list, click the desired button............. `Alt`+`D`, `↓`, `↑`
7. Drag the desired button out of the Customize dialog box and onto the desired toolbar.

   ✓ *A thick I-beam indicates the location where the button will be placed on the toolbar.*

8. Release the mouse button.
9. Click **Close** to close the Customize dialog box ...... `Enter`

### Remove a toolbar button:

1. Display the toolbar from which you want to remove a button.
2. Click **Tools** ................. `Alt`+`T`

   OR

   Right-click any toolbar.

   OR

   a. Click **View** .............. `Alt`+`V`

   b. Click **Toolbars** .............. `T`

   OR

   a. Click **Toolbar Options** button `▾` on any toolbar.

   b. Select **Add or Remove Buttons**......................... `A`

3. Click **Customize**................. `C`

   ✓ *If necessary drag the Customize dialog box to move it away from the toolbars.*

---

4. Drag the desired button off of the toolbar where it is currently located.

   ✓ *The mouse pointer resembles a button attached to an arrow with an X.*

5. Release the mouse button.
6. Click **Close** to close the Customize dialog box. ...... `Enter`

### Change toolbar button size:

1. Click **Tools**.................. `Alt`+`T`

   OR

   Right-click any toolbar.

   OR

   a. Click **View** .............. `Alt`+`V`

   b. Click **Toolbars** .............. `T`

   OR

   a. Click **Toolbar Options** button `▾` on any toolbar.

   b. Select **Add or Remove Buttons** ......................... `A`

2. Click **Customize** ................. `C`
3. Click **Options** tab ........ `Alt`+`O`
4. Select **Large Icons** check box .................... `Alt`+`L`

   ✓ *Icons size changes immediately on-screen.*

5. Click **Close** to close dialog box, leaving icons large.... `Enter`

   OR

   a. Deselect **Large Icons** check box............... `Alt`+`L`

   b. Click **Close** ................ `Enter`

### Create a new toolbar:

1. Click **Tools**.................. `Alt`+`T`

   OR

   Right-click any toolbar.

   OR

   a. Click **View** .............. `Alt`+`V`

   b. Click **Toolbars** .............. `T`

   OR

   a. Click **Toolbar Options** button `▾` on any toolbar.

b. Select **Add or Remove**
   **Buttons** ........................... Ⓐ

2. Click **Customize** ................. Ⓒ

3. Click **Toolbars** tab ....... Ⓐⓛⓣ+Ⓑ

4. Click **New** ..................... Ⓐⓛⓣ+Ⓝ

5. Type toolbar name.

6. Click **OK** ........................... Enter

   ✓ *New toolbar is displayed as*
   *floating palette on-screen; you*
   *can move it or dock it.*

7. Follow steps to add buttons to
   a toolbar.

**Delete a custom toolbar:**

1. Click **Tools** ................. Ⓐⓛⓣ+Ⓣ

   OR

   Right-click any toolbar.

   OR

   a. Click **View** ............. Ⓐⓛⓣ+Ⓥ

   b. Click **Toolbars** .............. Ⓣ

   OR

   a. Click **Toolbar Options**
      button on any toolbar.

   b. Select **Add or Remove**
      **Buttons** ......................... Ⓐ

2. Click **Customize** ................. Ⓒ

3. Click **Toolbars** tab ...... Ⓐⓛⓣ+Ⓑ

4. Select toolbar to delete.

5. Click **Delete** ............... Ⓐⓛⓣ+Ⓓ

6. Click **OK** ........................ Enter

7. Click **Close** .................... Enter

# Exercise Directions

1. Start Word, if necessary.

2. Open ⌨**SALE** or open 💿**22SALE**.

3. Save the document as **SALEREV**.

4. Add a button for opening the Symbol dialog
   box to the Standard toolbar.

   a. Open the Customize dialog box.

   b. Click the Commands tab.

   c. Select the Insert category

   d. Drag the Insert Symbol button Ω on to the
      Standard toolbar.

5. Create a new toolbar named **Font Effects**.

6. Add the following buttons to the new toolbar

   a. Word Underline Ⓦ.

   b. Small Caps ᴀʙᴄ.

   c. Changing case ᴀᴀₐ.

   d. Opening the Font dialog box Ⓐ.

7. Dock the toolbar at the top of your screen.

8. Follow the steps below to create the document
   shown in Illustration A.

   a. Insert the Wingdings symbol of a bell (#37) at
      the beginning of the first line of text. Size the
      symbol to 72 points and adjust the character
      spacing position to raise the symbol by 8 points.

   b. Apply Small Caps formatting to the store name
      on the first line, format the entire line (including
      the symbol) with a Shadow text effect and
      change the font color to Sea Green.

   c. Apply a Word Only underline in Sea Green to
      the second line of text.

   d. Move the three lines of text that comprise the
      store address to follow the second occurrence of

the store name, replacing the text **Flowers,**
**Plants, and More**

e. Change the text **ANNUAL SUMMER**
   **CLEARANCE SALE** to title case, in regular
   (no bold or italic) 22-point Jokerman font.

f. Insert ten of the Wingdings symbol of a flower
   (#123) on the line below the text **Annual**
   **Summer Clearance Sale**. Size the symbols
   to 26 points, change the font color to Orange,
   and center the line horizontally.

   ✓ *If you do not have the Wingdings font set, select*
   *a comparable symbol from one of the other font*
   *sets.*

g. Horizontally center the paragraph beginning
   **Take advantage of special savings...**

h. Select the four sale items and change the left
   tab from 1" to .5".

i. Apply a solid underline to each sale item name.

j. Insert the Webdings symbol of a bouquet of
   flowers (#90) to the left of each sale item. Size
   the symbols to 36 points and change the font
   color to Sea Green.

k. Copy the line of symbols you inserted in
   step f and paste it on the blank line below the
   last sale item.

l. Change the second occurrence of the store
   name to 28 points, Small Caps, Shadow, in
   Sea Green.

m. Insert the Wingdings symbol of a bell (#37) at
   the beginning of the second occurrence of the
   store name. Size the symbol to 36 points, and
   adjust the character spacing position to raise the
   symbol by 8 points.

9. Move the Insert Symbol button from the Standard toolbar to the new Font Effects toolbar.

10. Hide the Font Effects toolbar.

11. Check the spelling and grammar in the document.

12. Display the document in Print Preview. It should look similar to Illustration A. If necessary, adjust the line spacing.

13. Print the document.

14. Close the document, saving the changes.

15. Exit Word.

*Illustration A*

## Liberty Blooms

*Flowers, Plants, And More*

Announcing the

### Annual Summer Clearance Sale

Take advantage of special savings on everything in the store, including the following items:

Topiaries ........................................$9.95 and up

Bonsai Trees..............................$24.99 and up

Hanging Planters ........................$10.00 and up

Dried Floral Arrangements .......$7.50 and up

 Liberty Blooms

345 Chestnut Street
Philadelphia, PA 19106
Phone: (215) 555-2837

*Liberty Blooms conducts free classes and seminars on a wide range of topics. For a complete schedule give us a call, or look us up on-line at www.libertyblooms.net.*

# On Your Own

1. Open the document **OWD21**, the document you created in Exercise 21, or open ⊘ **22INVITE**.

2. Save the document as **OWD22**.

3. Create a new custom toolbar that you can use to format documents. For example, create an Underlining toolbar that includes buttons for applying different types of underlines.

4. Use the buttons on the toolbar to format the document.

5. Use symbols to enhance the document. For example, use symbols as separators between words or paragraphs, or use them to decorate or emphasize the document.

6. Try different symbol fonts.

7. Try changing the font size for a symbol inserted in a document.

8. Try repeating a symbol to create a line across the page.

9. Check the spelling in the document.

10. Preview and print the document.

11. Ask a classmate to review the document and offer suggestions and comments.

12. Incorporate the suggestions into the document.

13. Close the document, saving all changes.

# Exercise 23

## Skills Covered:

### ◆ Bulleted Lists ◆ Numbered Lists ◆ Sort

## On the Job

Lists are an effective way to present items of information. Use a bulleted list when the items do not have to be in any particular order, like a grocery list or a list of objectives. Use a numbered list when the order of the items is important, such as directions or instructions. Use Sort to organize a list into alphabetical or numerical order.

As the Manager of a StyleEyes eyewear franchise, you want to make sure employees understand the proper check-in procedure for customers. In this exercise, you will edit and format a memo document using a bulleted list and a numbered list. You will also sort the bulleted list into alphabetical order.

## Terms

**Bullet** A dot or symbol that marks an important line of information or designates items in a list.

**Sort** To organize items into a specified order.

## Notes

### Bulleted Lists

- Use **bullets** to mark lists when the order of items does not matter.
- Word has seven built-in bullet symbols.
- The default bullet symbol is a simple black dot, indented .25" from the left margin. The symbol is followed by a .5" left tab, and the text on subsequent lines is indented to .5".
- You can create a customized bullet by changing the font and/or paragraph formatting of one of the built-in bullet styles, or by selecting a different bullet symbol.
- Once you apply a bullet style, that style becomes the default until you apply a different one.
- Word automatically carries bullet formatting forward to new paragraphs in a list.

*Select a bullet style in the*
*Bullets and Numbering dialog box*

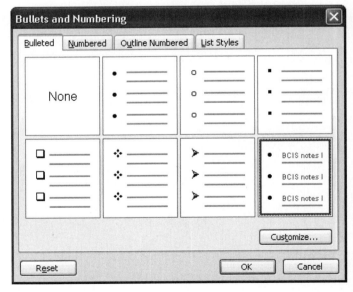

## Numbered Lists

- Use numbers to mark lists when the order of items matters, such as with directions or how-to steps.

- Word automatically renumbers a list when you add or delete items.

- Word comes with seven numbering styles, but the default numbering style is an arabic numeral followed by a period.

- You can select a different number style in the Bullets and Numbering dialog box or customize the formatting to create a new style.

- Word automatically carries number formatting forward to new paragraphs in a list.

- You can restart numbering in the middle of a list.

*Select a number style in the*
*Bullets and Numbering dialog box*

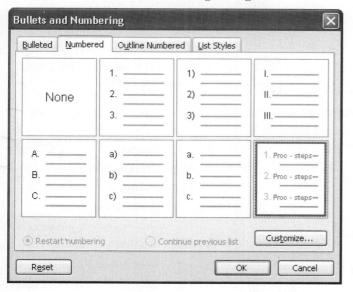

## Sort

- Word can automatically **sort** items into alphabetical, numerical, or chronological order.

- A sort can be ascending (A to Z or 0 to 9) or descending (Z to A or 9 to 0).

- The default sort order is alphabetical (ascending).

- Although the Sort command is on the Table menu, sorting is useful for arranging lists, paragraphs, or rows of regular text as well as in a table.

# Procedures

## Create Bulleted List

### Use the default bullet:

1. Position insertion point where you want to start list.
   OR
   Select paragraphs you want in the list.
2. Click **Bullets** button 🗒️.

### Select a different bullet:

1. Position insertion point where you want to start list.
   OR
   Select paragraphs you want in the list.
2. Click **F**ormat ............... `Alt`+`O`
3. Click **Bullets and Numbering** ........................... `N`
4. Click **B**ulleted page tab ..................... `Alt`+`B`
5. Click desired bullet style ...... `↓`, `↑`, `→`, `←`
6. Click **OK** ........................... `Enter`

### Use a symbol as a bullet:

1. Position insertion point where you want to start list.
   OR
   Select paragraphs you want in list.
2. Click **F**ormat ............... `Alt`+`O`
3. Click **Bullets and Numbering** ........................ `N`
4. Click **B**ulleted tab ....... `Alt`+`B`
5. Click desired bullet style ...... `↓`, `↑`, `→`, `←`
6. Click **Cus**t**omize** ......... `Alt`+`T`
7. Click **C**haracter .................. `C`
8. Click desired symbol .... `Tab`, `↓`, `↑`, `→`, `←`
   - ✓ *You may select any symbol from any font set. Refer to Exercise 22 for more information.*
9. Click **OK** ........................... `Enter`
10. Click **OK** ........................... `Enter`

### Use a picture as a bullet:

1. Position insertion point where you want to start list.
   OR
   Select paragraphs you want in list.
2. Click **F**ormat ............... `Alt`+`O`
3. Click **Bullets and Numbering** ........................... `N`
4. Click **B**ulleted page tab ..................... `Alt`+`B`
5. Click desired bullet style ....... `↓`, `↑`, `→`, `←`
6. Click **Cus**t**omize** .......... `Alt`+`T`
7. Click **P**icture ..................... `P`
8. Click desired picture ..... `Tab`, `↓`, `↑`, `→`, `←`
9. Click **OK** ........................... `Enter`
10. Click **OK** ........................... `Enter`

### Customize bullet formatting:

1. Position insertion point where you want to start list.
   OR
   Select paragraphs you want in list.
2. Click **F**ormat ............... `Alt`+`O`
3. Click **Bullets and Numbering** ........................... `N`
4. Click **B**ulleted page tab ..................... `Alt`+`B`
5. Click desired bullet style ....... `↓`, `↑`, `→`, `←`
6. Click **Cus**t**omize** .......... `Alt`+`T`
7. Click **I**ndent **a**t ...................... `A`
8. Type value to set bullet indent.
9. Click **Ta**b **space after** .. `Alt`+`B`
10. Type value to set left tab following bullet.
11. Click **I**ndent at ............. `Alt`+`I`
12. Type value to set text indent.
13. Click **F**ont ................... `Alt`+`F`
14. Select font formatting options.

15. Click **OK** ........................... `Enter`
16. Click **OK** ........................... `Enter`

### Turn off bullets:

- Click **Bullets** button 🗒️.
   - ✓ *To remove existing bullets, select bulleted list then click Bullets button.*

## Create Numbered List

### Use default number style:

1. Position insertion point where you want to start list.
   OR
   Select paragraphs you want in list.
2. Click **Numbering** button 🗒️.

### Select different number style:

1. Position insertion point where you want to start list.
   OR
   Select paragraphs you want in list.
2. Click **F**ormat ............... `Alt`+`O`
3. Click **Bullets and Numbering** ........................ `N`
4. Click **N**umbered page tab ..................... `Alt`+`N`
5. Click number style ............... `↓`, `↑`, `→`, `←`
6. Click **OK** ........................... `Enter`

### Turn off numbering:

- Click **Numbering** button 🗒️.
   - ✓ *To remove numbers, select numbered list, then click Numbering button.*

### Customize a numbered list:

1. Position insertion point where you want to start list.
   OR
   Select paragraphs you want in list.
2. Click **F**ormat ............... `Alt`+`O`
3. Click **Bullets and Numbering** ........................ `N`

4. Click **Numbered**
   page tab......................`Alt`+`N`
5. Click number
   style ..............`↓`, `↑`, `→`, `←`
6. Click **Customize**..........`Alt`+`T`
7. Set desired options:
   - Click **Number**
     **format**...................`Alt`+`O`
     to type a different character.
   - Click **Font**...............`Alt`+`F`
     to change font formatting.
   - Click **Number**
     **style** ......................`Alt`+`N`
     to select a different style
     from drop-down list.
   - Click **Start at**..........`Alt`+`S`
     to enter the number to
     start at.
   - Click **Number**
     **position**.................`Alt`+`U`
     to select location of the
     number in relation to
     the text.
   - Click **Aligned at** .....`Alt`+`A`
     to enter the horizontal
     location at which to align
     the number.
   - Click **Tab space**
     **after**.......................`Alt`+`B`
     to enter the tab stop setting
     between the number and
     the text.
   - Click **Indent at**.......`Alt`+`I`
     to enter an indent setting
     for text.
8. Click **OK**...................`Enter`
9. Click **OK**...................`Enter`

**Restart numbering in a list:**
1. Right-click number in list.
2. Click **Restart Numbering**....`R`

OR
1. Position insertion point in
   numbered paragraph.
2. Click **Format**...............`Alt`+`O`

3. Click **Bullets and**
   **Numbering** ........................`N`
4. Click **Numbered**
   page tab ....................`Alt`+`N`
5. Click **Restart numbering**
   option button...............`Alt`+`R`
6. Click **OK** .........................`Enter`

**Continue a previous list:**
1. Right-click number.
2. Click **Continue**
   **Numbering** ........................`C`

OR
1. Position insertion point in
   numbered paragraph.
2. Click **Format** ..............`Alt`+`O`
3. Click **Bullets and**
   **Numbering** ........................`N`
4. Click **Numbered**
   page tab ....................`Alt`+`N`
5. Click **Continue previous**
   **list** option button .........`Alt`+`C`
6. Click **OK** .........................`Enter`

## Quickly Change Formatting of Number or Bullets in a List
1. Click first number or bullet.
   - ✓ *All numbers or bullets appear shaded.*
2. Select desired formatting.
   - ✓ *For example, select a new color or size.*

## Reset Customized Bullets or Numbers to Default Formatting
1. Position insertion point in
   formatting list.
   OR
   Select paragraphs in list.
2. Click **Format** ..............`Alt`+`O`
3. Click **Bullets and**
   **Numbering** ........................`N`

4. Click **Numbered**
   page tab ....................`Alt`+`N`
   OR
   Click **Bulleted** page
   tab ..........................`Alt`+`B`
5. Click style
   to reset ................`↓``↑``→``←`
6. Click **Reset** ...............`Alt`+`E`
7. Click **Yes**.........................`Y`
8. Click **OK**.........................`Enter`

## Sort a List

**Use default sort order:**
1. Select the paragraphs you
   want sorted.
2. Click **Table**.................`Alt`+`A`
3. Click **Sort**..........................`S`
4. Click **OK**..........................`Enter`

**Use a numerical or chronological sort:**
1. Select the paragraphs you
   want sorted.
2. Click **Table**.................`Alt`+`A`
3. Click **Sort**..........................`S`
4. Click **Type**
   drop-down arrow .........`Alt`+`Y`
5. Click **Number**...........`↓`, `Enter`
   OR
   Click **Date** ................`↓`, `Enter`
6. Click **OK**..........................`Enter`

**Reverse the sort order:**
1. Select the paragraphs you
   want sorted.
2. Click **Table**.................`Alt`+`A`
3. Click **Sort**..........................`S`
4. Click **Descending** .......`Alt`+`D`
5. Click **OK**..........................`Enter`

# Exercise Directions

1. Start Word, if necessary.
2. Open ⊚ **23CHECKIN**.
3. Save the document as **CHECKIN**.
4. Set fonts, font sizes, tabs, and alignments as shown in Illustration A.
   - ✓ *Use the default 12 point Times New Roman unless otherwise marked.*
5. Insert the symbol as shown.
6. Apply the default numbering style to the five items in the first list.
7. Select a different number style.
8. Change back to the default number style.
9. Apply the default bullet style to the five items in the second list.
10. Change the bullet to the one shown in the Illustration.
11. Sort the bulleted list into ascending alphabetical order.
12. Check the spelling and grammar in the document.
13. Display the document in Print Preview. It should look similar to the one in the illustration.
14. Print the document.
15. Close the document, saving all changes.
16. Exit Word.

# On Your Own

1. Create a new document in Word.
2. Save the file as **OWD23**.
3. Type a bulleted list of five things you'd like to accomplish in the next year. These can be goals for school, work, or personal development. Examples might include earning a better grade in math, completing a project on the job, or getting in better shape by exercising and eating right.
4. Sort the list in alphabetical order.
5. Using a different font, type a numbered list that includes at least five steps describing how you expect to accomplish one of the items in the bulleted list.
6. Change the sort order of the bulleted list to descending order.
7. Resort the list back into ascending order.
8. Save the changes and then print the document.
9. Ask a classmate to review the document and make suggestions and comments.
10. Incorporate the suggestions and comments into the document.
11. Save your changes, close the document, and exit Word.

*Illustration A*

*Arial,*
*centered*

# StyleEyes —— 28 points

## "Fashion Eyewear at Affordable Prices" —— 18 points

### 754 Erieside Avenue 👁 Cleveland, Ohio 44114 —— 14 points

*Webdings symbol # 78*

# MEMO —— *24-point*
*Arial*

To:            All employees
From:        Your Name          } *Left tab at 1"*
Date:         Today's date
Re:            Customer Check-in

I would like to make sure we are all on the same page when it comes to customer check-in. This is a very important procedure, because it is our initial contact with most customers, and we want to make sure that the experience is a positive one. If you are working the front desk, please use the following steps when greeting all customers:

1. Ask the customer how you may help him or her.
2. If the customer has an appointment, check the name of the appointment list. Otherwise, enter the name on the waiting list.
3. Ask the customer to fill out the registration form.
4. Notify the appropriate employee that the customer has arrived.
5. Ask the customer to have a seat until he or she is called.

*Numbered list*

Of course, there may be situations when you must deviate from the above steps. Just remember the following points and everyone should be satisfied:

➢ A customer in person has priority over a phone call.
➢ Be cheerful.
➢ Listen carefully to what the customer has to say.
➢ The customer is always right.
➢ When in doubt, call the manager.

*Bullet list in alphabetical order*

I appreciate your cooperation with the customer check-in procedure. If you have any questions, please contact me.

# Exercise 24

## Skills Covered:

◆ **Apply Styles** ◆ **Create a Style**
◆ **Modify a Style** ◆ **Reapply Direct Formatting**
◆ **Check Formatting** ◆ **Clear Formatting**

## On the Job

Word provides many ways to apply and remove formatting in documents. Use styles to apply a collection of formatting settings to characters or paragraphs. Styles help ensure continuity in formatting throughout a document. You can also set Word to check for formatting inconsistencies in much the same way it checks for spelling and grammatical errors.

As the owner of Liberty Blooms, a flower shop, you want to distribute a document listing classes you are offering in the coming months. In this exercise, you will use styles and direct formatting to apply consistent formatting to the document.

## Terms

**Style** A collection of formatting settings that can be applied to characters or paragraphs.

**Style sheet** A list of available styles.

**Direct formatting** Individual font or paragraph formatting settings applied directly to text, as opposed to a collection of settings applied with a style.

## Notes

### Apply Styles

- **Styles** make it easy to apply a collection of formatting settings to characters or paragraphs all at once.

- Word includes built-in styles for formatting body text, headings, lists, and other parts of documents.

- Different Word templates have different **style sheets** depending on formatting required for the document.

  ✓ *To see the list of all available styles press and hold Shift and click the Style drop-down arrow on the Formatting toolbar.*

*The Style list for the Normal template style sheet*

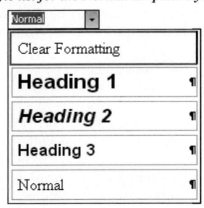

- You can apply a style to existing text, or select a style before you type new text.
- You can select a style from the drop-down style list on the Formatting toolbar or from the Styles and Formatting task pane.
- By default, the Styles and Formatting task pane displays a list of styles in use in the current document. You can select to display all available styles (styles attached to the style sheet even if they are not in use), or all styles attached to all style sheets. You can also customize the style list if you want.
- The styles are listed alphabetically in both the drop-down style list and the Styles and Formatting task pane.

*The Styles and Formatting task pane*

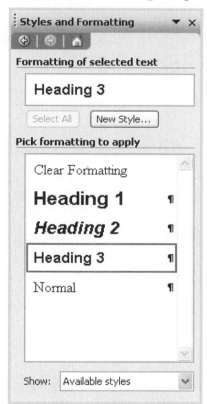

## Create a Style

- You can create new styles for formatting your documents.
- Styles can contain font and/or paragraph formatting.
- Style names should be short and descriptive.
- The style will be added to the style sheet for the current document.

## Modify a Style

- You can modify an existing style.
- When you modify a style that has already been applied to text in the document, the formatted text automatically changes to the new style.
- If you modify a style and give it a new name, it becomes a new style; the original style remains unchanged.

## Reapply Direct Formatting

- By default, Word keeps track of **direct formatting** that you apply to text or paragraphs.
- When you apply direct formatting, Word automatically adds the information to the name of the current style in the Style box on the Formatting toolbar.
- The direct formatting is also added to the Style drop-down list and to the list of available formatting in the Styles and Formatting task pane.
- For example, if you apply italics to text formatted with the Normal style, Word displays a plus sign followed by the word Italic in the Style list box and the Styles and Formatting task pane.
- You can use the Styles and Formatting task pane or the Style list to reapply direct formatting that you have already used in a document to selected text.
- This feature is similar to the Format Painter, but you do not have to scroll through the document from the formatted text to the text you want to format.
- You can disable the track formatting option to keep Word from adding direct formatting to the style list.

## Check Formatting

- Use Word's Format Checker to ensure consistent formatting throughout a document.
- As with the spelling and grammar checker, you can have Word check formatting while you work. Word underlines formatting inconsistencies with a wavy blue underline.
- You can ignore the blue lines and keep typing, or you can use a shortcut menu to correct the formatting error.
- The automatic Format Checker is off by default; you must turn it on to use it.
- If the wavy underlines distract you from your work, you can turn off the automatic Format Checker.

## Clear Formatting

- You can quickly remove all formatting from selected text.

- Clearing the formatting from text removes both direct formatting and styles.

- You can clear formatting using the Style list, or the Styles and Formatting task pane.

- After you clear the formatting, text is displayed in the default normal style for the current document. For the default document, that means single spaced 12-point Times New Roman, flush left.

- To quickly remove direct character formatting from selected text, press Ctrl+Spacebar; to remove direct paragraph formatting, press Ctrl+Q.

# Procedures

### Apply a Style

1. Click in the paragraph.
   OR
   Select the text.
2. Click the **Style** drop-down arrow `Normal` on the Formatting toolbar.
3. Select style to apply ............. ↑, ↓, Enter

### Apply a Style Using the Task Pane

1. Click in the paragraph.
   OR
   Select the text.
2. Click the **Styles and Formatting** button 🔠 on the Formatting toolbar.
   OR
   a. Click **Format** .......... Alt+O
   b. Click **Styles and Formatting** .................... S
3. Click style to apply in **Pick formatting to apply** list.
   ✓ If necessary, scroll through the list to find the desired formatting.

### Change the list of Displayed Styles

1. Open the Styles and Formatting task pane.
2. Click **Show:** drop-down arrow.
3. Click desired list:

- **Available formatting** to display all direct formatting in the current style sheet.
- **Formatting in use** to display all direct formatting currently in use in the document.
- **Available styles** to display all styles in the current style sheet.
- **All styles** to display all existing styles.
- **Custom** to open the Format Settings dialog box.
   ✓ Use the options in the Format Settings dialog box to select specific styles and formatting to display.

### Create a Style

**Use the Style drop-down list:**
1. Format text or paragraph.
2. Select formatted text or paragraph.
3. Click in the **Style** box `Normal` on the Formatting toolbar.
4. Type style name.
5. Press **Enter** .................... Enter

**Use the Styles and Formatting task pane:**
1. Format text or paragraph.
2. Select formatted text or paragraph.
3. Open the Styles and Formatting task pane.

4. Click the **New Style** button .
5. Type style name.
6. Select formatting options as desired.
   ✓ Use options displayed in New Style dialog box just as you would use regular formatting options. Click the Format button for more formatting options.
7. Click **OK** .......................... Enter

### Modify a Style

1. Change formatting of text or paragraph formatted with the style.
2. Select modified text or paragraph.
3. Open the Styles and Formatting task pane.
4. Click style to modify.
5. Click **Update to Match Selection** ......... Alt+U
   OR
   a. Click **Modify** .......... Alt+M
   b. Select formatting options as desired.
      ✓ Use options displayed in Modify Style dialog box just as you would use regular formatting options. Click the Format button for more formatting options.
   c. Click **OK** ....................

## Reapply Direct Formatting

1. Click in the paragraph.
   OR
   Select the text.
2. Click the **Style** drop-down
   arrow `Normal ▾` on the
   Formatting toolbar.
   OR
   Open the Styles and
   Formatting task pane.
3. Click direct formatting to apply.
   ✓ *If necessary, scroll through the
   list to find the desired formatting.*

## Disable the Track Formatting Option

1. Click **Tools** ................. `Alt`+`T`
2. Click **Options** ..................... `O`
3. Click the **Edit** tab ....... `Ctrl`+`Tab`
4. Deselect **Keep track
   of formatting**
   check box..................... `Alt`+`K`
   ✓ *A checkmark indicates the
   option is selected.*
5. Click **OK**.......................... `Enter`

## Turn on Automatic Format Checking

1. Click **Tools** ................. `Alt`+`T`
2. Click **Options** ..................... `O`
3. Click the **Edit** tab ........ `Ctrl`+`Tab`
4. Select **Keep track
   of formatting**
   check box. ................... `Alt`+`K`
   ✓ *A checkmark indicates this
   option is already selected.*
5. Select **Mark formatting
   inconsistencies**
   check box ................... `Alt`+`F`
6. Click **OK** .......................... `Enter`

## Check Formatting as You Type

1. Right-click formatting
   inconsistency marked with
   blue, wavy underline.
2. Click desired correct formatting
   option on shortcut menu.
   OR
   Click **Ignore Once** to
   hide this occurrence ............ `I`
   OR
   Click **Ignore Rule** to
   hide all occurrences ............ `U`

## Clear Formatting

1. Select text.
2. Click the **Style** drop-down
   arrow `Normal ▾` on the
   Formatting toolbar.
   OR
   Open the Styles and
   Formatting task pane.
3. Select **Clear
   Formatting** ........`↑`, `↓`, `Enter`
   ✓ *Clear Formatting is usually
   found at the top of the drop-
   down Style list or at the top of
   the alphabetical list of styles in
   the Pick formatting to apply list.*

# Exercise Directions

1. Start Word, if necessary.

2. Open ⊙**24CLASSES**.

3. Save the document as **CLASSES**.

4. Enable the formatting checker and make sure that Word is set to track formatting.

5. Format the store name in 36-point Jokerman, centered. If Jokerman is not available on your system, select a different decorative font.

   ✓ *Notice the direct formatting is displayed in the Style box on the Formatting toolbar. If the Styles and Formatting task pane is open, you see the direct formatting displayed there as well.*

6. Create a new style based on the formatted store name. Name the style **Liberty**.

7. Apply the new Liberty style to the text **Class Schedule**.

8. Change the font size of the text **Class Schedule** to 24 points.

9. Apply the Heading 3 style to the store address.

10. Center the store address and apply a solid underline.

11. Reapply the Heading 3 + Centered + Underline direct formatting to the names of the classes.

12. Apply the Heading 2 style to names of the months.

13. Format the paragraph describing the Flower Arranging class in 12-point Comic Sans MS.

14. Create a style named **Class** based on the formatting of the class description.

15. Select the paragraph describing the class All About Herbs and change the formatting to 12 point Comic Sans MS.

    ✓ *Notice that Word displays the wavy blue underline indicating a problem with the paragraph formatting.*

16. Right-click the paragraph and select the option to replace direct formatting with the Class style.

17. Apply the Class style to the paragraph describing the Perennial Garden Design class.

18. Modify the Class style to justify the horizontal alignment.

    ✓ *Notice that all of the paragraphs formatted with the style are updated to reflect the change.*

19. Move the insertion point to the end of the document and press Enter twice to leave a blank line.

20. Clear all formatting from the new line, then type **Space is limited for all classes and seminars. For more information or to register, call 215-555-2837 or visit our Web site www.libertyblooms.net.**

21. Check the spelling and grammar in the document.

22. Display the document in Print Preview. It should look similar to the one in Illustration A.

23. Print the document.

24. Close the file, saving all changes.

*Illustration A*

# Liberty Blooms —— *Liberty style*

*Heading 3 +*
*Underline,* —— **345 Chestnut Street, Philadelphia, PA 19106**
*Centered*

# Class Schedule —— *Liberty + 24 points*

## *January* —— *Heading 2 style*

### Introduction to Flower Arranging —— *Heading 3 + Underline, Centered*

*Class style* { Brighten up the winter doldrums with a lesson on flower arranging! We'll work with a variety of cut flowers such as daisies, irises, and roses as well as greenery and accent stems to create beautiful bouquets. This entry-level class is open to everyone.

## *February* —— *Heading 2 style*

### All About Herbs —— *Heading 3 + Underline, Centered*

*Class style* { Get ready for spring with a fun-filled class all about herbs! We'll learn about the types of herbs that are easy to grow indoors and out, how to identify herbs by appearance and smell, and how to use fresh and dried herbs in a variety of ways. For example, we might use herbs to scent a sachet, or to flavor a pot of stew.

## *March* —— *Heading 2 style*

### Perennial Garden Design —— *Heading 3 + Underline, Centered*

*Class style* { A successful perennial garden enhances blooms all season long, year after year. This seminar will cover the basics of planning a perennial garden. Learn how to determine the amount of space you need, how to lay out the garden, and how to select the right types of plants. Time permitting, we will discuss soil composition and planting techniques.

Space is limited for all classes and seminars. For more information or to register, call } *Normal style* 215-555-2837 or visit our Web site www.libertyblooms.net.

# On Your Own

1. Open **OWD23**, the document you created in the On Your Own section of Exercise 23, or open 📀**24GOALS**.

2. Save the document as **OWD24**.

3. Clear all formatting from the document.

4. Use styles to format the document. You can use existing styles, modify existing styles, or create new styles.

5. Apply some direct formatting for emphasis, then reapply the formatting to other text in the document.

6. Check the spelling, grammar, and formatting in the document.

7. Save changes and then print the document.

8. Ask a classmate to review the document and offer comments and suggestions.

9. Incorporate the suggestions into the document.

10. Close the document, saving all changes, and exit Word.

# Exercise 25

Now that you have learned more about how to format document text, you can create a more elaborate flyer advertising the grand opening of the Cleveland StyleEyes. In this exercise, you will type and format a new flyer, including font effects, text effects, underlines, color, styles, symbols, and lists.

## Exercise Directions

1. Start Word, if necessary.
2. Create a new document.
3. Save the document as **NEWAD**.
4. Use the following steps to type and format the document shown in Illustration A.
5. Center the first line and type the word **Announcing** in red, 16-point Wide Latin font, or a font that is similar to Wide Latin.
6. Select the text and create a style named **StyleEyes Subtitle**.
7. On the second line, also centered, type **StyleEyes'** using the same font in Blue, 36 points.
8. Select the text and create a style named **StyleEyes Title**.
9. On the third line, apply the StyleEyes Subtitle style and type **Grand Opening Sale!**.
10. Select the text and apply a wave underline.
11. Press Enter twice to leave a blank line and clear all formatting from the new line.
12. Flush left, in black 16-point Comic Sans MS or a similar font, type **Huge savings on our full line of Fashion Eyewear and Accessories including:**.
13. Create the bullet list shown in the illustration, using 18-point Comic Sans MS in Blue: **Sunglasses, Eyeglass holders, Clip-ons, Cleaning solutions, Goggles, Eyeglass cases**.
14. Customize the bullet marker using an appropriate symbol (Webdings #78 is used in the illustration).
15. Increase the size of the bullet so it is clearly visible in the document.
16. Sort the list into ascending alphabetical order.
17. Leave a blank line—clearing all formatting— and then, using the same formatting as in step 12, type **Additional savings on:**.
18. Create the second bullet list shown in the illustration, using a right tab with dot leaders to align the text at the end of each line.
    - ✓ *Use the same formatting as the previous list, or copy the formatting from the previous list to the new list.*
19. Leave a blank line—clearing all formatting— and then type **Subscribe to our mailing list!**.
20. Copy the formatting from the third line of the document to the new text.
21. Type the numbered list shown in the illustration, using 18-point Comic Sans MS in Blue. You may have to clear all formatting from the new line, first.
22. On the next line, use the StyleEyes Title style to format the text **StyleEyes**.
23. Use the StyleEyes Subtitle style to type the slogan and address shown in the illustration.
24. Modify the font size of the slogan and address to 12 points.
25. Preview the document. It should look similar to Illustration A. If necessary, use Shrink to Fit to make the document fit on a single page.
26. Print the document.
27. Save the document and close it.
28. Exit Word.

# Announcing

# StyleEyes'

## Grand Opening Sale!

Huge savings on our full line of Fashion Eyewear and Accessories, including:

- Cleaning solutions
- Clip-ons
- Eyeglass cases
- Eyeglass holders
- Goggles
- Sunglasses

Additional savings on:

- Designer frames ............................ all types
- Colored contact lenses ................. all colors
- Eye exams.........................new patients only

## Subscribe to our mailing list!

1) Stop in.
2) Sign our guest register.
3) Receive notification of special savings and promotions via e-mail or snail mail.

# StyleEyes

**"Fashion Eyewear at Affordable Prices"**
**754 Erieside Avenue**
**Cleveland, OH 44114**
**216-555-1228**

# Lesson 5

## Document Formatting

# Exercise 26

## On the Job

Format documents using the right amount of space between lines, paragraphs, and words to make the pages look better and the text easier to read. Use indents to call attention to a paragraph, to achieve a particular visual effect, or to leave white space along the margins for notes or illustrations.

Potential students have been asking about the instructors for the classes sponsored by Liberty Blooms. In this exercise, you will use line spacing, paragraph spacing, and indents to format a document that includes information about the classes and the instructors.

## Terms

**Line spacing** The amount of white space between lines of text in a paragraph.

**Leading** Line spacing measured in points.

**Paragraph spacing** The amount of white space between paragraphs.

**Indent** A left and/or right margin for lines or paragraphs.

## Notes

### Line Spacing

- **Line spacing** sets the amount of vertical space between lines. By default, line spacing in Word is set to single space. Line spacing can be measured in either lines (single, double, etc.) or in points.

- When line spacing is measured in points, it is sometimes called **leading** (pronounced *ledding*).

> By default, Word uses leading that is 120% of the current font size. For a 10-point font, that means 12-point leading. This paragraph is formatted with the default leading for a 12-point font (14.4 pts.).

> Increase leading to make text easier to read. In this paragraph, the font is still 12 points, but the leading has been increased to exactly 16 points.

> Decrease leading to fit more lines on a page. In this paragraph, the leading has been set to exactly 10 points, while the font size is still 12 points. Keep in mind that decreasing leading makes text harder to read.

✓ *You should never decrease leading so much that the text is difficult to read, as shown above.*

- Line spacing measured in lines can be set to single spaced, 1.5 spaced, or double spaced.

- Set line spacing using options in the Paragraph dialog box.

*The Paragraph dialog box*

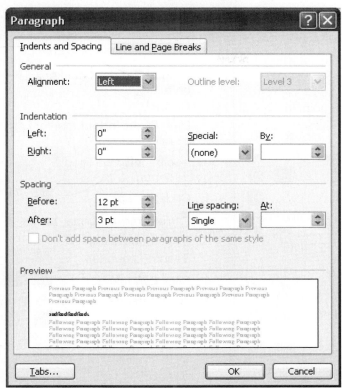

## Paragraph Spacing

- **Paragraph spacing** can affect space before or after paragraphs.
- The amount of space can be specified in lines or in points. The default is points.
- Use increased paragraph spacing in place of extra returns or blank lines.
- Set paragraph spacing using options in the Paragraph dialog box.

## Indent Text

- There are five types of **indents**:
  - *Left* indents text from the left margin.
  - *Right* indents text from the right margin.
  - *Double* indents text from both the left and right margins.
  - *First line* indents just the first line of a paragraph from the left margin.
  - *Hanging* indents all lines but the first line from the left margin.
- Indent markers on the horizontal ruler show where current indents are set.
- Set indents using options in the Paragraph dialog box or the indent markers on the horizontal ruler.

*Indents in a document*

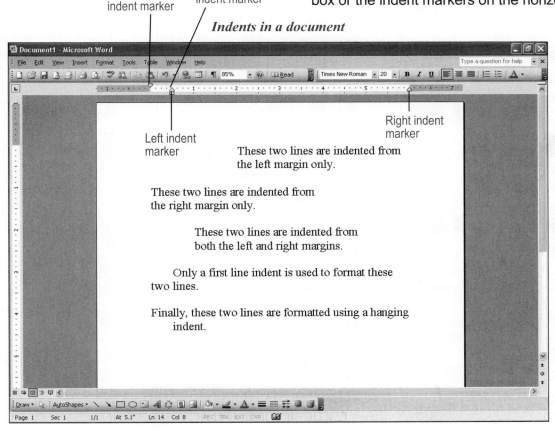

# Procedures

## Set Line Spacing
### *(Ctrl+1, Ctrl+2, Ctrl+5)*

1. Position insertion point where text will be typed.

   OR

   Position insertion point in paragraph to change.

   OR

   Select paragraphs to change.

2. Click **Line Spacing** button [↕≡] drop-down arrow on Formatting toolbar.

3. Click desired spacing option.

   ✓ *Click More to open the Paragraph dialog box.*

OR

1. Position insertion point where text will be typed.

   OR

   Position insertion point in paragraph to change.

   OR

   Select paragraphs to change.

2. Click **F**o**rmat**............... [Alt]+[O]

3. Click **P**aragraph ................. [P]

4. Click **I**ndents and **Spacing** page tab ....... [Alt]+[I]

5. Click **Li**n**e** spacing ..... [Alt]+[N]

6. Select a line spacing option:.......... [↓], [Enter]
   - Single
   - 1.5 lines
   - Double

   OR

   a. Select leading option................... [↓], [Enter]
      - **At least** to set a minimum leading.
      - **Exactly** to set an exact leading.
      - **Multiple** to specify a number of times to increase leading.

   b. Click **A**t box ........... [Alt]+[A]

   c. Type value in points.

7. Click **OK**........................... [Enter]

## Set Paragraph Spacing

1. Position insertion point where text will be typed.

   OR

   Position insertion point in paragraph to change.

   OR

   Select paragraphs to change.

2. Click **F**o**rmat**............... [Alt]+[O]

3. Click **P**aragraph ................. [P]

   ✓ *To open the Paragraph dialog box quickly, right-click paragraph to format, then click P*aragraph*.*

4. Click **I**ndents and **Spacing** page tab ........ [Alt]+[I]

5. Click **B**e**fore** text box... [Alt]+[B]

   OR

   Click **Af**t**er** text box ...... [Alt]+[E]

6. Type amount of space to leave.

   ✓ *Type li after value to specify lines instead of points.*

7. Click **OK** .......................... [Enter]

## Indent Text

### Indent from the left:

1. Position insertion point where text will be typed.

   OR

   Position insertion point in paragraph to change.

   OR

   Select paragraphs to change.

2. Click **Increase Indent** button [≣→].

   OR

   Click **Decrease Indent** button [≣←].

   OR

   Drag **Left-indent** marker [⧗] on ruler.

### Indent from the left and/or right:

1. Position insertion point where text will be typed.

   OR

   Position insertion point in paragraph to change.

OR

Select paragraphs to change.

2. Drag **Left-indent** marker [⧗] on ruler.

   **AND/OR**

   Drag **Right-indent** marker [△] on ruler.

### Set precise left and/or right indents:

1. Click **F**o**rmat** ............... [Alt]+[O]

2. Click **P**aragraph.................. [P]

3. Click **I**ndents and **Spacing** page tab........ [Alt]+[I]

4. Click **L**eft text box ....... [Alt]+[L]

5. Type distance from left margin.

6. Click **R**ight text box..... [Alt]+[R]

7. Type distance from right margin.

8. Click **OK** ........................... [Enter]

### Indent first line only *(Tab)*:

1. Position insertion point where text will be typed.

   OR

   Position insertion point in paragraph to change.

   OR

   Select paragraphs to change.

2. Drag **First Line indent** marker [▽].

   OR

   a. Click **F**o**rmat** .......... [Alt]+[O]

   b. Click **P**aragraph ............ [P]

   c. Click **I**ndents and Spacing page tab ................ [Alt]+[I]

   d. Click **S**pecial drop-down arrow .... [Alt]+[S]

   e. Click **First line** ..... [↓], [Enter]

   f. Click **B**y text box .... [Alt]+[Y]

   g. Type amount to indent.

   h. Click **OK** ...................... [Enter]

**Insert hanging indent** *(Ctrl+T):*

1. Position insertion point where text will be typed.

   **OR**

   Position insertion point in paragraph to change.

   **OR**

   Select paragraphs to change.

2. Drag **Hanging indent** marker △.

   **OR**

   a. Click **Format** ........... `Alt`+`O`

   b. Click **Paragraph**............. `P`

   c. Click **Indents and Spacing** page tab ................. `Alt`+`I`

   d. Click **Special** drop-down arrow .... `Alt`+`S`

   e. Click **Hanging**...... `↓`, `Enter`

   f. Click **By** text box .... `Alt`+`y`

   g. Type amount to indent.

   h. Click **OK**..................... `Enter`

# Exercise Directions

1. Start Word, if necessary.

2. Create a new document and type the document text shown in Illustration A, or open 💿**26CLASSREV**.

3. Save the document as **CLASSREV**.

4. Format the first four lines as follows:
   - Line 1: Centered, 28-point Jokerman. If you do not have Jokerman on your computer system, select a different decorative font.
   - Line 2. Centered, 12-point Comic Sans MS.
   - Line 3. Centered, 18-point Comic Sans MS, 6 pts. of space before and after.
   - Line 4. 12-point Arial, bold, flush left. Right tab set at 6" to align class name with right margin. Leave 6 pts of space before and after.

5. Justify the description of the Flower Arranging class, and indent it .5" from both the left and right margins.

6. Copy the formatting from line 4 to the other lines with the months and course names.

7. Copy the formatting of the Flower Arranging class description to the other two class descriptions.

8. Copy the formatting from the third line in the document to the heading **Instructors**.

9. Format the list of instructors as follows:
   - Apply an underline to the month names.
   - Align the paragraphs flush left with a hanging indent of .75".
   - ✓ Notice that the tab aligns the instructor information with the hanging indent.
   - Use 1.5 line spacing.

10. Format the final paragraph as follows:
    - Use a first line indent of .5".
    - Double-space the lines.
    - Leave 12 points of space before the paragraph.

11. Check the spelling and grammar in the document.

12. Preview the document. It should look similar to the illustration. If necessary, use Shrink to Fit to make the document fit on a single page.

13. Print the document.

14. Close the document, saving all changes.

# Liberty Blooms

## 345 Chestnut Street Philadelphia, PA 19106

## Training Schedule

**January**                                   **Introduction to Flower Arranging**

Brighten up the winter doldrums with a lesson on flower arranging! We'll work with a variety of cut flowers such as daisies, irises, and roses as well as greenery and accent stems to create beautiful bouquets.

**February**                                              **All About Herbs**

Get ready for spring with a fun-filled class all about herbs! We'll learn about the types of herbs that are easy to grow indoors and out, how to identify herbs by appearance and smell, and how to use fresh and dried herbs in a variety of ways.

**March**                                          **Perennial Garden Design**

This seminar will cover the basics of planning a perennial garden. Learn how to determine the amount of space you need, how to lay out the garden, and how to select the right types of plants.

## Instructors

<u>January:</u>    The instructor for the introductory Flower Arranging class is Mary Beth Longrin. Mary Beth has been an employee of Liberty Blooms for three years. She specializes in centerpieces for special occasions.

<u>February:</u>    Frank Smiley, owner of Smiley's Catering Service, has agreed to lead All About Herbs. Frank uses many home grown herbs in his catering business.

<u>March:</u>    The Perennial Garden Design seminar leader is Vicky Devereaux, the director of the Mid Atlantic Horticultural Association. Vicky is considered an authority on garden planning and design.

Classes are free and open to the public. However, due to the limited space at Liberty Blooms, we must restrict all class sizes. To register, or for more information about these and other events at Liberty Blooms, call 215-555-2837 or visit our Web site www.libertyblooms.net.

# On Your Own

1. Think of some documents that could benefit from line spacing, paragraph spacing, and indent formatting. For example, many instructors require reports and papers to be double spaced. A resume can be set up neatly using spacing and indent features, as can a reference list.

2. Plan a document that will contain brief (one paragraph each) descriptions of three types of technology used in business.

   a. Start by selecting three items, such as software programs, hardware devices, or the Internet.

   b. If necessary, research the items using a library or the Internet so that you have the information you need to write the descriptions.

3. Create a new document in Word.

4. Save the file as **OWD26**.

5. Type a title or headline at the top of the document, and a brief introduction.

6. Type the paragraphs describing each of the three items. Include a definition of each item, and explain its function or purpose. Include information about what tasks the item should be used for. Use proper grammar and punctuation.

7. Format the document using line and paragraph spacing and indents, as well as font formatting, tabs and alignments.

8. Save the changes and print the document.

9. Ask a classmate to review the document and offer comments and suggestions.

10. Incorporate the suggestions into the document.

11. Save your changes, close the document, and exit Word.

# Exercise 27

## Skills Covered:

◆ **Format a One-page Report** ◆ **Set Margins**
◆ **Set Page Orientation** ◆ **Vertical Alignment**

## On the Job

Format a one-page report so that when you print the report it looks good on the page. Set margins to meet expected requirements and to improve the document's appearance and readability. For example, leave a wider margin in a report if you expect a reader to make notes or comments; leave a narrower margin to fit more text on a page. Align text vertically to make the best use of white space and to improve readability.

New clients may want to know the history of a company. In this exercise, you'll create a one-page report providing background information about Blue Sky Dairy Co. The report will be used as part of an information package sent to media outlets and prospective purveyors of Blue Sky Dairy products.

## Terms

**Gutter** Space added to the margin to leave room for binding.

**Margins** The amount of white space between the text and the edge of the page on all four sides.

**Section** In Word, a segment of a document defined by a section break. A section may have different page formatting from the rest of the document.

**Portrait orientation** The default position for displaying and printing text horizontally across the shorter side of a page.

**Landscape orientation** Rotating document text so it displays and prints horizontally across the longer side of a page.

**Vertical alignment** The position of text in relation to the top and bottom page margins.

## Notes

### Format a One-page Report

■ Traditionally, a one-page report is set up as follows:

- The title is positioned 1" from the top of the page.
- The report title is centered and all uppercase.
- Spacing following the title ranges from ¾" (54 pts.) to 1" (72 pts.).
- Unbound reports have left and right margins of 1".
- A **gutter** on bound reports makes the left margin wider than right margin.

✓ *Use the Mirror margins option to set gutter width on inside margin of each page.*

- Text is justified.
- Lines are double spaced.
- First-line indents are .5" or 1".

### Set Margins

- **Margins** are measured in inches.
- Default margins in Word are 1.25" on the left and right and 1" on the top and bottom.
- You can also set a gutter width to leave room for binding multiple pages.

- Margin settings affect an entire document, or the current **section**.
  - ✓ *To set margins for a paragraph that are different from the page margins, use indents as described in Exercise 26.*

- On the rulers, areas outside the margins are shaded gray, while areas inside the margins are white.
  - ✓ *To see both vertical and horizontal rulers, use Print Layout view.*

- Light gray bars mark the margins on the rulers.

- Set margins in the Page Setup dialog box or by dragging the margin markers on the horizontal ruler.

*The Page Setup dialog box*

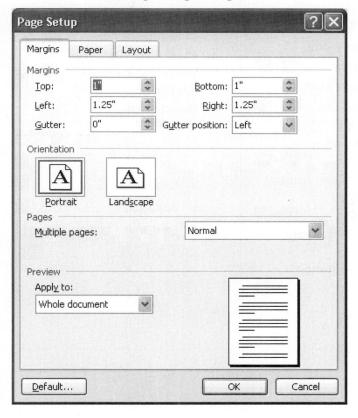

## Set Page Orientation

- There are two page orientations available:
  - **Portrait**
  - **Landscape**

- Portrait is the default orientation and is used for most documents, including letters, memos, and reports.

- Use landscape orientation to display a document across the wider length of the page. For example, if a document contains a table that is wider than the standard 8.5" page, Word will split it across two pages in Portrait mode. When you change to landscape orientation, the table may fit across the 11" page.

- Note that in landscape mode, the default margins are 1" on the left and right and 1.25" on the top and bottom.

- Select page orientation in the Page Setup dialog box.

## Vertical Alignment

- **Vertical alignment** is used to adjust the position of all text on a page in relation to the top and bottom margins.

- There are four vertical alignments:
  - *Top:* Text begins below the top margin. Top is the default vertical alignment.
  - *Center:* Text is centered between the top and bottom margins.
  - *Justified:* Paragraphs are spaced to fill the page between the top and bottom margins.
  - *Bottom:* The last line of text begins just above the bottom margin.

- Centering vertically can improve the appearance of some one-page documents, such as flyers or invitations.

- Vertical justification improves the appearance of documents that contain nearly full pages of text.

- Set vertical alignment on the Layout tab of the Page Setup dialog box.

# Procedures

## Set Margins in Print Layout View

1. Move the mouse pointer over the margin marker on the ruler.

   ✓ *The mouse pointer changes to a double-headed arrow ↔, and the ScreenTip identifies the margin.*

2. Drag the margin marker to new location.

   ✓ *Press and hold the Alt key while you drag to see the margin width.*

## Set Margins in Any View

1. Click **File**...................`Alt`+`F`
2. Click **Page Setup**.................`U`

   ✓ *To quickly open the Page Setup dialog box, double-click on a ruler.*

3. Click **Margins** tab .......`Ctrl`+`Tab`
4. Click **Top** text box........`Alt`+`T`
5. Type top margin width.
6. Click **Bottom** text box........................`Alt`+`B`
7. Type bottom margin width.
8. Click **Left** text box........`Alt`+`L`
9. Type left margin width.
10. Click **Right** text box .....`Alt`+`R`
11. Type right margin width.
12. Click **Gutter** text box ...`Alt`+`G`
13. Type gutter width.
14. Click **Gutter position** drop-down arrow..........`Alt`+`U`
15. Select desired gutter location.
16. Click the **Apply to** drop-down arrow..........`Alt`+`Y`
17. Select **This point forward**.
    OR
    Select **Whole document**.
18. Click **OK** ........................`Enter`

## Set Page Orientation

1. Click **File** .....................`Alt`+`F`
2. Click **Page Setup**...............`U`
3. Click **Margins** tab.......`Ctrl`+`Tab`
4. Click **Portrait**...............`Alt`+`P`
   OR
   Click **Landscape** ........`Alt`+`S`
5. Click **OK** ..........................`Enter`

## Align Vertically

1. Click **File** .....................`Alt`+`F`
2. Click **Page Setup**...............`U`
3. Click **Layout** tab.........`Ctrl`+`Tab`
4. Click **Vertical alignment** .....`Alt`+`V` drop-down arrow.
5. Select **Vertical alignment** option: ...............`↑`, `↓`, `Enter`
   • **Top**...............................`T`
   • **Center**..........................`C`
   • **Justified** ......................`J`
   • **Bottom** .........................`B`
6. Click **OK** ..........................`Enter`

# Exercise Directions

1. Start Word, if necessary.
2. Type the document shown in Illustration A, or open ☞**27DAIRY**.
3. Save the file as **DAIRY**.
4. Use the following steps to format the document as shown in the illustration.
5. Set 1" margins on the top, left, and right and .75" on the bottom.
6. Format the title in 16 point Arial, centered.
7. Change the spacing to leave 1" (72 pts.) of space after the title.
8. Justify and double space all body text paragraphs, and apply a .5" first line indent.
9. Apply the Heading 3 style to the subheadings.
10. Vertically center the document.
11. Check the spelling and grammar.
12. Change the page orientation to Landscape.
13. Display the document in Print Preview. It should extend on to two pages.
14. Print the document.
15. Change the page orientation back to Portrait.
16. Preview the document the again. It should look similar to Illustration A.
17. Print the document.
18. Close the document, saving all changes.
19. Exit Word.

# On Your Own

1. Create a new document in Word.
2. Save the file as **OWD27**.
3. In the third person, draft a one-page report about yourself. For example, draft a document that you could include in a directory for an organization of which you are a member. Think of the *About the Author* paragraphs found in books and magazines, or the *About the Performers* paragraphs found in a theater program.
4. Double space the report.
5. Use correct document formatting for a one-page report.
6. Use other formatting effects, if appropriate, including fonts, styles, lists, and symbols.
7. Adjust the vertical alignment to improve the appearance of the document.
8. Change the orientation to Landscape.
9. Check the spelling and grammar, then save and print the document.
10. Change back to Portrait orientation.
11. Ask a classmate to review the document and offer comments and suggestions.
12. Incorporate the suggestions into the document.
13. Save your changes.
14. Preview and then print the report.
15. Close the document and exit Word.

*1" top margin*

# Blue Sky Dairy Co.

*16-point Arial, centered, 72 pts. after*

*Justified, double spaced, .5" first line indent*

Blue Sky Dairy has been producing quality milk, ice cream, and other dairy products for over 100 years. It is a family-owned farm located in southern Wisconsin, not far from Lake Ripley. In the late 19th century, John and Marie Thomson settled in Wisconsin and started the dairy with a herd of ten cows. Today, Jack and Kimberly Thomson have a thriving business anchored by a herd of 200 pampered Holstein dairy cows.

← *1" right margin*                              *1" right margin* →

## The Facility

Blue Sky Dairy uses a combination of grazing and confinement. Some of the herd is set out to pasture, while some are housed in free stalls. There are two milking parlors and an ice cream manufacturing facility. Ice cream is the only item currently produced on the farm. The dairy has approximately 55 employees in agriculture, manufacturing, distribution, and support services.

*Heading 3*

## The Products

Blue Sky Dairy is famous for its wholesome, refreshing ice cream products, including prepackaged ice cream and novelties. It sells ice cream direct from its farm stand, and also distributes its products to supermarkets and specialty stores throughout the United States. Blue Sky Dairy has won numerous awards for its ice cream and for its environmentally friendly policies.

For more information about Blue Sky Dairy and its products, contact Kimberly or Jack Thomson at 608-555-2697, or visit the Blue Sky Dairy Web site at www.blueskydairy.net.

*.75" bottom margin*

# Exercise 28

## On the Job

Use the AutoFormat feature to automatically apply styles and other common formatting options to a document. AutoFormat can save you time and help insure consistent formatting throughout a document.

The Marketing Director at Blue Sky Dairy has given you a document about Holstein cows that she would like to be able to distribute to dairy visitors and school groups. In this exercise, you will use AutoFormat to format the report.

## Terms

**Em dash (—)**  A symbol that is approximately the width of the typed letter M.

**Straight quotes (")**  Quotation marks that drop straight down instead of curving to the left or right.

**Smart quotes (" ")**  Quotation marks that curve left or right toward enclosed text.

## Notes

### Use AutoFormat

- The AutoFormat feature automatically applies styles such as headings and lists to an entire document.

- In addition, it replaces typed characters with symbols. For example, it replaces a double hyphen with an **em dash** and **straight quotes** with **smart quotes**.

- By default, Word applies formatting for a general document, such as a report, but you can specify formatting for a letter or e-mail message.

- You can also select to mark each change so that you can review them individually using Word's Track Changes feature.

  ✓ *You learn about tracking changes in Exercise 65.*

- Select AutoFormat options on the AutoFormat page of the AutoCorrect dialog box.

  ✓ *Note that if AutoFormat is turned on, it has been automatically applying formatting to your text all along. For example, it may be replacing straight quotation marks with smart—or curved—quotes.*

*The AutoFormat page of the AutoCorrect dialog box*

## AutoFormat As You Type

- You can set Word to automatically format a document as you type.

- When AutoFormat as you type is active, Word applies the selected styles and replaces typed characters with symbols as soon as you enter the text in the document.

- For example, if you type two hyphens, a word, and then press the spacebar, or type two hyphens, press the spacebar, type a word, and then press Enter, Word automatically replaces the hyphens with a dash.

*The AutoFormat As You Type page of the AutoCorrect dialog box*

# Procedures

### Set AutoFormat Options

1. Click **F**ormat .............. `Alt`+`O`
2. Click **A**utoFormat .............. `A`
3. Click **O**ptions .................... `O`

   OR

   a. Click **T**ools ............ `Alt`+`T`
   b. Click **A**utoCorrect
      **O**ptions ......................... `A`
   c. Click **A**utoFormat
      page tab ................ `Ctrl`+`Tab`
4. Click options as desired.

   ✓ *A checkmark in a check box indicates option is selected. Click it to remove the checkmark and deselect the option.*
5. Click **OK** .......................... `Enter`
6. Click **Cancel** ...................... `Esc`

### Use AutoFormat

1. Click **F**ormat .............. `Alt`+`O`
2. Click **A**utoFormat .............. `A`
3. Make sure **AutoFormat now** ................................ `A`
   option button is selected
4. Click **Please select a document type to help improve the Formatting process** drop-down arrow ... `P`
5. Click desired document type ................... `↓`, `↑`, `Enter`
6. Click **OK** ......................... `Enter`

### Turn On AutoFormat as You Type

1. Click **F**ormat ............... `Alt`+`O`
2. Click **A**utoFormat .............. `A`
3. Click **O**ptions .................... `O`

   OR

   a. Click **T**ools ............. `Alt`+`T`
   b. Click **A**utoCorrect
      **O**ptions ......................... `A`
4. Click **AutoFormat As You Type** page tab ............ `Ctrl`+`Tab`
5. Click options as desired.

   ✓ *A checkmark in a check box indicates option is selected. Click it to remove the checkmark and deselect the option.*
6. Click **OK** .......................... `Enter`
7. Click **Cancel** ...................... `Esc`

# Exercise Directions

1. Start Word, if necessary.

2. Open 💿 **28HOLSTEINS**.

3. Save the document as **HOLSTEINS**.

4. Open the AutoFormat page of the AutoCorrect dialog box.

5. Select all available options in the Apply section and the Replace section.

6. Switch to the AutoFormat As You Type page.

7. Make sure the options to replace straight quotes with smart quotes, ordinals with superscript, and hyphens with dashes are selected, and that other options are not selected.

8. Use AutoFormat to format the document.

9. Insert a new line at the end of the document.

10. Type the subhead **Cow Visits** and format it in the Heading 1 style.

11. Start a new line and type the following paragraph:

    **You are welcome to visit the Holsteins at Blue Sky Dairy. Dairy tours are offered the 1st and 3rd Saturdays of each month -- no reservations are required. Stops on each tour include the milking parlor, the barn, and the ice cream manufacturing facility. Tours start at the main visitor's center and conclude at the gift shop.**

12. Notice as you type that Word replaces the ordinal (1st) with superscript ($1^{st}$), the double hyphen (--) with a dash (–), and the straight apostrophe with a smart apostrophe.

13. Change the margins to 1" on all sides.

14. Double-space all Body Text paragraphs.

15. Check the spelling and grammar in the document.

16. Display the document in Print Preview. It should look similar to Illustration A.

17. Print the document.

18. Close the document, saving all changes.

# On Your Own

1. Open **OWD27** the document you created in the On Your Own section of Exercise 27, or open 💿 **28BIO**.

2. Save the document as **OWD28**.

3. Clear all formatting from the document and make sure the vertical alignment is set to Top.

   ✓ *For example, select all text in the document, then select Clear Formatting from the style list. Check the vertical alignment setting in the Page Setup dialog box.*

4. Select all AutoFormat options.

5. Use AutoFormat to format the document.

6. Check the spelling and grammar in the document.

7. Print the document.

8. Ask a classmate to review the document and make suggestions and comments.

9. Incorporate the suggestions and comments into the document.

10. Close the document, saving your changes, and exit Word.

# Holsteins—America's Dairy Cows

There are many types of dairy cows, including Guernsey, Jersey, and Brown Swiss, but Holsteins are the most common dairy cow in America. Holsteins are good-natured attractive to look at and they are excellent milk producers. Read on to learn more about the wonderful Holstein!

## Cow Appearance

Holsteins are well known for their black and white markings, although some Holsteins have red and white markings instead. You may think all cows look alike, but a Holstein's markings are like a fingerprint—which means no two are exactly alike. A Holstein is one of the largest breeds of dairy cow. A milking Holstein weighs between 1,100 and 1,500 pounds and may stand up to 58 inches tall at the shoulder. A healthy Holstein calf weighs 90 pounds or more at birth.

## Cow Output

The average dairy cow produces about 19,825 pounds of milk each year which is about 2,300 gallons. Top producing Holsteins have been known to produce up to 67,914 pounds of milk in a year! It takes about 12 pounds of milk to make one gallon of ice cream. That means that each day, a Holstein produces enough milk to make five gallons of ice cream! Most Holsteins produce milk for three to four years. They may live to be 20 years old.

## Cow Visits

You are welcome to visit the Holsteins at Blue Sky Dairy. Dairy tours are offered the 1st and 3rd Saturdays of each month – no reservations are required. Stops on each tour include the milking parlor, the barn, and the ice cream manufacturing facility. Tours start at the main visitor's center and conclude at the gift shop.

# Exercise 29

◆ **Create Footnotes and Endnotes**

## On the Job

Include footnotes or endnotes in documents to provide information about the source of quoted material, or to supplement the main text.

You have been working on the document about Holstein dairy cows for Blue Sky Dairy. In this exercise, you will insert footnotes and endnotes into a version of the document you created in Exercise 28.

## Terms

**Footnote** An explanation or reference to additional material printed at the bottom of a page.

**Endnote** An explanation or reference to additional material printed at the end of a document.

**Citation** A reference to the source of quoted material.

**Note reference mark** A number or character inserted in the document to refer to footnote or endnote text.

**Note text** The text of the footnote or endnote citation.

## Notes

### Create Footnotes and Endnotes

■ **Footnotes** or **endnotes** are required in documents that include quoted source material, such as research papers.

■ Standard footnotes and endnotes include the following **citation** information:

- The author of the quoted material (first name first) followed by a comma.

- The title of the book (in italics), article (in quotation marks), or Web page (in quotation marks), followed by a comma.

- The name of the publication if it is a magazine or journal (in italics).

- The publication volume, number and/or date (the date in parentheses), followed by a colon.

- The page number(s) where the material is located, followed by a period.

- If the source is a Web page, the citation should also include the URL address, enclosed in angle brackets <>, and the date you accessed the information.

  ✓ *There are other styles used for footnotes and endnotes. For example, some use periods between parts instead of commas. If you are unsure which style to use, ask your instructor for more information.*

■ Footnotes or endnotes can also provide explanations or supplement text. For example, an asterisk footnote might provide information about where to purchase a product mentioned in the text.

■ When you insert a footnote, Word first inserts a **note reference mark** in the text, then a separator line following the last line of text on the page, and finally inserts the note number corresponding to the note mark below the separator line. You then type and format the **note text**.

✓ *The note mark should be positioned after closing punctuation.*

### *Footnotes at the bottom of a page*

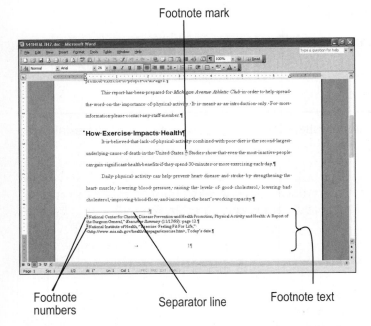

Footnote mark

Footnote numbers

Separator line

Footnote text

- Endnotes include the same parts as footnotes but are printed on the last page of a document.

- In a one-page document, the endnotes are printed at the end of the text, and the footnotes are printed at the bottom of the page. If you want your endnotes to begin on a separate page, you can insert a page break at the end of the document.

  ✓ *Page breaks are covered in Exercise 51.*

- It is easiest to insert footnotes or endnotes in Print Layout view.

- Footnotes and endnotes are not displayed in Normal view; to see them, use Print Preview or Print Layout view.

- Notes can be displayed in a ScreenTip by resting the mouse pointer on the note reference mark.

- Word uses Arabic numerals for footnote marks; if endnotes are used in the same document, the endnote marks are roman numerals.

- You can select a different number format or a symbol for the note mark.

- By default, numbering is consecutive from the beginning of the document. You can set Word to restart numbering on each page or each section. You can also change the starting number if you want.

- Word automatically updates numbering if you add or delete footnotes or endnotes, or rearrange the document text.

### *Footnote and Endnote dialog box*

# Procedures

## Footnotes and Endnotes

### To insert footnotes in Print Layout view:

1. Position insertion point after text to footnote.
   - ✓ *If necessary, position insertion point after closing punctuation.*
2. Click **Insert** .................. `Alt`+`I`
3. Click **Reference** .................. `N`
4. Click **Footnote** .................. `N`
5. Click the **Footnotes** option button .................. `Alt`+`F`
6. Click **Insert** .................. `Alt`+`I`
7. Type note text.
8. Click in document text .................. `Shift`+`F5`

### To insert endnotes in Print Layout view:

1. Position insertion point after text to endnote.
   - ✓ *If necessary, position insertion point after closing punctuation.*
2. Click **Insert** .................. `Alt`+`I`
3. Click **Reference** .................. `N`
4. Click **Footnote** .................. `N`
5. Click the **Endnotes** option button .................. `Alt`+`E`
6. Click **Insert** .................. `Alt`+`I`
7. Type note text.
8. Click in document text .................. `Shift`+`F5`

## Display Note Text in ScreenTip

- Rest mouse pointer on note reference mark in text.
  - ✓ *If ScreenTip is not displayed, you may have the option disabled.*

### Enable ScreenTips:

1. Click **Tools** .................. `Alt`+`T`
2. Click **Options** .................. `O`
3. Click **View** tab .................. `Ctrl`+`Tab`
4. Select **ScreenTips** check box .................. `Alt`+`N`
5. Click **OK** .................. `Enter`

## Edit a Footnote or Endnote

1. Double-click note reference mark in text.
   - ✓ *The insertion point automatically moves to the note text.*
2. Edit footnote or endnote text.
3. Click in document text .. `Shift`+`F5`

## Delete a Footnote or Endnote

1. Position insertion point to the right of note reference mark in text.
2. Press **Backspace** .................. `Backspace`
   - ✓ *Mark is selected.*
3. Press **Backspace** .................. `Backspace`
   - ✓ *Note is deleted.*

## Change the Footnote or Endnote Mark in Print Layout View

1. Position insertion point after text to footnote.
2. Click **Insert** .................. `Alt`+`I`
3. Click **Reference** .................. `N`
4. Click **Footnote** .................. `N`
5. Click **Footnotes** option button .................. `Alt`+`F`

   OR

   Click **Endnotes** .................. `Alt`+`E`
   option button.
6. Click the **Custom mark** text box .................. `Alt`+`U`
7. Type character in text box.

   OR

   a. Click **Symbol** .................. `Alt`+`Y`
   b. Select desired font .................. `Alt`+`F`, `↓`, `Enter`
   c. Click symbol to use.
   d. Click **OK** .................. `Enter`
8. Click **Insert** .................. `Alt`+`I`
9. Type note text.
10. Click in document text .................. `Shift`+`F5`

# Exercise Directions

1. Start Word, if necessary.

2. Open ⊙**29COWS**.

3. Save the file as **COWS**.

4. Position the insertion point after the first paragraph under the heading **Cow Appearance**, and insert a footnote as follows:
   **Deborah Richardson, "All About Dairy Cows," page 11, <http://www.nal.usda.gov>, today's date**

   ✓ *Word may automatically format the URL address as a hyperlink and remove the angle brackets. If so, use the Undo command to remove the automatic formatting. Alternatively, right-click the hyperlink text and choose Remove Hyperlink from the shortcut menu, then retype the brackets.*

5. At the end of the of the fourth sentence under the heading **Cow Output**, insert the following footnote:
   **"Moomilk FAQs," 2002: <http://www.moomilk.com/faq.htm>, today's date.**

6. After the first sentence in the first paragraph, insert the following endnote:
   **Consult the Web site <www.amsi.okstate.edu/BREEDS/cattle/> for more information about different types of dairy cows.**

   • Again, remove the hyperlink and retype the angle brackets, if necessary.

7. Check the spelling and grammar in the document and correct errors as necessary.

8. Display the document in Print Preview. It should look similar to the one in Illustration A.

9. Close Print Preview.

10. Print the document.

11. Delete the endnote.

12. Print the document.

13. Close the document, saving all changes.

# On Your Own

1. Open the document **OWD28** that you used in the On Your Own section of Exercise 28, or open ⊙**29BIO**.

2. Save the document as **OWD29**.

3. Insert at least two footnotes or endnotes to provide citations or to supplement text with additional information.

4. If necessary, adjust the margins so the document still fits on one page.

5. Check the spelling and grammar in the document and then print it.

6. Ask a classmate to review the document and make comments and suggestions.

7. Incorporate the suggestions into the document.

8. Close the document, saving all changes, and exit Word.

*Illustration A*

# Holsteins—America's Dairy Cows

There are many types of dairy cows, including Guernsey, Jersey, and Brown Swiss, but Holsteins are the most common dairy cow in America.[i] Holsteins are good-natured animals which may be one reason they are so popular. They are also attractive to look at and they are excellent milk producers. Read on to learn more about the wonderful Holstein!

## Cow Appearance

Holsteins are well known for their black and white markings, although some Holsteins have red and white markings instead. You may think all cows look alike, but a Holstein's markings are like a fingerprint—which means no two are exactly alike. Holsteins are one of the largest dairy cows. A milking Holstein weighs between 1,100 and 1,500 pounds and may be up to 58 inches tall at the shoulder. In contrast, a Jersey cow usually weighs between 700 and 1,000 pounds. A healthy Holstein calf weighs 90 pounds or more at birth.[1]

## Cow Output

The average dairy cow produces about 19,825 pounds of milk each year which is about 2,300 gallons. Top producing Holsteins have been known to produce up to 67,914 pounds of milk in a year! It takes about 12 pounds of milk to make one gallon of ice cream. That means that each day, a Holstein produces enough milk to make five gallons of ice cream![2] Most Holsteins produce milk for three to four years. They may live to be 20 years old.

---

[i] Consult the Web site <www.amsi.okstate.edu/BREEDS/cattle/> for more information about different types of dairy cows.

---

[1] Deborah Richardson, "All About Dairy Cows," page 11, <http://www.nal.usda.gov>, today's date.
[2] "Moomilk FAQs," 2002: <http://www.moomilk.com/faq.htm>, today's date.

# Exercise **30**

## Skills Covered:

### ◆ **Create Hyperlinks**

## On the Job

Create a hyperlink to connect related documents to each other, to connect a Word document to a Web site, or to connect one location in a document to another location in the same document. For example, create hyperlinks from a table of contents in a report to each chapter heading or from a report topic to an Internet site where more information can be found. Hyperlinks let you expand the boundaries among documents and among computers because, in effect, you can link to information stored anywhere on the Internet.

In this exercise, you will work with a variation of the classes document you created for the Liberty Blooms flower shop. You will insert hyperlinks to help readers navigate through the document. You will also insert a hyperlink to an existing Word document describing what employees should expect from in-house training.

## Terms

**Hyperlink** Text or graphics linked to a destination file or location. Click the link to jump to the destination.

**Hyperlink destination** The location displayed when the hyperlink is clicked.

**Hyperlink source** The document where the hyperlink is inserted.

**Bookmark** A nonprinting character that you insert and name so that you can quickly find a particular location in a document.

## Notes

### Create Hyperlinks

- **Hyperlinks** can be used to link locations within a single document, to link two documents, or to link a document to an e-mail address.

- A **hyperlink destination** does not have to be in the same file format as the **hyperlink source** document. For example, you can link a Word document file to a Web page file or to an Excel file.

- The hyperlink destination can be a file stored on your computer, on your company intranet, or a site on the Internet.

- You can create a hyperlink within a document for moving to the top of the document, to a specific heading, or to a **bookmark**.

  ✓ *Bookmarks are covered in Exercise 53.*

- When you access a hyperlink to an e-mail address, Word starts your e-mail program and displays a new e-mail message. The address and subject are filled in with the hyperlink information.

  ✓ *You learn about using e-mail in Word in Exercise 67.*

- You can change existing text to a hyperlink or type new text to create a hyperlink.

  ✓ *When you format text as a hyperlink, Word automatically applies the Hyperlink style, which usually uses a blue font and a solid underline.*

  ✓ *Once you access the hyperlink, the font color changes to indicate that the hyperlink has been used at least once.*

*The Insert Hyperlink dialog box*

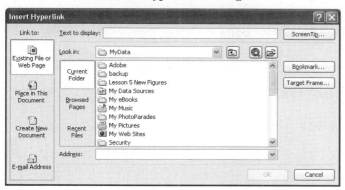

- By default, in Word documents you must press Ctrl and click the hyperlink in order to go to the hyperlink destination. This helps you avoid accidental access.
- You can change the setting so that you don't have to press Ctrl.
- You can edit and format hyperlink text the same way you edit and format regular text.
- If you change the setting so that you don't have to press Ctrl to click to follow a hyperlink, you must select the hyperlink before you can edit it or format it.
- You can change a hyperlink destination.
- You can remove a hyperlink completely.

# Procedures

### Insert a Hyperlink Within a Document (*Ctrl+K*)

1. Position insertion point where you want to insert hyperlink.
   OR
   Select text to change to a hyperlink.
2. Click **Insert Hyperlink** button 🔗.
   OR
   a. Click **Insert**.............Alt+I
   b. Click **Hyperlink**..............I
3. Click **Place in This document** in Link to bar................Alt+A
4. In the **Select a place in this document list**, click hyperlink destination ............Alt+C, ↓
   ✓ If necessary click the expand symbol + to expand the list to show additional headings and/or bookmarks.
5. Click **OK**...........................Enter
   ✓ If existing text is not selected, Word uses the destination name as the hyperlink text.

### Insert a Hyperlink to a Different Document

1. Position insertion point where you want to insert hyperlink.
   OR

Select text to change to a hyperlink.
2. Click **Insert Hyperlink** button 🔗.
   OR
   a. Click **Insert**.............Alt+I
   b. Click **Hyperlink**..............I
3. Click **Existing File or Web Page** in the Link to bar...................Alt+X
4. In the **Address** text box, type the hyperlink destination file name....................Alt+E, *type file name*
   ✓ Word automatically completes the file name as you type based on recently used file names; stop typing to accept the entry or keep typing to enter the name you want.
   OR
   a. Click **Current Folder**...................Alt+U
   to display a list of files stored in the current folder.
   b. Click the file name in the list of files.
   OR
   a. Click **Browsed Pages** to display a list of recently viewed Web pages ....................Alt+B

   b. Locate and click file name.
   OR
   a. Click **Recent Files**. Alt+C to display a list of recently used files.
   b. Click the file name in the list of files.
5. Edit **Text to display**...........Alt+T
   ✓ Word displays this text as the hyperlink in the document.
6. Click **OK**...........................Enter

### Insert a Hyperlink to a Web Page

1. Position insertion point where you want to insert the hyperlink.
   OR
   Select text to change to a hyperlink.
2. Click **Insert Hyperlink** button 🔗.
   OR
   a. Click **Insert** ............Alt+I
   b. Click **Hyperlink**..............I
3. Click **Existing File or Web Page** in Link to bar......Alt+X
4. In the **Address** text box, type the hyperlink destination URL............Alt+E, *type URL*

✓ Word automatically completes the URL as you type based on other URLs you have typed in the past. Stop typing to accept the entry, or keep typing to enter the URL you want.

OR

a. Click **Browsed Pages** .................... `Alt`+`B`

   to display a list of Web pages you have recently accessed.

b. Click the URL or site name you want in the list of files.

5. Edit **Text to display**........................ `Alt`+`T`

   ✓ Type the text you want displayed for the hyperlink. Word displays this text as the hyperlink.

6. Click **OK**........................... `Enter`

## Insert a Hyperlink to an E-Mail Address

1. Position insertion point where you want to insert the hyperlink.
   OR
   Select text to change to a hyperlink.

2. Click **Insert Hyperlink** button 🖳.
   OR

   a. Click **Insert**............ `Alt`+`I`

   b. Click **Hyperlink** .............. `I`

3. Click **E-mail address** in Link to bar................... `Alt`+`M`

4. In the **E-mail address** text box, type the e-mail address........................ `Alt`+`E`

   ✓ This address will be inserted in the To line of the e-mail message.

   OR

   a. Click the address in the **Recently** used e-mail addresses list......... `Alt`+`C`, `↓`, `Enter`

   b. In the **Subject** text box, type the text you want displayed in the e-mail Subject text box... `Alt`+`U`, *type text*

5. Click **OK** .......................... `Enter`

## Remove a Hyperlink

1. Right-click hyperlink text.

2. Click **Remove Hyperlink** .... `R`

   ✓ This removes hyperlink, not the text.

## Change a Hyperlink Destination

1. Right-click hyperlink text.

2. Click **Edit Hyperlink** .......... `H`

3. Select new destination.

4. Click **OK** .......................... `Enter`

## Set Word to Follow Hyperlink On Click

1. Click **Tools**................. `Alt`+`T`

2. Click **Options**..................... `O`

3. Click **Edit** tab.............. `Ctrl`+`Tab`

4. Deselect **Use CTRL+Click to follow hyperlink** check box ...................................... `H`

5. Click **OK** .......................... `Enter`

## Select a Hyperlink

1. Right-click hyperlink text.

2. Click **Select Hyperlink** ....... `S`

# Exercise Directions

1. Start Word, if necessary.

2. Open 💿 **30TEACHERS**.

3. Save the file as **TEACHERS**.

4. Insert a new line at the end of the document and clear all formatting from it.

5. Set paragraph spacing to leave 72 points of space before the line and after the line.

6. Change the font to 18-point Comic Sans MS, then type the text **RETURN**.

7. Close the document, saving all changes.

8. Open the file 💿 **30CLASS**.

9. Save the file as **CLASSLINK**.

10. Use the following steps to insert hyperlinks to create the document shown in Illustration A.

11. Position the insertion point at the end of the heading **Training Schedule** and press Enter.

12. Clear all formatting from the new line and then type **January** and press Enter.

13. Type **February** and press Enter.

14. Type **March** and press Enter twice.

15. Type **Click here for information about our instructors**.

16. Insert a hyperlink from the text **January** that you typed in step 12 to the heading **January**.

17. Insert a hyperlink from the text **February** that you typed in step 13 to the heading **February**.

18. Insert a hyperlink from the text **March** that you typed in step 14 to the heading **March**.

19. At the end of each course description paragraph, press Enter and type **Return to Top.** (Include the ending period, as shown in the illustration.)

20. Insert hyperlinks from each occurrence of **Return to Top** to the top of the document.

21. Insert a hyperlink from the text you typed in step 15 to the **TEACHERS** document.

22. Increase the font size of all hyperlink text to 14 points.

23. Check the spelling and grammar in the document.

24. Display the document in Print preview. It should look similar to Illustration A.

25. Print the document.

26. Test the hyperlinks to navigate through the **CLASSLINK** document.

   ✓ Word's Web toolbar may be displayed.

27. Test the hyperlink to go to the **TEACHERS** document.

28. Word should open the document and display it on-screen.

29. Insert a hyperlink from the text **RETURN** at the bottom of the **TEACHERS** document, back to the **CLASSLINK** document.

30. Test the hyperlink to return to the **CLASSLINK** document.

31. Close the **CLASSLINK** document, saving all changes.

32. Close the **TEACHERS** document, saving all changes.

# On Your Own

1. Open the document 📟**SOWD29**, the one-page report about yourself that you used in the On Your Own section of Exercise 29, or open 💿**30BIO**.

2. Save the file as **OWD30-1**.

3. Open the document **OWD17**, the resume you created in the On Your Own section of Exercise 17, or open 💿**30RESUME**.

4. Save the file as **OWD30-2**, and then close it.

5. Create a hyperlink from the **OWD30-1** report document to the **OWD30-2** resume document.

6. Test the link.

7. Create a link back to the **OWD30-1** report from the resume.

8. Test the link.

9. Create a link from the bottom of the **OWD30-1** document to the top of the document.

   ✓ If you have access to the Internet, you might want to try linking the report to a Web site that you like. You learn more about linking to Web sites in Lesson 10.

10. Test the links.

11. Check the spelling and grammar in each document.

12. Preview each document.

13. Print each document.

14. Ask a classmate to review the documents and offer comments and suggestions.

15. Incorporate the suggestions as necessary.

16. Close all open documents, saving all changes, and exit Word.

# Liberty Blooms

345 Chestnut Street Philadelphia, PA 19106

## Training Schedule

January
February
March

Click here for information about our instructors.

**January**                                    **Introduction to Flower Arranging**

Brighten up the winter doldrums with a lesson on flower arranging! We'll work with a variety of cut flowers such as daisies, irises, and roses as well as greenery and accent stems to create beautiful bouquets. This entry-level class is open to everyone.

Return to Top.

**February**                                                    **All About Herbs**

Get ready for spring with a fun-filled class all about herbs! We'll learn about the types of herbs that are easy to grow indoors and out, how to identify herbs by appearance and smell, and how to use fresh and dried herbs in a variety of ways. For example, we might use herbs to scent a sachet, or to flavor a pot of stew.

Return to Top.

**March**                                            **Perennial Garden Design**

A successful perennial garden enhances blooms all season long, year after year. This seminar will cover the basics of planning a perennial garden. Learn how to determine the amount of space you need, how to lay out the garden, and how to select the right types of plants. Time permitting, we will discuss soil composition and planting techniques.

Return to Top.

Classes are free and open to the public. However, due to the limited space at Liberty Blooms, we must restrict all class sizes. To register, or for more information about these and other events at Liberty Blooms, call 215-555-2837 or visit our Web site www.libertyblooms.net.

# Exercise 31

## ◆ Critical Thinking

The Marketing Director at Long Shot, Inc. has asked you to prepare an agenda for a meeting next Friday. He wants to approve the agenda before it is distributed to the meeting attendees, and it must be distributed at least two days in advance. He also needs you to complete a one-page report about golf balls that will be distributed at the meeting. Although he wants to see the report before the meeting, it does not need to be distributed in advance. You must first determine the priority for each document to decide which one you should complete first. You then prepare the documents using the skills you have learned in this lesson paying particular attention to speed and accuracy.

## Exercise Directions

Before starting Word, consider which document should take priority over the other. Both are needed for the meeting next Friday, but the agenda must be distributed in advance. Therefore, you should complete the agenda first. While the marketing director proofs the agenda, you can begin work on the report.

### Prepare the Agenda

1. Start Word, if necessary.
2. Open ☾**31AGENDA**.
3. Save the document as **AGENDA**.
4. Change the orientation to Landscape.
5. Make editing and formatting changes as marked to create the document shown in Illustration A.
   a. Apply font formatting and styles as shown.
   b. Adjust paragraph spacing as shown.
   c. Apply indents as shown.
   d. Set tabs and tab leaders as shown.
   e. Change vertical alignment to Center.
6. Check the spelling and grammar in the document.
7. Display the document in Print Preview. It should look similar to Illustration A.
8. Print the document.
9. Show the document to someone in the class for review.

10. When you receive the document back, address all comments and make changes as necessary.

### Prepare the One-Page Report

1. Open ☾**31DIMPLES**.
2. Save the document as **DIMPLES**.
3. Change the margins to 1" on the top, left, and right, and .75" on the bottom.
4. Make sure all AutoFormat options are selected.
5. Use AutoFormat to format the report.
6. Modify the formatting of Body Text paragraphs as follows:
   - Justify, double-space, first-line indent by .5", and set paragraph spacing to leave 0 points before and after.
7. Modify the formatting of Heading 1 paragraphs to leave 0 points of space before and 3 points of space after.
8. Insert the following footnotes:
   a. At the end of the first Body Text paragraph: **Marshall Brain, "How Things Work," <http://www.howstuffworks.com/question37.htm>, today's date**.
   b. At the end of the fifth sentence under the heading Featheries: **"A History of the Golf Ball," <http://www.golfeurope.com>, today's date**.

c. At the end of the second sentence under the heading Gutta Perchas: **"The Origin of the Golf Ball,"** <**http://www.kidzworld.com/site/p445.htm**>, **today's date**.

d. At the end of the second sentence under the heading Modern Golf Balls: **"A History of the Golf Ball,"** <**http://www.golfeurope.com**>, **today's date**.

9. Check the spelling and grammar in the document.

   ✓ *Ignore the spelling of the types of golf balls or add them to the dictionary.*

10. Display the document in Print Preview. It should look similar to Illustration B. If necessary, use Shrink to Fit to make the document fit on a single page.

11. Print the document.

## Link the Two Documents

1. Create a hyperlink from the text **RETURN** on the last line of the **DIMPLES** document to the **AGENDA** document.

2. Test the hyperlink.

3. Create a hyperlink from the text **Why Golf Balls Have Dimples** in the **AGENDA** document to the **DIMPLES** document.

4. Test the hyperlink.

5. Close all open documents, saving all changes, and exit Word.

*Illustration A*

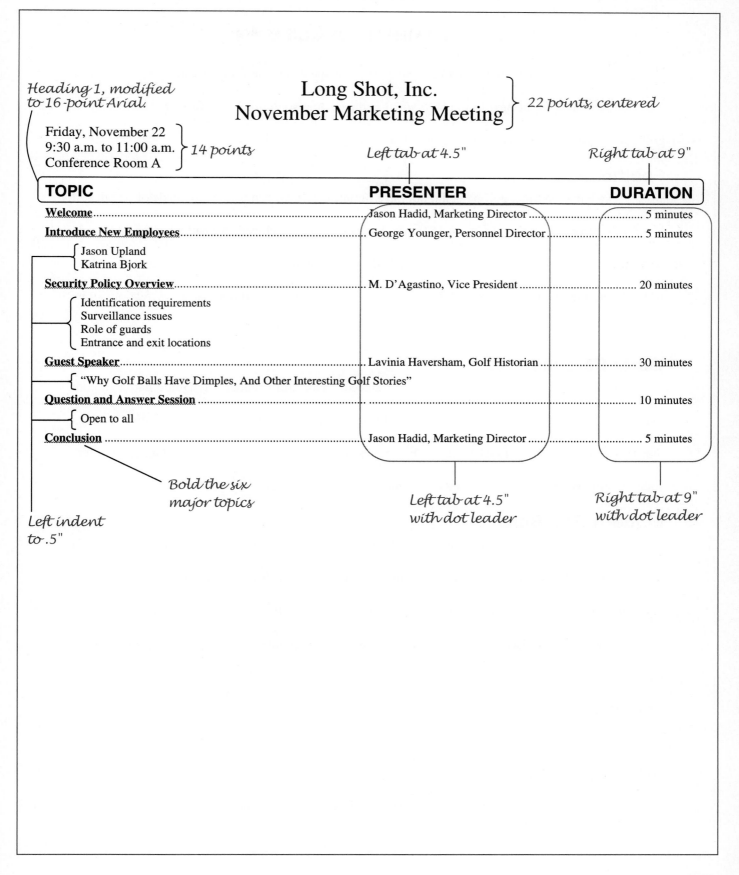

Heading 1, modified to 16-point Arial.

# Long Shot, Inc.
## November Marketing Meeting

22 points, centered

Friday, November 22
9:30 a.m. to 11:00 a.m.
Conference Room A

14 points

Left tab at 4.5"

Right tab at 9"

| TOPIC | PRESENTER | DURATION |
|---|---|---|
| **Welcome** | Jason Hadid, Marketing Director | 5 minutes |
| **Introduce New Employees** | George Younger, Personnel Director | 5 minutes |
| Jason Upland Katrina Bjork | | |
| **Security Policy Overview** | M. D'Agastino, Vice President | 20 minutes |
| Identification requirements Surveillance issues Role of guards Entrance and exit locations | | |
| **Guest Speaker** | Lavinia Haversham, Golf Historian | 30 minutes |
| "Why Golf Balls Have Dimples, And Other Interesting Golf Stories" | | |
| **Question and Answer Session** | | 10 minutes |
| Open to all | | |
| **Conclusion** | Jason Hadid, Marketing Director | 5 minutes |

Bold the six major topics

Left indent to .5"

Left tab at 4.5"
with dot leader

Right tab at 9"
with dot leader

# A (Brief) History of Golf Balls

Why do golf balls have dimples? Scientifically speaking, the dimples induce turbulence in the boundary layer of air next to the ball, which reduces drag so the ball flies further. The history of golf balls illustrates how dimples came to be the standard.[1]

## Featheries

Once upon a time, golf balls did not have dimples. The earliest balls were made of wood, and had a solid, smooth surface. In about 1618, the Featherie was introduced. A Featherie was handmade from wet leather horse or cow hide tightly packed with wet goose feathers. The leather got smaller as it dried, and the feathers got stiffer.[2] The result was a hard, uneven ball that had imperfections in its surface.

## Gutta Perchas

In 1848 the Gutta Percha ball was introduced. Made from rubber, the Guttie had a smooth exterior and was cheaper to manufacture and to buy than the Featherie.[3] However, golfers noticed that new Gutties did not travel as far as Featheries, or even as far as old, beat-up Gutties. Golfers soon determined that the extra distance was due to the uneven surface.

## Modern Golf Balls

After 1880, manufacturers added patterns to the rubber balls in an attempt to make them travel further. At first, patterns were raised. In 1905, William Taylor applied a dimple pattern to golf balls, and that has been the tradition ever since.[4] Over the years there have been many variations on the number, size, and placement of the dimples in order to help golfers pick up a few extra yards off the tee.

RETURN

---

[1] Marshall Brain, "How Things Work," <http://www.howstuffworks.com/question37.htm>, today's date.
[2] "A History of the Golf Ball," <http://www.golfeurope.com>, today's date.
[3] "The Origin of the Golf Ball," <http://www.kidzworld.com/site/p445.htm>, today's date.
[4] "A History of the Golf Ball," <http://www.golfeurope.com>, today's date.

# Lesson 6

## Manage Documents

# Exercise 32

## On the Job

Word offers many options for opening a document. For example, open a document as read-only when you do not want revisions to affect the original file. (You must save the file with a new name in order to save changes.) You can use Windows features to open a document and start Word at the same time, and you can use Word to open files created with different programs.

The owner of Liberty Blooms has asked you to update the class list. In addition to making the changes she has requested, you want to propose changing the course names. In this exercise, you will open the document using Windows. You will make the required changes and then close the document. You will then open the document as read-only, so that you cannot make changes accidentally. You will modify the file, and then save it in text only format so it can be opened using a different program.

## Terms

**Read-only** A mode of operation in which revisions cannot be saved in the original document.

**File type** The format in which the file is stored. Usually, the file type corresponds to the program used to create the file.

**File extension** A dot followed by three or four characters attached to a file name, used to indicate the file type. For example, a *.doc* file extension indicates a Word document file.

**File icon** The icon used to represent a file type in a file list, such as Windows Explorer or Word's Open dialog box.

**Compatible file type** A file type that Word can open, even though it was created and saved using a different program.

**XML** An abbreviation and file extension for Extensible Markup Language, which is an industry standard file format.

## Notes

### Open a Document as Read-only

- Opening a document as **read-only** is a safeguard against accidentally making changes.

- Word prompts you to use Save As to save revisions made to a document opened as read-only in a new document with a different file name.

- The words *Read-Only* appear in the title bar of a document opened as read-only.

### Open a Document from Windows

- Use the Windows Start Menu to open a document and start Word at the same time.

- Click My Recent Documents on the Start menu to select from a menu of recently used files.

- Locate and open any document using Windows Explorer.

- You can also open a Word document using the Open Office Document dialog box accessed from the Windows All Programs menu.

## File Types

- Files are saved in different **file types**, depending on the application used to create, save, and open the file.

- In Windows and Windows applications, file types can be identified by the **file extension** and by the **file icon**.

- Word can open documents saved in **compatible file types**. For example, Word can open text files, Web page files, **XML** files, and files created with other versions of Word.

- You can save a compatible file in its original file type or as a Word document file.

- Some common file types include the following:
  - Word document files .doc
  - Word template files .dot
  - Text files .txt
  - Web pages .htm
  - Excel workbooks .xls
  - Access databases .mdb
  - PowerPoint presentations .ppt

- Word can also open many other types of files depending on the file conversion features you have installed. For example, you may be able to open WordPerfect files and rich text format files.

  ✓ *File conversion features are installed during setup.*

# Procedures

### Open a Document as Read-only *(Ctrl+O)*

1. Click **Open** button 📂.
   OR
   a. Click **File**................. Alt + F
   b. Click **Open**.................... O
2. Click document name.
3. Click **Open** drop-down arrow Open ▼.
4. Click **Open Read-Only** ........ R

### Open a Word Document from the Documents Menu

1. Click **Start** button 🏁 start
2. Select **My Recent Documents** ......................... D
3. Click document name.

### Open a Word Document From Windows Explorer (⊞+E)

1. Right-click **Start** button 🏁 start.
2. Click **Explore**
3. Select drive where folder/file is located.
4. Open folder.
5. Double-click document name that you want to open.

### Open a Word Document From Windows All Programs Menu

1. Click **Start** button 🏁 start ........ 🏁
2. Click **All Programs** ............. P
3. Click **Open Office Document**
4. Click **Look in** drop-down arrow ......... Alt + I
5. Select drive or folder where document is stored.
   ✓ *If necessary double-click folder name.*
   OR
   Click folder in Places Bar to open it.
6. Double-click document name.
   OR
   a. Click document name.
   b. Click **Open** ..................... O

### Open a Compatible File Type in Word *(Ctrl+O)*

1. Click **File** ..................... Alt + F
2. Click **Open** ......................... O
3. Click the **Look in** drop-down arrow ......... Alt + I
4. Select the disk or folder.
   ✓ *Alternatively, click the folder you want to open in the Places bar.*
5. Click the **Files of type** drop-down arrow ......... Alt + T

6. Click the file type.
7. Click the desired file name.
8. Click **Open** ................. Alt + O
   ✓ *If the File Conversion dialog box is displayed, click OK.*

### Save a Compatible File *(Ctrl+S)*

1. Open the compatible file.
2. Click **File** ..................... Alt + F
3. Click **Save** ........................... S
4. Click **Yes** ........................... Y
   to save the file in its original format.
   OR
   Click **No** ............................ N
   to save the file as a Word document.

### Save a Compatible File as a New File in Word Format

1. Open the compatible file.
2. Click **File** ..................... Alt + F
3. Click **Save As** ..................... A
4. Click the **Save as type** drop-down arrow ......... Alt + T
5. Click **Word Document (\*.doc)**.
6. Click the **File name** text box ..................... Alt + N
7. Type the new file name.
8. Click **Save** ................. Alt + S

# Exercise Directions

1. Without starting Word, open the document ⊚**32CLASSES**.
2. Save the file as **NEWCLASS1**.
3. Edit the months **January**, **February**, and **March** to **April**, **May**, and **June**.
4. Close the document, saving all changes.
5. Open the document as read-only.
6. Change the April course title to **Flower Arranging for All**.
7. Change the May course title to **Growing Herbs**.
8. Change the June course title to **All About Perennials**.

9. Try to save the changes.
   - ✓ *Word will display the Save As dialog box.*
10. Cancel the dialog box.
11. Save the document in plain text format, with the name **NEWCLASS2**.
    - ✓ *If Word displays a warning or a file conversion dialog box, click OK.*
12. Close the document, saving all changes. If prompted, remember to save the file in text format, not Word format.
13. Open the **NEWCLASS2.TXT** document in Word. The text file should look similar to the one in illustration A.
14. Close the file, saving all changes.

# On Your Own

1. Open ⌨**OWD26**, the file you created in the On Your Own section of Exercise 26, or open ⊚**32PROGRAMS**.
2. Save the document as **OWD32-1**.
3. Change some formatting in the document.
4. Print the file and then close it, saving all changes.
5. Ask a classmate to review the file and offer comments and suggestions.
6. Open the file as read-only.

7. Incorporate the comments and suggestions into the document.
8. Try saving the document.
9. Save the file in plain text format as **OWD32-2**.
10. Close the document, saving all changes.
11. Open the text file in Word.
12. Print the file.
13. Close the file, saving all changes, and exit Word.

*Illustration A*

Liberty Blooms
345 Chestnut Street Philadelphia, PA 19106
Training Schedule
April Flower Arranging for All
Brighten up the winter doldrums with a lesson on flower arranging! We'll work with a variety of cut flowers such as daisies, irises, and roses as well as greenery and accent stems to create beautiful bouquets. This entry-level class is open to everyone.
May    Growing Herbs
Get ready for spring with a fun-filled class all about herbs! We'll learn about the types of herbs that are easy to grow indoors and out, how to identify herbs by appearance and smell, and how to use fresh and dried herbs in a variety of ways. For example, we might use herbs to scent a sachet, or to flavor a pot of stew.
June  All About Perennials
A successful perennial garden enhances blooms all season long, year after year. This seminar will cover the basics of planning a perennial garden. Learn how to determine the amount of space you need, how to lay out the garden, and how to select the right types of plants. Time permitting, we will discuss soil composition and planting techniques.
Classes are free and open to the public. However, due to the limited space at Liberty Blooms, we must restrict all class sizes. To register, or for more information about these and other events at Liberty Blooms, call 215-555-2837 or visit our Web site www.libertyblooms.net.

# Exercise 33

◆ **Use Split Screen View**

◆ **Open Multiple Documents** ◆ **Arrange Documents on Screen**

## On the Job

Use Split Screen view to see different sections of the same document on screen at the same time. For example, you may want to see a table of contents at the beginning of a document while you work in a section at the end of the document. Open multiple documents when you need to work with more than one document at a time. For example, if you are planning a meeting, you may need to work with an agenda and a list of attendees at the same time.

As the Manager of a StyleEyes franchise, you often have many different tasks to attend to at the same time. Today you must modify a letter to a supplier regarding an incomplete order and make sure the correct version of a press release about the grand opening is sent out. In this exercise, you will first open the letter to the supplier and use Split Screen view to make the necessary changes. You will save the changes and print the letter. When the letter is complete, you will move on to the press release. You will arrange all versions of the press release on-screen and select the two you believe are the most accurate. You will then compare the two side by side to determine which is correct. You will then print the correct press release.

## Terms

**Active document** The document in which the insertion point is currently located. Commands and actions occur in the active document.

**Tile** Arrange windows so they do not overlap on-screen.

**Synchronous scrolling** A feature that links the scroll bars in two windows so that when you scroll in one window the other window scrolls as well.

**Independent scrolling** The ability to scroll a window without affecting the display in other open windows.

## Notes

### Use Split Screen View

- Split the screen into two panes so you can see and work in different sections of a single document.
- Word tiles the panes one above the other within the program window.
- Each pane has its own scroll bars so you can scroll each section independently from the other.
- Each pane also has its own rulers.

- There is only one menu bar, one title bar, and one set of toolbars.
- Commands affect the active pane. For example, you can change the zoom in the top pane without affecting the bottom pane.
- You can make edits and formatting changes in either pane.
- Use the mouse to move the insertion point from one pane to the other.

*One document in Split Screen view*

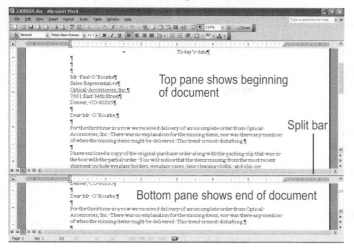

Top pane shows beginning of document

Split bar

Bottom pane shows end of document

## Open Multiple Documents

- You can open multiple Word documents at the same time.

- By default, each open document is represented by a button on the Windows taskbar.

- However, if there is not enough room on the taskbar to show all buttons, they are grouped into one Word button.

- By default, the **active document** is displayed on-screen while other open documents are hidden.

- Only one document can be active at the same time. You can identify the active document window by the following:

  - The active document contains the insertion point.

  - The active document window has a brighter colored title bar than other open document windows.

  - The active document window is represented by the "pressed in" taskbar button.

## Arrange Documents On-screen

- You can arrange all open documents on-screen at the same time.

- Word **tiles** up to three open documents one above the other.

- If there are more than three open documents, Word fits them on-screen by tiling some of them side by side as well.

- The more open documents there are, the smaller each document window is on-screen. Therefore, editing with more than two documents arranged on-screen may be difficult.

✓ To keep a document from being arranged on-screen with other open documents, minimize it.

*Multiple documents tiled on-screen*

Active title bar

Windows tiled horizontally

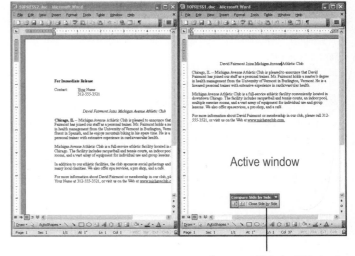

Group taskbar button

Windows tiled vertically

## Compare Documents Side by Side

- You can select to compare the active document with another open document by arranging them side by side.

- By default, both windows are set to use **synchronous scrolling**, but you can use **independent scrolling** if you want.

- Changes you make to the view in one window affect the other window as well.

- If the windows move or are resized on the desktop, you can reset their position to side by side.

*Compare documents side by side*

Active window

Compare Side by Side toolbar

# Procedures

## Open Split Screen View

- Double-click **Split box** at top of vertical scroll bar.

OR

1. Click **Window** ............. `Alt`+`W`
2. Click **Split** .......................... `S`

   ✓ *Mouse pointer changes to a resizing pointer and a dark gray bar extends horizontally across the screen.*

3. Click at location where you want to split the screen.

## Remove Split Screen View:

- Double-click **Split bar** that divides window.

OR

1. Click **Window** ............. `Alt`+`W`
2. Click **Remove Split** ........... `S`

## Resize Split Screen Panes

1. Position mouse pointer so it touches **Split bar**.

   ✓ *Pointer changes to a resizing pointer.*

2. Press and hold **left mouse button**.
3. Drag **Split bar** up or down to desired position.

## Open Multiple Documents
*(Ctrl+O)*

1. Open first document.
2. Open second document.
3. Continue opening documents as desired.

## Arrange Documents On-screen:

1. Open all documents.
2. Click **Window** ............. `Alt`+`W`
3. Click **Arrange All** ................ `A`

## Display active document only:

- Click active document's **Maximize** button `▢`.

## Switch among open documents:

1. Click **Window** ............. `Alt`+`W`
2. Click desired document name.

OR

- Click in desired document window.

OR

- Press `Ctrl`+`F6` until desired document is active.

OR

- Click taskbar button representing desired document.

   ✓ *If there is a group taskbar button, click the button, then click desired document.*

## Compare Documents Side by Side

1. Open both documents.
2. Click **Window** ............. `Alt`+`W`
3. Click **Compare Side by Side with *documentname*** .......... `B`

## If more than two documents are open:

1. Click **Window** ............. `Alt`+`W`
2. Click **Compare Side by Side with** ........................ `B`
3. Click name of file to compare ........................ `↓`
4. Click **OK** ........................... `Enter`

## Toggle Synchronous Scrolling:

- Click **Synchronous Scrolling** button `▤↕` on Compare Side by Side toolbar.

   ✓ *If button is highlighted, synchronous scrolling is set. Click it again to allow independent scrolling.*

## Reset Windows:

- Click **Reset Window Position** button `▦` on Compare Side by Side toolbar.

## Remove side by side arrangement:

1. Click **Window** ............. `Alt`+`W`
2. Click **Close Side by Side** ... `B`

OR

- Click **Close Side by Side** `Close Side by Side` on Compare Side by Side toolbar.

# Exercise Directions

## Letter

1. Start Word, if necessary.
2. Open 🖭 **33ORDER**.
3. Save the file as **ORDER**.
4. Insert today's date.
5. Display the document in Split Screen view.
6. Adjust the zoom in the top pane to Page Width.
7. Adjust the contents of the top pane to display from the inside address through the first paragraph of the letter.
8. Click in the bottom pane and adjust the zoom to Text Width.
9. Scroll down in the bottom pane and position the insertion point at the beginning of the paragraph beginning **Please contact me as soon as possible...**
10. Type the recipient's name. Refer to the information in the top pane to make sure you use the correct name and spelling.
11. Use correct grammar and punctuation. For example, make sure to include a comma after the name and to change the uppercase **P** at the beginning of the sentence to lowercase. When you have made the changes, your screen should look similar to Illustration A.
12. Remove the split screen.
13. Check the spelling and grammar in the document.
14. Preview the document.
15. Print the document.
16. Close the document, saving all changes.

## Press Release

1. In Word, open the file 🖭 **33PRESS1**.
2. Open the file 🖭 **33PRESS2**.
3. Open the file 🖭 **33PRESS3**.
4. Arrange all three documents on the screen at the same time.
5. Make **33PRESS1** active. This is clearly the oldest of the three. It does not have as much information or detail as the others.
6. Close **33PRESS1** without saving any changes.
7. Arrange the remaining two documents on the screen.
8. Make **33PRESS2** active.
9. Select to compare it side by side with **33PRESS3**.
10. Set the zoom to Text Width. Your screen should look similar to Illustration B.
11. The press releases look similar, but are not the same. Read one and then the other to determine which is more complete.
12. If necessary, adjust the zoom to increase the size of the text on-screen.
13. Close the side by side display.
14. Close **33PRESS2** without saving any changes.
15. Maximize **33PRESS3** and then save it as **FINALPRESS**.
16. Replace the text **Your Name** with your name.
17. Check the spelling and grammar in the document.
18. Preview the document.
19. Print the document.
20. Close the document, saving all changes.

## Illustration A

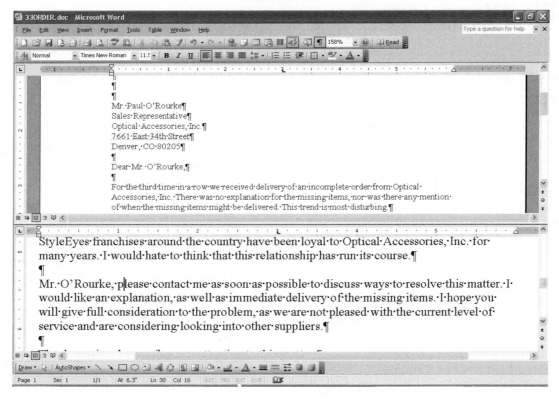

## Illustration B

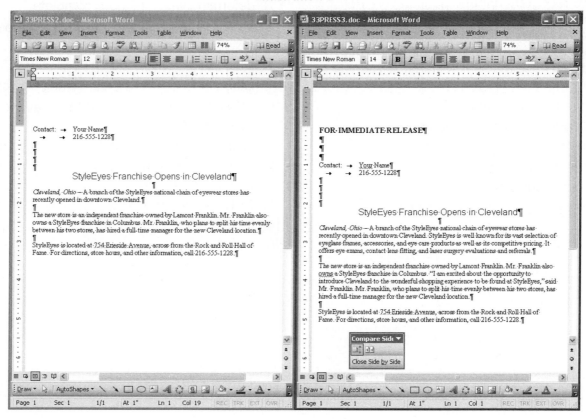

# On Your Own

1. Look around your classroom and note the types of technology that you have available. For example, the hardware may include desktop computers, printers, network drives, CD-ROM drives, monitors, keyboards, and so on. The software may include the Microsoft Office 2003 programs as well as other programs.

2. In addition, consider how each item is used for a different purpose or to accomplish specific tasks.

3. Create a new document in Word.

4. Save the document as **OWD33**.

5. Create a document listing the available hardware and software and the appropriate use for each item. For example, you might use an inkjet printer for printing color documents. You might have a floppy disk drive for storing small files that you need to take to a different computer. You use Word to create text-based documents and PowerPoint to create presentations.

6. Include a heading for the entire document, such as Available Technology, and headings for each category: Hardware and Software.

7. Use tabs to separate the items on the left from the appropriate tasks on the right.

8. As your list gets longer, use Split Screen view to make sure you don't duplicate items that you have already entered.

9. When you believe the list is complete, check the spelling and grammar and then print the document.

10. Close the document, saving all changes.

11. Get together with a classmate who also completed the assignment.

12. Open both your document and his or her document in Word.

13. Working together, compare the two documents side by side to see if you have missing items, or have incorrect information about appropriate usage.

    ✓ *The documents may have the same name; if they are stored in different locations, you can open them both at the same time. Alternatively, you may have to add your initials to the file name to distinguish between the two.*

14. Using a different font or font style, make changes to the documents as necessary.

    ✓ *With the different font, you'll be able to see the information you had originally, and the information you added based on your collaboration with a classmate.*

15. Close all open documents, saving all changes, and exit Word.

# Exercise 34

◆ **Preview a Closed Document** ◆ **Print Files without Opening Them**

## On the Job

Preview a document before opening it or printing it to make sure it is the correct file. Print files without opening them to save time or to print more than one document at once.

The owner of Blue Sky Dairy has asked you to type a letter to a prospective employee confirming a job offer. In this exercise, you will preview, open, and revise a one-page report about the dairy, and then you will create a letter to the applicant. Finally, you will print both documents.

## Notes

### Preview a Closed Document

- By default, Word displays a simple list of files in the Open dialog box.
- You can change the display in the dialog box to show a preview of the document selected in the file list.
- Files are sorted in the files list based on when they were created or modified.
- Previewing is useful for making sure a document is the one you want before you open it or print it.
- Most documents are too large to be displayed completely in the dialog box; use the scroll arrows in the preview area to scroll up and down.
- If you don't want to display a preview, you can set the Open dialog box to display large or small file icons, the default file list, file details, such as size, type, and date last saved, or document properties.

*Preview a document in the Open dialog box*

Selected file　　　　　Preview area　　Views button

### Print Files without Opening Them

- To save time, you can print a document from the Open dialog box without opening it.
- Print without opening when you are certain the document is ready for printing.
  - ✓ *You can also print a document without opening it from the Open Office dialog box or from Windows Explorer.*
- You can select more than one file at a time for printing in the Open dialog box.
- Selecting multiple files for printing sends them all to the printer, where they will be printed one after the other.
- All selected files must be in the same folder.

# Procedures

### Preview a Closed Document

1. Click **File**......................Alt + F
2. Click **Open**..........................O
3. Click **Views** button drop-down arrow ⊞ ▾.
4. Click **Pre_view**.......................V
5. Click document name to preview.

   ✓ *If necessary, select drive and/or folder to locate document.*

### To turn preview off:

1. Click **File**......................Alt + F
2. Click **Open**..........................O
3. Click **Views** button drop-down arrow ⊞ ▾.
4. Select another view:

- Click **Thumbnails** 🔲 .... T
- Click **Tiles** ☑ ............... S
- Click **Icons** ⬚ ............. N
- Click **List** ▤ ............... L
- Click **Details** ▦ ............ D
- Click **Properties** ▦ ...... R

  ✓ *Or click the Views button repeatedly to cycle through the Views options.*

### Print a File Without Opening It

1. Click **File** .....................Alt + F
2. Click **Open** .........................O
3. If necessary, select drive and/or folder to locate document.
4. Select the document.

5. Click **Tools** button

   Tools ▾
   .........................Alt + L
6. Click **Print** .......................... P

### Print Multiple Files

1. Click **File** ...................Alt + F
2. Click **Open** ......................... O
3. Click the first document name.
4. Press and hold **Ctrl**............Ctrl
5. Click each additional document name.
6. Click **Tools** button

   Tools ▾
   .........................Alt + L
   OR
   Right-click selection.
7. Click **Print** .......................... P

# Exercise Directions

1. Start Word, if necessary.
2. In the Open dialog box, preview 📖**DAIRY**, the document you created in Exercise 27, or preview 💿**34DAIRY**.
3. This should be a brief report about Blue Sky Dairy.
4. Change the Open dialog box to display details instead of the preview.
5. Open the document and save it as **INFO**.
6. Make revisions as indicated in Illustration A.
7. If necessary, shrink the document so it fits on one page.

8. Check the spelling and grammar in the document.
9. Close the document, saving all changes.
10. Create a new document and type the letter shown in Illustration B, or open 💿**34LETTER**.
11. Save the document as **LETTER**, and then close it.
12. Preview the document **LETTER** in the Open dialog box.
13. Print both the **INFO** and **LETTER** documents without opening them.

# Blue Sky Dairy Co.

*Co.*

Blue Sky Dairy has been producing quality milk, ice cream, and other dairy products for over 100 years. It is a family-owned farm located in southern Wisconsin, not far from Lake Ripley. In the late 19th century, John and Marie Thomson settled in Wisconsin and started the dairy with a herd of ten cows. Today, Jack and Kimberly Thomson have a thriving business anchored by a herd of 200 pampered Holstein dairy cows.

## The Facility

*to raise happy and productive cows.*

Blue Sky Dairy uses a combination of grazing and confinement. Some of the herd is set out to pasture, while some are housed in free stalls. There are two milking parlors and an ice cream manufacturing facility. Ice cream is the only item currently produced on the farm. The dairy has approximately 55 employees in agriculture, manufacturing, distribution, and support services.

*Additional Blue Sky products are produced at other facilities in Wisconsin.*

## The Products

Blue Sky Dairy is famous for its wholesome, refreshing ice cream products, including prepackaged ice cream and novelties. It sells ice cream direct from its farm stand, and also distributes its products to supermarkets and specialty stores throughout the United States. Blue Sky Dairy has won numerous awards for its ice cream and for its environmentally friendly policies.

For more information about Blue Sky Dairy and its products, contact Kimberly or Jack Thomson at 608-555-2697, or visit the Blue Sky Dairy Web site at www.blueskydairy.net.

*Illustration B*

Today's date

Ms. Gretchen Handel
6733 51st Street
St. Louis, MO 63101

Dear Ms. Handle,

This letter is to confirm the offer of employment as a marketing assistant at Blue Sky Dairy. Blue Sky only hires the most qualified candidates, and I sincerely hope that you will join our staff. Your credentials seem impeccable, and your references all gave you glowing reports.

I have enclosed a brief report about Blue Sky Dairy. If you have any questions, please feel free to call me at any time. I would like to set up an appointment to discuss salary and benefits. I am confident that we can put together a package that you will find suitable.

Again, I hope you will accept our offer. Blue Sky is a great place to work. It has a warm, friendly atmosphere that makes it vibrant and fun. Thank you very much for considering Blue Sky.

Sincerely,

Kimberly Thomson
Owner
Kt/yo

Enclosure

# On Your Own

1. Start Word.
2. Preview some of the documents that you have created for the On Your Own sections of previous exercises, or preview ⊚ **34RESUME**, ⊚ **34BIO**, and ⊚ **34GOALS**.
3. Display details instead of the preview.
4. Display small icons.
5. Display the preview again.
6. Print at least two of the documents without opening them.
7. When you are finished, exit Word.

# Exercise 35

**Skills Covered:**

◆ **Document Properties** ◆ **Use Basic Search to Find a File**

## On the Job

Use document properties to identify important information about a file, such as the name of the author and the main topic. Use a basic search to locate a file so you can open it in Word.

Liberty Blooms is preparing for a new sale. Instead of creating a flyer from scratch, the owner has asked you to locate the old sale flyer and modify it. In this exercise, you will use a basic search to locate the old flyer. You will open and modify the flyer, and save it with a new name. You will enter document properties to help differentiate the new flyer from the old flyer.

## Terms

**Document properties** Categories of information about a document.

**Keywords** Important words found in a document. Keywords can be used to classify a document.

**Wildcard characters** Typed characters that represent one or more other characters. For example, an asterisk (*) is used to represent any other character or string of characters.

## Notes

### Document Properties

- With the **Document Properties** feature you can save information that is unique to a particular document.

- Using document properties can help you identify a document, or differentiate it from another similar document.

- Document properties lets you enter information in five categories:
  - *General properties.* Allows you to view the type of document, its size, its location, when it was created, last accessed, and last modified. Use General properties to check file storage and access information.
  - *Summary properties.* Allows you to enter a document title, subject, author, **keywords**, and comments. Use Summary properties to save summary information with a document.

  - *Statistics properties.* Word automatically updates statistical information including the number of pages, paragraphs, lines, words, and characters in the document. Use Statistics properties to check the size length, or word count in a document.
  - *Contents properties.* Displays the headings in a document if the Save preview picture check box is selected on the Summary tab of the Document Properties dialog box.
  - *Custom properties.* Allows you to specify a name, type and value which you can use to find and link files.

- You can set Word to display the Properties dialog box automatically the first time you save a document.

*The Summary page of the Properties dialog box*

## Use Basic Search to Find a File

- Word has a Search feature that can help you find a file stored anywhere on your computer system, even if you can't remember the file name.

- Use a basic search to locate a file that contains specified text in its title, contents, or properties.

- Enter text in the Search text box to locate files containing that text. The text may be in the body of the file, or in the document properties.

  - Word finds files containing various forms of the search text. For example, if you enter *run*, Word finds documents containing *run*, *running*, or *ran*.

  - You can use **wildcard characters** in the search text.

    - ◆ * represents one or more characters.
    - ◆ ? represents any single character.

- Before starting a search, select the disks or folders to search, as well as the types of files to search for. These can be on your hard drive or on a network.

  - If you know the folder to search, type it in the Search in box.

  - Alternatively, select the check box beside the folder(s) to search.

- In the Results should be box, select the types of files to find:

  - Anything. Finds all file types.

  - Office Files. Finds all files created with Microsoft Office programs. You can select the specific program type.

- Outlook Items. Finds only files created with Microsoft Office Outlook.

- Web Pages. Finds only Web page files.

- You can search using the Search task pane, or by opening the Search dialog box from the Open dialog box. Both methods offer you the same options in slightly different formats.

*Search task pane*

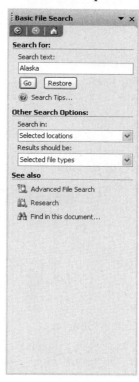

- Word displays files matching your criteria in the Search Results list.

*Search Results in task pane*

# Procedures

## Use Document Properties

1. Click **F**ile ..................... `Alt`+`F`
2. Click **Proper**t**i**es ................ `I`
3. Select desired
   tab ............................. `Ctrl`+`Tab`
4. Enter data as necessary.
5. Click **OK** .......................... `Enter`

## Automatically Display Properties Dialog Box

1. Click **T**ools .................. `Alt`+`T`
2. Click **O**ptions ..................... `O`
3. Click **Save** tab ............. `Ctrl`+`Tab`
4. Select **Prompt for document properties** check
   box ............................. `Alt`+`I`
5. Click **OK** .......................... `Enter`

## Search for Files from the Search Task Pane

1. Click **F**ile ..................... `Alt`+`F`
2. Click **File Search** ............... `H`
3. Type search text in **Search text** box.
   - ✓ *If necessary, delete existing text, first.*
4. Click **Search in**: drop-down arrow to open list.
5. Select folders as follows:
   - Click **plus sign** to
     expand list ....................... `→`
   - Click check box to
     select folder ................ `Space`
   - Click check box twice to select folder and all subfolders

- Click check box three times to select only subfolders
- Click check box four times to deselect subfolders

6. Click **Search in**: drop-down arrow to close list.
7. Click **Results should be**: ............. `Tab`, `Space`
8. Click plus sign to
   expand list ................... `↓`, `→`
9. Click desired file
   type(s) .............. `↑`, `↓`, `Space`
10. Click **Results should be** drop-down arrow to close it.
11. Click **Go** button `Go`.
12. Click file to open.
    OR
    - Click **Modify** button `Modify` to display Basic Search Task Pane again.
    - ✓ *To interrupt a search before it is complete, click the Stop button `Stop`.*

## Search for Files from the Open Dialog Box

1. Click **F**ile ..................... `Alt`+`F`
2. Click **O**pen ........................... `O`
3. Click the **Look in**
   drop-down arrow .......... `Alt`+`I`
4. Select the disk, folder, or network.
   - ✓ *Alternatively, click the folder you want to open in the Places bar.*
5. Click **Tools** drop-down
   arrow `Tools ▾` ............... `Alt`+`L`
6. Click **S**earch ....................... `S`

7. Click **Basic** tab, if
   necessary .................. `Ctrl`+`Tab`
8. Type search text in
   **Search** t**ext** box .......... `Alt`+`T`
   - ✓ *If necessary, delete existing text, first.*
9. Click **Search in**:
   drop-down arrow ......... `Alt`+`I`
10. Select folders as follows:
    - Click plus sign
      to expand list ................. `→`
    - Click check box to select
      folder ........... `↑`, `↓`, `Space`
    - Click check box twice to select folder and all subfolders
    - Click check box three times to select only subfolders
    - Click check box four times to deselect subfolders
11. Click **Results should** b**e**:
    drop-down arrow ......... `Alt`+`B`
12. Click plus sign to expand list
13. Click desired file
    type(s) ... `↑`, `↓`, `Space`, `Enter`
14. Click **Go** button `Go` ... `Alt`+`S`
15. Double-click file to open.
    OR
    a. Click file to open.
    b. Click **OK** ..................... `Enter`
    c. Word displays Open dialog box.
    d. Click **O**pen ............. `Alt`+`O`

# Exercise Directions

✓ *Before beginning this exercise, make sure that the* ⊙**35OLDSALE** *file is stored somewhere on your computer or computer network. Ask your instructor for more information.*

1. Start Word, if necessary.

2. Search your computer for ⊙**35OLDSALE**, the old sale flyer, using the following steps:

   a. Open the Search task pane or the Search dialog box.

   b. Enter the Search text **Summer Clearance Sale**.

   c. Select the folder(s) to search. For example, if the file is stored locally, choose to search drive C, or My Computer. If the file is stored on a network, choose the network drive. The more you can narrow down the location, the faster the search will be.

   d. Select Word Files in the Results should be list.

   e. Start the search.

3. Open the document from the Search Results list.

   ✓ *Word may find many files that contain the search text. Make sure you open the file* ⊙**35OLDSALE**.

4. Save the file as **NEWSALE**.

5. Close the task pane.

6. Make the revisions indicated in Illustration A.

7. Save the file.

8. Use the Properties dialog box to check the number of words in the document.

9. Enter the following summary information:

   Title: **Sale Flyer**

   Subject: **Fall Sale**

   Author: **Your name**

   Manager: **Your instructor's name**

   Company: **Liberty Blooms**

   Category: **Sale Flyer**

   Keywords: **Fall Sale, Promotions, Flyer**

   Comments: **Revised summer sale flyer for fall sale**.

10. Check the spelling and grammar in the document.

11. Print the document.

12. Close the document, saving all changes.

# On Your Own

1. Search for ⌨**OWD33**, the document you used in the On Your Own section of Exercise 33, or search for ⊙**35TECH**.

2. Open the file from the Search Results task pane.

3. Save the file as **OWD35**.

4. Check the number of words in the document.

5. Note the file size, date created, and date last modified.

6. Enter document properties, including Title, Subject, Manager, Company, Category, Keywords, and Comments.

7. Close the document and exit Word.

# Liberty Blooms

## Flowers, Plants, And More

Announcing the

Annual ~~Summer~~ ^Fall^ Clearance Sale

Take advantage of special savings on everything in the store, including the following items:

Topiaries ........................................ $~~9~~ ^5^.95 and up

*Silk Roses* ^
~~Bonsai Trees~~ ........................... $24.99 and up   2.99 per stem

Hanging Planters ....................... $10.00 and up

Dried Floral Arrangements ....... $~~7~~ ^9^.50 and up

# Liberty Blooms

345 Chestnut Street
Philadelphia, PA 19106
Phone: (215) 555-2837

*Liberty Blooms conducts free classes and seminars on a wide range of topics. For a complete schedule give us a call, or look us up on-line at www.libertyblooms.net.*

# Exercise 36

## ◆ Critical Thinking

The owner of Liberty Blooms has asked you to locate the press release used to announce the store's summer hours and modify it to announce extended hours for the fall sale. She also wants you to save a copy of it in text format so she can take it home and use it with a different computer program. Finally, she wants you to print copies of the new press release in both .rtf and .doc formats, and the sale flyer you created in the previous exercise in .doc format.

## Exercise Directions

1. Start Word, if necessary.

2. Search for and open the file 🞉**36HOURS** using the search text **Summer Hours**.

3. Open the file and save it as **SALEHOURS**.

4. Make changes to the document as marked on Illustration A.

5. Edit the information on the Document Properties summary tab as follows:

   Title: **Liberty Blooms Announces Sale Hours**
   Subject: **Extended hours for fall sale**
   Author: **Your name**
   Keywords: Edit **Summer Hours** to **Sale Hours**.

6. Check the spelling and grammar.

7. Save the changes.

8. Save the document in rich text format with the name **RTFHOURS**.

   ✓ *Unlike Plain Text format, Rich Text Format preserves some font formatting. It has an .rtf file extension.*

9. In the Open dialog box, locate and preview the **SALEHOURS** document

10. Open the **SALEHOURS** document as read-only.

11. Compare the **SALEHOURS** document side by side with the **RTFHOURS** document to see if using Rich Text Format caused any formatting problems.

12. Close side by side and then close both documents, saving changes if necessary.

13. In the Open dialog box, locate and preview the file 🖮**NEWSALE** or the file 🞉**36NEWSALE** to be sure it is the flyer for the fall sale.

14. Locate and preview the rich text format **RTFHOURS** document and the Word document **SALEHOURS**.

    ✓ *Remember, to display the RTFHOURS document in the Open dialog box you will have to select to display all file types.*

15. Print all three documents without opening them.

16. Exit Word.

**FOR IMMEDIATE RELEASE**

*duration of its Fall clearance sale by two
hours on Fridays, Saturdays, and Sundays.*

# Liberty Blooms Announces ~~Summer~~ Hours

*Sale*

***Philadelphia, PA*** – ~~Anticipating longer days and more foot traffic,~~ Liberty Blooms, an independently-owned flower shop on Chestnut Street, has extended its hours for the ~~summer months.~~ The longer hours will allow the shop to service more customers.

"It's been a long winter," remarked Kristin Dadarian, a store employee. "People are ready to stay out later and buy more flowers and plants." Ms. Dadarian said she believes the new hours will appeal to tourists as well as to the long-time clients who live or work in the area.

Liberty Blooms has been in business for eight years. It offers cut flowers, houseplants, floral arrangements for all occasions, and gift items with a floral theme. It is located at 345 Chestnut Street in Philadelphia. For more information, call 215-555-2837.

*"We want to be sure everyone has the opportunity to experience our annual fall sale," said Kristin Dadarian, a store employee. "This sale offers exceptional values on some of our most popular items." According to Ms. Dadarian, the sale includes everything from silk flowers to bonsai trees.*

# Lesson 7

## Creating Tables

# Exercise 37

## Skills Covered:

◆ **Insert a Table** ◆ **Move the Insertion Point in a Table**
◆ **Enter Data in a Table** ◆ **Format a Table**

## On the Job

Create tables to organize data into columns and rows. Any information that needs to be presented in side-by-side columns can be set up in a table. For example, a price list, an invoice, a resume, and a script are all types of documents for which you should use a table. The table format lets you align information side by side and across the page so the information is easy to read.

Long Shot, Inc. is offering the staff training courses. In this exercise, you will create a memo that includes a list of courses being offered. You will set up the course list in a table.

## Terms

**Table** A grid comprised of horizontal rows and vertical columns into which you can enter data.

**Column** A vertical series of cells in a table.

**Row** A horizontal series of cells in a table.

**Column markers** Markers on the horizontal ruler that indicate column borders.

**Dividers** The lines that indicate the edges of cells in a table. Dividers do not print, although they are indicated on-screen by either gridlines or borders.

**Border** A line drawn around the edges of an element, such as a table or a table cell. Borders can also be drawn around paragraphs and pages.

**Cell** The rectangular area at the intersection of a column and a row in a table, into which you enter data.

**Gridline** A nonprinting line that indicates the boundaries of cells in a table.

**End of row/cell marks** Nonprinting characters used to mark the end of a cell or a row in a table.

## Notes

### Insert a Table

■ **Tables** are easier to use than tabbed columns when setting up and organizing data in **columns** and **rows**.

■ You can insert a table in any Word document using either of the following methods:
  • The Insert Table button 🖩 on the Standard toolbar
  • The Insert, Table command on the Table menu

✓ *You can also draw a table using the Draw Table tool on the Tables and Borders toolbar. The Draw Table button is covered in Exercise 40.*

■ With either method, you specify the number of columns and rows you want in the table.

■ Word inserts the table at the insertion point location.

■ By default, Word sizes the columns equally across the width of the page.

■ **Column markers** on the horizontal ruler show the location of the right **divider** of each column.

■ By default, Word places a ½-pt. **border** around all **cells** in a table.

*A table with four columns and four rows*

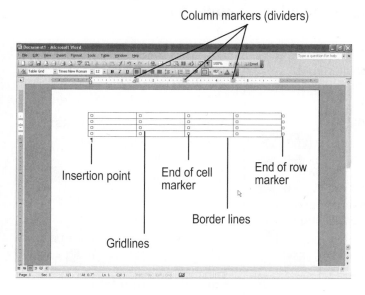

■ Tables have three unique nonprinting elements:
  • **Gridlines**
    ✓ *Gridlines are only displayed if there are no table borders and if you select the Show Gridlines command on the Table menu.*
  • **End of cell markers**
  • **End of row markers**

## Move the Insertion Point in a Table

■ You must position the insertion point in the table cell where you want characters to be entered.

■ You can move the insertion point with the keyboard or mouse.

## Enter Data in a Table

■ You enter data in the cells of a table.

■ Row height increases automatically to accommodate as much data as you type.

■ Column width does not change automatically. Text wraps at the right margin of a cell the same way it wraps at the right margin of a page.

■ When you press Enter in a cell, Word starts a new paragraph within the cell.

■ You can edit and format text within a cell the same way you do outside a table.

## Format a Table

■ By default, a table is formatted in the Table Grid style.

■ Format text within a table using standard Word formatting techniques. For example, use font formatting, alignments, spacing, and indents to enhance text in a table.

■ Apply formatting to new text, selected text, or to selected cells, columns, or rows.
    ✓ *You select text in a cell using the same techniques you use to select text outside a table. Learn about selecting table components such as cells, rows, and columns in Exercise 38.*

■ Select a table AutoFormat style to quickly apply formatting effects to an entire table.

■ AutoFormat styles include border lines, shading, color, fonts, and other formatting.

*The Table AutoFormat dialog box*

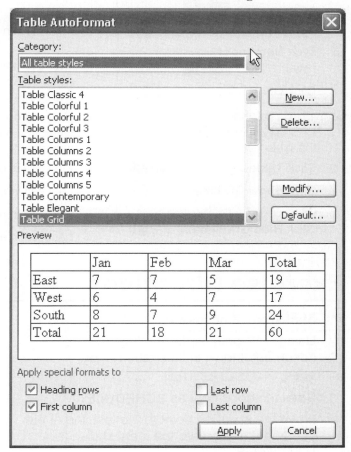

■ AutoFormat overrides existing formatting. Therefore, you should apply AutoFormat first, then apply additional formatting as needed.

# Procedures

## Insert a Table

**Use the toolbar button:**

1. Position insertion point.
2. Click **Insert Table** button ⊞.
3. Drag the mouse pointer across the grid to select desired number of columns and rows.
4. Release the mouse button.

**Use menu commands:**

1. Position the insertion point.
2. Click **T**able .................. `Alt`+`A`
3. Select **I**nsert ...................... `I`
4. Click **T**able .......................... `T`
5. Type **Number of** **c**olumns ....... `Alt`+`C`, *number*
6. Press **Tab** .......................... `Tab`
7. Type **Number of** **r**ows .............. `Alt`+`R`, *number*
8. Click **OK** ........................... `Enter`

**Show/Hide gridlines:**

1. Click anywhere within the table.
2. Click **T**able .................. `Alt`+`A`
3. Click **Show G**ridlines ......... `G`

   OR

   Click **Hide G**ridlines ........... `G`

## Move the Insertion Point in a Table

**With the mouse:**

- Click mouse pointer in cell where you want to position insertion point.

**With the keyboard:**

- One cell left ............... `Shift`+`Tab`

  or `Ctrl`+`↑`

  or `←`

  when insertion point is at beginning of cell.

- One cell right ..................... `Tab`

  or `Ctrl`+`↓`

  or `→`

  when insertion point is at beginning of cell.

- One cell up ......................... `↑`

  when insertion point is on first line of cell.

- One cell down ..................... `↓`

  when insertion point is on last line of cell.

- First cell in column ..... `Alt`+`Page Up`
- Last cell in column ...... `Alt`+`Page Down`
- First cell in row ........ `Alt`+`Home`
- Last cell in row .......... `Alt`+`End`

## Enter Data in a Table

1. Click in desired cell.
2. Type data.
3. Move to next cell.
4. Type data.
5. Repeat until all data is entered.

## Apply a Table AutoFormat

1. Click anywhere within the table.
2. Click **T**able .................. `Alt`+`A`
3. Click **Table AutoF**ormat ..... `F`
4. Select **T**able style ..................... `Alt`+`T`, `↓`
5. Click **A**pply ... `Alt`+`A` or `Enter`

## Format text in a table

1. Select text to format.
2. Apply formatting as with regular document text.

# Exercise Directions

1. Start Word, if necessary.
2. Using a 12-point serif font, type the document shown in Illustration A, or open ⊙ **37SCHEDULE**.
3. Save the document as **SCHEDULE**.
4. Move the insertion point to the last line of the document and create the table shown in Illustration B.

   a. Insert a table with three columns and five rows.

   b. Enter the data as shown.

   ✓ *To insert the em dash in the time, type two dashes; AutoFormat will replace them. Alternatively, insert the em dash special character from the Symbol dialog box.*

   c. Apply the Table Contemporary AutoFormat style to the table.

   d. Apply bold italics to all of the course names.

5. Check the spelling and grammar in the document.
6. Preview the document. It should look similar to Illustration B.
7. Print the document.
8. Close the document, saving all changes.

*Illustration A*

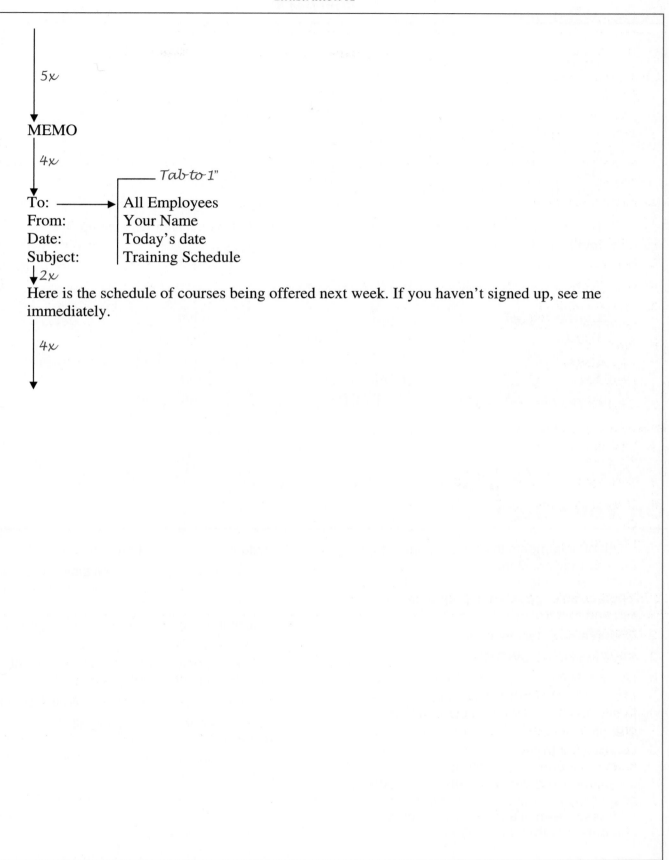

5x

MEMO

4x

Tab to 1"

To: ⟶ All Employees
From:       Your Name
Date:       Today's date
Subject:    Training Schedule

2x

Here is the schedule of courses being offered next week. If you haven't signed up, see me immediately.

4x

MEMO

To:              All Employees
From:          Your Name
Date:           Today's date
Subject:      Training Schedule

Here is the schedule of courses being offered next week. If you haven't signed up, see me immediately.

| Course Name | Location | Time |
|---|---|---|
| *Word 1* | Conference Room A | 8:30 – 11:45 |
| *Word 2* | Conference Room A | 1:30 – 3:30 |
| *Excel 3* | Conference Room B | 8:30 – 11:45 |
| *Intro to the Internet* | Media Lab | 1:30 – 3:30 |

# On Your Own

1. Think of documents that would benefit from table formatting. Some examples include a weekly schedule, meeting agenda, travel itinerary, sales report, telephone/address list, and roster.

2. Create a new document in Word.

3. Save the file as **OWD37**.

4. Use a table to set up the document as a telephone list. The list could include friends, family members, or members of a club or organization to which you belong.

5. Use at least three columns—one for the first name, one for the last name, and one for the telephone number. You may use more columns if you want to include mailing addresses, e-mail addresses, cell phone numbers, or other information.

6. Include at least eight names in the list.

7. Apply an AutoFormat to the table. If you are not satisfied with the results, try a different AutoFormat.

8. Check the spelling and grammar in the document, then print it.

9. Ask a classmate to review the document and offer comments or suggestions.

10. Incorporate the suggestions into the document.

11. Close the document, saving all changes, and exit Word.

# Exercise 38

## Skills Covered:

◆ **Select in a Table** ◆ **Insert Columns, Rows, or Cells**
◆ **Delete Columns, Rows, or Cells**

## On the Job

You can change the structure of a table to add or delete columns, rows, or cells. You can even delete the entire table. In order to make changes affecting the table structure, you must first select the elements you want to change.

The Training Director at Long Shot, Inc. wants you to change the training course schedule. In this exercise, you add a column to the schedule table and add and delete rows.

## Terms

**Table components**  Parts of a table, including columns, rows, and cells.

## Notes

### Select in a Table

- As with other Word features, you must select **table components** before you can affect them with commands.
- You select text within a cell using the standard selection commands.

  ✓ *Selecting text is covered in Exercise 9.*

- You can select one or more columns, one or more rows, one or more cells, or the entire table.
- Selected table components appear highlighted.

*A table with the third row selected*

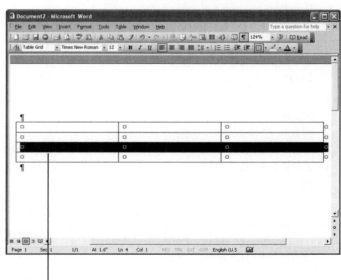

Row selected in a table

## Insert Columns, Rows, or Cells

- You can insert columns, rows, or cells anywhere in a table.
- If necessary, you specify where to insert the new component—above, below, to the left, or to the right of the current component.

## Delete Columns, Rows, or Cells

- You can delete any column, row, or cell.
- If necessary, you specify how to shift remaining components to fill in the area left by the deletion.
- You can delete an entire table.
- Data entered in a deleted column, row, or cell is deleted as well.

# Procedures

### Select in a Table

1. Position insertion point within table component to select.
   - ✓ *For example, click in cell if selecting cell; click anywhere in row if selecting row, etc.*
2. Click **Table**................. Alt + A
3. Click **Select**........................ C
4. Click one of the following:
   - **Table** ............................ T
   - **Column** ........................ C
   - **Row** .............................. R
   - **Cell** ............................... E

### Select with the Mouse

**Column:**

1. Position mouse pointer at top of column until pointer resembles a small, black, down-pointing arrow ↓.
2. Click.

**Row:**

1. Position mouse pointer to left of row until pointer resembles a white right-pointing arrow with a black outline ⇗.
2. Click.

**Cell:**

1. Position mouse pointer to right of left cell border until pointer resembles a small, black, right-pointing arrow ➚.
2. Click.

### Select adjacent components:

1. Select first component.
2. Press and hold **Shift**.......... Shift
3. Click in last component to select.
   - ✓ *This method enables you to select adjacent columns, adjacent rows, or adjacent cells.*

### Select nonadjacent components:

1. Select first components.
2. Press and hold **Ctrl** ........... Ctrl
3. Click in next component to select.
4. Repeat until all desired components are selected.

### Insert Columns, Rows, or Cells

1. Position insertion point within table.
   - ✓ *To insert more than one component, select as many as you want to insert. For example, to insert two columns, select two columns.*
2. Click **Table** ................. Alt + A
3. Click **Insert**........................... I
4. Click one of the following:
   - **Columns to the Left**...... L
   - **Columns to the Right** ... R
   - **Rows Above**.................. A
   - **Rows Below** ................. B
   - **Cells**.............................. E
     - a. Select option for shifting existing cells to make room for new cells.
     - b. Click **OK** ............... Enter

### Delete Columns, Rows, or Cells

1. Select cells, or click in the row or column to delete.
2. Click **Table** ................. Alt + A
3. Click **Delete**........................ D
4. Click one of the following:
   - **Columns**...................... C
   - **Rows** ........................... R
   - **Cells** ........................... E
     - a. Select option for shifting existing cells to make room for new cells.
     - b. Click **OK**................ Enter

### Delete Entire Table

1. Click anywhere in table.
2. Click **Table** ................. Alt + A
3. Click **Delete**........................ D
4. Click **Table** ........................ T

# Exercise Directions

1. Start Word, if necessary.

2. Open ⌨SCHEDULE or open ⊙38SCHEDULE.

3. Save the document as **SCHEDULE2**.

4. Select the last two rows in the table.

5. Insert two new rows above the selected rows.

6. Enter the following data in the new rows:

   **Word 3    Conference   8:30–11:45**
   **           Room A**

   **Excel 2   Conference   3:00–4:30**
   **           Room B**

7. Insert another new row between the Word 3 and Excel 2 rows, and enter the following data:

   **Excel 1   Conference   1:30–3:30**
   **           Room B**

8. Insert a new column between the Location column and the Time Column.

9. Enter the following data in the new column:
   **Days**
   **Monday, Wednesday**
   **Monday, Wednesday**
   **Tuesday, Thursday**
   **Tuesday, Thursday**
   **Tuesday, Thursday**
   **Monday, Wednesday**
   **Friday**

10. Delete the row for the Word 1 course.

11. Apply the Table 3D effects 2 AutoFormat style to the table.

12. Check the spelling and grammar in the document.

13. Preview the document. It should look similar to the one in Illustration A.

14. Print the document.

15. Close the document, saving all changes.

# On Your Own

1. Open ⌨OWD37, the document you created in the On Your Own section of Exercise 37, or open ⊙38TABLE.

2. Save the document as **OWD38**.

3. Add two new rows to the table.

4. Add a new column.

5. Fill in the data for the new rows and column.

6. Delete one row.

7. Apply a different AutoFormat to the table.

8. Save the changes and print the document.

9. Ask a classmate to review the document and offer comments and suggestions.

10. Incorporate the comments and suggestions into the document.

11. Save the document, close it, and exit Word.

MEMO


To:          All Employees
From:        Your Name
Date:        Today's date
Subject:     Training Schedule

Here is the schedule of courses being offered next week. If you haven't signed up, see me immediately.


| Course Name | Location | Days | Time |
|---|---|---|---|
| *Word 2* | Conference Room A | Monday, Wednesday | 1:30 – 3:30 |
| *Word 3* | Conference Room A | Tuesday, Thursday | 8:30 – 11:45 |
| *Excel 1* | Conference Room B | Tuesday, Thursday | 1:30 – 3:30 |
| *Excel 2* | Conference Room B | Tuesday, Thursday | 3:00 – 4:30 |
| *Excel 3* | Conference Room B | Monday, Wednesday | 8:30 – 11:45 |
| *Intro to the Internet* | Media Lab | Friday | 1:30 – 3:30 |

# Exercise 39

## On the Job

Use alignment options and tabs to make tables easy to read. Numbers are usually aligned flush right in a cell, while text can be flush left, centered, or justified. You can vertically align data in a cell as well. Decimal tabs are especially useful in tables for aligning dollar values. Other ways to improve the appearance of a table include aligning the table horizontally on the page, and adjusting column width and row height.

The owner of the StyleEyes franchise in Cleveland, Ohio has asked you to create a flyer announcing clearance sale prices. In this exercise, you will create a document listing sale price information. You will use different alignment options to set up the data in the table. You will also set row heights and column widths, and you will align the table horizontally on the page.

## Terms

**Column width** The width of a column in a table, measured in inches.

**Row height** The height of a row in a table, measured in inches.

## Notes

### Set Alignments within Table Cells

- You can set horizontal alignment within a cell the same way you set alignment in a document by using paragraph formatting and tabs.

- In a table, numbers are usually right aligned, and text is either left aligned or centered.

- All tab stops can be used within a table cell, but the most useful is the decimal tab stop.

- Decimal tab stops automatically align numbers such as dollar values within a cell or a column.

- You can vertically align data at the top of the cell, centered in the cell, or at the bottom of the cell. The default is at the top.

*Aligned text in a table*

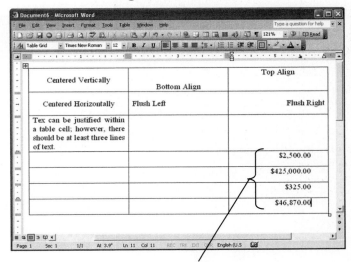

Aligned on a decimal tab

193

## Align Table on the Page

- You can left align, right align, or center a table on the page.

*Table tab of the Table Properties dialog box*

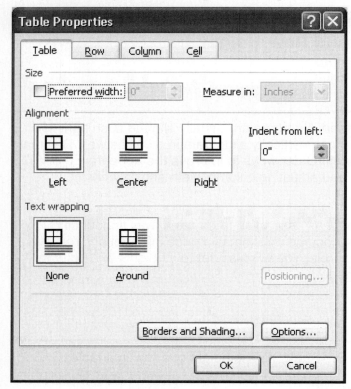

## Column Width and Row Height

- By default, Word creates columns of equal **column width**, sized so the table extends from the left margin to the right margin.

- Rows are sized according to the line spacing on the line of the document where the table is inserted.

- By default, **row height** automatically increases to accommodate lines of text typed in a cell.

- You can drag column dividers to increase or decrease column width.

  ✓ *Press and hold the* **Alt** *key as you drag to see the column width measurements displayed on the ruler.*

- In Print Layout view, you can drag row dividers to increase or decrease row height.

  ✓ *You cannot drag row dividers In Normal view.*

- Set precise measurements for columns, rows, cells, and entire tables in the Table Properties dialog box.

# Procedures

## Set Horizontal Alignment in a Cell

1. Position insertion point in cell.
   **OR**
   Select component(s) to format.
2. Click desired alignment button on Formatting toolbar:
   - **Align Left** 📄.
   - **Center** 📄.
   - **Align Right** 📄.
   - **Justify** 📄.

## Set Tabs in a Cell

1. Position insertion point in cell.
   **OR**
   Select component(s) to format.
2. Click Tab box at left end of horizontal ruler to select tab stop type.
3. Click desired position on horizontal ruler.

   ✓ *For more information on tabs, refer to Exercise 13.*

## Advance insertion point one tab stop within a table cell:

- Press **Ctrl+Tab** ........... `Ctrl`+`Tab`

## Set Vertical Alignment in a Cell

1. Position insertion point in cell.
   **OR**
   Select component(s) to format.
2. Click **T**a**ble**.................... `Alt`+`A`
3. Click **Table P**roperties ........ `R`
4. Click the **C**ell tab ........ `Alt`+`E`
5. Click desired Vertical Alignment option:
   - **Top** ⬜. ................. `Alt`+`P`
   - **C**enter ▤ ............. `Alt`+`C`
   - **B**ottom ▤ ............ `Alt`+`B`
6. Click **OK** .......................... `Enter`

## Align a Table Horizontally

1. Select table.
2. Click desired alignment button on Formatting toolbar:
   - **Center** 📄.
   - **Align Right** 📄.
   - **Align Left** 📄.

   **OR**
1. Click anywhere in table.
2. Click **T**able .................. `Alt`+`A`
3. Click **Table P**roperties ........ `R`
4. Click the **T**able tab ...... `Alt`+`T`
5. Click desired Alignment option:
   - **L**eft ⊞ ................ `Alt`+`L`
   - **C**enter ⊞ ........... `Alt`+`C`
   - **Rig**h**t** ⊞ ............. `Alt`+`H`
6. Click **OK** .......................... `Enter`

## Change Column Width

1. Position mouse pointer on column divider.

   ✓ *Pointer changes to a double-vertical line with arrows pointing left and right* ↔.
2. Drag divider left or right.

   ✓ *Press* `Alt` *at the same time that you drag the divider to see the width displayed on the horizontal ruler.*

   **OR**
1. Click in column.
2. Click **T**able .................. `Alt`+`A`
3. Click **Table P**roperties ........ `R`
4. Click **Column** tab ........ `Alt`+`U`
5. Select **Preferred Width** check box ......... `Alt`+`W`
6. Press **Tab** .......................... `Tab`
7. Type column width in inches.
8. Click **OK** .......................... `Enter`
   **OR**
   Click **Next Column**
   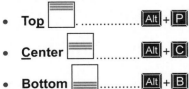 ..... `Alt`+`N`

## OR
Click **Previous Column**
 ..... `Alt`+`P`

9. Repeat steps 5-8 to set additional column widths.
10. Click **OK** .......................... `Enter`

## Change Row Height

1. Change to Print Layout view.
2. Position mouse pointer on row divider.

   ✓ *Pointer changes to a double-vertical line with arrows pointing up and down* ⬍.
3. Click and drag divider up or down.

   ✓ *Press* `Alt` *at the same time that you drag the divider to see the height displayed on the vertical ruler.*

   **OR**
1. Click in row.
2. Click **T**able .................. `Alt`+`A`
3. Click **Table P**roperties ....... `R`
4. Click **R**ow tab ............................... `Alt`+`R`
5. Select **Specify Height** check box .................. `Alt`+`S`
6. Press **Tab** .......................... `Tab`
7. Type row height in inches.

   ✓ *Select Exactly in Row height is box to fix row height at specified size.*
8. Click **OK** .......................... `Enter`
   **OR**
   Click **Next Row**
   ` Next Row ⯯ ` ..... `Alt`+`N`
   **OR**
   Click **Previous Row**
   ` ⯭ Previous Row ` ..... `Alt`+`P`
9. Repeat steps 5-8 to set additional column widths.
10. Click **OK** .......................... `Enter`

# Exercise Directions

1. Start Word, if necessary.
2. Type the document shown in Illustration A, or open ⊙ **39SALE**.
3. Save the file as **SALE2**.
   - ✓ *If you type the document, you must clear the formatting from the current line before inserting the table. If you do not clear the formatting, the text in the table will have the current font formatting, and the table itself will have the current paragraph formatting.*
4. Format the table as follows:
   a. Set column 1 to be 2" wide.
   b. Set the other columns to be 1" wide.
   c. Set row 1 to be at least .75" high.
   d. Set all remaining rows to be exactly .5" high.
   e. Make the text in the first row bold, italic, and 18 points.
5. Set alignment in the table as follows:
   a. Center the data in the first row vertically and horizontally.
   b. Vertically align all other rows with the bottom of the cells.
   c. Right align the data in the **In Stock?** column.
   d. Use decimal tabs to align the prices in both the **Regular Price** and the **Sale Price** columns.
6. Center the entire table horizontally on the page.
7. Check the spelling and grammar in the document.
8. Preview the document. It should look similar to Illustration B.
9. Print the document.
10. Close the document, saving all changes.

# On Your Own

1. Open ⌨**OWD38**, the document you used in the On Your Own section of Exercise 38, or open ⊙ **39TABLE**.
2. Save the document as **OWD39**.
3. Adjust the column widths and row heights by dragging the table borders.
4. Set precise column widths and row heights.
5. Use different alignments in the table.
6. Center the table on the page.
7. Save the changes and print the document.
8. Ask a classmate to review the document and make comments and suggestions.
9. Incorporate the comments and suggestions into the document.
10. Close the document, saving all changes, and exit Word.

*Illustration A*

72-point Arial ——— # StyleEyes

18-point Arial ——— "Fashion Eyewear at Affordable Prices"

12-point Arial, 48 pts of space after ——— 754 Erieside Avenue 👁 Cleveland, OH 44114 👁 216-555-1228

Webding symbol #78

Centered

18-point Times New Roman, 24 pts of space after ——— CLEARANCE SALE

| Item | In Stock? | Regular Price | Sale Price |
|---|---|---|---|
| Oakley frames | No | $195.00 | $155.00 |
| Nike frames | No | $188.00 | $149.00 |
| Colored contact lenses | Yes | $75.00 | $65.00 |
| Lens solution | Yes | $5.99 | $4.49 |
| Glasses holders | Yes | $3.99 | $1.99 |
| Glasses cases | Yes | $5.99 | $3.49 |
| Clip-on sunglasses | Yes | $19.99 | $14.99 |
| Cleaning cloths | Yes | $3.29 | $1.99 |

# StyleEyes

### "Fashion Eyewear at Affordable Prices"
754 Erieside Avenue ☯ Cleveland, OH 44114 ☯ 216-555-1228

## CLEARANCE SALE

| Item | In Stock? | Regular Price | Sale Price |
|---|---|---|---|
| Oakley frames | No | $195.00 | $155.00 |
| Nike frames | No | $188.00 | $149.00 |
| Colored contact lenses | Yes | $75.00 | $65.00 |
| Lens solution | Yes | $5.99 | $4.49 |
| Glasses holders | Yes | $3.99 | $1.99 |
| Glasses cases | Yes | $5.99 | $3.49 |
| Clip-on sunglasses | Yes | $19.99 | $14.99 |
| Cleaning cloths | Yes | $3.29 | $1.99 |

# Procedures

## Display Tables and Borders Toolbar

- Click **Tables and Borders** button 📝 on the Standard toolbar.

OR

1. Click **View**.....................Alt+V
2. Click **Toolbars**....................T
3. Click **Tables and Borders**.

OR

1. Right-click any toolbar.
2. Click **Tables and Borders**.

## Draw a Table

1. Click **Table**..................Alt+A
2. Click **Draw Table** ................W

OR

Click **Draw Table** button 📝 on Tables and Borders toolbar.

  ✓ *The mouse pointer resembles a pencil.*

3. Click where you want to position the upper-left corner of the table.
4. Drag diagonally down and to the right.
5. Release mouse button where you want to position the lower-right corner of the table.

  ✓ *This draws one cell.*

6. Click and drag the mouse pointer to draw horizontal borders and vertical borders.

  ✓ *As you drag, Word displays a dotted line where the border will be. Once you drag far enough, Word completes the line when you release the mouse button.*

7. Click **Esc**.............................Esc to turn off Draw Table.

OR

Click **Draw Table** button 📝.

## Merge Cells

1. Select cells to merge.
2. Click **Merge Cells** button 📑.

OR

a. Click **Table** ............Alt+A
b. Click **Merge Cells** ..........M

## Merge Cells and Erase Table Dividers

1. Click **Eraser** button 📝 on the Tables and Borders toolbar.
2. Click on border to erase.
3. Click **Esc** ............................Esc to turn off Eraser.

OR

Click **Eraser** button 📝.

## Split Cells

1. Select cell to split.
2. Click **Split Cells** button 📰.

OR

a. Click **Table** .............Alt+A
b. Click **Split Cells** .............P

3. Enter **Number of columns** to create ............Alt+C, *number*
4. Enter **Number of rows** to create ............Alt+R, *number*
5. Click **OK** ........................... Enter

## Apply Cell Borders

1. Position insertion point in cell to format.

OR

Select component(s) to format.

2. Click **Borders** drop-down arrow 📑.
3. Click border style.

  ✓ *Border buttons are toggles— click to display border; click again to hide border.*

## Apply Line Styles

1. Click cell to format.

OR

Select component(s) to format.

2. Click **Line Style** drop-down arrow ⬚.
3. Click desired line style.

  ✓ *Click No Border to remove border lines.*

4. Apply cell border(s) as desired.

## Apply Line Weight

1. Click cell to format.

OR

Select component(s) to format.

2. Click **Line Weight** drop-down arrow ½.
3. Click desired line weight.
4. Apply cell border(s) as desired.

## Apply Line Color

1. Click cell to format.

OR

Select component(s) to format.

2. Click **Border Color** button 📝.
3. Click desired color.
4. Apply cell border(s) as desired.

## Apply Cell Shading

1. Position insertion point in cell to format.

OR

Select component(s) to format.

2. Click **Shading Color** drop-down arrow 🪣.
3. Click desired color.

  ✓ *Click No Fill to remove shading or color.*

## Align Data in Cells

1. Position insertion point in cell to format.

OR

Select component(s) to format.

2. Click Align drop-down arrow ▦.
3. Click desired alignment option.

# Exercise Directions

1. Start Word, if necessary.

2. Type the document shown in Illustration A, or open 💿 **40REGIONS**

3. Save the document as **REGIONS**.

4. Move the insertion point to the last line of the document.

5. Use the Draw Table tool to draw a cell approximately 4" wide and 4" high.

   ✓ *Use the rulers as guides to measure the height and width of cells as you draw, but don't worry if the table components are not sized exactly. You can adjust column width and row height as necessary.*

6. Divide the cell into two columns by drawing a vertical line through the cell. Try to size the columns as follows:

   Column 1 – 1.5" wide
   Column 2 – 2.5" wide

7. Divide the table into four rows, about 1" high each.

8. Merge the cells in the top row to create one cell the width of the table.

9. Leaving the top row intact, use the Split Cells tool to divide each of the cells in the right column into two rows (refer to Illustration B to see the desired result).

   ✓ *Split each cell into one column and two rows.*

10. Enter the text shown in Illustration B, using the following formatting and alignments to achieve the desired result:

    a. Row 1 (Table title): 18-point sans serif, bold. Centered both horizontally and vertically. Apply a 12.5% gray shading and a 3 pt. solid black line border across the bottom of the cell.

    b. Chapter names: 14-point serif, bold, aligned left and centered vertically. Apply a 5% gray shading to each cell containing a chapter name.

    c. Locations and dates: 14-point serif, centered horizontally and aligned vertically with the cell bottom. Replace the solid line border between the locations and the dates with a ½ pt. dashed line border in red.

    d. Apply a 2¼ pt. double line border in black around the outside of the entire table

11. Center the entire table horizontally on the page.

12. Check the spelling and grammar in the document.

13. Preview the document. It should look similar to the one in the Illustration B.

14. Print the document.

15. Close the document, saving all changes.

# On Your Own

1. Create a new document and save it as **OWD40**.

2. Create a weekly schedule for yourself by drawing a table. For example, the first column may be time periods or class blocks, and you may enter days across the top row of the schedule.

3. Fill in the schedule using uneven columns and rows.

4. If necessary, merge and split cells to create the schedule correctly.

5. Use different alignments in the table.

6. Apply borders and shading to improve the appearance and readability of the schedule.

7. Center the table on the page.

8. Save the document and print it.

9. Ask a classmate to review the document and make suggestions and comments.

10. Incorporate the suggestions and comments into the document.

11. Close the document, saving all changes, and exit Word.

*Illustration A*

24-pt. Arial — # Horticultural Shop Owners Association

12-point Arial, 24 points of space after — 452 Cathedral Street - Baltimore, MD 21201

*Centered*

22-point Arial, 24 points of space after — ## MEMORANDUM

*Tab to 1"*

| | |
|---|---|
| Date: ——→ | Today's date |
| To: | Ms. Knowlton |
| From: | Your Name |
| Subject: | Regional Meetings |

*12 points of space*

Below are the dates and locations of the three regional meetings scheduled in the coming months. Let me know if you would like to attend any of the meetings and I will make the travel arrangements.

*12 points of space*

*Insert table here*

*12-point Times New Roman*

# Horticultural Shop Owners Association

452 Cathedral Street - Baltimore, MD 21201

## MEMORANDUM

Date:        Today's date
To:          Ms. Knowlton
From:        Your Name
Subject:     Regional Meetings

Below are the dates and locations of the three regional meetings scheduled in the coming months. Let me know if you would like to attend any of the meetings and I will make the travel arrangements.

| HSOA Regional Meetings | |
| --- | --- |
| **Mid Atlantic Chapter** | August 14 – 18 <br> Philadelphia, Pennsylvania |
| **Mid West Chapter** | August 27 – 31 <br> Cleveland, Ohio |
| **Southeast Chapter** | September 9 – 13 <br> Phoenix, Arizona |

# Exercise 41

◆ **Move and Resize Tables** ◆ **Rotate Text** ◆ **Wrap Text**

## On the Job

You can position and format a table in a text document so it complements the document text. Once a table is in place in a document, you can easily move it and resize it. You can set Word to wrap document text around the table, and you can rotate text in table cells to achieve the exact effect you need.

Ms. Knowlton, the Director of the Horticultural Shop Owners Association, wants to send the information about regional meetings to other association volunteers and employees. In this exercise, you will modify the memo, including the table. You will move and resize the table, rotate text in the table, and set the memo text to wrap around the table.

## Terms

**Table move handle** A rectangle with a four-headed arrow in it, displayed at the upper-left corner of a table, and used to move the table.

**Sizing handle** A rectangle displayed somewhere along the sides of an object, used to resize the object. A table's sizing handle is displayed at the lower-right corner of the table.

**Rotate text** Shift the position of text so it runs top to bottom or bottom to top, instead of left to right.

**Wrap** Control the way text flows around an object, such as a table.

## Notes

### Move and Resize Tables

- You can drag the **table move handle** to move the table anywhere on the page.
- You can drag the **sizing handle** to change the table size.

*Table anchor and sizing handle*

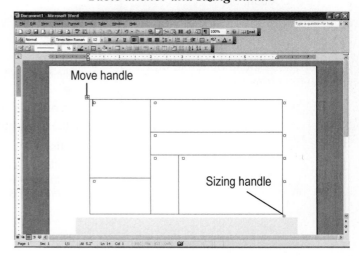

## Rotate Text

- **Rotate text** direction within a cell so text runs from left to right, from top to bottom, or from bottom to top.

*Rotate text in a table*

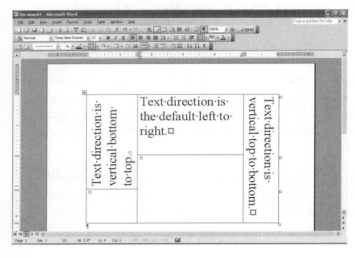

## Wrap Text

- By default, tables are inserted on a blank line above or below existing text.
- You can set Word to **wrap** text around the table.
- Wrapping text around a table integrates the table object into the text so text appears above, below, or on either side of the table.

*Wrap text around a table*

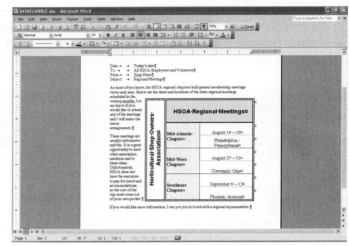

# Procedures

## Move a Table

1. Rest mouse pointer on table so handles are displayed.
   - ✓ *You must be in Print Layout view for the sizing handle and table anchor to be available.*
2. Click and drag table anchor to new location.
   - ✓ *A dotted outline moves with the mouse pointer to show new location.*
3. Release mouse button to drop table in new location.

## Resize a Table

1. Rest mouse pointer on table so handles are displayed.
2. Click and drag sizing handle to increase or decrease table size.
   - ✓ *A dotted outline moves with the mouse pointer to show new size.*
3. Release mouse button to resize table.

## Rotate Text

1. Click in cell to format.
   OR
   Select components to format.
2. Click **Change Text Direction** button ▐▌.
   - ✓ *Click the button to toggle through the three available directions.*

## Wrap Text Around a Table

1. Click in table.
2. Click **Table** .................. `Alt`+`A`
3. Click **Table Properties** ........ `R`
4. Click **Table** tab ................... `T`
5. Click **Around** .............. `Alt`+`A`
6. Click **OK** .......................... `Enter`

# Exercise Directions

1. Start Word, if necessary.

2. Open ⌨**REGIONS** or open 💿**41REGIONS**.

3. Save the document as **REGIONS2**.

4. Replace the name **Ms. Knowlton** on the To: line with the text: **All HSOA Employees and Volunteers**.

5. Add the following sentence to the beginning the existing paragraph:

   **As most of you know, the HSOA regional chapters hold general membership meetings twice each year**.

6. Position the insertion point on the blank line after the existing paragraph and type the following:

   **These meetings are usually informative and fun. It is a great opportunity to meet other association members and to share ideas. Unfortunately, HSOA does not have the resources to pay for travel and accommodations, so the cost of the trip must come out of your own pocket.**

   **If you would like more information, I can put you in touch with a regional representative**.

7. Use the Draw Table tool to draw a new cell on the left side of the table. Size the new cell to the full height of the table and approximately .75" wide.

8. If necessary, apply a 2¼ pt. double-line border around the new cell.

9. In the new cell, set the text to run vertically bottom to top.

10. Type the association name, **Horticultural Shop Owners Association**, in a bold, 18-point sans serif font.

11. Center the name horizontally and vertically.

12. Align the table on the right side of the page.

13. Set text to wrap around the table.

14. Resize the table to set its width and height to about 4.5".

15. Move the table up so the text wraps around it (refer to Illustration A).

16. Check the spelling and grammar in the document.

17. Display the document in Print Preview. It should look similar to the one in Illustration A.

18. Print the document.

19. Close the document, saving all changes.

# On Your Own

1. Create a new document in Word.

2. Save the file as **OWD41**.

3. Type a personal business letter to an employer or to your parents explaining why you need a raise. Write at least two paragraphs about why you deserve the raise and what you plan to do with the additional funds. Include information about how you spend the money you receive now.

4. To illustrate your point, draw a table in the letter and list items that you have purchased in the past two weeks. For example, include CDs, books, meals, movie tickets, and other expenses. The table should have at least three columns—for the date, the item, and the cost. List at least four items.

5. Add a column along either side of the table where you can type a title using vertical text.

6. Use different alignments in the table cells.

7. Set the text in the letter to wrap around the table.

8. Try moving and resizing the table to improve the appearance of the letter.

9. When you are satisfied with the appearance of the table and the letter, check the spelling and grammar and print the document.

10. Ask a classmate to review the document and offer comments and suggestions.

11. Incorporate the suggestions into the document.

12. Close the document, saving all changes, and exit Word.

# Horticultural Shop Owners Association

452 Cathedral Street - Baltimore, MD 21201

# MEMORANDUM

Date:         Today's date
To:           All HSOA Employees and Volunteers
From:         Your Name
Subject:      Regional Meetings

As most of you know, the HSOA regional chapters hold general membership meetings twice each year. Below are the dates and locations of the three regional meetings scheduled in the coming months. Let me know if you would like to attend any of the meetings and I will make the travel arrangements.

These meetings are usually informative and fun. It is a great opportunity to meet other association members and to share ideas. Unfortunately, HSOA does not have the resources to pay for travel and accommodations, so the cost of the trip must come out of your own pocket.

If you would like more information, I can put you in touch with a regional representative.

| Horticultural Shop Owners Association | HSOA Regional Meetings | |
|---|---|---|
| | **Mid Atlantic Chapter** | August 14 – 18<br>Philadelphia, Pennsylvania |
| | **Mid West Chapter** | August 27 – 31<br>Cleveland, Ohio |
| | **Southeast Chapter** | September 9 – 13<br>Phoenix, Arizona |

# Exercise 42

## Skills Covered:

### ◆ Calculate in a Table ◆ Number Formats ◆ Sort Rows

## On the Job

Perform basic calculations in tables to total values in a column or row. If the values change, you can update the result without redoing the math! At the same time, you can format the calculation results with one of Word's built-in number formats. Sorting rows, like sorting paragraphs or lists, helps you keep your tables in order.

Liberty Blooms is offering a special Mother's Day basket. In this exercise, you will create a document to advertise the package. You will use a table to organize the information and to calculate costs. You will also sort the data.

## Terms

**Spreadsheet** An application, such as Microsoft Office Excel, used for setting up mathematical calculations.

**Function** A built-in **formula** for performing calculations, such as addition in a table.

**Formula** A mathematical equation.

**Field** A placeholder used to insert information that changes, such as the date, the time, a page number, or the results of a calculation.

**Header row** A row that contains a title or column headings.

## Notes

### Calculate in a Table

- Word tables include basic **spreadsheet functions** so you can perform calculations on data entered in tables.

- By default, Word assumes you want to add the values entered in the column above the current cell, or in the row beside the current cell.

- Word enters the calculation result in a **field** so it can be updated if the values in the table change.

- For anything other than basic calculations, use an Excel worksheet, not a Word table.

*The Formula dialog box set up to total a row*

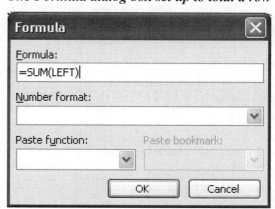

## Number Formats

- When you set up a calculation in a table you can select a number format to use to display the result.
- Number formats include features such as dollar signs, commas, percent signs, and decimal points.

*The Number format list*

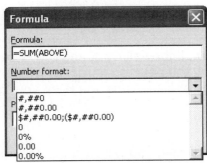

## Sort Rows

- Sort rows in a table the same way you sort lists or paragraphs.
  - ✓ See Exercise 23.
- Rows can be sorted according to the data in any column.
- Word rearranges the rows in the table but does not rearrange the columns.
- You can sort by more than one column if you want.
- For example, in a table of names and addresses, rows can be sorted alphabetically by name, by city, or numerically by ZIP Code, or they can be sorted by all three.
- If a table includes a **header row**, you can exclude it from the sort.

# Procedures

### Total Values in a Column or Row

1. Click in cell where you want the total to be displayed.
2. Click **Table** ................. Alt + A
3. Click **Formula** ...................... O
   - ✓ By default, Word enters the formula for totaling the values in the cells in the column above or the row to the left.
4. Click **Number format** drop-down arrow .......................... Alt + N
5. Click desired format ..... ↑, ↓
6. Click **OK** ........................... Enter

### Update the Total

1. Select the cell where the total is displayed.
2. Press **F9** ........................... F9

OR

1. Right-click cell where the total is displayed.
2. Click **Update Field** ............. U
   - ✓ You must update the total each time one of the values used in the formula is changed. The total is not updated automatically.

### Sort Rows

1. Display the Tables and Borders toolbar.
2. Position the insertion point in the column by which you want to sort.
3. Click **Sort Ascending** button A↓Z on the Tables and Borders toolbar to sort from A to Z or from 0 to 9.

OR

   Click **Sort Descending** button Z↓A on the Tables and Borders toolbar to sort from Z to A or from 9 to 0.
   - ✓ If the sort does not include the first row, click Table, Sort and select the No header row option button, then click OK.

OR

1. Click **Table** ................. Alt + A
2. Click **Sort** ........................... S
3. Click **Sort by** ............. Alt + S
4. Click desired column.
5. Click **Type** ................. Alt + Y
6. Click either:
   - **Text**
   - **Number**
   - **Date**

7. Click either:
   - **Ascending** ............. Alt + A
   - **Descending** ........... Alt + D
   - ✓ If the sort should not include the first row, make sure the My list has Header row option button is selected.
8. Click **OK** ........................... Enter

### Sort by Multiple Columns

1. Click **Table** ................. Alt + A
2. Click **Sort** ........................... S
3. Click **Sort by** ............. Alt + S
4. Click desired column.
5. Click **Type** ................. Alt + Y
6. Click either:
   - **Text**
   - **Number**
   - **Date**
7. Click either:
   - **Ascending** ............. Alt + A
   - **Descending** ........... Alt + D
8. Click **Then by** ............. Alt + T
9. Click desired column.
10. Click **Type** ................. Alt + P

11. Click either:
    - **Text**
    - **Number**
    - **Date**
12. Click either:
    - As<u>c</u>ending ............ `Alt`+`C`
    - Desce<u>n</u>ding .......... `Alt`+`N`

13. Click Then <u>by</u> .............. `Alt`+`B`
14. Click desired column.
15. Click Typ<u>e</u> .................. `Alt`+`E`
16. Click either:
    - **Text**
    - **Number**
    - **Date**

17. Click either:
    - Ascend<u>i</u>ng ............ `Alt`+`I`
    - Descendin<u>g</u> .......... `Alt`+`G`
    - ✓ *If the sort should not include the first row, make sure the My list has Header row option button is selected*
18. Click **OK** .......................... `Enter`

# Exercise Directions

1. Start Word, if necessary.
2. Type the document shown in Illustration A, or open 💿 **42BASKET**.
3. Save the document as **BASKET**.
4. Align all dollar values with a decimal tab set at approximately 4" on the horizontal ruler.
5. Sort all rows except the header row in descending order according to the values in the **Regularly** priced column.
6. Insert a new row at the end of the table.
7. In the first cell in the new row, type **Total**.
8. In the last cell of the new row, insert a formula to calculate the total cost.
   - ✓ *Select the currency format showing two decimal places.*
9. Insert a new row above the **Total** row.
10. In the left column, type **1 quart fresh orange juice**.
11. In the right column, type **$2.50**
12. Update the calculation result.
13. Set all rows to be at least .5" high.
14. Set column 1 to be at least 2.5" wide and column 2 to be at least 2" wide.
15. Apply the Table Grid 8 AutoFormat to the table.
16. Increase the font in row 1 to 16 points, and change the alignment to centered horizontally and vertically aligned on the bottom.
17. Align rows 2 through 7 on the bottom vertically and flush left horizontally.
18. Center the table horizontally on the page.
19. Check the spelling and grammar in the document.
20. Preview the document. It should look similar to the one in Illustration B.
21. Print the document.
22. Close the document, saving all changes.

# On Your Own

1. Open the document **OWD41**, the letter that you wrote in the On Your Own section of Exercise 41, or open 💿 **42TABLE**.
2. Save the file as **OWD42**.
3. If necessary, use a decimal tab to align the dollar values in the table.
4. Sort the rows in the table into descending numerical order, according to the amount of the expenses.
   - ✓ *Depending on how you formatted the first row in the table, you may have to delete it before you can sort the remaining rows.*
5. Add a row to the bottom of the table.
6. Label the row **Total**.
7. Calculate the total amount of expenses in the table. Make sure the result is displayed in dollar format.
8. Change one or more of the values in the table.
9. Update the calculation.
10. Format the table using cell borders and shading. For example, use borders and shading or an AutoFormat.
11. Check the spelling and grammar, then print the document.
12. Ask a classmate to review the document and offer comments and suggestions.
13. Incorporate the suggestions into the document.
14. Close the document, saving all changes, and exit Word.

*22-point Comic Sans MS, centered* ———————

# Liberty Blooms

## Good Morning Mother's Day Gift Basket
## Specially Priced at $39.99

*16-point Comic Sans MS, centered*

*12-point Comic Sans MS, justified*

Celebrate Mother's Day by sending someone a beautiful gift basket filled with exceptional items perfect for starting the day right. The basket includes everything listed below, and we guarantee delivery by 9:30 a.m. Call now to order this wonderful wake-up surprise!

| Basket includes: | Regularly priced: |
|---|---|
| Assortment of breakfast sweets | $10.99 |
| 2 - 8 oz. all natural fruit preserves | $5.99 |
| 1 dozen long stem roses | $24.99 |
| 1 lb. Gourmet Columbian coffee | $11.99 |

*12-point Times New Roman*

*Illustration B*

# Liberty Blooms
## Good Morning Mother's Day Gift Basket
## Specially Priced at $39.99

Celebrate Mother's Day by sending someone a beautiful gift basket filled with exceptional items perfect for starting the day right. The basket includes everything listed below, and we guarantee delivery by 9:30 a.m. Call now to order this wonderful wake-up surprise!

| Basket includes: | Regularly priced: |
|---|---|
| 1 dozen long stem roses | $24.99 |
| 1 lb. Gourmet Columbian coffee | $11.99 |
| Assortment of breakfast sweets | $10.99 |
| 2 - 8 oz. all natural fruit preserves | $5.99 |
| 1 quart fresh orange juice | $2.50 |
| **Total** | **$ 56.46** |

# Exercise 43

## Skills Covered:

◆ **Convert Text to a Table** ◆ **Convert a Table to Text**
◆ **Use AutoFit**

## On the Job

Convert existing text into a table or an existing table into document text in order to save time retyping. Use AutoFit to automatically adjust column width and row height.

You have been coordinating travel plans for employees and volunteers who wish to attend regional chapter meetings. The Director of the Horticultural Shop Owners Association is not sure which regional chapter meeting to attend. You have gathered some information about each host city and the other people attending meetings that you think will help her make up her mind. You can make the information easier to read by reformatting it. In this exercise, you will convert existing tables into document text and existing text into a table. You will also use AutoFit to format the table.

## Terms

**Separator character** A character such as a comma or a tab used to delineate the location where text should be divided into columns and/or rows.

## Notes

### Convert Text to a Table

- You can easily convert existing document text into a table format.
- Word automatically divides text into columns based on the location of a specified **separator character** such as a comma or tab.
- Word starts a new row at each paragraph mark.
- When you convert the text into a table, you can specify a column width, and you can choose to apply an AutoFormat.

## Convert a Table to Text

- Convert an entire table or selected table rows into regular document text.
- Word inserts the specified separator character into the text at the end of each column.
- Word starts a new paragraph at the end of each row.
  - ✓ *If document text is set to wrap around a table, when you convert the table to text Word inserts the text in a text box. For more information about working with text boxes, refer to Exercise 80.*
  - ✓ *Because most Web pages are formatted using tables, converting tables to text is useful when you copy data from a Web page into a Word document. For more information on working with Web pages, refer to Lesson 10.*

## Use AutoFit

- Use the AutoFit command on the Table menu to automatically adjust the width of table columns.
  - Select the AutoFit to Contents command to adjust column width to accommodate the widest contents.
  - Select the AutoFit to Window command to set column width to fit within the current window size. This is particularly useful when you are working with tables on Web pages.
  - Select the Fixed Column Width command (the default) if you do not want the column width to adjust automatically.
- You can also use AutoFit to automatically distribute columns and rows evenly.
  - Distributing columns makes them all the same width.
  - Distributing rows makes them all the same height.

# Procedures

### Convert Text to a Table

1. Insert separator characters in text where you want new columns to begin.
2. Select text to convert.
3. Click **T**able ................... `Alt`+`A`
4. Select **Con**v**ert** .................... `V`
5. Click **Te**x**t to Table** .............. `X`
6. If necessary, enter the **Number of Columns** to create ......... `C`, *type number*
7. Select desired AutoFit behavior:
   - **Fixed column** w**idth** ..................... `Alt`+`W`
   - **AutoF**i**t to** **contents** ................ `Alt`+`F`
   - **AutoFit to** win**d**o**w** ................. `Alt`+`D`

8. If desired, click **AutoFormat** ................. `Alt`+`A`
   a. Select desired AutoFormat style ........................ `↓`, `↑`
   b. Click **OK** ..................... `Enter`
9. Select desired separator character:
   - **P**aragraphs ........... `Alt`+`P`
   - **T**abs ...................... `Alt`+`T`
   - **Co**m**mas** ............... `Alt`+`M`
   - **O**ther .................... `Alt`+`O`, *type character*
10. Click **OK** ......................... `Enter`

### Convert a Table to Text

1. Select table to convert.
   OR
   Select rows to convert.
2. Click **T**able ................ `Alt`+`A`
3. Select **Con**v**ert** ................. `V`
4. Click **Ta**b**le to Text** ............. `B`
5. Click desired separator character:
   - **P**aragraph marks .. `Alt`+`P`
   - **T**abs ...................... `Alt`+`T`
   - **Co**m**mas** ................ `Alt`+`M`
   - **O**ther ................... `Alt`+`O`, *type character*
6. Click **OK** ......................... `Enter`

## Use AutoFit to Adjust Column Width

1. Position insertion point in table
2. Click **T**able .................. `Alt`+`A`
3. Click **A**utoFit ...................... `A`
4. Click desired option:
   - **AutoF**it to **Contents** ............... `Alt`+`F`
   - **AutoFit to Window** ................. `Alt`+`W`
   - **Fi**xed Column **Width** ................... `Alt`+`X`

## Distribute Columns Evenly

1. Click in table to format.
2. Click **Distribute Columns Evenly** button ⊞ on Tables and Borders toolbar.
   OR
   a. Click **T**able ............. `Alt`+`A`
   b. Click **A**utoFit ................. `A`
   c. Click **Distribute Columns Evenly** ........................... `Y`

## Distribute Rows Evenly

1. Click in table to format.
2. Click **Distribute Rows Evenly** button ⊞ on Tables and Borders toolbar.
   OR
   a. Click **T**able ............. `Alt`+`A`
   b. Click **A**utoFit ................. `A`
   c. Click **Distribute Rows Eve**n**ly** ........................... `N`

# Exercise Directions

1. Start Word, if necessary.
2. Open ⊚ **43TRAVEL**.
3. Save the document as **TRAVEL**.
4. Convert all three tables to document text, separating the text with paragraph marks.
5. Select the list of people attending meetings at the end of the document.
6. Convert the text to a table, separate the text at commas, and apply the Table Contemporary AutoFormat.
7. Remove the Bold from the first row in the table.
8. Use AutoFit to automatically resize the table columns to fit the contents.
9. Center the table horizontally on the page.
10. Check the spelling and grammar in the document.
11. Preview the document. It should look similar to Illustration A.
12. Print the document.
13. Close the document, saving all changes.

# On Your Own

1. Think of a directory list that could be used by someone visiting your school. The list should include at least ten items, with three bits of information about each item. For example, a directory of teachers might include the teacher's name, classroom number, and subject.
2. Start Word and create a new document.
3. Save the document at **OWD43**.
4. Type the directory using tabs to separate each item of information.
5. In the same document, create a table in which you can type information in paragraph form about the directory. For example, in a directory of teachers, the first row might include the teacher's name and the second row might include information about a class he or she teaches, and a third might include a rating, such as four stars.
6. When the document is complete, check the spelling and grammar.
7. Exchange the document with a classmate.
8. Working in the document created by your classmate, convert the table to paragraph text and the tabbed directory into a table.
9. AutoFit the table columns to fit the contents.
10. Adjust spacing and formatting as necessary. For example, center the table horizontally, and use shrink to fit to make the document fit on one page.
11. Preview the document and print it.
12. Give it back to the author.
13. In your original document, make changes or corrections that you think are necessary.
14. Save the document, close it, and exit Word.

*Illustration A*

# Horticultural Shop Owners Association
452 Cathedral Street - Baltimore, MD 21201

# MEMORANDUM

Date:       Today's date
To:         Ms. Knowlton
From:       Your Name
Subject:    Regional Meetings

To help you decide which regional meeting to attend, here is the list of people already who have already signed up, and some information about one attraction in each host city that I found on the Internet.

### Cleveland, Ohio
Rock and Roll Hall of Fame
No trip to Cleveland would be complete without paying a visit to the Rock Hall! See exhibits and maybe catch a concert!

### Philadelphia, Pennsylvania
Independence Hall
A World Heritage Site where both the Declaration of Independence and the U.S. Constitution were created.

### Phoenix, Arizona
The Desert Botanical Garden
Combines desert plants with desert wildlife that can both be seen from short trails that are well marked.

These are the people who have already signed up to attend a regional meeting:

| Alyssa Jenkins | Volunteer | 410-555-5678 | Mid West |
| Stephen Knight | Volunteer Coordinator | 410-555-7890 | Southeast |
| Jessie Samsonov | Marketing Director | 410-555-4321 | Mid West |
| Debra Whist | Public Relations | 410-555-7654 | Mid Atlantic |
| Justin Bachman | Fundraising | 410-555-6534 | Mid Atlantic |

# Exercise 44

◆ **Critical Thinking**

You work in the Accounts Payable department at Blue Sky Dairy. You have been asked to design an invoice to send to a client. You've decided that this is a great opportunity to use your table skills.

## Exercise Directions

1. Start Word and create a new blank document.

2. Save the document as **INVOICE**.

3. Using either the Draw Table tool or the Insert Table command, create the table shown in Illustration A.

   - Size the cells as closely as possible to the sizes indicated on Illustration A.

   ✓ *If you use the Insert Table command, you will have to merge and split cells to achieve the desired results.*

4. Remove all borderlines from the table.

5. Display gridlines, if necessary, so you can see the cells on-screen.

6. Center the table horizontally on the page.

7. Enter the text shown in Illustration B, using the specified formatting and alignment.

8. In the right cell of the row labeled **Total**, use a formula to calculate the total amount owed. Format the result using the dollar number format.

9. Apply border lines as shown in Illustration B.

10. Check the spelling and grammar in the document.

11. Preview the document. It should look similar to the one in Illustration B.

12. Print the document.

13. Close the document, saving all changes, and exit Word.

*Illustration A*

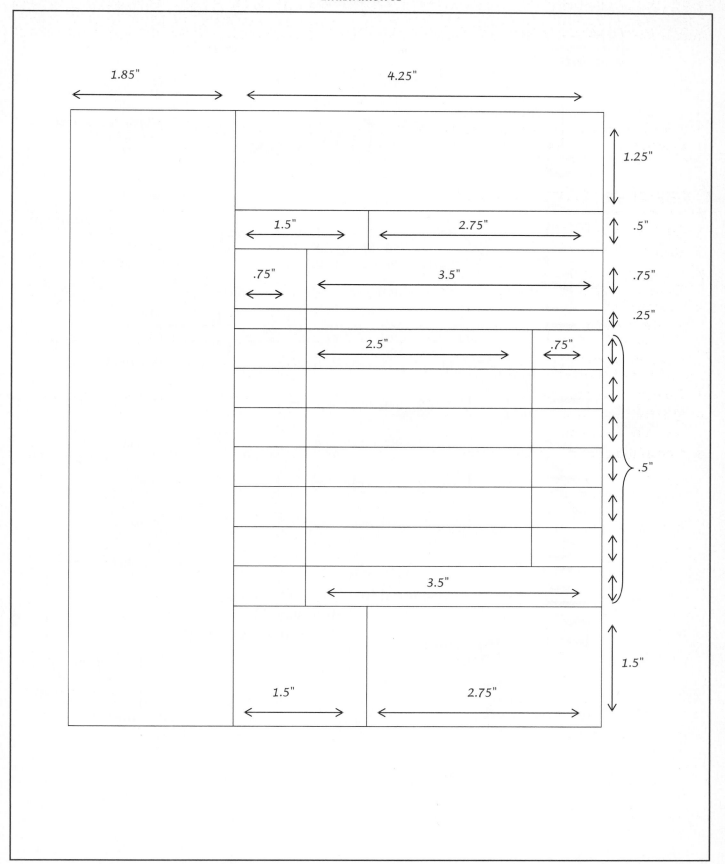

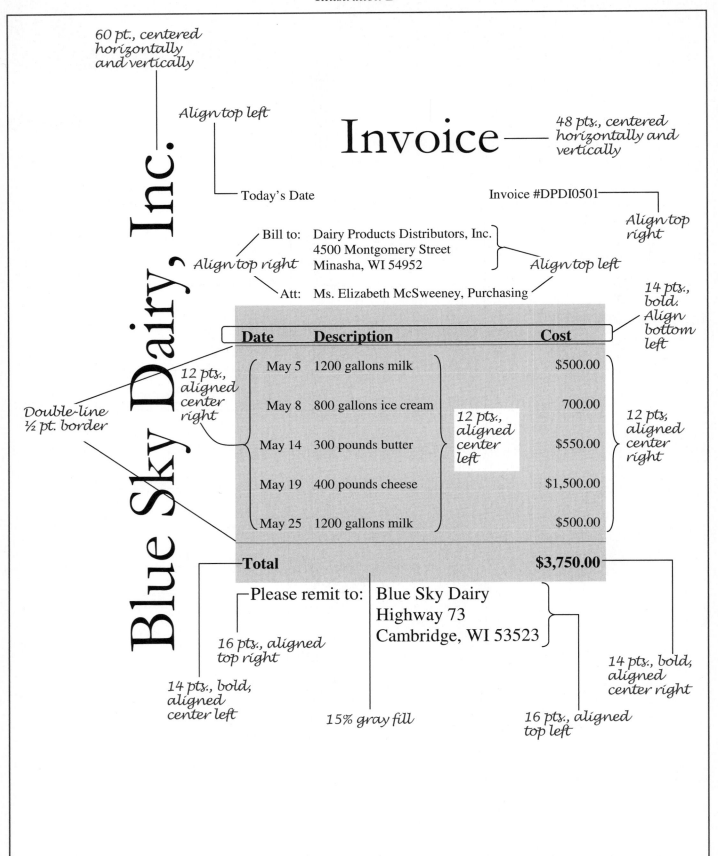

60 pt., centered horizontally and vertically

Align top left

Invoice

48 pts., centered horizontally and vertically

Today's Date

Invoice #DPDI0501

Align top right

Bill to:   Dairy Products Distributors, Inc.
4500 Montgomery Street
Minasha, WI 54952

Align top right

Align top left

Att:   Ms. Elizabeth McSweeney, Purchasing

14 pts., bold. Align bottom left

12 pts., aligned center right

Double-line ½ pt. border

Blue Sky Dairy, Inc.

| Date | Description | Cost |
|------|-------------|------|
| May 5 | 1200 gallons milk | $500.00 |
| May 8 | 800 gallons ice cream | 700.00 |
| May 14 | 300 pounds butter | $550.00 |
| May 19 | 400 pounds cheese | $1,500.00 |
| May 25 | 1200 gallons milk | $500.00 |
| Total | | $3,750.00 |

12 pts., aligned center left

12 pts, aligned center right

Please remit to:   Blue Sky Dairy
Highway 73
Cambridge, WI 53523

16 pts., aligned top right

14 pts., bold, aligned center left

15% gray fill

16 pts., aligned top left

14 pts., bold, aligned center right

# Lesson 8

## Merge

# Exercise 45

## Skills Covered:

◆ **Mail Merge Basics** ◆ **Use the Mail Merge Task Pane**
◆ **Create a New Address List** ◆ **Use Merge Fields**

## On the Job

Use Mail Merge to customize mass mailings. For example, with Mail Merge you can store a document with standard text, such as a form letter, and then insert personalized names and addresses on each copy that you generate or print. You can also use Mail Merge to generate envelopes, labels, e-mail messages, and directories, such as a telephone list.

A letter thanking those people who submitted entries to Blue Sky Dairy's Name that Flavor contest becomes a simple task using the Mail Merge feature. The form letter will be personalized with each person's name and address. In this exercise, you will create the letter document and the data source address list, and you will merge them to generate the letters.

## Terms

**Mail merge** A process that inserts variable information into a standardized document to produce a personalized or customized document.

**Main document** The document containing the standardized text that will be printed on all documents.

**Merge field** A placeholder in the main document that marks where and what will be inserted from the data source document.

**Merge block** A set of merge fields stored as one unit. For example, the Address block contains all of the name and address information.

**Data source** The document containing the variable data that will be inserted during the merge.

**Office address list** A simple data source file stored in Access file format that includes the information needed for an address list, such as first name, last name, street, city, state, and so on.

**Outlook contact list** Names, address, and other information stored as contacts for use in the Microsoft Office Outlook personal information manager program.

**Microsoft Office Access database** A file created with the Microsoft Office Access program used for storing information.

**Merge document** The customized document resulting from a merge.

**Field** One item of variable data, such as a first name, a last name, or a ZIP Code.

**Record** A collection of variable data about one person or thing. In a form letter merge for example, each record contains variable data for each person receiving the letter: first name, last name, address, city, state, and ZIP Code.

**Address list form** A dialog box used to enter mailing list information for a data source file.

# Notes

## Mail Merge Basics

- Use **Mail Merge** to create mass mailings, envelopes, e-mail messages, labels, or directories.

- To create a mail merge, you must have two files:

  - A **main document**, which contains information that won't change, as well as **merge fields** and **merge blocks**, which act as placeholders for variable information. For example, you might have a form letter that has merge fields where the address and greeting should be.

- During the merge, Word generates a series of **merge documents** in which the variable information from the data source replaces the merge fields entered in the main document.

- You can print the merge documents or save them in a file for future use.

- You can use the Mail Merge task pane or the buttons on the Mail Merge toolbar to access Mail Merge features and commands.

*A series of merge documents*

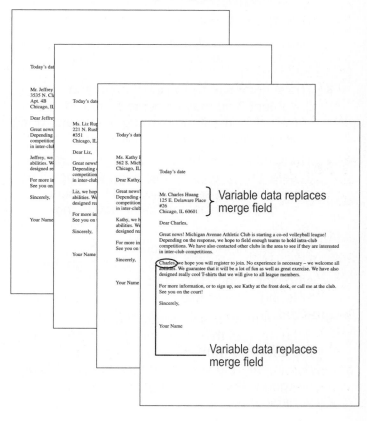

*A main document*

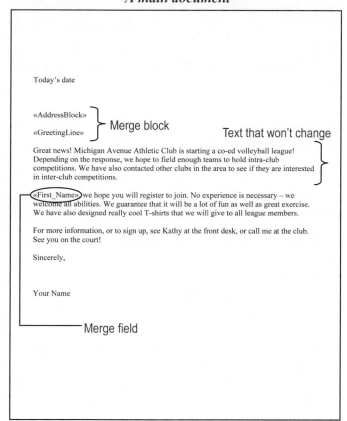

  - A **data source** file, which contains variable information such as names and addresses. Word lets you use many types of data source files for a merge, including an **Office address list**, an **Outlook contact list**, or a **Microsoft Office Access database**.

## Use the Mail Merge Task Pane

- The Mail Merge task pane prompts you through the process of conducting a merge.

- There are six steps to complete the merge:

  - The first step is to select the type of main document you want to create:

    | | |
    |---|---|
    | Letters | Used for letters or other regular Word documents such as reports, flyers, or memos. |
    | E-mail messages | Used to create messages to send via e-mail. |
    | Envelopes | Used to create personalized envelopes. |
    | Labels | Used to create personalized labels. |
    | Directory | Used for lists such as rosters, catalogs, or telephone lists. |

  - The second step is to select a starting document. You may select to start from the current document, an existing document, or a new document based on a template.

  - The third step in the Mail Merge task pane is to select recipients. In this step, you locate or create the data source file, and then select the individual recipients to include in the merge.

  - If you select to create a new list, the Mail Merge task pane prompts you through the steps for creating the data source file by entering the variable data for each recipient.

  - The fourth step is to create the main document. In this step, you type and format the data you want included in each merge document, and you insert the merge fields or merge blocks where Word will insert the variable data.

    - ✓ If the text is already typed in the document, you simply insert the merge fields and merge blocks in step 4.

  - The fifth step is to preview the merge documents. In this step you have the opportunity to see the merge documents before you print them. This lets you check for spelling, punctuation, and grammatical errors and make corrections.

  - The final step is to complete the merge. You have the option of printing the merge documents, or saving them in a new file for later use.

## Create a New Address List

- An Office address list is a simple data source file used to store all of the variable information required to complete a mail merge.

- The data is stored in a table format, with each column containing one **field** of information, and each row containing the **record** for one recipient.

- One merge document is created for each record in the data source document.

*The list of recipients stored in an address list*

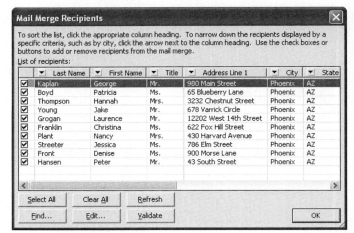

- You enter the data in an **address list form** that has already been set up to include the necessary fields.

- You must save the file the same way you save any Office file—by giving it a name and selecting a storage location.

- By default, Word stores the file in the My Data Sources folder, which is a subfolder of My Documents. You can store the file in any location you choose.

- If a field in the data source is blank, the information is left out of the merge document for that record.

- You can use an address list file many times, with different main documents.

■ You can sort the list, and you can select the specific recipients you want to include in the merge.

*An address list form*

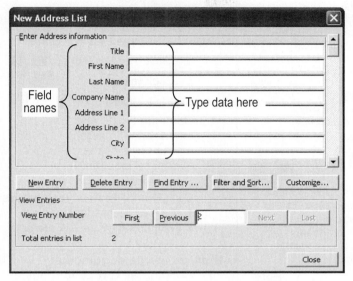

## Use Merge Fields

■ Word has a preset list of merge fields that correspond to variable information typically used in a mail merge, such as First Name, Last Name, and ZIP Code.

■ It also creates merge blocks for certain common sets of fields, such as a complete address, so that you can insert one merge block instead of inserting numerous merge fields.

■ You insert the merge fields or blocks in the main document at the location where you want the corresponding variable data to print.

■ You must type all spaces and punctuation between merge fields. Merge blocks, however, include standard punctuation and spacing, such as a comma following the city name in an address.

■ By default, when you insert a merge field, you see the field name enclosed in merge field characters (<< >>). The field may be shaded, depending on your system's field code option settings.

✓ *The field code option settings are found on the View tab in the Options dialog box. Select Options from the Tools menu, and then click the View tab.*

■ You may insert merge fields more than once in a document. For example, you can insert the name merge field in multiple locations in order to personalize a letter.

# Procedures

## Use the Mail Merge Task Pane to Generate a Form Letter Using a New Address List Data Source File

### Select the main document:

1. Open a new blank document.
2. Click **Tools**.................. **Alt** + **T**
3. Select **Letters and Mailings** ..................... **E**
4. Click **Mail Merge**................ **M**
   - ✓ *The Mail Merge task pane opens.*
5. Click the **Letters** options button in the Mail Merge task pane.
6. Click **Next: Starting document** in the Mail Merge task pane.
7. Click the **Use the current document** option button in the Mail Merge task pane.
8. Click **Next: Select recipients** in the Mail Merge task pane.

### Create an address list data source file:

1. Click the **Type a new list** option button in the Mail Merge task pane.
2. Click **Create**  in the Mail Merge task pane.
3. In the Title text box, type the title for the first person you want to add to the address list.
4. Press **Enter**...................... **Enter**
   or **Tab**................................. **Tab**
   - ✓ *Press Shift+Tab to move to previous field.*
5. Type the person's first name.
6. Press **Enter**...................... **Enter**
   or **Tab**................................. **Tab**
7. Continue typing variable data until record is complete.
   - ✓ *You may leave blank any fields for which information is not available or necessary.*
8. Click **New Entry**.......... **Alt** + **N**
   - ✓ *Word displays next blank address form.*

9. Repeat steps 3–8 until you have entered the information for all recipients.
   - ✓ *You can edit the data source file in the future. For example, you can add and delete records. For more information, refer to Exercise 47.*
10. Click **Close** .......................... **Esc**
    - ✓ *Word displays the Save Address List dialog box.*
11. Type file name.
12. Click **Save** button

     ............. **Alt** + **S**
    - ✓ *Word displays the Mail Merge Recipients dialog box. By default, all recipients are selected. For information on selecting specific recipients, refer to Exercise 48.*
13. Click **OK** ........................... **Enter**
14. Click **Next: Write your letter** in the Mail Merge task pane.
    - ✓ *Word displays the starting document, and a list of available merge blocks.*

### Create a form letter document:

1. In the main document, begin typing the letter, including all text and formatting as you want it to appear on each merge document. For example, insert the date and move the insertion point down four lines.
2. Position the insertion point at the location where you want the recipient's address displayed and then click **Address block** in the Mail Merge task pane.
   OR
   Click **Insert Address Block** button  on Mail Merge toolbar.
   - ✓ *Word displays the Insert Address Block dialog box.*
3. Select desired options.
4. Click **OK** .......................... **Enter**
   OR
   a. Click **More items** in the task pane.
      OR

- Click **Insert Merge Fields** button  on Mail Merge toolbar.
  - ✓ *Word displays the Insert Merge Field dialog box.*
  b. Click field to insert... ↑, ↓
  c. Click **Insert** ........... **Alt** + **I**
  d. Click **Close** .................. **Esc**
5. Continue typing and formatting letter, repeating steps to insert merge fields or merge blocks at desired location(s).
6. Save the document.
7. Click **Next: Preview your letters** in the Mail Merge task pane.
   - ✓ *Word displays the first merge document.*

### Preview merge documents:

1. Click the **Next recipient** button
   ▶▶ in the Mail Merge task pane.
   OR
   Click the **Next Record** button
   ▶ on the Mail Merge toolbar.
   OR
   Click the **Previous recipient** button ◀◀ in the Mail Merge task pane.
   OR
   Click the **Previous Record** button ◀ on the Mail Merge toolbar.
2. Click **Next: Complete the merge** in the Mail Merge task pane.

### Complete the merge:

- Click the **Print** button on the Mail Merge task pane to open the Merge to Printer dialog box to print the merge documents.
OR
1. Click **Edit individual letters** to create a new file containing all merged letters.
   - ✓ *Word displays the Merge to New Document dialog box.*
2. Click **OK** .......................... **Enter**
   to merge all letters to a new file.
   - ✓ *You can make changes to individual letters, and/or save the document to print later.*

# Exercise Directions

1. Start Word, if necessary.
2. Create a new blank document.
3. Save the file as **FORMLET**.
4. Start the Mail Merge task pane.
5. Select to create a letter, using the current document.
6. Create a new address list to use as a data source document.
7. Enter the recipients shown in Illustration A into the data source file.
8. Save the data source file as **SOURCE**.
9. Select to use all recipients in the merge, then close the Mail Merge Recipients dialog box.
10. Type the document shown in Illustration B, inserting the merge fields and merge blocks as marked.
11. Check the spelling and grammar in the document.
12. Preview the merged documents.
13. Complete the merge by generating a file containing all of the individual records.
14. Save the file as **LETTERS**.
15. Print the file.
16. Close all open documents, saving all changes.

*Illustration A*

| Title | First Name | Last Name | Address Line 1 | Address Line 2 | City | State | ZIP Code |
|-------|-----------|-----------|----------------|----------------|------|-------|----------|
| Mr. | Jeffrey | Levine | 2902 Karen Rd. | | Seaford | NY | 11786 |
| Ms. | Liz | Mohoney | 7865 Stuart Dr. | | Newton | MA | 01468 |
| Ms. | Melanie | Jackson | 89 Beaumont Ave. | Apt. 221E | San Francisco | CA | 94107 |
| Mr. | Alex | Daniels | 592 Roosevelt Parkway | | Auburn | ME | 04210 |
| Mr. | Suhail | Nakahmi | 73 Applewood Lane | | Jenkintown | PA | 19046 |

# On Your Own

1. Think of ways Mail Merge would be useful to you. For example, are you involved in any clubs or organizations that send out mass mailings? Do you send out "Holiday Letters" every year? Are you responsible for regular reports that contain variable data, such as sales reports or forecasts?
2. Use the Mail Merge task pane to create a form letter.
3. Save the main document as **OWD45-1**.
4. Create an address list data source file that includes at least five records.
5. Save the data source file as **OWD45-2**.
6. Type the letter, inserting merge fields and merge blocks as necessary.
7. Check the spelling and grammar in the document.
8. Merge the documents into a new file.
9. Save the merge document file as **OWD45-3**.
10. Print the letters.
11. Close all open documents, saving all changes, and exit Word.

Today's date

««AddressBlock»»

*Insert Merge blocks*

««GreetingLine»»

Thank you very much for your submission to Blue Sky Dairy's "Name that Flavor" contest. To date, we have received over 1,500 names from people all over the United States! To be perfectly honest, we are overwhelmed by the response.

This letter is simply a confirmation that we have received your submission. As stated in the official rules, we will announce the winners on June 1.

*Insert Merge fields* — «Title» «Last_Name», because we believe that every one of the submissions deserves recognition, we have decided to send you a specially designed T-shirt commemorating the contest. You should receive it in 6 – 8 weeks.

Again, thank you for taking the time to take part in Blue Sky Dairy's "Name that Flavor" contest.

Sincerely,


Your Name
Contest Director

# Exercise 46

## Skills Covered:

◆ **Merge with an Existing Address List** ◆ **Merge Envelopes**

## On the Job

If you have an existing data source document, you can merge it with any main document to create new merge documents. This saves you from retyping repetitive data. For example, using an existing Address List data source makes it easy to create envelopes to accompany a form letter merge that you previously created.

To mail out the form letters for Blue Sky Dairy, you need to print envelopes. In this exercise, you create an envelope main document and merge it with the same Address List file you used in Exercise 45.

## Terms

There is no new vocabulary in this exercise.

## Notes

### Merge with an Existing Address List

- Once you create and save an Office Address List data source file, you can use it with different main documents.

- In Step 3 of the Mail Merge task pane, you can locate and open the data source file you want to use.

- Alternatively, click the Open Data Source button
  ▨ on the Mail Merge toolbar to display the Select Data Source dialog box.

*The Select Data Source dialog box*

- You can also use existing data source files created with other applications, including Microsoft Office Access.

  ✓ *If you select a data source created with Access, you must specify which table or query to use, and the merge fields inserted in the Word document must match the fields used in the Access file.*

- Using an existing data source saves you the time and trouble of retyping existing data.

## Merge Envelopes

- To create envelopes using Mail Merge, select Envelopes as the main document type.

- The Mail Merge task pane prompts you to select envelope options so that the main document is laid out just like the actual paper envelopes on which you will print.

*The Envelope Options dialog box*

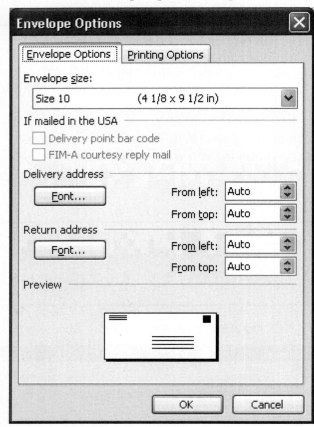

- When you select the size and format of the envelopes, Word changes the layout of the current document to match. Any existing data in the document is deleted.

- To generate the envelopes, you can create a new data source file (see Exercise 45) or use an existing data source file (as covered in this exercise).

- You can merge the envelopes to a printer or to a new document to save, edit, or use at a later time.

# Procedures

## Use the Mail Merge Task Pane to Generate Envelopes using an Existing Address List Data Source File

### Select the main document:

1. Open a new blank document.
2. Click **Tools** .................. Alt + T
3. Select **Letters and Mailings** ............................ E
4. Click **Mail Merge** .................. M
5. Click the **Envelopes** option button in the Mail Merge task pane.
6. Click **Next: Starting document** in the Mail Merge task pane.

### To select envelope options:

1. Click the **Change document layout** option button in the Mail Merge task pane.
2. Click **Envelope options** in the Mail Merge task pane.
   - ✓ Word displays the Envelope Options dialog box.
3. Click **Envelope size** .... Alt + S
4. Click desired size .................... ↑ , ↓ , Enter
5. Click **OK**............................ Enter
   - ✓ Word changes the layout of the current document. If a warning is displayed, click OK to continue or Cancel to cancel the change.
6. Click **Next: Select recipients** in the Mail Merge task pane.

### Select an existing Address List data source file:

1. Click the **Use an existing list** option button in the Mail Merge task pane.
2. Click **Browse**  in the Mail Merge task pane.
   - ✓ Word opens the Select Data Source dialog box.
3. Locate and select the desired data source file.
4. Click **Open**........................ Enter

- ✓ Word displays the Mail Merge Recipients dialog box. By default, all recipients are selected. For information on selecting specific recipients, refer to Exercise 48.

5. Click **OK** ........................... Enter
6. Click **Next: Arrange your envelope** in the Mail Merge task pane.
   - ✓ Word displays the starting document and a list of available merge blocks.

### Arrange the envelope:

1. In the main document, type any text you want to appear on each printed envelope. For example, type a return address in the upper-left corner.
2. Position the insertion point at the location where you want the recipient's address displayed.
   - ✓ By default, Word creates a text box on the envelope document where the address should print. If necessary, click Show/Hide ¶ to display non-printing characters so you can see where the text box is located.
3. Click **Address block**  in the Mail Merge task pane.
   OR
   Click **Insert Address Block** button 📄 on Mail Merge toolbar.
   - ✓ Word displays the Insert Address Block dialog box.
4. Select desired options.
5. Click **OK** ........................... Enter
   OR
   a. Click **More items** 📄 in the task pane.
      OR
      - Click **Insert Merge Fields** button 📄 on Mail Merge toolbar.
        - ✓ Word displays the Insert Merge Field dialog box.
   b. Click field to insert ... ↑ , ↓
   c. Click **Insert**............. Alt + I
   d. Click **Close**.................... Esc

6. Type any other standard text required on the envelope.
7. Insert additional fields or blocks as necessary.
8. Save the document.
9. Click **Next: Preview your envelopes** in the Mail Merge task pane.
   - ✓ Word displays the first merge document.

### Preview merge documents:

1. Click the **Next recipient** button ⏩ in the Mail Merge task pane.
   OR
   Click the **Next Record** button ▶ on the Mail Merge toolbar.
   OR
   Click the **Previous recipient** button ⏪ in the Mail Merge task pane.
   OR
   Click the **Previous Record** button ◀ on the Mail Merge toolbar.
2. Click **Next: Complete the merge** in the Mail Merge task pane.

### Complete the merge:

- Click **Print** 📇 on the Mail Merge task pane to open the Merge to Printer dialog box and print the merged documents.

OR

1. Click **Edit individual envelopes** 📑 to create a new file containing all merged envelopes.
   - ✓ Word displays the Merge to New Document dialog box.
2. Click **OK**............................ Enter
   to complete the merge.
   - ✓ You can make changes to individual envelopes, and/or save the document to print later.

# Exercise Directions

✓ In this exercise you will use ⌨ **SOURCE** the Office Address List file you created in Exercise 45. If that file is not available on your system, prior to starting the exercise copy the file 💿 **46SOURCE** and save the copy as **SOURCE**.

✓ To copy the file, right-click the file name and select Copy. Right-click the destination folder and select Paste. Right-click the copied file name and select Rename. Type the new file name and press Enter.

1. Start Word, if necessary.
2. Create a new blank document.
3. Save the document as **MAINENV**.
4. Start the Mail Merge task pane.
5. Select to create envelopes, using the current document.
6. Select envelope size 10.
7. Select to use an existing address list file as a data source document.
8. Locate and open the **SOURCE** data source file.
9. Close the Mail Merge Recipients dialog box.
10. Set up the envelope main document as shown in Illustration A.
    a. Type the return address.
    b. Insert the Address merge block.
11. Check the spelling and grammar in the document.
12. Preview the merged documents.
13. Complete the merge by generating a file containing all of the individual envelopes.
14. Save the file as **ENVELOPES**.
15. If requested by your instructor, print the merge documents.
    ✓ If you do not have actual envelopes, you can print the merge documents on regular paper.
16. Close all open files, saving all changes.

*Illustration A*

Blue Sky Dairy Co.
Highway 73
Cambridge, WI 53523

«AddressBlock»

# On Your Own

1. Create a new document in Word.
2. Save it as **OWD46-1**.
3. Use the Mail Merge task pane to create envelopes for the letters you merged in Exercise 45.
4. Use ⌨ **OWD45-2** (the data source document you used in Exercise 45) as the data source.

✓ If ⌨ **OWD45-2** is not available, copy 💿 **46OYOSOURCE** and save it as **OWD46-2** and use it as the data source.

5. Merge the envelopes to a new document.
6. Save the merge document as **OWD46-3**.
7. Close all open documents, saving all changes, and exit Word.

# Exercise 47

## Skills Covered:

◆ **Edit an Address List** ◆ **Customize Merge Fields**
◆ **Merge Labels**

## On the Job

You can easily edit a data source document to add or remove records, or to customize merge fields to include specialized information not included in the default Address List data source file. You can also use mail merge to generate mailing labels.

The T-shirts that you promised to the people who submitted a name for Blue Sky Dairy's Name that Flavor contest have arrived. In this exercise, you edit the address list data source and customize the merge fields. Finally, you use the Address List to print labels to use on the packages containing the T-shirts.

## Terms

There is no new vocabulary in this exercise.

## Notes

### Edit an Address List

- You can easily edit an existing Address List.
- You can change information that is already entered.
- You can add or delete information, including entire records.

### Customize Merge Fields

- Customize merge fields to change field names, delete unused fields, or add fields specific to your needs. For example, you might want to add a field for entering a job title.
- You can also move fields up or down in the field list.

*The Customize Address List dialog box*

## Merge Labels

- To create labels using Mail Merge, select Labels as the main document type.

- The Mail Merge task pane prompts you to select label options so that the main document is laid out just like the actual paper labels on which you will print.

- You must know the label manufacturer and the product number in order to select the correct label options.

- When you select the size and format of the labels, Word changes the layout of the current document to match. Any existing data in the document is deleted.

- You can create a new data source file as covered in Exercise 45, or use an existing data source file as covered in Exercise 46.

- You can merge the labels to a printer or to a new document to save, edit, or use at a later time.

*The Label Options dialog box*

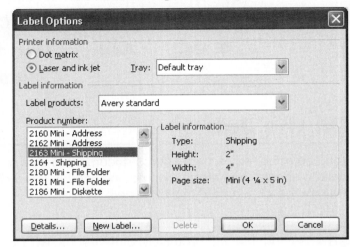

# Procedures

## Use the Mail Merge task pane to Generate Labels

### Select the main document:

1. Open a new blank document.
2. Click **Tools**................. [Alt]+[T]
3. Select **Letters and Mailings**............................ [E]
4. Click **Mail Merge**................. [M]
5. Click the **Labels** option button in the Mail Merge task pane.
6. Click **Next: Starting document** in the Mail Merge task pane.

### To select label options:

1. Click the **Change Document Layout** option button in the Mail Merge task pane.
2. Click **Label options** [icon] in the Mail Merge task pane.
   - ✓ *Word displays the Label Options dialog box.*
3. Select label options.

4. Click **OK** ........................... [Enter]
   - ✓ *Word changes the layout of the current document. If a warning is displayed, click OK to continue or Cancel to cancel the change.*
5. Click **Next: Select recipients** in the Mail Merge task pane.

### Select an Address List data source file:

1. Click the **Use an existing list** option button in the Mail Merge task pane and follow steps in Exercise 46 to locate and select desired list.
   OR
   Click the **Type a new list** option button and follow steps in Exercise 45 to create a new list.
2. When list is complete click **OK** ........................... [Enter]
3. Click **Next: Arrange your labels** in the Mail Merge task pane.
   - ✓ *Word displays the starting document, and a list of available merge blocks.*

### Arrange the labels:

1. In the main document, position the insertion point in the first label at the location where you want the recipient's address displayed.
2. Click **Address block** [icon] in the Mail Merge task pane.
   OR
   Click **Insert Address Block** button [icon] on Mail Merge toolbar.
   - ✓ *Word displays the Insert Address Block dialog box.*
3. Select desired options.
4. Click **OK** ........................... [Enter]
   OR
   Click **More items** [icon] in the task pane.
   OR
   Click **Insert Merge Fields** button [icon] on Mail Merge toolbar.
   - ✓ *Word displays the Insert Merge Field dialog box.*
   a. Click field to insert... [↑], [↓]
   b. Click **Insert** ............ [Alt]+[I]
   c. Click **Close** ................. [Esc]

5. Type any other standard text and/or punctuation required on the label.

6. Insert additional fields or blocks as necessary.

7. Click **Update all labels** button <kbd>Update all labels</kbd> in the task pane to copy the layout from the first label to all other labels.

   OR

   Click **Propagate Labels** button <kbd>🖾</kbd> on the Mail Merge toolbar.

8. Save the document.

9. Click **Next: Preview your labels** in the Mail Merge task pane.

   ✓ *Word displays the first merge document.*

**Preview merge documents:**

1. Click the **Next recipient** button <kbd>>></kbd> in the Mail Merge task pane.

   OR

   Click the **Next Record** button <kbd>▶</kbd> on the Mail Merge toolbar.

   OR

   Click the **Previous recipient** button <kbd><<</kbd> in the Mail Merge task pane.

   OR

   Click the **Previous Record** button <kbd>◀</kbd> on the Mail Merge toolbar.

2. Click **Next: Complete the merge** in the Mail Merge task pane

**Complete the merge:**

● Click **Print** <kbd>🖨</kbd> on the Mail Merge task pane to open the Merge to Printer dialog box and print the merged documents

   OR

1. Click **Edit individual labels** <kbd>🖺</kbd> to create a new file containing all merged labels.

   ✓ *Word displays the Merge to New Document dialog box.*

2. Click **OK** ......................... <kbd>Enter</kbd> to complete the merge.

   ✓ *You can make changes to individual labels, and/or save the document to print later.*

**Edit an Existing Address List**

1. Click **Mail Merge Recipients** button <kbd>🖾</kbd> on Mail Merge toolbar.

   OR

   In Step 3 or Step 5 of Mail Merge task pane, click **Edit recipient list** <kbd>🖾</kbd>.

2. Click **Edit** ...................... <kbd>Alt</kbd>+<kbd>E</kbd>

   ✓ *Word displays the Address List dialog box, with the record for the first recipient displayed.*

3. Do any of the following.

**To add a new record:**

   a. Click **New Entry** ..... <kbd>Alt</kbd>+<kbd>N</kbd>

   b. Enter variable information as covered in Exercise 45.

**To delete a record:**

   a. Click **Delete Entry** .. <kbd>Alt</kbd>+<kbd>D</kbd> to delete the entry currently displayed.

   b. Click **Yes** ................ <kbd>Alt</kbd>+<kbd>Y</kbd> to delete the entry.

   OR

   Click **No** ................... <kbd>Alt</kbd>+<kbd>N</kbd> to cancel the deletion.

   ✓ *You cannot undo an entry deletion.*

**To edit a record:**

   a. Display record to edit.

   ✓ *Use the Ne**x**t, **P**revious, **F**irst, and **L**ast buttons to scroll through the records.*

   b. Edit variable data as desired.

4. Click **Close** ..................... <kbd>Enter</kbd>

5. Click **OK** ......................... <kbd>Enter</kbd>

**Customize Merge Fields**

1. Click **Mail Merge Recipients** button <kbd>🖾</kbd> on Mail Merge toolbar.

   OR

   In Step 3 or Step 5 of Mail Merge task pane, click **Edit recipient list** <kbd>🖾</kbd>.

2. Click **Edit** ................... <kbd>Alt</kbd>+<kbd>E</kbd>

   ✓ *Word displays the Address List dialog box, with the record for the first recipient displayed.*

3. Click **Customize** ........ <kbd>Alt</kbd>+<kbd>Z</kbd>

   ✓ *Word displays the Customize Address List dialog box.*

4. Do any of the following.

**To add a field:**

   a. Click **Add** .............. <kbd>Alt</kbd>+<kbd>A</kbd>

   b. Type field name.

   c. Click **OK** .................... <kbd>Enter</kbd>

**To delete a field:**

   a. Click field to delete ........... <kbd>↑</kbd>, <kbd>↓</kbd>, <kbd>Enter</kbd>

   b. Click **Delete** ........... <kbd>Alt</kbd>+<kbd>D</kbd>

   c. Click **Yes** ............... <kbd>Alt</kbd>+<kbd>Y</kbd> to delete the field and all data entered in the field.

   OR

   Click **No** ................. <kbd>Alt</kbd>+<kbd>N</kbd> to cancel the deletion.

**To change the order of fields in the field list:**

   a. Click field to move ............ <kbd>↑</kbd>, <kbd>↓</kbd>, <kbd>Enter</kbd>

   b. Click **Move Up** ....... <kbd>Alt</kbd>+<kbd>U</kbd> to move the field up one line in list.

   OR

   Click **Move Dow_n_** ... <kbd>Alt</kbd>+<kbd>N</kbd> to move field down one line in list.

5. Click **OK** ........................... <kbd>Enter</kbd>

6. Click **Close** ..................... <kbd>Enter</kbd>

7. Click **OK** ........................... <kbd>Enter</kbd>

# Exercise Directions

✓ *Prior to starting the exercise, copy the file* ⌨**SOURCE** *or the file* 💿**47SOURCE** *and save the copy as* **SOURCE2**.

✓ *To copy the file, right-click the file name and select Copy. Right-click the destination folder and select Paste. Right-click the copied file name and select Rename. Type the new file name and press Enter.*

1. Start Word, if necessary.

2. Create a new blank document.

3. Save the file as **MAINLABEL**.

4. Start the Mail Merge task pane.

5. Select to create labels, using the current document.

6. Select Avery standard number 2163 Mini – Shipping labels.

7. Select to use an existing address list file as a data source document.

8. Locate and open **SOURCE2**.

9. Customize the merge fields as follows:

   a. Delete the Company Name field.

   b. Delete the Work Phone field.

   c. Add a T-Shirt Size field.

   d. Move the new field between the Country and the Home Phone fields.

   e. Add a Submission field.

   f. Move the new field between the T-Shirt Size and the Home Phone fields.

10. Add a new record to the address list using the following information:

    **Ms. Janine Flaherty**
    **39621 Gardendale Drive**
    **Tampa, FL 33624**
    T-Shirt Size: **M**
    Submission: **"Chocolate Sunrise"**

11. Fill in the new fields for all existing records using the information in the following table:

| | Size | Submission |
|---|---|---|
| Jeffrey Levine | XL | **"Sundae Delight"** |
| Liz Mohoney | S | **"Sea Foam"** |
| Melanie Jackson | M | **"Blue Sky Banquet"** |
| Alex Daniels | M | **"Danny's Dream"** |
| Suhail Nakhami | L | **"Sweet Sky"** |

12. Close the Mail Merge Recipients dialog box.

13. Set up the labels main document as shown in Illustration A.

    a. Insert the individual merge fields as shown.

       ✓ *Don't worry if the field names wrap onto multiple lines.*

       ✓ *Also, you may notice that Word changes the names of some fields when it displays field codes.*

    b. Type text, punctuation, and spacing as shown, including line breaks.

    c. Once you set up the first label, use Update all labels to set up the other labels.

14. Check the spelling and grammar in the document.

15. Preview the merged documents.

16. Complete the merge by generating a file containing all of the individual labels.

17. Save the file as **LABELS**.

18. Close all open files, saving all changes.

*Illustration A*

«Title» «First_Name» «Last_Name»
«Submission»
«Address_Line_1»
«Address_Line_2»
«City», «State» «ZIP_Code»

Enclosed shirt size: «TShirt_Size»


«Next Record»«Title» «First_Name» «Last_Name»
«Submission»
«Address_Line_1»
«Address_Line_2»
«City», «State» «ZIP_Code»

Enclosed shirt size: «TShirt_Size»

# On Your Own

1. Create a new document in Word.

2. Save it as **OWD47-1**.

3. Use the Mail Merge task pane to create labels for the letters you merged in Exercise 45.

4. Use OWD45-2 or **OWD46-2** (the data source documents you used in Exercises 45 and 46) as the data source.

   ✓ *If OWD45-2 or OWD46-2 is not available, copy ● **47OYOSOURCE** and save it as* **OWD46-2** *and use it for the merge.*

5. Add at least one new record to the data source.

6. Delete at least one field.

7. Add at least one field.

8. Fill in all missing information for the existing records.

9. Merge the labels to a new document.

10. Save the merge document as **OWD47-3**.

11. Close all open documents, saving all changes, and exit Word.

# Exercise 48

## Skills Covered:

◆ **Sort Recipients in an Address List** ◆ **Select Specific Recipients**
◆ **Filter Recipients** ◆ **Create a Directory with Mail Merge**

## On the Job

You can use Mail Merge to create a directory, such as a telephone directory, an address list, or a customer directory. Mail Merge makes it easy to select records in your data source file so you can include only specific recipients in a merge. You can also sort the data source file so that the merge documents are generated in alphabetical or numerical order.

As a service to clients, the StyleEyes franchise in Cleveland wants to provide a list of its doctors. You have an existing Office Address List file that includes all employees. In this exercise, you will use the existing address list data source file, which you will filter in order to select the records you need. You will also sort the list before generating the directory.

## Terms

**Column heading** The label displayed at the top of a column.

**Filter** To display records based on whether or not they match specified criteria.

**Criteria** Specific data used to match a record or entry in a data source file or list.

**Directory** A single document listing data source file entries.

## Notes

### Sort Recipients in an Address List

- You can quickly change the order of records in an address list using the data entered in any column in the list.

- Simply click any **column heading** in the Mail Merge Recipients dialog box to sort the records into ascending order.

- Click the column heading again to sort the records into descending order.

### Select Specific Recipients

- By default, all recipients in an address list are selected to be included in a merge.

- You can select the specific recipients you want to include. For example, you might want to send letters only to the people who live in a specific town.

- To indicate that a recipient is selected, Word displays a check in the check box at the left end of the recipient's row in the Mail Merge Recipients dialog box.

- You click the check box to clear the check, or click the empty box to select the recipient again.

*An address list with only some recipients selected*     *A list filtered to show entries with the Title Ms.*

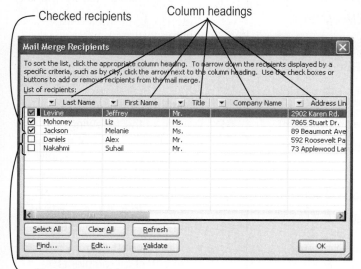

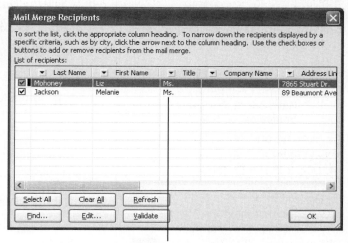

Filtered to show Ms. recipients

## Filter Recipients

- You can **filter** the records in an address list in order to display records that match specific **criteria**.

- The records that match the criteria are displayed, while those that don't match are hidden.

- Only the displayed records are used in the merge.

## Create a Directory with Mail Merge

- Use Mail Merge to create a **directory**, such as a catalog, an inventory list, or a membership address list.

- When you merge to a directory, Word creates a single document that includes the variable data for all selected recipients.

- You arrange the layout for the first entry in the directory; Mail Merge uses that layout for all entries.

- When you preview the directory document you will see each entry on a single page. Once you complete the merge, all entries are listed on one page.

- You may type text, spacing, and punctuation, and you can include formatting. For example, you might want to include labels such as *Name:*, *Home Phone:*, and *E-Mail:*.

- Word does not give you the option of printing the directory in step 6 of the Mail Merge task pane; however, you may print the merged document the same way you would print any document.

# Procedures

**Use the Mail Merge task pane to Generate a Directory Using an Existing Address List Data Source File**

**Select the main document:**

1. Open a new blank document.
2. Click **Tools** .................. Alt + T

3. Select **Letters and Mailings** ............................. E
4. Click **Mail Merge** ................. M
5. Click the **Directory** option button in the Mail Merge task pane.

6. Click **Next: Starting document** in the Mail Merge task pane.
7. Click the **Use the current document** option button in the Mail Merge task pane.
8. Click **Next: Select recipients** in the Mail Merge task pane.

## Select an existing Address List data source file:

1. Click the **Use an existing list** option button in the Mail Merge task pane.

2. Click **Browse**  in the Mail Merge task pane.

   ✓ *Word opens the Select Data Source dialog box.*

3. Locate and select the desired data source file.

4. Click **Open** button

    ........... **Alt**+**O**

   ✓ *Word displays the Mail Merge Recipients dialog box.*

5. Click **OK**........................ **Enter**

6. Click **Next: Arrange your directory** in the Mail Merge task pane.

   ✓ *Word displays the starting document and a list of available merge blocks.*

## Arrange the directory:

1. In the main document, position the insertion point at the location where you want the first entry in the directory displayed.

2. Insert the merge fields or merge blocks as necessary to set up the first entry.

3. Type any additional text, spacing, or punctuation you want in the entry.

   ✓ *Typed data will be repeated as part of each entry in the directory.*

4. Save the document.

5. Click **Next: Preview your directory** in the Mail Merge task pane.

   ✓ *Word displays the first entry in the document.*

## Preview merge documents:

1. Click the **Next recipient** button

    in the Mail Merge task pane.

   **OR**

   Click the **Next Record** button

    on the Mail Merge toolbar.

   **OR**

   Click the **Previous recipient**

   button  in the Mail Merge task pane.

   **OR**

   Click the **Previous Record**

   button  on the Mail Merge toolbar.

2. Click **Next: Complete the merge** in the Mail Merge task pane.

## Complete the merge:

1. Click **To New Document**

   button  to create the directory document.

   ✓ *Word displays the Merge to New Document dialog box.*

2. Click **OK** .......................... **Enter**

   ✓ *You can make changes to the document and/or save the document to print later.*

## Sort Recipients in an Address List

1. Click **Mail Merge Recipients**

   button  on Mail Merge toolbar.

   **OR**

   In Step 3 or Step 5 of Mail Merge task pane, click **Edit recipient list** .

2. Click column heading by which you want to sort.

   ✓ *To sort in descending order, click column heading again.*

3. Click **OK** .......................... **Enter**

   ✓ *Records will be merged in current sort order.*

## Select Specific Recipients

1. Click **Mail Merge Recipients** button on Mail Merge toolbar.

   **OR**

   In Step 3 or Step 5 of Mail Merge task pane, click **Edit recipient list** .

2. Do one of the following:
   - Click check box at left end of row to deselect recipient.
   - Click blank check box to select recipient.
   - Click **Clear All**........ **Alt**+**A** to deselect all recipients.
   - Click **Select All** ...... **Alt**+**S** to select all recipients.

3. Click **OK**.......................... **Enter**

## Filter Recipients

1. Click **Mail Merge Recipients** button on Mail Merge toolbar.

   **OR**

   In Step 3 or Step 5 of Mail Merge task pane, click **Edit recipient list** .

2. Click filter arrow ▼ on column heading by which you want to filter.

   ✓ *Word displays a list of data.*

3. Select data to filter by.

   ✓ *Word displays only those entries that match the selected data.*

   **OR**

   Select one of the following:
   - **(All)** to display all entries.

     ✓ *Use this option to remove an existing filter.*
   - **(Blanks)** to display entries in which the current field is blank.
   - **(Nonblanks)** to display entries in which the current field is not blank.

     ✓ *The filter arrow on the column heading changes to blue so you know which column is used for the filter.*

4. Click **OK**.......................... **Enter**

# Exercise Directions

1. Make a copy of the Office Address List file ☉**48JOBDATA**, and name the copy **JOBDATA**.

   ✓ *To copy the file, right-click the file name and select Copy. Right-click the destination folder and select Paste. Right-click the copied file name and select Rename. Type the new file name and press Enter.*

2. Start Word, if necessary.

3. Create a new blank document.

4. Save the document as **MAINDIR**.

5. Start the Mail Merge task pane.

6. Select to create a directory, using the current document.

7. Select to use an existing address list file as a data source document.

8. Locate and open **JOBDATA**.

9. Deselect all records.

10. Filter the list to display only doctors.

    a. Click the filter arrow on the Title column heading.

    b. Click *Dr.*

11. Select all of the doctors.

12. Sort the list in ascending order by Last Name.

13. Close the Mail Merge Recipients dialog box.

14. Using a bold, 14 point serif font, set up the directory main document as shown in Illustration A.

15. Preview the directory.

16. Complete the merge by generating a new directory document.

17. Save the directory document in a new file, named **DIRECTORY**.

18. Edit the file as shown in Illustration B.

    a. Insert five new lines at the beginning of the document.

    b. Centered on line 1, type **StyleEyes** in a 36-point serif font.

    c. Centered on line 2, type the address as shown in a 14-point serif font.

    d. Leave line 3 blank.

    e. Centered on line 4, type **Directory of Doctors** in a 26-point serif font.

19. Check the spelling and grammar in the document.

20. Display the document in Print Preview. It should look similar to the one shown in Illustration B.

21. Print the directory.

22. Close all open files, saving all changes.

# On Your Own

1. Create a new document in Word.

2. Save it as **OWD48-1**.

3. Use the Mail Merge task pane to create a directory for the recipients entered in your data source file.

4. Use ▭**OWD45-2**, **OWD46-2**, or **OWD47-2** (the data source documents you used in exercises 45, 46, or 47) as the data source.

   ✓ *If ▭**OWD45-2**, ▭**OWD46-2**, or ▭**OWD47-2** is not available, copy ☉**48OYOSOURCE**, save it as **OWD48-2** and use it for the merge.*

5. Filter the list.

6. Select to include only certain entries.

7. Sort the list.

8. Merge the directory to a new document.

9. Save the directory as **OWD48-3**.

10. Edit the directory document to include a title.

11. Check the spelling and grammar.

12. Print the directory.

13. Close all open documents, saving all changes, and exit Word.

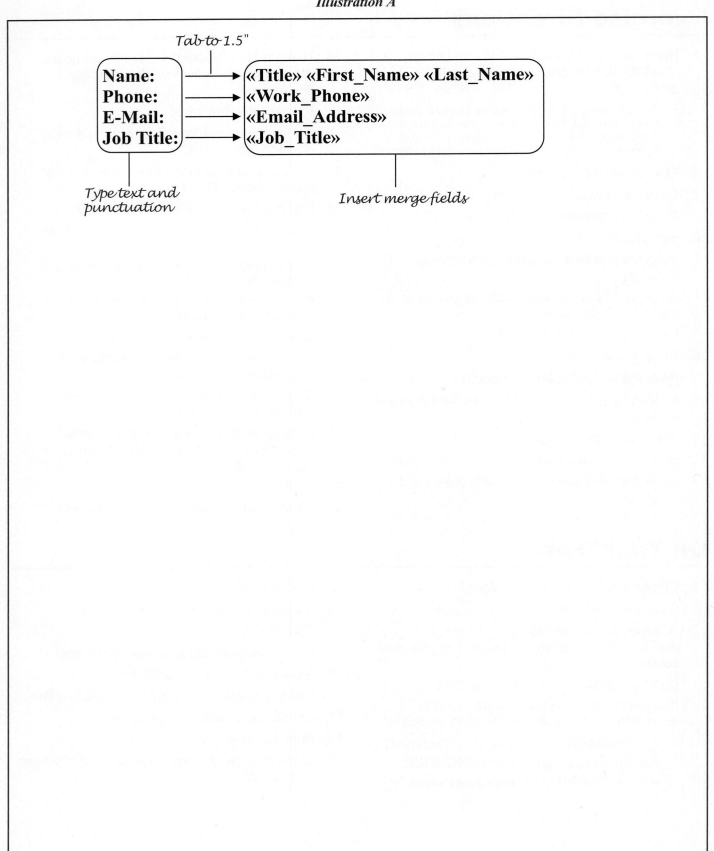

*Illustration B*

# StyleEyes

754 Erieside Avenue, Cleveland, Ohio 44114

## Directory of Doctors

| | |
|---|---|
| **Name:** | **Dr. Finn Broderbund** |
| **Phone:** | **216-555-2928** |
| **E-Mail:** | **finn@styleeyes.net** |
| **Job Title:** | **Optometrist** |

| | |
|---|---|
| **Name:** | **Dr. Francis Dorsky** |
| **Phone:** | **216-555-2924** |
| **E-Mail:** | **dorsky@styleeyes.net** |
| **Job Title:** | **Ophthamologist** |

| | |
|---|---|
| **Name:** | **Dr. William Doyle** |
| **Phone:** | **216-555-2927** |
| **E-Mail:** | **wdoyle@styleyes.com** |
| **Job Title:** | **Optometrist** |

| | |
|---|---|
| **Name:** | **Dr. Amanda Josephson** |
| **Phone:** | **216-555-2923** |
| **E-Mail:** | **josephson@styleeyes.net** |
| **Job Title:** | **Optometrist** |

| | |
|---|---|
| **Name:** | **Dr. Clarissa Joubert** |
| **Phone:** | **216-555-2929** |
| **E-Mail:** | **cjoubert@styleeyes.net** |
| **Job Title:** | **Ophthamologist** |

# Exercise 49

## ◆ Critical Thinking

Long Shot, Inc. wants you to create class lists for three upcoming in-house training courses so the instructors know how many people to expect. In addition, you need to send out memos to all enrollees confirming their course selection. In this exercise, you will use Mail Merge to create the memos and the directories. You will create a new data source file that you can use for all merges. The file will need to be customized to include fields specific to your needs. It will also need to be filtered and sorted to complete each merge.

# Exercise Directions

## Generate a Memo with Mail Merge

1. Start Word, if necessary.
2. Create a new blank document.
3. Save the file as **CONFIRM**.
4. Start Mail Merge.
5. Select to create a letter, using the current document.
6. Create a new address list to use as a data source document.
7. Customize the address list as follows:
   a. Rename the Company field to **Department**.
   b. Delete all of the fields pertaining to address (Address Line 1, Address Line 2, City, State, ZIP Code, and Country).
   c. Add a field named **Course**.
   d. Delete the Home Phone field.
8. Enter the recipients from the table in Illustration A on the following page into the data source file.
9. Save the data source file as **NAMES**.
10. Sort the data source file into ascending order by Department.
11. Select to use all recipients in the merge, then close the Mail Merge Recipients dialog box.
12. Type the document shown in Illustration B, inserting the merge fields as marked.
13. Check the spelling and grammar in the document.
14. Preview the merged documents.

15. Complete the merge by generating a new file containing all merged records.
16. Save the file as **MEMOS**.
17. Print the file.
18. Close all open documents, saving all changes.

## Create a Directory with Mail Merge

1. Create a new blank document.
2. Save the file as **ENROLLED**.
3. Start the Mail Merge Wizard.
4. Select to create a directory, using the current document.
5. Use the **NAMES** address list as the data source file.
6. Sort the list alphabetically by last name.
7. Filter the list to display only the people enrolled in the Word 1 course.
8. Set up the directory as shown in Illustration C.
9. Preview the directory.
10. Generate the directory and save it in a new file named **WORD1**.
11. Add the title **Word 1 Class List** in a 24-point sans serif font at the top of the Word 1 directory.
12. Check the spelling and grammar in the document.
13. Print the document.
14. Close the document, saving all changes.
   ✓ *The Enrolled document should still be open on-screen, with the Mail Merge Wizard displaying Step 6.*

15. Go back through Mail Merge to step 5.

16. Edit the Recipient list to change the filter from Word 1 to Word 2.

17. Preview the directory.

18. Generate the directory and save it in a new file named **WORD2**.

19. Add the title **Word 2 Class List** in a 24-point sans serif font at the top of the Word 2 directory.

20. Check the spelling and grammar in the document.

21. Print the document.

22. Close the document, saving all changes.

23. Repeat steps 15–22 to create a directory for the Word 3 class.

24. Close the **ENROLLED** document, saving all changes, and exit Word.

*Illustration A*

| Mr. Gary Dubin | Human Resources | Word 3 | 555-3232 | gdubin@longshot.net |
|---|---|---|---|---|
| Ms. Elizabeth Doone | Design | Word 1 | 555-3233 | lizdoone@longshot.net |
| Ms. Janice Loring | Accounting | Word 2 | 555-3234 | jloring@longshot.net |
| Mr. Antonio DiBuono | Marketing | Word 1 | 555-3235 | antonio@longshot.net |
| Ms. Katharine Peterson | Human Resources | Word 2 | 555-3236 | kpeterson@longshot.net |
| Ms. Marianne Flagg | Design | Word 3 | 555-3237 | mflagg@longshot.net |
| Mr. Howard Jefferson | Customer Support | Word 2 | 555-3238 | hjefferson@longshot.net |
| Mr. Julian Lovett | Design | Word 3 | 555-3239 | jullovett@longshot.net |
| Ms. Christina Bottecelli | Accounting | Word 1 | 555-3240 | chrisbott@longshot.net |
| Ms. Rose Mekalian | Marketing | Word 3 | 555-3241 | rosemekalian@longshot.net |
| Mr. Dana Teng | Design | Word 2 | 555-3242 | dteng@longshot.net |
| Mr. Luis Martinez | Accounting | Word 1 | 555-3243 | lmartinez@longshot.net |

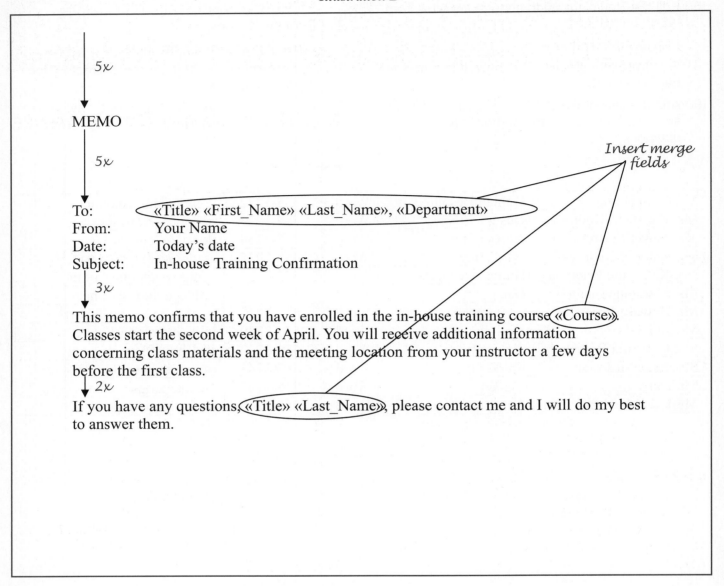

5x

MEMO

5x

Insert merge fields

To:         «Title» «First_Name» «Last_Name», «Department»
From:       Your Name
Date:       Today's date
Subject:    In-house Training Confirmation

3x

This memo confirms that you have enrolled in the in-house training course «Course». Classes start the second week of April. You will receive additional information concerning class materials and the meeting location from your instructor a few days before the first class.

2x

If you have any questions, «Title» «Last_Name», please contact me and I will do my best to answer them.

*Illustration C*

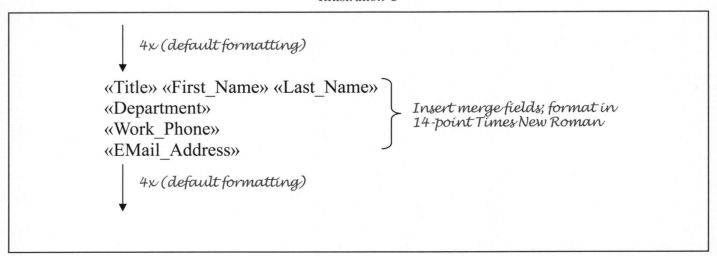

4x (default formatting)

«Title» «First_Name» «Last_Name»
«Department»
«Work_Phone»
«EMail_Address»

Insert merge fields; format in 14-point Times New Roman

4x (default formatting)

# Lesson 9

## Multiple-Page Documents

**Exercise 50**

- ◆ Create an Outline
- ◆ Edit an Outline
- ◆ Collapse and Expand Outlines
- ◆ Number an Outline

**Exercise 51**

- ◆ Set Margins for Multiple Page Documents
- ◆ Insert Hard Page Breaks
- ◆ Insert Section Breaks
- ◆ Control Text Flow
- ◆ View the Word Count

**Exercise 52**

- ◆ Create Headers/Footers
- ◆ Different First Page Headers/Footers
- ◆ Different Odd/Even Headers/Footers
- ◆ Different Section Headers/Footers
- ◆ Insert Page Numbers

**Exercise 53**

- ◆ Find and Replace
- ◆ Insert Bookmarks
- ◆ Use Browse Objects
- ◆ Use AutoSummarize

**Exercise 54**

- ◆ Use Reading Layout View
- ◆ Use Document Map
- ◆ Use Thumbnails
- ◆ Preview Multiple Pages
- ◆ Copy or Move Text from One Page to Another
- ◆ Print Specific Pages

**Exercise 55**

- ◆ Create a Master Document
- ◆ Work with Subdocuments

**Exercise 56**

- ◆ Insert a Cross-reference
- ◆ Insert a Caption
- ◆ Create an Index
- ◆ Modify an Index

**Exercise 57**

- ◆ Create a Table of Contents
- ◆ Create a Table of Figures
- ◆ Create a Table of Authorities
- ◆ Update a Table of Contents, Table of Figures, or Table of Authorities

**Exercise 58**

- ◆ Critical Thinking

# Exercise 50

## Skills Covered:

◆ **Create an Outline** ◆ **Edit an Outline**
◆ **Collapse and Expand Outlines** ◆ **Number an Outline**

## On the Job

Create an outline to organize ideas for any document that covers more than one topic, such as an article, a report, a presentation, or a speech. For example, you might create an outline to list the chapters or headings in a report or to arrange main subjects for a presentation. The outline serves as a map you can follow as you complete the entire document.

Liberty Blooms wants to publish a report to use as a handout for a class about roses. In this exercise, you will create an outline for that document.

## Terms

**Outline** A document that lists levels of topics.

**Promote** To move up one level in an outline.

**Demote** To move down one level in an outline.

**Collapse** To hide subtopics in an outline.

**Expand** To show subtopics in an outline.

## Notes

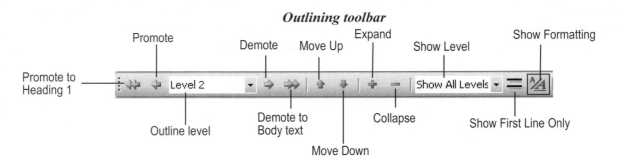

*Outlining toolbar*

### Create an Outline

■ Use Outline view to create and edit **outlines**.

■ When you switch to Outline view, the Outlining toolbar is displayed; use the Outlining toolbar buttons to organize and format an outline.

> ✓ *The ten buttons on the right end of the Outlining toolbar are used for working with Master documents. You learn about Master documents in Exercise 55.*

■ Outline topics are set up in levels, which are sometimes called *headings*: Level 1 is a main heading, Level 2 is a subheading, Level 3 is a sub-subheading, and so on up to 9 heading levels.

■ Word automatically applies different styles to different levels in an outline.

- Levels that have sublevels under them are preceded by an Expand Outline symbol ⊕.
- Levels that do not have sublevels are preceded by a Collapse Outline symbol ⊟.
- Regular document text is called *Body text.*
- In Outline view, the document is displayed the way it will print.
- When you display an unnumbered outline in Normal view, Print Layout view, or Print Preview, it retains its style formatting, but not the indented levels.
- To print an unnumbered outline with the indented levels, it must be displayed in Outline view when you select the Print command.

## Edit an Outline

- You can edit an outline using the same techniques you use to edit regular document text. For example, you can insert and delete text at any location.
- To reorganize an outline, you can **promote** or **demote** heading levels. For example, you can demote a Level 1 paragraph to a Level 2 paragraph.
- You can also move headings and subheadings up or down the outline to reorganize the outline.

## Collapse and Expand Outlines

- When you want to work with only some heading levels at a time you can **collapse** the outline.
- Collapsing an outline hides lower heading levels.
- To see hidden or collapsed levels, you can **expand** the outline.

## Number an Outline

- Traditional outlines are numbered using a multilevel numbering scheme, with different number and letter styles used to represent different levels.
- Word comes with seven built-in outline numbering styles.
- You can select a numbering style before or after typing the outline.
- Once an outline is numbered, it retains its indented levels in any view.

*Select an outline numbering style in the Bullets and Numbering dialog box*

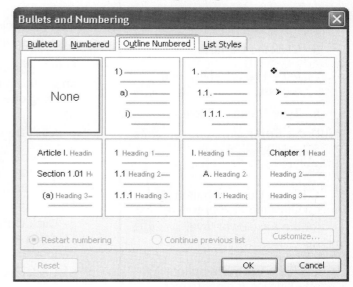

# Procedures

## Create an Outline

1. Click the **Outline View** button ▦.

   OR

   a. Click **V**iew............. `Alt`+`V`

   b. Click **O**utline................. `O`

2. Type Heading 1 text.

3. Press **Enter**..................... `Enter`

   ✓ *Heading level is carried forward to the new paragraph.*

4. Type more Heading 1 text.

   OR

   a. Click the **Demote** button ⇨ on Outlining toolbar........................... `Tab`

   b. Type Heading 2 text.

5. Press **Enter**..................... `Enter`

6. Type Heading 2 text.

   OR

   Click the **Demote** button ⇨ on Outlining toolbar to type text for the next lower level ....... `Tab`

   OR

   Click the **Promote** button ⇦ on Outlining toolbar to type text for the next higher level ........................... `Shift`+`Tab`

7. Press **Enter**..................... `Enter`

8. Continue until outline is complete.

## Type body text:

1. Position insertion point where you want to type Body text.

2. Click **Demote to Body Text** button ⇒ on Outlining toolbar................ `Ctrl`+`Shift`+`N`

3. Type text.

## Edit an Outline

### Select headings:

1. Click outline symbol preceding the heading ⊞ or ⊟.

   ✓ *The heading and all subheadings are selected.*

2. Make desired changes.

### Change heading levels:

1. Position insertion point anywhere on heading line.

   OR

   Select heading.

2. Click **Promote** button ⇦ ................. `Shift`+`Tab` on Outlining toolbar to promote heading one level.

   OR

   • Click **Demote** button ⇨ ................... `Tab` on Outlining toolbar to demote heading one level.

   OR

   a. Click **Outline Level** drop-down arrow on Outlining toolbar.

   b. Click desired level.

### Move headings:

1. Position insertion point anywhere on the heading line.

   OR

   Select heading to move.

2. Drag outline symbol up or down to a new location.

   OR

   Click **Move Up** ⬆ on Outlining toolbar to move heading up one line.

   OR

   Click **Move Down** ⬇ on Outlining toolbar to move heading down one line.

## Collapse and expand an outline:

1. Click **Outline Level** drop-down arrow on Outlining toolbar.

2. Click desired level.

   OR

   • Double-click **outline symbol** preceding heading.

## Number an Outline

1. Position the insertion point where the outline will begin.

   OR

   Select headings to number.

2. Click **F**ormat ............... `Alt`+`O`

3. Click **Bullets and Numbering** ......................... `N`

4. Click O**u**tline Numbered page tab ..................... `Alt`+`U`

5. Select numbering style.

   ✓ *Select None to remove numbering.*

6. Click **OK** ........................... `Enter`

# Exercise Directions

1. Start Word, if necessary.
2. Create a new document, or open
   💿 **50OUTLINE**.
3. Save the document as **OUTLINE**.
4. Change to Outline view.
5. Type the outline shown in Illustration A, or, if you are using the existing file, apply outline levels as shown in the Illustration.
   a. Press Tab or click Demote to demote a level.
   b. Press Shift+Tab, or click Promote to promote a level.
   c. Press Ctrl+Shift+N or click Demote to Body Text to type regular text.
   d. Apply the Numbering style used in the illustration.

6. Collapse the outline to show only levels 1 and 2.
7. Display all levels.
8. Move the heading **Caring for Cut Roses** and its subheadings down so it becomes heading E.
   ✓ *Notice that Word renumbers the outline automatically.*
9. Promote the subheading **Garden Roses** to level 3.
10. Demote the subheading **Natural Options** to level 5.
11. Check the spelling in the document.
12. Print the document.
13. Close the document, saving all changes.

# On Your Own

1. Begin planning a research report on a topic of your choice.
   - Start by selecting a topic. You may want to base the report on something you are learning in a class at school, or you may want to research something new. Think of three to five possible topics, and then ask your instructor to approve one of them.
2. Perform some preliminary research that will help you organize the report. You may use books, magazine articles, or the Internet to locate useful information.
   ✓ *Remember to record all sources for use in a bibliography, source list, or for footnote references.*
3. Create a new document in Word.
4. Save the file as **OWD50**.

5. Using the preliminary research, create an outline for the report. The outline will help you organize the topics you plan to include. Try to list at least four headings in the outline, along with the necessary subheadings.
6. Number the outline if you want.
7. Examine the outline and make sure all headings are at the correct level. Change the levels if necessary.
8. Try rearranging the headings to see if you can improve the organization.
9. Check the spelling in the outline, save changes, and print it.
10. Ask a classmate to review the outline and offer comments and suggestions.
11. Incorporate the suggestions into the outline.
12. Close the document, saving all changes, and exit Word.

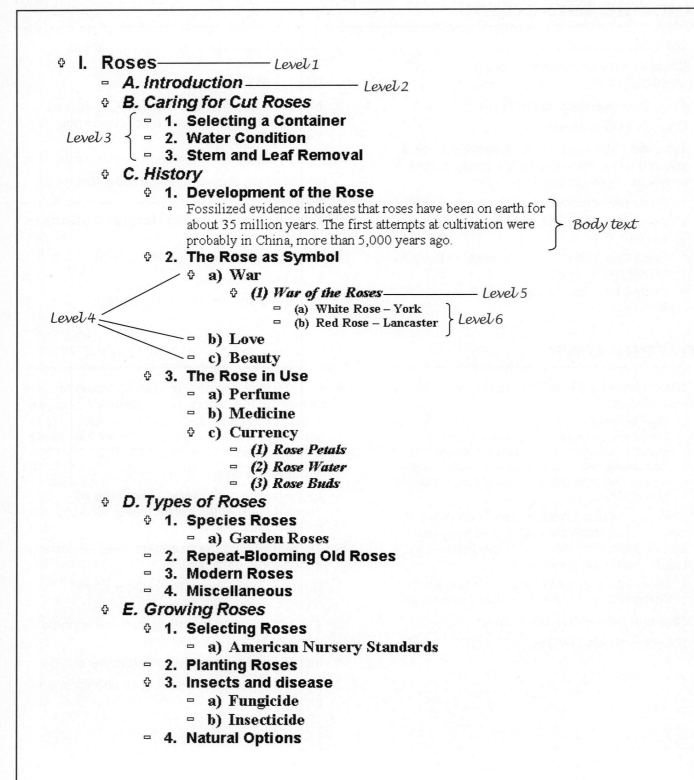

I. **Roses** — *Level 1*
  - A. *Introduction* — *Level 2*
  - B. *Caring for Cut Roses*
    - *Level 3*
      - 1. **Selecting a Container**
      - 2. **Water Condition**
      - 3. **Stem and Leaf Removal**
  - C. *History*
    - 1. **Development of the Rose**
      - Fossilized evidence indicates that roses have been on earth for about 35 million years. The first attempts at cultivation were probably in China, more than 5,000 years ago. — *Body text*
    - 2. **The Rose as Symbol**
      - *Level 4*
        - a) War
          - (1) *War of the Roses* — *Level 5*
            - (a) White Rose – York — *Level 6*
            - (b) Red Rose – Lancaster
        - b) Love
        - c) Beauty
    - 3. **The Rose in Use**
      - a) Perfume
      - b) Medicine
      - c) Currency
        - (1) *Rose Petals*
        - (2) *Rose Water*
        - (3) *Rose Buds*
  - D. *Types of Roses*
    - 1. **Species Roses**
      - a) Garden Roses
    - 2. **Repeat-Blooming Old Roses**
    - 3. **Modern Roses**
    - 4. **Miscellaneous**
  - E. *Growing Roses*
    - 1. **Selecting Roses**
      - a) American Nursery Standards
    - 2. **Planting Roses**
    - 3. **Insects and disease**
      - a) Fungicide
      - b) Insecticide
    - 4. **Natural Options**

# Exercise 51

## Skills Covered:

◆ **Set Margins for Multiple Page Documents**
◆ **Insert Hard Page Breaks** ◆ **Insert Section Breaks**
◆ **Control Text Flow** ◆ **View the Word Count**

## On the Job

Make a long document easier to read and work in by inserting page breaks, section breaks, and page numbers. Page breaks let you control where a new page should start, avoiding page layout problems such as headings at the bottom of a page. Section breaks let you change page formatting in the middle of a document. Text flow options let you control the way text flows from the end of one page or line to the beginning of the next. View the Word Count to find out if your document meets length requirements.

You have a document about selecting roses that you want to use as a handout for a class sponsored by Liberty Blooms. In this exercise, you will use a section break to create a title page and a page break to add a page for a list of sources. You will add a gutter for binding the pages at the top, and you will use options to control text flow.

## Terms

**Gutter** Space added to a margin to leave room for binding.

**Binding** Securing pages using stitching, staples, wire, plastic, tape, or glue.

**Mirror margins** Margins set on facing pages so that the inside margin on both pages are the same and the outside margin on both pages are the same.

**Facing pages** A left and a right page set to open opposite each other. Also called mirrored pages or a two-page spread.

**Inside margins** Margins along the side of the page where binding is placed. Usually, the left side of right pages and the right side of left pages.

**Outside margins** Margins along the side of the page opposite the binding. Usually, the left side of left pages and the right side of right pages.

**Soft page break** The place where Word automatically starts a new page when the current page is filled with text.

**Hard page break** A nonprinting character that tells Word to start a new page, even if the current page is not filled with text.

**Section** A portion of a document.

**Section break** A nonprinting character that tells Word to start a new section within a document. For example, a section break can separate a one-column from a two-column format.

**Widow line** The last line of a paragraph printed alone at the top of a page.

**Orphan line** The first line of a paragraph printed alone at the bottom of a page.

**Hard line break** A nonprinting character that tells Word to wrap text to a new line, even if the current line has not reached the right margin. Sometimes called a *text wrapping break*.

# Notes

## Set Margins for Multiple Page Documents

- Adjust the **gutter** width of a document to leave room for **binding** multiple pages.

- You can position the gutter on either side of a page or across the top, depending on where you plan to place the binding.

- Use **mirror margins** to set up **facing pages** when you plan to bind double-sided documents.

- With mirror margins, you set **inside margins** for the side of the page along the binding and **outside margins** for the side away from the binding.

    ✓ *For more information about setting margins, refer to Exercise 27.*

## Insert Hard Page Breaks

- A standard 8.5" by 11" sheet of paper with 1" top and bottom margins has 9" of vertical space for entering text.

    ✓ *The number of lines depends on the font size and line spacing settings.*

- Word inserts a **soft page break** to start a new page when the current page is full.

- Soft page breaks adjust automatically if text is inserted or deleted, so a break always occurs when the current page is full.

- Insert a **hard page break** to start a new page before the current page is full. For example, insert a hard page break before a heading that falls at the bottom of a page; the break forces the heading to the top of the next page.

- Breaks move like characters when you insert and delete text. Therefore, you should insert hard page breaks after all editing is complete to avoid having a break occur at an awkward position on the page.

- In Normal view, a soft page break is marked by a dotted line across the page.

- By default, in Print Layout view page breaks are indicated by a space between the bottom of one page and the top of the next page; if you have nonprinting characters displayed, the space where you insert a hard page break is marked by a dotted line with the words *Page Break* centered in it.

    ✓ *Click on the space between pages to replace it with a solid black line. Click on the solid line between pages to show the space again.*

- In Normal view, a hard page break is marked by a dotted line with the words Page Break centered in it.

*Page breaks in Normal view*

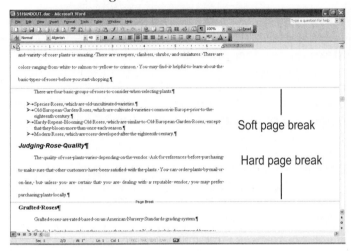

*Page breaks in Print Layout view*

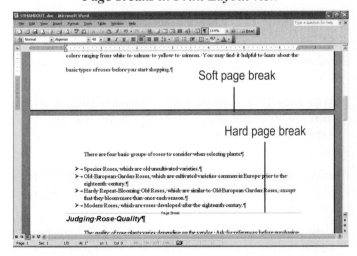

## Insert Section Breaks

- A default Word document contains one **section**.

- You can divide a document into multiple sections to apply different formatting to each section. For example, you can set different margins, headers, or footers for each section.

254

- There are four types of **section breaks**:
  - *Next page* inserts a section break and a page break so that the new section will start on the next page.
  - *Continuous* inserts a section break so that the new section will start at the insertion point.
  - *Even page* inserts a section break and page breaks so the new section will start on the next even-numbered page.
  - *Odd page* inserts a section break and page breaks so the new section will start on the next odd-numbered page.

*Break dialog box*

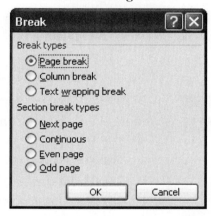

- In Normal view, section breaks are displayed as dotted double lines across the width of the page with the words Section Break in the middle, followed by the type of break in parentheses.
- In Print Layout view section breaks are displayed only if nonprinting characters are displayed.

## Control Text Flow

- Use text flow options to control the way Word breaks paragraphs and lines at the end of a page. For example, you can control whether or not a heading stays on the same page as the paragraph that follows it.
- You can access the following text flow options in the Paragraph dialog box:
  - **Widow/Orphan** control, for preventing either the first or last line of a paragraph from printing on a different page.
  - Keep lines together, for preventing a page break within a paragraph.
  - Keep with next, for preventing a page break between the current paragraph and the following paragraph.

- Page break before, for forcing a page break before the current paragraph.
- You can also use shortcut keys or the Break dialog box to manually insert a **text wrapping—** or **hard line—break**.
- A hard line break forces Word to wrap text before reaching the right margin.
- To see hard line breaks on screen, display nonprinting characters.
  - If you insert a hard line break using the Break dialog box, it is displayed as an arrow between two lines $\boxed{\leftarrow\!\shortmid}$; if you use shortcut keys it is displayed as an arrow $\boxed{\hookleftarrow}$.

## View the Word Count

- Word keeps track of statistics such as how many words you have typed in a document.
- There are three ways to view the word count:
  - Use the Word Count command on the Tools menu to check the document statistics.

*Word Count dialog box*

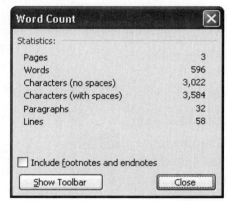

- Use the Word Count toolbar to have access to the current word count while you work.
  - ✓ *The Word Count toolbar can be set to display words, characters with spaces, characters without spaces, lines, pages, or paragraphs.*

*Word Count toolbar*

- Use the Statistics page of the Properties dialog box.
  - ✓ *See Exercise 35 for information about Document Properties.*

# Procedures

## Set a Gutter

1. Double-click ruler.
   OR
   a. Click **F**ile ............... `Alt`+`F`
   b. Click **Page Set**u**p** ......... `U`
2. Click **Margins** tab ....... `Ctrl`+`Tab`
3. Click **G**utter text box ... `Alt`+`G`
4. Type gutter width.
5. Click **Gutter position**
   drop-down arrow ......... `Alt`+`U`
6. Select desired gutter location.
7. Click the **Apply** t**o**
   drop-down arrow ......... `Alt`+`Y`
8. Select **This point forward**.
   OR
   Select **Whole document**.
   OR
   Select **This section**.
9. Click **OK** ........................... `Enter`

## Set Mirror Margins

1. Double-click ruler.
   OR
   a. Click **F**ile ............... `Alt`+`F`
   b. Click **Page Set**u**p** ......... `U`
2. Click **Margins** tab ....... `Ctrl`+`Tab`
3. Click **Multiple pages**
   drop down ................. `Alt`+`M`
4. Click **Mirror**
   margins ............ `↓`, `↑`, `Enter`
5. Click **T**op text box ....... `Alt`+`T`
6. Type top margin width.
7. Click **B**ottom text
   box ........................... `Alt`+`B`
8. Type bottom margin width.
9. Click **In**side text box ... `Alt`+`N`
10. Type inside margin width.
11. Click **O**utside text
    box ........................... `Alt`+`O`
12. Type outside margin width.

13. Click **G**utter text box ... `Alt`+`G`
14. Type gutter width.
15. Click the **Apply** t**o**
    drop-down arrow ......... `Alt`+`Y`
16. Select **This point forward**.
    OR
    Select **Whole document**
    OR
    Select **This section**
17. Click **OK** ...................... `Enter`

## Insert a Hard Page Break
### (*Ctrl+Enter*)

1. Click **I**nsert ................. `Alt`+`I`
2. Click **B**reak ..................... `B`
3. Click the **Page break**
   option button ............... `Alt`+`P`
4. Click **OK** ........................ `Enter`

## Delete a Hard Page Break

1. In Normal view, position
   insertion point on hard
   page break.
2. Press **Delete** .................... `Del`

## Insert a Section Break

1. Click **I**nsert ................. `Alt`+`I`
2. Click **B**reak ..................... `B`
3. Click the option button for
   desired break:
   • **N**ext page ............. `Alt`+`N`
   • **Con**t**inuous** .......... `Alt`+`T`
   • **E**ven page ............. `Alt`+`E`
   • **O**dd page ............. `Alt`+`O`
4. Click **OK** ........................ `Enter`

## Delete a Section Break

1. In Normal view, position
   insertion point on section break.
2. Press **Delete** key .............. `Del`

## Control Text Flow

1. Click **F**ormat ............. `Alt`+`O`
2. Click **P**aragraph ................. `P`
3. Click **Line and P**age
   **Breaks** tab ................. `Alt`+`P`
4. Select or deselect desired
   option(s):
   • **Widow/Orphan**
     **control** ................. `Alt`+`W`
   • **K**eep lines
     together ............... `Alt`+`K`
   • **Keep with ne**x**t** ...... `Alt`+`X`
   • **Page break**
     before ................. `Alt`+`B`
5. Click **OK** ...................... `Enter`

## Insert a Soft Line Break
### (*Shift+Enter*)

1. Click **I**nsert ................. `Alt`+`I`
2. Click **B**reak ...................... `B`
3. Click the **Text w**rapping **break**
   option button ......... `Alt`+`W`
4. Click **OK** ........................ `Enter`

## View Word Count

1. Click **T**ools ................. `Alt`+`T`
2. Click **W**ord Count ............... `W`
3. Click **Close** button
   `Close` to close dialog
   box when done ................. `Esc`
   OR
1. Click **V**iew ................. `Alt`+`V`
2. Click **T**oolbars ................. `T`
3. Click **Word Count**.
4. Click **<Click Recount to**
   **view>** drop-down arrow.
5. Click **Words** ...... `↓`, `↑`, `Enter`
   ✓ *Select one of the other items to*
     *count, if desired.*
6. Click **Recount** button
   `Recount` ............... `Alt`+`C`
   to update word count
   calculation.

# Exercise Directions

1. Start Word, if necessary.

2. Open ⊙ **51HANDOUT**.

3. Save the document as **HANDOUT**.

4. Replace the sample text **Student's Name** with your own name.

5. Replace the sample text **Today's date** with the current date.

6. Position the insertion point at the beginning of the heading **Selecting Roses**.

7. Insert a next page section break.

8. Move the insertion point to the beginning of the document.

9. Vertically center the text in the first section (the first page).

10. Position the insertion point at the beginning of the heading **Types of Roses**.

11. Insert a continuous section break.

12. Move the insertion point up into the second section (anywhere in the heading **Selecting Roses** or the two paragraphs following).

13. Change the margins for the second section to 1.25" on the left and the right.

14. Move the insertion point to the heading **Judging Rose Quality** at the bottom of the page.

15. Apply Keep with next formatting to the heading to make sure it stays on the same page as the following paragraph.

16. Position the insertion point at the beginning of the heading **List of Sources**.

17. Insert a page break.

18. In the second and third items in the list of sources, insert a text wrapping break or a line break between the date and the Web page address.

19. Apply a .5" gutter along the top of the whole document

20. Open the Word Count dialog box to check the number of words in the document.

21. Display the Word Count toolbar and close the dialog box.

22. Delete the first sentence from the first paragraph in the document (**Roses are prized by gardeners around the world.**).

23. Update the word count, and then close the Word Count toolbar.

24. Check the spelling and grammar in the document.

25. Preview the document. It should look similar to the one in Illustration A.

26. Print the document.

27. Close the document, saving all changes.

*Illustration A (Page 1 of 4)*

# ROSES

Prepared by
Student's Name
for
Liberty Blooms Flower Shop
345 Chestnut Street
Philadelphia, PA
Today's date

# Selecting Roses

While some roses have a reputation as being difficult to grow or care for, many variations exist that are resistant to disease, offer beautiful blooms and fragrances, and blend easily into suburban landscapes. With a little thought and preparation, anyone can select and grow magnificent roses.

When selecting plants you should consider the size of the garden and the growing conditions as well as the color, shape, and fragrance of the roses. Draw a garden plan so you can determine the location of each plant. You can then consider how each plant will relate to the others as well as to the garden as a whole. It is also important to educate yourself about the different types of plants that are available, how to judge the quality of plants, and how to identify, prevent, and cure diseases and insect problems.

## Types of Roses

Your first trip to a garden shop in search of roses may prove to be overwhelming. The number and variety of rose plants is amazing. There are creepers, climbers, shrubs, and miniatures. There are colors ranging from white to salmon to yellow to crimson. You may find it helpful to learn about the basic types of roses before you start shopping.

There are four basic groups of roses to consider when selecting plants:

➢ Species Roses, which are old uncultivated varieties.
➢ Old European Garden Roses, which are cultivated varieties common in Europe prior to the eighteenth century.
➢ Hardy Repeat-Blooming Old Roses, which are similar to Old European Garden Roses, except that they bloom more than once each season.
➢ Modern Roses, which are roses developed after the eighteenth century.

## *Judging Rose Quality*

The quality of rose plants varies depending on the vendor. Ask for references before purchasing to make sure that other customers have been satisfied with the plants. You can order plants by mail or on-line, but unless you are certain that you are dealing with a reputable vendor, you may prefer purchasing plants locally.

## Grafted Roses

Grafted roses are rated based on an American Nursery Standards grading system:

➤ Grade 1 plants have at least three canes that are about 3/4 of an inch in diameter and have no more than four inches between the graft union and the top of the roots. They also have a large well developed root system. They must be 2 years old when harvested for sale.
➤ Grade 1 1/2 roses have two strong canes and should quickly catch up to grade 1 plants in size and quality.
➤ Grade 2 roses are inferior quality plants with very small canes. They are usually sold as bargain roses.

## Bare-Root and Potted Roses

Bare-root—dormant plants sold with no soil around the roots—and potted plants have no official standard of grading. You must judge the quality by sight. Bare root plants should have canes that are plump and green, with smooth bark. They should feel heavy, because a light plant is likely to be dried out and brittle.

Potted plants generally have an extensive root system, although if they are called *containerized*, they may simply be bare root plants that the garden center has potted. If so, they may be young and have an immature root system.

## List of Sources

Stack, Greg. <u>Our Rose Garden</u>. University of Illinois Extension Web site. Current date.
<http://www.urbanext.uiuc.edu/roses/history.html>.

<u>A Brief History of Roses</u>. Current date.
<http://www.rosefarm.com/history_of_roses.asp>.

<u>The Flower of Love</u>. Current date.
<http://www.direct-roses.com/history-of-roses.asp>.

# On Your Own

1. Continue working on the report you started in the On Your Own section of Exercise 50.

2. Use sources such as the Internet or library to research your topic, remembering to record the source information.

3. Start Word and open **OWD50**, the outline you created in Exercise 50.

4. Save the document as **OWD51**.

5. Change to Normal view or Print Layout view and start writing the first draft of your report.

6. Keep track of the word count. Your instructor may ask for a minimum or maximum number of words.

7. Use proper formatting for the report. For example, your instructor may want you to double-space the body text paragraphs and use a first line indent.

8. Set appropriate margins. If you plan to bind the report using staples or a clip folder, leave room for the binding.

9. Insert page breaks if necessary so that headings or paragraphs start at the top of a page instead of at the bottom of one.

10. Use text flow control options as necessary.

11. Insert section breaks as necessary. For example, you may want to have a different header or footer in section 2.

12. When you have completed the first draft, ask a classmate to review it and offer comments and suggestions.

13. Incorporate the comments and suggestions into the document.

14. Check the spelling and grammar in the document.

15. Print the document.

16. Close the document, saving all changes, and exit Word.

# Exercise 52

## Skills Covered:

◆ **Create Headers/Footers** ◆ **Different First Page Headers/Footers**
◆ **Different Odd/Even Headers/Footers**
◆ **Different Section Headers/Footers** ◆ **Insert Page Numbers**

## On the Job

Use headers and footers when you need to print information on the top or bottom of every page. You can customize documents by creating different headers and footers on the first page, on odd and even pages, and for different sections. Using different headers and footers helps readers identify different sections of a document.

In this exercise, you will add headers and footers to a version of the Roses document.

## Terms

**Header** Repetitive text or graphics printed at the top of pages in a document.

**Footer** Repetitive text or graphics printed at the bottom of pages in a document.

## Notes

### Create Headers/Footers

- Create a **header** and/or **footer** to print repetitive information such as page numbers, dates, author, or subject on every page of a document.

- Headers and footers are not displayed in Normal view. Use Print Preview or Print Layout view to see them on the screen.

- By default, headers print .5" from the top of the page, and footers print .5" from the bottom of the page.

- You can apply headers and footers to the entire document or to the current section.

- Use Header and Footer toolbar buttons to customize headers and footers.

*Header and Footer toolbar*

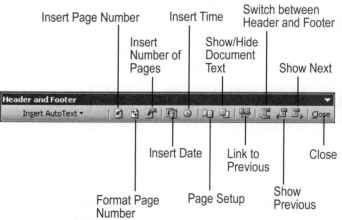

### Different First Page Headers/Footers

- Set Word to print a different header/footer on the first page of a document or section.

- Leave the first page header/footer blank to omit the header/footer from the first page.

## Different Odd/Even Headers/Footers

- Print different headers on odd and even pages.

- Using different headers/footers on odd and even pages gives you an opportunity to include information such as a chapter or section name and number and to customize the appearance of a document.

## Different Section Headers/Footers

- By default, new sections have the same header/footer as the previous section.

- You can change the header/footer for every section in a document.

## Insert Page Numbers

- You can insert page numbers in a Word document using either the Header and Footer toolbar, or the Insert, Page Numbers command.

- Use the Insert, Page Numbers command when you don't want to create an entire header or footer and to use the options for formatting and positioning the page numbers on the page.

- By default, page numbers print on the bottom right of each page.

- Set options to control page number placement:

*Page Numbers dialog box*

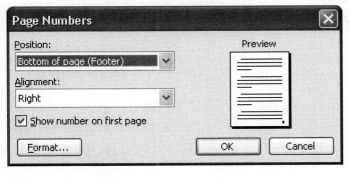

- *Position* sets numbers at the top or bottom of page.

- *Alignment* sets numbers left, right, centered, inside (along binding), or outside (along outer edge) of the page.

- *Show number on first page* shows or suppresses the page number on the first page.

- You can change the page number format to select a different number style, to include chapter numbers, or to restart numbering in a new section.

- Restarting the numbering is useful when your document has a title page that you do not want numbered.

  - Insert a Next Page section break between the title page and the first page of the document. That makes the title page the first section.

  - Then, click the Format button in the Page Numbers dialog box to display the Page Number Format dialog box.

  - Select the option to restart the page numbers for the second section, then click OK to return to the Page Numbers dialog box, or -- if you originally inserted the page number using the Header and Footer toolbar, click Close.

  ✓ *If you click OK instead of Close, you may insert two page numbers on each page. Click Undo and try again.*

*Page Number Format dialog box*

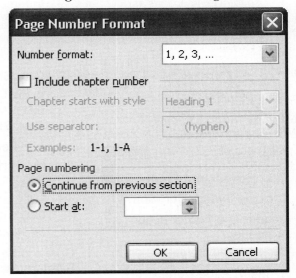

# Procedures

## Create Headers/Footers

### Create a header on every page:

1. Click **View** .................. Alt + V
2. Click **Header and Footer** ... H
3. In the Header box, type header text.
   - ✓ Use formatting options as desired, including fonts, font effects, alignment, tabs, and spacing.
4. Click **Close** button Close .............. Alt + C on the Header and Footer toolbar.

### Create a footer on every page:

1. Click **View** .................. Alt + V
2. Click **Header and Footer** ... H
3. Click the **Switch Between Header and Footer** button.
4. In the Footer box, type footer text.
   - ✓ Use formatting options as desired, including fonts, font effects, alignment, and tabs.
5. Click **Close** button Close .............. Alt + C on the Header and Footer toolbar.

### Insert page numbers, date, and/or time in a header/footer:

1. Click **View** .................. Alt + V
2. Click **Header and Footer** ... H
3. Click the **Switch Between Header and Footer** button as needed.
4. Click desired toolbar button(s):
   - **Insert Page Number**
   - **Insert Date**
   - **Insert Time**
5. Click **Close** button Close .............. Alt + C on the Header and Footer toolbar.

---

- ✓ Combine text and page numbers, date, or time to achieve different effects. For example, type Page, press the spacebar once to leave a space, then insert page number.

### Create first page header/footer:

1. Click **View** .................. Alt + V
2. Click **Header and Footer** .... H
3. Click the **Page Setup** button.
4. Click the **Layout** tab ... Ctrl + Tab
5. Select the **Different first page** check box .......... Alt + P
6. Click **OK** .......................... Enter
7. In First Page Header box, type first page header text.
   - ✓ Leave blank to suppress header on first page.
8. Click **Switch Between Header and Footer** button.
9. In First Page Footer box, type first page footer text.
   - ✓ Leave blank to suppress footer on first page.
10. Click **Show Next** button.
11. In the Footer box, type text for other footers.
12. Click **Switch Between Header and Footer** button.
13. In the Header box, type other header text.
14. Click **Close** button Close .............. Alt + C on Header and Footer toolbar.

### Create different odd and even headers/footers:

1. Click **View** .................. Alt + V
2. Click **Header and Footer** .... H
3. Click the **Page Setup** button.
4. Click the **Different odd and even** check box .......... Alt + O
5. Click **OK** .......................... Enter

---

6. In Even Page Header box, type even page header text.
   - ✓ If Odd Page Header box displays first, click Show Next button to display Even Page Header.
7. Click the **Switch Between Header and Footer** button.
8. In Even Page Footer box, type even page footer text.
9. Click the **Show Next** button or **Show Previous** button.
10. In Odd Page Footer box, type odd page footer text.
11. Click the **Switch Between Header and Footer** button.
12. In Odd Page Header box, type odd page header text.
13. Click **Close** button Close .............. Alt + C on Header and Footer toolbar.

### Create different headers/footers in sections:

1. Create sections.
2. Position insertion point in section where you want header/footer.
3. Click **View** .................. Alt + V
4. Click **Header and Footer** .... H
5. Click the **Switch Between Header and Footer** button as necessary.
6. Click **Link to Previous** button.
   - ✓ By default, Link to Previous button is toggled on. Click it to toggle it off. If button is already toggled off, skip step 6.
7. Enter header/footer information.
8. Click **Close** button Close .............. Alt + C on Header and Footer toolbar.

## Insert Page Numbers Only

1. Click **Insert** ................. Alt + I
2. Click **Page Numbers** .......... U
3. Click the **Position** drop-down arrow .......... Alt + P
4. Select **Bottom of page (Footer)** .......... ↓, Enter

   OR

   **Top of page (Header)** ................ ↑, Enter
5. Click the **Alignment** drop-down arrow ............ Alt + A
6. Select alignment option: ................ ↓, ↑, Enter
   - **Right**
   - **Left**
   - **Center**
   - **Inside**
   - **Outside**
7. Select **Show number on first page** if desired ............. Alt + S
8. Click **OK** .......................... Enter

## Change Page Number Formatting

1. Click **Insert** ................ Alt + I
2. Click **Page Numbers** .......... U
3. Click **Format** ............... Alt + F
4. Click the **Number format** drop-down arrow ........ Alt + F
5. Select format ............ ↓, Enter
   - **Arabic numerals** .. 1, 2, 3, 4, 5, etc.
   - **Arabic numerals with dashes** . -1-, -2-, -3-, -4-, etc.
   - **Lowercase letters** .... a, b, c, d, e, f, etc.
   - **Uppercase letters** A, B, C, D, E, F, etc.
   - **Lowercase Roman numerals** ....i, ii, iii, iv, v, etc.
   - **Uppercase Roman numerals** . I, II, III, IV, V, etc.

6. Click **OK** .......................... Enter
   to close Page Number Format dialog box.
7. Click **OK** .......................... Enter
   to close Page Numbers dialog box and insert page numbers.

   OR

   Click **Close** [ Close ] to close Page number box without inserting additional page numbers.

# Exercise Directions

1. Start Word, if necessary.
2. Open ☉ **52HANDOUT**.
3. Save the file as **HANDOUT2**.
4. Make sure the document is displayed in Print Layout view and that Show/Hide Paragraph marks is turned on, so you can see where breaks occur.
5. Position the insertion point within section 2 (pages 2 and 3).
6. Use the Page Number Format dialog box to set Word to restart numbering in section 2.
   a. Click Insert, Page Numbers.
   b. Click the Format button.
   c. Select the Start at option button and make sure the number is set at 1.
   d. Click OK to close the Page Number Format dialog box.
   e. Click Close to close the Insert Numbers dialog box.
   ✓ *Make sure you click Close and not OK in the Insert Numbers dialog box.*

7. Create different headers for the odd and even pages in each section.
8. Leave the section 1 header and footer blank.
9. Remove the default settings linking the section 2 headers and footers to the previous headers and footers.
10. Remove the default settings linking the section 3 header to the previous header, but leave the section 3 footer linked to the previous footer.
11. Go back to the Section 2 Odd Page Header.
12. Type the class name **All About Roses** flush left and the text **Prepared by** followed by your name flush right.
    ✓ *If necessary, adjust the right tab stop in the header to align with the right margin.*
13. Switch to the Section 2 Odd Page Footer.
14. Flush left, type the word Page, leave a space, and then insert the page number.
15. Go to the Section 2 Even Page Footer.

16. Flush right type the word Page followed by a space and then insert the page number.

   ✓ *Again, if necessary, adjust the right tab stop in the footer to align with the right margin.*

17. Switch to the Section 2 Even Page Header.

18. Type the shop name **Liberty Blooms** flush left and the insert the current date flush right.

   ✓ *Adjust the right tab stop if necessary.*

19. Switch to the Section 3 Odd Page Header.

20. Type the class name **All About Roses** flush left and the text **List of Sources** flush right.

   ✓ *Adjust the right tab stop if necessary.*

21. Switch to the Section 3 Footer. The same information already entered in the previous footer should be entered.

22. Close the Header and Footer toolbar.

23. Check the spelling and grammar in the document.

24. Preview the document. Sections 2 and 3 should look similar to the following illustrations.

   ✓ *Word may automatically insert a blank page between sections 1 and 2.*

25. Print the document.

26. Close the document, saving all changes.

# On Your Own

1. Continue working on your research report by improving the first draft. Add information and rewrite existing information.

2. Start Word and open **OWD51**.

3. Save the document as **OWD52**.

4. Create headers and footers for the document. Include your name and the date in the header, and center the page numbers in the footer.

5. You may want to have different headers and footers for different sections or pages.

6. When you have completed the second draft, ask a classmate to review it and offer comments and suggestions.

7. Incorporate the comments and suggestions into the document.

8. Check the spelling and grammar in the document.

9. Print the document.

10. Close the document, saving all changes, and exit Word.

*Illustration A (Page 1 of 3)*

All About Roses                                     Prepared by Student's Name

# Selecting Roses

While some roses have a reputation as being difficult to grow or care for, many variations exist that are resistant to disease, offer beautiful blooms and fragrances, and blend easily into suburban landscapes. With a little thought and preparation, anyone can select and grow magnificent roses.

Your first trip to a garden shop in search of roses may prove to be overwhelming. The number and variety of rose plants is amazing. There are creepers, climbers, shrubs, and miniatures. There are colors ranging from white to salmon to yellow to crimson. You may find it helpful to learn about the basic types of roses before you start shopping.

When selecting plants you should consider the size of the garden and the growing conditions as well as the color, shape, and fragrance of the roses. Draw a garden plan so you can determine the location of each plant. You can then consider how each plant will relate to the others as well as to the garden as a whole. It is also important to educate yourself about the different types of plants that are available, how to judge the quality of plants, and how to identify, prevent, and cure diseases and insect problems.

## *Types of Roses*

There are four basic groups of roses to consider when selecting plants:

➢ Species Roses, which are old uncultivated varieties.
➢ Old European Garden Roses, which are cultivated varieties common in Europe prior to the eighteenth century.
➢ Hardy Repeat-Blooming Old Roses, which are similar to Old European Garden Roses, except that they bloom more than once each season.
➢ Modern Roses, which are roses developed after the eighteenth century.

Page 1

Liberty Blooms                                                    Today's Date

## *Judging Rose Quality*

The quality of rose plants varies depending on the vendor. Ask for references before purchasing to make sure that other customers have been satisfied with the plants. You can order plants by mail or on-line, but unless you are certain that you are dealing with a reputable vendor, you may prefer purchasing plants locally.

## Grafted Roses

Grafted roses are rated based on an American Nursery Standards grading system:

➤ Grade 1 plants have at least three canes that are about ¾ of an inch in diameter and have no more than four inches between the graft union and the top of the roots. They also have a large well developed root system. They must be two years old when harvested for sale.
➤ Grade 1 ½ roses have two strong canes and should quickly catch up to Grade 1 plants in size and quality.
➤ Grade 2 roses are inferior quality plants with very small canes. They are usually sold as bargain roses.

## Bare-Root and Potted Roses

Bare-root—dormant plants sold with no soil around the roots—and potted plants have no official standard of grading. You must judge the quality by sight. Bare root plants should have canes that are plump and green, with smooth bark. They should feel heavy, because a light plant is likely to be dried out and brittle.

Potted plants generally have an extensive root system, although if they are called *containerized*, they may simply be bare root plants that the garden center has potted. If so, they may be young and have an immature root system.

Page 2

*Illustration A (Page 3 of 3)*

All About Roses                                        List of Sources

## List of Sources

Stack, Greg. <u>Our Rose Garden</u>. University of Illinois Extension Web site. Current date.
  <http://www.urbanext.uiuc.edu/roses/history.html>.

<u>A Brief History of Roses</u>. Current date.
  <http://www.rosefarm.com/history_of_roses.asp>.

<u>The Flower of Love</u>. Current date.
  <http://www.direct-roses.com/history-of-roses.asp>.

Page 3

# Exercise 53

## Skills Covered:
◆ **Find and Replace** ◆ **Insert Bookmarks**
◆ **Use Browse Objects** ◆ **Use AutoSummarize**

## On the Job

Use the Find, Bookmark, and Browse Object features to locate specific parts of a document, including text, graphics, paragraph marks, etc. Use Find and Replace when you want to automatically replace existing text or formatting with something different. When you need to briefly summarize a paper or report, use AutoSummarize.

> In this exercise, you will edit a longer version of the Roses document. You will use the Find and Replace commands to improve the text. You will also insert bookmarks into the document and use different browse objects to move through the document. Finally, you will create a summary of the document.

## Terms

**Bookmark** A nonprinting character that you insert and name so that you can quickly find a particular location in a document.

**Browse object** A specified element that Word locates and displays when you scroll through a document.

**Executive Summary** or **Abstract** The key points and main ideas of a document, paper, or report.

## Notes

### Find and Replace

- Use Word's Find command to locate specific text, nonprinting characters, formatting, graphics, objects, and other items in a document.

- You can use Find to scroll one by one through each occurrence of the Find text, or you can find and select all occurrences at once.

*Find tab of the Find and Replace dialog box*

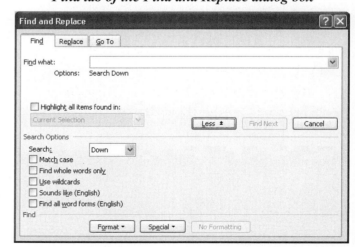

- Combine Find with Replace to replace items.

- The Find and Replace commands are useful for correcting errors that occur several times in a document, such as a misspelled name.

- In addition to text, you can find and replace formatting, symbols, and special characters such as paragraph marks.

- By default, not all options are displayed in the Find and Replace dialog box; click the More button ⌊ More ⤓ ⌋ to expand the box to show all options, then click the Less button ⌊ Less ⤒ ⌋ to collapse the box.

*Replace tab of the Find and Replace dialog box*

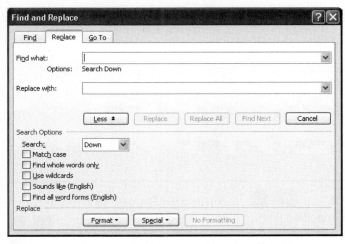

## Insert Bookmarks

- Use a **bookmark** to mark a specific location in a document, such as where you stopped working or where you need to insert information.

- You can use many bookmarks in one document.

- Use descriptive bookmark names to make it easier to find the bookmark location that you want.

- Use the Go To feature to go directly to a bookmark.

*Go To tab of Find and Replace dialog box*

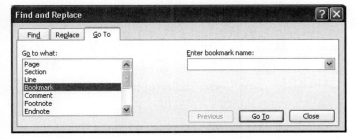

## Select Browse Object

- Use **browse object** to scroll to specific points in a document.

- There are twelve browse objects from which to choose; rest the mouse pointer on an object to see its name across the top or bottom of the object palette.

- When you choose the Go To browse object, you must specify the object to go to.

- When you choose the Find browse object, you must enter text to Find and/or Replace.

*The browse object palette*

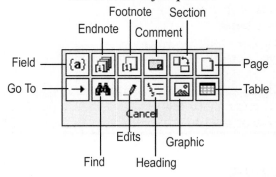

## Use AutoSummarize

- Use the AutoSummarize feature to identify key points in a document.

- Word determines the key points by ranking sentences based on how many times frequently used words are included in the sentence.

- You specify the length of the summary as a percentage of the original document; the higher the percentage, the more detail is included in the summary.

- Alternatively, choose a maximum number of words or sentences to include in the summary.

- You can choose to display the summary in four ways:

  - Highlight the key points in the document.

  - Hide all text except the key points.

  - Create an **executive summary** or **abstract** at the beginning of the document.

  - Create an executive summary or abstract in a new document.

*The AutoSummarize dialog box*

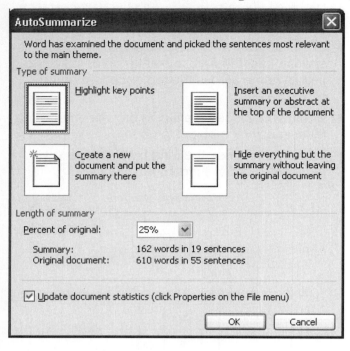

- If you select to highlight key points or to hide all text except key points, the AutoSummarize toolbar is displayed.
- Use buttons on the AutoSummarize toolbar to switch between highlighting key points or showing only the summary, adjusting the length of the summary, or to close AutoSummarize and display the original document.

*The AutoSummarize toolbar*

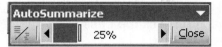

# Procedures

## Find Text *(Ctrl+F)*

1. Position the insertion point at the beginning of the document ................ `Ctrl`+`Home`

   ✓ *You may start searching at any point in the document, or you may search selected text. However, to be sure to search the entire document, start at the top.*

2. Click **E**dit ..................... `Alt`+`E`
3. Click **F**ind........................... `F`
4. Click **Fi**n**d** what .......... `Alt`+`N`
5. Type text to find.
6. Click **More** (if necessary) .............. `Alt`+`M`
7. Select options:
   - **Match case** .......... `Alt`+`H` to find only words in same case as text to find.
   - **Find whole words onl**y ...................... `Alt`+`Y` to find text as a whole word, not as part of a longer word.
   - **Use wildcards** ...... `Alt`+`U` to find words specified with wildcard characters.
   - **Sounds like** ........... `Alt`+`K` to find homonyms.
   - **Find all **w**ord forms** .................... `Alt`+`W` to find all grammatical forms of text.

8. Click **F**ind Next .......... `Alt`+`F`

   ✓ *Word highlights first occurrence of text in document. You can click in the document to edit or format the text, while leaving the Find and Replace dialog box open.*

9. Repeat step 8 until finished.

   ✓ *Click Cancel at any time to close the dialog box.*

10. Click **OK** ......................... `Enter`
11. Click **Cancel** ...................... `Esc`

## Find and Select Text

1. Click **E**dit..................... `Alt`+`E`
2. Click **F**ind...................... `F`
3. Click **Fi**n**d** what........... `Alt`+`N`
4. Type text to find.
5. Click **Highligh**t **all items found in:**...................... `Alt`+`T`

   ✓ *Default is to highlight items in main document only; you may select Headers and Footers from the drop-down list if desired.*

6. Click **F**ind **All** .............. `Alt`+`F`

   ✓ *Word finds and selects all occurrences of the specified text.*

7. Click **Close**........................ `Esc`

## Replace Text *(Ctrl+H)*

1. Click **E**dit..................... `Alt`+`E`
2. Click **R**eplace..................... `E`
3. Click **Fi**n**d** what........... `Alt`+`N`
4. Type text to find.

5. Press **Tab** .......................... `Tab`
   OR

   Click **Replace with** ...... `Alt`+`I`

   ✓ *To replace with nothing (delete), leave the Replace with text box blank.*

6. Type replacement text.

7. Click **More**
   (if necessary) .............. `Alt`+`M`

8. Select options.

9. Click **Find Next** ........... `Alt`+`F`

10. Click **Replace** ............. `Alt`+`R`
    OR

    Click **Replace All** ........ `Alt`+`A`

11. Repeat steps 9–10 until done.

    ✓ *Click Cancel at any time to close the dialog box.*

12. Click **OK** ........................... `Enter`

13. Click **Cancel** ...................... `Esc`

## Find and Replace Special Characters *(Ctrl +H)*

1. Click **Edit** .................... `Alt`+`E`

2. Click **Replace** ................... `R`

3. Click **Find what** .......... `Alt`+`N`

4. Click **More** .................. `Alt`+`M`

5. Click **Special** .............. `Alt`+`E`

6. Select special character.

7. Press **Tab** .......................... `Tab`
   OR

   Click **Replace with** ...... `Alt`+`I`

   ✓ *To replace with nothing (delete), leave Replace with text box blank.*

8. Click **Special** .............. `Alt`+`E`

9. Select special character.

10. Click **Find Next** ........... `Alt`+`F`

11. Click **Replace** ................... `R`
    OR

    Click **Replace All** ....... `Alt`+`A`

12. Repeat steps 10–11 until done.

    ✓ *Click Cancel at any time to close the dialog box.*

13. Click **OK** ........................... `Enter`

14. Click **Cancel** ...................... `Esc`

## Insert a Bookmark

1. Position the insertion point where you want the bookmark.

2. Click **Insert** ................. `Alt`+`I`

3. Click **Bookmark** ................. `K`

4. Click in the **Bookmark name** text box ...................... `Alt`+`B`

5. Type bookmark name.

6. Click **Add** ................... `Alt`+`A`

## Go To Bookmark *(Ctrl+G)*

1. Press **F5** ........................... `F5`
   OR

   a. Click **Edit** ............... `Alt`+`E`

   b. Click **Go To** ................... `G`

2. Click Bookmark in the **Go to what** list ........... `Alt`+`O`

   ✓ *Select any object in the Go to what list to browse directly to that object.*

3. Click **Enter bookmark name** ...................... `Alt`+`E`

4. Type bookmark name.
   OR

   Select bookmark name from drop-down list.

5. Click **Go To** ................. `Alt`+`T`

6. Click **Close** ...................... `Esc`

## Browse by Object *(Alt + Ctrl + Home)*

1. Click the **Select Browse Object** button `⊙`.

2. Click the desired browse object.

   ✓ *If you select Find or Go To, the Find and Replace dialog box is displayed.*

3. Click the **Previous** button `⬆` to scroll up to the previous browse object.

   ✓ *The screen tip for the Previous button includes the name of the current browse object.*

   OR

   Click the **Next** button `⬇` to scroll down to the next browse object.

   ✓ *The ScreenTip for the Next button includes the name of the current browse object.*

## Use AutoSummarize

1. Click **Tools** ................. `Alt`+`T`

2. Click **AutoSummarize** ........ `U`

3. Select type of summary:

   • **Highlight key points** .................. `Alt`+`H`

   • **Insert an executive summary or abstract at the top of the document** .............. `Alt`+`I`

   • **Create a new document and put the summary there** ..................... `Alt`+`R`

   • **Hide everything but the summary without leaving the original document** .............. `Alt`+`D`

4. If necessary, click **Percent of original** drop-down arrow ........................... `Alt`+`P`

5. Select desired percentage or maximum length.

6. Click **OK** ........................... `Enter`

## Use the AutoSummarize Toolbar

• Click **Highlight/Show Only Summary** button `⁄` to toggle between highlighting key points and hiding all but key points.

• Click increment arrows or drag the sliders on **Percent of Original** box `◀  25%  ▶` to change the length of the summary.

• Click **Close** button `Close` to close AutoSummarize.

# Exercise Directions

1. Start Word, if necessary.
2. Open the document ⊘ **53ROSES**.
3. Save the file as **ROSES2**.
4. Starting with the insertion point at the beginning of the document, use the Find command to locate the first occurrence of the word **rose**.
   - ✓ *Word should highlight the letters Rose in the report title.*
5. Locate the next occurrence of the word.
   - ✓ *Word should highlight the letters* rose *within the word* roses *in the first sentence of the document.*
6. Move the insertion point back to the beginning of the document.
7. Set the Find command to use the Whole Words Only and Match Case options so that it finds whole words in lowercase letters.
8. Locate the first occurrence of the word **rose**.
9. This time, Word should highlight the word **rose** in the third sentence of the first paragraph.
10. Use the Find command to select all occurrences of the word **rose**.
11. Close the Find dialog box, and format all selected words with bold italics.
12. Use Find and Replace to replace all occurrences of **eighteenth** with **18**th.
    - ✓ *Don't forget to remove the Match Case and Whole Words Only options from the Find dialog box.*
13. Replace all occurrences of **seventeenth** with **17**th.
14. Replace all occurrences of **fifteenth** with **15**th.
15. Replace all occurrences of the complete word **rose** formatted with bold italic with the word **rose** with no bold or italic (regular font style).
16. Use the Browse by Heading browse object to move the insertion point to the heading **Types of Roses** and insert a bookmark named **rosetypes**.
17. Use the Browse by Heading browse object to move the insertion point to the heading **Diseases and Insects** and insert a bookmark named **trouble**.
18. Use Go To browse object to go to the **rosetypes** bookmark.
19. Use the Go To browse object to go to the **trouble** bookmark.
20. Check the spelling and grammar in the document and correct errors as necessary.
21. Use AutoSummarize to highlight the key points in the document.
    - ✓ *Use the default 25% of the original setting.*
22. Close AutoSummarize.
23. Use AutoSummarize to create an executive summary in a new document. Set the summary to be 10% of the original document.
24. Save the new document as **SUMMARY**.
25. Display the document in Print Preview. It should look similar to the one in the illustration.
    - ✓ *If there are blank lines at the end of the document, delete them.*
26. Close Print Preview.
27. Print the document.
28. Close all open documents, saving all changes.

*Illustration A*

# ROSES

### *The Rose as Symbol*

## Selecting Roses

### *Types of Roses*

There are four basic groups of roses to consider when selecting plants:

Species Roses
Old European Garden Roses
Hardy Repeat-Blooming Old Roses
Modern Roses

Species Roses are uncultivated varieties. The oldest group of cultivated roses is

Old European Garden Roses. Hardy Repeat-Blooming Old Roses offer qualities similar

to the Old European Garden Roses, but they will bloom more than once each season,

while modern roses are rose varieties developed after the 18th century.

### *Judging Rose Quality*

### Grafted Roses

Grade 2 roses are inferior quality plants with very small canes. They are usually sold as
bargain roses.

### Bare-Root and Potted Roses

## Caring for Cut Roses

Cut roses are ideal for bringing a garden inside. Following are guidelines for maintaining

cut roses:

# On Your Own

1. Continue working to improve your research report by adding citations and marking text that needs additional work.

2. Open the document **OWD52** that you used in the On Your Own section of Exercise 52.

3. Save the document as **OWD53**.

4. Use Find to locate text that requires citations.

5. Insert footnotes or endnotes to provide citations or to supplement text with additional information.

6. Use Browse to check your citations.

7. If necessary, use Find and Replace to locate and replace specific text, such as an abbreviation or acronym.

8. Insert bookmarks to mark text that needs additional work. For example, you may want to mark a fact for which you need to check a citation, or a paragraph that you think needs to be rewritten.

9. Make edits as necessary, and save your changes.

10. Ask a classmate to review the document and make comments or suggestions.

11. Incorporate the suggestions into the paper.

12. Create an executive summary that is 10% of the original document in a separate document.

13. Save the summary document as **OWD53-2**.

14. Print both documents.

15. Close the documents, saving all changes.

# Exercise 54

**Skills Covered:**

◆ **Use Reading Layout View** ◆ **Use Document Map**
◆ **Use Thumbnails** ◆ **Preview Multiple Pages**
◆ **Copy or Move Text from One Page to Another** ◆ **Print Specific Pages**

## On the Job

Reading Layout view makes it easier to read a document on-screen. Preview multiple pages to see how an entire multipage document will look when it is printed. For example, when you preview more than one page at a time, you can see headers and footers on every page and determine whether the text flow from one page to the next looks professional. The Document Map helps you quickly locate sections of a long document without spending time scrolling through pages. Printing specific pages or selected text is an option that can save paper and time if you find that you only need hard copies of parts of a document.

In this exercise, you will preview, proofread, and edit the document about roses. You will use the Document Map to navigate through the document to find headings and paragraphs. You will move text from one page to another. You will preview multiple pages to determine whether page breaks are in the correct locations. Finally, you will print selected pages of the document.

## Terms

**Document Map** A vertical pane that opens on the left side of the document window to show the major headings and sections in a document; click a topic in the pane to go to it.

**Thumbnails** Miniature image of a document page.

**Magnifier** The mouse pointer used to zoom in or out on a page in Print Preview.

## Notes

### Use Reading Layout View

- Use Reading Layout view to read documents on screen.

- When you switch to Reading Layout view, the document text is formatted to display by the screen—not by the page.

- Also, only the Reading Layout and the Reviewing toolbars are displayed.

- By default, only one screen of text is displayed, but you can select to view two screens if you want.

- You can also select to display an actual page instead of a screen.

- You can increase or decrease the size of the text on screen without changing the size of the font in the document.

- Some visual elements—such as tables and pictures—may not display properly in Reading Layout view.

- You can edit and format text in Reading Layout view. To view the results of your changes, switch to Print Layout view or Print Preview.

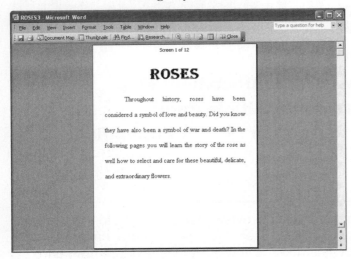

## Use Document Map

- **Document Map** is useful for navigating through long documents.
- Word displays the Document Map in a pane on the left side of the document window.
- The Document Map shows headings and major topics in an outline format.
- If there are no headings or major topics, the Document Map is empty.
- You can expand and collapse the Document Map as you would an outline to show the headings you need.

*The Document Map*

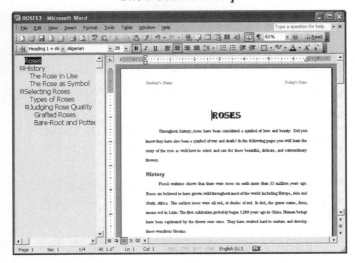

## Use Thumbnails

- **Thumbnails** are also useful for navigating in a longer document.
- Word displays thumbnails in a pane on the left side of the screen.
- In Normal view, Print Layout view, Outline view, and Web Layout view, each thumbnail represents one document page.
- In Reading Layout view, each thumbnail represents one screen.

*Thumbnails in Print Layout view*

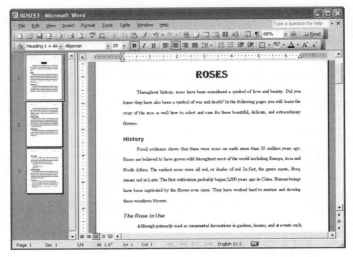

## Preview Multiple Pages

- By default, Print Preview displays one page at a time.
- You can change the Print Preview display to show multiple pages at one time.
- Preview multiple pages to get an overall view of the document, not to edit or format text.
  - ✓ *You can edit in Print Preview, but it is difficult if the pages are small.*
- You can select the number of pages you want to display using the Multiple Pages button on the Print Preview toolbar.
  - ✓ *You can also select a setting from the Zoom drop-down list. For more on the Zoom feature, refer to Exercise 3.*
- The more pages displayed, the smaller the pages appear on the screen, so the harder it is to read the text.
- Use the **Magnifier** tool to zoom in or out on a page in Print Preview.

*A four-page document in Print preview*

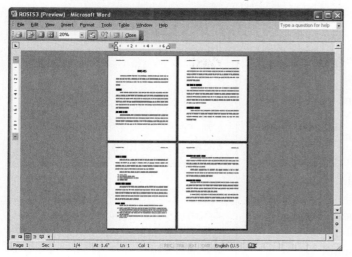

## Copy or Move Text from One Page to Another

- Use standard copy and move techniques to copy or move text from one page in a document to another page.

  ✓ *Moving text is covered in Exercise 17; Copying text is covered in Exercise 18.*

- Use Cut and Paste to move text.
- Use Copy and Paste to copy text.
- If you can see both locations on the screen at the same time, use the drag-and-drop method.

- Copying and/or moving text may affect hard page breaks or section breaks already inserted in a document. For example, if you cut text before a hard page break, the break may occur high up on the page.

## Print Specific Pages

- Select Print options to print a specific page, several pages, selected text, or the current page.

- In the Print dialog box, you can specify consecutive pages or nonconsecutive pages. You can also specify pages to print by page number.

*Set print options in the Print dialog box*

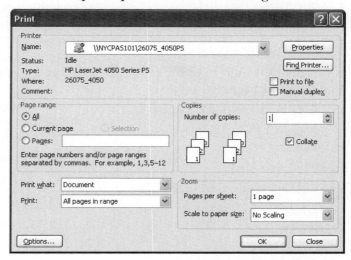

# Procedures

## Use Reading Layout View

### To switch to Reading Layout view (*Alt+R*):

1. Click **View**................... Alt + V
2. Click **Reading Layout** ........ R

OR

- Click **Read** button [📖 Read] on Standard toolbar.

OR

- Click **Reading Layout** view button [📖].

### To display actual pages:

- Click **Actual Page** button [📄] on Reading Layout toolbar.

### To display two screens/pages:

- Click **Allow Multiple Pages** button [📑] on Reading Layout toolbar.

### To adjust text size:

- Click **Increase Text Size** button [🔍] on Reading Layout toolbar.

OR

- Click **Decrease Text Size** button [🔍] on Reading Layout toolbar.

### To close Reading Layout view (*Alt+C*):

1. Click **View**................... Alt + V
2. Click desired view.

OR

- Click **Close** button [📖 Close] on Reading Layout toolbar.

## Use Document Map

### Display Document Map:

1. Click **View**................... Alt + V
2. Click **Document Map** ......... D

OR

- Click **Document Map** button [📑] on the Standard toolbar.

### Hide Document Map:

1. Click **View**................... Alt + V
2. Click **Document Map** .......... D

OR

- Click **Document Map** button [📑] on the Standard toolbar.

### Move insertion point to a heading:

- Click desired heading in Document Map.

### Expand/collapse headings:

1. Right-click anywhere in Document Map.
2. Click level of heading to Expand/Collapse.

OR

Click **Expand** (plus sign) or **Collapse** (minus sign) next to heading in Document Map.

## Use Thumbnails

### To display Thumbnails:

1. Click **View**................... Alt + V
2. Click **Thumbnails**............... B

OR

- Click **Thumbnails** button [📋] on Reading Layout toolbar.

### To hide Thumbnails:

1. Click **View**................... Alt + V
2. Click **Thumbnails**............... B

OR

- Click **Thumbnails** button [📋] on Reading Layout toolbar.

### To jump to a page:

- Click thumbnail representing desired page.

## Preview Multiple Pages

1. Click **Print Preview** button [📄].

OR

a. Click **File** ................ Alt + F
b. Click **Print Preview** ........ V

2. Click **Multiple Pages** button [▦].
3. Drag across number of rows and pages to display.
4. Release mouse button.

## Change Back to One-Page Preview

- Click **One Page** button .

## Zoom In in Print Preview

1. If necessary, click in document to position the insertion point.
2. Position the magnifier mouse pointer over the area to enlarge [🔍].
   - ✓ *The magnifier is selected by default. If the magnifier pointer is not displayed, click Magnifier button on Print Preview toolbar to toggle the option on.*
3. Click mouse once.
4. Click again to zoom out [🔍].
   - ✓ *To cancel the magnifier so you can edit a document, click the Magnifier button on Print Preview toolbar to toggle the option off.*

## Use Copy and Paste to Copy Text from One Page to Another (*Ctrl+C, Ctrl+V*)

1. Select the text to copy.
2. Click **Copy** button [📋].

OR

a. Click **Edit** .............. Alt + E
b. Click **Copy** ..................... C

3. Display other page and position insertion point in new location.
4. Click **Paste** button [📋].

OR

a. Click **Edit** .............. Alt + E
b. Click **Paste**.................... P

## Use Drag-and-Drop Editing to Copy Text

1. Display multiple pages on-screen in Print Preview, Print Layout or Reading Layout view.

   ✓ *If necessary, click the magnifier button to turn off zoom feature.*

2. Select text to copy.
3. Move mouse pointer anywhere over selected text.
4. Press and hold **Ctrl** ............. `Ctrl`
5. Drag selection to new

   location `⊞`.
6. Release mouse button.
7. Release **Ctrl** ...................... `Ctrl`

## Move Text from One Page to Another

1. Select text to move.
2. Press **F2** ............................. `F2`
3. Display other page and position insertion point at new location.
4. Press **Enter** ...................... `Enter`

## Use Cut and Paste to Move Text *(Ctrl+X, Cltr+V)*

1. Select text to move.
2. Click **Cut** button `✂`.

   OR

   a. Click **Edit** ................ `Alt`+`E`
   b. Click **Cut** ......................... `T`

3. Display other page and position insertion point at new location.
4. Click **Paste** button `📋`.

   OR

   a. Click **Edit** ................ `Alt`+`E`
   b. Click **Paste** .................... `P`

## Use Drag-and-Drop Editing to Move Text

1. Display multiple pages on-screen in Print Preview, Print Layout, or Reading Layout view.
2. Select text to move.

   ✓ *If necessary, click the magnifier button to turn off zoom feature.*

3. Move mouse pointer anywhere over selected text.
4. Drag selection to new

   location `🖫`.
5. Release mouse button when the insertion point is in new location.

## Print Specified Pages *(Ctrl+P)*

### Print single page:

1. Click **File** ..................... `Alt`+`F`
2. Click **Print** .......................... `P`
3. Click **Pages** ................. `Alt`+`G`
4. Type page number.
5. Click **OK** ......................... `Enter`

### Print consecutive pages:

1. Click **File** ..................... `Alt`+`F`
2. Click **Print** .......................... `P`
3. Click **Pages** ................. `Alt`+`G`
4. Type page range as follows: first page number, hyphen, last page number. For example: 3-5

   ✓ *Do not type spaces.*

5. Click **OK** .......................... `Enter`

### Print nonconsecutive pages:

1. Click **File** ..................... `Alt`+`F`
2. Click **Print** .......................... `P`
3. Click **Pages** ................. `Alt`+`G`
4. Type each page number separated by commas. For example: 3,5,7

   ✓ *Do not type spaces.*

5. Click **OK** .......................... `Enter`

   ✓ *You can combine consecutive and nonconsecutive pages. For example, 2-5,7,10.*

### Print current page:

1. Click **File** ..................... `Alt`+`F`
2. Click **Print** .......................... `P`
3. Click **Current page** ..... `Alt`+`E`
4. Click **OK** .......................... `Enter`

### Print selected text:

1. Select text to print.
1. Click **File** ..................... `Alt`+`F`
2. Click **Print** .......................... `P`
3. Click **Selection** ........... `Alt`+`S`
4. Click **OK** .......................... `Enter`

# Exercise Directions

1. Start Word, if necessary.
2. Open 💿 **54ROSES**.
   - ✓ *This is a version of the report used in previous exercises.*
3. Save the file as **ROSES3**.
4. Edit the header to change the text **Student's Name** to your own name, and to display the actual date instead of the text Today's Date.
5. Change to Reading Layout view.
6. Display Thumbnails.
7. Go to page 4.
8. Display actual pages instead of screens.
9. Go to page 1.
10. Print the current page.
11. Switch back to displaying screens.
12. Close Reading Layout view.
13. Display the Document Map.
14. Using the Document Map, go to the heading **The Rose in Use** and change the formatting to leave 12 points of space after.
15. Repeat step 14 for each heading 2 in the document.

16. Change to Print Preview to display two pages at the same time.
17. Zoom in on the bottom of page 2.
18. Toggle the magnifier off and then select the second paragraph under the heading Selecting Roses.
19. Display all pages of the document on-screen at the same time.
20. Drag the selection to the end of the document.
21. Zoom in on the bottom of page 2 again.
22. Toggle the magnifier off, then insert a hard page break to move the heading **Types of Roses** to the top of page 3.
23. Zoom out to display all pages again.
24. Close Print Preview.
25. Go to the heading **Judging Rose Quality**.
26. Select the heading and all text from the heading to the end of the page and print the selection.
27. Print pages 2 and 4.
28. Close the Document Map, if necessary.
29. Close the document, saving all changes.

# On Your Own

1. Continue working on your research report using the skills you learned in this exercise to edit and improve the document.
2. Open the document ⌨ **OWD53** that you used in the On Your Own section of Exercise 53.
3. Save the document as **OWD54**.
4. Change to Reading Layout view and proofread the document.
5. Use the Document Map or Thumbnails to navigate through the document.
6. Make edits and corrections as you work.
7. When you have completed proofreading the document, close Reading Layout view.
8. Preview multiple pages of the document at one time.

9. If necessary, move or copy text from one page in the document to another to improve the flow of the report. (You can always use Undo to revert back, if necessary.)
10. Preview all pages at once.
11. If necessary, adjust page and section breaks.
12. Print one page of the document and ask a classmate to read it and offer comments and suggestions.
13. If there is a particular part of the document that you feel needs work, select it, print it, and ask another classmate to read it and offer comments and suggestions.
14. Use the feedback you get from your classmates to make changes and corrections to improve the report.
15. Close the document, saving all changes, and exit Word.

# Exercise 55

## On the Job

When you need to organize and manage long documents, you can create a master document with subdocuments. For example, use a master document to manage a book that has multiple chapters, or a report that has many sections.

The Marketing Director at Blue Sky Dairy has asked you to write a lengthy report about dairy cows. You are just getting started on the project and have decided that using a master document will help you stay organized. In this exercise, you will create a master document from an existing outline, insert an additional subdocument into the master document, and edit a subdocument. Finally, you will print the master document.

## Terms

**Master document** A document that contains a set of related documents.

**Subdocument** A document contained in a master document.

## Notes

### Create a Master Document

■ Use a **master document** to organize and manage a long document by dividing it into **subdocuments**.

■ For example, you can use subdocuments to renumber pages, footnotes, or endnotes, in a manuscript that contains multiple chapters.

■ To create a master document, simply designate headings in an outline as subdocuments.

✓ *For information about working with outlines, see Exercise 50.*

■ Word automatically saves each designated heading, its subheadings, and its body text as a separate document.

■ Word inserts sections breaks between subdocuments in a master document and displays a gray border around each subdocument.

■ You can view and edit the subdocuments in the master document, or you can open a subdocument separately.

■ Once you create subdocuments, the master document outline is displayed in Master Document view.

■ In Master Document view, Word displays additional buttons on the Outlining toolbar.

■ A subdocument icon 🖳 is displayed to the left of each subdocument in Master Document view.

   • Click the subdocument icon to select the entire subdocument.

   • Double-click the subdocument icon to quickly open the subdocument. The subdocument opens in a separate window.

■ You can create a master document from a new document, or convert an existing document into a master document.

- You can also insert an existing document into an existing master document as a subdocument.

- You can expand, collapse, and rearrange a master document or the contents of a subdocument using Outline view, just as you would a regular Word outline.

## Work with Subdocuments

- You can edit and format subdocuments the same way you do any Word document.

- In Master Document view, you can expand and collapse subdocuments using buttons on the Outlining toolbar.

- Collapsed subdocuments are displayed as hyperlinks in the master document outline. When you Ctrl+Click the hyperlink, the subdocument opens.

- When subdocuments are collapsed, a lock icon is displayed under the subdocument icon.

- Word automatically names subdocument files based on the first text in the subdocument heading. You can rename subdocument files.

- You can rearrange subdocuments by rearranging the master document outline.

- You can remove a subdocument from a master document. Removing the subdocument does not delete the contents of the file.

- When you print an expanded master document, all subdocuments are printed as well.

*Expanded Master Document*

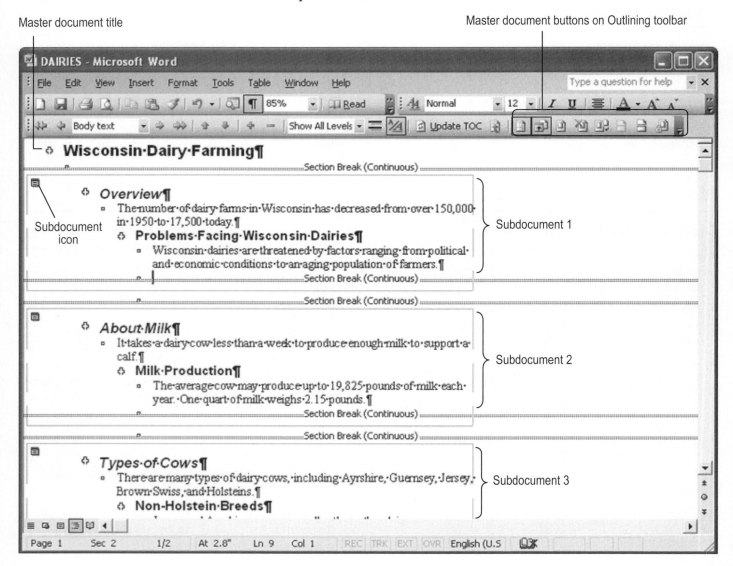

Subdocument icon

*Collapsed Master document*

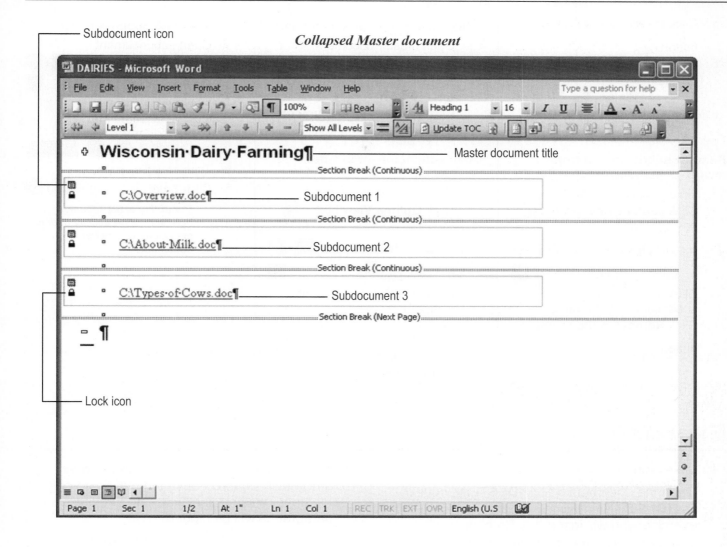

Lock icon

# Procedures

## Create a Master Document

**Use a new document:**

1. Create a new Word document.
2. Click **Outline View** button 📄.
   OR
   a. Click **View**..............Alt+V
   b. Click **Outline** ..................O
3. Type document title in heading 1 style.
4. Type all subdocument titles in heading 2 style.
5. Type any additional text or headings.
6. Select all subdocuments.
7. Click **Create Subdocument** button 📄.

## Use an existing document:

1. Open existing document.
2. Click **Outline View** button 📄.
   OR
   a. Click **View** ..............Alt+V
   b. Click **Outline** ..................O
3. Apply same heading level to all subdocument titles.
4. Select each subdocument.
5. Click **Create Subdocument** button 📄.

## Work with Subdocuments

**Insert subdocument in master document:**

1. Open master document.
2. Click **Outline View** button 📄.
   OR
   a. Click **View**..............Alt+V
   b. Click **Outline**..................O
3. Position insertion point on blank line in master document.
   ✓ *Be sure that the insertion point is not within the box defining an existing subdocument. If it is, you will end up creating a subdocument of the existing subdocument.*

4. Click **Insert Subdocument** button .

5. Select file to insert from **Look in** drop-down list ........ `Alt`+`|`, `↑`, `↓` `Enter`

6. Click **Open** button

   [ Open ] ........... `Alt`+`O`

**Remove subdocument from master document:**

1. Open master document.

2. Click **Outline View** button 🔲.
   OR
   a. Click **View** ............. `Alt`+`V`
   b. Click **Outline** ................. `O`

3. Click anywhere in subdocument to be removed.

4. Click **Remove Subdocument** button 🔲.

**Collapse/expand subdocuments:**

1. Open master document.

2. Click **Collapse Subdocuments** button 🔲.
   OR
   Click **Expand Subdocuments** button 🔲.

**Open subdocument in a new window:**

1. Open master document.

2. Click **Outline View** button 🔲.
   OR
   a. Click **View** ............. `Alt`+`V`
   b. Click **Outline** ................. `O`

3. Double-click subdocument icon.
   OR
   a. Collapse master document.
   b. **Ctrl+click** subdocument hyperlink.

**Rename a subdocument file:**

1. Open subdocument.

2. Click **File** ..................... `Alt`+`F`

3. Click **Save As** ..................... `A`

4. If necessary, select storage location from **Save in** drop-down list........ `Alt`+`|`, `↑`, `↓` `Enter`

5. Type new file name.

6. Click **Save** ................. `Alt`+`S`

   ✓ *Renaming a subdocument does not automatically update the link to the master document.*

# Exercise Directions

1. Start Word, if necessary.

2. Open the document 💿 **55HOLSTEIN**, save it as **HOLSTEIN** and close it. Later in this exercise, you will insert this file as a subdocument in a master document.

3. Open 💿 **55DAIRIES** and save it as **DAIRIES**.

4. Change to Outline view.

5. Make sure that paragraph marks and other hidden characters are displayed.

6. Format the first line in the document— **Wisconsin Dairy Farming**—as Heading 1. This will be the Master Document title.

   ✓ *You may format the headings using the Style drop-down list on the Formatting toolbar or by promoting them using the Outline toolbar buttons.*

7. Apply Heading 2 to the **Overview**, **About Milk**, and **Types of Cows** headings. These will be the subdocuments.

8. Apply Heading 3 to the following:

   **Problems Facing Wisconsin Dairies**
   **Milk Production**
   **Non Holstein Breeds**
   ✓ *All remaining text paragraphs should be at the body text level.*

9. Select Show Level 3 from the Show Level drop-down list to collapse the outline so only the headings are displayed (the body text paragraphs will be hidden).

10. Select all of the heading 2 and 3 levels (all but the first heading in the document).

11. Click the Create Subdocument button on the Outlining toolbar. Word creates the three subdocuments in the master document and displays them in Master Document view.

12. Select Show All Levels from the Show Levels drop-down list to display the entire contents of the Master document.

13. Click the Collapse Subdocuments button to collapse the subdocuments. (Click OK if Word prompts you to save the master document.)

14. Open the second subdocument, **About Milk**, by resting the mouse pointer on the hyperlink and pressing Ctrl+Click.

    ✓ *The document opens in Print Layout view.*

15. Move the insertion point to the end of the last paragraph before the section break (display paragraph marks if necessary), insert a new paragraph formatted as Heading 3, and type the following: **Dairy Products**.

16. Following the new heading, insert a paragraph formatted as body text in the Normal style as follows:

    **It takes 10 pounds of milk to make 1 pound of cheese. It takes 12 pounds of milk to make 1 gallon of ice cream.**

17. Save the file and close it. The master document should still be open on-screen.

18. Click the Expand Subdocuments button on the Outlining toolbar to expand the subdocuments in the master document.

19. Move the insertion point to the blank line at the end of the master document, after the last section break, and insert the file **HOLSTEIN** as a subdocument.

20. Collapse the subdocuments, saving changes as prompted.

21. Expand the subdocuments.

22. Check the spelling and grammar in the master document.

23. Print the master document.

24. Close the master document, saving all changes.

# On Your Own

1. Working in a group or team, plan a research project. Agree on a topic and then assign each group member a subtopic. Establish a timeline for completing each stage of the project. For example, set a deadline for research, set a deadline for a rough draft, and so on.

2. When each team member has completed a rough draft of his or her subtopic, get together and create a master document.

3. Start Word and create a new document.

4. Save the document as **OWD55**.

5. Change to Outline view and create an outline for the project, entering the headings for each subtopic.

6. Insert the subdocuments provided by each group member.

7. Save the master document.

8. Collapse the subdocuments.

9. Working together, open each subdocument in turn and review the content. Make suggestions and revisions as necessary.

10. Save the changes.

11. Display the entire contents of the master document.

12. Print the master document.

13. Close the document and exit Word.

14. Present your project to your classmates.

# Exercise 56

## Skills Covered:
◆ **Insert a Cross-reference** ◆ **Insert a Caption**
◆ **Create an Index** ◆ **Modify an Index**

## On the Job

Sometimes it may be difficult for readers to locate the specific information they need in long or complex documents. To quickly refer a reader from one location to another related location, you can create a cross-reference. To help readers identify illustrations such as tables or figures, you can insert captions. To help readers find the page containing specific information, you can create an index in which topics and subtopics are listed; Word automatically fills in the correct page number.

You have almost completed the document on roses for the Liberty Blooms flower shop. In this exercise, you will create cross-references in the report and insert captions. You will also generate an index to help readers locate specific topics in the document quickly and easily.

## Terms

**Cross-reference** Text that refers a reader to a different location in a document.

**Cross-reference text** The information entered in a document to introduce a cross-reference.

**Cross-reference type** The type of object which is being referred to, such as a bookmark or heading.

**Field code** The instructions inserted in a field that tell Word what results to display.

**Field results** The information displayed in a field.

**Caption** A text label that identifies an illustration such as a figure, table, or picture.

**Index** An alphabetical list of topics and/or subtopics in a document along with the page numbers where they appear.

**Tab leaders** Characters inserted to the left of text aligned with a tab stop, such as page numbers in an index.

## Notes

### Insert a Cross-reference

- A **cross-reference** is text that directs a reader to another location in the same document for more information. For example, "*For more information, see page 22*" is a cross-reference.

  ✓ *To reference a location in a different document, make both documents subdocuments of a master document. For information on creating master documents and subdocuments, see Exercise 55.*

- You can create cross-references to existing headings, footnotes, bookmarks, captions, numbered paragraphs, tables, and figures.

- When you create a cross-reference with Word, you enter the **cross-reference text**, and then select the **cross-reference type**.

- After you select the reference type, you select whether you want Word to reference the item by page number, text, or paragraph. This is the information Word will automatically insert in the document.

- Word enters the reference as a field, so it can be updated if necessary. This means that if you reference a heading and then move the heading to another location in the document, you can update the cross-reference to reflect the change.

- By default Word inserts a cross-reference as a hyperlink. Ctrl+click the cross-reference to jump to the specified destination.

- You can change the setting if you do not want the cross-reference inserted as a hyperlink.

  ✓ *See Exercise 30 for more information on hyperlinks.*

- If the cross-reference **field code** is displayed in your document instead of the **field results**, you must deselect the Field Codes check box on the View tab of the Tools, Options dialog box.

## Insert a Caption

- Insert a **caption** to label an item.

- Each caption includes a text label and a number field.

- By default, Word comes with labels for tables, figures, and equations.

- You can create new labels for other items or to use different label text. For example, you might want to label a figure as *Illustration*.

- By default, Word uses Arabic numbers and positions the captions below the item. You can customize the number format, and select to position the caption above the item.

- Word automatically updates the numbers for each caption entered; however, if you delete or move a caption, you must manually update the remaining captions.

- You can insert a caption manually or set Word to automatically insert captions.

*The Caption dialog box*

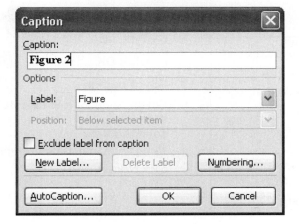

## Create an Index

- An **index** lists topics and subtopics contained in a document, along with the page numbers where they appear.

- Word automatically generates an alphabetical index based on index entries you mark in the document text.

- Word comes with a selection of index formats.

- Other index layout options include the number of columns in the index and whether subtopics should be run in on the same line or if each subtopic should be indented. The default setting is for two columns and indented subtopics.

- You can also choose to right-align page numbers and to precede page numbers with **tab leaders**.

*Select options for creating an index*

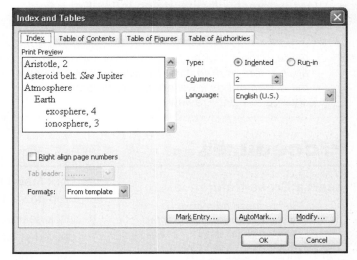

- You can index a single character, a word, a phrase, or a topic that spans multiple pages.

- You can mark all occurrences of the same text, or mark a single occurrence. Keep in mind that Word only marks all occurrences of *exactly* the same text. That means that the formatting, capitalization, tense, etc. must be exactly the same.

- Index entries can cross-reference a different index entry. For example, *Cats, see Pets* is a cross-referenced index entry.

- If you index many subtopics, you can use a multi-level index. For example, *Pets* may be the main index topic, with *Cats, Dogs,* and *Goldfish* as subtopics.

- To mark entries for an index, you select an item you want marked for inclusion in the index, then open the Mark Index Entry dialog box and type the entry text as you want it displayed in the index.

- You can type the entry text using any formatting; it does not have to match the selected text in the document. However, if you are marking all items, only the items that appear exactly as the *selected text* will be marked. It doesn't matter what you type in the Main entry text box.

- If the selected item is exactly as you want it to appear in the index, you do not have to retype the entry text.

- If the entry is for a subtopic, you type the main entry topic under which the subtopic should be listed, then the subentry text as you want it displayed.

- Word automatically inserts an Index Entry field in the document following the selected item.

    ✓ *If hidden text is displayed, you see the Index Entry fields in the document. This makes the document appear longer than it will be when printed. To see the document as it will print, hide hidden text or change to Print Preview.*

*Keep the Mark Index Entry dialog box open while marking multiple entries*

## Modify an Index

- You can edit existing index entries by editing the text in the Index Entry field.

- If you add, delete, or move indexed items in the document, you must update the index so that Word changes the page numbers.

# Procedures

### Insert a Cross-Reference

✓ *Before inserting a cross-reference, make sure that the item which is being referenced—such as the heading, bookmark, or footnote—already exists.*

1. Position insertion point where you want cross-reference to appear.

2. Type cross-reference text, followed by a space and any necessary punctuation.

    ✓ *For example, type the text: For more information see.*

3. Click **Insert** ................. Alt + I

4. Click **Reference** ................. N

5. Click **Cross-reference** ........ R

6. Click **Reference type:** drop-down arrow ......... Alt + T

7. Click desired reference type ................... ↑, ↓, Enter

8. Click **Insert reference to:** drop-down arrow .......... Alt + R

9. Click desired reference option ................ ↑, ↓, Enter

10. Select specific item in **For which** list ....... Alt + W, ↑, ↓

    ✓ *If you do not want cross-reference inserted as a hyperlink, deselect the Insert as hyperlink check box.*

11. Click **Insert** button

    Insert ................ Alt + I

12. Click **Close** button Close .

### Update a Cross-reference

1. Select cross reference to update.

2. Press **F9** ............................ F9

    OR

    a. Right-click cross-reference to update.

    b. Click **Update Field** ......... U

### Insert a Caption Manually

1. Select item to caption

2. Click **Insert** ................. Alt + I

3. Select **Reference** ............... N

4. Click **Caption** .................... C

5. Click **Label** drop-down arrow ......................... Alt + L

6. Select desired label.

    OR

    a. Click **New Label** .... Alt + N

    b. Type label name.

    c. Click **OK** .................... Enter

7. Click **Position** .................... P

8. Select either **Below selected item** (default) or **Above selected item**.

9. To customize number format, click **Numbering** ................ U

10. Click **Format** drop-down
    arrow..............................`F`
11. Click format to use.
12. Click **OK**..........................`Enter`
13. Click **OK**..........................`Enter`

### Insert a Caption Automatically

1. Click **Insert** ............`Alt`+`I`
2. Select **Reference** ................`N`
3. Click **Caption**......................`C`
4. Click **AutoCaption** ..............`A`
5. In **Add caption when inserting** list, click check box(es) for item(s) you want to label ............... `↑`, `↓`, `Space`
6. Click **Use label** ....................`L`
7. Click desired label.
   OR
   a. Click **New Label** .....`Alt`+`N`
   b. Type label name.
   c. Click **OK**.
8. Click **Position**......................`P`
9. Click desired position.
10. To customize number format, click **Numbering**..................`U`
11. Click **Format** drop-down
    arrow....................................`F`
12. Click format to use.
13. Click **OK**..........................`Enter`
14. Click **OK**..........................`Enter`

### Create an Index

#### Mark index entries:

1. Click **Insert** ..................`Alt`+`I`
2. Click **Reference**..................`N`
3. Click **Index and Tables** .......`D`
4. Click **Index** tab............`Alt`+`X`
5. Click **Mark Entry** button
   `Mark Entry...` ............`Alt`+`K`
6. In document, select text to mark.
   ✓ *Mark Entry dialog box remains open while you select text to mark. If necessary, move Mark Entry dialog box out of the way.*

7. Click **Main entry** text box.
8. Type main index entry text.
9. Click **Subentry**
   text box......................`Alt`+`S`
10. Type subentry text if necessary.
11. Click **Mark** button
    `Mark` ..............`Alt`+`M`
    to mark selected occurrence only.
    OR
    Click **Mark All** button
    `Mark All` ..............`Alt`+`A`
    to mark all occurrences of selected text in document.
12. Repeat steps 6-11 until all entries are marked.
13. Click **Close**.

#### Mark a cross-references entry:

1. Click **Insert**..................`Alt`+`I`
2. Click **Reference** ..................`N`
3. Click **Index and Tables**.......`D`
4. Click **Index** tab ............`Alt`+`X`
5. Click **Mark Entry** button
   `Mark Entry...` ..........`Alt`+`K`
6. In document, select text to mark.
   ✓ *Mark Entry dialog box remains open while you select text to mark. If necessary, move Mark Entry dialog box out of the way.*

7. Click **Main entry**
   text box......................`Alt`+`E`
8. Type main index entry text.
9. Click **Cross-reference**
   option button................`Alt`+`C`
10. Type desired main entry text to refer to.
11. Click **Mark** button
    `Mark` ..............`Alt`+`M`
12. Repeat steps 6–11 until all entries are marked.
13. Click **Close**.

#### Generate index:

1. Position insertion point in document where you want index displayed.
2. Click **Insert** ................`Alt`+`I`
3. Click **Reference**..................`N`
4. Click **Index and Tables** ......`D`
5. Click **Index** tab............`Alt`+`X`
6. Click **Formats**
   drop-down arrow .........`Alt`+`T`
7. Click desired
   format..................`↑`, `↓`, `Enter`
8. Select any other desired options.
9. Click **OK**..........................`Enter`

#### Update index:

1. Click in index.
2. Press **F9**..............................`F9`
   OR
   a. Right-click index.
   b. Click **Update Field**.........`U`

# Exercise Directions

1. Start Word, if necessary.
2. Open the document ⚙**56ROSES**.
3. Save the document as **ROSES4**.
4. Replace the text **Student's Name** in the header with your own name.
5. Replace the text **Today's Date** in the header with the current date.

## Insert Captions

1. Select the first table in the document.
2. Insert a caption to label the table. Use the label text **Table**, the default numbering scheme, and position the caption above the table.
3. Insert a page break before the caption.
4. Select the second table in the document.
5. Insert a caption to label the table, using the same options that you used to create the first caption.
6. Insert a page break before the caption.

## Insert Cross References

1. Position the insertion point at the end of the first paragraph under the heading **History**.

   ✓ *You may want to use the Document Map to navigate through the document.*

2. Type the following cross-reference text: (**For information on types of roses, refer to the section .**) Be sure to leave a space between the last word and the period.
3. Position the insertion point to the left of the period you just typed, and insert a hyperlinked cross-reference to the heading **Types of Roses**.
4. Scroll down to the heading **Selecting Roses** on page 2 (or use the cross-reference hyperlink you inserted in step 3).
5. At the end of the paragraph under the heading Types of Roses, type the following cross-reference text: **For a description of common types of roses, refer to**
6. Position the insertion point to the right of the space after the word to, and insert a hyperlinked cross-reference to the entire caption for Table 1.

7. Position the insertion point after the cross-reference field, type a space followed by the text **on page .**
8. Position the insertion point to the left of the period and then insert a hyperlinked cross-reference to the page number on which Table 1 is located.
9. Ctrl+click the page number to go to the table.
10. Move the insertion point to the end of the sentence under the heading **Grafted Roses** and type the following cross-reference text **For information about the grading system, refer to**
11. Position the insertion point to the right of the space after the word to, and insert a hyperlinked cross-reference to the entire caption for Table 2.
12. Position the insertion point after the cross-reference field, type a space followed by the text **on page .**
13. Position the insertion point to the left of the period and then insert a hyperlinked cross-reference to the page number on which Table 2 is located.
14. Check the spelling and grammar in the document.
15. Display the document in Print Preview. Page 3 should look similar to Illustration A.

    ✓ *If you have the Field shading option set to Always on the View page of the Tools, Options dialog box, the table number and cross-reference text will be shaded with gray as shown.*

## Create an Index

1. Close Print Preview and then press Ctrl+Home to move the insertion point to the beginning of the document.
2. Mark entries for an index as follows:

   ✓ *You might want to use the Find command to locate the specified text.*

   a. Select the text **roses** in the first sentence of the introduction, open the Mark Index Entry dialog box and mark all entries of the text **roses,** changing the entry to start with a capital R.
   b. Select the text **symbol**, and mark all entries, again, changing the entry to start with a capital S.

c. Mark all entries of the text **cultivation, types**, **varieties**, and **hybrids** (start all entries with a capital letter).

d. Select the text **ornamental decorations** in the first sentence under the heading **The Rose in Use**. Edit the text in the Main entry box to Usage, and then type ornamental decoration in the Subentry box. Mark the entry.

e. Select the text **confetti**, and again, edit the Main entry text to Usage, and then type the text confetti in the Subentry box. Mark the entry.

f. Continue entering the following as subentries for the Main entry Usage: **Egyptian mummies**, **perfume**, **medicine**, and **currency**.

g. Select the text **white rose** under the heading **The Rose as Symbol**. Edit the main entry text to capitalize the initial letter in each word Type **York** as the Subentry text. Select the Cross-reference option button, and type **Symbol** after the word See in the Cross-reference box, then mark the entry.

h. Select the text **red rose**. Edit the main entry text to capitalize the phrase. Type **Lancaster** as the Subentry text. Select the cross reference option button and type **Symbol** after the word See in the Cross-reference box, then mark the entry.

i. Mark the phrase **War of the Roses**.

j. Mark the phrase **American Nursery Standards**.

k. Mark all occurrences of the following words: **disease**, **quality**, and **insects**, remembering to capitalize the main entry text.

l. Mark the first occurrence of the word **pests** with a cross-reference to Insects.

m. Mark the

n. When you have finished marking the necessary entries, close the Mark Index Entry dialog box.

3. Press Ctrl+End to move the insertion point to the end of the document.

4. Insert a page break.

5. At the top of the new page, type **Index**, and format it with the Heading 1 style.

6. Press Enter to move the insertion point to a blank line.

7. Generate the index as follows:

a. Select the Classic style.

b. Right align page numbers.

c. Use a dotted tab leader.

d. Use two columns.

e. Indent the subtopics.

8. When the index is inserted in the document, save the changes.

9. Preview the document.

10. Close Print Preview and mark all occurrences of the text **rose water** as a main index entry (capitalize the text).

11. Update the index to reflect the change.

12. Preview the index page. It should look similar to Illustration B.

13. Close the document, saving all changes.

# On Your Own

1. Start Word and open ⌨**OWD54**, the research report you have been working on.

2. Save the document as **OWD56**.

3. If possible, create tables to illustrate the text and then insert captions for the tables.

4. Insert cross-references in the document as necessary. Try using different cross-reference types. For example, select a heading for one cross-reference and a footnote or table for another.

5. Create an index for the document. Mark main entries and subentries.

6. Insert the index on a new page at the end of the document. Try different formatting options, such as the fancy format with dashed tab leaders.

7. Preview the document and insert page breaks as necessary.

8. Update the index and the cross-references if necessary.

9. Print the document. Ask a classmate to review the document and offer comments or suggestions.

10. Incorporate the comments and suggestions into the document.

11. Close the document, saving all changes, and exit Word.

Student's Name                                              Today's Date

**Table 1**

| | |
|---|---|
| **Species Roses** | These are uncultivated varieties. They are Usually hardy and disease resistant. They come in a wide variety of types and colors. |
| **Old European Garden Roses** | These are the oldest group of cultivated roses. They are hybrid groups common in European gardens prior to the 18th century. They usually have a strong fragrance and can withstand cold winters, but are susceptible to heat, drought, and disease. |
| **Hardy     Repeat-Blooming     Old Roses** | These plants are similar to the Old European Garden Roses but they will bloom more than once each season. |
| **Modern Roses** | These include the varieties developed after the 18th century. |
| **Miniature Roses** | Small plants that are extremely useful for small gardens and container planting. |
| **Shrub Roses** | Plants that are noted for their rounded shape, winter hardiness and disease resistance. Shrub roses tend to be free-flowering, which means they provide blooms all season long, and are suitable for using as hedges and in border gardens. |

## *Judging Rose Quality*

The quality of rose plants varies depending on the vendor. Ask for references before purchasing to make sure that other customers have been satisfied with the plants. You can order plants by mail or on-line, but unless you are completely certain that you are dealing with a reputable vendor, you may prefer purchasing plants locally, so you can see them before you buy, and so that you can return them if necessary.

### Grafted Roses

Grafted roses are rated based on an American Nursery Standards grading system. For information about the grading system, refer to Table 2 on page 4.

*Illustration B*

Student's Name                                              Today's Date

# Index

**A**

American Nursery Standards.............................................. 4

**C**

Cultivation ........................................................................ 1

**D**

Disease ...................................................................... 2, 4, 5

**H**

Hybrids.............................................................................. 1

**I**

Insects............................................................................... 5

**P**

Pests...............................................................See Insects

**Q**

Quality...................................................................... 4, 5

**R**

Red Rose
    Lancaster ...................................................... *See* Symbol

Rose Water ..................................................................... 2
Roses ................................................................. 1, 2, 3, 4, 5

**S**

Symbol ......................................................................... 1, 2

**T**

Types ......................................................................... 1, 3, 4

**U**

Usage
    confetti ...................................................................... 1
    currency .................................................................... 2
    Egyption mummies .................................................. 2
    medicine................................................................... 2
    ornamental decoration............................................. 1
    perfume .................................................................... 2

**V**

Varieties ...................................................................... 1, 4

**W**

War of the Roses .............................................................. 2
White Rose
    York .............................................................*See* Symbol

Page 5

# Exercise 57

◆ **Create a Table of Contents** ◆ **Create a Table of Figures**
◆ **Create a Table of Authorities**
◆ **Update a Table of Contents, Table of Figures, or Table of Authorities**

## On the Job

A table of contents helps readers locate information they need in a long document by listing headings and the page numbers where each heading starts. Likewise, a table of figures lists the page numbers where tables are located. A table of authorities is used specifically in a legal document to list references such as cases, statutes, and rules. Use Word to automatically generate a table of contents, table of figures, or table of authorities. If the page numbers change, you can update the table.

You have just about completed the Roses document for Liberty Blooms. The final touch is to add a table of contents and table of figures to help readers locate the information they need. In this exercise, you will generate the table of figures. You will check that all topics you want included in the table of contents are formatted with heading styles. Then, you will generate the table of contents. Finally, you will make some editing changes to the report, and update the tables to reflect the changes.

## Terms

**Table of contents** A list of topics and subtopics in a document, usually accompanied by the page numbers where the topics begin and placed before the main body of the document.

**Table of figures** A list of figures in a document, usually accompanied by the page numbers where the figures are located.

**Table of authorities** A list of citations in a legal document, usually accompanied by the page numbers where the references occur.

**Citation** A reference to previous court decisions or authoritative writings.

**Passim** A word used in citations of cases, articles, or books in a legal document to indicate that the reference is found in many places within the work.

## Notes

### Create a Table of Contents

■ Word generates a **table of contents** based on paragraphs formatted with the built-in heading styles.

■ You can create a table of contents using as many levels as you want, depending on how many levels of headings are used in the document.

■ You do not have to include all heading levels in the table of contents. For example, you may have paragraphs formatted with up to four heading levels, but select to include only two heading levels in the table of contents.

■ Paragraphs formatted with the same level of heading style will be listed at the same level in the table of contents.

- Word comes with a selection of table of contents formats which you can preview in the Index and Tables dialog box.

- You can also select whether to include page numbers and whether to right-align them.

- If you right-align page numbers, you can select a tab leader.

- By default, Word formats the headings in a table of contents as hyperlinks. Ctrl+click the heading in the table to jump to the destination.

- If you don't want to use hyperlinks in your table of contents, deselect the Use hyperlinks instead of page numbers check box on the Table of Contents tab of the Index and Tables dialog box.

*Table of Figures tab of the Index and Tables dialog box*

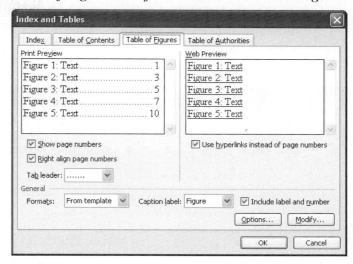

*Table of Contents tab of the Index and Tables dialog box*

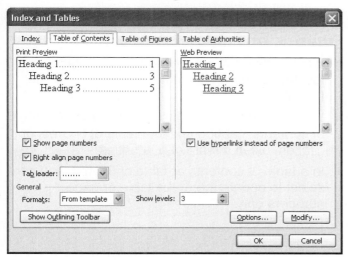

## Create a Table of Figures

- A **table of figures** includes a list of the captions used to identify items in a document.

- To create the table, specify the captions you want to include.

- Word sorts the captions by number and displays them in the table of figures.
  - ✓ *For information on inserting captions, refer to Exercise 56.*

## Create a Table of Authorities

- Create a **table of authorities** to list **citations** in a legal document, along with the page numbers where the references are located.

- If a citation appears on five or more pages, you may select to substitute the word **passim** for the page numbers.

- Word comes with built-in categories of common citations, such as cases, statutes, regulations, and rules. You can create new categories if you want.

- Use the Mark Citation dialog box to mark each citation in the document with a table of authorities field code.
  - ✓ *This process is similar to marking items for an index. For information on creating an index, refer to Exercise 56.*

- You can mark each occurrence manually, or automatically mark all occurrences.

- You can also specify a short version of a citation to mark automatically along with the long version.
  - ✓ *As with index entries, you see the field codes in the document if you have hidden text displayed. To see the document as it will print, hide hidden text or change to Print Layout view.*

- Word can automatically search through a document to find citations, or you can scroll through manually. To find citations, Word searches for the text **v**.

*Mark Citation dialog box*

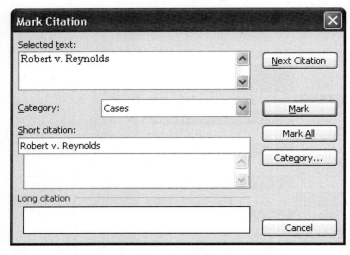

- When all items are marked, use the Table of Authorities tab of the Index and Tables dialog box to select options and generate the table.
- Word sorts the citations by category.

*Table of Authorities tab of the Index and Tables dialog box*

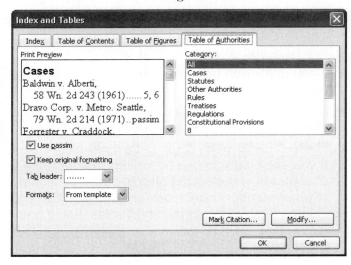

## Update a Table of Contents, Table of Figures, or Table of Authorities

- If the page numbers where items in a table are located change, you can automatically update the table.
- Likewise, you can update heading text in a table of contents, caption text in a table of figures, or citation text in a table of authorities.
- In a table of contents or table of figures, you can select to update the entire table or page numbers only.

# Procedures

### Create a Table of Contents

1. Apply heading styles to all paragraphs you want in table of contents.
2. Position insertion point where you want table of contents to appear.
3. Click **Insert** ................. `Alt`+`I`
4. Click **Reference** ................. `N`
5. Click **Index and Tables** ...... `D`
6. Click **Table of Contents** tab .............. `Alt`+`C`
7. Click **Formats**: list box ........................ `Alt`+`T`
8. Select desired format ................ `↑`, `↓`, `Enter`

9. Click **Show levels** text box ........................ `Alt`+`L`
10. Enter number of heading levels to include.
11. Select or deselect **Show page numbers** ........... `Alt`+`S`
12. Select or deselect **Right align page numbers** ... `Alt`+`R`
    - ✓ *If you select to right-align page numbers, select a tab leader option from **Tab leader** drop-down list.*
13. Select or deselect **Use hyperlinks instead of page numbers** .................... `Alt`+`H`
14. Click **OK** ......................... `Enter`

### Create a Table of Figures

1. Insert captions as desired.
2. Position insertion point where you want table to appear.
3. Click **Insert**................. `Alt`+`I`
4. Click **Reference** ................. `N`
5. Click **Index and Tables**....... `D`
6. Click **Table of Figures** tab ................. `Alt`+`C`
7. Click **Formats**: list box ........................ `Alt`+`T`
8. Select desired format ................ `↑`, `↓`, `Enter`
9. Click **Caption label** text box....................... `Alt`+`L`
10. Select label to include.

11. Select or deselect **Include label and number** ....... `Alt`+`N`

12. Select or deselect **Show page numbers** ..................... `Alt`+`S`

13. Select or deselect **Right align page numbers** ... `Alt`+`R`

   ✓ *If you select to right-align page numbers, select a tab leader option from Tab leader drop-down list.*

14. Select or deselect **Use hyperlinks instead of page numbers** ..................... `Alt`+`H`

15. Click **OK** ............................ `Enter`

## Create a Table of Authorities

### Mark entries:

1. Click **Insert** ................. `Alt`+`I`

2. Click **Refere**n**ce** ..................... `N`

3. Click **Index and Tables** ....... `D`

4. Click **Table of Authorities** tab ................................ `Alt`+`A`

5. Click **Mark Citation** button

   `Mark Citation...` ............ `Alt`+`K`

6. In document, select text to mark.

   ✓ *Mark Citation dialog box remains open while you select text to mark. If necessary, move dialog box out of the way.*

7. Click **Category** drop-down arrow .......................... `Alt`+`C`

8. Selected desired category ............. `↑`, `↓`, `Enter`

9. Click **Short citation** box ................................ `Alt`+`S`

10. Type short version of citation, if necessary.

11. If necessary, edit or format text in **Selected text** box. .............. `Alt`+`T`, edit text

12. Click **Mark** button

   `Mark` ................ `Alt`+`M`

   to mark selected occurrence only.

OR

Click **Mark All** button

   `Mark All` ............. `Alt`+`A`

to mark all occurrences of selected text in document.

13. Repeat steps 6-12 until all entries are marked.

   ✓ *To search for the next citation in the document, click the **Next Citation** button* `Next Citation`.

14. Click **Close** button

   `Close` ..................... `Enter`

### Generate table:

1. Position insertion point in document where you want table displayed.

2. Click **Insert** ................. `Alt`+`I`

3. Click **Refere**n**ce** ................. `N`

4. Click **Index and Tables** ....... `D`

5. Click **Table of Authorities** tab .............................. `Alt`+`A`

6. Click **Category** list ....... `Alt`+`G`

7. Click category to include .......................... `↑`, `↓`

   ✓ *Click All to include all citations.*

8. Click **Formats** drop-down arrow ......... `Alt`+`T`

9. Click desired format ............... `↑`, `↓`, `Enter`

10. Select or deselect **Use passim** ................ `Alt`+`P`

11. Select or deselect **Keep original formatting** ..... `Alt`+`R`

12. Click **Tab leader** drop-down arrow .......................... `Alt`+`B`

13. Click desired tab leader ............... `↑`, `↓`, `Enter`

14. Click **OK** .......................... `Enter`

## Update a Table

1. Position insertion point anywhere in table.

2. Press **F9**.

   OR

   a. Right-click anywhere in table.

   b. Click **Update Field** ......... `U`

3. For a table of contents or table of figures, select one of the following:

   • **Update page numbers only** ....... `Alt`+`P`

   OR

   • **Update entire table** ............ `Alt`+`E`

4. Click **OK** ............................ `Enter`

# Exercise Directions

1. Start Word, if necessary.
2. Open the document ⊙ **57ROSES**, a version of the report you have used in earlier exercises.
3. Save it as **ROSES5**.
4. Replace the text **Student's Name** in the header with your own name.
5. Replace the text **Today's Date** in the header with the current date.

## Generate a Table of Figures

1. Display page 5 and position the insertion point at the end of the last paragraph of text in the document.
2. Press Enter to insert a blank line after the document text but before the page break.
   - ✓ *Display paragraph marks, if necessary, so you can see the page break. However, be aware that displayed hidden text affects the position of text in the document.*
3. Using the Heading 1 style, type **Table of Figures**.
4. Press Enter to move the insertion point to a new blank line.
5. Generate a table of figures using the following options:
   a. Distinctive format.
   b. Caption label: Table.
   c. Show label and number.
   d. Show page numbers.
   e. Right align page numbers.
   f. Use a dot tab leader.
   g. Do not use hyperlinks.
6. Save the changes.
   - ✓ *If you do not have hidden text (including index entries) displayed, the table appears at the top of page 5.*
7. Press Ctrl+Home to move the insertion point to the beginning of the document.
8. Scroll through the document to verify that all headings are formatted with heading styles.
9. Press Ctrl+Home again to move the insertion point to the beginning of the document.
10. Insert two blank lines after the title.
11. Clear all formatting from the new blank lines.
12. On the first blank line type **Table of Contents** in 20-point Arial, centered
13. Position the insertion point on the second blank line.
14. Create a table of contents using the following options:
    - Distinctive format.
    - 3 heading levels.
    - Right-aligned page numbers.
    - Dot tab leader.
    - Use page numbers, not hyperlinks.
15. Preview the first page of the document. It should look similar to Illustration A.
    - ✓ *You can control when fields in the table of contents are shaded by using the Field shading: drop-down list on the View tab of the Tools, Options dialog box.*
16. Close Print Preview.
17. Change the heading **Diseases and Insects** from Heading 2 to Heading 1.
18. Update the entire table of contents to reflect the change.
19. Preview all pages of the document. Notice that there are now hard page breaks that are not necessary.
20. Delete the hard page breaks before table 1, table 2, and the heading Index.
21. Update the page numbers in the table of contents.
22. Update the page numbers in the table of figures.
23. Update the page numbers in the index.
24. Check the spelling and grammar in the document.
25. Print the document.
26. Close the document, saving all changes.

*Illustration A*

Student's Name                                                                                    Today's date

# ROSES

## Table of Contents

Throughout history, roses have been considered a symbol of love and beauty. Did you know they have also been a symbol of war and death? In the following pages you will learn the story of the rose as well how to select and care for these beautiful flowers.

## History

Fossil evidence shows that there were roses on earth more than 35 million years ago. Roses are believed to have grown wild throughout most of the world. The earliest roses were all red, or shades of red. In fact, the genus name, *Rosa*, means red in Latin. The first cultivation probably began 5,000 years ago in China. Human beings have been captivated by the flower ever since. They have worked hard to nurture and develop these wondrous blooms so that now there are hundreds of types

Page 1

# On Your Own

1. Start Word and open OWD56, the research report you have been working on.

2. Save the document as **OWD57**.

3. Complete the research project.

4. Finish adding and editing content as necessary.

5. Create a table of figures if appropriate.

6. Create a table of authorities if appropriate.

7. Create a table of contents.

8. Preview the document.

9. Adjust page breaks as necessary.

10. Update all tables.

11. Check the spelling and grammar.

12. Print the report.

13. Ask a classmate to review the report and make comments and suggestions.

14. Incorporate the comments and suggestions.

15. Update tables and adjust page formatting as necessary.

16. Close the document, saving all changes, and exit Word.

# Exercise 58

You have been working on a report about eye care for the elderly for StyleEyes. Your supervisor has decided the store should develop a directory that describes the different services it offers and that your report on eye care for seniors should be included. She has an outline of the directory and has asked you to organize the project.

In this exercise, you will modify a format a multi-page document about eye care for seniors. You will use the find and replace feature, create bookmarks, headers and footers, and captions. You will insert section and page breaks, control text flow as necessary, and insert cross-references. You will also create a table of figures, an index, and a table of contents. Finally, you will take an outline of the directory and convert it into a master document, and you will insert the modified document as a subdocument in the master document.

## Exercise Directions

### Use Find and Replace and Create a Summary Document

1. Start Word, if necessary.
2. Open the **SENIORS** subdocument.
3. Find and replace all occurrences of the text **the elderly** with the text **seniors**. Use the match case option.
4. Find and replace all occurrences of the text **the Elderly** with the text **Seniors**. Use the match case option.
5. Create an executive summary of the document in a new document. Set the summary to be 10% of the original document.
6. Save the summary document as **EYESUMMARY** and close it.

### Edit and Format the Document

1. In the **SENIORS** document, change to Reading Layout view.
2. Display Thumbnails.
3. Go to screen 3.
4. Go to screen 1.
5. Close Reading Layout view.
6. Display the Document Map.
7. Go to the heading **Nutrition**.

8. Insert a bookmark named **Nutrition**.
9. Go to the heading **Eye Site and Medication**.
10. Move the second paragraph under the heading **Eye Site and Medication** (it begins with the text **The U.S. Department of Agriculture**) and the list that follows it to the end of the section **Nutrition**.
11. Go to the section **Common Eye Ailments**.
12. Close the Document Map.

### Insert Cross-References, an Index, and a Table of Contents

1. Insert hyperlinked cross-references from the first four items in the bullet list of common eye ailments to the page numbers where the reader can find the corresponding heading.
2. Check the word count in the document.
3. Mark items to create an index for the document. Use your judgment as to which words to include. Include at least ten words. Include at least two cross-references. Include at least three subentries.
   ✓ *Refer to Illustration A to see suggested index entries.*
4. Insert a page break at the end of the document.
5. At the top of the last page, type the heading **Index** using the Heading 1 style, centered.

6. Below the new heading, create the index, using the Classic format, with page numbers right-aligned, using dot tab leaders, indented in two columns.

7. Display the index in Print Preview. It should look similar to Illustration A, depending on the entries you choose to include.

8. Insert a blank line before the heading **Overview** near the beginning of the document, and clear all formatting from it.

9. Generate a table of contents in the Classic format, with page numbers right-aligned, using dot tab leaders, with no hyperlinks.

10. Insert a next page section break between the table of contents and the heading **Overview**.

11. Set the margins in the first section of the document to be 1.5" on the left and right.

## Complete the Document

1. Insert a header on all but the first page that has your name flush left and the company name (**StyleEyes, Inc.**) flush right.
   ✓ *Adjust the right tab stop if necessary.*

2. Insert a footer on all pages that has today's date flush left and the page number in the format of **Page X of N** flush right.
   ✓ *Adjust the tab stops if necessary.*

3. Preview the second page of the document. It should look similar to Illustration B.

4. Preview all pages of the document at once.

5. Use the Keep with Next text flow option to keep all items in the bulleted list at the bottom of page 2 and the top of page 3 together on the same page.

6. Update the page numbers in cross-references, the table of contents, and the index.

7. Check the spelling and grammar in the document.

8. Display the document in Print Preview and make adjustments and corrections as necessary.

9. Print the document.

10. Close the file, saving all changes.

## Create a Master Document

1. Open ☉ **58SERVICES**, and save it as **SERVICES**.

2. Change to Outline view.

3. Format the document title as Heading 1.

4. Format the remaining headings as Heading 2:
   **Directory of Services**
   **Annual Eye Exams**
   **Eye Care for Children**
   **Emergency Eye Care**
   **Eye Glasses**
   **Contact Lenses**
   **Surgery Evaluation and Referral**
   **Preventative Care**
   **List of Resources**

5. Select all text in the document except the title and create subdocuments.

6. Insert the **SENIORS** document as a subdocument into the **SERVICES** master document between the Eye Care for Children subdocument and the Emergency Eye Care subdocument.

7. Save the **SERVICES** master document.

8. Close all open documents, saving all changes, and exit Word.

*Illustration A*

# Index

# Eye Care for Seniors

How Aging Affects the Health of Our Eyes

Prepared by
StyleEyes, Inc.

# Lesson 10

## The Internet

### Exercise 59
- Internet Basics
- Use Internet Features in Word
- Save a Web Page Locally
- Work with the Favorites Folder

### Exercise 60
- Search the Internet
- Print Web Page Information
- Copy Data from a Web Page into a Word Document
- Use the Research Tool

### Exercise 61
- Create a Web Page Document in Word
- Use Web Layout View
- Preview a Web Page
- Open a Web Page Document in Word

### Exercise 62
- Use Web Page Titles
- Apply a Background
- Apply a Theme

### Exercise 63
- Use Tables in Web Page Documents
- Insert a Link Bar in a Word Document
- Create a Frames Page

### Exercise 64
- Critical Thinking

# Exercise 59

## Skills Covered:

◆ **Internet Basics** ◆ **Use Internet Features in Word**
◆ **Save a Web Page Locally** ◆ **Work with the Favorites Folder**

## On the Job

Log on to the Internet to access information on any subject and to communicate with other people. Use Word's Internet features to make using the Internet easy and familiar.

Your supervisor at Long Shot, Inc. has to travel to Alaska on business. She will have one free day and has heard that the train ride up the White Pass is spectacular. She has asked you to locate some basic information, such as the schedule and prices. In this exercise, you will use the Internet to locate the White Pass Railroad site. You will add the site to your Favorites folder and save the page that has the information you need locally so you can read it offline in Word.

## Terms

**Internet** A worldwide network of computers.

**World Wide Web** A system for finding information on the Internet through the use of linked documents.

**Internet Service Provider (ISP)** A company that provides access to the Internet for a fee.

**Web browser** Software that makes it easy to locate and view information stored on the Internet. Common browsers include Microsoft Internet Explorer and Netscape Navigator.

**Shareware** Software that can be downloaded from the Internet for free or for a nominal fee.

**Web site** A set of linked Web pages.

**Web page** A document stored on the World Wide Web.

**Uniform Resource Locator (URL)** A Web site's address on the Internet.

**Hyperlinks or links** Text or graphics in a document set up to provide a direct connection with a destination location or document. When you click a hyperlink, the destination displays.

## Notes

### Internet Basics

- Anyone with a computer, an **Internet** connection, and communications software can access the Internet and the **World Wide Web**.

- For a fee, **Internet Service Providers (ISP)** provide you with an e-mail account, **Web browser** software, and Internet access.

- Microsoft Office 2003 comes with the Internet Explorer Web browser, although your computer may be set up to use a different browser.

  ✓ *This exercise assumes you are using Internet Explorer. If your computer is set up to use a different browser, ask your instructor for directions.*

■ Some things available via the Internet and the World Wide Web include e-mail communication, product information and support, reference material, shopping, stock quotes, travel arrangements, real estate information, **shareware**, and games.

## Use Internet Features in Word

■ If you have a connection to the Internet and Web browser software, you can use Word's Web toolbar to access the Internet.

■ Word remains running while you use the Internet, so you can go back and forth from Word to the Internet sites that you have opened on your browser.

■ To locate a **Web site**, **Web page**, or document, you enter its Internet address, or **Uniform Resource Locator (URL)**.

   ✓ *If you don't know the URL of a site, you can search the Web for the site you want. For information on searching the Web, refer to Exercise 60.*

■ Most sites provide **hyperlinks**, also called **links**, to related pages or sites. Text links are usually a different color and underlined to stand out from the surrounding text. Graphics may also be links.

■ When the mouse pointer rests on a link, the pointer changes to a hand with a pointing finger, and a ScreenTip shows the destination.

## Save a Web Page Locally

■ Use your browser's Save As command to save a Web page on your computer.

■ Once you save a Web page, you can access it while you are working offline.

   ✓ *Even though you can save a Web page, you still must consider copyright laws before you reuse the information.*

■ When you save a Web page you can select from four file types:

   ● Web page, complete. This saves all of the associated files needed to display the Web page, including graphics.

   ● Web Archive. Saves a snapshot of the current Web page in a single file.

   ● Web Page, HTML only. Saves the information on the Web page but does not save the associated files.

   ● Text Only. Saves the information in plain text format.

## Work with the Favorites Folder

■ Use the Favorites folder on your computer to store the URLs of Web sites you like to access frequently.

■ You can also add locally stored files and folders to your Favorites folder.

■ The easiest way to add a URL to the Favorites folder is by using your Web browser, but you can use Word as well.

■ Access the Favorites folder from Word or from Windows when you want to go directly to one of your favorite sites.

*Items in the Favorites Folder*

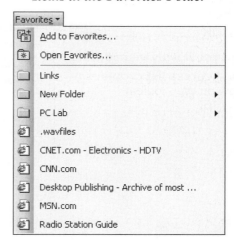

*The Web toolbar*

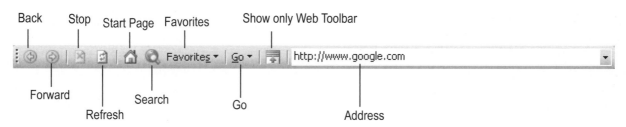

# Procedures

## Use Internet Features in Word

**To display the Web toolbar:**

1. Click **View** ................... `Alt`+`V`
2. Select **Toolbars** ................ `T`
3. Click **Web** .......... `↑`, `↓`, `Enter`

OR

- Right-click on any toolbar and select **Web** ......... `↑`, `↓`, `Enter`

   ✓ *Be sure to select the Web toolbar and not the Web Tools toolbar.*

**To go to a specific URL:**

1. Type URL in Address drop-down list box on Web toolbar.
2. Press **Enter** ....................... `Enter`

OR

1. Click **Go** button  ........................ `Alt`+`G`
2. Click **Open Hyperlink** button 📧 ........................ `O`
3. Type the URL in the **Address** list box.
4. Click **OK** .......................... `Enter`

**To go to a previously visited URL:**

1. Click **Address list drop-down arrow** on Web toolbar.
2. Click URL.

## To use a hyperlink:

1. Move mouse pointer to touch link.
2. Click left mouse button.

**To display the previously displayed page or document:**

- Click **Back** button [← Back] on the Browser's toolbar.

   ✓ *If the Back button is dimmed on the toolbar, there is no page to go to.*

**To display the next Web page:**

- Click **Forward** button [→] on the Browser's toolbar.

   ✓ *If the Forward button is dimmed on the toolbar, there is no page to go to.*

**Save a Web page locally:**

1. Open Web page in browser.
2. Click **File** ..................... `Alt`+`F`
3. Click **Save As** ..................... `A`
4. Type file name.
5. Select disk or folder.
6. Click **Save as type** ...... `Alt`+`T` drop-down arrow.
7. Click desired file type.
8. Click **Save** ................... `Alt`+`S`

## The Favorites Folder

**To use Internet Explorer to add a site to your Favorites folder:**

1. Open Internet site to add to Favorites.
2. Click **Favorites** ............ `Alt`+`A`
3. Click **Add to Favorites** ....... `A`
4. Type site name if necessary .................... `Alt`+`N`

   ✓ *Your browser automatically enters a site name; you can edit it if you want.*

5. Click **OK** .......................... `Enter`

**To use Word to add a file to your Favorites folder:**

1. Open file to add to Favorites.
2. Click **Favorites** button  .................. `Alt`+`S` on Web toolbar.
3. Click **Add to Favorites** ....... `A`

   ✓ *The Add to Favorites dialog box is similar to the Save As dialog box.*

4. Type a name.
5. Click **Add** ......................... `Enter`

**To go to a site from your Favorites folder:**

1. Click **Favorites** button [Favorites ▾] on Web toolbar.
2. Click site name.

   ✓ *If necessary, Word starts your Web browser to connect to the Internet and display the site.*

# Exercise Directions

✓ *You must have an Internet connection and an account with an ISP in order to search the Internet or Web. When prompted, you must enter an ID and/or password in order to gain access.*

1. Start Word, if necessary.

2. Create a new, blank document.

3. Display the Web toolbar.

4. In the Address line type the following and press Enter: **whitepassrailroad.com**

   ✓ *The Web site may have changed or may no longer be available. If this site is not available, refer to Excise 60 to learn how to search for a Web site and search for information on train rides that go up the White Pass in Alaska.*

5. Use your Web browser to add the page to your Favorites folder.

6. Click the <u>Schedule</u> link on the Welcome page.

   ✓ *Click the Graphics Enhanced link first, and then click the Schedule link.*

7. Click the <u>General Information</u> link.

   ✓ *The available links may be different. You may simply scroll through the page to read the Information, or test the links at the top of the page, then skip to step 11.*

8. Click the <u>Top</u> link.

9. Click the <u>White Pass Summit Excursion</u> link.

10. Click the <u>Top</u> link.

11. Save the page in Web archive format with the name **TRAIN**.

12. Click the Back button enough times to return to Word.

13. Open the **TRAIN** document in Word.

    ✓ *If the document is not listed in Word's Open dialog box, change the list to display all file types.*

14. Display the document in Print Preview.

15. Use Word to add the **TRAIN** document to your Favorites folder.

16. Close the document, saving all changes.

17. Disconnect from the Internet, if necessary.

# On Your Own

1. If you have access to the Internet, use it to explore a Web site about something that interests you. You can find the URL for most sites on advertisements, packaging, or in the yellow pages. For example, go to the Web site for your hometown, a sports team that you follow, or a writer, musician, or artist you admire.

2. When you get to a site you like, add it to your Favorites folder.

3. Save one of the pages you find as a single file Web page document so you can spend more time reading it offline. Save it as **OWD59**.

4. If you want, try saving it in one or more of the other available formats to see the difference between them.

5. In Word, open ⌨**OWD59** or open ⊚ **59WEB**.

6. Read the document in Word.

7. Close the document and exit Word.

8. Disconnect from the Internet, if necessary.

# Exercise 60

◆ **Search the Internet** ◆ **Print Web Page Information**
◆ **Copy Data from a Web Page to a Word Document**
◆ **Use the Research Tool**

## On the Job

Search the Internet when you do not know the URL of the Web site you need. Use Word to select a search engine that can display a list of Web sites that match the information you are looking for. You can also use Word's Research tool to locate information about a specific topic. When a Web page is displayed on your computer, print it for future reference or to pass along to someone else. If you don't need to print the entire page, you can copy the data you need into a Word document to save or print for future use.

Your supervisor has asked you to locate a hotel in Skagway, Alaska in case she needs to spend the night there. In this exercise, you will search the Internet for lodging in Skagway. You will print some of the information that you find, and you will copy some of the information into a Word document to save for future use.

## Terms

**Search engine** Software available on the Internet that searches for Web sites containing the information you are looking for.

## Notes

### Search the Internet

■ The Internet and World Wide Web contain millions of pages of information.

■ If you do not know the URL for a Web site, you can use one of a number of available **search engines** to locate the site.

■ Search engines prompt you to enter information, and then they display a hyperlinked list of Web sites containing that information.

■ Some search engines are designed for specific purposes, such as finding a business, or locating an e-mail address.

■ Others are for more general use. Some general purpose search engines include Yahoo!, About.com, Google.com, and Ask.com.

■ Your ISP (Internet Service Provider) might have its own search engine, it might suggest a specific search engine when you select the Search option, or it might give you a choice of search engines.

■ You can also access a specific search engine site by entering its URL in the Address bar. For example, to go to the Google search engine site, enter www.google.com.

■ The search results vary depending on the information you type and the search engine you use.

■ For a successful search, enter specific information, such as a full company name.

## Print Web Page Information

- You can print a Web page displayed in Word or displayed in your browser.

- The commands for printing a Web page are the same as for printing a regular Word document.

- Many Web sites contain graphics, such as photographs and artwork. Some printers may not be able to print the graphical content of a Web page.

- Some Web pages offer a link to display a print-friendly version of the page that has fewer graphics elements, or a text-only version.

## Copy Data from a Web Page to a Word Document

- You can use the Copy and Paste commands to copy data from a Web page into a Word document.

- The commands may be accessed from a shortcut menu, or from the Edit menu in your Web browser.

- Remember that copying someone else's work and using it without attribution is plagiarism.

- If you use Web page data in a report or other project, you must cite the source in a footnote, bibliography, or other list of sources.

- It is also important to know whether or not the source is reputable.

- You can copy a URL from an Address bar and paste it into a Word document. This is useful for recording a Web page address that you will need to use in a footnote or bibliography.

## Use the Research Tool

- Use the Research task pane to start a search of online research and reference services.

- By default, Word searches the dictionary and thesaurus, but you can select the specific reference tool or service to use.

  ✓ *For information on using the dictionary or thesaurus, refer to Exercise 11.*

- The results of the search are displayed in the Research task pane. Click a link to go to the destination.

- You can add and remove Web sites and intranet sites to the list of available reference and research locations. For example, you can add the Microsoft Encarta Encyclopedia to the list.

  ✓ *Some research services require that you sign up for a subscription.*

# Procedures

### Access a Search Engine Web Site

  ✓ *You must have an Internet connection and an account with an ISP in order to search the Internet or Web. When prompted, you must enter an ID and/or password in order to gain access.*

1. In Word, display the Web toolbar.
2. Click **Search the Web** button .
   **OR**
   a. Click **Go** button
      `Go ▾` ...................... Alt + G
   b. Click **Search the Web** .... W

   ✓ *The Search site options will vary depending on ISP.*

3. Type search topic in Search text box.

4. Click **Search** button.

   ✓ *The name on the search button (Find It, Go Get It, etc.) will vary depending on the search site.*

5. Click a hyperlink on the Search Results page to go to that site.

**OR**

1. Display the Web toolbar.
2. Type search engine URL in Address bar.

   ✓ *For example, type www.google.com to go to the Google search engine home page, or type www.ask.com to go to the Ask Jeeves search engine home page.*

3. Press **Enter** ..................... Enter

### Print Web Page Information (*Ctrl+P*)

1. Display the desired Web page.
2. Click the **Print** button on your browser's toolbar.
   **OR**
   a. Click **File** ............... Alt + F
   b. Click **Print** ..................... P
   c. Click **OK** ..................... Enter

### Copy Data from a Web Page into a Word Document (*Ctrl + C/Ctrl + V*)

1. Display the desired Web page.
2. Select data to copy.
3. Right-click selection.
4. Click **Copy** ......................... C
5. Open Word document.

6. Position insertion point at desired location.

7. Right-click and click **Paste**.. [P]

OR

1. Display the desired Web page.

2. Select data to copy.

3. Click **Edit** .................. [Alt]+[E]

4. Click **Copy** ......................... [C]

5. Open Word document.

6. Position insertion point at desired location.

7. Click **Edit** .................... [Alt]+[E]

8. Click **Paste**. ....................... [P]

### Use the Research Task Pane

1. Click **Tools** ................. [Alt]+[T]

2. Click **Research** .................... [R]

   ✓ *The Research task pane opens.*

3. Enter desired word or phrase in Search for box.

4. Click **Show results from:** drop-down arrow.

5. Select desired research tool or reference service.

6. Click **Start Searching** button [→] ......................... [Enter]

7. Click link in Research task pane to display information.

# Exercise Directions

1. Start Word, if necessary.

2. Create a new blank document and name it **LODGING**.

3. Display the Web toolbar.

4. In the Address line type the following and press Enter: **altavista.com**

5. In the Search text box type **Skagway Alaska Lodging**.

6. Click the Find button.

   ✓ *Remember, the name of the button may vary depending on the actual search site you use.*

7. Notice that the search engine lists the page name, the first few lines of text from the page, and the page's URL. Click a link with hotel information.

8. Look for information for the At the White House bed and breakfast.

   ✓ *If you can't find information on this B&B, either open* 💿 *60whitehouse.htm or search on another hotel.*

9. Locate and select the telephone and address information at the bottom of the page and copy it to the Clipboard.

10. Click the Back button on your browser's toolbar until you return to the **LODGING.doc** document.

11. On the first line of the document, type **The White House in Skagway, Alaska**, and then press Enter.

12. Paste the data into the document.

13. Click the Forward button on the Web toolbar to return to the AltaVista site, and then click the Forward button on your browser's toolbar to return to that last page you visited at The White House site.

14. Click the <u>Next</u> link twice.

15. Select the text on the page beginning with the line above the table (**Rates based upon single/double occupancy**) and ending with the last line on the page (**Open year round. Off-season rates October through April.**), and copy the selection to the Clipboard.

   ✓ *If you have trouble locating the page, you may go directly to www.atthewhitehouse.com/White%20House3.html.*

   ✓ *If you cannot locate the information, then open* 💿 *60whitehouse2.htm.*

   ✓ *The Web site may have changed since the printing of this book.*

16. Exit the Internet.

17. Insert a new line in the **LODGING** document, and paste the data from the Clipboard.

18. Display the document in Print Preview.

19. Close the document, saving all changes.

# On Your Own

1. If you have access to the Internet, use the Web toolbar in Word to access a search engine.

2. Search for a Web site about a place in the world you would like to visit. It may be a city, a country, or a vacation destination.

3. Test a few links from the search results list.

4. Add one that you like to your Favorites folder.

5. Go the Web site and print a Web page.

6. Create a new Word document and save it with the name **OWD60**.

7. Copy at least one paragraph of information about the destination to the Word document.

8. Try copying the URL from the address bar into the Word document as well, so you know where you found the information.

9. If available, use the Research tool to look up information about the destination in the Encarta encyclopedia. Copy the information from Encarta into the **OWD60** Word document.

10. Notice that at the bottom of the page, Encarta provides information about how to cite the article. Copy this information to the Word document, as well.

11. When you are finished, disconnect from the Internet, and exit Word, saving all changes.

# Exercise 61

◆ **Create a Web Page Document in Word** ◆ **Use Web Layout View**
◆ **Preview a Web Page** ◆ **Open a Web Page Document in Word**

## On the Job

Save Word documents in HTML, XML, or MHTML format so that you can display them on the World Wide Web or on a company intranet. You can create new Web page documents, or save existing documents in a Web page format. You can use Word features and tools to edit and format the documents.

The owner of Liberty Blooms has asked you to create a document that can serve as a Web page for the store's new Web site. In this exercise, you will create a new Web page document. You will also save an existing document as a Web page and use hyperlinks to link the two to each other.

## Terms

**Web server** A computer connected to the Internet used to store Web page documents.

**MHTML** A format used for storing Web pages as single files so they can be easily transmitted over the Internet.

**HTML** Hypertext Markup Language. A file format used for storing Web pages.

**XML** Extensible Markup Language. A file format used for displaying and exchanging data via the World Wide Web.

**Microsoft Office tags** Codes embedded in a Web Page document created with a Microsoft Office program. The codes enable you to edit the document using the original program.

## Notes

### Create a Web Page Document in Word

- You can save an existing Word document as a Web page so it can be stored on a **Web server** and viewed online.

- You can also create a new blank Web page document.

- By default, when you create a new Web page in Word the file is saved as a single file in **MHTML** format.

- When you save an existing document as a Web page you can choose from four Web page formats:

- Single File Web Page. Saves a Web page and all associated text and graphics in a single file in MHTML format. This is the default option.

- Web Page. Saves the document in **HTML** format. Associated graphics files such as bullets, lines, and pictures are stored in a separate folder that is linked to the HTML file.

  ✓ *The folder has the same name as the HTML file, followed by an underscore and the word files, like this: Filename_files. Use caution when moving or renaming the graphics files or the folder they are stored in. If Word cannot identify the files, the page will display without graphics elements.*

- **XML** Document. Saves a file in XML format.

- Web Page, Filtered. Saves a file in HTML format without **Microsoft Office tags**. This reduces the file size, but limits some functionality for editing the file.

  ✓ *This option is recommended for advanced users only.*

*The Save As Web Page dialog box*

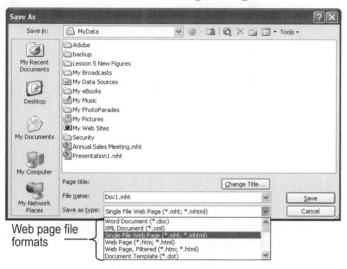

Web page file formats

## Use Web Layout View

- Web Layout view displays documents in Word as they will look on the Web.

- Word automatically switches to Web Layout view when you save a document as a Web page, when you create a new Web page document, or when you open an existing Web page document.

- You can also switch to Web Layout view using the View menu or the View buttons.

- Web Layout view lets you edit a document for viewing on-screen, instead of for printing on a page.

- Features of Web Layout view include:
  - Word wrapping to fit the window, not a page.
  - Graphics positioned as they would be in a Web browser.
  - Backgrounds (if there are any) displayed as they would be in a browser.

## Preview a Web Page

- Use Web Page Preview to see how a Word document will look in a Web browser.

- You can display regular Word documents or Web page documents in Web Page Preview.

- When you preview a Web page document, Word opens the document in your default browser.

- You cannot edit a document in Web Page Preview; however, you can test hyperlinks and other interactive features.

## Open a Web Page Document in Word

- Use the Open dialog box to open a Web page document in Word the same way you open a regular Word document.

- The document displays in Web Layout view.

- When you save the document, it remains in its original Web page format.

- By default, if you try to open a Web page document from Windows, the document displays in your Web browser, not in Word.

  ✓ *Use the Open With command in Windows to open the Web page document with Word: right-click the file in Windows, select Open With, and then click Microsoft Word.*

# Procedures

### Create a New Blank Web Page Document

1. Click **File**.......................`Alt`+`F`
2. Click **New**............................`N`
3. Click **Web page** in New Document task pane.
4. Click **File**.......................`Alt`+`F`
5. Click **Save As**.......................`A`

6. Type file name.
   ✓ *If necessary, open the folder, disk, or server where the file will be stored.*
7. Click **Save as type** drop-down arrow ..........................`Alt`+`T`
8. Click desired file format ...............`↑`, `↓`, `Enter`
9. Click **Save** button
    ............`Alt`+`S`

### Save a Document as a Single File Web Page

1. Open the document.
2. Click **File** ....................`Alt`+`F`
3. Click **Save as Web Page**....`G`
4. Type file name.
   ✓ *If necessary, open the folder, disk, or server where the file will be stored.*
5. Click **Save** button
    ............`Alt`+`S`

## Save a Document in a Different Web Page Format

1. Open the document.
2. Click **File** ..................... `Alt`+`F`
3. Click **Save as Web Page** .... `G`
4. Type file name.
   - ✓ *If necessary, open the folder, disk, or server where the file will be stored.*
5. Click **Save as type** drop down arrow ................. `Alt`+`T`
6. Click desired file format ................ `↑`, `↓`, `Enter`
7. Click **Save** button

   `Save` ............ `Alt`+`S`

## Change to Web Layout View

1. Open Web page document in Word.
2. Click **Web Layout view** button .

   OR

1. Click **View** ................... `Alt`+`V`
2. Click **Web Layout** .............. `W`

## `Use Web Page Preview

1. Click **File** ..................... `Alt`+`F`
2. Click **Web Page Preview** .... `B`

## Close Web Page Preview

1. Click **File** ..................... `Alt`+`F`
2. Click **Close** ......................... `C`

## Open a Web Page Document in Word

1. Click **File** ..................... `Alt`+`F`
2. Click **Open** ......................... `O`
3. Click file name.
   - ✓ *If necessary, open the folder or disk where the file is stored.*
4. Click **Open** button

   `Open` ............... `Alt`+`O`

# Exercise Directions

1. Start Word, if necessary.
2. Create a new blank Web page document.
3. Save the document as **BLOOMWEB**.
4. Type and format the document shown in Illustration A.
5. Check the spelling and grammar in the document.
6. Display the document in Web Page Preview. It should look similar to Illustration A.
   - ✓ *If your browser displays smart tags (small purple dots) under certain information on the page, ignore them. You learn more about smart tags in Exercise 92.*
7. Close Web Page Preview.
8. Open the file ⊛**61ONLINEAD**, a version of the advertisement you created for Liberty Blooms in an earlier exercise.
9. Save the file as a single file Web page with the name **ONLINEAD**.
   - ✓ *Click Continue if Word warns you that some formatting may not be preserved.*

10. Press Ctrl+End to move the insertion point to the end of the document.
11. Insert a new blank line and then type the text **HOME**.
12. Select the text **HOME** and insert a hyperlink to the **BLOOMWEB** document.
    - ✓ *For a refresher on inserting hyperlinks, refer to Exercise 30.*
13. Switch to the **BLOOMWEB** document.
14. Insert a hyperlink from the text **Special Online Savings Offers!** to the **ONLINEAD** document.
15. Test the link.
16. Test the <u>HOME</u> link back to the **BLOOMWEB** document.
17. Close all open files, saving all changes.

*Illustration A*

36-pt. decorative font, centered, all caps.

# LIBERTY BLOOMS ONLINE

Wingdings symbol #37, 36 pts.

### Flowers, Plants, And More

18-pt. decorative font, centered, 36 pts after.

18-pt, serif, centered, all caps, 18 pts. after

WELCOME TO THE NEW WEB SITE FOR

## LIBERTY BLOOMS FLOWER SHOP

28-pt. serif, all caps, centered, bold, 18 pts. after

Check this Web site daily for information about:

Classes

Growing tips and other useful information

Special Online Savings Offers!

16-pt. serif, flush left, 18 pts. after

This site is new. Please let us know what other information you would like to see posted here. We will do our best to respond to your requests.

14-pt. serif, flush left

# On Your Own

1. Plan a personal Web page. Decide the information you would like to include and how you want the page to look. For example, you should include your name, what you like to do, who your favorite musicians and sports teams are, where you go to school or where you work. You might include favorite sayings, upcoming events in your life, or fun things your family or friends plan to do. If you have a connection to the Internet, you might browse other pages to get some ideas.

   ✓ *Never include your home address, phone number, or photo on a Web site.*

2. When you are ready, create a new document in Word.

3. Save the file as **OWD61-1**.

4. Use this document to design a Web page and enter the text.

5. Save the changes, and then save the document as a Single File Web page with the name **OWD61-2**.

6. Use Web Page Preview to look at your new Web page in your browser software.

7. Ask a classmate to view the Web page and to offer comments or suggestions.

8. Close Web Page Preview.

9. Incorporate the suggestions into the document.

10. Close the document, saving all changes, and exit Word.

# Exercise 62

◆ **Use Web Page Titles**

◆ **Apply a Background** ◆ **Apply a Theme**

## On the Job

The title of a Web page is displayed at the top of the screen in your Web browser. You can enter any title you want. You can enhance and edit Web page documents by adding elements such as a background and by applying a theme.

The owner of Liberty Blooms wants you to improve the appearance of the Web pages you already designed. In this exercise, you change the page titles for both pages. You apply a theme to one page and a background to the other page. You edit the hyperlinks and then test the pages in your browser.

## Terms

**Background** The color, pattern, or fill displayed on the page behind data in a document.

**Fill effect** A texture, shading, picture, or pattern used as a background.

**Theme** A unified set of design elements and colors that can be applied to a document.

**Web bullets** Graphics files inserted as bullet markers.

**Graphics lines** Graphics files inserted as horizontal rules or dividers.

## Notes

### Use Web Page Titles

- Web page titles are displayed in the Web browser title bar when the page is displayed.

- By default, Word uses the file name or the first line of document text as the Web page title.

- You can set or change the page title name by accessing the Set Page Title dialog box from the Save As dialog box.

*Set Page Title dialog box*

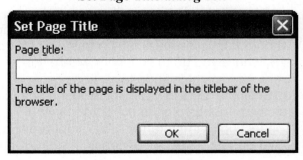

320

## Apply a Background

- By default, Word documents—including Web pages—have a plain white **background**.
- Add visual interest or create an effect by applying a color, pattern, **fill effect**, or picture to a document background.

*Fill Effects dialog box*

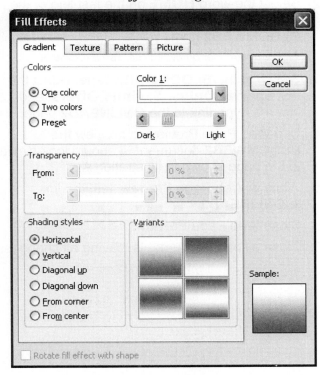

## Apply a Theme

- Word comes with built-in **themes** you can use to format any Word document.
- Each theme includes a background, font formatting, and graphics elements such as **Web bullets** and **graphics lines**.
- You can select a theme to apply consistent formatting to a document.
- Themes can be used with any Word document, but they are particularly useful for formatting Web pages.

- You should coordinate backgrounds for pages in a Web site to establish continuity.

# Procedures

## Set a Web Page Title

1. Click **File** ..................... `Alt`+`F`
2. Click **Save As** ..................... `A`
3. Click **Change Title** button

   Change Title... ............. `Alt`+`C`
4. Type new title.
5. Click **OK**.
6. Click **Save** button

   Save ............. `Alt`+`S`

## Apply a Background

1. Open file to format.
2. Click **Format** .............. `Alt`+`O`
3. Click **Background** .............. `K`
4. Click desired color.
   OR
   a. Click **Fill Effects** ............. `F`
   b. Click desired page tab ................ `Ctrl`+`Tab`
   c. Select desired effect.
   d. Click **OK** .................... `Enter`

## Apply a Theme

1. Open file to format.
2. Click **Format** .............. `Alt`+`O`
3. Click **Theme** ........................ `H`
4. Select desired **Theme** .......... `Alt`+`T`, `↑`, `↓`
5. Click **OK** .......................... `Enter`

✓ *Not all themes are installed automatically. If a theme you select is not installed, use the Setup disk to install it, or select a different theme.*

# Exercise Directions

1. Start Word, if necessary.

2. In Word, open the document ⌨BLOOMWEB or open ⊙62BLOOMWEB.

3. Save the file as BLOOMWEB2.

4. Change the Web Page Title to LIBERTY BLOOMS HOME PAGE.

5. Apply the Eclipse theme.

   ✓ If the Eclipse theme is not available, select a different theme.

6. Change Classes, Growing tips and other useful information, and Special Online Savings Offers! into a bulleted list, using the default bullet style.

7. Apply the Heading 1 style to the third and fourth lines in the document, and then center them.

8. In Word, open the document ⌨ONLINEAD or open ⊙62ONLINEAD.

9. Save it as ONLINEAD2.

10. Change the Web Page Title to LIBERTY BLOOMS SPECIAL SALE PAGE.

11. Apply the Newsprint background texture to the page.

12. Select the word HOME on the last line of the document and insert a hyperlink to the BLOOMWEB2 home page.

    ✓ For a refresher on hyperlinks, see Exercise 30.

13. Switch to the BLOOMWEB2 page, select the text Special Online Savings Offers! and insert a hyperlink to the ONLINEAD2 page.

14. Use Web Page Preview to preview the BLOOMWEB2 document. It should look similar to the page shown in Illustration A.

15. While in Web Page Preview, test the link to ONLINEAD2.

16. Close Web Page Preview.

17. Close all open documents, saving all changes.

*Illustration A*

# LIBERTY BLOOMS ONLINE

### Flowers, Plants, And More

## WELCOME TO THE NEW WEB SITE FOR

## LIBERTY BLOOMS FLOWER SHOP

Check this Web site daily for information about:

■ Classes

■ Growing tips and other useful information

■ Special Online Savings Offers!

This site is new. Please let us know what other information you would like to see posted here. We will do our best to respond to your requests.

## On Your Own

1. Start Word and open ⌨OWD61, the Web page you created in the On Your Own section of Exercise 61, or open 💿62WEB.

2. Save the document as **OWD62**.

3. Change the Web Page title to **YOUR NAME'S WEB PAGE**. (Substitute your own name.)

4. Apply a theme.

5. If there is not already a bulleted list on your Web page, create one.

6. Apply headings to format some of the text.

7. Try a different theme.

8. Keep trying themes until you find one you like.

9. Try changing just the background on the page.

10. If you don't like the background you apply, use Undo to remove it.

11. Use Web Page Preview to preview the document.

12. Close the document, saving all changes.

# Exercise 63

## Skills Covered:

◆ **Use Tables in Web Page Documents**
◆ **Insert a Link Bar in a Word Document** ◆ **Create a Frames Page**

## On the Job

Use tables and frames in a Web page document to organize and align data. Tables let you set up data in columns and rows as in a regular Word document and define different areas on a page using cell formatting. Frames let you create sections on a Web page for displaying different information. Insert a link bar to aid in navigation.

You are designing a Web site for Blue Sky Dairy. In this exercise, you will design a Start page for the Web site using two frames. You will use tables to create a home page, a page for the online store, and a header frame page. You will then link the start page to the other pages in the Web site.

## Terms

**Link bar** A Web page element that automatically creates buttons which can be clicked to move to specified links.

**Frames page** A Web page that contains one or more frames.

**Frame** A section or subwindow on a frames page that can display Web content independently from other frames on the page.

## Notes

### Use Tables in Web Page Documents

- Tables are common features in Web page documents.

- Tables can be used in a Web page just as they are used in a regular document—to set up information in columns and rows. For example, you can use a table in a Web page that lists a schedule.

- You can also use a table in a Web page to organize the page into independent areas. Since each cell can be formatted separately, you can create visual effects that might otherwise be unavailable.

- Steps for creating, modifying, and formatting tables in Web page documents are the same as in regular Word documents.

- You can insert more than one table on a Web page. You can also insert a table within a table.

*Tables can be used to define areas on a Web page*

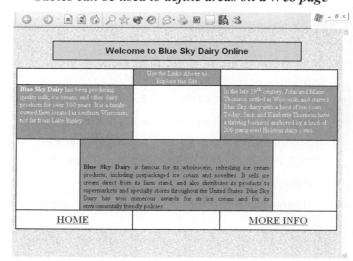

## Insert a Link Bar in a Word Document

- If you save a Word document as a Web page on a Web server that has the Microsoft FrontPage 2002 Server Extensions, or the SharePoint Team Services from Microsoft, you can automatically insert a **link bar**.

  ✓ *Saving Word documents to a Web server is not covered in this book.*

- A link bar lists hyperlinked buttons that help you navigate through a Web site. You can select to insert a link bar with Back and Next buttons (for moving to the previous or next pages in a site), or you can create customized buttons.

- Once you create a link bar, you can insert it in multiple documents.

- You can select to display a link bar across the top or along the left side of the Web page.

## Create a Frames Page

- Create a **frames page** to include multiple **frames** on a Web page.

- Each frame is an independent section that can display the contents of a Web page. That means that multiple Web pages can be displayed at once.

- Common uses for frames include displaying a table of contents, site map, or a header.

- When you create a frames page, you start with a Web page (sometimes called the parent page) in which you insert and size frames and then set frame properties.

- Each frame is saved as a separate MHTML Web page document.

  ✓ *Make sure to store all frames page documents in the same location as the parent page.*

- Set frame properties to specify the initial Web page displayed in the frame as well as options such as whether or not to display scroll bars in a frame, and whether or not to display borders around the frame.

*Frame Properties dialog box*

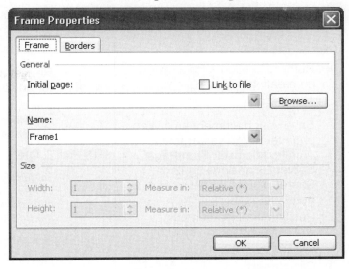

- Use menu commands or buttons on the Frames toolbar to insert and delete frames and to open the Frame Properties dialog box.

- Use the Set Target Frame dialog box to specify which frame you want a hyperlink destination to open in. For example, a user may click a link in the table of contents in the left frame to open information in the right frame; the table of contents will still be displayed in the left frame.

*Set Target Frame dialog box*

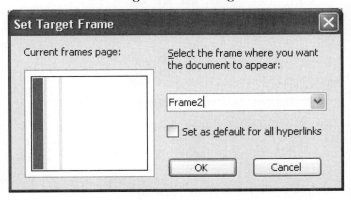

- You can also specify a link to open in a new browser window or in the original Web page.

- Word can automatically create a table of contents on a frames page based on heading styles used in a document. This looks and functions like the document map – click a heading in the table of contents frame to jump to that section in the document in a different frame.

  ✓ *For information on the Document Map, refer to Exercise 54.*

# Procedures

## Create Tables

- Refer to Lesson 7 for a review on creating tables.

## Insert a Link Bar

1. Save your document as a Web page to a Web server that is running Microsoft FrontPage Server Extensions 2002 or SharePoint Team Services from Microsoft.

2. Position the insertion point where you want to place the link bar.

3. Click **Insert** ................. `Alt`+`I`

4. Click **Web Component**....... `W`

5. Select Link Bars in the **Component type** list ................. `Alt`+`T`, `↑`, `↓`

6. Select desired bar type in the **Choose a bar type** list ................. `Alt`+`H`, `↑`, `↓`

7. Click **Next** ................... `Alt`+`N`

8. Select desired style .............. `Alt`+`H`, `↑`, `↓`

9. Click **Next** ................... `Alt`+`N`

10. Select desired orientation ................... `↑`, `↓`

11. Click **Finish**................. `Alt`+`F`

    ✓ The Link Bar Properties dialog box is displayed.

12. Do one of the following:
    - Select an existing link bar.
    OR
    a. Click **Create New** .. `Alt`+`C`
    b. Type new link bar name
    c. Click **OK**..................... `Enter`
    d. Click **Add link**........ `Alt`+`A`

       ✓ The Add to Link Bar dialog box appears.

    e. Select destination for first button on link bar.
    f. In **Text to Display** box, type text to display on link bar button.

g. Click **OK** .................... `Enter`

h. Repeat steps d through g for additional buttons.

    ✓ If necessary, use the Move Up and Move Down buttons to rearrange the link bar buttons.

13. Click **OK** .......................... `Enter`

    ✓ To quickly access the Link Bar Properties dialog box so you can add or modify links, click the Edit Links link.

## Create a Frames Page

1. Create and save a new Web Page document.
   OR
   Open an existing Web page document.

2. Click **Format**................ `Alt`+`O`

3. Select **Frames**.................... `R`

4. Click **New Frames Page** ..... `N`

    ✓ The Frames toolbar is displayed.

5. Click a button on the Frames toolbar to insert a frame:
   OR
   a. Click **Format** .......... `Alt`+`O`
   b. Select **Frames**................ `R`
   c. Click desired option:
      - **New Frame Left**
        `New Frame Left` ......`L`
      - **New Frame Right**
        `New Frame Right` ......`G`
      - **New Frame Above**
        `New Frame Above` .... `M`
      - **New Frame Below**
        `New Frame Below` .....`B`

    ✓ The insertion point is positioned in the new frame.

6. Drag frame border to size frame as desired.

7. Save frames page.

8. Repeat steps 5–7 to create additional frames.

## Set Frame Properties

1. Position insertion point in desired frame.

2. Click **Frame Properties** button 🔲 on Frames toolbar.
   OR
   a. Click **Format** ......... `Alt`+`O`
   b. Select **Frames** .............. `R`
   c. Click **Frame Properties** ..................... `P`

3. Click **Initial page** box.......... `P`

4. Type page to display in frame at startup.
   OR
   a. Click **Browse** ................ `R`
   b. Locate and select desired page.
   c. Click **Open** .................... `O`

5. Click **Name** box................... `N`

6. Type desired frame name

    ✓ A frame name may be useful when setting target frame hyperlinks.

7. Set size options as desired.

8. Click **Borders** tab................ `B`

9. Set border options as desired.

10. Click **OK** .......................... `Enter`

## Set Target Frame Hyperlinks

1. Create hyperlink.
   OR
   a. Right-click existing hyperlink.
   b. Click **Edit Hyperlink** ...... `H`

2. In Hyperlink dialog box, click **Target Frame**.............. `Alt`+`G`

3. Click **Select the frame where you want the document to appear** drop-down arrow ......... `Alt`+`S`

4. Click desired frame ................ `↑`, `↓`, `Enter`

5. If desired, click the **Set as default for all hyperlinks** check box............................[D] to set selected frame as default.

6. Click **OK**............................[Enter]

7. Click **OK**............................[Enter]

**Create Table of Contents Frame**

1. Open document with headings formatted using heading styles.

2. Save document as a Web page.

3. Click **Table of Contents in Frame** button 🔲 on Frames toolbar.
   OR
   a. Click **F**ormat ..........[Alt]+[O]
   b. Select **F**rames ...............[R]
   c. Click **T**able of Contents in Frame ........................[T]

4. Save frames page.

**Delete a Frame**

1. Position insertion point in frame to delete.

2. Click **Delete Frame** button 🔳 on Frames toolbar.
   OR
   a. Click **F**ormat ..........[Alt]+[O]
   b. Select **F**rames ...............[R]
   c. Click **D**elete Frame........[D]

   ✓ There is no confirmation of the deletion, and the Undo command is not available to reverse the action.

# Exercise Directions

1. Start Word, if necessary.

2. Open the document 💿**63HOLSTEINS** and save it as a single file Web page with the name **BSDHOLSTEINS** and the Web page title **About Holsteins**.

3. Close the document.

4. Open the document 💿**63CONTEST** and save it as a single file Web page with the name **BSDCONTEST** and the Web page title **Name That Flavor Contest**.

5. Close the document.

## Create Web Pages with Tables

1. Create a new blank Web page document and save it as **BSDHOME** with the Web page title **Blue Sky Dairy Home Page**.

2. Type and format the document shown in Illustration B.
   a. Create a table with one row and one column.
   b. Enter the text **Welcome to Blue Sky Dairy Online**.
   c. Format the text as Heading 1, then center it horizontally and vertically.
   d. Change the font color to white and the cell fill color to black.
   e. If necessary, size the cell to approximately 9" wide by .5" high.
   f. Leave a blank line and then create another table, three rows by three columns.

g. Using the normal style, type the text as shown in Illustration A on page 329.

h. Format the text as white font on black fill.

i. Fill the cells that do not contain text with white.

j. If necessary, size the columns to 3" wide. The row height should adjust automatically, but if necessary you can set the height for row 1 to be at least .25" and rows 2 and 3 to be at least 1.5".

k. Apply a Sky Blue background to the page. The document should look similar to illustration B.

3. Check the spelling and grammar in the document.

4. Save the changes and close the document.

5. Create a new blank Web page document and save it as **BSDSTORE** with the Web page title **Online Store**.

6. Type and format the document shown in Illustration C.
   a. On the first line of the document, type the text **Blue Sky Dairy Online Store**.
   b. Format the text in the Heading 1 style, then center it on the page.
   c. Leave a blank line and then insert a table with eleven rows and three columns.
   d. Merge the cells in the first row.
   e. Type the text **Online Merchandise Specials** in the first row, formatted with Heading 1 and centered horizontally.

    f.  Type the text as shown in row 2, formatted as Heading 2 and centered horizontally.

    g.  Type the remaining text in 16-point Times New Roman. Columns 1 and 2 should be flush left and column 3 should be flush right.

    h.  Apply fill colors as shown, including white.

    i.  Apply a 1½ pt. solid white line border around and between all cells.

    j.  Apply a 1½ pt. solid black line border across the bottom of row 1.

    k.  Center the table horizontally on the page.

    l.  Apply a Sky Blue background to the page.

7.  Check the spelling and grammar in the document.

8.  Save the changes and close the document.

9.  Create a new blank Web Page document.

10.  Save the document as **BSDHEADER** with no Web page title.

11.  Create a table as follows:

    a.  Create the table with four columns and one row.

    b.  In cell 1, type **HOME,** in bold, centered horizontally and vertically.

    c.  In cell 2, type **CONTEST INFORMATION,** in bold, centered horizontally and vertically.

    d.  In cell 3, type **ONLINE STORE,** in bold, centered horizontally and vertically

    e.  In cell 4, type **ABOUT HOLSTEINS,** in bold, centered horizontally and vertically.

    f.  Center the table on the page horizontally.

    g.  Apply a Sky Blue background.

    h.  Apply a white 1½ pt. border around and between all cells in the table.

12.  Save and close the document.

13.  Create a new blank Web page and save it as **BSDSTART**.

14.  In 24-point Arial Black, centered, type **Click Here to Enter the Wonderful World of Blue Sky Dairy!**

15.  Apply a Sky Blue Background.

16.  Save and close the document.

## Create a Frames Page

1.  Create a new blank Web page and save it as **BSDFRAMES**.

2.  Create a Frames page.

3.  Create a Frame Above.

4.  In the lower frame, set the initial page to **BSDSTART**.

5.  Name the frame **Start Frame**.

6.  In the upper frame, set the initial page to **BSDHEADER**.

7.  Name the frame **Header Frame**.

8.  Size the frame to 20%.

9.  Save the changes to the **BSDFRAMES** document.

## Set Hyperlink Targets

1.  With the **BSDFRAMES** page open, insert a hyperlink from the text in the lower frame to the **BSDHOME** page; set the Target Frame to the **Start Frame**.

2.  Insert a hyperlink from the text **HOME** in the upper frame to the **BSDHOME** document.

3.  Set the Target Frame to **Start Frame**, and make it the default for all hyperlinks on the page.

    ✓  *Once you set the default, you do not have to set the target frame for other hyperlinks on the page.*

4.  Insert a hyperlink from the text **CONTEST INFORMATION** to the document **BSDCONTEST**.

5.  Insert a hyperlink from the text **ONLINE STORE** to the document **BSDSTORE**.

6.  Insert a hyperlink from the text **ABOUT HOLSTEINS** to the document **BSDHOLSTEINS**.

7.  Save the document and then close it.

8.  Open the document in your Web browser. It should look similar to Illustration D.

9.  Test the links.

10.  Close your browser.

11.  Close all open documents, saving all changes.

*Illustration A*

| | | |
|---|---|---|
| | Welcome to Blue Sky Dairy Online | |
| | Use the Links Above to Explore this Site | |
| Blue Sky Dairy has been producing quality milk, ice cream, and other dairy products for over 100 years. It is a family-owned farm located in southern Wisconsin, not far from Lake Ripley. | | In the late 19th century, John and Marie Thomson settled in Wisconsin and started Blue Sky dairy with a herd of ten cows. Today, Jack and Kimberly Thomson have a thriving business anchored by a herd of 200 pampered Holstein dairy cows. |
| | Blue Sky Dairy is famous for its wholesome, refreshing ice cream products, including prepackaged ice cream and novelties. It sells ice cream direct from its farm stand, and also distributes its products to supermarkets and specialty stores throughout the United States. Blue Sky Dairy has won numerous awards for its ice cream and for its environmentally friendly policies. | |

*Illustration B*

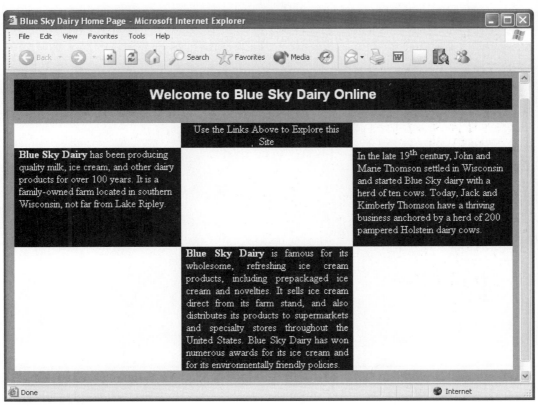

*Illustration C*

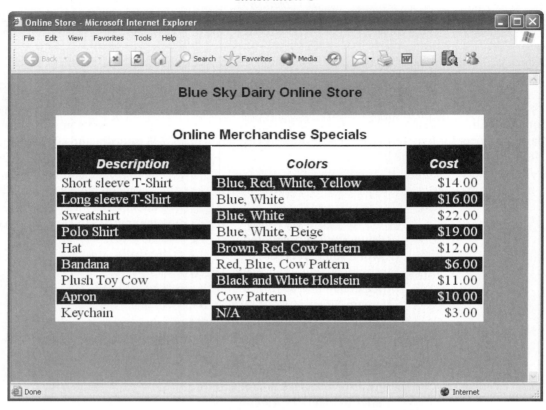

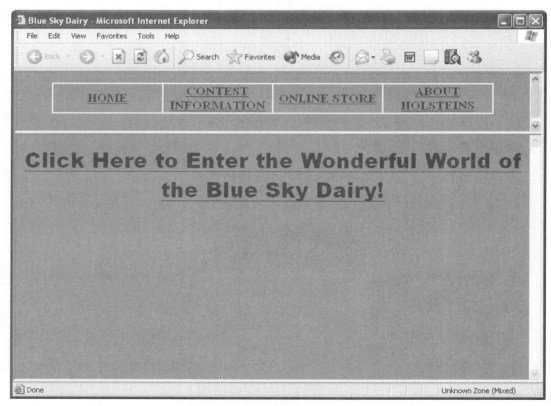

# On Your Own

1. Plan a Web site about yourself. For example, would you want to use a table of contents, a site map, or a header? Would you use tables to organize and lay out information on the page? Consider whether you have created any documents in other On Your Own exercises that you could link to your Web site. For example, you might want to link a resume and a class schedule to a start page.

2. When you are ready, start Word.

3. Create a frames page as follows:

   a. Create a new blank Web page and save it as **OWD63-1**.

   b. Design a start page to use for your Web site.

   c. Save and close the document.

   d. Create a new blank Web page and save it as **OWD63-2**.

   e. Using a table, design a page that provides links to the other documents you plan to use. For example, in each cell type text that can be used as a hyperlink to another page.

4. Save and close the document.

5. Create a new blank Web page and save it as **OWD63-3**.

6. Create a frames page and insert at least one frame.

7. Make the initial page for one frame the **OWD63-1** start page and make the initial page for another frame the **OWD63-2** links page.

8. Save the document.

9. Locate, open, and save as single file Web pages at least three existing documents you want to link to **OWD63-3**. For example, open **OWD62**, the Personal Web page you created in Exercise 62 and save it as **OWD63-4**, open the **OWD30-2**, the resume you created in Exercise 30 and save it as **OWD63-5**, and open **OWD40**, the class schedule you created in Exercise 40, and save it as **OWD63-6**. Alternatively, use the files provided: ⊙ **63WEB**, ⊙ **63RESUME**, and ⊙ **63SCHEDULE**.

   ✓ *If you use your own solution files, you may save each document as a Web page or as regular Word document. Also, if the files contain hyperlinks, remove them before linking the documents to the frames page.*

10. Format and edit the documents as desired. For example, apply a background or theme, and change the page title.

11. Close each document once you have named them and saved them.

12. Insert hyperlinks to link the **OWD63-3** frame page to the other documents. Set the target frames as necessary.

13. Save and close the page.

14. Open **OWD63-3** in your Web browser.

15. Test the links.

16. Close your browser.

17. Close all open documents, saving all changes, and exit Word.

# Exercise 64

### ◆ Critical Thinking

You have been hired by StyleEyes, Inc. to develop a Web site. The company is particularly interested in how other company's handle customer satisfaction regarding online sales. In this exercise, you will browse the Internet looking at customer satisfaction policies on existing Web sites. So that you can review the information offline, you will save one page locally and copy data from another page into a Word document. You will create and format new Web page documents, and save existing documents in Web page format. Finally, you will create a frames page to which you link the other Web pages.

## Exercise Directions

✓ *You will need Internet access to complete the first part of this exercise.*

### Locate Information on the Internet

1. Start Word, if necessary.
2. Create a new blank document and save it as **RETURN**.
3. Display the Web Toolbar.
4. In the Address line type the following and press Enter: **google.com**
5. Type **eyewear** in the search box and click Google Search.
6. Scroll down the page and note the links.
7. Go back to Word.
8. Go to the URL www.eyewear.com.
9. Click the Price Guarantee link.
   ✓ *The available links may be different. If these links are no longer available, explore the site on your own.*
10. Save the page locally in Web Archive format with the name **GUARANTEE**.
11. Click the Return Policy link.
12. Select the first two paragraphs under the heading **Return Policy** and copy them to the Clipboard.
13. Switch back to Word and paste the selection into the **RETURN** Word document.
14. Save and close the document.
15. Switch back to the eyewear.com Web site.
16. Close Internet Explorer.

### Save Word Documents in Web Page Format

1. Open the file ⌨**DIRECTORY** that you last used in Exercise 48, or open 💿**64DIRECTORY**.
2. Save the file as a single file Web page with the name **DOCTORS** and the Web page title **StyleEyes Directory of Doctors**.
3. Apply the Recycled Paper background texture to the document.
4. On a new blank line at the bottom of the document, type the text **RETURN TO START PAGE**.
5. Save and close the document.
6. Open the file ⌨**FINALPRESS** that you last used in Exercise 33, or open 💿**64FINALPRESS**.
7. Save the file as a single file Web page with the name **INTHENEWS** and the Web page title **StyleEyes In the News**.
8. Replace the sample text **Your Name** with your own name.
9. Apply the Recycled Paper background texture to the document.
10. On a new blank line at the bottom of the document, type the text **RETURN TO START PAGE**.
11. Save and close the document.
12. Open the file ⌨**SALE2** that you last used in Exercise 39, or open 💿**64SALE**.

13. Save the file as a single file Web page with the name **SPECIALS** and the Web page title **StyleEyes Online Specials**.

    ✓ *If Word displays a message about changing formatting settings, click Continue.*

14. Apply the Recycled Paper background texture to the document.

15. On a new blank line at the bottom of the document, type the text **RETURN TO START PAGE**.

16. Save and close the document.

## Create New Web Page Documents

1. Create a new Web page document in Word.

2. Save the file as **EYESPAGE** with the page title **StyleEyes Home Page**.

3. Apply the Quadrant theme to the document.

4. Insert a table with three columns and four rows, and center it horizontally on the page.

5. Merge the cells in row 1.

6. Type and format the document shown in Illustration A.

7. Check the spelling and grammar in the document.

8. Display the file in Web Page Preview. It should look similar to the one in the illustration.

9. Close Web Page Preview and close the **EYESPAGE** document.

10. Create a new blank Web Page document.

11. Save the document as **EYESMAP** with no Web page title.

12. Apply the Quadrant theme.

13. Create a table as follows (refer to the left frame in illustration B to see the result. Keep in mind that the hyperlinked text in the illustration has been clicked, so it may be displayed in a different color.):

    a. Create the table with one column and seven rows.

    b. Size the column to approximately 2.5" wide.

    c. In row 1, type **HOME**.

    d. Leave row 2 blank.

    e. In row 3, type **DIRECTORY OF DOCTORS**.

    f. Leave row 4 blank.

    g. In row 5, type **SPECIALS**.

    h. Leave row 6 blank.

    i. In row 7, type **IN THE NEWS**.

    j. Apply bold, 14 point formatting to the text.

    k. Apply the default bullet to the text.

    l. Remove all border lines in the table.

14. Save and close the document.

15. Create a new blank Web page and save it as **EYESSTART**.

16. Apply the Quadrant theme to the document.

17. In Heading 1 style, centered, type **Click Here to Enter the StyleEyes of Chicago Web Site.**

18. Save and close the document.

## Create the Frames Page

1. Create a new blank Web page and save it as **EYESFRAMES**.

2. Create a Frames page.

3. Create a new frame on the left.

4. In the right frame, set the initial page to **EYESSTART**.

5. Name the frame **Start Frame**.

6. In the left frame, set the initial page to **EYESMAP**.

7. Name the frame **Map Frame**.

8. Size the frame to 20%.

9. Save the changes to the **EYESFRAMES** document.

## Insert Hyperlinks

1. With the **EYESFRAMES** page open, insert a hyperlink from the text in the right frame to the **EYESPAGE** page; set the Target Frame to the **Start Frame**.

2. Insert a hyperlink from the text **HOME** in the left frame to the **EYESPAGE** document.

3. Set the Target Frame to **Start Frame**, and make it the default for all hyperlinks on the page.

    ✓ *Once you set the default, you do not have to set the target frame for other hyperlinks on the page.*

4. Insert a hyperlink from the text **DIRECTORY OF DOCTORS** to the document **DOCTORS**.

5. Insert a hyperlink from the text **SPECIALS** to the document **SPECIALS**.

6. Insert a hyperlink from the text **IN THE NEWS** to the document **INTHENEWS**.

7. Save the document.

8. Insert a hyperlink from the text **RETURN TO START PAGE** on the **DOCTORS**, **SPECIALS**, **INTHENEWS**, and **EYESPAGE** pages to the **EYESSTART** document, with the Start Frame as the target.

9. Display the **EYESFRAMES** document in Web Page Preview.

10. It should look similar to Illustration B.

11. Test all links.

12. Close Web Page Preview.

13. Close all open documents, saving all changes, and exit Word.

*Illustration A*

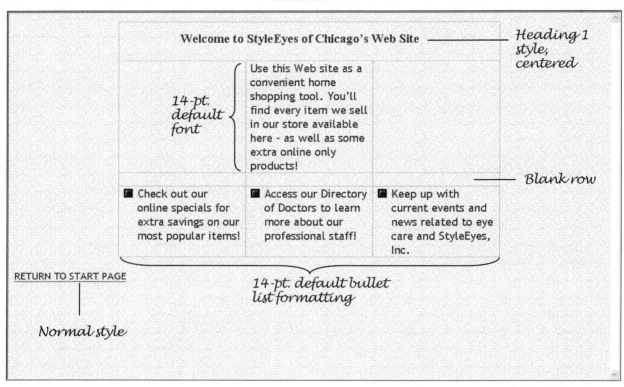

*Illustration B*

# Lesson 11

## Collaboration

# Exercise 65

◆ **Insert Comments** ◆ **Track Changes** ◆ **Customize Revision Marks**
◆ **Compare and Merge Documents** ◆ **Accept/Reject Changes**

## On the Job

Insert comments in a document when you want to include a private note to the author, another reader, or to yourself, in much the same way you might attach a slip of paper to a hard copy print out. Track changes made to a document to monitor when and how edits are made. Tracking changes lets you consider revisions before incorporating them into a document. If you agree with the change, you can accept it, but if you disagree with the change you can reject it. You can track changes made by one person, or by many people, which is useful when you are collaborating on a document with others. When you compare and merge documents, differences between the two are marked like revisions.

The owner of Liberty Blooms has asked you to revise a document listing seminars and classes. In this exercise, you will use the Track Changes feature while you edit the document and insert comments. You will then review the document to accept or reject the changes. Finally, you will compare the document to an earlier version. When you are satisfied with the document you will print it.

## Terms

**Comment** A note attached to a document for reference.

**Comment balloon** An area in the right margin in which comment text is displayed.

**Reviewing pane** A window where revisions and comments are displayed.

**Comment mark** Color-coded brackets that mark the location in the document where a comment was inserted. In Normal view, the reviewer's initials and a number are also displayed.

**Revision marks** Formatting applied to text in a document to identify where insertions, deletions, and formatting changes have been made.

**Revision balloon** An area in the right margin in which revisions are displayed.

**Ink annotations** Comments, notes, and other marks added to a document using a tablet PC or other type of pen device.

## Notes

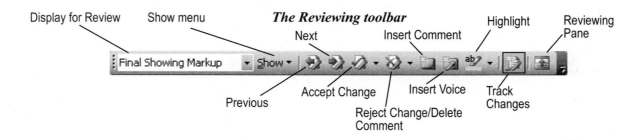

*The Reviewing toolbar*

Display for Review — Show menu — Next — Insert Comment — Highlight — Reviewing Pane

Final Showing Markup — Show

Previous — Accept Change — Reject Change/Delete Comment — Insert Voice — Track Changes

## Insert Comments

- Insert **comments** to annotate text, communicate with readers, or to attach reminders or questions.

- By default, in Print Layout and Web Layout views you can type and edit comments in either the **comment balloon** or in the **Reviewing pane**. In Normal view, you must use the Reviewing pane, and in Reading Layout view you must use the comment balloon.

- When you create a comment, Word inserts **comment marks** around the word to the left of the current insertion point location, or around selected text.

- In Print Layout, Reading Layout, and Web Layout views, the mark is connected to the comment balloon by a dashed line.

- The comment balloons are displayed in the page margin; Word automatically adjusts the appearance of the margin width and the document text on-screen to accommodate the balloons.

- In the Reviewing pane, comments are organized according to where they occur in the document. For example, they may be listed under Main Document, or Header and Footer.

- Both the comment marks and comment balloons are color coded by reviewer.

- You can choose to hide or show comments on-screen.

- Comments can be printed with a document.

### A comment in Print Layout view

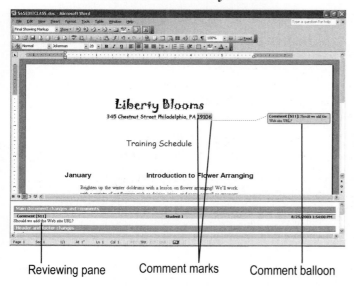

Reviewing pane    Comment marks    Comment balloon

## Track Changes

- Turn on Word's Track Changes feature to apply **revision marks** to all insertions, deletions, and formatting changes in a document.

- When Track Changes is active, the TRK button on the status bar is bold and Word applies revision marks as you edit a document.

- The way that revisions are marked on-screen depends on the current view and on the selected Display for Review option:

  - Final Showing Markup (default). This option displays inserted text in color with an underline, and all formatting changes are applied. In Print Layout and Web Layout views deleted text is moved into a **revision balloon**; while in Normal view, deleted text is marked in color with a strikethrough effect.

  - Final. In all views, this option displays the document as it would look if all of the revisions that had been entered were incorporated in the document.

  - Original Showing Markup. This option displays deleted text in color with a strikethrough effect. In Print Layout and Web Layout views inserted text and formatting are displayed in a revision balloon, while in Normal view inserted text is marked in color with an underline.

  - Original. In all views, this option displays the document as it would look if no revisions had been made.

- Like comments, revisions are color coded by reviewer.

- By default, Word also inserts a vertical line to the left of any changed line to indicate where revisions occur in the document.

- In any view, you can view descriptions of all revisions in the Reviewing pane.

- You can select which changes you want displayed on-screen. For example, you can display insertions and deletions, but not formatting.

- You can even set Word to show only the changes made by one reviewer at a time.

  ✓ *Word 2003 also supports the use of **ink annotations**.*

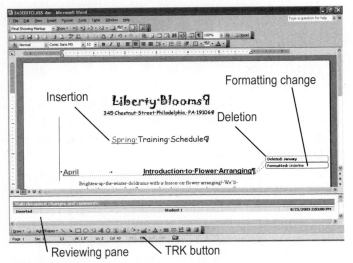

*Tracking changes in Normal view*

Insertion — Liberty Blooms¶
345 Chestnut Street Philadelphia, PA 19106¶

Formatting change

Spring Training Schedule¶

Deletion

Deleted: January
Formatted: Underline

·April → **Introduction to Flower Arranging**¶

Brighten up the winter doldrums with a lesson on flower arranging! We'll

Main document changes and comments
Inserted                              Student 1                    8/25/2003 2:03:00 PM

Reviewing pane          TRK button

## Customize Revision Marks

- You can customize revision marks in the Track Changes dialog box as follows:
  - You can select the color you want to use.
  - You can select the formatting used to indicate changes. For example, you can mark formatting changes with a double-underline, or insertions with color only instead of color and an underline.
  - You can customize the location of the vertical bar used to mark lines that have been changed.
  - You can also customize the way balloons are displayed in a document.

## Compare and Merge Documents

- You can compare two or more documents to mark the differences between them.
- When you compare documents, Word uses revision marks to indicate where text has been inserted, deleted, or formatted.
- Comparing and merging documents is useful if you have more than one version of a document and need to see what changes have been made, if more than one person has edited a document, or if someone has edited a document without using the track changes features.
- You can merge the documents into the original document, the current document, or into a new document.

## Accept/Reject Changes

- Revision marks remain stored as part of a document until the changes are either accepted or rejected.
- To incorporate edits into a document file, accept the changes.
- To cancel the edits and erase them from the file, reject the changes.
- You can also reject comments to delete them from the file.

*Track Changes dialog box*

# Procedures

## Display Reviewing Toolbar

1. Click **View**.................... `Alt`+`V`
2. Select **Toolbars**.................. `T`
   OR
   Right-click any toolbar.
3. Click **Reviewing**.

## Display Reviewing Pane

- Click **Reviewing Pane** button `▣` on Reviewing toolbar.

OR

1. Click **Show**
   drop-down arrow.......... `Alt`+`S`
   on Reviewing toolbar.
2. Click **Reviewing Pane**......... `P`
   ✓ *Repeat steps to hide reviewing pane.*

OR

1. Right-click **TRK** button `TRK` on Status bar.
2. Click **Reviewing Pane** button `▣`.

## Show/Hide Balloons

1. Click **Show**
   drop-down arrow.......... `Alt`+`S`
   on Reviewing toolbar.
2. Click **Balloons** .................... `B`
3. Click desired option:
   - **Always** ......................... `A`
   - **Never**............................. `N`
   - **Only for Comments/ Formatting**.................. `O`

   ✓ *A check mark next to option indicates it is already selected.*

## Insert a Comment
*(Alt + Ctrl + M)*

1. Position insertion point where you want to insert comment.
   OR
   Select text to comment on.
2. Click **New Comment** button `▣` on Reviewing toolbar.

OR

a. Click **Insert**............ `Alt`+`I`
b. Click **Comment**.............. `M`
3. Type comment text.
   ✓ *Click back in the document to continue working.*

## Edit a Comment

1. Click in comment balloon.
   OR
   a. Display Reviewing pane.
   b. Scroll up or down to locate comment.
   OR
   a. Right-click commented text.
   b. Click **Edit Comment** ...... `E`
2. Edit comment text.

## Delete a Comment

1. Right-click comment balloon.
   OR
   Right-click or commented text.
   OR
   Right-click comment in Reviewing pane.
2. Click **Delete Comment** ....... `M`

OR

1. Click anywhere in comment text.
2. Click **Reject Change/Delete Comment** drop-down arrow `⊗ ▾` on the Reviewing toolbar.
3. Click **Reject Change/Delete Comment**.......................... `R`

## Turn Track Changes On or Off
*(Ctrl+Shift+E)*

- Double-click **TRK** button `TRK` on Status bar to toggle feature on and off.

OR

- Click **Track Changes** button `▣` on Reviewing toolbar.

OR

1. Right-click **TRK** button `TRK` on Status bar.

2. Click **Track Changes** button `▣`.

OR

1. Click **Tools**................. `Alt`+`T`
2. Click **Track Changes**.......... `T`
   ✓ *Repeat steps to turn feature off.*

## Select a Display for Review

1. Click **Display for Review** drop-down arrow on Reviewing toolbar.
2. Click desired option: ...................... `↓`, `Enter`
   - **Final Showing Markup**
   - **Final**
   - **Original Showing Markup**
   - **Original**

## Compare and Merge Documents

1. Open edited document.
2. Click **Tools**................. `Alt`+`T`
3. Click **Compare and Merge Documents**.................... `D`
4. Locate and select original document.
5. Click **Merge** button drop-down arrow
   `Merge ▾` ............ `Alt`+`M`
6. Click desired option:
   - **Merge** .......................... `M`
     to merge changes into original document.
   - **Merge into current document**.................. `C`
     to merge changes into document opened in step 1.
   - **Merge into new document**.................... `N`
     to merge changes into a new document.

## Print Comments and Revisions *(Ctrl + P)*

1. Click **File** .................. `Alt`+`F`
2. Click **Print**......................... `P`

3. Click **Print what**
   drop-down arrow ......... `Alt`+`W`
4. Click **Document showing markup** to print comment and revision balloons with the document
   - ✓ *If you select this option, the size of the printed document is reduced in order to accommodate the balloons on the page.*

   OR

   Click **List of markup** to print a list of comments and revisions separately.
5. Click **OK** ........................... `Enter`

## Select Revision Display Options

1. Click **Show** drop-down arrow on Reviewing toolbar .. `Alt`+`S`
2. Select Desired option:
   - **Comments** ................... `C`
   - **Ink Annotations** ........... `T`
   - **Insertions and Deletions** ...................... `I`
   - **Formatting** ................... `F`
   - ✓ *Repeat to select additional options.*

### To select which reviewers' marks to display:

1. Click **Show** drop-down arrow on Reviewing toolbar .. `Alt`+`S`
2. Select **Reviewers** ............... `R`
3. Click **All Reviewers** ........... `A` to display marks for all reviewers.

   OR

   Click desired reviewer name.
   - ✓ *Repeat to select additional reviewers.*

## Customize Revision Marks

1. Click **Show** drop-down arrow on Reviewing toolbar ... `Alt`+`S`

   OR

   Right-click **TRK** button `TRK` on Status bar.
2. Click **Options** ...................... `O`

   OR

   a. Click **Tools** ............. `Alt`+`T`
   b. Click **Options** ................. `O`
   c. Click **Track Changes** tab ...................... `Ctrl`+`Tab`
3. Select options as desired.
4. Click **OK** ......................... `Enter`

## Accept/Reject Changes One by One

1. Right-click revision in document.

   OR

   Right-click revision in balloon.
2. Click **Accept Insertion** (or **Deletion**) ........................ `E`

   OR

   Click **Reject Insertion** (or **Deletion**) ........................ `R`

   OR

1. Click **Next** button ▶ on Reviewing toolbar to browse forward from insertion point.

   OR

   Click **Previous** button ◀ to browse back from insertion point.
2. Click **Accept Change** button 🖊 to incorporate highlighted change into document.

   OR

   Click **Reject Change** button 🗑 to delete highlighted change from document.

## Accept Changes All At Once

1. Click **Accept Change** drop-down arrow 🖊▾ on Reviewing toolbar
2. Click **Accept All Changes Shown** ................................ `S`

   OR

   Click **Accept All Changes in Document** ...................... `H`

## Reject Changes All At Once

1. Click **Reject Change/Delete Comment** drop-down arrow 🗑▾ on Reviewing toolbar
2. Click **Reject All Changes Shown** ................................ `S`

   OR

   Click **Reject All Changes in Document** ...................... `H`

# Exercise Directions

1. Start Word, if necessary.
2. Open ✆ **65EDITCLASS**.

   ✓ *This is a version of the course list document you worked with earlier in this book.*

3. Save the file as **EDITCLASS**.
4. Insert the comment shown in Illustration A.
5. Turn on the Track Changes feature.
6. Make sure Word is set to display comments, insertions, deletions, and formatting changes.
7. Customize the marks to show formatting changes with a double-underline and set the Changed lines color to red.
8. Switch to Normal view.
9. Make the insertions, deletions, and formatting changes shown in Illustration A.
10. Switch to Print Layout view.
11. Display the document as Final.
12. Display the document as Original Showing Markup.
13. Display the document as Final Showing Markup.
14. Print the document with the comments and changes.
15. Save the document.
16. Save a copy of the document as **EDITCLASS2**.
17. In the **EDITCLASS2** document, delete the comment.
18. Accept the insertion of the word **Spring**.
19. Accept the changes—both insertions and deletions—to the names of the months.
20. Reject all formatting changes.
21. Accept all editing changes to the last paragraph in the document.
22. Turn off the Track Changes feature.
23. Save the changes.
24. Compare the document to the original ✆ **65EDITCLASS**, merging the changes into the current document.
25. Accept all changes.
26. Check the spelling and grammar in the document.
27. Print the document.
28. Close the document, saving all changes.

# Liberty Blooms

## 345 Chestnut Street Philadelphia, PA 19106

*Insert comment: Should we add the Web site URL?*

*Spring*

# Training Schedule

*April*
### January

*Underline*
## Introduction to Flower Arranging

Brighten up the winter doldrums with a lesson on flower arranging! We'll work with a variety of cut flowers such as daisies, irises, and roses as well as greenery and accent stems to create beautiful bouquets. This entry-level class is open to everyone.

*May*
### February

*Underline*
## All About Herbs

Get ready for spring with a fun-filled class all about herbs! We'll learn about the types of herbs that are easy to grow indoors and out, how to identify herbs by appearance and smell, and how to use fresh and dried herbs in a variety of ways. For example, we might use herbs to scent a sachet, or to flavor a pot of stew.

*June*
### March

*Underline*
## Perennial Garden Design

A successful perennial garden enhances blooms all season long, year after year. This seminar will cover the basics of planning a perennial garden. Learn how to determine the amount of space you need, how to lay out the garden, and how to select the right types of plants. Time permitting, we will discuss soil composition and planting techniques.

*Due to limited space,*

Classes are free and open to the public. However, due to the limited space at Liberty Blooms we must restrict all class sizes. To register, or for more information about these and other events at Liberty Blooms, call 215-555-2837 or visit our Web site www.libertyblooms.net.

*Bold, italic.*

# On Your Own

1. Open **OWD28**, the one page autobiography you worked on earlier, or open ⊙ **65BIO**.

2. Save the document as **OWD65-1**.

3. Turn on the Track Changes feature.

4. Read the document carefully and critically, inserting comments and making revisions to improve the writing and formatting.

5. Save the document.

6. Exchange files with a classmate.

7. Customize revision marks.

8. Insert comments and make editing suggestions for improving the writing and formatting in your classmate's document.

   ✓ *Remember to use constructive criticism that shows respect for your classmate.*

9. Save the changes.

10. Print the document with comments and revision marks.

11. When you are both ready, exchange files to get your own back.

12. Save the document as **OWD65-2**.

13. Review your classmate's comments and suggestions and accept or reject them as necessary.

14. Review the comments and suggestions you made yourself and accept or reject them as necessary.

15. Proofread the entire document again.

16. Check the spelling and grammar.

17. When you are satisfied with the document, print it.

18. Close the document, saving all changes, and exit Word.

# Exercise 66

## On the Job

Word includes tools that make it easy to collaborate with others to create and generate documents. You can protect documents that you do not want others to change—and you can add digital signatures to verify the authenticity of a document. You can create multiple versions of a document so you know which one is the most up-to-date.

The Manager of Corporate Communications at Long Shot, Inc. wants her staff to collaborate on a new version of the company's mission statement. As the team leader for this project, she has asked you to create the first new version of the mission statement, which other members can then revise. In this exercise, you will first create a one-page report drafting the new mission statement. You will protect the document so that all changes are tracked with revision marks, and you will save multiple versions of the document. When the document is complete, you will authenticate it by attaching your own digital signature.

## Terms

**Version** An archived snapshot of a document saved in the same file as the original document.

**Workgroup** A group of individuals who work together on the same projects, usually connected via a network.

**Digital signature** An electronic, encryption-based, secure stamp of authentication on a macro or document.

**Digital certificate** An attachment for a file, macro project, or e-mail message that vouches for its authenticity, provides secure encryption, or supplies a verifiable signature.

## Notes

### Create Multiple Versions of a Document

- Save a **version** of a file when you want to keep track of documents passed around to multiple users.

- You can manually save a version of a document at any time, or you can set Word to automatically save a version every time a document is closed.

- Saving a version creates an archive of the document, not a copy.

- Word automatically marks each version with the name of the person who saves it, the date the version was last saved, and the time the version was saved.

- You can save multiple versions of a document; all saved versions are stored in one file.

- Add comments to a saved version to help identify it. For example, you can identify an original version, a version that has been edited by someone, or a version that incorporates changes.

*Word displays a list of all versions
saved with a document*

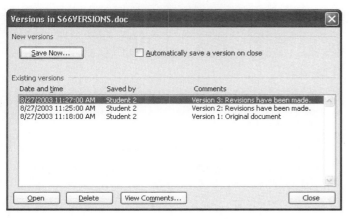

- When you display a list of saved versions, you can select to view the comments.

- You can open a saved version in a split-screen with the original file to compare the two.

- If you want to edit a saved version, you must use the Save As command to save the version as a separate file.

- When there are multiple versions of a file, Word displays the Versions icon 🖼 on the Status bar.

## Protect a Document

- Use the Protect Document task pane to protect a document from formatting changes and from editing changes.

- To protect formatting, you limit the ability of others to modify selected styles and apply direct formatting.

- When you open a protected document, the Protect Document task pane displays information about the changes you may or may not make to the document.

- To protect a document from editing changes, you may select from four options:
  - Tracked Changes. Use this option to automatically display changes to a document with revision marks.

✓ *Tracking changes is covered in Exercise 65.*

  - Comments. Use this option to allow **workgroup** members to enter comments without being able to edit document text.

✓ *Using comments is covered in Exercise 65.*

  - Filling in Forms. Use this option to allow changes in form fields only.

✓ *Forms and form fields are covered in Exercise 76.*

  - No changes (Read only). Use this option when you do not want to allow any changes at all.

*Protect Document task pane*

## Set Protection Exceptions

- By default, an entire document is protected from changes made by all users.

- If you set formatting, read only, or comments protection, you may specify exceptions by allowing some people or groups access to all or parts of the document.

- In order to allow access to parts of a document, the document must be divided into sections.

- To add a person to the exceptions list, you must know his or her e-mail address or Microsoft Windows user account name.

## Apply Password Protection

- To ensure that users cannot remove or change document protection, you can assign password protection. Only someone who enters the assigned password can change the document protection settings.

- You may also be able to select to encrypt the document so that only authenticated owners of the document can remove protection. Authenticity is based on use of a valid digital signature.

- You may also assign a password to restrict access to opening a file.

*The Start Enforcing Protection dialog box*

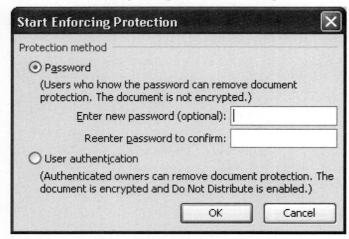

## Use Digital Signatures

- You can add a **digital signature** to a Word file in order to confirm the authenticity of the file.

- Word will not save changes to a file that has a digital signature, thereby insuring that the file has not been edited since the author attached the signature.

- If you try to save changes to a file that has a digital signature, Word prompts you to remove the digital signature.

- The signature is created using a **digital certificate**, and it certifies that the file has not been altered.

- You obtain a digital certificate from an authorized vendor or from the internal security administrator responsible for the computer system that you use.

- A list of digital certificates attached to a document is displayed in the Digital Signature dialog box.

*The Digital Signature dialog box*

- You can also create a digital signature for yourself.

  ✓ *Self-made digital signatures are considered unauthenticated and may trigger a security warning on some computers.*

- The text *(Signed)* is displayed in the title bar of a document that has a digital signature attached. If the certificate is not authorized, the word *Unverified* is displayed as well.

- Also, when there is a digital signature attached to a document, Word displays the Digital Signatures icon 🔒 on the Status bar.

# Procedures

## Save a Version of a Document

1. Click **File** ..................... `Alt`+`F`
2. Click **Versions** ..................... `R`
3. Click **Save Now** button

   | Save Now... | .......... `Alt`+`S`
4. Type desired comments.
5. Click **OK** ................. `Tab`, `Enter`

OR

1. Click **File** ..................... `Alt`+`F`
2. Click **Save As** ..................... `A`
3. Click **Tools** drop-down

   arrow | Tools ▾ | ..... `Alt`+`L`
4. Click **Save Version** ............. `V`
5. Type comments as desired.
6. Click **OK** ..................... `Enter`

## Set Word to automatically save versions:

1. Click **File** ..................... `Alt`+`F`
2. Click **Versions** ..................... `R`
3. Click **Automatically save a version on close**

   check box ..................... `Alt`+`A`
4. Click **Close** button | Close | .

## Display a list of saved versions:

1. Click **File** ..................... `Alt`+`F`
2. Click **Versions** ..................... `R`

## Display comments for saved versions:

1. Click **File** ..................... `Alt`+`F`
2. Click **Versions** ..................... `R`
3. Select desired version .. `↑`, `↓`
4. Click **View Comments** button

   | View Comments... | ........ `Alt`+`M`

## Open a saved version:

1. Click **File** ..................... `Alt`+`F`
2. Click **Versions** ..................... `R`
3. Select desired version .. `↑`, `↓`
4. Click **Open** button

   | Open | ............... `Alt`+`O`

## Delete a saved version:

1. Click **File** ..................... `Alt`+`F`
2. Click **Versions** ..................... `R`
3. Select desired version .. `↑`, `↓`
4. Click **Delete** button

   | Delete | ............... `Alt`+`D`
5. Click **Yes** ..................... `Y`

## Protect a Document from Formatting Changes

1. Open the document to protect.
2. Click **Tools** ................. `Alt`+`T`
3. Click **Protect Document** ..... `P`
4. Click **Limit formatting to a selection of styles**

   check box ..................... `M`
5. Click the **Settings** link.
6. Deselect the check boxes beside the styles which you want to restrict.

   ✓ *Selected styles may be modified.*

   OR

   Click one of the following:

   - **All** ........................... `Alt`+`L`
     to select all styles.
   - **Recommended Minimum** .............. `Alt`+`R`
     to allow modification of only user defined styles.
   - **None** ..................... `Alt`+`N`
     to deselect all styles so that none may be modified.
7. Click **OK** .......................... `Enter`

   ✓ *If the document contains formatting that you have deselected, Word may ask if you want to remove them from the document. Click Yes to remove the formatting or click No to preserve the existing formatting.*
8. Click **Yes, Start Enforcing Protection**

   | Yes, Start Enforcing Protection | .
9. Click **OK** ......................... `Enter`

## Protect a Document from Editing Changes

1. Open the document to protect.
2. Click **Tools** ................. `Alt`+`T`
3. Click **Protect Document** .... `P`
4. Click **Allow only this type of editing in the document** check box.
5. Click editing restrictions options drop-down arrow.
6. Select one of the following:
   - **Tracked changes**
   - **Comments**
   - **Filling in Forms**
   - **No changes (Read only)**
7. Click **Yes, Start Enforcing Protection**

   | Yes, Start Enforcing Protection | .
8. Click **OK** ..................... `Enter`

## Set Protection Exceptions

1. Open the document to protect.
2. Click **Tools** ................. `Alt`+`T`
3. Click **Protect Document** .... `P`
4. Click **Allow only this type of editing in the document** check box.
5. Click editing restrictions options drop-down arrow.
6. Select one of the following:
   - **Comments**
   - **No changes (Read only)**
7. If necessary, select sections of the document which may be edited.
8. Click the check box beside each individual or group who may edit the selected sections.
9. Click **Yes, Start Enforcing Protection**

   | Yes, Start Enforcing Protection | .
10. Click **OK** ........................... `Enter`

## Add users to the Exceptions list:

1. Open the document to protect.
2. Click **Tools**.................. `Alt`+`T`
3. Click **Protect Document** .... `P`
4. Click **Allow only this type of editing in the document** check box.
5. Click editing restrictions options drop-down arrow.
6. Select one of the following:
   - **Comments**
   - **No changes (Read only)**
7. Click the **More users** link.
8. Type name(s) to add.
   - ✓ *You may type multiple names. Separate the names using semicolons.*
9. Click **OK**............................ `Enter`

## Add password protection:

1. Open the document to protect.
2. Click **Tools**.................. `Alt`+`T`
3. Click **Protect Document** .... `P`
4. Select desired type of protection.
5. Click **Yes, Start Enforcing Protection**
   
   `Yes, Start Enforcing Protection`
6. Click **Enter new password** text box ........................ `Alt`+`E`
7. Type password.
8. Click **Reenter password to confirm** text box ......... `Alt`+`P`
9. Click **OK**............................ `Enter`

**OR**

1. Open document to protect.
2. Click **Tools**.................. `Alt`+`T`
3. Click **Options**...................... `O`
4. Click the **Security** tab .............................. `Ctrl`+`Tab`

5. Click **Password to open** text box ........................ `Alt`+`O`
6. Type password required to open document.
7. Click **Password to modify** text box ........................ `Alt`+`M`
8. Type password required to modify document.
9. Click **OK** .......................... `Enter`

## Add encryption protection:

1. Open the document to protect.
2. Click **Tools** .................. `Alt`+`T`
3. Click **Protect Document** ..... `P`
4. Select desired type of protection.
5. Click **Yes, Start Enforcing Protection**
   
   `Yes, Start Enforcing Protection`
6. Click **User authentication** option button................ `Alt`+`I`
7. Click **OK** .......................... `Enter`

## Remove document protection:

1. Click **Tools** .................. `Alt`+`T`
2. Click **Unprotect Document** .......................... `P`
   - ✓ *If password protection has been applied, Word will prompt you to enter the correct password.*
3. Deselect protection options as necessary.

## Add a Digital Signature to a Document

1. Save document to certify.
2. Click **Tools**.................. `Alt`+`T`
3. Click **Options**...................... `O`
4. Click the **Security** tab .............................. `Ctrl`+`Tab`
5. Click the **Digital Signatures** button
   
   `Digital Signatures...` ..... `Alt`+`D`
6. Click **Add** button
   
   `Add...` .......... `Alt`+`A`
7. Select certificate to use.
8. Click **OK**............................ `Enter`
9. Click **OK**............................ `Enter`
10. Click **OK**............................ `Enter`

## Create Your Own Digital Certificate

1. Click **Start** button
   
   `start` ...............
2. Click **All Programs** ............. `P`
3. Select the **Microsoft Office** folder icon.
4. Select **Microsoft Office Tools**.
5. Click **Digital Certificate for VBA Projects**.
6. Type certificate name.
7. Click **OK**............................ `Enter`
   - ✓ *If the Digital Certificate for VBA Projects option is not available, it may not be installed on your system. Run Office setup to install it.*

# Exercise Directions

1. Start Word, if necessary.
2. Open the file ◉**66MISSION**.
3. Save the document as **VERSIONS**.
4. Save a version of the document with the comment: **Version 1: Original document**.
5. Set editing restrictions so that all changes will be displayed with revision marks.
6. Do not enter a password.
7. Make the following edits to the document (refer to Illustration A to see the end results):
   - On a new line at the beginning of the document insert the title **Long Shot, Inc. Mission Statement** in the Heading 1 style.
   - Insert a blank line, and then type the text **Customer Satisfaction** using the Heading 2 style.
   - Edit the first paragraph to read: **Long Shot, Inc. is committed to providing quality service to all of our clients at every level of our organization. Our ultimate goal is to hear our clients say, "Thank you. That is just what we wanted."**
   - Insert a blank line, and then type the text **Employee Well-Being** using the Heading 2 style.
   - Edit the second paragraph the read: **Second only to customer satisfaction is the happiness and well-being of our employees. The employees at Long Shot, Inc. are encouraged to set personal and professional goals. We respect all employees as individuals and believe that fostering a strong**

   - **community within the workplace strengthens our position in the marketplace.**
   - Insert a blank line, and then type the text **Conclusion** using the Heading 2 style.
   - Type the following: **At Long Shot, Inc. we vow to maintain the highest standards, pursue the extraordinary, and guarantee customer satisfaction. We are confident that our commitment to quality will make us leaders in our industry.**

8. Check the spelling and grammar in the document.
9. Save the changes.
10. Save another version of the document with the comment: **Version 2: Revisions have been made**.
11. Remove document protection.
12. Accept all changes to the document.
    ✓ *See Exercise 65 for information about accepting and rejecting revisions.*
13. Check the spelling and grammar in the document.
14. Save the changes.
15. Save another version of the document with the comment: **Version 3: Revisions have been made.**
16. Preview the document. It should look similar to the one in Illustration A.
17. Create your own digital certificate, using your own name.
18. Attach the digital certificate to the document as a digital signature.
19. Close the document.

# Long Shot, Inc. Mission Statement

## *Customer Satisfaction*

Long Shot, Inc. is committed to providing quality service to all of our clients at every level of our organization. Our ultimate goal is to hear our clients say, "Thank you. That is just what we wanted."

## *Employee Well-Being*

Second only to customer satisfaction is the happiness and well-being of our employees. The employees at Long Shot, Inc. are encouraged to set personal and professional goals. We respect all employees as individuals and believe that fostering a strong community within the workplace strengthens our position in the marketplace.

## *Conclusion*

At Long Shot, Inc. we vow to maintain the highest standards, pursue the extraordinary, and guarantee customer satisfaction. We are confident that our commitment to quality will make us leaders in our industry.

# On Your Own

1. Start Word and create a new document.

2. Save the document as **OWD66**.

3. Type three or four paragraphs describing a group, club, class, or organization to which you belong.

4. Check the spelling and save the changes.

5. Save a version of the file, identifying the version as the original document.

6. Protect the document so that only comments may be entered.

7. Exchange files with a classmate.

8. Read your classmate's document and insert at least two comments.

9. Save a version of the document, using your initials or name to identify that you worked on the version.

10. Protect the document to track changes.

11. Exchange files with another classmate.

12. Make editing and formatting changes to the document.

13. Save a third version of the document, again, using your initials or name to identify that you worked on the version.

14. Return the file to the original author. You should now have your original document back.

15. Review the different versions to see what changes your classmates made.

16. Remove all protection from the document.

17. Accept or reject the changes, and respond to the comments as necessary.

18. Save a final version of the document.

19. Attach your digital signature.

20. Close the document, and exit Word.

# Exercise 67

◆ **Create E-mail in Word**

◆ **Send a Word Document as E-mail**

◆ **Attach a Word Document to an E-mail Message**

◆ **Copy Data from a Word Document into an E-mail Message**

## On the Job

E-mail is suitable for jotting quick notes such as an appointment confirmation. You can create and format e-mail messages, then send the messages via Outlook directly from Word. When you need to communicate in more depth, you can attach a Word document to the message, or simply send a document as the message itself. You can exchange e-mail messages via the Internet or an intranet with anyone who has an e-mail account, including coworkers located down the hall, in a different state, or halfway around the world.

You have been compiling a list of employees willing to be judges for the Blue Sky Dairy Name that Flavor contest. In this exercise, you will use e-mail to communicate with the dairy owner about the contest. First, you will create and send an e-mail message into which you copy the list of judges. Then, you will send a message asking the dairy owner to review a memo you plan to distribute to the prospective judges.

## Terms

**Outlook** A personal information management program that includes e-mail features and that is included in the Microsoft Office 2003 suite.

**Outlook Express** An e-mail program that is included as part of the Microsoft Internet Explorer Web browser.

**E-mail (electronic mail)** A method of sending information from one computer to another across the Internet or intranet.

**Internet** A global network of computers.

**Intranet** A network of computers within a business or organization.

**Mail service provider** A company that maintains and controls e-mail accounts.

**Message header** Fields added to an e-mail message where you enter information such as the recipient's address.

**E-mail address** The string of characters that identifies the name and location of an e-mail user.

**To:** Mail notation that indicates to whom an e-mail message is addressed.

**Cc: (carbon copy)** Mail notation that indicates to whom you are sending a copy of the message.

**Subject** The title of an e-mail message.

**Introduction** The area in the message header of a Word document sent as e-mail, where a message may be typed.

**Attachment** A document attached to an e-mail message and sent in its original file format.

# Notes

## Create E-mail in Word

- If you use **Outlook** or **Outlook** Express as your default e-mail program, you can use Word to create **e-mail** messages.

- You can edit and format the messages with Word's editing and formatting features, including the spelling and grammar checkers, and AutoCorrect.

- To send e-mail messages you must have the following:
  - A connection to the **Internet** or to an **intranet**.
  - An account with a **mail service provider**.

- Every e-mail message has a **message header** that includes text boxes, or fields, for entering the following information:
  - The recipient's **e-mail address** is entered in the **To**: text box.
  - The addresses of other people receiving copies of the message are entered in the **Cc**: text box.
  - A title for the message is entered in the **Subject** text box.
  - There may also be a From: field that Word automatically fills with your e-mail address information.

- The body of the message is typed in the message window.

*E-mail in Word*

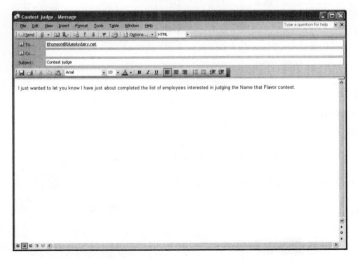

- By default, when you send the message from Word it is sent to the Outbox folder in Outlook. You must start Outlook and sign in to your mail service provider in order to transmit the message.

- The Internet connection remains online in the background until you disconnect.

## Send a Word Document as E-mail

- If you use Outlook as your default e-mail program, you can send an existing Word document as an e-mail message.

- The original document remains stored on your computer, and a copy is transmitted as e-mail.

- By default, the transmitted document is sent in HTML format so it retains its original formatting when opened in the recipient's e-mail application.

  ✓ *Using Outlook, you can select to send the document in plain text or rich text format.*

## Attach a Word Document to an E-mail Message

- You can attach a Word document to an e-mail message.

- The original document remains stored on your computer, and a copy is transmitted as the **attachment**.

- An attached document is sent in its original file format.

- The message recipient can open the attached Word document on his or her computer in Word, or in another application that is compatible with Word.

- You can also send a Word document as an attachment for review.

- When you send a document for review, Word creates a new message with the text "Please review *filename*" in the Subject text box in the message header, and the text "Please review the attached document." in the message body.

*Send a document as an attachment for review*

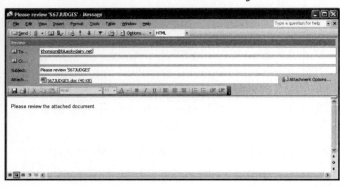

## Copy Data From a Word Document into an E-mail Message

■ If you don't want to send or attach an entire document, you can paste a selection from the document into the e-mail message.

■ Use the Copy and Paste commands to copy the data from the Word document and paste it into the e-mail message.

# Procedures

### Create E-mail Message in Word

1. Click **File**.................... 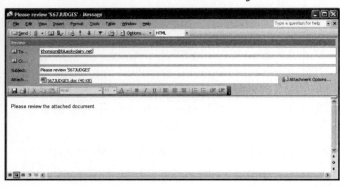Alt+F
2. Click **New**........................... N
3. Click **E-mail message** ✉ in the New Document task pane.

   ✓ *If E-mail message is not an option in the New Document task pane, Outlook is not installed, or is not set as your default e-mail program.*

4. Fill in **To:** information..........*type recipient's address*
5. Press **Tab**........................... Tab
6. Fill in **Cc:** information ..........*type additional recipients' addresses*
7. Press **Tab**........................... Tab
8. Fill in **Subject** information ......*type subject title*
9. Press **Tab**........................... Tab
10. Type and format message text.
11. Click **Send** button

    Send .......................... Alt+S

   ✓ *Log on to transmit the message as necessary.*

### Attach a Word Document to an E-mail Message

1. Compose an e-mail message.
2. Click **Insert File** button 📎.
3. Locate and select file to attach.
4. Click **Insert**.................. Alt+S

   ✓ *Word adds a new text box to the message heading called Attach: and enters the document name.*

5. Click **Send** button

   Send .......................... Alt+S

**OR**

1. Open or create the document to attach.
2. Click **File**.................... Alt+F
3. Highlight **Send To**............... D
4. Click **Mail Recipient (as Attachment)**................. A
5. Compose e-mail message.

   ✓ *By default, Word enters the document name in the Attach text box.*

6. Click **Send** button

   Send .......................... Alt+S

### Send a Word Document for Review

1. Open or create document to send.
2. Click **File**.................... Alt+F
3. Highlight **Send To**............... D
4. Click **Mail Recipient (for Review)**...................... C
5. Complete message header information.
6. Click **Send** button

   Send .......................... Alt+S

   ✓ *Log on to transmit the message as necessary.*

### Send a Word Document as E-mail

1. Open or create document to send.
2. Click **E-mail** button 🖼.

   **OR**

   a. Click **File**................ Alt+F
   b. Select **Send To**............. D
   c. Click **Mail Recipient**...... M

   ✓ *If the E-mail button and/or the Send To, Mail Recipient options are not available, Outlook is not installed, or is not set as your default e-mail program.*

3. Fill in **To**: information..........*type recipient's address*

4. Press **Tab** ........................... `Tab`

5. Fill in **Cc**: information .........*type additional recipients' addresses*

6. Press **Tab** ........................... `Tab`

7. Fill in **Subject** information ......*type subject title*

   ✓ *By default, Word enters the document name in the Subject text box. You can edit it if necessary.*

8. Press **Tab** ........................... `Tab`

9. Click **Send a Copy** button

   `📧 Send a Copy` .............. `Alt`+`S`

   ✓ *If you change your mind about sending the document as e-mail, simply click the **E-Mail** button* `🖨️` *again. Word removes the message heading and displays the document.*

## Copy Data from a Word Document into an E-mail Message

1. Compose an e-mail message.
2. Open Word document containing data to copy.
3. Select data to copy.
4. Click **Copy** button `📋`.

   **OR**

   a. Click **Edit**............... `Alt`+`E`
   b. Click **Copy** .................... `C`

   **OR**

   a. Right-click selected text.
   b. Click **Copy** .................... `C`

5. Display e-mail message and position insertion point in new location.
6. Click **Paste** button `📋`.

   **OR**

   a. Click **Edit**............... `Alt`+`E`
   b. Click **Paste**.................... `P`

   **OR**

   a. Right-click where you wish to insert text.
   b. Click **Paste**.................... `P`

## Send E-mail from Outlook

1. Click **Start** button

   `start` ................. `📇`

2. Click **All Programs**............. `P`
3. Select **Microsoft Office**.
4. **Click Microsoft Office Outlook 2003**.

   ✓ *Alternatively, you may use a shortcut icon to start Outlook from the desktop or taskbar. For more information about starting applications, refer to Exercise 87.*

   ✓ *Outlook may automatically connect to your mail service provider and download new messages. Enter account name and password if prompted.*

5. Click **Send/Receive** button

   `📧 Send/Receive` .......... `Alt`+`C`

   **OR**

   a. Click **Tools** ............ `Alt`+`T`
   b. Select **Send/Receive**..... `E`
   c. Click **Send/Receive All** . `A`

   ✓ *If not already online, Outlook will automatically connect to your mail service provider and send all messages. If prompted, enter your account name and password.*

## Disconnect Outlook from Internet

1. Click **File** .................... `Alt`+`F`
2. Click **Work Offline**.............. `W`
3. Click **Yes**............................. `Y`

# Exercise Directions

✓ *This exercise uses a fictitious e-mail address. If you try to send the messages, they will be returned as undeliverable. If directed by your teacher, use another student's address.*

1. Start Word, if necessary.
2. Open the document 💿 **67JUDGES**.
3. Save the document as **JUDGES**.
4. Compose an e-mail message as follows:
   a. Enter the address:
   **jthomson@blueskydairy.com**
   b. Skip the Cc box.
   c. Enter the subject: **Contest Judges**
   d. Using a 14-point serif font, such as Times New Roman, enter the message: **Here is the list of employees who have expressed an interest in judging the Name that Flavor contest. I am working on a memo to send out letting them know what they're in for. I'll send it to you for review as soon as it is complete.**
5. Press Enter twice, then copy the table from the document **JUDGES** and paste it on the last line of the e-mail message.
6. Check the spelling and grammar in the message (ignore all proper names). It should look similar to Illustration A.

7. Send the message, or save it and close it.
8. Open the document 💿 **67CONGRATS**.
9. Save the document as **CONGRATS**.
10. Replace the sample text **Your Name** with your own name, and the sample text **Today's date** with the correct date.
11. Insert the following at the end of the **CONGRATS** document:

    **We would like to hold our first judges meeting next week. At that time we will lay out a schedule and distribute assignments. The deadline for submissions is March 1, so that is when we will have a good idea of how long it will take to go through them all and select the winner. Thanks for your help.**
12. Check the spelling and grammar in the document.
13. Save the changes.
14. Prepare to send the **CONGRATS** document as e-mail for review to **jthomson@blueskydairy.com**.
15. Send the message, or save it and close it.
16. Close all open documents, saving all changes.

*Illustration A*

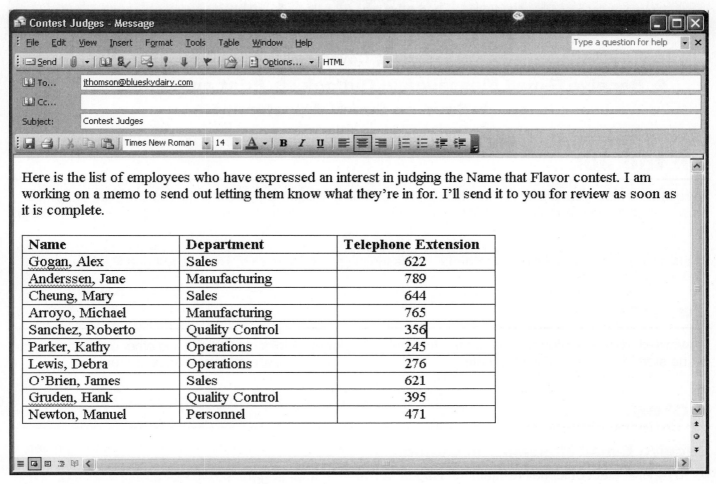

## On Your Own

1. Look up and record e-mail addresses for friends, coworkers, and companies.

2. Send an e-mail message to a friend or co-worker and ask him or her to send one back to you.

3. Create a new document and save it as **OWD67**.

4. Type a letter to someone else whose e-mail address you have. For example, type a letter to a teacher requesting a missed homework assignment, or to your employer.

5. Attach the document to an e-mail message and send it.

6. Check your e-mail to see if you received a reply.

7. When you are finished, close all open documents, and exit all open applications.

# Exercise 68

◆ **Receive E-mail Messages in Outlook** ◆ **Print an E-mail Message**
◆ **Save an E-mail Attachment**

## On the Job

To receive e-mail, you use an e-mail application such as Microsoft Office Outlook. You can print an e-mail message using your e-mail application, and save documents attached to e-mail messages to open in Word.

In this exercise, you will exchange e-mail messages with the Director of Training at Long Shot, Inc.

## Terms

**Download** Retrieve information from the Internet and store it locally on your computer.

**Inbox** A folder in Outlook and other e-mail programs where new e-mail messages are received.

## Notes

### Receive E-mail Messages in Outlook

- To receive electronic mail (e-mail) messages with Microsoft Office Outlook you must have a connection to the Internet or to an intranet and an account with a mail service provider.

  ✓ *To exchange e-mail, Outlook must be correctly configured with your e-mail account information.*

- When you connect to the Internet, the e-mail application **downloads** new messages into a folder called **Inbox**.

- You can read the downloaded messages immediately, while still online, or after you disconnect and are working offline.

- Messages remain in the Inbox folder until you move them or delete them.

  ✓ *You can use the File, Save As command to save e-mail messages in HTML or text format to open in Word.*

### Print an E-mail Message

- You can use Outlook to print any e-mail message.

- Your computer must be connected to a printer, and the printer must be on and loaded with paper in order to print an e-mail message.

### Save an E-mail Attachment

- Documents attached to e-mail messages in Outlook have a paper clip icon next to them in the Inbox.

- You can save a document attached to an e-mail message so you can open it in another application later.

- An attachment is saved in its original file format. For example, a Word document attached to an e-mail message is saved in Word document format.

- The attachment is saved with its original file name. You select the disk and/or folder where you want to store the file.

  ✓ *E-mail is often used to spread computer viruses, so you should use care when downloading and opening e-mail attachments. Make sure you know and trust the sender. If you are unsure, delete the message and attachment before opening, or leave it in the Inbox folder until you can verify that it does not contain a virus.*

# Procedures

## Receive E-mail Messages in Outlook (*F9*)

1. Click **Start** button

    ..................

2. Click **All Programs**.............. P
3. Select **Microsoft Office**.
4. **Click Microsoft Office Outlook 2003**.

   ✓ *Alternatively, you may use a shortcut icon to start Outlook from the desktop or taskbar. For more information about starting applications, refer to Exercise 87.*

   ✓ *Outlook may automatically connect to your mail service provider and download new messages. Enter account name and password if prompted.*

5. Click **Send/Receive** button

   Send/Receive .............Alt + C

   OR

   a. Click **Tools** .............Alt + T
   b. Select **Send/Receive** .....E
   c. Click **Send/Receive All** ..A

   ✓ *If not already online, Outlook will automatically connect to your mail service provider and send all messages. If prompted, enter your account name and password.*

   ✓ *You may read messages online, or disconnect from the Internet to read messages offline.*

## Open Mail Items in Outlook

1. In Outlook, click folder where mail is stored.
2. Double-click mail item in Mail Pane.

   OR

   a. Click mail item in Mail Pane.

   ✓ *The selected item may be displayed in the Outlook Preview Pane.*

   b. Click **File** ...............Alt + F
   c. Click **Open** .....................O
   d. Click **Selected Items** .....S
3. Click window **Close** button ☒ to close message when done..................Alt + F4

## Disconnect Outlook from Internet

1. Click **File** ....................Alt + F
2. Click **Work Offline** ..............K
3. Click **Yes** ............................Y

## Print an E-mail Message (*Ctrl + P*)

1. Select message.
2. Click **File** ....................Alt + F
3. Click **Print** .........................P
4. Click **OK** ..........................Enter

## Save an E-mail Attachment in Outlook

1. Select message.
2. Click **File** .....................Alt + F
3. Select **Save Attachments** .. N
4. Click file name to save.
5. Select storage location (disk and/or folder) in **Save Attachment** dialog box.
6. Click **Save** button

   Save ...........Alt + S

# Exercise Directions

✓ *You must have access to the Internet and an active e-mail account in order to complete the steps in this exercise.*

1. Start Word, if necessary.

2. Compose an e-mail message as follows:

    ✓ *Click E-mail message on the New Document task pane.*

    a. In the To: box, enter your own e-mail address, or the address of a classmate.

    b. Enter the subject: **Intro to Net Enrollment**

    c. Enter the message: **Hi. I am assigning classroom space for the fall training classes and would like to know how much interest there is in the Intro to the Internet course. Do you have an enrollment list that you could send me? Reply by e-mail as soon as possible. Thanks.**

3. Check the spelling and grammar in the message.

4. Send the message.

    ✓ *For information on composing and sending e-mail messages, see Exercise 67.*

5. Launch or switch to Outlook.

6. Send all messages.

7. Download new messages.

8. Locate and open the Intro to Net Enrollment message.

9. Print the message.

10. Exit your e-mail program and disconnect from the Internet, if necessary.

11. Close all open documents, saving all changes.

# On Your Own

1. Use Word to compose an e-mail message to someone and ask him or her to send you an e-mail message with a Word document attached to it. If you don't know anyone who can do this, send one to yourself.

2. Download the new message and save the attachment.

3. Open the attachment in Word.

4. When you are finished, close the document, saving all changes, and exit Word. Disconnect from the Internet, if necessary.

# Exercise 69

### ◆ Merge to an E-Mail Message

## On the Job

Use Word's mail merge feature to create and distribute a customized e-mail message to a group of recipients. You can merge a message or send the merged document as an attachment.

As a training assistant at Long Shot, Inc., you want to increase the enrollment in the new Introduction to the Internet class. In this exercise, you will send a message to the students who have taken other training classes to see if you can interest them in the new class.

## Terms

There is no new vocabulary in this exercise.

## Notes

### Merge to an E-Mail Message

- Use Word's Mail Merge to set up and complete a merge using e-mail messages as the main document.

  ✓ *For a refresher on using Mail Merge, refer to Lesson 8.*

- You type the standard text that will be the same in every message into a document, and then insert merge fields or merge blocks to customize the message.

- You can use an existing document as the message, or you can create a new document.

- You can use an existing data source file such as an Office Address List or an Outlook Contacts list, or you can create a new data source file.

- You must be sure your data source includes a field for an e-mail address; the information entered in the e-mail address field will be inserted as the recipient's address in the message header.

- You select options for merging to e-mail in the Merge to E-mail dialog box. For example, you may enter the text that will be displayed in the Subject field of the message header, and select the format to use for the message—either HTML, plain text, or as an attachment.

*Merge to E-mail dialog box*

- When you merge to e-mail, Word does not create a merge document as it does when you merge letters, envelopes, or labels. Instead, the customized messages are created and sent to your e-mail program's Outbox folder.

- To successfully complete a merge to e-mail, you must have a MAPI-compatible e-mail program, such as Microsoft Office Outlook, installed and set up for use with Microsoft Word.
  - ✓ Refer to Exercise 67 for information on sending e-mail.

# Procedures

## Use Mail Merge to Merge to E-Mail, Using an Existing Data Source Document

**Select the main document:**

1. Open a new blank document.
2. Click **Tools**.................. Alt+T
3. Select **Letters and Mailings**............................. E
4. Click **Mail Merge**................. M
5. Click the **E-mail messages** option button in the Mail Merge task pane.
6. Click **Next: Starting document** in the Mail Merge task pane.
7. Click the **Use the current document** option button in the Mail Merge task pane.
8. Click **Next: Select recipients** in the Mail Merge task pane.

**Select an existing Address List data source file:**

1. Click the **Use an existing list** option button in the Mail Merge task pane.
2. Click **Browse** button ▦ in the Mail Merge task pane.
   - ✓ Word opens the Select Data Source dialog box.
3. Locate and select the desired data source file.
4. Click **Open** [ Open ].
   - ✓ Word displays the Mail Merge Recipients dialog box.

5. Click **OK** ......................... Enter
6. Click **Next: Write your e-mail message** in the Mail Merge task pane.
   - ✓ Word displays the starting document in Web Layout view, and a list of available merge blocks.

**Arrange the message:**

1. In the current document, type the message text as you want it to appear on each e-mail message.
2. Insert the merge fields or merge blocks as necessary to complete the message.
3. Click **Next: Preview your e-mail message** in the Mail Merge task pane.
   - ✓ Word displays the first entry in the document.

**Preview e-mail messages:**

1. Click the **Next recipient** button  in the Mail Merge task pane.

   OR

   Click the **Next Record** button ▶ on the Mail Merge toolbar.

   OR

   Click the **Previous recipient** button ◀◀ in the Mail Merge task pane.

   OR

   Click the **Previous Record** button ◀ on the Mail Merge toolbar.
2. Click **Next: Complete the merge** in the Mail Merge task pane.

**Complete the merge:**

1. Click **Electronic Mail** button.
   - ✓ Word displays the Merge to E-mail dialog box.
2. Click **To**: drop-down arrow ........................... Alt+O
3. Select field that specifies recipient's e-mail address.
4. Click **Subject line** box .............................. Alt+S
5. Type text you want displayed in message header subject line.
6. Click **Mail format** drop-down arrow ........................... Alt+M
7. Select desired format.
8. Select other options as desired.
9. Click **OK** ........................... Enter
   - ✓ Messages are sent to your Outbox. If necessary, start your e-mail program, sign on to the Internet, and send the messages.

# Exercise Directions

1. Make a copy of the Office Address List file 💿 **69LSIDATA.mdb** and name the copy **LSIDATA**.

    ✓ *To copy the file, right-click the file name and select Copy. Right-click the destination folder and select Paste. Right-click the copied file name and select Rename. Type the new file name and press Enter.*

2. Start Word, if necessary.

3. Create a new blank document.

4. Save the document as **MAINMAIL**.

5. Open the Mail Merge task pane.

6. Select to create e-mail messages, using the current document.

7. Select to use an existing address list file as a data source document.

8. Locate and open the **LSIDATA** data source file.

9. Close the Mail Merge Recipients dialog box.

10. Set up the e-mail message main document as shown in Illustration A, inserting the GreetingLine merge block and the Course merge field as indicated.

11. Check the spelling and grammar in the document.

12. Preview the messages.

13. Select to complete the merge as follows:

    a. Select to merge Electronic Mail.

    b. In the Merge to E-mail dialog box, leave Email_Address as the option in the To: box.

    c. Type **Announcing a New Training Class** in the Subject line box.

    d. Leave HTML as the option in the Mail format box.

    e. Select to send All records.

    f. Click OK.

14. Start your e-mail program to see if the messages are in the Outbox.

    ✓ *The e-mail addresses are fictitious and will not work. If you try sending the messages you will receive an undeliverable message for each one.*

15. Exit your e-mail program.

16. Close all open files, saving all changes.

# On Your Own

1. Create a new document in Word.

2. Save it as **OWD69-1**.

3. Use Mail Merge to create e-mail messages. You may create a new data source document, or use 📇**OWD45-2**, **OWD46-2**, or **OWD47-2** (the data source documents you used in the On Your Own sections of exercises 45, 46 or 47) as the data source.

    ✓ *If 📇OWD45-2, 📇OWD46-2, or 📇OWD47-2 is not available, copy 💿 69DATA to use, saving the copy as OWD69-2.*

4. If necessary, edit the list to fill in the e-mail address information for all records.

5. Type the e-mail message, inserting merge fields as necessary.

6. Check the spelling and grammar.

7. Complete the merge.

8. If you have an Internet connection, send the messages.

9. Close all open documents, saving all changes, and exit Word.

«GreetingLine»

I hope that you enjoyed the «Course» class that you took last spring. I would like to take this opportunity to invite you to join a new class that we are offering in September: Introduction to the Internet. It promises to be very exciting and informative. We are planning to limit the class size, so please let me know as soon as possible if you are interested.

Sincerely,


Your Name
Training Assistant

# Exercise 70

## ◆ Critical Thinking

The designers of the Web site for StyleEyes have been asking for the copy they need to put on the Customer Satisfaction page. In this exercise, you will open the original document and save a version. You will protect it and send it as an attachment to a message asking for input from the legal department. You will open a version of the document that includes revisions suggested by the legal department and reject or accept the changes. You will compare the revised copy to the original, saving versions of each one. Finally, you will attach a digital signature to the final copy and send it as e-mail to the Web site designers.

## Exercise Directions

✓ *The steps in this exercise use fictitious e-mail addresses. If you try sending the messages, you will receive a warning that they are undeliverable. You may select to substitute the addresses with your own or a classmate's address in order to use a live Internet and e-mail connection.*

1. Start Word, if necessary.

2. Compose a new e-mail message as follows:

   a. Enter the address: **legal@styleeyes.net**

   b. Enter the subject: **Request input**

   c. Using 14-point Arial, type the message: **I will be sending along a document with the text I think should go on the customer satisfaction page of the Web site. Please review the document when you receive it, and send it back to me as soon as possible. Thanks.**

3. Check the spelling and grammar in the message.

4. Save the message and send it, or close it without sending.

5. Open the document ⊚**70PROMISE** and save it as **PROMISE**.

6. Insert the following comment at the word **Promise** in the title: **Is it OK to use the word "Promise?"**

7. Protect the document for tracked changes.

8. Save a version of the document with the comment: **Original sent to legal for input.**

9. Send the document for review to **legal@styleeyes.net**.

10. Save the message and send it, or close it without sending.

11. Open the document ⊚**70LEGAL** and save it as **LEGAL**. This is a version of the document that includes some tracked changes.

12. Unprotect the document.

13. Accept and reject changes as follows:

    a. Delete both comments.

    b. Accept the changes in the first paragraph.

    c. Accept the changes to the fourth paragraph.

    d. Reject the change in the last paragraph.

14. Save the document.

15. Unprotect the **PROMISE** document.

16. Compare the **LEGAL** document to the **PROMISE** document, merging the changes into the **PROMISE** document.

17. Save the changes to the **PROMISE** document and then save a version with the comment: **Tracked changes made by Legal Department**.

18. Delete the comment.

19. Accept all other changes.

20. Check the spelling and grammar in the document.

21. Save the document.

22. Preview the document. It should look similar to the one in Illustration A.

23. Print the document.

24. Attach your digital signature to the document.

25. Send the document as e-mail using the following message heading:

   a. Enter the address:
      **webdesign@styleeyes.net**

   b. Enter the subject: **Customer Satisfaction Copy**

26. Send the document.

27. Close the document, and exit all open programs.

*Illustration A*

---

### A Promise to Our Online Customers

StyleEyes takes customer satisfaction seriously. If you are not completely satisfied, we promise to exchange the merchandise or refund your purchase price along with shipping and handling charges.

We promise that we will match your prescription!
If the lenses you receive do not match your prescription, we will exchange them at no cost.

We promise to supply eyeglasses that look good!
If you are not satisfied with the style or color of your eyeglasses, we will exchange them for a pair you like better.

We promise to provide products that last!
If the eyeglasses do not hold up well under normal use, we will exchange them for a pair that does. Normal use is defined as everyday wear and tear according to the manufacturer's recommendations. Eyewear used for purposes other than intended cannot be guaranteed.

To obtain a full refund, customer must return eyeglasses in like-new condition within 30 days, accompanied by a copy of the original receipt. Exchanges due to manufacturing errors may be made at the discretion of StyleEyes Online management.

# Lesson 12

## Desktop Publishing and Automation

# Exercise 71

Skills Covered:

◆ **About Desktop Publishing** ◆ **About Document Production**
◆ **Create Newsletter Columns** ◆ **Set Column Width**
◆ **Insert Column Breaks** ◆ **Balance Columns**

## On the Job

Designing a document with columns lets you present more information on a page, as well as create a visually interesting page. Newsletter-style columns are useful for creating documents such as newsletters, pamphlets, articles, or brochures.

Liberty Blooms wants to send a newsletter to customers. In this exercise, you will create a newsletter to send to people who have signed a store register.

## Terms

**Desktop publishing** The process of designing and printing a document using a desktop computer and printer.

**Publish** Output a document so it can be distributed to readers.

**Commercial printer** A business that provides printing, copying, and publishing services.

**Newsletter-style columns** Columns in which text flows from the bottom of one column to the top of the next column.

**Gutter** The space between column margins.

## Notes

### About Desktop Publishing

■ **Desktop publishing** refers to designing and producing printed documents using a desktop computer.

■ Some common documents you can create with desktop publishing include reports, newsletters, brochures, booklets, manuals, and business cards.

■ Most word processing programs, such as Microsoft Office Word, include desktop publishing features that are sufficient for producing many types of published documents.

■ Some programs, such as Microsoft Office Publisher, are designed exclusively for desktop publishing applications. These programs offer more sophisticated features for designing documents for publication.

■ Many documents can be **published** using the computer, printer, and software that you already have at home, work, or school.

■ If you have complex publishing requirements such as color matching or binding, you may be able to design the document on your own equipment, but you may need to use a **commercial printer** to produce the final product.

■ A third alternative for publishing a document is to create a file and then have it reproduced at a copy shop.

## About Document Production

■ There are three basic steps to producing any business document: planning, creating, and publishing.

■ The planning stage requires you to think about such questions as the type of document you want to create, who will receive the document, and whether there are any special publishing requirements.

■ For example, you might consider what paper to print on, if color ink should be used, how many copies to print, or whether you will need to print on both sides of a page.

■ During the planning stage you should create a schedule that includes milestones, such as how long it will take to gather the information you need, when the first draft will be complete, how long it will take for a review process, and when the final document will be complete.

■ The creation stage involves selecting page and document settings, such as margins and page size, and entering and formatting the text and graphics.

■ The publishing stage involves outputting the document using either your desktop printer or a commercial printer. In some cases, the document may be published electronically on a Web site.

## Create Newsletter Columns

■ By default, a Word document has one column, the width of the page from the left margin to the right margin.

■ Use Word's Columns feature to divide a document into more than one **newsletter-style column**.

   ✓ *Use tables to create side-by-side columns; use the Columns feature to create newsletter-style columns; use tabs to align data along a single line in a document.*

■ You can apply column formatting to existing text or you can set column formatting before typing new text.

■ You can apply column formatting to an entire document or to the current section.

■ By dividing a document into sections using section breaks, you can combine different numbers of columns within a single document.

■ For example, you can create a headline banner across the top of the page using one column, then insert a continuous section break and divide the remainder of the page into two or more columns.

■ Multiple columns are not displayed in Normal view. Switch to Print Layout view or Print Preview to see the column formatting in a document.

*Newsletter columns*

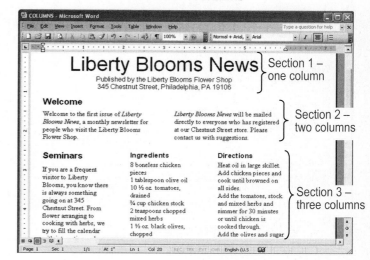

## Set Column Width

■ By default, Word creates columns of equal width.

■ You can change the width of any column. Select from Word's five preset column width arrangements or set precise column widths.

Select a preset width    *Columns dialog box*

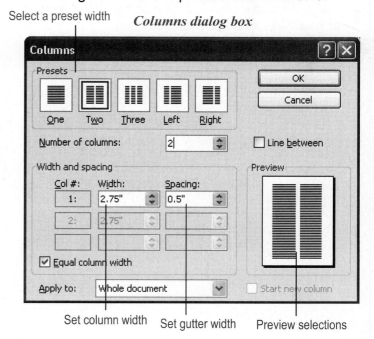

Set column width    Set gutter width    Preview selections

- You can also use the Columns dialog box, or drag the column margins, to adjust the amount of space in the **gutter** between columns.

*Drag column margins to adjust gutter*

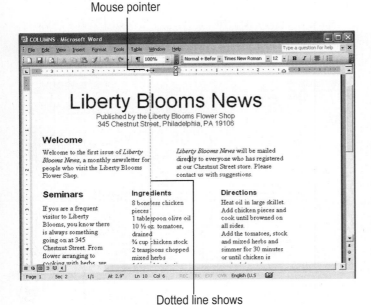

Mouse pointer

Dotted line shows new margin

## Insert Column Breaks

- By default, text flows to the top of the next column when the current column is filled.
- Use a column break to force text to flow to the top of the next column before the current column is filled.
- Column breaks are useful for moving headings or headlines to the top of a column.

## Balance Columns

- If there is not enough text to fill the last column in a document, the columns will be uneven, which does not look professional.

*Unbalanced columns*

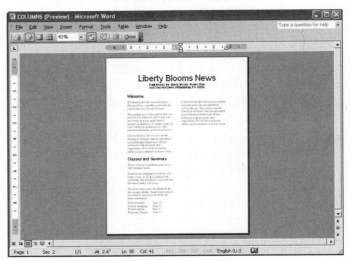

- Balance the amount of text in multiple columns on a page by inserting a continuous section break at the end of the last column.

*Balanced columns*

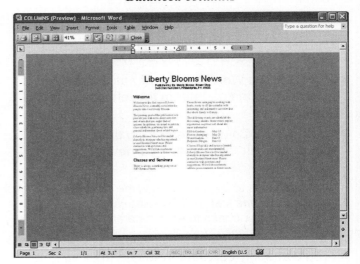

# Procedures

## Create Columns of Equal Width

1. Click the **Columns** button ▦.
2. Drag across the number of columns to create.
3. Release mouse button.

OR

1. Click **Format**............... `Alt`+`O`
2. Click **Columns**................ `C`
3. Click **Number of columns**............. `Alt`+`N`
4. Type the number of columns to create.
5. Click **OK**............................ `Enter`

## Select a Preset Column Format

1. Click **Format**............... `Alt`+`O`
2. Click **Columns**................ `C`
3. Click the desired Preset option:
   - **One**....................... `Alt`+`O`
   - **Two** ....................... `Alt`+`W`
   - **Three**.................... `Alt`+`T`
   - **Left** ...................... `Alt`+`L`
   - **Right** .................... `Alt`+`R`
4. Click **OK**............................ `Enter`

## Return to One Column Formatting

1. Click the **Columns** button ▦.
2. Drag across one column only.
3. Release mouse button.

OR

1. Click **Format** ............... `Alt`+`O`
2. Click **Columns** .................. `C`
3. Click **One**.................... `Alt`+`O`

OR

   a. Click **Number of columns** ........... `Alt`+`N`
   b. Type **1** .......................... `1`
4. Click **OK** .......................... `Enter`

## Create Columns of Any Width

1. Click **Format** ............... `Alt`+`O`
2. Click **Columns** .................. `C`
3. Click **Number of columns** ............... `Alt`+`N`
4. Type the number of columns to create.
5. For column 1, do the following:
   a. Type column **Width** ..................... `Alt`+`I` in inches.
   b. Type gutter **Spacing** ................ `Alt`+`S` in inches.

6. Deselect **Equal column width** check box.......... `Alt`+`E`
7. Repeat step 5 for additional columns.
8. Click **OK**........................... `Enter`

## Adjust Gutter Spacing

1. Position mouse pointer on column margin marker.
   ✓ When positioned correctly, the ScreenTip shows either Left Margin or Right Margin.
2. Drag left or right.

## Insert Column Break

1. Position insertion point where you want the break.
2. Click **Insert** ................ `Alt`+`I`
3. Click **Break** ........................ `B`
4. Click **Column break** .......... `C`
5. Click **OK**........................... `Enter`

## Balance Columns

1. Position insertion point at end of last column.
2. Click **Insert** ................ `Alt`+`I`
3. Click **Break** ........................ `B`
4. Click **Continuous** .............. `T`
5. Click **OK**........................... `Enter`

# Exercise Directions

1. Start Word, if necessary.
2. Open ⊙**71COLUMNS**.
3. Save the file as **COLUMNS**.
4. Format the document as follows:
   a. Center the title in 36-point sans serif.
   b. Center the company name and address (lines 2 and 3) in 12-point sans serif.
   c. Leave 12 points of space after address.
   d. Format the three headlines (**Welcome**, **Classes and Seminars**, and **Recipe Showcase**) using the Heading 1 style.
   e. Format all occurrences of **Liberty Blooms News** in the body of the newsletter in italics.
   f. Insert 6 points of space before and 6 points of space after all body text paragraphs in the first two articles. (Do not include the list of classes and dates.)

g. Format the recipe title and serving information (**Chicken with Tomatoes and Herbs** and **Yield: Four Servings**) with the Heading 2 style.

h. Insert a right tab stop on that line to align the serving information at the 6" mark on the horizontal ruler.

i. Apply the Heading 3 style to the text **Ingredients** and **Directions**.

j. Format the directions as a numbered list.

5. Format the entire document into three columns of equal width.

6. Preview the document.

7. Close Print Preview and return to one column formatting.

8. Insert a continuous section break before the headline **Welcome**.

   ✓ *There are now two sections in the document.*

9. Insert another continuous section break before the headline **Recipe Showcase**.

   ✓ *There are now three sections in the document.*

10. Insert another continuous section break before the heading **Ingredients**.

    ✓ *There are now four sections in the document.*

11. Format the second section (from the headline **Welcome** to the **Recipe Showcase**) into two columns of equal width.

12. Leave the third section as one column (the section containing the headline **Recipe Showcase**).

13. Format the fourth section (from the heading **Ingredients** to the end of the document) using the Left preset column arrangement.

14. In the fourth section, increase the width of the left column to 1.85" and decrease the gutter space between the columns to .25".

15. Preview the document. It should look similar to the one in Illustration A.

16. Check the spelling and grammar in the document.

17. Print the document.

18. Close the document, saving all changes.

# On Your Own

1. Research the types of technologies available for desktop publishing. For example, look up information about different software programs, the types of printers that might be appropriate and other equipment that might be useful.

2. Start Word and create a new document.

3. Save the document as **OWD71**.

4. Create a newsletter.

5. Set the newsletter up so it has a one-column title at the top. You may want to include a subtitle or motto as well as a line for the date or volume number.

6. Divide the rest of the document into either two or three columns.

7. Write two or three articles for the newsletter, including one that explains what you have learned about desktop publishing technology. The others might include information about your classes, job, movies or television shows you enjoy, or a trip you have taken recently.

8. Try adjusting the widths of the columns.

9. Try changing the number of columns.

10. Insert column breaks as necessary.

11. Balance the columns if necessary.

12. Check the spelling and grammar in the document.

13. Ask a classmate to review the document and make comments or suggestions.

14. Incorporate the suggestions into the document.

15. Print the document.

16. Close the document, saving all changes, and exit Word.

*Illustration A*

# Liberty Blooms News

Published by the Liberty Blooms Flower Shop
345 Chestnut Street, Philadelphia, PA 19106

## Welcome

Welcome to the first issue of *Liberty Blooms News*, a monthly newsletter for people who visit the Liberty Blooms Flower Shop. The primary goal of this publication is to provide you with news about activities and events that you might find of interest. In addition, we intend to publish class schedules, gardening tips, and general information about related topics.

*Liberty Blooms News* will be mailed directly to everyone who has registered at our Chestnut Street store. Please contact us with questions and suggestions. We will do our best to address your comments in future issues.

## Classes and Seminars

If you are a frequent visitor to Liberty Blooms, you know there is always something going on at 345 Chestnut Street. From flower arranging to cooking with herbs, we try to fill the calendar with interesting and informative activities that the whole family will enjoy.

The following events are scheduled for the coming months. Some events require registration, so please call ahead for more information.

| | |
|---|---|
| Edible Gardens | May 13 |
| Flower Arranging | May 21 |
| Water Gardens | June 3 |
| Potpourri Designs | June 11 |

## Recipe Showcase

### *Chicken with Tomatoes and Herbs*      *Yield: Four Servings*

### Ingredients

8 boneless chicken pieces
1 tablespoon olive oil
10 ½ oz. tomatoes, drained
¾ cup chicken stock
2 teaspoons mixed herbs, chopped
1 ½ oz. black olives, chopped
1 teaspoon sugar
Fresh basil to garnish

### Directions

1. Heat oil in large skillet.
2. Add chicken pieces and cook until browned on all sides.
3. Add the tomatoes, stock and mixed herbs and simmer for 30 minutes or until chicken is cooked through.
4. Add the olives and sugar and simmer for an additional 5 minutes.
5. Garnish with fresh basil and serve with rice or pasta.

# Exercise 72

◆ **About Layout and Design** ◆ **Use Dropped Capitals**
◆ **Enhance a Document with Borders and Shading**

## On the Job

Dropped capital letters, borders, and shading can call attention to a single word, a line, a paragraph, or an entire page. They make a document visually appealing and interesting to the reader, so the reader will be more likely to take the time to read and remember the text.

StyleEyes has asked you to create a one-page flyer to distribute to its customers. You'll use newsletter-style columns for the flyer, and you will enhance the document with dropped capitals, borders, and shading.

## Terms

**Page layout** The way text, graphics, and space are organized on a document page.

**Contrast** A basic principle of design that describes the way objects with opposite or complementary features are positioned in relation to each other in order to create visual interest.

**Balance** A basic principle of design that describes the visual weight of objects on a page and the way the objects are arranged in relation to each other.

**Consistency** The use of repetition to create a uniform and predictable design or layout.

**Dropped capital** An enlarged capital letter that drops below the first line of body text in the paragraph.

**Border** A line placed on one or more sides of a paragraph(s), page, or text box.

**Shading** A color or pattern applied to a paragraph(s), page, or text box.

**3D** A perspective added to a border to give the appearance of three dimensions.

**Shadow** An effect designed to give the appearance of a shadow behind a border.

## Notes

### About Layout and Design

- The way you set up a page effects the way the reader sees and interprets the textual information.

- Effective **page layout** uses the basic principles of design, including **contrast**, **balance**, and **consistency** to highlight the text and capture the reader's attention.

- In addition to newsletter columns, you can use features such as tables, borders, font formatting, lists, alignment, pictures, and spacing to create interesting and informative documents.

### Use Dropped Capitals

- **Dropped capital** letters, called *drop caps,* are used to call attention to opening paragraphs.

- Drop caps can be placed in the margin to the left of the paragraph, or within the paragraph.

- Drop caps can be in the same font as the surrounding text or in a different font.
- Selecting a different, more decorative font can enhance the drop-cap effect.
- In Normal view, drop caps will not appear exactly as they will in a printed document. Use Print Layout view or Print Preview to display the drop cap correctly.

*Drop Cap dialog box*

*Borders and Shading dialog box: Borders tab*

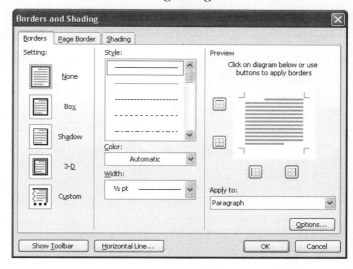

*Borders and Shading dialog box: Page Border tab*

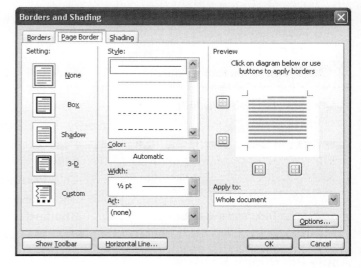

## Enhance a Document with Borders and Shading

- Apply **borders** and/or **shading** to a paragraph, selected paragraphs, or an entire page.
- Basic border and shading options are similar to those for tables, including line style, line weight (width), and line color.
- Additional border options include **3D** or **Shadow** effects.
- Apply page borders to the whole document or to specified section(s).
- In addition to using basic border options, Word has a built-in list of artwork designed for page borders. Art borders are useful for stationery, invitations, and other informal, decorative documents.
- You can apply paragraph and page borders and shading using the Borders and Shading dialog box; you can also apply paragraph borders and shading using the Tables and Borders toolbar.
  - ✓ *Using the Tables and Borders toolbar is covered in Exercise 40.*

*Borders and Shading dialog box: Shading tab*

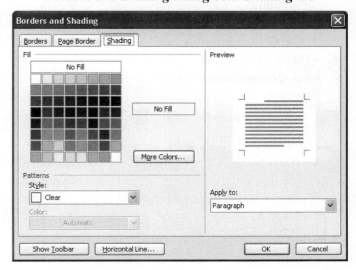

# Procedures

## Create a Dropped Capital

1. Position insertion point in the paragraph.
2. Click **Format** ............... `Alt`+`O`
3. Click **Drop Cap** ................... `D`
4. Select one of the following:
   - **Dropped** ............... `Alt`+`D`
   - **In margin** ............... `Alt`+`M`
   - ✓ Click *None* to remove an existing drop cap.
5. If desired, do the following:
   a. Click the **Font** drop-down arrow ............ `Alt`+`F`
   b. Select font to apply.
   c. Click **Lines to drop** .................. `Alt`+`L`
   d. Type the number of lines to drop capital letter.
      - ✓ The default is three.
   e. Click **Distance from text** ............... `Alt`+`X`
   f. Type the distance from text to position dropped capital (in inches).
      - ✓ The default is zero.
6. Click **OK** ........................... `Enter`

## Apply Paragraph Borders

1. Position insertion point in the paragraph.
   OR
   Select paragraphs.
2. Click **Format** ............... `Alt`+`O`
3. Click **Borders and Shading** ........................... `B`
4. Click the **Borders** tab . `Alt`+`B`
5. Click a Setting option:
   - **Box** ⬚ ................. `Alt`+`X`
   - **Shadow** ⬚ .......... `Alt`+`A`
   - **3-D** ⬚ ................. `Alt`+`D`
   - **Custom** ⬚ ............ `Alt`+`U`
   - ✓ Click *None* ⬚ to remove existing border.
6. Click desired **Style** .................. `Alt`+`Y`, `⇳`
7. Click desired **Color** ........ `Alt`+`C`, `⇕`, `Enter`
8. Click desired **Width** ........ `Alt`+`W`, `⇳`, `Enter`
9. For a custom border, click the desired button in the preview area to position border:
   - **Top** button ⬚.
   - **Bottom** button ⬚.
   - **Left** button ⬚.
   - **Right** button ⬚.
10. Click **OK** ........................... `Enter`

## Apply Page Borders

1. Position insertion point on the page.
2. Click **Format** ............... `Alt`+`O`
3. Click **Borders and Shading** ........................... `B`
4. Click the **Page Border** tab .......................... `Alt`+`P`
5. Click a **Setting** option:
   - **Box** ⬚ ................. `Alt`+`X`
   - **Shadow** ⬚ .......... `Alt`+`A`
   - **3-D** ⬚ ................. `Alt`+`D`
   - **Custom** ⬚ ............ `Alt`+`U`
   - ✓ Click *None* ⬚ to remove existing border.
6. Click desired **Style** .................. `Alt`+`Y`, `⇳`
7. Click desired **Color** ........ `Alt`+`C`, `⇕`, `Enter`
8. Click desired **Width** ....... `Alt`+`W`, `⇳`, `Enter`
   OR
   Select desired **Art** ........... `Alt`+`R`, `⇳`, `Enter`
   - ✓ If the art borders are not installed on your system, Word prompts you to insert the setup disk.
9. For a custom border, click the desired button in the preview area to position border:
   - **Top** button ⬚.
   - **Bottom** button ⬚.
   - **Left** button ⬚.
   - **Right** button ⬚.
10. Select section(s) to **Apply to** ... `Alt`+`L`, `⇳`, `Enter`
11. Click **OK** ........................... `Enter`

## Apply Shading

1. Position insertion point in paragraph.
   OR
   Select paragraphs.
2. Click **Format** ............... `Alt`+`O`
3. Click **Borders and Shading** ........................... `B`
4. Click the **Shading** tab .............................. `Alt`+`S`
5. Click desired **Fill color** .................... `Tab`, `⇕`
6. If desired:
   - Select Patterns **Style** ... `Alt`+`Y`, `⇳`, `Enter`
   - Select Patterns **Color** ... `Alt`+`C`, `⇕`, `Enter`
7. Click **OK** ........................... `Enter`

# Exercise Directions

1. Start Word, if necessary.

2. Open ⊙ **72EYENEWS**.

3. Save the file as **EYENEWS**.

4. Apply a 48-point sans serif font to line 1 (the company name).

5. Apply a 20-point sans serif font to line 2 (the address).

6. Apply formatting to leave 6 points of space after line 2.

7. On line 3, set a right tab stop flush with the right page margin (6" on the horizontal ruler). This will right-align the date, **Fall/Winter**, while leaving the text **Customer Newsletter** flush left.

8. Apply formatting to leave 12 points of space after line 3.

9. Apply the Heading 1 style to the headlines: **Eye Care Symposium**, **Expanded Hours**, **New Associate**, and **Report Available**.

10. Modify the formatting of all headlines so that there is no space left before.

11. Leave 6 points of space before and after all body text paragraphs. (Do not modify the items in the list of topics in the **Report Available** article at the end of the document.)

12. Insert a continuous section break before the headline **Eye Care Symposium**.

13. Format section 2 into three newsletter-style columns, of equal width, with .25" of gutter space between columns.

14. Insert a column break before the headline **Report Available**.

15. Apply the default dropped capital formatting to the first character under the headlines **Eye Care Symposium**, **New Associate**, and **Report Available**.

16. Select the headline **Expanded Hours** and the paragraph following it, and apply a 1½ point solid line shadow border and a 12.5% gray shading.

17. Justify the text in the paragraph.

18. In the article **Report Available**, italicize both occurrences of the report title **Eye Care for Seniors**.

19. Apply bullet list formatting to the topics listed as being included in the report (if necessary, change the paragraph formatting so there is no space before or after the bulleted items).

20. Select the bulleted list and apply a ½ point solid line outside border.

21. Display the Tables and Borders toolbar.

22. Apply the borders shown in Illustration A along the top and bottom of line 3.
    a. Select the top line style (unequal double-line with the thinner line on the bottom).
    b. Select the line weight (3 points).
    c. Select Top Border from the Border drop-down palette.
    d. Select the bottom line style (unequal double-line with the thinner line on the top).
    e. Select the line weight (3 points).
    f. Select Bottom Border from the Border drop-down palette.

23. Apply a 10% gray shading to line 3, as shown in Illustration A.

24. Apply the Stars page border (select the border from the Art drop-down list) to the entire document.

25. Check the spelling and grammar.

26. Display the document in Print Preview. It should look similar to the one in Illustration A.

27. Print the document.

28. Close the document, saving all changes.

# StyleEyes, Inc.

## 754 Erieside Avenue, Cleveland, OH 44114

Customer Newsletter                                      Fall/Winter

## Eye Care Symposium

On Sunday, March 10, our very own Dr. Finn Broderbund will be the featured speaker at the annual Cleveland Eye Care Breakfast Symposium.

The symposium, which is sponsored by a consortium of eye care providers, is held every year in March. It is intended to foster awareness of the importance of eye care, and to provide an opportunity for eye care professionals to meet and discuss the industry. This year, Dr. Broderbund will speak about current advances in eye surgery as well as providing a peak at some of the technologies that will aid eye care in the future.

Tickets are still available. If you are interested in attending, call the office as soon as possible.

## Expanded Hours

As of January 1, StyleEyes, Inc. of Cleveland will be open until 8:00 p.m. Monday through Friday and until 6:00 p.m. on Saturdays and Sundays.

## New Associate

StyleEyes of Cleveland is pleased to welcome Dr. Cynthia Ramirez.

Dr. Ramirez studied medicine at Ohio State University. She became a certified Opthamologist in 1998. She has extensive experience working with geriatric patients, and she specializes in senior eye care. She is fluent in English, Spanish, and Portuguese.

We know that Dr. Ramirez will be an excellent addition to our staff. Please call the office for more information.

## Report Available

The associates at StyleEyes have been hard at work researching and writing *Eye Care for Seniors*, a report that we hope offers useful information for the elderly and their caregivers.

The report takes a straight forward approach to providing information in regards to managing the eye care needs of our senior citizens.

*Eye Care for Seniors* includes information about the following topics:

- An overview of eye care issues
- Common eye ailments
- How to maintaining eye health
- Eye sight and medication

The report is now available. Call the office for more information or to request a copy.

# On Your Own

1. Open ⌨OWD71, the newsletter document you created in the On Your Own section of Exercise 71, or open ⊙**72NEWS**.

2. Save the file as **OWD72**.

3. Apply dropped capitals to the first paragraph of each article.

4. Use borders to call attention to paragraphs. Try different effects, such as different line styles, shadows, and 3-D. You might want to insert a border between the single column section and the multi-column section.

5. Apply a page border.

6. If necessary, adjust column breaks and balance columns to improve the appearance of the newsletter.

7. Check the spelling and grammar in the document.

8. Preview the document.

9. Print the document.

10. Ask a classmate to review the document, paying particular attention to the layout and design, and to offer comments and suggestions.

11. Incorporate the suggestions into the document.

12. Close the document, saving all changes, and exit Word.

# Exercise 73

## Skills Covered:

◆ **Use Templates** ◆ **Use Wizards** ◆ **Save a Document as a Template**
◆ **Set Default File Location for Workgroup Templates**

## On the Job

Templates and wizards help you create similar documents efficiently—and time after time. Templates include page setup and formatting settings to insure that new documents will be uniform. In many cases they include standard text and graphics as well. Wizards are automated templates that prompt you to provide information that can be used to customize the resulting document. Because workgroups often share templates for creating documents, you can store the templates in a location that everyone can access easily.

As an account representative at Long Shot, Inc. you are planning a business trip to a new client. In this exercise, you will save a document as a template, and then use it to create a memo telling the client when you will arrive. You will then use a Wizard to create a fax cover sheet, which you could use when transmitting the memo to the client.

## Terms

**Template** A Word document on which new documents are based. Templates include formatting settings, text, and graphics used to create the new documents.

**.dot extension** The file extension assigned by Word to template files.

**Normal.dot** The default template used to create new documents in Word.

**Wizard** An automated template.

**Workgroup** A group of individuals who work together on the same projects, usually connected via a network.

## Notes

### Use Templates

- All new Word documents are based on a **template**.
- Templates include formatting settings, such as margins, font, and font size.
- Some templates include boilerplate text and graphics that are part of new documents.
- All new documents based on the same template will have the same default formatting settings and will display any boilerplate text and graphics entered in the template file.

- Some templates include editing directions and sample text for completing the document. You replace sample text, fill in missing information, and customize the document using standard editing and formatting commands.
- Word comes with built-in templates for creating common documents such as memos, letters, and resumes.
- You can preview built-in templates in the Templates dialog box.

*Templates dialog box*

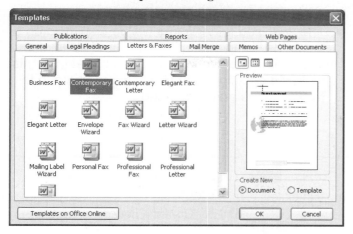

- You can also download templates from the Microsoft Office Online Web site.
- Recently used templates are listed in the New Document task pane.

*New Document task pane*

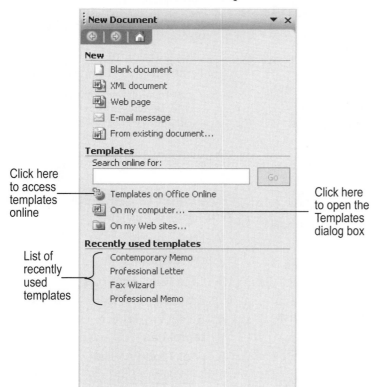

Click here to access templates online

Click here to open the Templates dialog box

List of recently used templates

- Templates are usually available in several styles, which means they offer different formatting settings for different situations. For example, a letter in the Professional template may be suitable for business correspondence, while the Elegant template may be more suitable for personal correspondence.

- Document templates are stored in the Templates folder on your computer system; if they are not stored in the Templates folder they may not be available to use to create new documents.
  - ✓ *Not all templates are installed by default.*
- Template files have a **.dot extension**. The default template for creating a blank document is called **Normal.dot**.

## Use Wizards

- Use a **Wizard** to create a customized new document.
- Wizards prompt you through a series of dialog boxes to enter information that can be incorporated into the document.
  - ✓ *The flowchart in the first dialog box indicates how many dialog boxes there are.*
- For example, a memo Wizard might prompt you for the recipient's name and the memo subject. When Word creates the document, the recipient's name and the memo subject will be entered automatically.
- You can customize documents created with a Wizard using standard editing and formatting commands.
- Wizards are listed along with templates in the Templates dialog box; recently used Wizards are listed in the New Document task pane.

## Save a Document as a Template

- Create your own templates that include boilerplate text as well as formatting settings.
- For example, you can create a template that includes a business letterhead, a specific font, margins, and paragraph spacing. By default, every document you create based on your template will have the same text and formatting.
- To create your own templates, simply save a document using the template file type.
- As soon as you select the Document Template file type in the Save As dialog box, Word switches to the Templates folder.
- You can create a new folder within the Templates folder to store your templates. The new folder name will be listed on a tab in the Templates dialog box, and your templates will be displayed on that tab. If you do not create a new folder, the templates will be displayed on the General tab.

## Set Default File Location for Workgroup Templates

- Members of a **workgroup** are often expected to use the same templates to create new documents.

- Documents created with the same template will be consistent in layout and design.

- You can use Word to specify a folder where workgroup file templates are stored.

- The specified folder name will be displayed on a tab in the Templates dialog box, and templates stored in the folder will be listed on that tab. This makes it easy for everyone in the workgroup to find the templates they need.

# Procedures

### Create a Document Using a Template

1. Click **File** ..................... `Alt`+`F`
2. Click **New** ........................... `N`

    ✓ *The New Document task pane opens.*

3. Click **On my computer** `W` in the Templates section of the task pane.

    ✓ *If desired template is listed in the Recently used templates list, click it and skip to step 7.*

4. Click the desired tab ... `Ctrl`+`Tab`
5. Select the desired template icon ............... `↑`, `↓`
6. Click **OK** ........................... `Enter`
7. Replace directions and prompts with text.
8. Edit and format document as desired.
9. Name and save document ..................... `Ctrl`+`S`

### Create a Document Using a Wizard

1. Click **File** ..................... `Alt`+`F`
2. Click **New** ........................... `N`

    ✓ *The New Document task pane opens.*

3. Click **On my computer** `W` in the Templates section of the task pane.

    ✓ *If desired Wizard is listed in the Recently used templates list, click it and skip to step 7.*

4. Click the desired tab ... `Ctrl`+`Tab`
5. Click the desired Wizard icon ................. `↑`, `↓`

6. Click **OK** ......................... `Enter`
7. Respond to prompts in dialog box.
8. Click **Next** ................... `Alt`+`N`
    OR
    Click **Back** to return to previous dialog box to change responses ................... `Alt`+`B`
    OR
    Click **Finish** to create document with default settings ....... `Alt`+`F`
9. Repeat steps 7 and 8 until last dialog box is displayed.
10. Click **Finish** ................. `Alt`+`F`
11. Edit and format document as desired.
12. Save document ........... `Ctrl`+`S`

### Access Templates Online

1. Establish a connection to the Internet.
2. Click **File** ..................... `Alt`+`F`
3. Click **New** ........................... `N`

    ✓ *The New Document task pane opens.*

4. Click **Templates on Office Online** button `📇` in the Templates section of the task pane.
5. Locate and select desired template.
6. Click **Download Now** button.

    ✓ *If necessary, read the license agreement and click Accept button.*

7. Follow steps to complete download.

    ✓ *If cookies are not enabled on your computer system, you will not be able to complete the download.*

### Save a Document as a Template

1. Create a new document.
2. Enter and format text as desired.
3. Set page, paragraph, and font formatting.
4. Click **File** ..................... `Alt`+`F`
5. Click **Save** ........................... `S`
6. Type file name................... *type*
7. Click **Save as type** box ........................... `Alt`+`T`
8. Click **Document Template**............ `↑`, `↓`, `Enter`

    ✓ *Word automatically switches to the Templates folder. Select the desired subfolder or create a new folder as necessary.*

9. Click **Save** button

    `Save` ........... `Alt`+`S`

### Set Default Location for Workgroup File Templates

1. Click **Tools** ................... `Alt`+`T`
2. Click **Options** ...................... `O`
3. Click **File Locations** tab ........................... `Ctrl`+`Tab`
4. Select **Workgroup templates** ................... `↑`, `↓`
5. Click **Modify** button

    `Modify...` ........... `Alt`+`M`

6. Select desired folder using Look in drop-down list.

    ✓ *If necessary, create new folder as described in Exercise 6.*

7. Click **OK** ......................... `Enter`
8. Click **OK** ......................... `Enter`

# Exercise Directions

## Work with Templates

1. Start Word, if necessary.

2. Set the Workgroup Templates folder as the default Workgroup template file location.

   ✓ *If necessary, create a new folder named Workgroup Templates. Make sure that the folder is stored in your Word Templates directory, for example, in the C:\Documents and Settings\UserName\Application Data\Microsoft\Templates\Workgroup Templates directory. If necessary, ask your instructor for more information.*

3. Open the document ⊘**73LONGSHOT** and save it as a template named **LONGSHOT** in the Workgroup Templates folder.

4. Close the **LONGSHOT** template file.

5. Create a new document based on the **LONGSHOT** template. Note that the letterhead text is already entered in the document, because it is part of the template file.

   ✓ *The template should be displayed on the Workgroup Templates tab of the Templates dialog box. If it is not, you did not store the folder in the correct template directory.*

6. Save the new document as **LSIMEMO**.

7. Type the document shown in Illustration A.

8. Check the spelling and grammar in the document.

9. Display the document in Print Preview. It should look similar to the one in Illustration A.

10. Print the document.

11. Close the document, saving all changes.

## Use a Wizard

1. Use the Fax Wizard to create a fax cover sheet.

2. Complete the prompts in the Wizard dialog boxes as follows:

   - In the Document to Fax screen, select the option to create just a cover sheet with a note.

   - Specify that you want to print the document and send it from a separate fax machine.

   - Use the following information:

     Recipient's name: **Harold Cantor**

     Recipient's fax number: **941-555-2598**

     Use the Professional style.

     Sender: **Your Name**

     Sender's company: **Long Shot, Inc.**

     Mailing address: **234 Simsbury Drive, Ithaca, NY 14850**

     Phone: **607-555-9191**

     Fax: **607-555-9292**

3. Replace all remaining sample text in the document as shown in Illustration B.

   ✓ *Double-click in the Please Reply box to insert the check mark.*

4. Save the document as **FAXCOVER**.

5. Check the spelling and grammar in the document.

6. Display the document in Print Preview. It should look similar to the one in Illustration B.

7. Print the document.

8. Close the document, saving all changes.

# Long Shot, Inc.

## 234 Simsbury Drive ⚑ Ithaca, NY 14850

**Telephone: 607-555-9191** ⚑ **Fax: 607-555-9292** ⚑ **E-mail: mail@longshot.net**

MEMO

To:         Harold Cantor
From:       Your Name
Date:       Today's date
Subject:    Travel Plans

I have finalized my travel plans and will be arriving on flight 6234 at 9:55 a.m. on Friday the 13th. Assuming the traffic is light, I should reach your office by 11:00 a.m.

I look forward to meeting you on the 13th. Please contact me if you have any questions. Also, if you are able to arrange a tee time for Friday afternoon, I will be happy to bring along my golf gear.

*Illustration B*

234 Simsbury Drive
Ithaca, NY 14850
Phone: 607-555-9191
Fax: 607-555-9292

**Long Shot, Inc.**

| | | | |
|---|---|---|---|
| **To:** | Harold Cantor | **From:** | Your Name |
| **Fax:** | 941-555-2598 | **Date:** | Today's date |
| **Phone:** | 941-555-2500 | **Pages:** | 2 (including cover) |
| **Re:** | Travel Plans | **CC:** | |

☐ **Urgent**    ☐ **For Review**    ☐ **Please Comment**    ☑ **Please Reply**    ☐ **Please Recycle**

•**Comments:** Please review the memo and respond as soon as possible.

Thanks.

# On Your Own

1. Word includes templates for a wide variety of documents, including publications such as manuals and brochures. In this exercise, think of a task for which you could create an instruction manual. The task might be school or class related, or might be extracurricular. For example, you might create a manual about how to fill out a course registration form, how to throw a shot put, prepare a science fair exhibit, or use a self-serve gas pump.

2. Once you select a task, gather all of the information you need. Decide how many chapters or sections you will need, what the titles will be, and map out the precise steps the reader will have to follow to complete the task.

3. When you are ready, start Word and use the Manual template to create a new document.

   ✓ You will find the template on the Publications tab of the Templates dialog box.

4. Save the document as **OWD73**.

5. Scroll through the document to see the components of the manual. Note that the Manual template creates a complex document that includes a table of contents, an index, and a lot of sample text and instructions. As you work, you can delete the sections, text, and graphics you don't need, and retain those that you want to use.

   ✓ To delete an object such as a picture or text box, click it then press the Delete key. Working with graphics objects is covered in Lesson 13.

6. Replace the sample text, headings, and graphics with your own information. Simply type your text, and insert graphics or symbols to illustrate the document.

7. Save your document frequently so that you do not accidentally lose information.

8. Include a table of contents and an index.

9. When you have entered all of the information, and have deleted the sample information that you don't need, check the spelling and grammar in the document.

10. Print the document.

11. Ask a classmate to review the manual and offer suggestions and comments on both the content and the design.

12. Incorporate the suggestions into the document.

13. Close the document, saving all changes.

# Exercise 74

### ◆ Insert a File in a Document ◆ Use AutoText

## On the Job

Insert a file into another file to save time retyping existing text. When you insert a file, the entire contents of the file become part of the current document, while the original file remains unchanged. Use AutoText to quickly insert words or phrases you type often, such as the closing to a letter.

As an assistant at Blue Sky Dairy, you want to show that you are resourceful. In this exercise, you will design a letterhead that you will save as AutoText. You can then insert it at the top of a press release you will write announcing the winners of the Name that Flavor contest. You also need to include the names of the contest judges in the press release. Since you already have a document containing the names of the judges, you can simply insert it directly into the press release.

## Terms

**AutoText** A feature of Word that lets you automatically insert a selection of stored text or graphics.

## Notes

### Insert a File in a Document

- Insert one file into another file to incorporate the first file's contents into the second file.
- The entire contents are saved as part of the second file.
- The first file remains unchanged.
- Inserting a file is different from copying and pasting, because you do not have to open the file to insert it and the entire file contents are inserted—no selecting is necessary.
  - ✓ *To mark where a file is inserted into an existing document, turn on the Track Changes feature before the insertion.*

### Use AutoText

- **AutoText** is part of Word's AutoCorrect feature.
  - ✓ *Using AutoCorrect is covered in Exercise 9.*
- AutoText eliminates repetitive typing by automatically inserting saved blocks of text or graphics.
- By default, Word recognizes AutoText entries once you type four characters and displays the entry name in a ScreenTip.
- You can insert the entry or continue typing.
- An unlimited amount of text or graphics may be stored in an AutoText entry.
- Word comes with a built-in list of AutoText entries, including standard letter closings and salutations.

- You can add entries to the AutoText list.
- AutoText entry names can have up to 31 characters, including spaces.
- Use descriptive names when creating new entries.
- You can delete an entry when you don't need it anymore.

*The AutoText tab of the AutoCorrect dialog box*

## Procedures

### Insert a File

1. Position the insertion point where you want file inserted.
2. Click **Insert** ................. Alt+I
3. Click **File** ........................... L
4. Select file to insert........ ↓, ↑
5. Click **Insert** button

    [ Insert ] ............... Alt+S

### Use AutoText

**To create an AutoText entry**
*(Alt+F3):*

1. Select text or graphics.
2. Click **Insert**. ................ Alt+I
3. Select **AutoText**.................. A
4. Click **New**........................... N
5. Type the entry name.
6. Click **OK**............................ Enter

**To insert an AutoText entry:**

1. Type entry name.
2. Press **F3** ............................. F3

    OR

    Wait until ScreenTip is displayed and press
    **Enter** ............................. Enter

    OR

1. Click **Insert**................. Alt+I
2. Select **AutoText**.................. A

    ✓ *Recently used AutoText entries are displayed on the AutoText submenu.*

3. Click desired AutoText entry on submenu.

    OR

1. Click **Insert**................. Alt+I
2. Select **AutoText**................. A

3. Click **AutoText**.................... X
4. Select desired AutoText entry.
5. Click **Insert**................. Alt+I

**Delete an AutoText entry:**

1. Click **Insert**................. Alt+I
2. Select **AutoText**................. A
3. Click **AutoText**.................... X

    ✓ *The AutoCorrect dialog box is displayed, with the AutoText tab active.*

4. Locate and select entry to delete in list of entries.

    ✓ *You can type the entry in the text box at the top of the list to quickly scroll to it.*

5. Click **Delete**................. Alt+D
6. Click **OK**........................... Enter

# Exercise Directions

1. Start Word, and create a new document.

2. Design the letterhead shown at the top of Illustration A.

   a. Type the company name in a bold, 28-point serif font with the small caps effect (Garamond is used in the illustration), flush right.

   b. Type the address using the same font formatting in 18 points, also flush right.

   c. Type the phone numbers using the same font formatting in 10 points, also flush right.

   d. Leave 48 points of space after the last line in the letterhead.

   e. Insert a diamond shaped Wingding symbol to separate parts of the address and phone numbers.

   f. Apply a 20% gray shading behind the three lines of the letterhead.

   g. Apply a triple-line border above and below the letterhead, as shown.

3. Save the letterhead as an AutoText entry named **dairyhead**.

   a. Press Ctrl+A to select everything in the document.

   b. Click Insert, AutoText, New.

   c. Type the name **dairyhead** in the Create AutoText dialog box.

   d. Click OK.

4. Close the document without saving any changes.

5. Open ☞ **74WINNERS**.

6. Save the file as **WINNERS**.

7. Position the insertion point at the beginning of the document, and then insert the **dairyhead** AutoText entry.

   ✓ Once you insert the entry, your instructor may ask you to delete the dairyhead entry from the AutoText list.

8. Move the insertion point to the end of the document and insert the file ☞ **74JUDGES**.

9. Check the spelling and grammar in the document.

10. Display the document in Print Preview. It should look similar to the one in Illustration A.

11. Print the document.

12. Close the file, saving all changes.

# On Your Own

1. Start Word, and create a new document.

2. Design a letterhead for yourself suitable for using at the top of stationery or other document.

3. Save the letterhead as an AutoText entry with a descriptive name, such as **MYNAME**.

4. Close the document without saving the changes.

5. Create another new document.

6. Save the document as **OWD74-1**.

7. Type a brief biography. The biography should be no more than two paragraphs, and it should be appropriate for inclusion in a document such as a yearbook, a team or club roster, or a theater program.

8. Check the spelling and grammar in the document.

9. Close the document, saving all changes.

10. Create another new document, and save it as **OWD74-2**.

11. Insert your letterhead AutoText entry at the top of the document.

12. Type a letter to the yearbook editor, a club president, or whoever is responsible for printing the collection of biographies. Somewhere in the body of the letter, insert the **OWD74-1** document.

13. Check the spelling and grammar in the document.

14. Display the document in Print Preview.

15. Print the document.

16. Ask a classmate to review the document and offer comments and suggestions.

17. Incorporate the suggestions into the document.

18. Close the document, saving all changes, and exit Word.

# BLUE SKY DAIRY COMPANY

## HIGHWAY 73 ❖ CAMBRIDGE, WISCONSIN 53523

TELEPHONE: (608) 555-2697 ❖ FACSIMILE: (608) 555-2698 ❖ E-MAIL: MAIL@BLUESKYDAIRY.NET

FOR IMMEDIATE RELEASE

Blue Sky Dairy Announces Contest Winners

**Cambridge, Wisconsin** – Blue Sky Dairy is pleased to announce the winners of its first Name that Flavor contest. Over 3,500 entries were received from all over the world, and the judges were hard pressed to pick a winner. After much deliberation, a grand prize winner and two honorable mention winners were selected. They are:

Grand Prize:  "Blue Sky Banquet" submitted by Melanie Jackson of San Francisco, California

Honorable Mention: "Chocolate Sunrise" submitted by Janine Flaherty of Tampa, Florida
"Sundae Delight" submitted by Jeffrey Levine of Seaford, New York

All participants received commemorative T-Shirts and discount coupons for use wherever Blue Sky Dairy products are sold.

List of Judges for the Blue Sky Dairy Name that Flavor contest:

| Name | Department | Telephone Extension |
|------|------------|---------------------|
| Gogan, Alex | Sales | 622 |
| Anderssen, Jane | Manufacturing | 789 |
| Cheung, Mary | Sales | 644 |
| Arroyo, Michael | Manufacturing | 765 |
| Sanchez, Roberto | Quality Control | 356 |
| Parker, Kathy | Operations | 245 |
| Lewis, Debra | Operations | 276 |
| O'Brien, James | Sales | 621 |
| Gruden, Hank | Quality Control | 395 |
| Newton, Manuel | Personnel | 471 |

# Exercise 75

## On the Job

Macros let you simplify tasks that ordinarily require many keystrokes or commands, such as creating a header or footer, or changing line spacing and indents for a paragraph. Once you record a macro, you can run it at any time to repeat the recorded actions. You can use macros for tasks as simple as opening and printing a document, or for more complicated tasks, such as creating a new document, inserting a table, entering text, and applying an AutoFormat.

As an administrative assistant at Long Shot, Inc., you frequently have to format documents by changing the margins to 1" on all sides and by inserting a standard header and footer. In this exercise, you will create macros for setting the margins and creating a header and footer. You will then use the macros to format a press release.

## Terms

**Macro** A series of commands and keystrokes that you record and save together. You can run the macro to replay the series.

**Shortcut key** A combination of keys (including Alt, Ctrl, and/or Shift, and a regular keyboard key) that you assign to run a macro.

**Visual Basic Editor (VBE)** The programming environment used to write new VBA code or to edit existing VBA code.

**Visual Basic for Applications (VBA)** A macro language version of the Microsoft Visual Basic language used to program Windows applications.

## Notes

### Record a Macro

■ Record a **macro** to automate tasks or actions that you perform frequently.

■ By default, new macros are stored in the Normal template, so they are available for use in all new documents created with the Normal template.

✓ *You can specify a different template if you want.*

■ Macros can save time and help eliminate errors.

■ A single macro can store an unlimited number of keystrokes or mouse actions.

■ You can record mouse actions that select commands in menus and dialog boxes; however, you cannot record mouse actions that select text or position the insertion point.

■ As soon as you start recording, everything you input into your computer is stored in the macro.

✓ *When recording a macro, the mouse pointer changes to an arrow with a cassette tape icon* 📼.

■ A macro is different from AutoText because a macro can store actions and commands as well as text and graphics.

■ You can assign a **shortcut key** combination including Alt, Ctrl, and/or Shift and a regular keyboard key to a macro when you record it to use to play the macro back at any time.

- Word indicates whether the combination is unassigned or already assigned to a Word command in the Customize Keyboard dialog box.

*The Customize Keyboard dialog box*

Shortcut key is unassigned

- If you use a combination that is already assigned, the original purpose of the combination is replaced. For example, if you assign the combination Ctrl+S, you will no longer be able to use that combination to save a file.

✓ You can also create a toolbar button to assign to the macro.

- If a macro doesn't work the way you want, you can delete it and record it again, or edit it using the **Visual Basic Editor**.

- Macros created in Word are recorded using the **Visual Basic for Applications (VBA)** programming language, but you do not need to know how to use VBA to record a macro.

- If you do know how to use VBA you can create a macro by entering code in the Visual Basic Editor (VBE).

- The VBE includes the tools you need to find syntax, logic, and run-time errors in VBA code and to fix them.

- To start the VBE from Word, click Tools, Macro, Macros, select the template or document in which you want to store the macro, type a name for the macro, and then click Create.

## Run a Macro

- Once you have recorded a macro, you can run it any time you are using the template with which it is stored.

- When you run a macro, Word executes the recorded commands and actions in the current document.

- Use the key combination (or toolbar button) you assigned when you recorded the macro to run the macro.

- To perform the macro on part of a document, be sure to select the part first.

# Procedures

### Record a Macro

1. Position the insertion point where you want it to be when you start recording the macro.
2. Double-click **REC** button `REC` on the Status bar.

   **OR**

   a. Click **Tools** ............. `Alt` + `T`
   b. Click **Macro** ..................... `M`
   c. Click **Record New Macro** ............................. `R`
3. Type a macro name.
4. Click **Description** ........ `Alt` + `D`
5. Type a description of the macro, or replace the default description.
6. Click **Keyboard** ........... `Alt` + `K`
7. Press a shortcut key combination.
8. Click **Assign** ........ `Tab`, `Alt` + `A`
9. Click **Close** button

   `    Close    ` .................... `Enter`
10. Perform actions to record.

**To stop recording a macro:**

- Click the **Stop** button `▫` on the Stop Recording toolbar.

**OR**

1. Click **Tools** ................. `Alt` + `T`
2. Click **Macro** ........................ `M`
3. Click **Stop Recording** ......... `R`

   **OR**

   - Double click **REC** button `REC` on Status bar.

### Run a Macro *(Alt+F8)*

- Press assigned key combination.

**OR**

1. Click **Tools** ................. `Alt` + `T`
2. Select **Macro** ..................... `M`
3. Click **Macros** ....................... `M`
4. Click the name of macro to run ..................... `↑`, `↓`
5. Click **Run** button

   `    Run    ` ......... `Alt` + `R`

### Delete a Macro *(Alt+F8)*

1. Click **Tools** ................. `Alt` + `T`
2. Click **Macro** ........................ `M`
3. Click **Macros** ..................... `M`
4. Click the name of macro to delete ........... `↑`, `↓`
5. Click **Delete** button

   `    Delete    ` ........ `Alt` + `D`
6. Click **Yes** button

   `    Yes    ` ...................... `Y`
7. Click **Close** button

   `    Close    ` ................. `Enter`

# Exercise Directions

1. Start Word, if necessary.

2. In a new blank document create the following macros:

   a. Open the Record Macro dialog box.

   b. Name the macro **Margins**.

   c. Enter the description: **Sets all margins to 1"**.

   d. Assign the macro to the key combination Alt+M.

      ✓ *If Alt+M is already assigned to a command or macro, use a different key combination, such as Alt+Ctrl+M.*

   e. Click Assign and then Close to begin recording the macro keystrokes.

   f. Perform the steps to set all page margins to 1".

   g. Stop recording the macro.

3. Open the Record Macro dialog box and create a second macro as follows:

   a. Name the macro **Header**.

   b. Include the description: **Creates a header and footer in Long Shot documents**.

   c. Assign the macro to the key combination Alt+H.

      ✓ *If Alt+H is already assigned to a command or macro, use a different key combination, such as Alt+Shift+H.*

   d. Click Assign and then Close to begin recording the macro keystrokes.

   e. Create a header with the company name— **Long Shot, Inc.**—flush left and today's date flush right.

      ✓ *If necessary, move the right tab stop so that the date is flush with the right margin.*

   f. Create a footer with your name flush left and the word **Page** followed by a space then the page number flush right.

      ✓ *If necessary, move the right tab stop to align with the margin.*

   g. Close the Header/Footer toolbar.

   h. Stop recording the macro.

4. Close the blank document without saving any changes.

5. Open ☺ **75DIMPLES**. This is a version of a one page document you worked with in Exercise 31.

6. Save the file as **DIMPLES2**.

7. Run the Header macro.

8. Run the Margins macro.

9. Preview the document. It should look similar to the one in Illustration A.

      ✓ *At this point, your instructor may ask you to delete the Header and Margins macros from the macro list.*

10. Check the spelling and grammar in the document.

11. Print the document.

12. Close the document, saving all changes.

*Illustration A*

Long Shot, Inc.                                                        Today's date

# A (Brief) History of Golf Balls

Why do golf balls have dimples? Scientifically speaking, the dimples induce turbulence in the boundary layer of air next to the ball, which reduces drag so the ball flies further. The history of golf balls illustrates how dimples came to be the standard.[1]

## Featheries

Once upon a time, golf balls did not have dimples. The earliest balls were made of wood, and had a solid, smooth surface. In about 1618, the Featherie was introduced. A Featherie was handmade from wet leather horse or cow hide tightly packed with wet goose feathers. The leather got smaller as it dried, and the feathers got stiffer.[2] The result was a hard, uneven ball that had imperfections in its surface.

## Gutta Perchas

In 1848 the Gutta Percha ball was introduced. Made from rubber, the Guttie had a smooth exterior and was cheaper to manufacture and to buy than the Featherie.[3] However, golfers noticed that new Gutties did not travel as far as Featheries, or even as far as old, beat-up Gutties. Golfers soon determined that the extra distance was due to the uneven surface.

## Modern Golf Balls

After 1880, manufacturers added patterns to the rubber balls in an attempt to make them travel further. At first, patterns were raised. In 1905, William Taylor applied a dimple pattern to golf balls, and that has been the tradition ever since.[4] Over the years there have been many variations on the number, size, and placement of the dimples in order to help golfers pick up a few extra yards off the tee.

---

[1] Marshall Brain, "How Things Work," <http://www.howstuffworks.com/question37.htm>, today's date.
[2] "A History of the Golf Ball," <http://www.golfeurope.com>, today's date.
[3] "The Origin of the Golf Ball," <http://www.kidzworld.com/site/p445.htm>, today's date.
[4] "A History of the Golf Ball," <http://www.golfeurope.com>, today's date.

Student's Name                                                        Page 1

# On Your Own

1. Start Word and open ⌨OWD74, the brief biography you created in the On Your Own section of Exercise 74, or open 💿75BIO.

2. Save the document as **OWD75-1**, and then close it.

3. Create a new blank document.

4. Create a new macro named **Insertbio** and assign it to a shortcut key combination, such as Alt+I.

5. Record the keystrokes for inserting the **OWD75-1** file into the open document.

6. After you stop recording the macro, close the current document without saving the changes.

7. Create a new blank document and save it as **OWD75-2**.

8. Type a document in which you can include your biography. You might type a letter to someone other than the person you wrote to in Exercise 74, or you might type part of a program or yearbook page.

9. At the appropriate location, use the Insertbio macro to insert the **OWD75-1** file into the **OWD75-2** document.

   ✓ *If you want to work in groups, each classmate could insert his or her bio file into the same document, thereby creating a complete document such as a program or yearbook.*

10. Check the spelling and grammar in the document.

11. Preview the document.

12. Print the document.

13. Ask a classmate to review the document and offer comments or suggestions.

14. Incorporate the suggestions into the document.

   ✓ *Your instructor may ask you to delete the Insertbio macro from the macro list.*

15. Close the document, saving all changes, and exit Word.

# Exercise 76

## Skills Covered:

◆ **Create a Form** ◆ **Insert Form Fields** ◆ **Set Form Field Options**
◆ **Fill Out a Form** ◆ **About Legal Documents**

## On the Job

Use forms to collect information such as names and addresses for product registrations, data for surveys, or products and pricing for invoices or purchase orders. With Word, you can create forms that can be printed and filled out by hand, by typewriter, or with a computer printer. You can also store forms on a computer so they can be filled out on-screen.

As the Manager of in-house training at Long Shot, Inc., you have decided to survey the employees to find out what types of training classes they are interested in. In this exercise, you will create a form that employees can fill out indicating their class preferences, time preferences, whether they have ever taken an in-house training class, and, if so, whether they were satisfied with the class. You will print the form, and, finally, you will test the form by filling it out on the computer.

## Terms

**Form** A document used to collect and organize information.

**Protected** Locked so that unauthorized changes cannot be made.

**Form field** A field inserted in a form document where users can enter information.

**Text box form field** A field inserted on a form in which users can enter data such as text and numbers.

**Check box form field** A rectangular box-shaped field inserted on a form for users to select or deselect.

**Drop-down form field** A field inserted on a form from which users can display a list and select an option.

## Notes

### Create a Form

■ In Word, you store **forms** as template files.

■ To use the form, you create a document based on the template.

■ Forms are **protected** so that users can enter data in the **form fields**, but cannot change any other parts of the document.

■ You can print the document and fill out the form on paper, or you can fill out the form on your computer and store it on a disk.

■ You can save a new Word document as a form, or you can save an existing Word document as a form.

■ In some ways, Word forms are similar to mail merge documents. They contain standard text and graphics that appear the same on every document, and they contain form fields where users can enter variable data.

## Insert Form Fields

- There are three basic types of form fields:
  - **Text box form fields**
  - **Check box form fields**
  - **Drop-down form fields**
- Use the buttons on the Forms toolbar to insert form fields.
- When inserting form fields, give some consideration to the form layout. You may want to use a table or tab stops to be sure fields are aligned to look good on the page and so that it will be easy for users to fill out the form.
- Also, it is important to keep in mind that when a user fills out a form on-screen, Word moves the insertion point from form field to form field based on the order in which fields are inserted in the document.
- To ensure a logical order for users filling out the form, you should give some thought to the order in which you insert the form fields.

## Set Form Field Options

- By default, Word inserts form fields using basic settings. For example, text form fields are set to allow users to enter an unlimited number of text characters.
- You can customize the form field options to control the way data may be entered in the field. For example, you can set text form field options to limit users to entering valid dates, or no more than ten characters.
- You must set properties for drop-down form fields in order to enter the drop-down list items.

## Fill Out a Form

- To fill out a form manually, simply print it.
- To fill out a form on-screen, create a new document based on the form template, enter data in the form fields, then save the document.
- You can leave form fields blank.

## About Legal Documents

- Legal documents are used to insure the legal rights of people, groups, or organizations.
- Legal documents may be as simple as a handwritten note that is signed by all concerned parties and witnessed by a third party.
- Alternatively, legal documents may be long, complex, and written using legal terms and language.
- Many legal documents are forms that combine text and blank spaces or form fields where you may enter customized information.
- Other legal documents are reports, case studies, or opinions that include references to legal authorities.
  - ✓ *Creating a table of authorities is covered in Exercise 57.*
- Some common legal forms include the following:
  - Bill of Sale
  - Last Will and Testament
  - Rental Agreement
  - General Release
  - Living Will
- The laws governing legal documents vary from state to state.
- You may be able to find legal document forms on the Internet.

# Procedures

## Create a Form

1. Create a new Word document.
   OR
   Open an existing document.
2. Display Forms toolbar.
3. Type standard text that will appear on all forms.
4. Delete variable text that will not appear on all forms.
5. Insert form fields as necessary.
   - ✓ *Refer to Insert Form Fields procedures for step-by-step instructions on inserting form fields.*
6. Click **Protect Form** button 🔒 on Forms toolbar.
   OR
   a. Click **Tools** ............. `Alt`+`T`
   b. Click **Protect Document** ...................... `P`
   c. Click **Allow only this type of editing in the document**: check box.
   d. Click **Editing restrictions** drop-down arrow.
   e. Click **Filling in forms**.
   f. Select exceptions as necessary.
   g. Click **Yes, Start Enforcing Protection**.
      - ✓ *For more information on protecting documents, refer to Exercise 66.*
7. Click **File** ...................... `Alt`+`F`
8. Click **Save As** ...................... `A`
9. Click **Save as type** drop-down arrow .......... `Alt`+`T`
10. Select **Document Template** ................ `↕`, `Enter`
11. Select template folder where you want form template stored.
    - ✓ *In the Templates dialog box, the form template will be displayed on the tab with the name of the folder where it is stored.*
12. Click **File name** .......... `Alt`+`N`

13. Type desired file name.
14. Click **Save** button
    Save ............ `Alt`+`S`
15. Click **File** .................... `Alt`+`F`
16. Click **Close** ........................ `C`

## Insert Form Fields

1. Open form template document.
2. Display Forms toolbar.
3. If necessary, click **Protect Form** button 🔒 on Forms toolbar to unprotect the form.
   OR
   a. Click **Tools** ............. `Alt`+`T`
   b. Click **Unprotect Document** ...................... `P`
4. Position insertion point where you want to insert first form field.
   - ✓ *Remember, users will tab through form fields in the order in which form fields are inserted.*
5. Click desired button on Forms toolbar:
   - Click **Text Form Field** button `ab|` to insert text form field.
   - Click **Check Box Form Field** button ☑ to insert check box field.
   - Click **Drop-Down Form Field** button to insert drop-down field.
6. Repeat steps 4 and 5 until all form fields are inserted.
   - ✓ *You can toggle form field shading off and on using the Form Field Shading button `a` on the Forms toolbar.*
7. Click **Protect Form** button 🔒 on Forms toolbar.
   OR
   a. Click **Tools** ............. `Alt`+`T`
   b. Click **Protect Document** ...................... `P`

c. Click **Allow only this type of editing in the document**: check box.
   d. Click **Editing restrictions** drop-down arrow.
   e. Click **Filling in forms**.
   f. Select exceptions as necessary.
   g. Click **Yes, Start Enforcing Protection**.
8. Click **Save** button
   Save ............ `Alt`+`S`
9. Click **File** .................... `Alt`+`F`
10. Click **Close** ........................ `C`

## Set Form Field Properties

**Text form fields:**

1. Open form template document.
2. If necessary, click **Protect Form** button 🔒 on Forms toolbar.
   OR
   a. Click **Tools** ............ `Alt`+`T`
   b. Click **Unprotect Document** ...................... `P`
3. Click desired text form field.
4. Click **Form Field Options** button on Forms toolbar.
   OR
   a. Right-click desired form field.
   b. Click **Properties** ............ `R`
5. Select desired options as follows:
   - Select type of text allowed from **Type** drop-down list ....... `Alt`+`P`, `↕`, `Enter`
   - Enter default text to display in **Default text** text box .................. `Alt`+`E`
   - Enter number of characters allowed in **Maximum length** text box ...... `Alt`+`M`
   - Select format from (*Type*) **format** drop-down list ........ `Alt`+`F`

✓ *Name of format box changes depending on the type of text selected from* **Type** *drop-down list.*

6. Click **OK**..........................`Enter`

7. When all changes are complete, click **Protect Form** button 🔒 on Forms toolbar.
   OR

   a. Click **Tools** ...........`Alt`+`T`

   b. Click **Protect Document** .....................`P`

   c. Click **Allow only this type of editing in the document**: check box.

   d. Click **Editing restrictions** drop-down arrow.

   e. Click **Filling in forms**.

   f. Select exceptions as necessary.

   g. Click **Yes, Start Enforcing Protection**.

## Check box form fields:

1. Open form template document.

2. If necessary, click **Protect Form** button 🔒 on Forms toolbar.
   OR

   a. Click **Tools** ............`Alt`+`T`

   b. Click **Unprotect Document** .....................`P`

3. Click desired check box form field.

4. Click **Form Field Options** button 🖳 on Forms toolbar.
   OR

   a. Right-click desired form field.

   b. Click **Properties** ...........`R`

5. Set size options as follows:

   • Select **Auto** option button ..........`Alt`+`A` to set size according to current font size.

   • Select **Exactly** option button ..........`Alt`+`E` type desired font size.

6. Set default value options as follows:

   • Select **Not checked**.................`Alt`+`K` to display check box not checked by default.

   • Select **Checked** .....`Alt`+`D` to display check box checked by default.

7. Click **OK** ...........................`Enter`

8. Click **Protect Form** button 🔒 on Forms toolbar.
   OR

   a. Click **Tools** ............`Alt`+`T`

   b. Click **Protect Document**.....................`P`

   c. Click **Allow only this type of editing in the document**: check box.

   d. Click **Editing restrictions** drop-down arrow.

   e. Click **Filling in forms**.

   f. Select exceptions as necessary.

   g. Click **Yes, Start Enforcing Protection**.

## Drop-down form fields:

1. Open form template document.

2. If necessary, click **Protect Form** button 🔒 on Forms toolbar.
   OR

   a. Click **Tools** ............`Alt`+`T`

   b. Click **Unprotect Document**.....................`P`

3. Click desired drop-down form field.

4. Click **Form Field Options** button 🖳 on Forms toolbar.
   OR

   a. Right-click desired form field

   b. Click **Properties**.............`R`

5. Click **Drop-down item**: text box.......................`Alt`+`D`

6. Type first option.

7. Click **Add**.....................`Alt`+`A`

8. Repeat steps 5-7 until all drop-down options are entered.

9. Click **OK**..........................`Enter`

10. Click **Protect Form** button 🔒 on Forms toolbar.
    OR

    a. Click **Tools**.............`Alt`+`T`

    b. Click **Protect Document** .....................`P`

    c. Click **Allow only this type of editing in the document**: check box.

    d. Click **Editing restrictions** drop-down arrow.

    e. Click **Filling in forms**.

    f. Select exceptions as necessary.

    g. Click **Yes, Start Enforcing Protection**.

## Fill Out a Form

1. Start Word.

2. Click **File** ....................`Alt`+`F`

3. Click **New** ..........................`N`

4. Click **On my computer** in the Templates section of the New task pane.

5. Click tab where form template is stored.......`Ctrl`+`Tab`

6. Double-click desired form template.

   ✓ *First form field is selected.*

7. Enter data in first form field as follows:

   • Type text in text form field.

   • Click check box form field ...........................`Space` to select or deselect check box.

   • Click drop-down form field arrow, then click desired option ..`Alt`+`↓`, `↗↙`, `Enter`

8. Press **Tab**...........................`Tab` to move to next form field.

9. Repeat steps 7–8 until form is complete.

   ✓ *You do not have to enter data in every field.*

10. Save and name document.

# Exercise Directions

1. Start Word, if necessary.

2. Create a new blank document based on the Longshot document template you created in Exercise 73.

3. Save the document as a new template with the name **SURVEY**.

   ✓ *Ask your instructor where to store the new template file.*

4. Insert a table in the document as shown in Illustration A. Keep gridlines displayed, but do not use any borders.

   ✓ *Use the Draw table features and the Tables and Borders toolbar to create the table as shown. Cell sizes are approximate. For a refresher on drawing tables, see Exercise 40.*

5. Using a 16-point serif font, type the text in the table shown in Illustration A.

6. Center the words **Yes**, **No**, and **Maybe** in their cells.

7. Check the spelling and grammar in the document.

8. Preview the document. It should look similar to Illustration A.

   ✓ *Gridlines are displayed in the illustration so you can see the size of columns and rows; they will not be displayed in Print Preview.*

9. Print the document.

10. In row 1, column 2, insert a text form field using default properties.

11. In row 2, column 2, insert another text form field, using default properties.

12. In row 3, column 2, insert a third text form field. Set the type property to *Current date*, and select the *MM/dd/yy* format.

13. In rows 5 and 6, insert check box form fields under the text **Yes** and **No** in columns 2 and 3.

    ✓ *Press Enter after the text in each column to position the insertion point centered on the next line in the cell.*

14. In row 7, column 2, insert a text form field.

15. In row 8, insert check box form fields under the text **Yes**, **No**, and **Maybe** in columns 2, 3, and 4.

16. In row 9, insert a drop-down form field. Enter the following three drop-down list items: **Corporate Headquarters, Local Office, Off-site Training Center**.

17. In row 10, column 2, insert a text form field.

18. Display form field shading if it is not already displayed.

19. Form protect the template.

20. Preview the document. It should look similar to the one in Illustration B.

21. Close the template document, saving all changes.

22. Create a new document based on the **SURVEY** form template.

23. Save the document as **SURVEY1**.

24. Fill out the form as follows:

    • Enter your name in the first text form field.

    • Enter **Marketing** in the second text form field.

    • Skip the date field, which should fill in the current date automatically.

    • Select *Yes* for whether or not you have attended in-house training classes.

    • Select *No* for whether or not you were satisfied.

    • For the reason why you were not satisfied, type that you thought the course was not challenging enough.

    • Select *Maybe* for whether or not you are interested in future classes.

    • Select *Off-site Training Center* as the location you would prefer.

    • Enter any comments you would like in the final text form field.

25. Print the document.

26. Close the document, saving all changes.

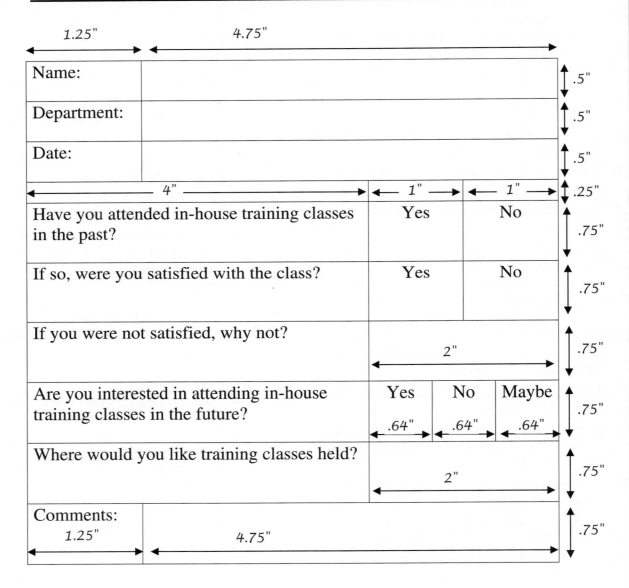

# Long Shot, Inc.

**234 Simsbury Drive ⚑ Ithaca, NY 14850**

**Telephone: 607-555-9191 ⚑ Fax: 607-555-9292 ⚑ E-mail: mail@longshot.net**

| | |
|---|---|
| Name: | |
| Department: | |
| Date: | |

| | | |
|---|---|---|
| Have you attended in-house training classes in the past? | Yes | No |
| If so, were you satisfied with the class? | Yes | No |
| If you were not satisfied, why not? | | |
| Are you interested in attending in-house training classes in the future? | Yes / No / Maybe | |
| Where would you like training classes held? | | |
| Comments: | | |

*Illustration B*

# Long Shot, Inc.

**234 Simsbury Drive ⚑ Ithaca, NY 14850**

**Telephone: 607-555-9191 ⚑ Fax: 607-555-9292 ⚑ E-mail: mail@longshot.net**

Name:

Department:

Date: mm/dd/yy

| | | |
|---|---|---|
| Have you attended in-house training classes in the past? | Yes ☐ | No ☐ |
| If so, were you satisfied with the class? | Yes ☐ | No ☐ |

If you were not satisfied, why not?

Are you interested in attending in-house training classes in the future?   Yes ☐   No ☐   Maybe ☐

Where would you like training classes held?   Corporate Headquarters

Comments:

# On Your Own

1. Plan a form that could be used as a legal document for a club or organization to which you belong. For example, a field trip permission slip is a legal form. If the organization rents or loans equipment, you might create a rental form. Decide the form fields you would need on the form, as well as the standard text. Plan the layout and design of the form.

2. Start Word and create a new document.

3. Save the document as a template with the name **OWD76-1**.

4. Enter all of the standard text you want on your form. Use a table if it helps you line up the information neatly on the page.

5. Enter the form fields you will need on your form. Remember to enter them in the order in which you want users to fill them out.

6. Check the spelling and grammar in the document.

7. Form protect the document.

8. Print the document.

9. Ask a classmate to review the document and offer comments and suggestions.

10. Incorporate the comments and suggestions into the form template.

11. Save the template and close it.

12. Create a new document based on the **OWD76-1** template.

13. Save the document as **OWD76-2**.

14. Fill out the form on the screen, or print it and fill it out manually.

15. Save the form, close it, and exit Word.

# Exercise 77

### ◆ Critical Thinking

The Blue Sky Dairy Name that Flavor contest was such a success that the company wants to continue sponsoring contests throughout the year and has hired you as the Contest Coordinator. You have decided to design some documents that can be used for all promotional material. In this exercise, you will create an AutoText entry with your name and new job title so you can insert it in all letters, memos, and other documents you generate.

You will also design a newsletter template that you can use to issue contest information to Dairy employees on a monthly basis, and you will create a registration form that employees can use to offer their services as contest judges. You will use the newsletter template to create the first monthly update, inserting a file that already contains some text you want to use. You will also test the registration form by filling it out on-screen.

## Exercise Directions

### Create AutoText and a Macro

1. Start Word, if necessary.
2. Create a new document.
3. Create an AutoText entry named **mysignature** from the following text:

   **Your Name**
   **Contest Coordinator**
   **Blue Sky Dairy Co.**
   **Highway 73**
   **Cambridge, WI 53523**
   **608-555-2697**
   **mail@blueskydairy.net**

4. Once the AutoText entry is saved, delete the text from the document.
5. Record a macro that inserts a continuous section break and then divides the second section into two columns of equal width.
   - Name the new macro **Columns**.
   - Type the description: **Applies newsletter formatting**.
   - Assign the key combination Alt+C, if it is available, or another combination if necessary.
   - Record the necessary keystrokes, and then stop recording.
6. Close the current document without saving it.

### Create a Template

1. Create a new blank document.
2. Save the document as a template with the name **DIARY**.
3. Design the document as follows (refer to Illustration A to see the completed letterhead):
   a. On the first line of the document, type **DAIRY DIARY** centered in a 48 point sans serif font. (Tempus Sans ITC is used in the illustration.)
   b. On the second line, use the same font in 16 points to type **The Monthly Update for all Blue Sky Dairy Contests**
   c. Leave the third line blank, and remove all formatting from it.
   d. Apply a ¾ pt. triple line border below the second line.
   e. Apply a ¾ triple line page border around the entire document.
4. Move the insertion point to the blank line at the end of the document and run the Columns macro.
5. Close the file, saving all changes.

## Create a Newsletter

1. Create a new document based on the **DIARY** template.
2. Save the file with the name **MONTH1**.
3. Move the insertion point to the end of the document and insert the file ⊙ **77UPDATE**.
4. Select the information about the prize winners (the paragraphs beginning **Grand Prize, Honorable Mention 1**, and **Honorable Mention 2**) and apply a hanging indent to align the information.
5. Move the insertion point to the end of the document and type: **For more information contact:**, and then press Enter.
6. Insert the *mysignature* AutoText entry.
7. Check the spelling and grammar in the document.
8. Preview the document. It should look similar to Illustration A. If necessary, insert a column break to move the heading **Registration Forms** to the top of the right column.
9. Print the document and then close it, saving all changes.

## Create a Form

1. Create a new blank document and save it as a template with the name **REGFORM**.
2. Type and format the document shown in Illustration B.
   - ✓ *Do not include any table border lines. The gridlines are shown so you can see the cell sizes.*
   - ✓ *Cell measurements are approximate.*
3. Insert form fields as follows:
   - First Name: Text field with default properties.
   - Last Name: Text field with default properties.
   - Department: Drop down field with options for **Administration**, **Field**, **Manufacturing**, **Marketing**, **Personnel**, **Quality Control**, **Sales**, **Other**.
   - Phone Extension: Text field, set to accept numbers only, in the general format, with a maximum length of 4 characters.
   - Email Address: Text field with default properties.
   - Contest for which you would like to be a judge: Drop-down field with options for **Art**, **Contest Ideas**, **Essay**, **Games**, **Name that Flavor**.
   - Yes: Check box.
   - No: Check box.
   - Comments: Text field with default properties.
4. Check the spelling and grammar.
5. Display field shading.
6. Form protect the document.
7. Preview the document. It should look similar to Illustration B, without the border lines.
   - ✓ *If there are border lines in your document, remove them.*
8. Print the form.
9. Close the document, saving all changes.
10. Create a new document based on the **REGFORM** template.
11. Save the document as **MYREG**.
12. Fill out the form.
13. Print the document.
14. Close the document, saving all changes, and exit Word.

*Illustration A*

# DAIRY DIARY

## The Monthly Update for all Blue Sky Dairy Contests

### Name that Flavor Contest a Huge Hit

The success of the Name that Flavor contest was overwhelming! Entries came in from around the world, and the judges had a hard time selecting a winner. As a result, Blue Sky has committed to sponsoring additional contests throughout the year. A contest coordinator has been appointed (see the end of the newsletter), and a budget has been set aside.

Since we can't come out with a new flavor every month, we'll be running many different types of contests, designed for people of all ages, talents, and abilities. We hope to have essay contests, art contests, guessing games, and more. We may even have a contest to generate ideas for new contests! Stay tuned to the Dairy Diary for the latest contest information.

### Judge Training

Also in the works is a training plan for judges. With the advent of new contests, we will need more employees to volunteer to help with selecting the winners. We hope that experienced judges will help train newcomers. Although it may take some time, judging can be a lot of fun.

### Registration Forms

Finally, we are in the process of formalizing a judge's registration form. It will be made available on the company's Web site as well as in our main office. Employees interested in judging any contest to fill out and return the form.

### Name that Flavor Contest Winners

Grand Prize: "Blue Sky Banquet" submitted by Melanie Jackson of San Francisco, California

Honorable Mention 1: "Chocolate Sunrise" submitted by Janine Flaherty of Tampa, Florida

Honorable Mention 2: "Sundae Delight" submitted by Jeffrey Levine of Seaford, New York

All participants received commemorative T-Shirts and discount coupons for use in any Blue Sky retail outlet.

For more information contact:
Student's Name
Contest Coordinator
Blue Sky Dairy Co.
Highway 73
Cambridge, WI 53523
608-555-2697
mail@blueskydairy.net

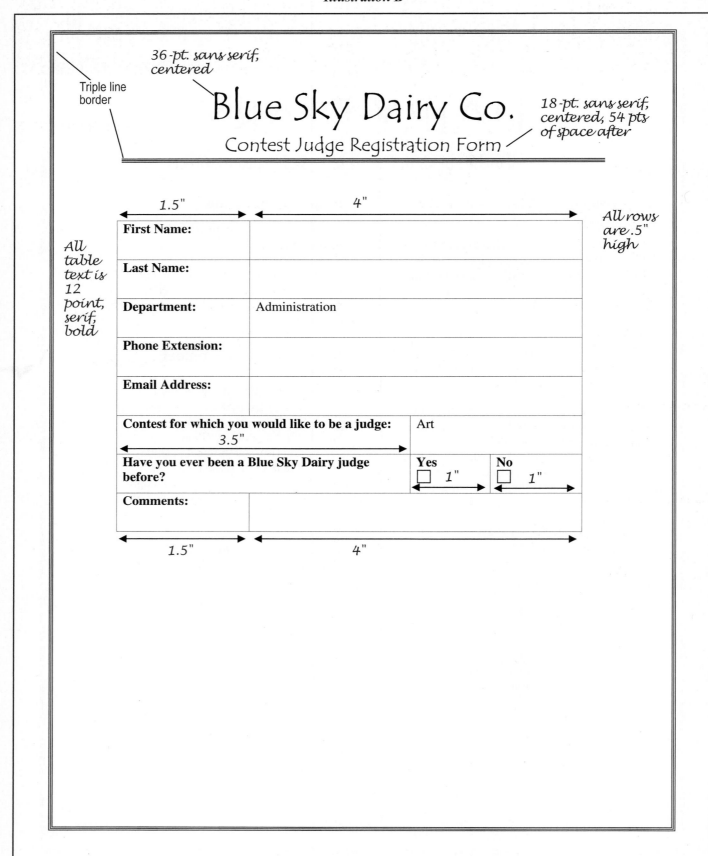

36-pt. sans serif, centered

Triple line border

# Blue Sky Dairy Co.

18-pt. sans serif, centered, 54 pts of space after

## Contest Judge Registration Form

All table text is 12 point, serif, bold

1.5"    4"

All rows are .5" high

| First Name: | |
| --- | --- |
| Last Name: | |
| Department: | Administration |
| Phone Extension: | |
| Email Address: | |
| Contest for which you would like to be a judge:<br>3.5" | Art |
| Have you ever been a Blue Sky Dairy judge before? | Yes ☐ 1"   No ☐ 1" |
| Comments: | |

1.5"    4"

# Lesson 13

## Graphics

# Exercise 78

**Skills Covered:**

◆ **About Graphics Objects** ◆ **Insert Drawing Objects**
◆ **Use the Drawing Canvas** ◆ **Select Objects** ◆ **Move Drawing Objects**
◆ **Set Text Wrap Options**

## On the Job

Use graphics such as shapes and text boxes to illustrate and enhance text documents. You can integrate the objects into the document, making the document easier to read and more interesting for the reader.

You want to improve the appearance of the Liberty Blooms newsletter. In this exercise, you will make the document more visually interesting by inserting and positioning drawing objects.

## Terms

**Graphics object** A picture, chart, shape, or other element that can be inserted into a Word document.

**Drawing object** A shape or line created in Word and saved as part of the Word document.

**Picture object** A graphics object created using a different application and then inserted into a Word document.

**AutoShape** Built-in shapes you select from a palette to insert in a Word document.

**Text box** A rectangular drawing object in which text or graphics images can be inserted and positioned anywhere on a page.

**Clip art** Picture files that can be inserted into a document.

**Floating object** A graphics object that is positioned independently from the document text.

**Drawing canvas** A drawing object that defines an area in a document in which you can insert other drawing objects.

**Sizing handles** Rectangular boxes around the edges of a selected object that you use to resize the object.

**In-line** An object positioned within the text with other characters.

**Bounding box** A nonprinting border around the outside of an object. When the object is selected, the bounding box is sometimes called the selection box, or selection rectangle.

## Notes

### About Graphics Objects

■ You can insert two types of **graphics objects** into a Word document: **drawing objects** and **pictures**.

- Common drawing objects include **AutoShapes**, diagrams, and **text boxes**.
- Common pictures include photographs and **clip art**.
  - ✓ *Using clip art is covered in Exercise 80.*

## Insert Drawing Objects

■ Use the tools on the left side of Word's Drawing toolbar to insert drawing objects into a document.

■ There are two basic types of drawing objects:
- Closed shapes. Closed shapes include rectangles and ovals as well as more complex shapes such as hexagons, hearts, stars, and lightning bolts.
- Lines. Lines include straight lines, curved lines, freeform lines, and arrows.

■ To draw objects you simply select the type of shape and then drag the mouse pointer to draw the shape in the document.

■ You can draw your own objects using the rectangle, oval, line, or arrow tools, or you can insert AutoShapes.

■ You can insert a single drawing object, or combine multiple objects to create a larger drawing.

■ By default, Word inserts drawings as **floating objects** in a document so they can be positioned anywhere on a page.

■ You must move the object to position it where you want it.

■ Floating objects cannot be displayed in Normal view. Use Print Layout view to insert and edit drawing objects.

## Use the Drawing Canvas

■ Word automatically inserts a **drawing canvas** when you select the drawing object you want to insert.

■ You can insert the object on the canvas, or in the document outside the canvas.

■ If you insert the object outside the canvas area, Word automatically deletes the canvas.
- ✓ *If you drag an object off of the canvas, the canvas is not automatically deleted.*

■ You can move and resize the entire canvas, which is useful if your drawing includes multiple objects that you want to keep together.

■ If you want to work with a single object at a time, you can drag the object off the canvas.

■ You must select and delete the canvas manually to remove it from the document.

■ By default, the canvas has no border or fill; you can apply formatting if you want the canvas to be visible in the finished document.
- ✓ *Refer to Exercise 82 for information on applying borders and fills to objects.*

■ You can delete an unused canvas from a document.

■ You can create a blank canvas.

■ You can set Word so that it does not automatically create a drawing canvas.

*Drawing Objects on a Drawing Canvas*

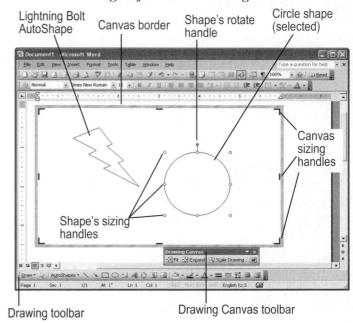

## Select Objects

■ You must select objects in order to change them.

■ **Sizing handles** are displayed around selected objects.

■ To select a single object you click it. You can also select more than one object at a time; changes will affect all selected objects.

## Move Drawing Objects

■ Drag a floating object to position it anywhere on the page.

■ Use drag-and-drop or the Cut and Paste commands to move an **in-line** object as you would a regular text character.
- ✓ *If you have nonprinting characters displayed, you will see an anchor icon displayed near the object. See Exercise 79 for information on anchors.*

## Set Text Wrap Options

- You can change the way text wraps around an object to affect the way the object is integrated into the document.

- Text wrapping options are available in the Format dialog box, or from the menu that's displayed when you click the Draw button on the Drawing toolbar.

- Graphics objects can be integrated with text in seven ways:

  - *In-line with text:*    Object is positioned on a line with text characters.
  - *Square:*    Text is wrapped on all four sides of the object's **bounding box**.
  - *Tight:*    Text is wrapped to the contours of the image.

  - *Behind text:*    Text continues in lines over the object, obscuring the object.
  - *In front of text:*    Text continues in lines behind the object, which may obscure the text.
  - *Top and Bottom*    Text is displayed above and below object but not on left or right sides.
  - *Through*    Text runs through object

  ✓ *You cannot set different wrapping options for individual objects on a drawing canvas.*

# Procedures

## Insert Blank Drawing Canvas

1. Click **Insert** ................. [Alt]+[I]
2. Click **Picture** ..................... [P]
3. Click **New Drawing** ............. [N]

## Display the Drawing Toolbar

- Click **Drawing** button 🖼️ on Standard toolbar.

  ✓ *By default, the Drawing toolbar is usually displayed along the bottom of the screen.*

OR

1. Click **View** .................. [Alt]+[V]
2. Click **Toolbars** ................... [T]
3. Click **Drawing**.

## Draw Closed Shapes

### Draw rectangle:

1. Click **Rectangle** button 🔲 on Drawing toolbar.

   ✓ *Mouse pointer changes to a cross hair.*

2. Position mouse pointer on canvas where you want shape to begin.

✓ *If you do not want to use the canvas, click in the document outside the canvas area.*

3. Click and drag diagonally to draw shape.
4. Release mouse button when shape is desired size.

   ✓ *Alternatively, simply click where you want to insert the shape. Word creates the shape in a default size, which can be resized and positioned as necessary.*

### Draw square:

1. Click **Rectangle** button 🔲 on Drawing toolbar.

   ✓ *Mouse pointer changes to a cross hair.*

2. Press and hold **Shift** key ... [Shift]
3. Position mouse pointer in document where you want shape to begin.
4. Click and drag diagonally to draw shape.
5. Release mouse button and then release Shift key when shape is desired size.

✓ *Alternatively, simply click where you want to insert the shape. Word creates the shape in a default size, which can be resized and positioned as necessary.*

### Draw oval:

1. Click **Oval** button 🔘 on Drawing toolbar.

   ✓ *Mouse pointer changes to a cross hair.*

2. Position mouse pointer in document where you want to begin shape.
3. Click and drag to draw shape.
4. Release mouse button when shape is desired size.

   ✓ *Alternatively, simply click where you want to insert the shape. Word creates the shape in a default size, which can be resized and positioned as necessary.*

### Draw circle:

1. Click **Oval** button 🔘 on Drawing toolbar.

   ✓ *Mouse pointer changes to a cross hair.*

2. Press and hold **Shift** key ... `Shift`
3. Position mouse pointer in document where you want shape to begin.
4. Click and drag to draw shape.
5. Release mouse button when shape is desired size.
6. Release **Shift** key .............. `Shift`

   ✓ *Alternatively, simply click where you want to insert the shape. Word creates the shape in a default size, which can be resized and positioned as necessary.*

## Draw Lines

### Draw straight lines:

1. Click **Line** button `\` on Drawing toolbar.

   ✓ *Mouse pointer changes to a cross hair.*

2. Position mouse pointer in document where you want line to begin.
3. Click and drag to point where you want line to end.
4. Release mouse button.

### Draw arrows:

1. Click **Arrow** button `↘` on Drawing toolbar.

   ✓ *Mouse pointer changes to a cross hair.*

2. Position mouse pointer in document where you want arrow to begin.

   ✓ *This end will not have an arrowhead.*

3. Click and drag to point where you want arrow to end.
4. Release mouse button.

   ✓ *Word adds an arrowhead to end of line.*

## Select AutoShape Tool

1. Click **AutoShapes** button `AutoShapes ▾` on Drawing toolbar...........................`Alt`+`U`
2. Select desired AutoShapes palette:

   • **Lines** ..............................`L`

   • **Connectors** ....................`N`
   • **Basic Shapes** ................`B`
   • **Block Arrows** ................`A`
   • **Flowchart** ......................`F`
   • **Stars and Banners**........`S`
   • **Callouts** ........................`C`

3. Click desired AutoShape button.

## Insert Closed AutoShape

1. Select desired AutoShape.

   ✓ *Mouse pointer changes to cross hair.*

2. Click on canvas where you want to insert shape.
   OR
   Click and drag to draw shape.

## Insert AutoShape Line or Arrow or Double-arrow

1. Select desired AutoShape.

   ✓ *Mouse pointer changes to cross hair.*

2. Position mouse pointer where you want line or arrow to begin.
3. Click and drag to point where you want line or arrow to end.
4. Release mouse button.

## Insert AutoShape Curve

1. Select **Curve** AutoShape `S` from Lines palette.

   ✓ *Mouse pointer changes to cross hair.*

2. Click where you want line to begin.
3. Release mouse button.
4. Click at point where you want line to curve.
5. Repeat step 4 at each point where you want line to curve.
6. Double-click to end line.

## Insert Freeform Line

1. Select **Freeform** AutoShape `⌓` from Lines palette.
2. Click where you want line to begin.

   ✓ *Mouse pointer changes to pencil icon.*

3. Drag to draw freehand as if you were using a pencil.
   OR
   Release mouse button and click to draw straight lines.
4. Double-click to end line.

## Insert AutoShape Scribble Line

1. Select **Scribble** AutoShape `⸙` from Lines palette.
2. Click where you want line to begin.

   ✓ *Mouse pointer changes to pencil icon.*

3. Drag to draw freehand as if you were using a pencil.
4. Release mouse button to end line.

## Select Object

• Click object to select.

## Select Multiple Objects

1. Click first object to select.
2. Press and hold **Shift** ..........`Shift`
3. Click next object to select.
4. Repeat until desired objects are selected.
5. Release **Shift**....................`Shift`
   OR
   a. Click **Select Objects** button `↖` on Drawing toolbar.
   b. Click and drag to draw a box around all objects to select.
   c. Release mouse button.
   d. Click **Select Objects** button `↖` to turn feature off.

## Move a Floating Object

1. Click object to select it.
2. Move mouse pointer over object.

   ✓ *Mouse pointer changes to four-headed arrow.*

3. Drag object to new location.

   ✓ *Use this method to move an object off the drawing canvas.*

## Move an In-Line Object
(*Ctrl + X, Ctrl + V*)

1. Select object.
2. Click **Cut** button ✂.
3. Position insertion point in new location.
4. Click **Paste** button 📋.

## Wrap Text around an Object

1. Click object to select it.
2. Click **Draw** .................. `Alt`+`D` on Drawing toolbar.
3. Click **Text Wrapping** button 🔲 .......................... `T`

   ✓ *If the Drawing Canvas or Picture toolbar is displayed, you may click the Text Wrapping button on the toolbar.*

4. Click desired wrapping option.
   - **In Line With Text** .......... `I`
   - **Square** ........................... `S`
   - **Tight** ............................ `T`
   - **Behind Text** .................. `D`
   - **In Front of Text** ........... `N`
   - **Top and Bottom** ........... `O`
   - **Through** ....................... `H`

OR

1. Click object to select it.
2. Click **Format** .............. `Alt`+`O`
3. Click object type:
   - **Text Box** ...................... `O`
   - **AutoShape** ................... `O`
   - **Drawing Canvas** .......... `D`
4. Click **Layout** tab ........ `Ctrl`+`Tab`
5. Click desired wrapping style:
   - **In line with text** ..... `Alt`+`I`
   - **Square** ................... `Alt`+`Q`
   - **Tight** ...................... `Alt`+`T`
   - **Behind text** .......... `Alt`+`B`
   - **In front of text** ...... `Alt`+`F`
6. Click **OK** .......................... `Enter`

## Set Word to Not Create a Drawing Canvas

1. Click **Tools** .................. `Alt`+`F`
2. Click **Options** ..................... `O`
3. Click the **General** tab . `Ctrl`+`Tab`
4. Deselect the **Automatically create drawing canvas when inserting AutoShapes** check box ........................ `C`
5. Click **OK** .......................... `Enter`

## Delete an Object

1. Select the object.
2. Press **Del** ........................ `Del`

   ✓ *When you delete a drawing canvas, all objects on the canvas are deleted as well.*

# Exercise Directions

1. Start Word, if necessary.
2. Open ⌨COLUMNS or open 💿**78COLUMNS**.
3. Save the file as **COLUMNS2**.
4. Insert the Smiley Face AutoShape from the Basic Shapes palette into the first article in the newsletter.
   a. Select the Smiley Face shape on the Basic Shapes palette
      ✓ *Word inserts the drawing canvas.*
   b. Click in the document within the text of the first article.
      ✓ *Word deletes the canvas and inserts the shape.*
      ✓ *If you insert the shape on the canvas, simply drag it off, and then delete the canvas. If you cannot see the canvas, click where you think it is located to select it.*
5. Move the shape so the bottom of the circle is at the 4" mark on the vertical ruler and so that the left side of the circle is at the 1.5" mark on the horizontal ruler (refer to the illustration).
6. Set text wrapping for the shape to square.
7. Insert a 5-point star from the Stars and Banners palette into the letterhead of the newsletter.
   a. Select the 5-point Star shape on the Stars and Banners palette.
   b. Click in the document within the letterhead.
      ✓ *If you insert the shape on the drawing canvas, simply drag it off, and then delete the canvas.*
8. Move the shape so the top-right point of the star is even with the right margin of the document and the bottom points align with the third line of text (refer to the illustration).
9. Set text wrapping for the shape to square. Notice that the text moves to leave more room around the shape.
10. Set text wrapping for the shape to Behind Text.
11. Preview the document. It should look similar to Illustration A.
12. Check the spelling and grammar in the document.
13. Print the document.
14. Close the file, saving all changes.

*Illustration A*

# Liberty Blooms News

Published by the Liberty Blooms Flower Shop
345 Chestnut Street, Philadelphia, PA 19106

## Welcome

Welcome to the first issue of *Liberty Blooms News*, a monthly newsletter for people who visit the Liberty Blooms Flower Shop. The primary goal of this publication is to provide you with news about activities and events that you might find of interest. In addition, we intend to publish class schedules, gardening tips, and general information about related topics.

*Liberty Blooms News* will be mailed directly to everyone who has registered at our Chestnut Street store. Please contact us with questions and suggestions. We will do our best to address your comments in future issues.

## Classes and Seminars

If you are a frequent visitor to Liberty Blooms, you know there is always something going on at 345 Chestnut Street. From flower arranging to cooking with herbs, we try to fill the calendar with interesting and informative activities that the whole family will enjoy.

The following events are scheduled for the coming months. Some events require registration, so please call ahead for more information.

Edible Gardens      May 13
Flower Arranging    May 21
Water Gardens       June 3
Potpourri Designs   June 11

## Recipe Showcase

### *Chicken with Tomatoes and Herbs*                    *Yield: Four Servings*

### Ingredients

8 boneless chicken pieces
1 tablespoon olive oil
10 ½ oz. tomatoes, drained
¾ cup chicken stock
2 teaspoons mixed herbs, chopped
1 ½ oz. black olives, chopped
1 teaspoon sugar
Fresh basil to garnish

### Directions

1. Heat oil in large skillet.
2. Add chicken pieces and cook until browned on all sides.
3. Add the tomatoes, stock and mixed herbs and simmer for 30 minutes or until chicken is cooked through.
4. Add the olives and sugar and simmer for an additional 5 minutes.
5. Garnish with fresh basil and serve with rice or pasta.

# On Your Own

1. Open ⌨OWD72, the newsletter document you used in the On Your Own section of Exercise 72, or open 💿78NEWS.

2. Save the file as **OWD78**.

3. Insert at least two drawing objects in the newsletter. For example, insert a lightning bolt AutoShape, or try drawing a shape of your own.

4. Position the shapes for the best effect.

5. Try different text wrapping options, and select the one that looks best.

6. Check spelling and grammar in the document.

7. Preview the document.

8. Adjust column breaks and balance columns as necessary.

9. Print the document.

10. Ask a classmate to review the document and offer comments and suggestions, particularly about the layout and design.

11. Incorporate the suggestions into the document.

12. Close the document, saving all changes, and exit Word.

# Exercise 79

**Skills Covered:**

◆ **Resize Objects**   ◆ **Use a Text Box**
◆ **Use Frames**   ◆ **Copy an Object**   ◆ **Align Drawing Objects**

## On the Job

Insert a text box in a document so you can position and format text independently from the rest of the document. Resize and align objects to improve the appearance of the document. Copy objects to save time and to insure consistency between similar objects in a document.

It is time to create a flyer announcing the essay contest for Blue Sky Dairy. In this exercise, you will open an existing flyer and edit it for the new contest. You will use text boxes and shapes to make the flyer interesting.

## Terms

**Scale** To change the size of an object by a percentage of the original size. For example, to double the size of an object, you would set the scale to 200%.

**Text box** A rectangular drawing object in which text or graphics images can be inserted and positioned anywhere on a page.

**Frame** A placeholder for text; similar to a text box.

**Anchor** An element in a document, such as the margin or the page itself, relative to which you can position an object.

## Notes

### Resize Objects

- Resize graphics objects to make them larger or smaller.

- Resize the height and width evenly to keep the object in proportion, or unevenly to distort it.

- **Scale** an object to increase or decrease the size proportionally to the original size. For example, to double the height, set the scale to 200%.

- Drag the sizing handles to resize an object, or use the appropriate Format dialog box to set precise measurements.

*A text box on the drawing canvas*

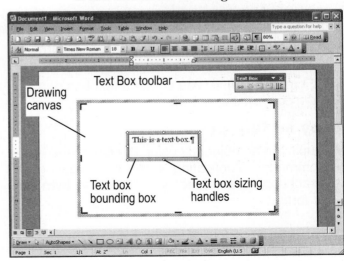

## Use a Text Box

- Insert a **text box** to position blocks of text on a page or to give text a different orientation from other text in the document.

- You can insert a new text box and then type in text, or you can insert a text box around existing text.

- Format text within a text box using the same commands as you would to format regular text. For example, you can select the font, font size, font color, and so on.

- You can also change the direction of the text so it runs top to bottom or bottom to top instead of left to right.

- By default, a new text box has a ½ point single line border around it. You learn how to change the borders around objects in Exercise 82.

- When a text box is selected, the Text Box toolbar is displayed.

- You can also add text to an AutoShape. This inserts a text box around the AutoShape, but the text box cannot be selected separately from the AutoShape.

## Use Frames

- In early versions of Word, text to be integrated with graphics was inserted in a **frame** instead of in a text box.

- Frames are still available in Word and must be used in place of a text box in certain circumstances.

- For example, you must use a frame if you want to include comments, footnotes or endnotes, or certain fields, such index entry fields, with the text.

- Frames do not support many features of text boxes. For example, you cannot change the text direction in a frame and you cannot format a frame.

- To create a frame, you create a text box and then convert it to a frame.

## Copy an Object

- Duplicate an object by using the Copy and Paste commands. Duplicating is useful for creating an exact copy of an object, which you can then edit or format.

- When you duplicate a floating object you cannot control where Word will insert the new copy; drag the copy to move it to its new location.

## Align Drawing Objects

- Use alignment options on the Layout tab of the appropriate Format dialog box to align a floating object horizontally on the page.

- Use the Advanced layout options to position the object precisely, or to customize text wrapping.

- On the Picture Position tab, you can select from three horizontal alignment options and two vertical alignment options. Each option has its own set of parameters:

- For horizontal alignment, select:
  - *Alignment* to align the object left, right, or centered relative to the selected anchor (margin, page, column, or character).
  - *Book layout* to align the object on the inside or outside of the anchor (margin or page).
  - *Absolute position* to specify the precise distance (in inches or points) that you want to leave between the left edge of the object and the anchor (margin, page, column, or character).

- For vertical alignment, select:
  - *Alignment* to align the object on the top, bottom, inside, outside, or centered relative to the anchor (margin, page, or line).
  - *Absolute position* to specify the precise distance (in inches or points) that you want to leave between the top edge of the object and the anchor (margin, page, paragraph, or line).

- An anchor icon ⚓ indicates the **anchor** location in the document. Click the anchor to select the object.

- This is useful if you have trouble selecting an object because it is behind another object or text.

- By default, the object moves with the anchor text if you insert or delete text or graphics in the document.

- You can set Word so the object stays in place even if the surrounding text moves, and you can lock the anchor to keep the object in its same position relative to the page, even if it moves to a different page.

# Procedures

## Resize an Object

1. Click object to select it.
2. Drag a corner sizing handle to resize both height and width.
   - ✓ *Press and hold Shift while dragging a corner to maintain original proportions.*

   **OR**

   Drag a side sizing handle to resize height or width only.

   **OR**

1. Select object.
2. Click **Format**..............`Alt`+`O`
3. Click object type:
   - **Text Box**........................`O`
   - **AutoShape**.....................`O`
   - **Drawing Canvas**...........`D`
4. Click the **Size** tab........`Ctrl`+`Tab`
5. Click **Height**................`Alt`+`E`
6. Type new height measurement.
   - ✓ *If the Lock aspect ratio check box is selected, Word automatically enters the appropriate Width measurement to keep the object proportioned.*
7. Click **Width**.................`Alt`+`D`
8. Type new width measurement.
9. Click **OK**..........................`Enter`

## Scale an Object

1. Select object.
2. Click **Format**................`Alt`+`O`
3. Click object type:
   - **Text Box**........................`O`
   - **AutoShape**.....................`O`
   - **Drawing Canvas**...........`D`
4. Click the **Size** tab........`Ctrl`+`Tab`
5. Click **Height**................`Alt`+`H`
6. Type new height percentage.
   - ✓ *If the Lock aspect ratio check box is selected, Word automatically enters the appropriate Width size to keep the object proportioned.*

7. Click **Width**...................`Alt`+`W`
8. Type new width percentage.
9. Click **OK**..........................`Enter`

## Insert a Text Box

1. Click **Text Box** button `[A]` on Drawing toolbar.

   **OR**

   a. Click **Insert**............`Alt`+`I`
   b. Click **Text Box**...............`X`
   - ✓ *Word inserts the Drawing Canvas and the mouse pointer changes to a cross hair.*
2. Position the mouse pointer where you want the upper-left corner of the text box to be.
3. Click and drag diagonally to draw the text box.
4. Release the mouse button.
5. Type text.

## Insert a Text Box Around Existing Text

1. Select paragraph(s).
2. Click **Text Box** button `[A]` on Drawing toolbar.

   **OR**

   a. Click **Insert**............`Alt`+`I`
   b. Click **Text Box**...............`X`

## Change Direction of Text in Text Box

1. Select text box.
2. Click **Change Text Direction** button `[IIↁ]` on Text Box toolbar.
3. Type text.
   - ✓ *Click Change Text Direction button again to cycle through available text directions.*

   **OR**

1. Select text box.
2. Click **Format** ...............`Alt`+`O`
3. Click **Text Direction**............`X`
4. Click desired orientation....................`↑`+`↓`
5. Click **OK** ..........................`Enter`

## Add Text to an AutoShape

1. Insert AutoShape.
2. Right-click shape.
3. Click **Add Text**....................`X`
   - ✓ *A text box is inserted around the AutoShape. It cannot be selected separately from the AutoShape.*
4. Type and format text.

## Convert a Text Box to a Frame

1. Select text box.
   - ✓ *Text box must be off of the Drawing Canvas.*
2. Click **Format** ..............`Alt`+`O`
3. Click **Text Box** ...................`O`
4. Click **Text Box** tab ......`Ctrl`+`Tab`
5. Click **Convert to Frame**......`F`
6. Click **OK** ..........................`Enter`

## Align an Object

1. Select object.
   - ✓ *Object must be off of the Drawing Canvas.*
2. Click **Format** ...............`Alt`+`O`
3. Click object type:
   - **Text Box**........................`O`
   - **AutoShape**.....................`O`
   - **Drawing Canvas**...........`D`
4. Click **Layout** tab..........`Ctrl`+`Tab`
5. Click desired alignment setting:
   - **Left** ........................`Alt`+`L`
   - **Center** ...................`Alt`+`C`
   - **Right**........................`Alt`+`R`
   - ✓ *Other is selected by default when object is manually positioned on page by dragging. Note that these alignment options are not available if the text wrapping is set to In line with text.*

## Use Advanced Alignment Options

**Set picture position options:**

1. Select object.
2. Click **F**o**rmat** ............... `Alt`+`O`
3. Click object type:
   - **Text B**o**x** ........................ `O`
   - **Aut**o**Shape** .................. `O`
   - **D**r**awing Canvas** .......... `D`
4. Click **Layout** tab ......... `Ctrl`+`Tab`
5. Click **A**d**vanced** button
   `Advanced...` ..... `Alt`+`A`
6. Click **Picture Position** tab .............. `Ctrl`+`Tab`
7. Do one of the following to set horizontal position:
   a. Click **A**l**ignment** option button .......... `Alt`+`A`
   b. Select desired alignment from drop-down list:
      - **Left**
      - **Centered**
      - **Right**
   c. Click **r**elative to ..... `Alt`+`R`
   d. Select desired anchor:
      - **Margin**
      - **Page**
      - **Column**
      - **Character**

   OR
   a. Click **B**ook layout option button .......... `Alt`+`B`
   b. Select desired position:
      - **Inside**
      - **Outside**
   c. Click **o**f ................... `Alt`+`O`
   d. Select desired anchor:
      - **Margin**
      - **Page**

   OR
   a. Click **Absolute position** option button .......... `Alt`+`P`
   b. Enter amount of space to leave.

c. Click **t**o the **right of** ................. `Alt`+`T`
d. Select desired anchor:
   - **Margin**
   - **Page**
   - **Column**
   - **Character**

8. Do one of the following to set vertical position:
   a. Click **A**l**ignment** option button .......... `Alt`+`I`
   b. Select desired alignment from drop-down list:
      - **Top**
      - **Centered**
      - **Bottom**
      - **Inside**
      - **Outside**
   c. Click **r**elative to ...... `Alt`+`E`
   d. Select desired anchor:
      - **Margin**
      - **Page**
      - **Line**

   OR
   a. Click **Absolute position** option button ........... `Alt`+`S`
   b. Enter amount of space to leave.
   c. Click **belo**w ............ `Alt`+`W`
   d. Select desired anchor:
      - **Margin**
      - **Page**
      - **Paragraph**
      - **Line**

9. Select desired check box options:
   - **Move object with text** ................ `Alt`+`M`
   - **Lock anchor** .......... `Alt`+`L`
   - **Allow o**v**erlap** ........ `Alt`+`V`
   - **Layout in table cell** ...................... `Alt`+`C`
10. Click **OK** ...................... `Enter`
11. Click **OK** ...................... `Enter`

**Set text wrapping options:**

1. Select object.
2. Click **F**o**rmat** ............... `Alt`+`O`
3. Click object type:
   - **Text B**o**x** ........................ `O`
   - **Aut**o**Shape** .................... `O`
   - **D**r**awing Canvas** .......... `D`
4. Click **Layout** tab ........ `Ctrl`+`Tab`
5. Click **A**d**vanced** button
   `Advanced...` ...... `Alt`+`A`
6. Click **Text Wrapping** tab ............................ `Ctrl`+`Tab`
7. Select desired text wrapping style:
   - **In line with text** ..... `Alt`+`I`
   - **S**q**uare** .................. `Alt`+`Q`
   - **Tight** .................... `Alt`+`T`
   - **Behind text** .......... `Alt`+`B`
   - **In front of text** ...... `Alt`+`F`
   - **T**o**p and bottom** .... `Alt`+`O`
   - **Through** ................. `Alt`+`H`
8. For Square, Through, and Tight styles, select desired text wrapping options:
   - **Both sides** ............. `Alt`+`S`
   - **Left only** ............... `Alt`+`L`
   - **Right only** ............. `Alt`+`R`
   - **Largest only** .......... `Alt`+`A`
9. For Square, Through, Top and bottom, and Tight styles, set distance from text options:
   - **Top** ...................... `Alt`+`P`
   - **Bottom** ................. `Alt`+`M`
   - **Left** ...................... `Alt`+`E`
   - **Right** .................... `Alt`+`G`
   - ✓ *Not all distance options will be available for all styles.*
10. Click **OK** ...................... `Enter`
11. Click **OK** ...................... `Enter`

## Copy an Object

1. Select object.
2. Click **Copy** button
3. Click **Paste** button .
4. Drag copy to new location.

# Exercise Directions

1. Start Word, if necessary.

2. Open ⊙ **79ESSAY**.

3. Save the file as **ESSAY**.

4. Insert the Explosion 1 shape from the Stars and Banners palette.

    ✓ *If you create the shape on the drawing canvas, drag it off, and then delete the canvas.*

5. Resize the shape to 2.25" high by 2.75" wide.

6. Align the shape horizontally left relative to the margin.

7. Align the shape vertically .5" below the page.

8. Set the text wrapping to Behind text.

9. Save the document.

10. Position the insertion point on the 10th line in the document: the topic **Breaking Away from the Herd**.

    ✓ *This positions the object's anchor.*

11. Insert a text box approximately .66" high and 1.75" wide.

    ✓ *If you create the box on the drawing canvas, drag it off, and then delete the canvas.*

12. Centered in the text box, in 16-point Arial, type:
    **Junior Division**
    **Grades 1- 4**

13. Position the text box 12 pts. below the topic line where the anchor is located.

    ✓ *If necessary, display hidden characters to see the anchor.*

    ✓ *The default measurement for positioning objects is inches. To set the measurement to points, type pt following the value (in this case 12) in the Absolute position increment box on the Picture Position tab.*

14. Set the text wrapping to square and align the box on the left horizontally.

15. Copy the text box and position the copy 12 pts. below the topic line, centered horizontally.

    ✓ *If necessary, drag the object's anchor to the topic line.*

16. Edit the text in the box to:
    **Middle Division**
    **Grades 5 - 9**

17. Copy the text box again. Position the third text box 12 pts. below the same topic line, aligned right horizontally.

18. Edit the text to:
    **Senior Division**
    **Grades 10 - 12**

19. Save the changes.

20. Insert the 5-point Star AutoShape from the Stars and Banners palette.

    ✓ *If you create the shape on the drawing canvas, drag it off, and then delete the canvas.*

21. Resize it to 2.75" high by 3" wide.

22. Center the shape relative to the page, and position it vertically 4.5" below the margin.

23. Set the text wrapping to Top and bottom.

24. Add the following text to the shape, using 14-point Arial in bold and centered: **Winners will be announced June 1!**.

    ✓ *The text should wrap within the shape.*

25. Save the document.

26. Check the spelling and grammar.

27. Display the document in Print Preview. It should look similar to Illustration A.

28. Print the document.

29. Close the file, saving all changes.

## BLUE SKY DAIRY CO.

### Proudly Announces
### Its First Ever

## ESSAY CONTEST

### Topic:

# BREAK AWAY FROM THE HERD

| Junior Division Grades 1 - 4 | Middle Division Grades 5 - 9 | Senior Division Grades 10 - 12 |
|---|---|---|

Winners will be announced June 1!

The Grand Prize winner will receive a $2,500 scholarship and a personal computer. Other prizes include gift certificates, computer equipment, travel vouchers, and more. For more information call: 608-555-2697, or consult the dairy's Web site: www.blueskydairy.net.

# On Your Own

1. Open ⌨**OWD78**, the newsletter document you used in the On Your Own section of Exercise 78, or open 💿**79NEWS**.

2. Save the file as **OWD79**.

3. Insert a text box and type in a headline, quotation, or other important information you want to stand out in the document. Alternatively, insert a text box around existing text.

4. Align the text box so it overlaps the two columns, and set text wrapping to square.

5. Try resizing one of the AutoShapes already in the newsletter.

6. Copy a shape and position the copy somewhere else in the document.

7. Check spelling and grammar in the document.

8. Preview the document.

9. Adjust column breaks, balance columns, and otherwise edit or reformat the document as necessary.

10. Print the document.

11. Ask a classmate to review the document and make comments and suggestions, paying particular attention to layout and design.

12. Incorporate the suggestions as necessary.

13. Close the document, save all changes.

# Exercise 80

## Skills Covered:

◆ **About Clip Art** ◆ **Insert Clip Art** ◆ **Use the Clip Organizer**
◆ **Download Clips from the Web**

## On the Job

Insert clip art into documents to illustrate and enhance your text. In addition to pictures such as drawings and cartoons, you can even insert sound, video, and photograph clips. Download graphic objects from the World Wide Web to supplement the objects in the Clip Organizer. You can download clip art, sounds, photos, and videos suitable for regular Word documents as well as for Web page documents.

You want to jazz up the StyleEyes newsletter. In this exercise, you insert clip art pictures into the document you created in Exercise 72.

## Terms

**Clip art** Files such as pictures, sounds, and videos, created, copyrighted, and made available for use with other programs such as Word.

**Brightness** The amount of white or black added to a color. Sometimes called tint.

**Contrast** The degree of separation of color values within a picture.

**Clip collection** A folder used to store clip files.

**Microsoft Clip Organizer** A folder that comes with Office. It contains drawings, photographs, sounds, videos, and other media files that you can insert and use in Office documents.

**Download** Copy a file from the Internet and store it locally on your computer.

**Thumbnail** A miniature representation of a graphic object.

## Notes

### About Clip Art

- Insert **clip art** to illustrate and decorate your Office documents.

- Clip art files include pictures, sounds, and videos created in different programs that can be inserted and edited in Word.

- Clip art files come with many programs, including Microsoft Office. They can be also purchased on CD or downloaded from the Web.

- You can edit and format clip art pictures using many of the same commands you use for editing and formatting drawing objects. For example, you can resize, move, and set text wrapping options.

- You can change the **brightness** and **contrast** of colors, and you can crop the pictures to remove edges you don't need.

- By default, clip art pictures are inserted in-line with text; you must change the text wrapping settings if you want them to float.

## Insert Clip Art

- Use the Clip Art task pane to locate and insert clip art.
- Search for files based on a keyword, category, and/or type.
- Word displays thumbnail-sized previews of each matching clip in the task pane.
- Small icons on the thumbnails indicate if the clip file is stored on a CD or online, or if it is an animation.
- To access a clip stored on a CD, the CD must be inserted in the appropriate CD drive. To access a clip stored on a Web site, you must have a connection to the Internet.
- You can also use the Insert, Picture, From File command to insert clip art, as well as photographs and other graphics files that you create using a scanner, digital camera, or graphics program.
- This is useful when you know where the file you need is stored on your system.

*Clip Art task pane*

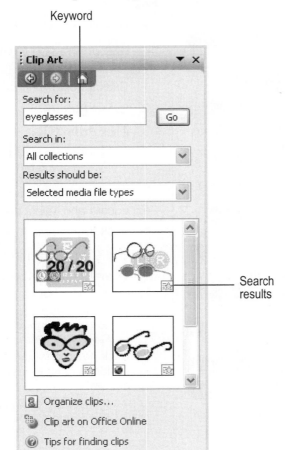

## Use the Clip Organizer

- To make it easy to find the clips you want, Office sorts the files into **clip collections** and stores them in the **Microsoft Clip Organizer**.
- By default, the Clip Organizer includes the following clip collections:
  - *My Collections*, which includes clips that you have stored on your system and sorted into folders such as *Favorites*. It may also include a Windows folder containing clips that come with Windows, other Windows programs, or clips that you had installed before you installed Microsoft Office 2003.
  - *Office Collections*, which includes the clips that come with Office. They are sorted into folders such as *People, Animals, Emotions,* and *Food.*
  - *Web Collections*, which automatically uses an open Internet link to access clips stored on the Microsoft Office Online Clip Art and Media Web site.
- You can use the Clip Organizer to browse through clip collections, create new collections, add clips from other locations, and copy or move clips from one collection to another.

*The Clip Organizer*

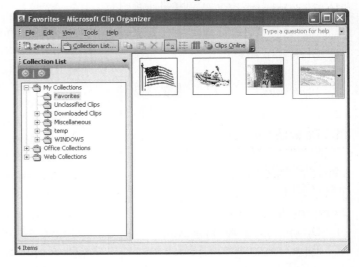

## Download Clips from the Web

- If you have access to the Internet, you can locate and **download** clip art, photos, sounds, and video clips from the Clip Art and Media page of the Microsoft Office Online Web site.

- The Clip Art and Media page offers collections of clips. Click a collection to view **thumbnails** of the clips.

*Microsoft Office Online's Clip Art and Media page*

Search box

Featured collections

Links

- Alternatively, search for the clips you need based on keyword, category and/or clip type.
- Click a thumbnail to display a preview of the clip in a separate window.
  - ✓ *Animations and sounds play in a separate window.*
- Word stores downloaded clip art in the Downloaded Clips collection of the Clip Organizer.
  - ✓ *There are other clip art Web sites that you may use for a fee or for free. To locate a clip art Web site, log on to the Internet and use a search engine to search for the key term* clip art.

# Procedures

## Open the Clip Art Task Pane

- Click **Insert Clip Art** button on Drawing toolbar.

OR

1. Click **I**nsert .................. **Alt** + **I**
2. Select **P**icture ..................... **P**
3. Click **C**lip Art ..................... **C**

OR

1. Click **V**iew .................. **Alt** + **V**
2. Click Tas**k** Pane ................. **K**
3. Click **Other Task Panes** drop-down arrow.
4. Click **Clip Art**.

## Insert Clip Art

**Using the task pane:**

1. Open the Clip Art task pane.
2. Type search text in Search for text box.
   - ✓ *If necessary, delete existing text first.*
3. Click **Search in** drop-down arrow.
4. Select and deselect collection folders as necessary, using the follows methods:
   - Click **plus sign** to expand list ..................... **→**

- Click **minus sign** to collapse list ..................... **←**
- Click check box to select or deselect folder ........... **Space**
- Click check box twice to select or deselect folder and all subfolders ............ **Space** 2X
- Click check box three times to select only subfolders ........... **Space** 3X
- Click check box four times to deselect subfolders ............ **Space** 4X

5. Click outside expanded list to close list ......................... **Tab**
6. Click **Results should be** drop-down arrow ..... **Tab**, **Space**
7. Click **plus sign** to expand list .......................... **→**
8. Deselect clip type(s) you don't need ......... **↑**, **↓**, **Space**
9. Click **Go** button  ..... **Enter**
   - ✓ *Word displays clips that match your criteria.*
10. Click clip to insert.

## Using the Insert Picture dialog box:

- Click **Insert Picture** button on Drawing toolbar

OR

1. Click **I**nsert ................. **Alt** + **I**
2. Select **P**icture ..................... **P**
3. Click **F**rom File ................... **F**
   - ✓ *Word displays the Insert Picture dialog box, with the contents of the My Pictures folder displayed by default.*
4. Locate and select desired file.
5. Click In**s**ert ......................... **S**

## Use the Clip Organizer

1. Open the Clip Art task pane.
2. Click **Organize clips...**
   - ✓ *The Microsoft Clip Organizer window opens with the My Favorites Collection displayed.*
3. Click desired folder in Collection List to view its contents.
   - ✓ *If necessary, click plus sign next to a folder to expand list.*

**To insert a clip:**

1. Open collection containing desired clip.
2. Drag clip from Organizer to desired location in document.
   OR
   a. Click clip.
   b. Click clip's drop-down arrow.
   c. Click **Copy** ..................... `C`
   d. Position insertion point in document where you want to insert clip.
      ✓ *Move Clip Organizer out of the way if necessary.*
   e. Click **Edit** ................ `Alt`+`E`
   f. Click **Paste** ..................... `P`

**To copy a clip to a different collection:**

1. Open collection containing desired clip.
2. Click clip.
3. Click clip's drop-down arrow.
4. Click **Copy to Collection** .... `Y`
   ✓ *The Copy to Collection dialog box opens.*
5. Select collection to copy to.
   OR
   a. Click **New** .............. `Alt`+`N` to create a new collection.
   b. Type new collection name.
   c. Click **OK** ..................... `Enter`
6. Click **OK** .......................... `Enter`

**To move a clip to a different collection:**

1. Open collection containing desired clip.
2. Click clip.
3. Click clip's drop-down arrow.
4. Click **Move to Collection** .... `M`
   ✓ *The Move to Collection dialog box opens.*
5. Select collection to move to.
   OR
   a. Click **New** .............. `Alt`+`N` to create a new collection.
   b. Type new collection name.
   c. Click **OK** ..................... `Enter`
6. Click **OK** .......................... `Enter`

**To add a clip to the Clip Organizer:**

1. Open collection in which you want to store clip.
2. Click **File** ..................... `Alt`+`F`
3. Select **Add Clips to Organizer** ........................... `A`
4. Do one of the following:
   a. Click **Automatically** ....... `M` to have Word automatically locate and add clips stored on your system.
   b. Click **OK** to begin ....... `Enter`
   OR
   a. Click **On My Own** .......... `O` to manually select clips to add.
   b. Locate and select desired clip file(s).
   c. Click **Add** .............. `Alt`+`A`
   OR
   • Click **From Scanner or Camera** .......................... `S` to upload a clip from a scanner device or camera device attached to your system.

**To delete a clip from the current folder:**

1. Open collection containing desired clip.
2. Click clip.
3. Click clip's drop-down arrow.
4. Click **Delete from "Collection Name"** ................ `F`

**To delete a clip from the Clip Organizer:**

1. Open collection containing desired clip.
2. Click clip.
3. Click clip's drop-down arrow.
4. Click **Delete from Clip Organizer** ........................... `D`
5. Word warns you that it is about to delete the clip.
6. Click **OK** .......................... `Enter`

**Download Clips from the Web**

1. If necessary, log on to Internet.
2. Open the Clip Art task pane.

3. Click **Clip art on Office Online**.
   ✓ *You may also use the **Clips Online** button in the Clip Organizer dialog box.*
4. Click a collection displayed on main page.
   OR
   a. Do one or more of the following:
      • Select clip type from Search drop down list.
      • Type search text in **Search for** box.
   b. Click **Click to search** arrow ➜ ..................... `Enter`
5. Click check box under each desired clip.
   ✓ *Use Next and Previous arrows in right corners of window to scroll through all clips.*
6. Click **Download "number" items** icon ⬇.
   OR
   a. Click **Review basket** link on left side of page to view selected clips.
   b. Click **Download "number" items** icon ⬇.
   ✓ *Microsoft may prompt you to install the Microsoft Office Template and Media Control program. If so, ask your instructor for information on how to proceed.*
7. Click the **Download Now** button `Download Now`.
   ✓ *You may be prompted to accept an end user license agreement.*
8. If the File Download dialog box is displayed, do one of the following:
   • Click **Open** ..................... `O`
      ✓ *The clips are downloaded and stored in the Downloaded Clips collection in the Clip Organizer. The Clip Organizer opens on-screen.*
   OR
   a. Click **Save** ..................... `S`

b. Select storage location for downloaded files.

c. Click **OK**......................Enter

✓ *The clips are downloaded and stored as a Clip Organizer Media Package file. Open the file to display the clips in the Clip Organizer.*

9. If necessary, disconnect from the Internet.

## Crop a Picture

1. Select picture in Word document.

✓ *Picture toolbar is displayed.*

2. Click **Crop** button .

✓ *The mouse pointer changes to include crop marks* 中.

3. Drag desired sizing handle toward center of picture.

✓ *Dotted lines indicate the new edge of the picture.*

4. Release mouse button to remove area outside dotted lines.

5. Click **Crop** button to turn crop feature off.

## Adjust Picture Brightness and/or Contrast

1. Select picture in Word document.

✓ *Picture toolbar is displayed.*

2. Do one of the following:

- Click **More Brightness** button to increase brightness.
- Click **Less Brightness** button to decrease brightness.
- Click **More Contrast** button to increase contrast.
- Click **Less Contrast** button to decrease contrast.

3. Repeat step 2 as necessary to achieve desired effect.

# Exercise Directions

1. Start Word, if necessary.

2. Open 🖮**EYENEWS** or open 💿**80EYENEWS**.

3. Save the file as **EYENEWS2**.

4. Position the insertion point at the end of the first line in the document.

5. Use the Clip Art task pane to search for clip art files in all collections with the keyword **eyeglasses**.

✓ *If you have an open connection to the Internet, Word searches for clips online as well as for clips on a CD or stored on your system.*

6. Insert the clip shown in the illustration.

✓ *If you cannot locate the same clip, use the Insert, Picture, From File command to insert the file* 💿***GLASSES1.wmf*** *supplied with this book, or select any eyeglass-related file you want.*

7. Resize the picture so it is 1.5" wide (the Lock aspect ratio check box is selected by default, so the height will adjust automatically to keep the picture in proportion).

8. Set the text wrapping for the picture to Behind text.

9. Right-align the picture.

10. Position the insertion point at the beginning of the heading New Associate.

11. Use the Clip Art task pane to search for clip art files in all collections with the keyword **doctor**.

12. Insert the clip shown in the illustration.

✓ *If you cannot locate the same clip, use the Insert, Picture, From File command to insert the file* 💿***DOCTOR1.wmf*** *supplied with this book.*

13. Crop approximately .75" from the bottom edge of the clip (refer to the illustration).

14. Resize the clip so it is .75" high (the width will adjust automatically).

15. Set text wrapping for the picture to Tight.

16. Position the picture horizontally at -.33 to the right of the column and -.05 below the line.

✓ *Setting the position value to a negative number moves the picture up relative to the anchor—in this case, the column horizontally and the line vertically. If the picture moves to an unexpected location, the horizontal anchor may be in the right column. Display nonprinting characters and locate the anchor icon in the document. The picture should be anchored to the heading* **Report Available**. *If not, drag the anchor icon into position, and then try positioning the picture again. Or, delete the picture, and start over from step 10.*

17. Check the spelling and grammar in the document.

18. Display the document in Print Preview. It should look similar to the one in Illustration A.

19. Print the document.

20. Close the document, saving all changes.

*Illustration A*

# StyleEyes, Inc.

## 754 Erieside Avenue, Cleveland, OH 44114

| Customer Newsletter | Fall/Winter |
|---|---|

## Eye Care Symposium

On Sunday, March 10, our very own Dr. Finn Broderbund will be the featured speaker at the annual Cleveland Eye Care Breakfast Symposium.

The symposium, which is sponsored by a consortium of eye care providers, is held every year in March. It is intended to foster awareness of the importance of eye care, and to provide an opportunity for eye care professionals to meet and discuss the industry. This year, Dr. Broderbund will speak about current advances in eye surgery as well as providing a peak at some of the technologies that will aid eye care in the future.

Tickets are still available. If you are interested in attending, call the office as soon as possible.

## Expanded Hours

As of January 1, StyleEyes, Inc. of Cleveland will be open until 8:00 p.m. Monday through Friday and until 6:00 p.m. on Saturdays and Sundays.

## New Associate

StyleEyes of Cleveland is pleased to welcome Dr. Cynthia Ramirez.

Dr. Ramirez studied medicine at Ohio State University. She became a certified Opthamologist in 1998. She has extensive experience working with geriatric patients, and she specializes in senior eye care. She is fluent in English, Spanish, and Portuguese.

We know that Dr. Ramirez will be an excellent addition to our staff. Please call the office for more information.

## Report Available

The associates at StyleEyes have been hard at work researching and writing *Eye Care for Seniors*, a report that we hope offers useful information for the elderly and their caregivers.

The report takes a straight forward approach to providing information in regards to managing the eye care needs of our senior citizens.

*Eye Care for Seniors* includes information about the following topics:

- An overview of eye care issues
- Common eye ailments
- How to maintaining eye health
- Eye sight and medication

The report is now available. Call the office for more information or to request a copy.

# On Your Own

1. Start Word and open ⌨**OWD79**, the newsletter you have used in the previous exercises, or open 💿**80NEWS**.

2. Save the document as **OWD80**.

3. Insert one or more clip art pictures into the newsletter.

4. Select text wrapping that integrates the pictures effectively with the document text.

   ✓ *If necessary, delete one or more drawing objects or edit the text to make room for the clip art.*

5. Size and position the pictures so they enhance the document.

6. Crop the pictures if necessary.

7. Adjust the contrast and brightness to see if it improves the appearance of the document.

8. Preview the document.

9. Adjust column breaks and edit the text as necessary.

10. Check the spelling and grammar in the document.

11. Preview the document again.

12. Print the document.

13. Ask a classmate to review the document and make comments and suggestions, paying particular attention to the layout and design.

14. Incorporate the suggestions into the document as necessary.

15. Close the document, saving all changes, and exit Word.

# Exercise 81

## Skills Covered:

### ◆ Adjust Objects ◆ Rotate and Flip Objects

## On the Job

You can manipulate objects to make sure they are positioned the way you want in a document. You can rotate objects around an axis and flip them horizontally or vertically. Many drawing objects have adjustment handles, which you can use to alter the most prominent feature of the object. For example, you can change the mouth on a smiley face from a smile to a frown.

You've been hired to design a logo for Long Shot, Inc. The company president wants the logo suitable for use on everything from the letterhead and business cards to golf shirts and umbrellas. In this exercise, you will use text and two graphics objects—one AutoShape and one clip art picture—to create the logo. You will resize, adjust, and rotate the AutoShape and you will resize and flip the clip art picture.

## Terms

**Adjustment handle**  A small yellow diamond used to alter the most prominent feature of an AutoShape. The mouse pointer is an arrowhead when resting on an adjustment handle.

**Rotate**  Shift the position of an object in a circular motion around its axis, or center point.

**Rotation handle**  A small, green circle used to drag an object around in a circle. The mouse pointer looks like a circular arrow when resting on a rotation handle.

**Flip**  Reverse the position of an object.

## Notes

### Adjust Objects

- Some AutoShapes have one or more **adjustment handles** that look like a small yellow diamond.
- When the mouse pointer touches an adjustment handle, it looks like an arrowhead ▷.
- You can drag an adjustment handle, if available, to alter the most prominent feature of the shape.
- For example, you can drag the adjustment handles on a block arrow AutoShape to change the width of the arrow body, or the length of the arrowhead.

*Adjust objects*

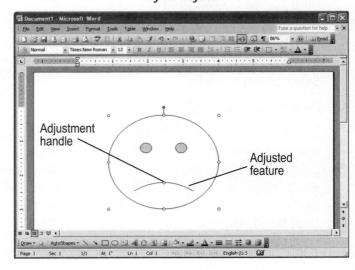

## Rotate and Flip Objects

- You can **rotate** an object to the left or right around its center point, or axis.

- When an object is selected, a green **rotation handle** is displayed.

  ✓ *Not all objects have a rotation handle. For example, arrows and lines do not. If there is no rotation handle, you can still rotate the object by using the Rotate Left, Rotate Right, or Free Rotate command.*

- When the mouse pointer touches the rotation handle, it looks like a circular arrow ↻.

- Drag the handle to freely rotate the object in either direction, or hold down the Shift key while you drag to rotate in 15 degree increments.

  ✓ *You can also select the Free Rotate command to display rotation handles around the object.*

- Alternatively, use the Rotate Left or Rotate Right command to rotate the object by 90 degree increments in the specified direction.

- You can also select the Size tab of the object's Format dialog box to set a precise rotation amount for the selected object, relative to its original position.

- For example, enter 90 to rotate the object 90 degrees—or ¼ turn—to the right; enter 270 to rotate the object 270 degrees—or ¾ turn.

  ✓ *Enter negative values to rotate the object to the left. For example, -90 rotates the object to the same position as 270.*

*Rotate or flip an object*

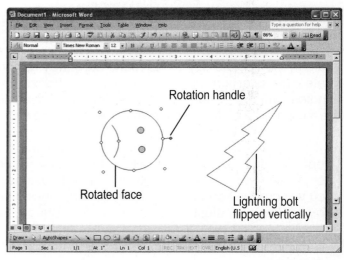

- You can **flip** an object horizontally (left to right) or vertically (top to bottom).

# Procedures

### Adjust Object

1. Select object to adjust.
2. Move mouse pointer over adjustment handle.

   ✓ *Mouse pointer changes to arrowhead ▷ .*

3. Drag adjustment handle to change feature's shape.

### Rotate Object

**Rotate left or right:**

1. Select object to rotate.
2. Click **Draw** button [Draw ▼] on Drawing toolbar........... [Alt]+[D]
3. Click **Rotate or Flip** ............ [P]
4. Click **Rotate Left** to rotate object 90 degrees to left...... [L]

   **OR**

   Click **Rotate Right** to rotate object 90 degrees to right ... [R]

**Free rotate:**

1. Select object to rotate.
2. Position mouse pointer over green rotation handle.

   ✓ *When pointer is positioned correctly, it resembles a circular arrow ↻ .*

   **OR**

   a. Click **Draw** button [Draw ▼] on Drawing toolbar ................... [Alt]+[D]
   b. Click **Rotate or Flip**........ [P]
   c. Click **Free Rotate**........... [T]
   d. Position mouse pointer over any green rotation handle.

3. Drag handle clockwise or counterclockwise.

   ✓ *Press and hold Shift key while dragging to rotate in 15 degree increments.*

4. Release mouse button when object is positioned as desired.
5. Click outside object to set rotation.

### Flip Object

1. Select object to flip.
2. Click **Draw** button [Draw ▼] on Drawing toolbar........... [Alt]+[D]
3. Click **Rotate or Flip** ............ [P]
4. Click **Flip Horizontal** to flip object left to right................ [H]

   **OR**

   Click **Flip Vertical** to flip object top to bottom............. [V]

# Exercise Directions

1. Start Word, if necessary.
2. Create a new document and save it as **LOGO**.
3. Insert three blank lines.
4. Using a sans serif font in a large font size in dark blue (Arial Rounded MT in 72 pts. is used in the illustration), type **LSI**.
5. Insert the 8-Point Star AutoShape from the Stars and Banners palette.
6. If necessary, drag it off the drawing canvas and delete the canvas.
7. Drag the adjustment handle toward the center of the star to make the points thinner (refer to the illustration).
8. Rotate the star 25 degrees to the right.
9. Resize the star so it is .75" high and .75" wide.
10. Position the star above the **I** in **LSI** as shown in the illustration.
    - ✓ *The absolute position shown in the illustration 1.06" to the right of the column and -0.4" below the paragraph.*
11. Open the Clip Art task pane and search for pictures related to golf.
12. Locate the picture of the golf ball and club head shown in the illustration.
    - ✓ *If you cannot locate the picture as shown, insert the file ✪GOLF1.wmf supplied with this book.*
13. Insert the clip into the **LOGO** document.
14. Flip the picture horizontally.
15. Resize the picture so it is 1" high (the width will adjust automatically).
16. Set the text wrapping for the picture to Behind text.
17. Position the picture so the bottom of the **S** in **LSI** is sitting in the middle of the golf ball.
    - ✓ *The absolute position shown is .38" to the right of the column and .43" below the paragraph.*
18. Preview the document. It should look similar to the one in Illustration A.
19. Make any adjustments necessary to the size and position of the objects.
20. Print the document.
21. Close the document, saving all changes.

# On Your Own

1. Start Word and create a new document.
2. Save the document as **OWD81**.
3. Use graphics objects and text to design a logo for yourself, a club, or organization.
4. Adjust, rotate, and flip the objects as necessary.
5. Resize and position the objects as necessary.
6. Preview the document and then print it.
7. Ask a classmate to review the document and offer suggestions and comments.
8. Incorporate the suggestions and comments into the logo as necessary.
9. Close the document, saving all changes, and exit Word.

# Exercise 82

## Skills Covered:

◆ **Line Color and Styles** ◆ **Fill Color** ◆ **Shadows and 3-D Effects**

## On the Job

Use color and special effects with drawing objects to create professional-looking graphics and pictures. You can change the color and style of the lines used to draw both closed shapes and lines, and you can enhance closed shapes by filling them with color or patterns. Shadows behind an object give a document the appearance of depth, while 3-D effects give depth to the object itself.

In this exercise, you will modify the graphics objects that you used in the flyer announcing the essay contest for Blue Sky Dairy. You will change the line color, style, and fill color of one shape, apply shadows to the text boxes, and apply a 3-D effect to the star.

## Terms

**Line style** The width and appearance of a line used to draw an object.

**Fill** Color or patterns used to fill a closed shape.

**Shadow** An effect applied to objects to make it look as if the object is casting a shadow.

**3-D Effect** An effect applied to objects to make them look as if they are three dimensional.

## Notes

### Line Color and Styles

- By default, drawing objects have a solid single line border on all sides.

- You can change the **line style** and color of existing closed shapes, lines, and arrows.

- The line style options are similar to those used for tables and paragraphs. For example, you can select a 3 pt., turquoise dashed border.

- Select line color and style from the palettes on the right end of the Drawing toolbar, or open the object's Format dialog box for additional options.

*Line Style palette*

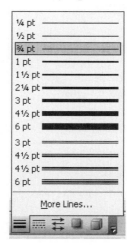

- You can also use the Drawing toolbar palettes to select the style of arrowheads used for arrow objects and to customize dashed lines.

**435**

## Fill Color

- Use the Fill Color palette on the Drawing toolbar or the object's Format dialog box to apply a **fill** color or effect to existing objects.

- When you use the dialog box, you can also set a transparency level to control whether the fill color is see-through or not; the higher the transparency level, the more see-through it is.

- Fill color options are similar to those available for table cells and paragraphs. For example, you can fill an object with a color or gray shading.

- Fill effect options are similar to those available for backgrounds. For example, you can select a geometric pattern or a texture.

*Fill Color palette*

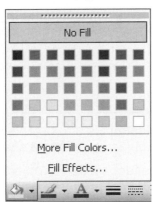

- Remember that color and textures are best used in documents designed to be viewed on-screen, such as Web pages, or documents that will be printed on a color printer.

## Shadows and 3-D Effects

- **Shadows** and **3-D effects** can be applied to any drawing object using the palettes available on the Drawing toolbar.

- You can customize the shadow effect by changing the shadow color and/or by adjusting the position of the shadow.

*Shadow Settings toolbar*

- You can customize the 3-D effect by changing the color, lighting, depth, direction, angle, and/or surface of the object.

*3-D Settings toolbar*

# Procedures

## Line Color and Style

### Select line color:

1. Select object.
2. Click **Line Color** button ![icon] drop-down arrow on Drawing toolbar.
   - ✓ *To quickly apply color displayed on Line Color button, simply click the button.*
3. Click desired color.
   - ✓ *Click No Line to remove color.*

   **OR**

   a. Click **Patterned Lines** ... `P`
   b. Click desired pattern.
   c. Click **OK** ..................... `Enter`

### Select line style:

1. Select object.
2. Click **Line Style** button ![icon] on Drawing toolbar.
3. Click desired line style.

   **OR**

   a. Click **More Lines** ............ `M`
   b. Click **Style** drop-down arrow ..................... `Alt`+`S`
   c. Click desired line style.
   d. Click **OK**.

### Select dash style:

1. Select object.
2. Click **Dash Style** button ![icon] on Drawing toolbar.
3. Click desired dash style.

### Select arrow style:

1. Select object.
2. Click **Arrow Style** button ![icon] on Drawing toolbar.
3. Click desired arrow style.

   **OR**

   a. Click **More Arrows** ........ `M`
   b. Click **Begin style** ... `Alt`+`B`
   c. Click desired arrow style for beginning of arrow.
   d. Click **Begin size** .... `Alt`+`I`
      - ✓ *For double-headed arrows only.*
   e. Click **End style** ...... `Alt`+`E`
   f. Click desired arrow style for end of arrow.

g. Click **End size** ........ `Alt`+`Z`

h. Click desired size for end of arrow.

i. Click **OK**.

## Fill Color

1. Select object.

2. Click **Fill Color** button [icon] drop-down arrow on Drawing toolbar.

   ✓ To quickly apply color displayed on Fill Color button, simply click the button.

3. Click desired color.

   ✓ Click No Fill to remove existing fill color.

   **OR**

   a. Click **Fill Effects** ............. `F`

   b. Click desired tab .... `Ctrl`+`Tab`

   c. Click desired option.

   d. Click **OK** ..................... `Enter`

### Set transparency:

1. Select object.

2. Click **Format** ............... `Alt`+`O`

3. Click object type:

   • **Text Box** ........................ `O`

   • **AutoShape** ..................... `O`

   • **Drawing Canvas** ............ `D`

4. Click **Colors and Lines** tab ............................... `Ctrl`+`Tab`

5. Click **Transparency** ..... `Alt`+`T`

6. Enter a value between 0 and 100.

   ✓ The higher the value, the more transparent the fill.

   **OR**

1. Drag the slider:

   • Right to increase the value

   • Left to decrease the value

2. Click **OK** ........................... `Enter`

### Use the Format dialog box to format lines and fills:

1. Select object.

2. Click **Format** ............... `Alt`+`O`

3. Click object type:

   • **Text Box** ........................ `O`

   • **AutoShape** .................. `O`

   • **Drawing Canvas** ........... `D`

4. Click **Colors and Lines** tab .............................. `Ctrl`+`Tab`

5. Click **Fill Color** drop-down arrow ........................ `Alt`+`C`

6. Click desired color.

   ✓ Click No Fill to remove existing fill.

7. Click **Line Color** drop-down arrow ........................ `Alt`+`O`

8. Click desired color.

   ✓ Click No Line to remove color.

   **OR**

   a. Click **Patterned Lines** .... `P`

   b. Click desired pattern.

   c. Click **OK** ..................... `Enter`

9. Click **Dashed** drop-down arrow ........................ `Alt`+`D`

10. Click desired dash style.

11. Click **Style** drop-down arrow ........................ `Alt`+`S`

12. Click desired line style.

13. Click **Weight** ............... `Alt`+`W`

14. Enter desired line weight .................... `↑`, `↓`

15. Click **Begin style** drop-down arrow ........................ `Alt`+`B`

16. Click desired arrow style for beginning of line.

17. Click **Begin size** drop-down arrow ........................ `Alt`+`I`

18. Click desired arrow size.

19. Click **End style** drop-down arrow ........................ `Alt`+`E`

20. Click desired arrow style for end of line.

21. Click **End size** drop-down arrow ........................ `Alt`+`Z`

22. Click desired arrow size.

23. Click **OK** ......................... `Enter`

## Shadows

### Apply shadows:

1. Select object.

2. Click **Shadow Style** button [icon] on Drawing toolbar.

3. Click desired effect.

   ✓ Click No Shadow to remove existing shadow.

### Shift shadow position:

1. Apply shadow to object.

2. Select object to change.

3. Click **Shadow Style** button [icon] on Drawing toolbar.

4. Click **Shadow Settings** ...... `S`

5. Click button as necessary:

   • **Nudge Shadow Up** [icon]

   • **Nudge Shadow Down** [icon]

   • **Nudge Shadow Left** [icon]

   • **Nudge Shadow Right** [icon]

### Change shadow color:

1. Apply shadow to object.

2. Select object to change.

3. Click **Shadow Style** button [icon] on Drawing toolbar.

4. Click **Shadow Settings** ...... `S`

5. Click **Shadow Color** button [icon] drop-down arrow.

6. Click desired color.

   ✓ To apply the color currently displayed on Shadow Color button, click the Shadow Color button.

### Close Shadow Settings toolbar:

• Click **Close** button `X` on Toolbar title bar.

   **OR**

1. Click **Shadow Style** button [icon] on Drawing toolbar.

2. Click **Shadow Settings** ...... `S`

## 3-D Effects

### Apply 3-D effects:

1. Select object.

2. Click **3-D Style** button [icon] on Drawing toolbar.

3. Click desired effect.

   ✓ Click No 3-D to remove existing effect.

**Shift 3-D angle:**

1. Apply effect to object.
2. Select object to change.
3. Click **3-D Style** button ▢ on Drawing toolbar.
4. Click **3-D Settings** .............. 🅱
5. Click button as necessary:
   - **Tilt Up** ↻
   - **Tilt Down** ↨
   - **Tilt Left** ⟷
   - **Tilt Right** ⟷

**Change 3-D color:**

1. Apply effect to object.
2. Select object to change.

3. Click **3-D Style** button ▢ on Drawing toolbar.
4. Click **3-D Settings** .............. 🅱
5. Click **3-D Color** button 🖊 drop-down arrow.
6. Click desired color.
   - ✓ *To apply the color currently displayed on 3-D Color button, click the button.*

**Change other 3-D settings:**

1. Apply effect to object.
2. Select object to change.
3. Click **3-D Style** button ▢ on Drawing toolbar.
4. Click **3-D Settings** .............. 🅱
5. Click desired button:

   - **Depth** 🔲
   - **Direction** 🔲
   - **Lighting** 🔲
   - **Surface** 🔲

6. Click desired option.

**Close 3-D Settings toolbar:**

- Click **Close** button ✖ on toolbar title bar.

OR

1. Click **3-D Style** button ▢ on Drawing toolbar.
2. Click **3-D Settings** .............. 🅱

# Exercise Directions

1. Start Word, if necessary.
2. Open ⌨**ESSAY** or open 💿**82ESSAY**.
3. Save the document as **ESSAY2**.
4. Select the explosion shape in the upper-left corner.
5. Change the line style to 3 pts.
6. Change the line color to Sky Blue.
7. Change the fill color to Pale Blue.
8. Select all three text boxes.
   - ✓ *Select the first box, press and hold Shift, then select the other two boxes.*
9. Apply the Shadow style 9 to the selected text boxes.
10. Select the Star shape.

11. Change the fill color to Light Turquoise.
12. Apply the 3-D Style 2.
13. Customize the 3-D effect as follows:
    - Click the 3-D Style button.
    - Click 3-D Settings.
    - Click the Tilt Right button three times.
    - Increase the depth to 48 pts.
    - ✓ *Click the Depth button, enter the value in the Custom box, then press Enter.*
14. Preview the document. It should look similar to the one in Illustration A.
15. Print the document.
16. Close the document, saving all changes.

# On Your Own

1. Start Word, and create a new blank document.
2. Save the document as **OWD82**.
3. Type an announcement for an event such as a birthday, graduation, performance, or meeting.
4. Insert graphics objects such as AutoShapes, text boxes, and clip art in the document.
5. Format the objects using line colors, styles, fills, and effects.
6. Resize and position the objects as necessary.

7. Set text wrapping options.
8. When you achieve the look you want, print the document.
9. Ask a classmate to review the document and offer comments and suggestions.
10. Incorporate the suggestions into the document as necessary,
11. Close the document, saving all changes, and exit Word.

*Illustration A*

BLUE SKY DAIRY CO.

**Proudly Announces
Its First Ever**

ESSAY CONTEST

**Topic:**

# BREAK AWAY FROM THE HERD

| Junior Division<br>Grades 1 - 4 | Middle Division<br>Grades 5 - 9 | Senior Division<br>Grades 10 - 12 |
|---|---|---|

**Winners
will be
announced
June 1!**

The Grand Prize winner will receive a $2,500 scholarship and a personal computer. Other prizes include gift certificates, computer equipment, travel vouchers, and more. For more information call: 608-555-2697, or consult the dairy's Web site: www.blueskydairy.net.

# Exercise 83

## ◆ Group and Ungroup Objects ◆ Layer Objects and Text

## On the Job

Integrate drawing objects with text to illustrate and enhance documents. Objects can be layered with each other and with text to create different effects. For example, you can design a letterhead with text layered on top of a logo created from drawing objects. You can group objects together to create one complete picture, and ungroup objects to edit them individually.

In this exercise, complete the logo you created for Long Shot, Inc. by grouping and layering objects and text. You will then copy the entire logo into a memo document.

## Terms

**Group** Select multiple objects and combine them into a single object.

**Ungroup** Separate a grouped object into individual objects.

**Regroup** Group objects that have been separated again.

**Layer** Position objects and/or text so they overlap on the page.

## Notes

### Group and Ungroup Objects

- **Group** objects together to create a single unified object.

- Sizing handles are displayed around the entire grouped object, not around the individual objects.

- The entire group has a single rotation handle.

- All changes are made to the entire group.

- You must **ungroup** the objects in order to edit them individually.

- You can ungroup pictures such as clip art images created with other programs in order to modify the individual elements.

  ✓ *After you ungroup objects that have been grouped, you can use the **Regroup** command to group them again without having to select them all again.*

*Multiple objects grouped together*

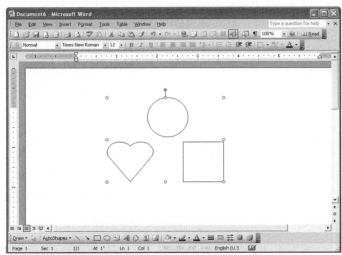

440

## Layer Objects and Text

*The heart is in front and the rectangle is in back*

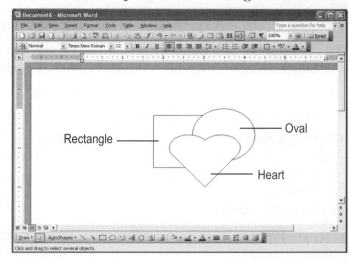

- **Layer** drawing objects with other objects or with document text to control the order in which text and objects overlap in a document.

- Elements layered in front of other elements appear to be on the top; elements layered behind—or in back of—other elements appear to be on the bottom.

- All text is always in the same layer. However, you can layer objects in front of or behind the text layer.

  - Layering an object in front of text is the same as setting the text wrapping for the object to the In front of text setting.

  - Layering an object behind text is the same as setting the text wrapping for the object to the Behind text setting.

*The oval is in front and the heart is in back*

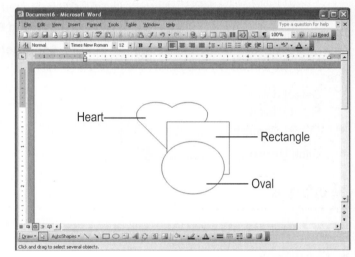

- Objects in layers can be rearranged layer by layer using the Bring Forward command to move an object forward one layer at a time or the Send Backward command to move an object backward one layer at a time.

- The Send to Back command lets you move the selected object in back of all other objects.

- The Bring to Front command lets you bring an object in front of all other objects.

  ✓ *Use the Send Behind Text or Bring in Front of Text commands to layer objects that combine text and graphics, such as text boxes and AutoShapes that have added text.*

# Procedures

## Group Objects

1. Select all objects to group.
2. Click **Draw** button `Draw ▾` on Drawing toolbar........... `Alt`+`D`
3. Click **Group** ........................ `G`

OR

1. Select all objects to group.
2. Right-click selection.
3. Select **Grouping** ............... `G`
4. Click **Group** ...................... `G`

## Ungroup Objects

1. Select grouped object.
2. Click **Draw** button `Draw ▾` on Drawing toolbar........... `Alt`+`D`
3. Click **Ungroup** ................... `U`

OR

1. Select grouped object.
2. Right-click selection.
3. Select **Grouping**............... `G`
4. Click **Ungroup** ................... `U`

## Layer Objects with Text

1. Select object.
2. Click **Draw** button `Draw ▾` on Drawing toolbar .......... `Alt`+`D`
3. Click **Order** ....................... `R`
4. Click desired option:
   - **Bring in Front of Text** ... `R`
   - **Send Behind Text** ......... `H`

OR

1. Select object.
2. Right-click selection.
3. Select **Order** ...................... `R`
4. Click desired option:
   - **Bring in Front of Text** ... `R`
   - **Send Behind Text** ......... `H`

## Layer Objects with Other Objects

1. Select object.
2. Click **Draw** button `Draw ▾` on Drawing toolbar .......... `Alt`+`D`
3. Click **Order** ....................... `R`
4. Click desired option:
   - **Bring to Front** ............... `T`
   - **Send to Back** ............... `K`
   - **Bring Forward** ............. `F`
   - **Send Backward** ........... `B`

OR

1. Right-click object.
2. Click **Order** ....................... `R`
3. Click desired option:
   - **Bring to Front** ............... `T`
   - **Send to Back** ............... `K`
   - **Bring Forward** ............. `F`
   - **Send Backward** ........... `B`

# Exercise Directions

1. Start Word, if necessary.
2. Open ⌨**LOGO** or open 💿**83LOGO**.
3. Save the document as **LOGO2**.
4. Select the golf ball and club head clip art object and the Star AutoShape object.
5. Group the two objects together.
6. Resize the grouped objects to 1.5" high by 1.18" wide.
7. Send the group behind the text.
8. Select the text and change the font size to 64 points.
9. Insert a text box around the text:
   a. Select the text.
   b. Click the Text Box button in the Drawing toolbar.
10. Resize the text box so it just fits around the text—approximately 1" high by 1.62" wide.
11. Set the transparency of the text box to 100%:
    a. Select the text box.
    b. Open the Format Text Box dialog box.
    c. Click the Colors and Lines tab.
    d. Drag the Transparency slider all the way to the right.
    e. Set the Line color to No Line.
12. Bring the text box to the front of all layers.
13. Set the Absolute position of the grouped object as follows:
    • Horizontally .5" to the right of the column
    • Vertically .15" below the paragraph
14. Preview the document.
15. If necessary, make adjustments to the position of the text box or the group.
16. When you are satisfied with the position of the objects, select both (the text box and the grouped shapes) and group them together. Now, you can copy, move, and otherwise manipulate the entire logo as one object.
17. Select the logo and copy it to the Clipboard.
18. Open the document ⌨**LSIMEMO** or open 💿**83LSIMEMO**.
19. Save the file as **LSIMEMO2**.
20. Paste the logo into the document.
21. Horizontally, center the object relative to the margins.
22. Vertically, align the object with the bottom margin.
23. Preview the memo document.
24. It should look similar to the one in Illustration A.
25. If necessary, make adjustments to the position of the logo.
26. Print the document.
27. Close all open documents, saving all changes.

# On Your Own

1. Start Word if necessary.
2. Open the file ⌨**OWD82** or open 💿**83ANNOUNCE**.
3. Save the file as **OWD83**.
4. Modify the document by layering objects and text. For example, overlap existing objects, or insert new objects in front of or behind existing objects.
5. Make use of line styles, color, fills and effects to achieve the look you want. Group objects to apply formatting to all of them.
6. If necessary, rotate, flip, and adjust objects so they look good on the page.
7. When you are satisfied the document, print it.
8. Ask a classmate to review the document and make comments and suggestions.
9. Incorporate the comments and suggestions as necessary.
10. Close the document, saving all changes, and exit Word.

# Long Shot, Inc.

### 234 Simsbury Drive ⚑ Ithaca, NY 14850

**Telephone: 607-555-9191 ⚑ Fax: 607-555-9292 ⚑ E-mail: mail@longshot.net**

MEMO

| | |
|---|---|
| To: | Harold Cantor |
| From: | Your Name |
| Date: | Today's date |
| Subject: | Travel Plans |

I have finalized my travel plans and will be arriving on flight 6234 at 9:55 a.m. on Friday the 13th. Assuming the traffic is light, I should reach your office by 11:00 a.m.

I look forward to meeting you on the 13th. Please contact me if you have any questions. Also, if you are able to arrange a tee time for Friday afternoon, I will be happy to bring along my golf gear.

# Exercise **84**

## Skills Covered:

◆ **Create WordArt** ◆ **WordArt Text** ◆ **WordArt Shapes and Formatting**

## On the Job

Use WordArt to transform text into artwork for letterheads, logos, brochures, and other documents. WordArt lets you create special effects using any text that you type. You can stretch characters, rotate them, reverse direction, and even arrange the text in shapes such as circles, waves, or arcs.

Liberty Blooms is opening a new store. In this exercise, you will design a flyer announcing the grand opening.

## Terms

**WordArt** A feature of Word used to transform text into a drawing object.

**WordArt text** The text included in a WordArt object.

**WordArt style** The shape and formatting characteristics of a WordArt object.

## Notes

### Create WordArt

- **WordArt** is a Word feature that you use to transform text into a drawing object.
- By default, WordArt objects are inserted in-line with text, but you can change the text wrapping to make them float.
- The WordArt Gallery includes a selection of styles you can quickly apply to any text.

*The WordArt Gallery*

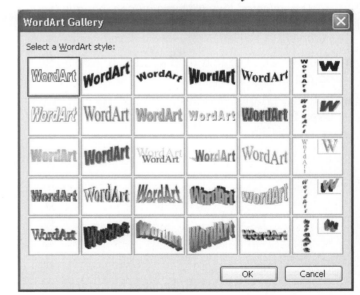

- You can customize WordArt objects to achieve the specific results you want.

## WordArt Text

- You enter **WordArt text** when you create the WordArt object.

- The placeholder text is: *Your Text Here,* which is replaced by any text you type.

- You can select text already typed in the document to use as the WordArt text.

  ✓ *The selected text will remain unchanged in the document, independent of the new WordArt object.*

- You can edit the text displayed in a WordArt object at any time.

- You can change the font, font size, and font style used for WordArt text.

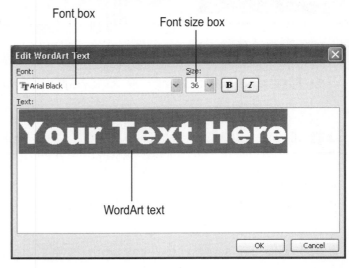

*The Edit WordArt Text dialog box*

Font box

Font size box

WordArt text

## WordArt Shapes and Formatting

- The **WordArt styles** in the WordArt Gallery include shape and formatting characteristics.

- When you select a WordArt object, the WordArt toolbar is displayed. Use the buttons on the WordArt toolbar to edit and format the object.

  - You can change the shape of a WordArt object by selecting a different shape from the WordArt Shape palette.

  - Rotate the WordArt object using the Free Rotate button.

  - Select a text wrapping option to integrate the WordArt object with existing document text.

  - Stretch lowercase letters to the same height as uppercase letters using the WordArt Same Letter Heights button.

  - Align WordArt text vertically using the WordArt Vertical Text button.

  - Align the entire WordArt object on the page using the WordArt Alignment button.

  - Adjust the spacing between characters in a WordArt object using the WordArt Character Spacing button.

- In addition to the commands on the WordArt toolbar, WordArt objects can be edited and modified using the same techniques used to edit other drawing objects, including moving and resizing, adjusting, rotating, flipping, shadow and 3-D effects, and layering.

# Procedures

## Create WordArt

1. Display Drawing toolbar.
2. Click the **WordArt** button [A] on the Drawing toolbar.
   
   OR
   
   a. Click **Insert** .............. `Alt` + `I`
   
   b. Click **Picture** ................... `P`
   
   c. Click **WordArt** ............... `W`
3. Click desired WordArt style.
4. Click **OK** ........................... `Enter`
5. Type WordArt text.
6. Click **OK** ........................... `Enter`

## WordArt Text

### Edit WordArt text:

1. Select WordArt object.
2. Click **Edit Text** button
   [Edit Text...] on WordArt
   toolbar ........................... `Alt` + `X`
3. Type new text.
4. Click **OK** ................... `Tab`, `Enter`

### Format WordArt text:

1. Select WordArt object.
2. Click **Edit Text** button
   [Edit Text...] on WordArt
   toolbar ........................... `Alt` + `X`
3. Click **Font** drop-down
   arrow ........................... `Alt` + `F`
4. Click desired font.
5. Click **Size** drop-down
   arrow ........................... `Alt` + `S`
6. Click desired size.
7. Click Font style buttons as desired:
   
   • **Bold** [B]
   
   • **Italic** [I]
8. Click **OK** ........................... `Enter`

## WordArt Shapes and Formatting

### Change WordArt style:

1. Select WordArt object.
2. Click **WordArt Gallery** button
   [icon] on WordArt toolbar.
3. Click desired style.
4. Click **OK** .......................... `Enter`

### Change WordArt shape:

1. Select WordArt object.
2. Click **WordArt Shape** button
   [A] on WordArt toolbar.
3. Click desired shape.

### Rotate WordArt object:

1. Select WordArt object.
2. Drag rotation handle to rotate object.
3. Release mouse button when object is in desired position.
   
   ✓ *You can rotate and flip WordArt objects using the commands on the Drawing toolbar.*

### Wrap text around a WordArt object:

1. Select WordArt object.
2. Click **Text Wrapping** button
   [icon] on WordArt toolbar.
3. Click desired text wrapping option.

### Adjust letter height:

1. Select WordArt object.
2. Click **WordArt Same Letter Heights** button [Aa] on WordArt toolbar.
   
   ✓ *Repeat to return text to normal height.*

### Align WordArt text vertically:

1. Select WordArt object.
2. Click **WordArt Vertical Text** button [Ab] on WordArt toolbar.
   
   ✓ *Repeat to return text to horizontal alignment.*

## Align WordArt object:

1. Select WordArt object.
2. Click **Format** .............. `Alt` + `O`
3. Click **WordArt** ..................... `O`
4. Click **Layout** tab .......... `Ctrl`, `Tab`
5. Click desired alignment option.
6. Click **OK** .......................... `Enter`

## Adjust character spacing:

1. Select WordArt object.
2. Click **WordArt Character Spacing** button [AV] on WordArt toolbar.
3. Click desired option.

# Exercise Directions

1. Start Word, if necessary.

2. Create a new document.

3. Save the document as **NEWSTORE**.

4. Using a 36-point script or handwriting font, type the following five lines of text:

   **Announces**
   **The**
   **Grand Opening**
   **of a**
   **New Store**

5. Center the five lines of text horizontally.

6. Display the Drawing toolbar.

7. Make sure there is no text selected in the document and then start WordArt.

8. Select the style in the fourth row of the second column (refer to Illustration A).

9. Using a 40-point sans serif font, enter the WordArt text: **Liberty Blooms**.

   ✓ *Click OK to create the WordArt object.*

10. Set Text Wrapping to Top and Bottom.

11. Resize the WordArt object to approximately 1" high and 5.5" wide.

    ✓ *You can resize the object using the sizing handles, or by entering precise measurements in the Format WordArt dialog box.*

12. Set the character spacing to Very Tight.

13. Center align the object horizontally, and set the vertical position to .5" below the margin.

    ✓ *You can set the vertical position in the Format WordArt dialog box, or by dragging and using the vertical rulers.*

14. Set paragraph formatting to leave 54 pts. of space before the first line of text (**Announces**).

15. Create another WordArt object using the arc style that is in the first row of the third column.

16. Using a 28-point serif font, type the following address and URL information on three separate lines, and then insert the object into the document:

    **345 Chestnut Street**
    **Philadelphia, PA**
    **http://www.libertyblooms.net**

    ✓ *Click OK to create the WordArt object.*

17. Change the text wrapping to Top and Bottom.

18. Change the WordArt object shape to Button (curve).

    a. Select the object.

    b. Click the WordArt Shape button on the WordArt toolbar.

    c. Click the Button (curve) shape (4th column, 2nd row in the Shape palette).

       ✓ *Use ScreenTips to identify the names of the shapes.*

19. Set the size of the WordArt object to approximately 2.5" by 3.25".

20. Center the object horizontally, and set the vertical position to 5.5" below the margin.

    ✓ *Depending on the font you use in step 3, you may have to adjust the vertical position to achieve the desired result. For example, you may need to set the position to 6" below the margin.*

21. Insert the Explosion 1 AutoShape from the Stars and Banners palette into the upper-left corner of the document.

    ✓ *If necessary, drag the object off the drawing canvas and delete the canvas.*

22. Resize the shape to approximately 2.5" by 2.5".

23. Fill it with Gray - 25%.

24. Position it over the beginning of the first WordArt object, as shown in the Illustration.

    ✓ *Set horizontal alignment to -.25" to the right of the margin and align it vertically with the top of the margin.*

25. Send the shape back behind the text.

26. Search for clip art images of roses.

27. Locate the image shown in Illustration A and insert it into the document.

    ✓ *If you cannot locate the image, use the* 🔊**ROSE1.wmf** *file provided with this book.*

28. Set the text wrap for the picture to Behind text.

29. Align the picture on the left horizontally and 4" below the margin vertically.

30. Create a copy of the picture, or insert a second copy.

31. Flip the copy horizontally.

32. Align the copy on the right horizontally and 4" below the margin vertically.

33. Apply an art page border of flowers around the page.

34. Preview the document. It should look similar to Illustration A.

35. If necessary, make adjustments to the size and position of all objects in the document.

36. Print the document.

37. Close the document, saving all changes.

# On Your Own

1. Start Word and create a new document.

2. Save the document as **OWD84**.

3. Use WordArt to create a logo for a business, club, or organization to which you belong.

4. Try different WordArt Shapes.

5. Try different formatting such as Same Letter Heights, Character Spacing, or Vertical Text.

6. Try applying effects such as 3-D or Shadows to the WordArt object.

7. See how rotating or adjusting the WordArt object affects its appearance.

8. When you are satisfied with the result, print the document.

9. Ask a classmate to review the document and offer comments and suggestions.

10. Incorporate the comments and suggestions into the document as necessary.

11. Close the document, saving all changes, and exit Word.

# Exercise 85

## On the Job

Place a watermark on almost any document to make an impression on readers, convey an idea, or provide a consistent theme. For example, a watermark on corporate stationery can create a corporate identity. Watermarks can be fun or serious, barely noticeable or strikingly bold. You can save a watermark as part of a template and use it on new documents.

Long Shot, Inc. is growing by leaps and bounds. To fill job vacancies, it is hosting an open house and career fair. In this exercise, you will create a notice announcing the event. You use a picture to create a watermark on the document.

## Terms

**Watermark** A pale or semi-transparent graphic object positioned behind text in a document.

## Notes

### Watermarks

- Insert text or graphics objects as a **watermark** to provide a background image for text-based documents.

- You can create a watermark from a picture object, such as clip art or a photograph file.

- You can also use drawing objects such as a text box, WordArt, or an AutoShape.

- To achieve a watermark effect, the inserted object is usually centered horizontally and vertically on the page, and its color is adjusted to make it appear faded.

  - Pictures should be formatted with the Washout color control.

  - Drawing objects should be formatted with at least a 50% transparency.

- To ensure that the object used as a watermark is not accidentally deleted or modified, insert the object in the document header. That way, to select the object you must first display the Header area.

✓ *For more information on headers, refer to Exercise 52.*

- Placing an object in the header also makes it easier to position and insures that it appears the same on all pages in the document.

- Use the Printed Watermark dialog box to automatically insert and format a picture or WordArt object as a watermark.

- In the Printed Watermark dialog box you can access a list of common text watermarks such as *ASAP* and *Confidential*.

- You can also type your own text, which Word will automatically convert into a WordArt object with the appropriate settings for a watermark.

- Watermarks are not displayed in Normal view. Use Print Layout view or Print Preview to see the watermark.

- Watermarks are a nice feature to add to a template because every document based on the template will display the same watermark.

# Procedures

## Automatically Create a Watermark from a Picture

1. Click **Format** .............. `Alt`+`O`
2. Select **Background** ........... `K`
3. Click **Printed Watermark** ... `W`
4. Click **Picture watermark** option button ...................... `I`
5. Click **Select Picture** button
   `Select Picture...` ........ `Alt`+`P`
6. Locate and select desired picture file.
7. Click **Insert** button
   `Insert` ............... `Alt`+`S`
8. Click **Scale** .................. `Alt`+`L`
9. Select desired size as a percentage of the original picture size.
   
   ✓ Select Auto (the default) to have Word automatically size the object to fit on the page.

10. Click **OK** .......................... `Enter`

## Automatically Create a Watermark from Text

1. Click **Format** .............. `Alt`+`O`
2. Select **Background** ........... `K`
3. Click **Printed Watermark** ... `W`
4. Click **Text watermark** option button .............. `Alt`+`X`
5. Click **Text** .................. `Alt`+`T`
6. Select desired text from drop-down list ..... `↑`, `↓`, `Enter`
   
   OR
   
   Type desired text.

7. Click **Font** .................. `Alt`+`F`

8. Select desired font .................. `↑`, `↓`, `Enter`
9. Click **Size** .................. `Alt`+`S`
10. Select desired font size ............ `↑`, `↓`, `Enter`
11. Click **Color** .................. `Alt`+`C`
12. Select desired font color ............ `↑`, `↓`, `Enter`
13. Click one of the following layout options:
    
    • **Diagonal** ................ `Alt`+`D`
      to position the text diagonally across the page.
    • **Horizontal** .............. `Alt`+`H`
      to position the text horizontally across the page.

14. Click **OK** .......................... `Enter`

## Manually Create a Watermark from a Picture

1. Click **View** .................. `Alt`+`V`
2. Click **Header and Footer** .... `H`
3. Insert picture.
4. Position and size picture as desired.
5. Click **Color** button 🔲 on Picture toolbar.
6. Click **Washout** .................. `W`
7. Click **Text Wrapping** button 🖼 on Picture toolbar.
8. Click **Behind Text** .............. `D`
   
   ✓ If the picture doesn't move behind the text, try selecting Behind Text from the Text Wrapping drop-down menu again.

OR

a. Click **View** .............. `Alt`+`V`
b. Click **Header and Footer** .................. `H`
c. Insert picture.
d. Click **Format** ......... `Alt`+`O`
e. Click **Picture** .................. `I`
f. Click **Picture** tab ... `Ctrl`+`Tab`
g. Click **Color** drop-down arrow .... `Alt`+`C`
h. Click **Washout**.
i. Click **Layout** tab.... `Ctrl`+`Tab`
j. Click **Behind text** .. `Alt`+`B`
k. Set position as desired.
l. Click **Size** tab ........ `Ctrl`+`Tab`
m. Set size as desired.
n. Click **OK** .................... `Enter`

## Manually Create a Watermark Using a Drawing Object

1. Click **View** .................. `Alt`+`V`
2. Click **Header and Footer** .... `H`
3. Insert object.
4. Format object using light colors or gray shading.
5. Position and size object as desired.
6. Set transparency to at least 50%.
7. Set Text wrapping to Behind text.

# Exercise Directions

1. Start Word, if necessary.

2. Create the document shown in Illustration A, or open 💿 **85JOBFAIR**.

   ✓ *If you are creating the document from scratch, use a 20-point sans serif font (Arial is used in the illustration) except where noted, and center all text.*

3. Save the file as **JOBFAIR**.

4. Display the header and footer.

5. Create a printed watermark using the picture file 💿 **SOAR.wmf** supplied with this book.

   ✓ *Alternatively, select a picture of an eagle or other soaring bird from the Clip Organizer.*

6. Select the object.

   ✓ *Remember that the object is in the header. View the header, then click the object to select it.*

7. Rotate the object approximately 70 degrees.

8. Resize the picture so the width is 10" (the height should adjust automatically).

9. Close the header and footer.

10. Check the spelling and grammar in the document.

11. Preview the document. It should look similar to the one in Illustration B.

12. Print the document.

13. Close the document, saving all changes.

# On Your Own

1. Start Word and open the document **OWD76-2**, the document template you last used in the On Your Own section of Exercise 76, or open the template 💿 **85FORM**.

2. Save it as a document template with the name **OWD85-1**.

3. Unprotect the document.

4. Locate a clip art picture or create your own object to use as a watermark for the form.

5. Insert and format the watermark.

6. Make sure the watermark is correctly sized and positioned on the page.

   ✓ *If you insert it manually, be sure to insert it into the header area.*

7. Check the spelling and grammar in the document.

8. Preview the template with the watermark.

9. Print the template.

10. Ask a classmate to review the document and offer comments and suggestions.

11. Incorporate the comments and suggestions into the document.

12. Protect the template.

13. Close the template, saving all changes.

14. Create a new document based on the template.

15. Save the document as **SOWD85-2**.

16. Fill in the form fields.

17. Print the document.

18. Close the document, saving all changes, and exit Word.

*72 pts.* ——

# SOAR

*24 pts.* ↓

to new heights
with

# Long Shot, Incorporated—— *36 pts.*

*24 pts.* ↓

Please Come to Our
Open House and Career Fair

*24 pts.* ↓

Saturday April 15th and Sunday April 16th
10:00 a.m. – 3:00 p.m.
234 Simsbury Drive
Ithaca, NY 14850

*24 pts.* ↓

Learn about
career opportunities in

*24 pts.* ↓

Manufacturing
Design
Marketing

*24 pts.* ↓

For more information call 607-555-0909.

*Illustration B*

# SOAR

to new heights
with

# Long Shot, Incorporated

Please Come to Our
Open House and Career Fair

Saturday April 15th and Sunday April 16th
10:00 a.m. – 3:00 p.m.
234 Simsbury Drive
Ithaca, NY 14850

Learn about
career opportunities in

Manufacturing
Design
Marketing

For more information call 607-555-0909.

# Exercise 86

◆ **Critical Thinking**

You've been asked to design an invitation to a luncheon honoring the judges of Blue Sky Dairy's Name that Flavor contest. The invitation will integrate a text box, an AutoShape, WordArt, and a watermark created from a clip art picture to create an effective, eye-catching document.

## Exercise Directions

1. Start Word, if necessary.
2. Create a new document and save it as **LUNCH**.

### Create a Text Box

1. In a 16-point script font, type the following lines of text (Brush Script MT is used in Illustration A):
   **You are cordially invited**
   **To attend a luncheon**
   **In honor of**
   **The Name that Flavor Judges**
   **Friday, October 19**
   **12:30 in the afternoon**
   **Blue Sky Dairy Bar**
   **Highway 73**
   **Cambridge, WI 53523**
   **RSVP (608) 555-2697**
2. Insert a text box around the text.
3. Set text wrap for the text box to Behind text.
4. Center the text box on the page horizontally and vertically.
5. Set the transparency for the text box to 100%.
6. Remove the border line from around the text box.

### Create WordArt

1. Create a WordArt object as follows:
   a. Select the style in the first row of the third column.
   b. Use a script font in 40 points (Brush Script MT is used in the illustration).
   c. For the WordArt text, type **Blue Sky Dairy**.
2. Set text wrapping to Top and Bottom.
3. Size the WordArt object to approximately 2" high by 7" wide.
4. Center the object horizontally between the margins and align it vertically 1" below the margin.
5. Set the line color to Dark Blue and the fill color to Pale Blue.
6. Create a second WordArt object as follows:
   a. Select the style in the second row of the fourth column.
   b. Use a serif font in 28 points (Garamond is used in Illustration A).
   c. Type **Contest Judges** as the WordArt text.
7. Set the text wrapping for the object to Square.
8. Size the new WordArt object to approximately .75" high by 4.5" wide.
9. Change the line color of the WordArt object to Pale Blue.
10. Change the shadow color of the WordArt object to Dark Blue.
11. Center the object horizontally between the margins and position it vertically 2" below the margin.

## Insert an AutoShape

1. Insert the Down Ribbon AutoShape from the Stars and Banners palette.
   - ✓ *If necessary, drag it off the canvas and delete the canvas.*
2. Size it to 2.25" high by 5.75" wide.
3. Center the shape horizontally between the margins and align vertically 6.5" below the top margin.
4. In a 20-point serif font, centered and in bold, add the following text to the AutoShape: **Honorees**.
5. Leave 6 points of space, and then type the following in a 14 point serif font, centered (use the Wingdings symbol 171 as the separator):

   **Alex Gogan ★ Oliver Tesini**
   **Marie Chang ★ Patty McKay**
   **Mikel Arroyo ★ Jonathan Zabriskie**
   **Chris Lewis ★ Sharon Zide**
   **Jackie Neuwirth ★ Larry Vieth**
   **Deb Bastion ★ Bob Sanchez**
   - ✓ *Do not leave extra space between the lines. Also, the word wrap should break each line after the second name. Only insert paragraph marks if necessary.*
6. Fill the AutoShape with Pale Blue.

## Create a Watermark

1. Create a Watermark using the ✍ **COW1.wmf** picture file supplied with this book. Or, select an appropriate clip.
2. Check the spelling and grammar in the document.
3. Preview the document. It should look similar to the one in Illustration A.
4. Print the document.
5. Close the document, saving all changes, and exit Word.

# Blue Sky Dairy

## Contest Judges

You are cordially invited
To attend a luncheon
In honor of
The Name that Flavor Judges
Friday, October 19
12:30 in the afternoon
Blue Sky Dairy Bar
Highway 73
Cambridge, WI 53523
RSVP (608) 555-2697

### Honorees

Alex Gogan ★ Oliver Tesini
Marie Chang ★ Patty McKay
Mikel Arroyo ★ Jonathan Zabriskie
Chris Lewis ★ Sharon Zide
Jackie Neuwirth ★ Larry Vieth
Deb Bastion ★ Bob Sanchez

# Lesson 14

## Integration

# Exercise 87

◆ **Microsoft® Office 2003** ◆ **Run Multiple Programs at the Same Time**
◆ **Arrange Multiple Program Windows**

## On the Job

If you use Microsoft Office 2003, you may find it necessary to work with more than one application at a time. For example, you might want to create a report detailing your department's decreased costs by combining a Word document with an Excel spreadsheet. Or, you might want to illustrate a Word letter using an Excel Chart. You can open multiple applications at the same time and easily switch among them. You can also arrange the open applications on the screen so you can quickly find the information you need.

The owners of Blue Sky Dairy are thinking about starting a home delivery service. You have been asked to coordinate a feasibility study, and the owners have sent you information prepared in Word, Excel, and PowerPoint. In this exercise, you will start Word and open a memo document. You will then start the other Office programs, open the other program files, arrange the windows on-screen, and switch among the open windows.

## Terms

**Software suite** A group of software applications sold as a single unit. Usually, the applications have common features that make it easy to integrate and share data among documents.

**Spreadsheet** A program used to organize data in columns and rows. Spreadsheets are often used for performing calculations, such as financial or budget analysis.

**Presentation graphics** A program used to create presentations, such as slide shows.

**Personal information manager (PIM)** A program that keeps track of such items as addresses and phone numbers, appointments and meetings, and things to do.

**Database** An organized collection of records, such as client records, a personal address book, or product inventory.

**Group button** A taskbar button that represents all open windows for one application.

**Active window** The window in which you are currently working.

**Tile** Arrange open windows on-screen so they do not overlap.

**Cascade** Arrange open windows on-screen so they overlap, with the active window displayed on top.

# Notes

## Microsoft® Office 2003

■ Microsoft Office 2003 is a **suite** of software programs designed to integrate with each other, the World Wide Web, and with other Microsoft programs.

■ Different versions of the suite are available to suit the needs of different people and businesses.

■ Each edition includes the following core Microsoft Office programs:

• Word, a word processing program.

• Excel, a **spreadsheet** program.

• PowerPoint, a **presentation graphics** program.

• Outlook, a **personal information manager** and communications program.

• Office tools, which include such features as the Clip Organizer, Search, and the spelling and grammar checker.

■ Some editions may include the following additional programs:

• Access, a **database** application.

• Publisher, a desktop publishing program.

• FrontPage, a Web site development program.

• OneNote, a note-taking and management program.

• InfoPath, an information gathering and management program.

## Run Multiple Programs at the Same Time

■ You can open multiple program windows at the same time. This is useful for comparing the data in different files, as well as for exchanging data between files.

■ Each open window is represented by a button on the Windows taskbar.

■ If there is not room on the taskbar to display buttons for each open window, Windows displays a **group button**.

■ Only one window can be active—or current—at a time.

■ The **active window** is displayed on top of other open windows. Its title bar is darker than the title bars of other open windows, and its taskbar button appears pressed in.

■ Switch among open windows to make a different window active.

■ Use Windows to start an Office program.

• Select a program name from the Programs menu to start the program and open a new blank file.

• Select a file name from the My Recent Documents menu to start the program and open the file at the same time.

• Locate and open any document using Windows Explorer.

• Locate and open an existing file using the Open Office Document command.

• Start a program and open a new file using the New Office Document command.

## Arrange Multiple Program Windows

■ **Tile** windows on-screen if you want to see all of them at the same time. Tiled windows do not overlap.

✓ *You can tile windows horizontally or vertically.*

*Windows tiled horizontally*

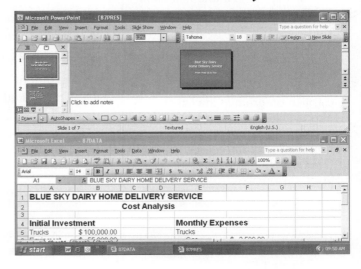

- **Cascade** windows if you want to see the active window in its entirety, with the title bars of all open windows displayed behind it.

*Cascaded windows*

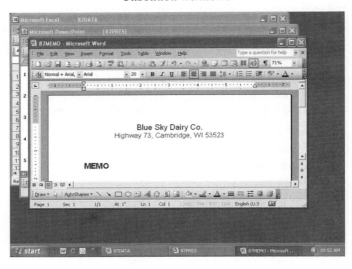

# Procedures

## Start Multiple Programs

✓ *Use any of the method procedures to start a program, then repeat to start additional programs.*

1. Click **Start** button
   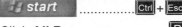 ...............Ctrl+Esc
2. Click **All** **P**rograms ........... P
3. Click the Microsoft Office folder icon.
4. Click the name of the Microsoft Office program.

**OR**

1. Click **Start** button
    ...............Ctrl+Esc
2. Click the name of the Microsoft Office program in the list of recently used programs.

**OR**

1. Double-click a program icon on the desktop:

   - **Word** shortcut icon to start Word.

   - **Excel** shortcut icon to start Excel.

   - **PowerPoint** shortcut icon
     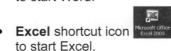 to start PowerPoint.

---

- **Access** shortcut icon
  to start Access.

- **Outlook** shortcut icon
  to start Outlook.

- **Publisher** shortcut icon
  to start Publisher.

**OR**

1. Click **Start** button
   ...............Ctrl+Esc
2. Click **All** **P**rograms ........... P
3. Click **New Office Document** .
4. Click desired page tab.....................Ctrl+Tab
5. Click desired document icon.
6. Click **OK** ......................... Enter

**OR**

1. Click **Start** button
   ...............Ctrl+Esc
2. Click **My Recent** **D**ocuments ......................... D
3. Click file name.

**OR**

1. Right-click **Start** button
   .

---

2. Click **E**xplore ...................... E
3. Select drive where folder/file is located.
4. Open folder.
5. Double-click name of file to open.

**OR**

1. Click **Start** button
   ...............Ctrl+Esc
2. Click **All** **P**rograms ........... P
3. Click **Open Office Document** .
4. Locate and select file to open.
5. Click **O**pen button
    ........... Alt+O

## Arrange Program Windows

1. Right-click on blank area of Windows taskbar.
2. Select desired option:

   - **Ca**scade Windows........ S
   - **Tile Windows H**orizontally................... H
   - **Tile Windows V**ertically ...................... E
   - **S**how the Desktop........ S

   ✓ *Maximize active window to display active window only.*

**Arrange Word document windows:**

1. Click **Window** .............. `Alt`+`W`
2. Click **Arrange All** ................. `A`

**Arrange Excel workbook windows:**

1. Click **Window** .............. `Alt`+`W`
2. Click **Arrange** ...................... `A`
3. Select desired option:
   - **Tiled**
   - **Horizontal**
   - **Vertical**
   - **Cascade**
4. Click **OK** ........................... `Enter`

**Arrange PowerPoint presentation windows:**

1. Click **Window** .............. `Alt`+`W`
2. Click **Arrange All** ................. `A`
   to tile windows vertically.
   OR
   Click **Cascade** ..................... `C`
   to cascade windows.

**Switch Between Open Windows**

- Click taskbar button of desired window.

  OR

- Click in desired window if it is visible on-screen.

  OR

1. Press and hold `Alt`.
2. Press `Tab` to cycle through open windows.
3. Release `Alt` when desired window is selected.

**Close Programs**

1. Click **Application Close** icon ⊠.
   OR
   a. Click **File** ............... `Alt`+`F`
   b. Click **Exit** ...................... `X`
   OR
   Click **Close** if Exit command is not available ..................... `C`
2. If prompted, click **Yes** ......... `Y`
   to save changes before closing.
   OR
   Click **No** ........................... `N`
   to close without saving.

# Exercise Directions

1. Start Word, if necessary, and open the file ⊙ **87MEMO.doc**.
2. Start Excel and open the file ⊙ **87DATA.xls**.
3. Start PowerPoint and open the file ⊙ **87PRES.ppt**.
4. Tile the windows vertically on-screen. They should look similar to Illustration A, although the order may vary.
5. Make the file ⊙ **87MEMO.doc** active.
6. Tile the windows horizontally.
7. Make the file ⊙ **87DATA.xls** active.
8. Cascade the windows.
9. Make the file ⊙ **87PRES.ppt** active.
10. Maximize the PowerPoint window.
11. Exit PowerPoint without saving any changes.
12. Exit Excel without saving any changes.
13. Exit Word without saving any changes.

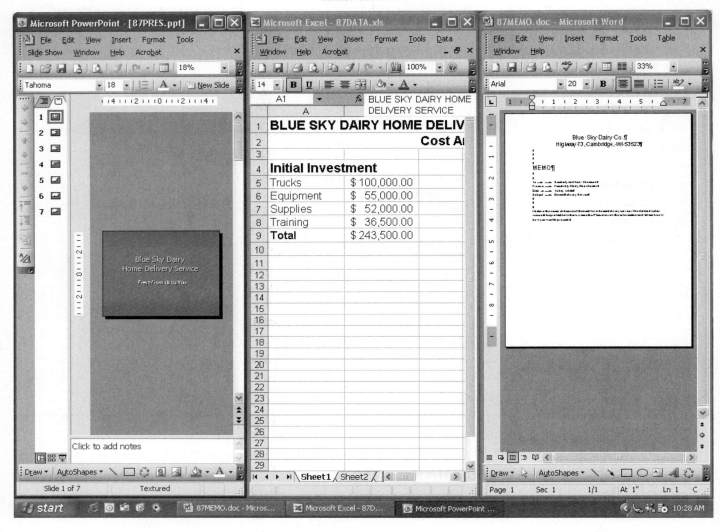

# On Your Own

1. Start Word and open the document **OWD83** or open ⊙**87ANNOUNCE**.

2. Start Excel with a blank workbook open.

3. Start PowerPoint with a blank presentation open.

4. Arrange the open windows in a cascaded fashion.

5. Arrange the windows in a tiled fashion.

6. Practice switching from window to window.

7. Maximize the Excel window.

8. Close the PowerPoint window without saving any changes.

9. Close the Excel window without saving any changes.

10. Exit Word without saving any changes.

# Exercise 88

## Skills Covered:

### ◆ Copy and Move Data from One Office Document to Another

## On the Job

You can use the standard copy and move commands to copy or move data from a document created with one program—such as an Excel worksheet—into a document created with a different program—such as a Word report. Copying or moving data from one application to another saves you the time and trouble of retyping.

The owners of Blue Sky Dairy have asked you for information about the costs of starting the home delivery service. In this exercise, you will copy data from an Excel worksheet into a memo you have written to them.

## Terms

**Source file** The file that contains the data to be copied.

**Destination file** The file where the data is pasted.

## Notes

### Copy and Move Data from One Office Document to Another

- Use the Windows Clipboard or drag-and-drop editing to copy or move data from one Office document to another.

- The **source file** contains the original data and the **destination file** is where the data is pasted.

- Data pasted into a destination file becomes part of the destination file. There is no link to the source file.

- Word may automatically format pasted data. For example, Excel data pasted into a Word document is displayed as a table, and a PowerPoint slide pasted into a Word document is formatted as a picture.

- You edit pasted data using standard commands for the destination application.

## Procedures

### Copy Data from One Office Document to Another
### (Ctrl+C, Ctrl+V)

**Use the Clipboard:**

1. Start programs.
2. Open source file.
3. Open destination file.
4. Select data to copy in source file.

5. Click **Copy** button 🖳.
   OR
   a. Click **Edit**............... Alt+E
   b. Click **Copy** ..................... C
   OR
   a. Right-click selection.
   b. Click **Copy** ..................... C
6. Make destination file active.

7. Position insertion point in the desired location.

8. Click **Paste** button 🖳.
   OR
   a. Click **Edit** ............... Alt+E
   b. Click **Paste** ................... P
   OR
   a. Right-click location.
   b. Click **Paste** ................... P

**Use drag-and-drop editing:**

1. Start programs.
2. Open source file.
3. Open destination file.
4. Right-click taskbar.
5. Choose **Tile Windows Vertically** ............................ V
6. Select data to copy in source document.
7. Scroll in destination document to display desired new location.
8. Move pointer to edge of selection.
9. Press and hold down **Ctrl** ... Ctrl
10. Drag selected data to correct position in destination file.

    ✓ *Word displays the copy pointer*

    *. A gray vertical bar indicates location where selection will be dropped.*

11. Release mouse button.
12. Release **Ctrl**.

**Move Data from One Office Document to Another**
*(Ctrl+X, Ctrl+V)*

**Use the Clipboard:**

1. Start programs.
2. Open source file.
3. Open destination file.
4. Select data to move in source file.
5. Click **Cut** button .
    OR
    a. Click **Edit** ................ Alt + E
    b. Click **Cut** ......................... T
    OR
    a. Right-click selection.
    b. Click **Cut** ......................... T
6. Make destination file active.
7. Position insertion point in the desired location.
8. Click **Paste** button .
    OR
    a. Click **Edit** ................ Alt + E
    b. Click **Paste** ..................... P

OR
    a. Right-click location.
    b. Click **Paste** ..................... P

**Use drag-and-drop editing:**

1. Start programs.
2. Open source file.
3. Open destination file.
4. Right-click taskbar.
5. Choose **Tile Windows Vertically** ............................ V
6. Select data to move in source document.
7. Scroll in destination document to display desired new location.
8. Move pointer to edge of selection.

    ✓ *Pointer changes to display selection arrow.*

9. Drag selected data to correct position in destination file.

    ✓ *Word displays the move pointer . A gray vertical bar indicates location where selection will be dropped.*

10. Release mouse button.

# Exercise Directions

✓ *This exercise assumes you know how to locate and select data in an Excel worksheet. If you do not, ask your instructor for more information.*

1. Start Microsoft Office Word.
2. Create the document shown in Illustration A, or open the document **88DELIVERY.doc**.
3. Save the document as **DELIVERY**.
4. Replace the text **Your Name** with your own name.
5. Replace the text **Today's date** with the current date.
6. Position the insertion point on the last line at the end of the document.
7. Start Microsoft Office Excel.
8. Open the worksheet **88COSTS.xls**.
9. Select cells A4 through B9.
    a. Click the cell in the fourth row of the first column (it contains the text **Initial Investment**).
    b. Press and hold Shift.
    c. Click the cell in the ninth row of the second column (it contains the value **$243,500.00**).

10. Copy the selected range of cells to the last line of the **DELIVERY** document.
    a. Click the Copy button.
    b. Switch to the **DELIVERY** document.
    c. Make sure the insertion point is on the last line.
    d. Click the Paste button.
11. Apply the Table 3D effects 2 AutoFormat to the table.
    ✓ *For a refresher on formatting tables, refer to Exercise 37.*
12. Center the table horizontally on the page.
13. Check the spelling and grammar in the document.
14. Preview the **DELIVERY** document. It should look similar to Illustration B.
15. Print the document.
16. Close the **88COSTS.xls** worksheet and exit Excel, without saving any changes.
17. Close **DELIVERY.doc**, saving all changes.

*Illustration A*

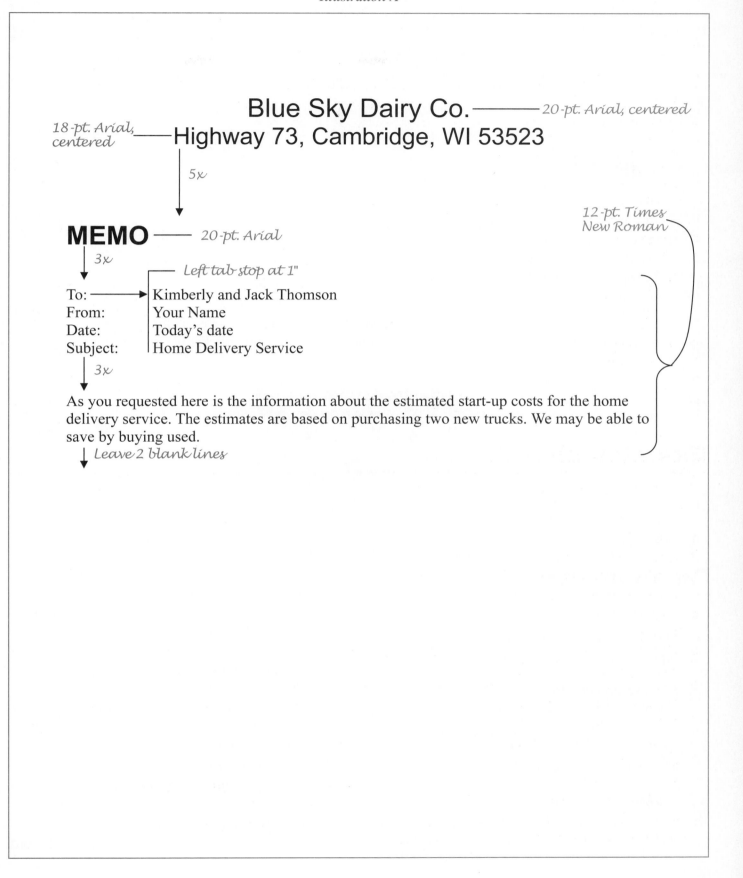

Blue Sky Dairy Co. ——— *20-pt. Arial, centered*

*18-pt. Arial, centered* ——— Highway 73, Cambridge, WI 53523

*5x*

**MEMO** ——— *20-pt. Arial*

*3x*

——— *Left tab stop at 1"*

*12-pt. Times New Roman*

To: —————▶ Kimberly and Jack Thomson
From:       Your Name
Date:       Today's date
Subject:   Home Delivery Service

*3x*

As you requested here is the information about the estimated start-up costs for the home delivery service. The estimates are based on purchasing two new trucks. We may be able to save by buying used.

*Leave 2 blank lines*

# Blue Sky Dairy Co.
## Highway 73, Cambridge, WI 53523

# MEMO

To:         Kimberly and Jack Thomson
From:       Your Name
Date:       Today's date
Subject:    Home Delivery Service

As you requested here is the information about the estimated start-up costs for the home delivery service. The estimates are based on purchasing two new trucks. We may be able to save by buying used.

| Initial Investment | |
|---|---|
| Trucks | $ 100,000.00 |
| Equipment | $ 55,000.00 |
| Supplies | $ 52,000.00 |
| Training | $ 36,500.00 |
| **Total** | $ 243,500.00 |

# On Your Own

1. Start Word and create a new document.

2. Save the document as **OWD88-1**.

3. Type a letter addressed to your friends and/or family telling them that you have made up a list of books and/or CDs that you would like to receive as birthday or holiday gifts.

4. Start Excel and create a new worksheet, or open the file ⊘ **88GIFTS.xls**.

5. Save the file as **OWD88-2**.

   ✓ *The steps for saving an Excel file are the same as those for saving a Word file.*

6. Create a worksheet listing the names and prices of CDs and/or books you would like to receive.

7. Select the Excel worksheet data and copy it to the Word document.

8. Format the data in the Word document to improve its appearance and make it easier to read.

9. Check the spelling and grammar in the document.

10. Print the document.

11. Ask a classmate to review the document and make comments or suggestions.

12. Incorporate the comments and suggestions into the document.

13. Close all files, saving all changes, and exit Word.

# Exercise 89

## On the Job

Link files when you have existing data in one file that you want to use in one or more other files. Whenever the original data is changed, the link ensures that it will be updated in all other files. Linking lets you maintain data in a single location, yet use it in other locations as well.

As the new Training Director at Long Shot, Inc., you have been asked to submit the department's expenses for the first quarter to the Director of Human Resources. However, you only have preliminary data available. In this exercise, you will link the preliminary data stored in an Excel worksheet into a Word memo. You will then change the data to reflect actual expenses, and update the data in the Word document.

## Terms

**Link**  To insert an object in a destination file. When the source file is edited, the linked object in the destination file is updated to reflect the change.

## Notes

### Link Files

- **Link** data to create a dynamic connection between two files. Linking enables you to keep files that include the same data up to date, without having to edit the data in every file.

- The source file contains the original data and the destination file contains the linked object.

- Source data can be linked to many destination files. For example, data in an Excel worksheet can be linked to multiple Word documents and to a PowerPoint slide.

- When you edit the source file, the linked object in the destination file(s) is changed as well.

- Use the Paste Special command with the Paste Link option enabled to link files.

- In the Paste Special dialog box you can also select how you want to format the selected object. The choices depend on the source program.

- A description of the selected format is displayed in the Result area of the dialog box.

*Paste Special dialog box*

Paste link option button

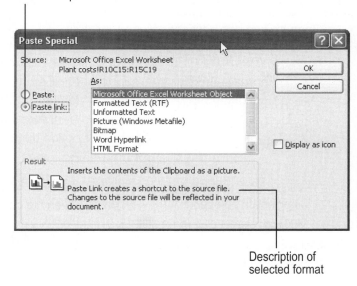

Description of selected format

**469**

## Edit a Linked Object

- To make sure that the original data is always up-to-date, you use the source program to edit a linked object.

- For example, if you have a linked Excel object in a Word memo you must use Excel to edit the object in the memo.

- When you double-click a linked object, the source program and file open so you can access the appropriate commands.

- Changes made to the original source file are reflected in the linked object when the link is updated.

- Although you cannot edit a linked object using the destination program, linked objects can be formatted, moved, and resized using many techniques you learned for working with graphics objects.

  ✓ *See Lesson 13 for information about working with graphics objects.*

## Update Links

- By default, links update automatically.

- When both the source and destination files are open, the linked object must be selected for the update to occur.

- When only the source file is open, the linked object is updated when you open the destination file.

- If there are many links in a file, automatic updating can slow down your system.

- You can turn off automatic updates and manually update links.

- If Word cannot locate the source file (for example, if it has been deleted, renamed, or moved) it will display a warning message telling you that it cannot update the link. You can use the Links dialog box to break the link or to change the location of the source file.

- Breaking the link leaves the object in the destination document without a link to a source document or program.

- Changing the source file in the Links dialog box links the object to a different source file.

*Links dialog box*

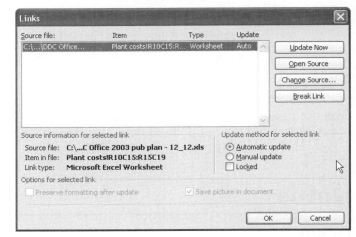

# Procedures

## Link Files

1. Open source and destination files.
2. Select data to be linked in source file.
3. Click **Copy** button.
   OR
   a. Click **Edit** .............. Alt+E
   b. Click **Copy** ..................... C
   OR
   a. Right-click selection.
   b. Click **Copy** ..................... C
4. Make destination file active.

5. Position insertion point in the desired location.
6. Click **Edit** ..................... Alt+E
7. Click **Paste Special** ............. S
8. Click **As** box to choose format ............ Alt+A, ↓, ↑
9. Click **Paste link** option button ............... Alt+L
10. Click **OK** ......................... Enter

## Edit Linked Object

1. Open file containing linked object.
2. Double-click linked object.
   ✓ *Source program and file open.*

3. Edit source file as desired.
4. Close source program and file, saving all changes.

## Update Links

**Turn off automatic updating:**

1. Click **Edit** ..................... Alt+E
2. Click **Links** ......................... K
3. Click **Manual update** option button ............... Alt+M
4. Click **OK** ......................... Enter

**Update links manually:**

1. Select object.
2. Press **F9** ............................. F9
   OR

1. Click **Edit** .................... `Alt`+`E`
2. Click **Links** ........................ `K`
3. Click **Update Now** button

   Update Now ...... `Alt`+`U`

**OR**
1. Right-click object.
2. Click **Update Link** .............. `D`

### Break a Link
1. Select object in document.
2. Click **Edit** .................... `Alt`+`E`
3. Click **Links** ......................... `K`
4. Click **Break Link** button

   Break Link ...... `Alt`+`B`
5. Click **OK** .......................... `Enter`

### Change a Link's Source
1. Select object in document.
2. Click **Edit** ................... `Alt`+`E`
3. Click **Links** ......................... `K`
4. Click **Change Source** button

   Change Source... ...... `Alt`+`N`
5. Locate and select desired source file.
6. Click **Open** button

   Open .............. `Alt`+`O`
7. Click **OK** .......................... `Enter`

# Exercise Directions

✓ *The steps in this exercise assume you know how to select and enter data in an Excel worksheet. If necessary, ask your instructor for more information.*

1. Start Word, if necessary.
2. Create the document shown in Illustration A, or open 💿 **89COSTMEMO**.
3. Save the document as **COSTMEMO**.
4. Replace the sample text **Your Name** with your own name.
5. Replace the sample text **Today's date** with the current date.
6. Position the insertion point on the blank line at the end of the document.
7. Start Excel and open the worksheet file 💿 **89Q1.xls**.
8. Save the file as **Q1**.

   ✓ *Use the File, Save As command just as you would in Word.*

9. Link the Excel worksheet data onto the last line of the **COSTMEMO** document.
   a. Select cells A5:E13 in the **Q1** worksheet.

      ✓ *Click cell A5, press and hold Shift, and then click cell E13.*

   b. Copy the selected range to the Clipboard.
   c. Switch to the **COSTMEMO** document.
   d. Make sure the insertion point is on the last line of the document.
   e. Select the Paste Special command from the Edit menu in Word.
   f. Select Microsoft Office Excel Worksheet Object as the format type.
   g. Select the Paste link option button.
   h. Click OK.

10. Center the object in the memo horizontally on the page.

    ✓ *Click the object to select it, then click the Center button on the Formatting toolbar. Alternatively, use the Format Object dialog box.*

11. Save the changes to the Word document.
12. Double-click the object in the Word document.

    ✓ *Excel opens the Q1 worksheet on-screen.*

13. In cell C9—**February Facility rentals** (the empty cell)—type **1,500** and then press Enter.

    ✓ *Excel is set to automatically format the data as currency.*

14. Close the worksheet, saving the changes.
15. Switch to the **COSTMEMO** document.
16. If necessary, press F9 to update the link.
17. Double-click the Excel object in the Word memo.

    ✓ *Excel starts and opens the Q1 worksheet.*

18. Click cell D12—**March Miscellaneous** expenses—and type **150** to edit the entry, and then press Enter.
19. Close the worksheet, saving the changes, and exit Excel.
20. If necessary, update the link in Word.
21. Preview the **COSTMEMO** document. It should look similar to Illustration B.
22. Close the document, saving all changes.

# Long Shot, Inc.

*36-pt. Arial, bold, centered*

↓ *3x*

## INTERDEPARTMENT MEMORANDUM

*16-pt. Arial, centered*

↓ *4x*

*Left tab stop at .5"*

To: → Director of Human Resources
From: Your Name
Date: Today's date
Re: Training Department Expenses

↓ *3x*

Per your request, here are the preliminary expense figures for the training department for the first quarter of the year. I will update the figures as soon as I receive the actual amounts.

↓ *Leave 2 blank lines*

*12-pt. Times New Roman*

*Illustration B*

# Long Shot, Inc.

## INTERDEPARTMENT MEMORANDUM

To:        Director of Human Resources
From:    Your Name
Date:     Today's date
Re:        Training Department Expenses

Per your request, here are the preliminary expense figures for the training department for the first quarter of the year. I will update the figures as soon as I receive the actual amounts.

| | January | February | March | Total |
|---|---|---|---|---|
| **Salaries** | $ 135,000.00 | $ 135,000.00 | $ 135,000.00 | $ 405,000.00 |
| **Overtime** | $ 30,000.00 | $ 32,000.00 | $ 29,000.00 | $ 91,000.00 |
| **Entertainment** | $ 1,500.00 | $ 1,750.00 | $ 1,200.00 | $ 4,450.00 |
| **Facility rentals** | $ 2,000.00 | $ 1,500.00 | $ 1,500.00 | $ 5,000.00 |
| **Books** | $ 500.00 | $ 250.00 | $ 500.00 | $ 1,250.00 |
| **Supplies** | $ 250.00 | $ 150.00 | $ 375.00 | $ 775.00 |
| **Miscellaneous** | $ 200.00 | $ 175.00 | $ 150.00 | $ 525.00 |
| **Total** | $ 169,450.00 | $ 170,825.00 | $ 167,725.00 | $ 508,000.00 |

# On Your Own

1. Start Word and open ⌨OWD88-1, the letter you created in the On Your Own section of Exercise 88, or open 💿89REQUEST.

2. Save the document as OWD89-1.

3. Delete the table from the document.

4. Start Excel and open the ⌨OWD88-2, the worksheet containing the list of books or CDs you created in the On Your Own section of Exercise 88, or open 💿89GIFTS.

5. Save the worksheet as OWD89-2.

6. Link the worksheet data to the Word document.

7. Change some of the data in the Excel worksheet.

8. Make sure the data updates in the Word document. Manually update the link, if necessary.

9. Close the Excel worksheet, saving all changes, and exit Excel.

10. Close the Word document, saving all changes, and exit Word.

# Exercise 90

## Skills Covered:
### ◆ Embed Objects ◆ Edit Embedded Objects

## On the Job

Embed data when you do not want a link between the source data and the embedded object. You can edit embedded data without the changes affecting the source. This is useful for illustrating changes that might occur, or for submitting information that might vary depending on the recipient, such as a proposal bid, or a contract.

As the new Training Director at Long Shot, Inc., you are planning a weekend training retreat for upper-level management. The Director of Human Resources has asked you to submit a preliminary budget for the event. In this exercise, you will embed an existing budget in a Word memo. You will then edit and format the object using Excel.

## Terms

**Embed** Insert an object in a file. The embedded object is not linked to a source file, but it is linked to the source application. You edit the object using the source application, but changes do not affect the source file data.

## Notes

### Embed Objects

- **Embedding** inserts an object into a destination file.

- There is no link between the original data in the source file and the embedded object; however, you can use all of the source program's commands to edit, format, and manipulate the embedded object.

- Use the Paste Special command to create an embedded object from existing data.

- Use the Insert, Object command to create a new embedded object.

- Embedding an object uses more disk space than linking an object, because the same data is stored in more than one file.

### Edit Embedded Objects

- Edit and format embedded objects using the source program.

- When you edit embedded objects in Word, the source application commands and toolbars are displayed in the Word window.

- Changes you make to the embedded object do not affect the original file.

*Edit an embedded Excel Worksheet object in Word*

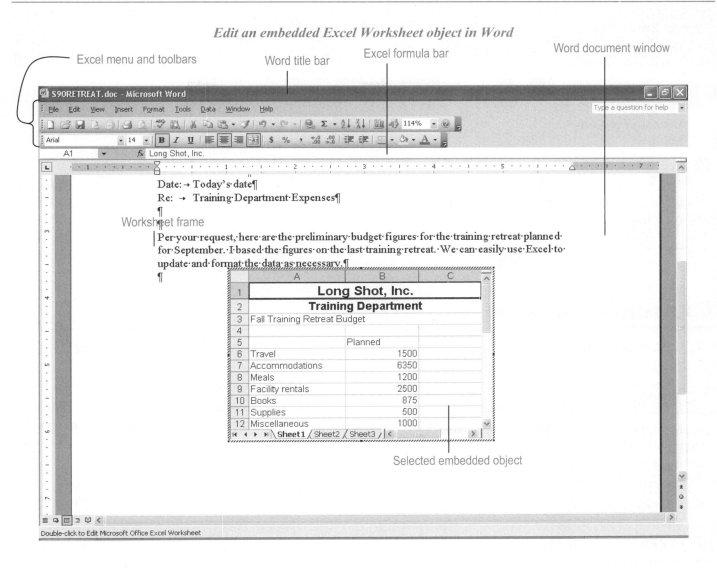

# Procedures

## Embed Selected Data

1. Open source file.
2. Select data to be copied.
3. Click **Copy** button.
   OR
   a. Click **Edit** .............. Alt + E
   b. Click **Copy** ..................... C
   OR
   a. Right-click selection.
   b. Click **Copy** .......... C , Enter
4. Make destination file active.
5. Position insertion point in the desired location.

6. Click **Edit** .................... Alt + E
7. Click **Paste Special** ........... S
8. Click **As** box to choose format ........... Alt + A , ↑ , ↓
9. Click **Paste** option button ............... Alt + P
10. Click **OK** ......................... Enter

## Embed a New Object

1. Open destination file.
2. Position insertion point.
3. Click **Insert** ................. Alt + I
4. Click **Object** ...................... O
5. Click **Create New** tab .. Alt + C

6. Click **Object type** list box ........................ Alt + O
7. Select object type. .................... Tab , ↑ , ↓
8. Click **OK** to create new object. ...................... Enter
   ✓ *Selected application opens.*
9. Enter, edit, or format data to create object as desired.
10. Click outside of object to close source application and display object in destination file.

## Embed Entire File

1. Open destination file.
2. Position insertion point.
3. Click **Insert** ................. `Alt`+`I`
4. Click **Object** ...................... `O`
5. Click **Create from File** tab ..................... `Alt`+`F`
6. Click **Browse** button

   [ Browse... ] ........ `Alt`+`B`

7. Locate and select file to insert.
8. Click **Insert** button

   [ Insert ] .............. `Alt`+`S`

9. Click **OK** ......................... `Enter`

## Edit Embedded Object

1. Open file containing embedded object.
2. Double-click embedded object.
   - ✓ *Source application menus and toolbars are displayed within destination application.*
3. Edit embedded data using source application commands.
4. Click outside embedded object to close source application.

# Exercise Directions

1. Start Word, if necessary.
2. Create the document shown in Illustration A, or open 🖸**90RETREAT**.
3. Save the document as **RETREAT**.
4. Replace the sample text **Your Name** with your name.
5. Replace the sample text **Today's date** with the current date.
6. Position the insertion point on the blank line at the end of the document.
7. Start Excel and open the file 🖸**90BUDGET.xls**.
8. Save the file as **BUDGET**.
9. Embed the cells A3:C13 as an Excel Worksheet Object on the last line of the Word document.
   a. Select cells A3 through C13.
      - ✓ *Click cell A3, press and hold Shift, and then click cell C13.*
   b. Copy the selection to the Clipboard.
   c. Position the insertion point at the end of the Word document.
   d. Choose the Edit, Paste Special command.
   e. Select the Microsoft Office Excel Worksheet Object as the format type.
   f. Select the Paste option button.
   g. Click OK.
10. Close the **BUDGET** file and exit Excel.
11. Double-click the Excel object in the Word document.
    - ✓ *Excel commands become available in Word.*
12. Edit the worksheet title from **Spring Training Retreat Budget** to **Fall Training Retreat Budget**.
    a. Click cell A3 in the embedded object.
    b. Type **Fall Training Retreat Budget** and press Enter, or click in the Formula bar, replace the text **Spring** with the text **Fall**, and then press Enter.
13. Delete all of the data from the Actual column.
    a. Select cells C5:C13.
    b. Press Delete.
14. Apply the 3D Effects 2 AutoFormat to the object.
    a. Select cells A3:C13.
    b. Click Format on the Excel menu bar.
    c. Click AutoFormat.
    d. Click 3D Effects 2.
    e. Click OK.
15. Increase the font size in the entire worksheet object to 12 points.
    a. Select cells A3:C13.
    b. Select 12 from Font Size drop-down list.
16. Increase the widths of columns A and B so all data is visible.
    - Drag borders between columns, or double-click borders between columns on worksheet frame.

17. Click outside the embedded object to close Excel.

18. Center the embedded object horizontally on the page.
   - Click the object to select it, and then click the Center button on the Word formatting toolbar.

19. Check the spelling and grammar in the document.

20. Save the document and preview it. It should look similar to the one in Illustration B.

21. Print the document.

22. Start Excel and open the worksheet **BUDGET**. Notice that the changes you made to the object in Word did not affect the original worksheet.

23. Close the worksheet and exit Excel.

24. Close the **RETREAT** document, saving all changes.

*Illustration A*

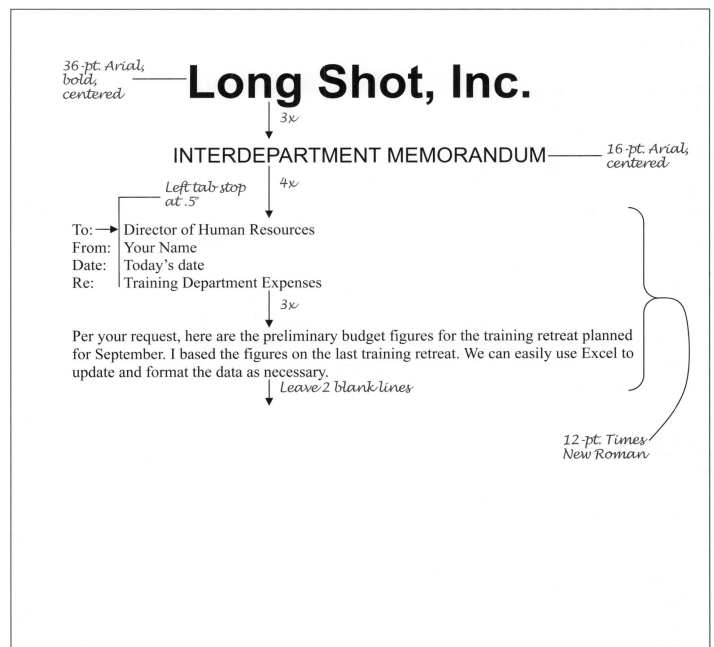

36-pt. Arial, bold, centered

# Long Shot, Inc.

↓ 3x

INTERDEPARTMENT MEMORANDUM —— 16-pt. Arial, centered

Left tab stop at .5"

↓ 4x

To: → Director of Human Resources
From: Your Name
Date: Today's date
Re: Training Department Expenses

↓ 3x

Per your request, here are the preliminary budget figures for the training retreat planned for September. I based the figures on the last training retreat. We can easily use Excel to update and format the data as necessary.

↓ Leave 2 blank lines

12-pt. Times New Roman

# Long Shot, Inc.

## INTERDEPARTMENT MEMORANDUM

To:      Director of Human Resources
From:   Your Name
Date:    Today's date
Re:      Training Department Expenses

Per your request, here are the preliminary budget figures for the training retreat planned for September. I based the figures on the last training retreat. We can easily use Excel to update and format the data as necessary.

**Fall Training Retreat Budget**

|  | Planned |
|---|---|
| Travel | $    1,500.00 |
| Accommodations | $    6,350.00 |
| Meals | $    1,200.00 |
| Facility rentals | $    2,500.00 |
| Books | $       875.00 |
| Supplies | $       500.00 |
| Miscellaneous | $    1,000.00 |
| **Total** | $  13,925.00 |

# On Your Own

1.  Start Word and open ⌨OWD89-1, the letter you created in the On Your Own section of Exercise 89, or open 💿90REQUEST.doc.

    ✓ *If Word prompts you to update links, click No.*

2.  Save the document as OWD90-1.
3.  Delete the linked object from the document.
4.  Start Excel and open ⌨OWD89-2, the worksheet containing the list of books or CDs you created in the On Your Own section of Exercise 89, or open 💿90GIFTS.xls.

5.  Save the file as OWD90-2.
6.  Embed the worksheet data into the Word document.
7.  Close the Excel worksheet and exit Excel.
8.  Use Excel to edit the data in the embedded object in the Word document.
9.  Apply formatting to the embedded object.
10. If you want, check to see that the original data has not changed.
11. Print the Word document.
12. Save and close the Word document, and exit Word.

# Exercise 91

## On the Job

Charts are an effective way to illustrate numeric data and trends. For example, you can use charts to plot sales over time, compare projected income to actual income, or to show a breakdown in revenue sources. You can create chart objects in a Word document using Microsoft Graph. You can enter new data to create the chart, or you can import data from an existing source, such as a table or even an Excel worksheet. You can also use Word's Drawing tools to create a diagram or organization chart.

As the person in charge of researching the feasibility of the home delivery service for Blue Sky Dairy, you have recently completed two surveys of people in your target areas. The first asked a group of 100 people how likely they were to use a dairy home delivery service. The second asked groups in each of four target areas whether they would be more likely to use a dairy home deliver service for milk, ice cream, eggs, or butter. In this exercise, you will create charts detailing this information and include them in a memo to the company owner. You will also include an organization chart for the project.

## Terms

**Microsoft Graph** A program that comes with Microsoft Office Word, used for creating charts.

**Chart object** A chart embedded in a Word document.

**Datasheet** A table comprised of columns and rows, in which you enter data you want to use to create a chart.

**Datasheet cell** The rectangular area at the intersection of a column and row where you enter data in a datasheet.

**Data label** Text that identifies the units plotted on the chart, such as months or dollar values.

**Data series** A range of values plotted in a chart.

**Chart title** The name of the chart.

**Data axis** The scale used to measure the data in the chart. The Y axis shows the vertical scale, and the X axis shows the horizontal scale.

**Legend** The key that identifies what each color or symbol in the chart represents.

**Delimited** A comma delimited file is one in which commas are used to separate sections of text.

**Diagram** A chart or graph used to illustrate a concept or describe the relationship of parts to a whole.

**Organization chart** A chart that depicts hierarchical relationships, such as a family tree or corporate management.

# Notes

## Create a Chart

- Word comes with a charting application called **Microsoft Graph**.

- You can use Microsoft Graph to embed **chart objects** in Word documents.

- When you start Microsoft Graph, its toolbars and menus replace the Word toolbars and menus, so you can use all of Microsoft Graph's features without closing Word.

  ✓ *For more information about working with embedded objects, see Exercise 90.*

### Create a chart with Microsoft Graph

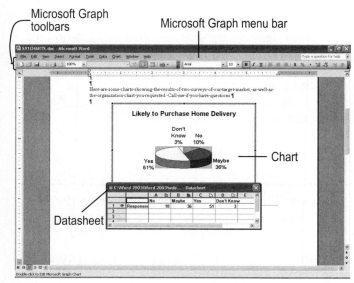

- Microsoft Graph opens with a sample chart selected and sample data entered in the **datasheet**.

- To create your own chart, you replace the sample data in the **datasheet cells**. Microsoft Graph automatically generates the chart.

- Typing in a datasheet is similar to typing in a Word table.

  ✓ *For more information on entering data in tables, see Exercise 37.*

- The top row in the datasheet is usually where the **data labels** for the columns are entered. For example, in the sample datasheet that opens when you start Microsoft Graph, the top row contains the placeholder column labels *1ˢᵗ Qrtr, 2ⁿᵈ Qrtr, 3ʳᵈ Qrtr,* and *4ᵗʰ Qrtr.*

- The left column in the datasheet is usually where the data labels for the rows are entered. For example, in the sample datasheet that opens when you start Microsoft Graph, the left column contains the placeholder row labels *East, West,* and *North*.

- Microsoft Graph comes with a wide selection of chart types and subtypes, which you can use to plot your data, including the following:

  - *Column* Compares values across categories.

  - *Bar* Compares values across categories.

  - *Line* Displays trends over time or categories.

  - *Pie* Displays the contributions of each value to a total value. Often used to show percentages of a whole.

  - *XY (Scatter)* Compares pairs of values.

  - *Area* Displays trends in values over time or categories.

- You can plot more than one **data series** on a chart, depending on the selected chart type.

## Modify a Chart

- Charts are linked to data entered in the Microsoft Graph datasheet, so when you edit the datasheet, the chart changes, too.

- To open Microsoft Graph to edit a chart, double-click the chart object.

- You can change the chart type by selecting a different type in the Chart Type dialog box.

- You can resize and position a chart object the same way you do other objects in a Word document.

  ✓ *For more information on working with objects, see Lesson 13.*

- You can select to display and format different elements of a chart, including the **chart titles**, the **data axis** names, the **legend**, gridlines, and the data labels.

## Import Data into a Chart

- You can use the Windows Clipboard to copy existing data from a Word table, an Excel worksheet, or an Access table into a datasheet in Microsoft Graph.

- You can also use the Import File command to import files into an existing chart.

- Microsoft Graph can import the following types of files:
  - Text files **delimited** by commas, spaces, or tabs
  - Excel files
  - Lotus 1-2-3 files

- When you import a file into a datasheet, you must select options to specify the data you want to import and how you want it imported.

- For example, you use the Import Options dialog box to specify the cells you want to import from a spreadsheet file, and you use the Text Import Wizard to specify how to organize the delimited data into columns and rows.

- You also specify whether the imported data should be added to existing data in a chart, or if it can replace existing data.

## Create Diagrams and Organization Charts

- Word includes a selection of five **diagrams** and an **organization chart** that you can insert in a document as drawing objects.
  - *Organization Chart*  Used to illustrate hierarchical relationships.
  - *Cycle Diagram*  Used to show a process that has a continuous cycle.
  - *Target Diagram*  Used to show steps toward a goal.
  - *Radial Diagram*  Used to show relationships of elements to a core element.
  - *Venn Diagram*  Used to show areas of overlap between and among elements.
  - *Pyramid Diagram*  Used to show foundation-based relationships.

- Unlike graphs, diagrams are not based on numerical values. Instead, they use shapes and text to illustrate concepts.

*Select a diagram type in the Diagram Gallery*

- When you create a diagram, it is inserted on the drawing canvas. You can move, resize, and format the drawing canvas using the same commands you use for other drawing objects.

- The Diagram and Organization Chart toolbars offer options for editing and formatting the current diagram.

*The Diagram toolbar*

*The Organization Chart toolbar*

- Alternatively, you can format the individual shapes that comprise the diagram by using standard shape-formatting techniques. For instance, you can select a fill or line style.

  ✓ *For information on working with drawing objects, refer to Lesson 13.*

# Procedures

## Create a Chart

1. Position insertion point in document.
2. Click **I**nsert ................ `Alt`+`I`
3. Click **O**bject ...................... `O`
4. Click **C**reate New tab.. `Alt`+`C` if necessary.
5. In Object type list box, select **Microsoft Graph Chart**.
6. Click **OK** ......................... `Enter`

   ✓ *Chart is created with sample data entered in datasheet.*

### Enter data in datasheet:

1. Click in datasheet cell.
2. Type new data.
3. Press **Tab** to move to next cell ......................... `Tab`
4. Type new data.
5. Repeat steps 3 and 4 until data is entered.

## Create a Chart from Existing Word Table Data

1. Select table in Word.

   ✓ *For best results, enter data labels in the first column and first row of the table.*

2. Click **I**nsert ................ `Alt`+`I`
3. Click **O**bject ...................... `O`
4. Click **C**reate New tab if necessary ........... `Alt`+`C`
5. In Object type list box, select **Microsoft Graph Chart**.
6. Click **OK** ......................... `Enter`

   ✓ *Chart is created with table data entered in datasheet.*

## Import Worksheet Data into a Chart

1. Double-click chart object.
2. Click cell in datasheet where inserted data should start.
3. Click **Import File** button 🖱 on Microsoft Graph toolbar.

4. Click **Files of type** list box ........................ `Alt`+`T`
5. Select desired file type ............. `↑`, `↓`, `Enter`
6. Locate and select desired file.
7. Click **O**pen button

   | Open | ............ `Alt`+`O`

   ✓ *Import Data Options dialog box is displayed.*

8. Select to import **Entire sheet** ................ `Alt`+`E`

   OR

   Select to import a specified **R**ange ....... `Alt`+`A`, *type range*
9. To replace existing data, select **O**verwrite existing cells check box (default) ...... `Alt`+`O`

   ✓ *Deselect the check box to add imported data to datasheet.*

10. Click **OK** ......................... `Enter`

## Import Delimited Text Data into a Chart

1. Double-click chart object.
2. Click cell in datasheet where inserted data should start.
3. Click **Import File** button 🖱 on Microsoft Graph toolbar.
4. Click **Files of type** list box ........................ `Alt`+`T`
5. Click **Text Files** . `↑`, `↓`, `Enter`
6. Locate and select desired file.
7. Click **O**pen button

   | Open | ............ `Alt`+`O`

   ✓ *The Text Import Wizard opens.*

8. Select **D**elimited option ........................... `Alt`+`D`
9. Click **N**ext ....................... `Enter`
10. Select type of delimiter(s) used in file:

    • **Tab** .............................. `T`
    • **S**pace ........................... `S`
    • **Se**micolon ..................... `M`

    • **C**omma ....................... `C`
    • **O**ther ...... `O`, *type delimiter*

11. Click **N**ext ...................... `Enter`
12. Select **G**eneral data format option ....... `Alt`+`G`
13. Click **F**inish ..................... `Enter`

## Modify a Chart

### Open Microsoft Graph:

• Double-click chart object.

### Change chart type:

1. Click **Chart Type** button drop-down arrow 📊 ▾.

   ✓ *If the button doesn't display on the toolbar, click the Toolbar Options button to display additional buttons.*

2. Click desired chart type.

   OR

1. Click **C**hart ................. `Alt`+`C`
2. Click Chart **T**ype ................ `T`
3. Click **Standard Types** tab .................. `Ctrl`+`Tab`
4. Click **C**hart type list box ........................ `Alt`+`C`
5. Click desired chart type ............................ `↑`, `↓`
6. Click **Chart sub type** list box ................ `Alt`+`T`
7. Click desired chart sub-type ...................... `↑`, `↓`

   ✓ *To view a sample of the selected chart, move mouse pointer to Press and Hold to View Sample button, then press and hold left mouse button. Release mouse button when done.*

8. Click **OK** ......................... `Enter`

## Set Chart Options

### Chart title and axis labels:

1. Double-click chart object.
2. Click **C**hart ................. `Alt`+`C`
3. Click **Chart O**ptions ........... `O`

4. Click **Titles** tab............ `Ctrl`+`Tab`
5. Click **Chart title**
   text box ....................... `Alt`+`T`
6. Type desired title.
7. Click **Category (X) axis**
   text box ....................... `Alt`+`C`
8. Type desired horizontal axis
   label.
9. Click **Value (Z) axis**
   text box ....................... `Alt`+`V`
10. Type desired vertical axis label.
11. Click **OK**....................... `Enter`

**Show/hide gridlines:**

1. Double-click chart object.
2. Click **Chart**................... `Alt`+`C`
3. Click **Chart Options** ........... `O`
4. Click **Gridlines** tab ..... `Ctrl`+`Tab`
5. For Horizontal axis gridlines
   (vertical lines) select or
   deselect the following:
   - **Major gridlines** .............. `M`
   - **Minor gridlines** .............. `I`
6. For Vertical axis gridlines
   (horizontal lines) select or
   deselect the following:
   - **Major gridlines** .............. `O`
   - **Minor gridlines** .............. `G`
7. Click **OK**........................... `Enter`

**Show/hide legend:**

1. Double-click chart object.
2. Click **Chart**................... `Alt`+`C`
3. Click **Chart Options** ........... `O`
4. Click **Legend** tab ........ `Ctrl`+`Tab`
5. Select or deselect **Show
   legend** check box ................ `S`
6. Select from the following
   placement options:
   - **Bottom** .......................... `M`
   - **Corner** ........................... `O`
   - **Top** ................................ `T`
   - **Right** ............................. `R`
   - **Left** ............................... `L`
7. Click **OK**........................... `Enter`

**Show/hide data labels:**

1. Double-click chart object.
2. Click **Chart** ................. `Alt`+`C`
3. Click **Chart Options**........... `O`
4. Click **Data Labels**
   tab .............................. `Ctrl`+`Tab`
5. Select from the following
   display options:
   - ✓ *Only the options for the
     selected chart type will be
     available.*
   - **None** ............................. `O`
   - **Show value** ................... `V`
   - **Show percent**............... `P`
   - **Show label** ................... `L`
   - **Show label and
     percent** ........................ `A`
   - **Show bubble sizes** ....... `U`
6. Select or deselect **Legend key
   next to label** check box ...... `K`
7. Click **OK** ......................... `Enter`

**Format chart elements:**

1. Right-click element in chart.
2. Select **Format** *element name*
   from shortcut menu.
3. Select desired formatting
   options.
4. Click **OK** ......................... `Enter`

**Show/Hide Datasheet**

- Click **View Datasheet** button
  📋 on Microsoft Graph
  toolbar.

**Insert a Diagram or
Organization Chart**

1. Click **Insert Diagram or
   Organization Chart** button
   📊 on Drawing toolbar.
   **OR**
   a. Click **Insert**............. `Alt`+`I`
   b. Click **Diagram** ............... `G`
2. Click desired diagram type
   button ......................... `→`,`←`
3. Click **OK** ......................... `Enter`
   - ✓ *Word inserts the diagram on
     the drawing canvas.*

**Enter Text in Diagram or
Organization Chart**

1. Click on diagram where text
   *Click to add text* is displayed.
2. Type text.
   - ✓ *Use Word's standard text editing
     and formatting commands to
     modify and enhance text.*

**Format Diagram or
Organization Chart**

1. Select shape to format.
2. Apply formatting.
   **OR**
   Use toolbar buttons to edit and
   format diagram as desired:
   - ✓ *Note that the options on the
     toolbar change, depending on
     the type of diagram you are
     formatting. Following are some
     of the typical options available.*
   - Click **Insert Shape** button
     Insert Shape ............ `Alt`+`N`
     to add a shape.
   - Click **AutoFormat** button
     to select from a list of
     styles.
   - Click **Text Wrapping** button
     to select a text
     wrapping option.
   - Click **Move Shape
     Backward** button to
     move selected shape back
     one layer in diagram.
   - Click **Move Shape
     Forward** button to
     move selected shape
     forward one layer in
     diagram.
   - Click **Reverse Diagram**
     button to flip the diagram.
   - Click **Layout** button
     Layout ▾ ................. `Alt`+`L`
     to select a new diagram layout.
   - Click **Change to** button
     Change to ▾ ............ `Alt`+`C`
     to select a different diagram
     type.
   - ✓ *Format the drawing canvas
     using standard drawing object
     commands, including the
     options in the Format, Drawing
     Canvas dialog box.*

# Exercise Directions

## Create Chart 1

1. Start Word, if necessary.
2. Create the document shown in Illustration A, or open ☻**91CHARTS**.
3. Save the document as **CHARTS**.
4. Position the insertion point on the blank line at the end of the document.
5. Insert a Microsoft Graph object.
6. Replace the sample data in the datasheet with the following:

|  | No | Maybe | Yes | Don't Know |
|---|---|---|---|---|
| **Responses** | 10 | 38 | 49 | 3 |

7. Delete the sample data not replaced by new data in rows 2 and 3.
8. Hide the Datasheet.
9. Change the chart type to Pie with a 3-D visual effect.
10. Add the title **Likely to Purchase Home Delivery** to the chart.
11. Hide the chart legend.
12. Display category names and percentages.
13. Display the datasheet and change the number of responses for **Maybe** to **36** and the number for **Yes** to **51**. Notice the changes in the chart.
14. Click anywhere in the document outside the chart area.
15. Center the chart horizontally on the page.
    - ✓ Click the object to select it, and then click the Center button on Word's formatting toolbar.

## Create Chart 2

1. Insert a new blank line at the end of the document.
2. Insert another new Microsoft Graph chart object.
3. Start Excel and open the file ☻**91SURVEY.xls**.
4. Copy the data in cells A4:E8 to the Clipboard.
    - ✓ Click cell A6, press and hold Shift, then click cell E10. Click the Copy button on the Formatting toolbar.
5. Close Excel.

6. Switch back to the Word document and position the insertion point in the upper-left cell of the datasheet.
    - ✓ If necessary, double-click the chart to open Microsoft Graph.
7. Paste the data from the Clipboard into the datasheet.
8. Hide the datasheet.
9. Drag the sizing handles to increase the height and width of the chart object so you can see all of the data series.
    - ✓ Size the chart to about 4.5" wide by 3" high. Use the rulers to judge the size.
10. Click the By Column button on the Microsoft Graph toolbar to change the display of data from rows to columns.
11. Add the title **Product Preference by Area** to the chart.
12. Click anywhere outside the chart to close Microsoft Graph.
13. If necessary, center the chart horizontally on the page.
14. Preview the document. It should look similar to Illustration B.

## Create Chart 3

1. Move the insertion point to the end of the document and insert a page break.
2. On the new page, type the following using a 22-point serif font, centered:
   **Home Delivery Service Organization Chart**
3. Leave two blank lines and then insert an Organization Chart.
4. Fill in the default shapes as follows:
   - Top: **Director of Services**
   - Second row left: **Driver Manager**
   - Second row middle: **Inventory Manager**
   - Second row right: **Customer Service Manager**
5. Add two subordinate shapes as follows:
   a. Select the Driver Coordinator shape.
   b. Click the Insert Shape drop-down arrow on the Organization Chart toolbar.

c. Click Subordinate.

d. Add the text: **Two Drivers**.

e. Select the Customer Service Manager shape.

f. Click the Insert Shape drop-down arrow on the Organization Chart toolbar.

g. Click Subordinate.

h. Add the text: **Two Customer Service Representatives**.

6. Format the chart as follows:

a. Click the AutoFormat button on the Organization Chart toolbar.

b. Select the 3-D Color style.

c. Click Apply.

7. Insert page numbers centered on the bottom of both pages in the document.

8. Check the grammar and spelling in the document.

9. Preview the document. Page 2 should look similar to Illustration C.

10. Print both pages of the document.

11. Close the document, saving all changes.

*Illustration A*

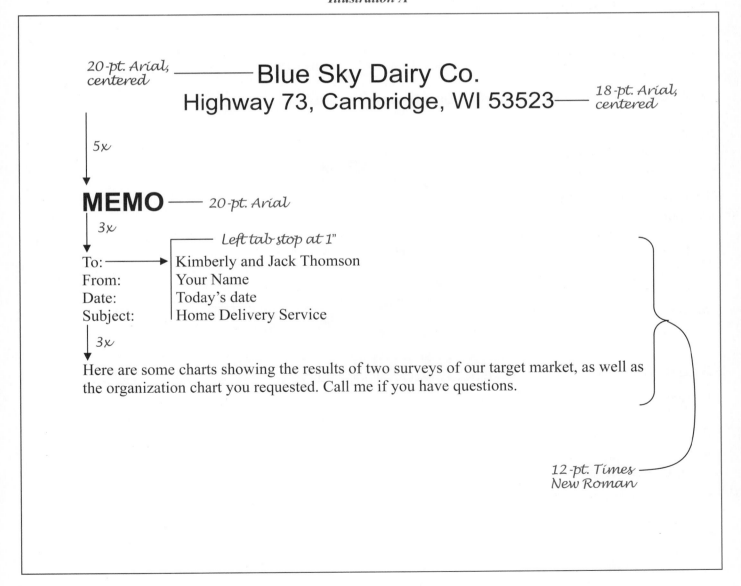

# Blue Sky Dairy Co.
## Highway 73, Cambridge, WI 53523

## MEMO

To:         Kimberly and Jack Thomson
From:       Your Name
Date:       Today's date
Subject:    Home Delivery Service

Here are some charts showing the results of two surveys of our target market, as well as the organization chart you requested. Call me if you have questions.

**Likely to Purchase Home Delivery**

**Product Preference by Area**

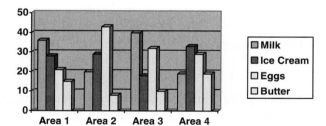

*Illustration C*

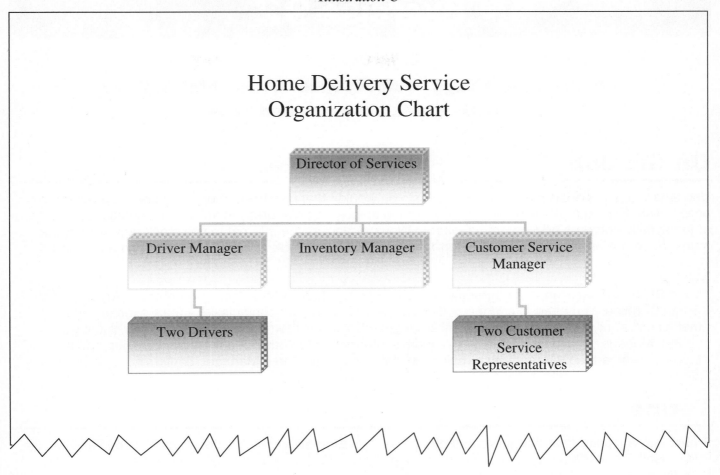

Home Delivery Service
Organization Chart

Director of Services

Driver Manager

Inventory Manager

Customer Service Manager

Two Drivers

Two Customer Service Representatives

# On Your Own

1. Start Word and create a new document.

2. Save the document as **OWD91**.

3. Type a letter, memo, or note to a friend or relative explaining that you are planning an event. The event might be a party, a graduation, a fundraiser, or anything you want. You can even use the same event you used in earlier On Your Own exercises.

4. Explain that you have surveyed people involved with planning or attending the event and that the results indicate when the event should be held. For example, some people might want the event in the morning, some in the afternoon, and some at night. Alternatively, explain that the survey indicates the type of event people want, such as a bowling party, a barbeque, or a dance.

5. Insert a chart in the memo to illustrate the results of your survey.

6. Enter the data in the datasheet; add a title and any necessary labels.

7. Select the chart type that best illustrates your data. For example, use a pie chart to show percentages of a whole, or a line chart to show values over time.

8. Save the document.

9. Preview it. If necessary, change the formatting of the chart.

10. Print the document.

11. Ask a classmate to review the document and make comments or suggestions.

12. Incorporate the comments and suggestions into the document.

13. Close the document, saving all changes, and exit Word.

# Exercise 92

## Skills Covered:
### ◆ Use Smart Tags  ◆ About XML  ◆ Use XML in Word
### ◆ Use XML Schemas and Tags

## On the Job

Use smart tags to perform actions in Word that you would otherwise have to open a different program to accomplish. For example, you can use a smart tag to look up an address in an Outlook contact list and then automatically enter the address into a letter in Word, or access the Internet to find stock quotes or street maps. Save a Word document in XML format to make data available to other programs and applications.

Long Shot, Inc. has signed an agreement to sponsor a golf tournament at a golf course in Myrtle Beach, South Carolina. You need to add the golf course Manager to your contacts list. In this exercise, you will make sure all of your smart tags options are enabled. You will then open an existing letter to the golf course Manager, and use a smart tag to add his information to your Outlook Contacts folder. You will then use a smart tag to create an e-mail message to the golf course Manager, confirming a meeting.

## Terms

**Smart tag**  A type of data that Word and other Microsoft Office 2003 programs recognizes and labels as available for use with other programs.

**Recognizer**  A type of data that Word identifies as a smart tag.

**XML (Extensible Markup Language)**  A file format based on the Standard Generalized Markup Language (SGML).

**XML schema**  A specification that defines the structure of an XML document.

**XML tags**  Codes that store information, such as properties and formatting.

**Elements**  The type of data allowed in an XML file, such as name or phone number.

**XSL Transformation (XSLT)**  A file used to transform—or display—an XML file in a particular format.

**Data View**  The way an XML file is displayed in Word.

**Namespace**  A unique identifier for elements defined by a schema.

**Alias**  A friendly, or plain English, name for a schema.

## Notes

### Use Smart Tags

- **Smart tags** are a feature of Microsoft Office 2003 that you can use to automatically integrate data entered in one program with another program.

✓ *You have already used one type of smart tag—the Paste Options button lets you select from a list of possible formatting options. Refer to Exercise 17 for more information about the Paste Options button.*

- For example, you can use smart tags to integrate Outlook contact information with your Word documents:

    - If you type a person's name into a Word document, you can use a smart tag to add the person to your Outlook contact list, or to insert the person's address from your contact list into the letter.

- Word comes set to recognize and label the following types of smart tags:

    ✓ *You can download additional smart tags from Microsoft and other vendors.*

    - Addresses

    - Financial symbols

    - Dates

    - Names

    - Places

    - Telephone numbers

    - Times

- You can select which of the **recognizers** you want Word to mark as smart tags in your documents.

- Word marks smart tags in a document using a purple dotted underline.

- When you rest the mouse pointer over the smart tag, the Smart Tag Actions button is displayed.

*Smart tag on a name*

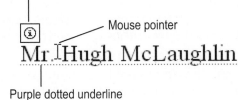

Smart Tag Actions button

Mouse pointer

Mr. Hugh McLaughlin

Purple dotted underline

- Move the mouse pointer over the button to display a drop-down arrow. Click the arrow to display a menu of available actions.

*Smart Tag Actions menu*

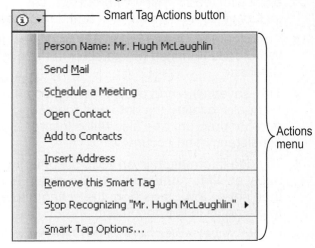

Smart Tag Actions button

Person Name: Mr. Hugh McLaughlin

Send Mail

Schedule a Meeting

Open Contact

Add to Contacts

Insert Address

Remove this Smart Tag

Stop Recognizing "Mr. Hugh McLaughlin" ▶

Smart Tag Options...

Actions menu

- The types of actions available on the menu depend on the type of recognizer.

- Smart tags are active by default, but you can turn them off.

- You can also select to hide the purple underline and still use the smart tag feature.

    ✓ *You can hide the Smart Tags Actions buttons as well.*

- You can save smart tags with your documents if you want to retain a link between the data in your Word document and the source data.

- If you don't need the link, you don't need to save the smart tag—the data remains saved in the document.

- If you don't need all of the smart tags in a document, you can select the specific smart tags you want to retain and the ones you want to discard.

- Saving smart tags with your document increases document size.

- If you want to use smart tags on Web pages created with Word, you must set Word to save the smart tags in XML format.

- You can also set Word to display smart tags in e-mail messages created with Outlook. That way, the message recipients can use the smart tags.

## About XML

- **XML (Extensible Markup Languag** format that lets you code informa of document so that the infor extracted and used in other

- XML formatted data can be updated, searched, and collected by many different sources, including automated servers and databases.

- For example, names coded in XML format in a Word document can be extracted for use in a database.

- This saves time and effort that might be spent manually locating the data and reentering it into another program and also helps insure consistency and accuracy.

- To code information in an XML document you apply an **XML schema** file to the document, and then select **XML tags** from the schema to apply to elements in the document.

  ✓ *XML schema files have an .XSD file extension.*

- The schema determines the **elements** allowed in the document and defines the structure of the data.

- Use the XML Structure task pane to view the elements available in the attached schema.

  ✓ *If the elements names are very long and complicated the namespace alias is probably displayed. Select Hide namespace alias in XML Structure task pane check box in the XML Options dialog box.*

*View XML elements in a Word document in the XML Structure task pane*

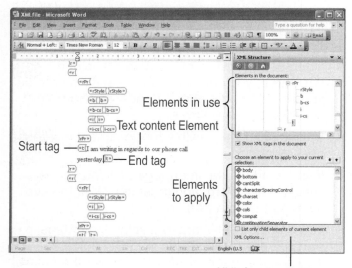

XML Structure task pane

## Use XML in Word

❧ There are two ways to apply XML in Word:
  - Save a Word document in XML format. Saving as XML applies Word's own XML

schema, WordML, to the document. Word automatically applies XML tags that store information, such as file properties; define the structure of the document, such as its paragraphs, headings, and tables; and store formatting and layout information.

  - Use the XML Schemas tab of the Templates and Add-ins dialog box to attach custom schemas that you obtain from outside sources. You then apply XML tags from that schema to the document content.

- You may also apply an **XSL Transformation (XSLT)** file to define the way the document is displayed—or **data view**.

- You can format documents with the WordML schema in any version of Microsoft Office Word 2003; however, other XML features are only available in Microsoft Office Professional 2003 or the standalone version of Microsoft Office Word 2003.

## Use XML Schemas and Tags

- Available schemas are stored in the Schema Library.

- You can add new schemas to the library at any time, and you can delete schemas you no longer need.

- When you add a schema you create a **namespace** and define options such as an **alias** for the schema as well as the XSLT files that are associated with the schema.

  ✓ *The namespace provides a unique identifier for all of the elements defined by the schema, so that if elements in different schema have the same name they do not conflict.*

- When you attach an XML schema to a document, the document becomes associated with the same namespace as the schema and with any auxiliary files that are also associated with the same namespace.

- You can modify schema settings and options at any time.

- XML tags include both a start tag and an end tag. They are inserted and removed as pairs.

- To insert a tag, you select the element in the document, then select the tag to insert in the XML Structure task pane.

- You can remove an XML tag without removing the content from the document.

# Procedures

## Turn Smart Tags Off or On

1. Click **Tools** .................. `Alt`+`T`
2. Click **AutoCorrect**
   **Options** ....................... `A`
3. Click the
   **Smart Tags** tab.......... `Ctrl`+`Tab`
4. Click the **Label text with**
   **smart tags** check box.......... `L`

   ✓ *If the check box is already*
   *selected, clicking it turns the*
   *feature off.*

5. Click **OK**.......................... `Enter`

## Select Smart Tag Recognizer(s)

1. Click **Tools** .................. `Alt`+`T`
2. Click **AutoCorrect**
   **Options** .......................... `A`
3. Click the
   **Smart Tags** tab.......... `Ctrl`+`Tab`
4. Click check box next to desired
   recognizer type.

   ✓ *If a check mark is already*
   *entered in the check box, Word*
   *is set to recognize that Smart*
   *Tag type.*

5. Click **OK**.......................... `Enter`

## Show/Hide Smart Tags Underlines

1. Click **Tools** .................. `Alt`+`T`
2. Click **Options** ...................... `O`
3. Click the **View** tab...... `Ctrl`+`Tab`
4. Click the **Smart tags**
   check box............................ `A`

   ✓ *If the check box is already*
   *selected, clicking it will hide the*
   *underlines.*

5. Click **OK**.......................... `Enter`

## Use a Smart Tag

1. Rest mouse pointer over smart
   tag in document.

   ✓ *Word displays the Smart Tag*
   *Actions button.*

2. Click the **Smart Tag Actions**
   button ⓘ▾ .
3. Click desired action.

## Show/Hide Smart Tags Action Button

1. Click **Tools** .................. `Alt`+`T`
2. Click **AutoCorrect**
   **Options** ......................... `A`
3. Click the
   **Smart Tags** tab .......... `Ctrl`+`Tab`
4. Click the **Show Smart**
   **Tag Actions buttons** check
   box................................... `B`

   ✓ *If the check box is already*
   *selected, clicking it will hide the*
   *Actions button.*

5. Click **OK** .......................... `Enter`

## Save Smart Tags with Document

1. Click **Tools** .................. `Alt`+`T`
2. Click **Options** ...................... `O`
3. Click the **Save** tab ...... `Ctrl`+`Tab`
4. Click the **Embed smart tags**
   check box ............................ `G`

   ✓ *If the check box is already*
   *selected, the option is enabled.*

5. Click **OK** .......................... `Enter`

## Save Smart Tags as XML in Web Pages

1. Click **Tools** .................. `Alt`+`T`
2. Click **Options** ...................... `O`
3. Click the **Save** tab ...... `Ctrl`+`Tab`
4. Click the **Save smart tags as**
   **XML properties in Web**
   **pages** check box. ................ `V`

   ✓ *If the check box is already*
   *selected, clicking it sets Word*
   *not to save the tags.*

5. Click **OK** .......................... `Enter`

## Turn Smart Tags On or Off for E-mail Messages

1. Click **Tools** .................. `Alt`+`T`
2. Click **Options** ...................... `O`
3. Click the **General** tab... `Ctrl`+`Tab`

4. Click the **E-mail Options**
   button ............................... `A`
5. Click the **General** tab .. `Alt`+`G`
6. Click the **Save smart tags**
   **in e-mail** check box .... `Alt`+`S`

   ✓ *If the check box is already*
   *selected, the option is enabled.*

7. Click **OK**.......................... `Enter`
8. Click **OK**.......................... `Enter`

## Remove a Smart Tag from a Document

1. Rest mouse pointer over smart
   tag in document.

   ✓ *Word displays the Smart Tag*
   *Actions button.*

2. Click the **Smart Tag Actions**
   button ⓘ▾ .
3. Click **Remove this Smart Tag**.

## Remove all Smart Tags

1. Click **Tools**................... `Alt`+`T`
2. Click **AutoCorrect**
   **Options** ............................ `A`
3. Click the **Smart Tags**
   tab ................................ `Ctrl`+`Tab`
4. Click **Remove Smart Tags**
   button [ Remove Smart Tags ]
5. Click **OK**.......................... `Enter`

## Create a New XML Document in Word

1. Click **File** .................... `Alt`+`F`
2. Click **New**........................... `N`
3. Click **XML document** in New
   Document task pane.

## Save a Document as XML

1. Click **File** .................... `Alt`+`F`
2. Click **Save As** ..................... `S`
3. Click **Save as type** drop-down
   arrow ........................... `Alt`+`T`
4. Click **XML Document** .. `↓`, `↑`
5. Change file name and select
   storage location as necessary.

6. To save XML data without Word formatting, select **Save data only** check box ... `Alt`+`D`

7. To apply a transform, do the following:

  a. Click **Apply transform** check box ............. `Alt`+`A`

  b. Click **Transform** button

  `Transform...` ........ `Alt`+`M`

  c. Locate and select desired XLST file.

  d. Click **Open** button

  `Open` ............. `Enter`

  ✓ *If you apply a transform while saving, Word saves only data that the XSLT file uses.*

8. Click **Save** button

  `Save` ................. `Enter`

## Attach a Schema to a Document

1. Open or create XML document.
2. Display XML Structure task pane.
3. Click **Templates and Add-Ins** link in XML Structure task pane.
4. If necessary, click **XML Schema** tab ............... `Ctrl`+`Tab`
5. Click check box for each XML schema to attach.

  ✓ *A check in the check box indicates schema is selected; a blank check box indicates schema is not selected.*

6. Click **OK** .......................... `Enter`

## Remove a Schema from a Document

1. Open XML document.
2. Display XML Structure task pane.
3. Click **Templates and Add-Ins** link in XML Structure task pane.
4. If necessary, click **XML Schemas** tab .............. `Ctrl`+`Tab`
5. Click check box for each XML schema to remove.

✓ *A check in the checkbox indicates schema is selected; a blank check box indicates schema is not selected.*

6. Click **OK** ......................... `Enter`

## Add an XML Schema to the Schema Library

1. Click **Tools** .................. `Alt`+`T`
2. Click **Templates and Add-Ins** ............................. `I`
3. Click **XML Schemas** tab.............................. `Ctrl`+`Tab`
4. Click **Add Schema** button

  `Add Schema...` ........ `Alt`+`C`

5. In Add Schema dialog box, locate and select desired schema file.
6. Click **Open** button

  `Open` ................. `Enter`

7. In Schema Settings dialog box, type desired Alias.
8. Click **OK** ......................... `Enter`

## Remove a Schema from the Schema Library

1. Click **Tools** .................. `Alt`+`T`
2. Click **Templates and Add-Ins** ............................. `I`
3. Click **XML Schema** tab.............................. `Ctrl`+`Tab`
4. Click **Schema Library** button

  `Schema Library...` ......... `Alt`+`L`

5. In list of schemas, click schema to remove ........ `↑`, `↓`
6. Click **Delete Schema** button

  `Delete Schema` ....... `Alt`+`D`

7. Click **Yes** ......................... `Enter`
8. Click **OK** ......................... `Enter`
9. Click **OK** ......................... `Enter`

## Change Schema Settings

1. Click **Tools** .................. `Alt`+`T`
2. Click **Templates and Add-Ins** ............................. `I`
3. Click **XML Schemas** tab.............................. `Ctrl`+`Tab`

4. Click **Schema Library** button

  `Schema Library...` ........ `Alt`+`L`

5. In list of schemas, click schema to change........ `↑`, `↓`
6. Click **Schema Settings** button

  `Schema Settings...` ...... `Alt`+`E`

7. Change settings as desired.
8. Click **OK** ......................... `Enter`
9. Click **OK** ......................... `Enter`
10. Click **OK** ......................... `Enter`

## Set XML Options

1. Click **Tools** .................. `Alt`+`T`
2. Click **Templates and Add-Ins**............................. `I`
3. Click **XML Schemas** tab .............................. `Ctrl`+`Tab`
4. Click **XML Options** button

  `XML Options...` ....... `Alt`+`P`

5. Select or deselect desired options:

  • **Save data only** ...... `Alt`+`D`

  • **Apply custom transform** .............. `Alt`+`T`

  ✓ *If you select to apply a custom transform, click the **Browse** button*

  `Browse...`,

  *locate and select the XLST file, then click OK.*

  • **Validate document against attached schemas**................ `Alt`+`V`

  • **Hide schema violations in this document** ...... `Alt`+`H`

  • **Ignore mixed content**................. `Alt`+`I`

  • **Allow saving as XML even if not valid** ............. `Alt`+`N`

  • **Hide namespace alias in XML Structure task pane**...................... `Alt`+`L`

  • **Show advanced XML error messages** .... `Alt`+`A`

  • **Show placeholder text for all empty elements** ............... `Alt`+`P`

6. Click **OK**............................. `Enter`

7. Click **OK**............................. `Enter`

## Apply XML Tags

1. Attach a schema to the document.

2. Open XML Structure task pane.

3. In document, select content to tag

4. In task pane, in Choose an element to apply to your current selection box, click desired element

   ✓ *Click the Shrink* ⬇ *or Grow* ⬆ *arrow to change the size of the Choose an element to apply box.*

5. If necessary, specify an attribute for the element as follows:

   a. In the Elements in the document box, right-click the element.

   b. Click **Attributes**.............. `A`

   c. Click desired attribute in the Available attributes list ............................ `↑`, `↓`

   d. Click **Value** box ...... `Alt`+`V`

   e. Type attribute value.

   f. Click **Add** button

   | Add | ............. `Enter` |

## Remove XML tags

1. Open document.

2. Open XML Structure task pane.

3. In task pane, select **Show XML tags in the document** check box .................... `Ctrl`+`Shift`+`X`

4. In document, right-click the Start of *Tag Name* tag to remove.

5. Click **Remove** *Tag Name* **tag** ....................................... `R`

## Show/Hide XML Tags in Word

1. Open document.

2. Open XML Structure task pane.

3. In XML task pane, select **Show XML tags in the document** check box .......... `Ctrl`+`Shift`+`X`

## Set Word to Print XML Tags with Documents

1. Click **Tools** ................. `Alt`+`T`

2. Click **Options** .................... `O`

3. Click **Print** tab ........... `Ctrl`+`Tab`

4. Click **XML tags** check box .................... `Alt`+`X`

5. Click **OK** ......................... `Enter`

## Specify a Solution

1. Click **Tools** ................. `Alt`+`T`

2. Click **Templates and Add-Ins** ............................. `I`

3. Click **XML Schemas** tab ............................ `Ctrl`+`Tab`

4. Click **Schema Library** button

   | Schema Library... | ........ `Alt`+`L` |

5. Select schema to modify ......................... `↑`, `↓`

6. Click the **Use solution with** drop-down arrow ........ `Alt`+`T`

7. Click Word .................. `↑`, `↓`

8. Click **Add Solution** button

   | Add Solution... | ...... `Alt`+`N` |

9. Locate and select desired XSLT file.

10. Click **Open** button

    | Open | ............... `Enter` |

11. In Solution Settings dialog box, type desired Alias.

12. Click **OK** ........................... `Enter`

13. Click **OK** ........................... `Enter`

14. Click **OK** ........................... `Enter`

# Exercise Directions

1. Start Word, if necessary.

2. Open the document 🖅**CONFIRM** that you used in Exercise 12, or open 💿**92CONFIRM**.

3. Save the document as **TAGS**.

4. Open the AutoCorrect dialog box and display the Smart Tags tab.

5. Make sure that smart tags are enabled and that all possible recognizers are selected.

6. Check the View tab of the Tools, Options dialog box to be sure that Word is set to display smart tags.

7. Move the mouse pointer over the smart tag under the recipient's street address in the **TAGS** document.

8. Click the Smart Tags Actions button and select Add to Contacts.

9. Word displays a Contact card from your Outlook Contacts folder. Note that the address is already filled in.

10. Fill in additional information for Hugh McLaughlin by typing the data into the fields.

    ✓ *You can use the Copy and Paste commands to copy data from the Word document into the fields in the Contact card.*

    ✓ *You do not have to fill in every field on the card.*

11. Include the following information:
    Full Name: **Mr. Hugh McLaughlin**
    Job Title: **Manager**
    Company: **Hideaway Golf Club and Resort**

Business Address: **2242 Ocean Boulevard**
**Myrtle Beach, SC 29577**
Business phone: **(843) 555-5432**
Business fax: **(843) 555-5434**
E-mail address: **Hugh@hideaway.net**

12. When you are done, it should look similar to Illustration A.

13. Close the Contact card, saving the changes.

14. In the **TAGS** document, move the mouse pointer over the smart tag under the recipient's name.

15. Click the Smart Tags Actions button and select Send Mail.

16. A new blank e-mail message with Hugh McLaughlin's name entered in the To: box is created.

17. Right-click the name in the To: box and select **Hugh McLaughlin (hugh@hideaway.net)**.

18. Enter the subject **Appointment Confirmation**.

19. Type the following message, in 12-point Arial:
**Mr. McLaughlin – Just a quick note to confirm our meeting for Monday. We will have a car and driver waiting for you at the airport. Thanks.**

20. Remove the smart tag from the recipient's name in the body of the message.

   ✓ *Click the Smart Tags Actions button, and then click Remove this Smart Tag.*

21. Check the grammar and spelling in the message. It should look similar to Illustration B.

22. Print the message.

   ✓ *The e-mail address is fictitious. If you try to send it you will receive a message saying it is undeliverable.*

23. Save the **TAGS** file in XML format with the name **TAGSXML**. Save the data and the tags and do not apply a transform.

24. Close all open documents, saving all changes.

*Illustration A*

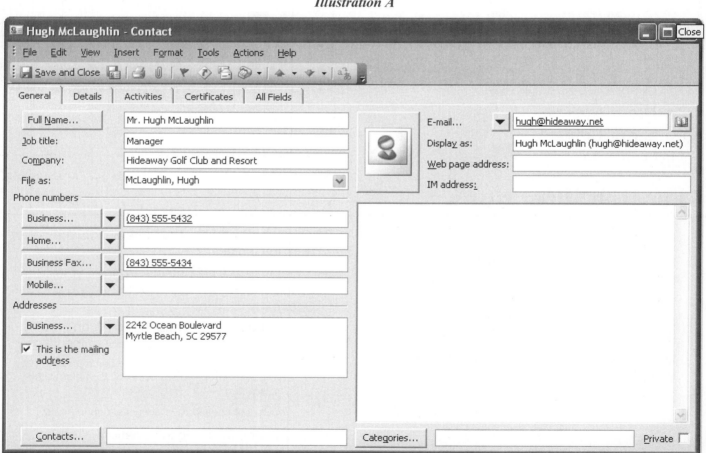

*Illustration B*

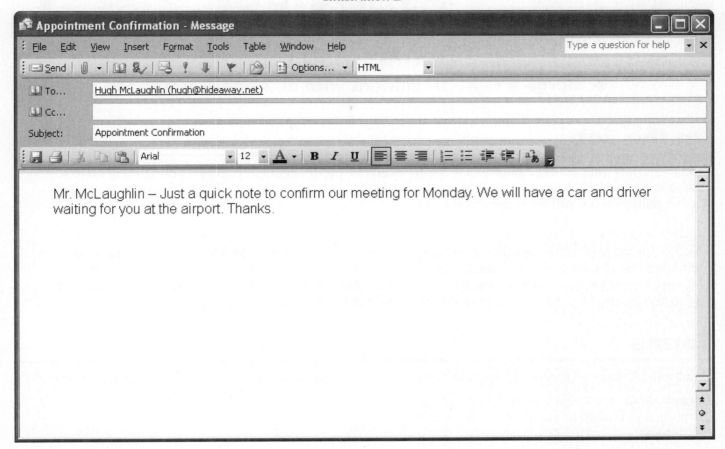

## On Your Own

1. Make sure you have at least one person entered in your Outlook Contact list.

   ✓ *If necessary, consult your instructor for more information on using the Outlook Contact list.*

2. Start Word and create a new document.

3. Save the document as **OWD92**

4. Type a letter to someone whose name is entered in your Outlook Contact list.

5. Use smart tags to insert the address.

6. When the letter is complete, check the spelling and grammar.

7. Preview the letter and print it.

8. Use a smart tag to create an e-mail message to the recipient.

9. Attach the letter to the e-mail message and send it via e-mail.

10. Close all open documents and exit all programs.

# Exercise 93

## Skills Covered:

◆ **Merge a Word Document with an Access Database**

## On the Job

Creating a new data source document in Word for a mail merge is unnecessary if you already have a database stored in a database application, such as Microsoft Office Access. You can easily merge the Access data with a Word main document.

As the Manager of in-house training at Long Shot, Inc., you want to send a letter to everyone who attended the Word 1 class last session to invite them to take the Word 2 class next session. The information for each student is already entered in an Access database. In this exercise, you will create a memo document in Word, and then merge it with data in the Access database.

## Terms

**Database** A file used to store records of data.

**Access table** An object organized in rows and columns and used to store data in an Access database.

**Access query** An object containing a subset of records in an Access database.

## Notes

### Merge a Word Document with an Access Database

- If you have an existing Access **database** file, you can use it as a data source for a Mail Merge in Word.

    ✓ *For information on using Mail Merge, refer to the exercises in Lesson 8.*

- To conduct the merge, you simply select the Access file as the data source in Step 3 of the Mail Merge task pane.

- If there is more than one **table** or **query** in the database file, Mail Merge prompts you to select the one you want to use.

- Complete the remaining steps in the Mail Merge task pane to complete the merge.

    ✓ *You can also start a merge from Access using the Tools, Office Links, Merge It with Microsoft Office Word command. Office starts Mail Merge and prompts you through the necessary steps.*

- You can sort and filter records in the Access data source file using the same methods you use when you create the data source using Word.

- You cannot edit the records using Word. To make changes, open the database file in Access.

    *Select the table or query to use as the data source*

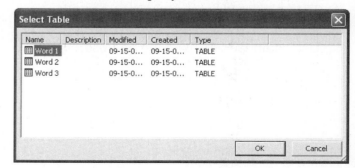

# 496

# Procedures

### Use an Access Database as a Data Source File for a Mail Merge

1. Open a new blank document.
2. Click **Tools** .................. Alt + T
3. Select **Letters and Mailings** .................... E
4. Click **Mail Merge** ................ M
5. Click the desired document type.
   - ✓ *For information specific to creating form letters, refer to Exercise 45. For information specific to creating envelopes, refer to Exercise 46. For information specific to creating labels, refer to Exercise 47. For information specific to creating a directory, refer to Exercise 48. For information specific to creating e-mail, refer to Exercise 69.*
6. Click **Next: Starting document**.
7. Select document to use.

8. If necessary, select options specific to the document type.
   - ✓ *For example, select envelope or label options.*
9. Click **Next: Select recipients**.
10. Click the **Use an existing list** option button.
11. Click **Browse** button .
    - ✓ *Word opens the Select Data Source dialog box.*
12. Locate and select the desired Access database file.
13. Click **Open** button 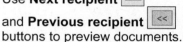.
    - ✓ *Word displays the Select Table dialog box.*
14. Click desired table or query.
15. Click **OK** .......................... Enter
    - ✓ *Word displays the Mail Merge Recipients dialog box. By default, all recipients are selected. For information on sorting, filtering, and selecting specific recipients, refer to Exercise 48.*

16. Click **OK** .......................... Enter
17. Click **Next: Write your letter**.
    - ✓ *Word displays the starting document and a list of available merge blocks.*
18. Type and format text as you want it to appear on each merge document.
19. Insert merge blocks and merge fields as necessary.
20. Save the document.
21. Click **Next: Preview your document type**.
    - ✓ *Word displays the first merge document.*
22. Use **Next recipient** >> and **Previous recipient** << buttons to preview documents.
23. Click **Next: Complete the merge**.
24. Print, edit, or save documents as desired.

# Exercise Directions

1. Make a copy of the Access database file ⊚**93STUDENTS.mdb**, and name the copy **STUDENTS**.
   - ✓ *To copy an Access database, right-click the file in the Window's Explorer window, and select Copy. Then go to where you wish to copy the file. Right-click on the destination folder, and select Paste. Right-click on the copied file and select Rename to rename the file.*
2. Start Word, and create a new blank document.
3. Save the document as **WORD1MEMO**.
4. Start Mail Merge.
5. Select to create form letters, using the current document.
6. Locate and select **STUDENTS** as the data source file.
7. Select to use the Word 1 query as the data source table.

8. Use all records in the query.
9. Create the document shown in Illustration A.
   a. Type and format the document text.
   b. Insert the merge fields.
10. Check the spelling and grammar in the document.
11. Preview the merge documents.
12. Complete the merge by merging all records to a new document.
13. Save the document as **WORD1MERGE**.
14. Print the merge documents.
15. Close all open files, saving all changes.

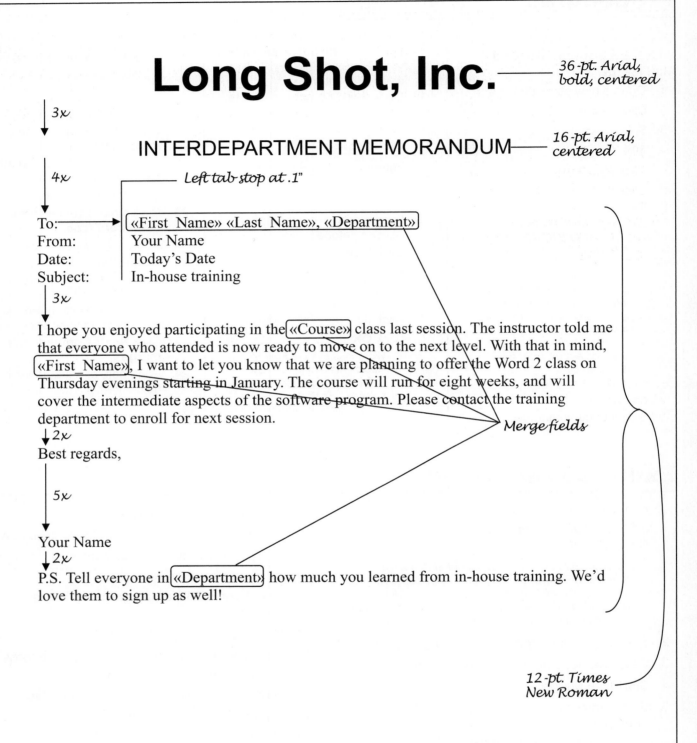

# Long Shot, Inc.

*36-pt. Arial, bold, centered*

↓ 3x

## INTERDEPARTMENT MEMORANDUM

*16-pt. Arial, centered*

↓ 4x

*Left tab stop at .1"*

To: → «First_Name» «Last_Name», «Department»
From: Your Name
Date: Today's Date
Subject: In-house training

↓ 3x

I hope you enjoyed participating in the «Course» class last session. The instructor told me that everyone who attended is now ready to move on to the next level. With that in mind, «First_Name», I want to let you know that we are planning to offer the Word 2 class on Thursday evenings starting in January. The course will run for eight weeks, and will cover the intermediate aspects of the software program. Please contact the training department to enroll for next session.

↓ 2x

Best regards,

↓ 5x

Your Name

↓ 2x

P.S. Tell everyone in «Department» how much you learned from in-house training. We'd love them to sign up as well!

*Merge fields*

*12-pt. Times New Roman*

# On Your Own

1. Create a form letter main document that you can send to relatives and friends thanking them for gifts you received recently for a birthday, holiday, or graduation. You can use graphics objects and formatting to make the document interesting to look at.

2. Save the document as **OWD93-1**.

3. Create an Access database file named **OWD93-2** that includes a table listing the names and addresses of the people you want to receive the letter. Include at least five records. Alternatively, make a copy of ⊙ **93GIFTLIST.mdb** and rename the copy **OWD93-2**.

4. Use the table in the **OWD93-2** database file as the data source for the **OWD93-1** form letter.

5. Merge the letters to a new document named **OWD93-3**.

6. Save and close all open files, and exit all open applications.

# Exercise 94

## Skills Covered:

◆ **Embed a PowerPoint Slide in a Word Document**

◆ **Export PowerPoint Slides and Notes to a Word Document**

◆ **Export PowerPoint Text to a Word Document**

## On the Job

Share information between two applications to save yourself work and to provide consistency between documents. If you have a PowerPoint presentation, for example, you can use the information in a Word document. You can embed PowerPoint slides in a Word Document as graphics objects, and you can export text and graphics from a PowerPoint presentation into a Word document.

You have been asked to present information about the Blue Sky Dairy home delivery service at a company meeting. You already have a PowerPoint presentation about the study. You can use pieces of the presentation to create documents to distribute as a package at the meeting. In this exercise, you will create a cover for the package using a slide from the PowerPoint presentation. You will then export the entire presentation to a Word document to use as a handout, leaving blank lines for writing notes. Finally, you will export the text from the presentation as an outline to use as a table of contents for the handout package.

## Terms

**Export** To send text or data from one application to another application. The original data remains intact.

## Notes

### Embed a PowerPoint Slide in a Word Document

- You can embed a slide in a Word document.
- The slide appears in Word in full color with graphics and text.
- Embedding a slide is similar to embedding an Excel object in a Word document.
  - ✓ *See Exercise 90 for information on embedding an Excel object in a Word document.*

### Export PowerPoint Slides and Notes to a Word Document

- You can **export** PowerPoint slides and notes to a Word document.
- When you export slides, miniatures of your slides are inserted in a table in the Word document.
- You can print slide notes with the slides, or leave blank lines for entering handwritten notes or comments.
- You can link the slides in the Word document to the source document so when you change the source document the linked document in Word updates automatically.

### Export PowerPoint Text to a Word Document

- You can export PowerPoint text to a Word document.

- Text will be saved in rich text format (.rtf).

- The text will be formatted using Outline heading levels.

- When you open the RTF file in Word, you can save it as a Word file.

# Procedures

### Embed a PowerPoint Slide in Word

1. Open presentation in PowerPoint.
2. Click **Slide Sorter View** button ⊞.
3. Select slide to copy.
4. Click **Copy** button ▤ .................... `Ctrl`+`C`
5. Switch to Word document and position insertion point.
6. Click **Paste** button ▤ .................... `Ctrl`+`V`

### Export PowerPoint Slides and Notes to Word

1. Open presentation in PowerPoint.
2. Click **File** .................... `Alt`+`F`
3. Click **Send To** .................... `D`
4. Click **Microsoft Office Word** .................... `W`
5. Select option for page layout in Word.
6. Select one of the following:
   - **Paste** .................... `Alt`+`P`
   - **Paste link** .................... `Alt`+`l`
7. Click **OK** .................... `Enter`

### Export PowerPoint Text to Word

1. Open presentation in PowerPoint.
2. Click **File** .................... `Alt`+`F`
3. Click **Save As** .................... `A`
4. Click **Save as type** ..... `Alt`+`T`
5. Select **Outline/RTF (\*.rtf)** ... `↓`
6. Click **Save** button
   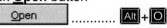 .......... `Alt`+`S`

### Open RTF File in Word

1. Click **File** .................... `Alt`+`F`
2. Click **Open** .................... `O`
3. Select **All Files** from **Files of type** drop-down list ............. `↑`
4. Select file in list.
5. Click **Open** button
   Open .......... `Alt`+`O`

# Exercise Directions

✓ *The steps in this exercise assume you know how to use a PowerPoint presentation file. If you do not, ask your instructor for more information.*

1. Start Word, if necessary.
2. Open 💿 **94COVER**.
3. Save the document as **COVER**.
4. Replace the sample text **Today's Date** with the current date.
5. Replace the sample text **Your Name** with your own name.
6. Start PowerPoint.
7. Open 💿 **94BSDPRES.ppt**.
8. Save it as **BSDPRES**.
9. Change to Slide Sorter view.
   - Click the Slide Sorter View button 🔲 or click View, Slide Sorter.
10. Copy slide 1 to the Clipboard.
    - Click slide 1 to select it, and then click the Copy button 📋 on the PowerPoint Standard toolbar.
11. Switch to the **COVER** document in Word.
12. Paste the slide from the Clipboard onto the last line in the document.
13. Center the picture object horizontally on the page.
    - Click the object to select it, then click the Center button on Word's Formatting toolbar.
14. Check the spelling and grammar in the document.

15. Preview the document. It should look similar to Illustration A.
16. Close the document, saving all changes.
17. Switch back to the **BSDPRES** PowerPoint presentation, and export the slides to a new Word document.
    - Click File, Send To, Microsoft Office Word.
    - Select the Blank lines next to slides option and the Paste option, and then click OK.
    - ✓ *It may take a minute or two for Word to set up the tables and insert the slides with lines.*
18. Save the document as **HANDOUT**.
19. Preview the document. The first page should look similar to Illustration B.
20. Close the document, saving all changes.
21. Switch back to the **BSDPRES** PowerPoint presentation.
22. Save the file in Outline/RTF format with the name **PRESOUT**.
23. Close the **BSDPRES** presentation file and exit PowerPoint. Do not save any changes.
24. Switch to Word and open the **PRESOUT.rtf** file.
25. Change to Outline view.
26. Preview the document. It should look similar to the one in Illustration C.
27. Close the document, saving all changes.

# On Your Own

1. Create a PowerPoint presentation about yourself or about a club or organization to which you belong, or open the presentation 💿 **94MYLIFE.ppt**.
2. Save the presentation with the name **OWD94-1**.
3. Create a report in Word by exporting the entire presentation to a new Word document. Include notes if there are any, or leave blank lines for hand writing notes.
4. Save the document with the name **OWD94-2**.
5. Insert a page break at the beginning of the document to create a new first page.
6. Enter and format text for a report title on the new first page.

7. Embed a slide from the presentation to illustrate the report cover.
8. Check the spelling and grammar in the document.
9. Print the document.
10. Ask a classmate to review the document and offer comments and suggestions.
11. Incorporate the suggestions and comment into the document.
12. Close all open documents, saving all changes.
13. Present the report along with the slide show to your class.

*Illustration A*

*Illustration B (Page 1 of 2)*

Slide 1

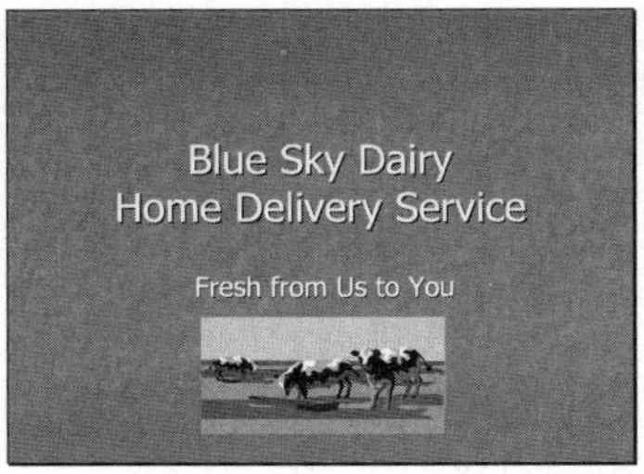
Blue Sky Dairy
Home Delivery Service
Fresh from Us to You

Slide 2

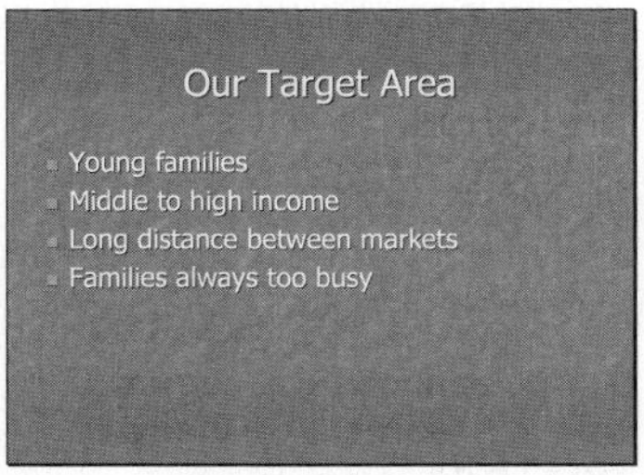
Our Target Area
Young families
Middle to high income
Long distance between markets
Families always too busy

Slide 3

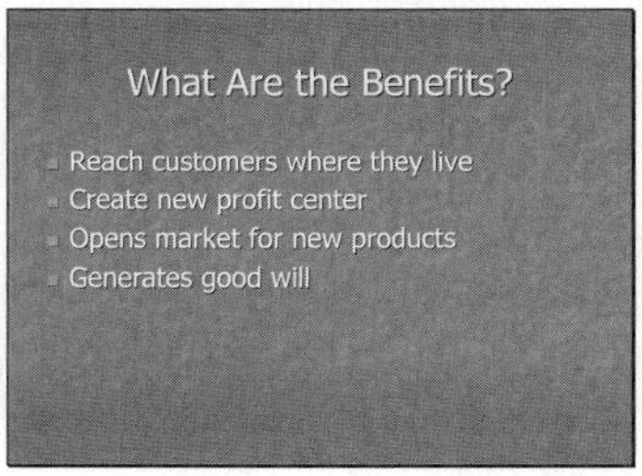
What Are the Benefits?
Reach customers where they live
Create new profit center
Opens market for new products
Generates good will

*Illustration C*

✧ **Blue Sky Dairy**
**Home Delivery Service**
- Fresh from Us to You
-

✧ **Our Target Area**
- ■ Young families
- ■ Middle to high income
- ■ Long distance between markets
- ■ Families always too busy

✧ **What Are the Benefits?**
- ■ Reach customers where they live
- ■ Create new profit center
- ■ Opens market for new products
- ■ Generates good will

- **Estimated Startup Costs**
- **Estimated Monthly Expenses**
✧ **Conclusion**
- ■ There is a market for this service
- ■ It creates a new profit center
- ■ It generates good-will

# Exercise 95

◆ **Critical Thinking**

The Horticultural Shop Owners' Association is sponsoring a trip to tour the Botanical Gardens in Montreal, Canada. The president of the association has asked you to create an information packet to send to members. She has sent you an Excel worksheet with financial information, a PowerPoint presentation about the trip, and an Access database that includes the names and addresses of the members. In this exercise, you will export the PowerPoint presentation to create a Word document. You will add a cover page to the document on which you will create a chart showing the satisfaction level of people who went on the trip last year, and you will add another page to the document on which you will embed financial information as an Excel worksheet object. Finally, you will use the Access database as a data source to create mailing labels so you can mail the packets to the members.

## Exercise Directions

✓ *The steps in this exercise assume you know how to use Excel, Access, and PowerPoint files. If you do not, ask your instructor for more information.*

### Export a PowerPoint Presentation to Word

1. Start PowerPoint and open the presentation file ⊙**95MONTREAL.ppt**.

2. Send the file to Word.
   - Paste the slides.
   - Select the layout that leaves blank lines next to each slide.

3. Save the Word document as **PACKET**.

### Create and Format a Graph Object

1. Insert a page break at the beginning of the document to create a cover page.

2. Move the insertion point to the beginning of the document and type the title **Tour the Botanical Gardens of Montreal**, using a 48-point sans serif font, centered.

3. Leave 2.5" of space and type the following paragraph using a 12-point sans serif font, justified:

   **Join the Horticultural Shop Owners' Association on an exciting four-day trip to the Botanical Gardens in Montreal, Canada. Last year, twenty members of the association joined a similar tour. When asked whether they were pleased with the experience, the overwhelming majority answered with a resounding "YES!"**

4. Insert two blank lines, and then insert a new Microsoft Graph chart object.

5. Enter the following data in the datasheet:

   |  | Happy | Unhappy | Ecstatic |
   |---|---|---|---|
   | **Responses** | 1 | 5 | 14 |

6. Delete any remaining sample data from the datasheet, then hide it.

7. Change the chart type to Exploded Pie with a 3-D visual effect.

8. Hide the legend.

9. Show the Category Name data labels and percentages.

10. Click outside the chart to close Microsoft Graph.

11. Increase the size of the chart object, and center it on the page.

   ✓ *You can increase the size of the entire object by dragging the sizing handles. You can also increase the size of individual chart elements, such as the plot area, or the data labels. Double-click the object to start Microsoft Graph, and then click the desired element to display a bounding box around it. Drag the sizing handles to increase the size. You can also move elements. For example, you can drag the labels away from the pie chart to reduce crowding.*

12. Save the changes.

## Embed Excel Worksheet Data

1. Move the insertion point to the end of the document and insert a page break.

2. On the new last page of the document, type the following title in the Heading 1 style, centered:

   **Breakdown of Costs for Montreal Trip**

3. Leave 1.5" of space between the title and a blank line.

4. Start Excel and open the file ⊛**95FINANCE.xls**.

5. Select cells A4:D8 and copy the selection to the Clipboard.

6. Switch back to **PACKET** and embed the data as a Microsoft Excel Worksheet object on the last line of the document.

7. Double-click the object in Word to make the Excel commands available.

8. Apply the 3D Effects 1 AutoFormat to the data.

9. Increase the font size of the entire selection to 12 points.

10. Increase the width of column D to show all of the data.

   ✓ *Double-click on the right border of the column in the worksheet frame, or drag the border to increase the column width. If you have trouble due to the size of the worksheet object, right-click the column letter in the worksheet frame, click Column Width, and then set the width to 12.14.*

11. Click outside the object to make the Word commands available again.

12. Center the object on the page.

13. Insert page numbers centered in the footer of all pages in the **PACKET** document.

14. Check the spelling and grammar in the document.

15. Preview the document. It should look similar to Illustration A.

16. Print the document.

17. Close the document, saving all changes.

## Merge with an Access Database

1. Create a new blank Word document and save it as **SETUP**.

2. Use Mail Merge to generate mailing labels.

3. Select the Avery Standard label number 5663.

4. Use the ⊛**95MEMBERS.mdb** Access database file as the data source.

5. Merge the labels to a new document.

6. Save the merge document as **MAILING**.

7. Print the document.

8. Close all open documents, saving all changes.

9. Exit all open applications.

# Tour the Botanical Gardens of Montreal

Join the Horticultural Shop Owners' Association on an exciting four-day trip to the Botanical Gardens in Montreal, Canada. Last year, twenty members of the association joined a similar tour. When asked whether they were pleased with the experience, the overwhelming majority answered with a resounding "YES!"

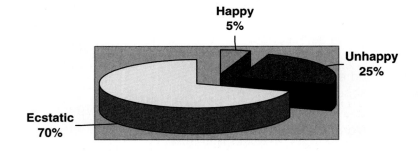

1

*Illustration A (Page 2 of 3)*

Slide 1

Slide 2

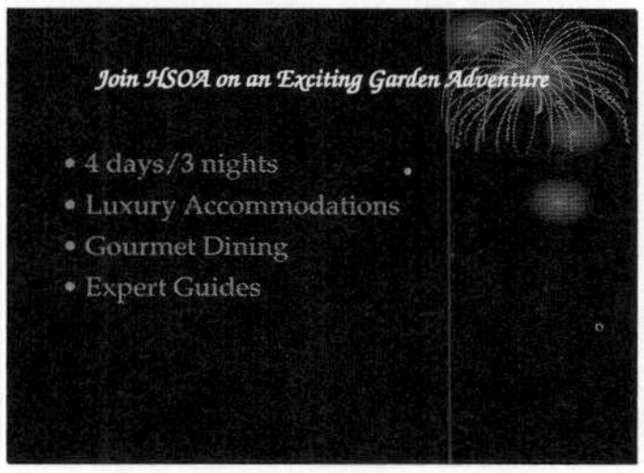

Slide 3

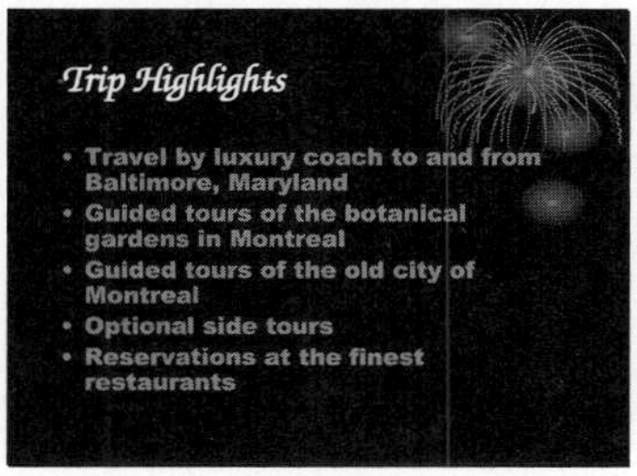

2

## Breakdown of Costs for Montreal Trip

| Transportation | $ | 250.00 |
|---|---|---|
| Lodging | $ | 320.00 |
| Meals | $ | 195.00 |
| Guides | $ | 250.00 |
| Total | $ | 1,015.00 |

3

# Lesson 15

## Challenge Exercises

### Exercise 96
- Link a Worksheet into a Word Document
- Locate Data on the Internet
- Edit Excel Worksheet
- Update Linked Object in a Word Document

### Exercise 97
- Save a Word Document as a Web Page
- Download Clip Art and Insert it on a Web Page
- Link Excel Data with a Web Page
- Update Linked Data

### Exercise 98
- Use an Access database as a merge data source
- Change the data source for a merge

### Exercise 99
- Locate Data on the Internet
- Make Web Data Available for use Offline
- Edit and Format a Table in a Word Document
- Send a Word Document via E-mail

### Exercise 100
- Create an Outline in Word
- Create a PowerPoint Presentation from a Word Outline
- Generate Presentation Handouts with Word
- Send Handouts via E-mail for Review

### Exercise 101
- Create a Home Page Using a Table
- Link the Home Page to Presentation Web Sites
- Link the Home Page to an Internet Site
- Add a Web Page to Your Favorites Folder
- Print a Web Page

### Exercise 102
- Plan a Team Project
- Complete a Research Report

### Exercise 103
- Use Smart Tags to Locate Financial Data on the Internet
- Copy Data from the Internet into an Excel Worksheet
- Use Excel Worksheet Data to Create a Word Table
- Attach a Word Document to an E-mail Message

### Exercise 104
- Import Data from Excel into Word
- Import Data from Access into Word

### Exercise 105
- Use Graphics Objects to Create a Double-sided Flyer
- Insert a File
- Apply Newsletter Formatting
- Use Mail Merge to Generate Mailing Labels

### Exercise 106
- Critical Thinking

# Exercise 96

**Skills Covered:**

◆ **Link a Worksheet into a Word Document**
◆ **Locate Data on the Internet** ◆ **Edit Excel Worksheet**
◆ **Update Linked Object in a Word Document**

You have been asked to organize a four-day trip to the Botanical Gardens in Montreal, Canada for the Horticultural Shop Owners Association. You have an Excel worksheet listing lodging costs in Canadian dollars. In this exercise, you will link the worksheet to a Word memo, then locate current exchange rates on the Web and edit the Excel worksheet to convert the costs to U.S. dollars. Finally, you will update the link to the Word document, and format the data in Word.

A Web page file with a currency exchange table is provided for use in this exercise. If you are connected to the Internet your instructor may ask you to access a live currency exchange Web site to locate the most current data available.

## Exercise Directions

1. Start Word, if necessary, and create the document shown in Illustration A, or open 💿 **96HSOATRIP**.

2. Save the file as **HSOATRIP**.

3. Start Excel and open the workbook 💿 **96LODGING**.

4. Save the file as **LODGING**.

5. Copy the range A1:D10 to the Clipboard.

6. Switch back to Word and link the worksheet object on to the last line of the **HSOATRIP** document.

7. Set the link for manual updating.

8. Open the Web page file 💿 **96EXCHANGE** in Internet Explorer.

   ✓ *If you have a connection to the Internet, your instructor may ask you to use a currency exchange Web site such as www.X-rates.com for up-to-date information.*

9. Locate the exchange rate for the number of Canadian dollars per one U.S dollar, and copy it to the Clipboard.

   ✓ *The first column lists the number of U.S. dollars per Canadian dollar; the second column lists the number of Canadian dollars per one U.S. dollar.*

10. Switch to the **LODGING** worksheet in Excel.

11. Paste the data from the Clipboard into cell C5, then copy it to cells C6, C7, and C8.

    ✓ *If necessary, ask your instructor for information about working with Excel.*

12. Disconnect from the Internet, if necessary.

13. In the Excel worksheet, create a formula in cell D5 to calculate the current cost in U.S. dollars of lodging in a four-star hotel.

    ✓ *Hint: Divide the cost in Canadian dollars by the exchange rate.*

14. Copy the formula to cells D6:D8.

15. Select cells A1:D10 and apply the Classic 2 AutoFormat.

16. Switch to the **HSOATRIP** document in Word.

17. Update the link.

18. Center the object horizontally.

19. Check the spelling and grammar in the document.

20. Preview the document. If should look similar to Illustration B.

21. Save and close all open documents, and exit all open applications.

*Illustration A*

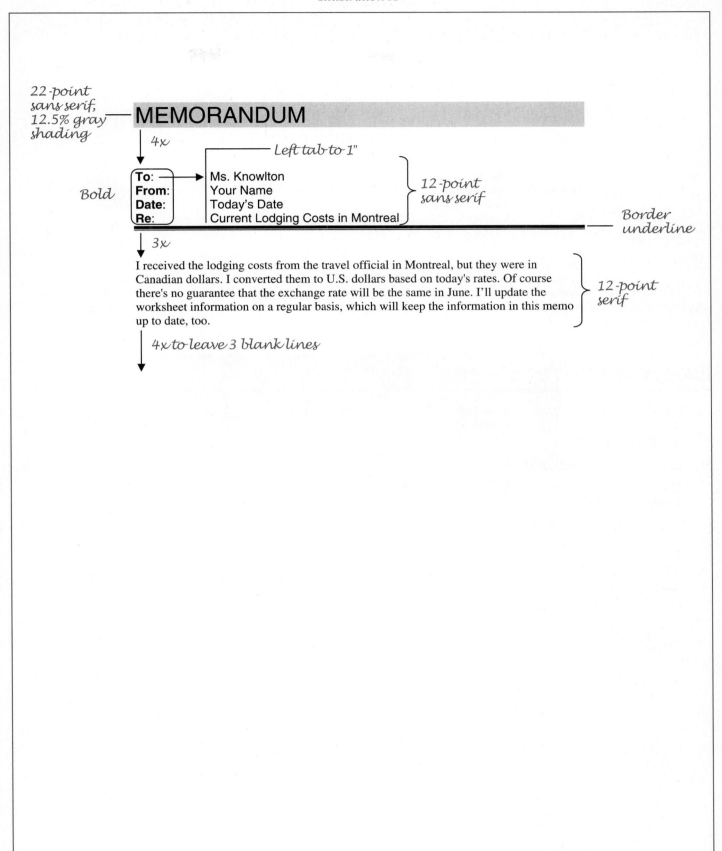

22-point sans serif, 12.5% gray shading

# MEMORANDUM

↓ 4x

Bold

**To:**
**From:**
**Date:**
**Re:**

Left tab to 1"

Ms. Knowlton
Your Name
Today's Date
Current Lodging Costs in Montreal

12-point sans serif

Border underline

↓ 3x

I received the lodging costs from the travel official in Montreal, but they were in Canadian dollars. I converted them to U.S. dollars based on today's rates. Of course there's no guarantee that the exchange rate will be the same in June. I'll update the worksheet information on a regular basis, which will keep the information in this memo up to date, too.

12-point serif

4x to leave 3 blank lines

## MEMORANDUM

**To**:      Ms. Knowlton
**From**:   Your Name
**Date**:   Today's Date
**Re**:      Current Lodging Costs in Montreal

I received the lodging costs from the travel official in Montreal, but they were in Canadian dollars. I converted them to U.S. dollars based on today's rates. Of course there's no guarantee that the exchange rate will be the same in June. I'll update the worksheet information on a regular basis, which will keep the information in this memo up to date, too.

**Lodging Packages; Four Days, Three Nights***
**Montreal, Canada**

| Accommodations | Cost (CAD) | Exchange Rate | Cost (USD) |
|---|---|---|---|
| Four Star | $  575.00 | 0.731689 | $  785.85 |
| Three Star | $  515.00 | 0.731689 | $  703.85 |
| Economy | $  465.00 | 0.731689 | $  635.52 |
| Budget | $  350.00 | 0.731689 | $  478.35 |

*Rates Based on Double Occupancy

# Exercise 97

Skills Covered:

◆ **Save a Word Document as a Web Page**

◆ **Download Clip Art and Insert it on a Web Page**

◆ **Link Excel Data with a Web Page** ◆ **Update Linked Data**

The president of the Horticultural Shop Owners Association wants you to make information about the trip to the botanical gardens in Montreal, Canada available on the organization's Web site. In this exercise, you will create a Word document about the trip and save it as a Web page. You will locate clip art and insert it on the Web page. You will also link worksheet information about lodging costs to the Web document, so if the conversion rate changes, the information on the Web site will remain current.

## Exercise Directions

1. Start Word if necessary and create the document shown in illustration A, or open ☉**97HSOATRIP2**.

2. Save the document as a Web page with the title **Botanical Gardens Tour** and the file name **HSOATRIP2**.

3. Apply the Edge theme to the Web page.

4. Use the Clip Art task pane to locate a suitable clip art image and photo and insert them into the **HSOATRIP2** Web page document. Suitable images might include flowers, plants, gardens, travel, or Montreal.

   ✓ *Alternatively, use the files ☉**CITY1.wmf** and ☉**GARDEN1.jpg** provided with this book.*

5. Set the text wrap around both graphics to Square.

6. Resize and position the objects so that in Web Page Preview the document looks similar to Illustration B.

7. Save the changes.

8. Start Excel and open the workbook ⌨**LODGING** or open ☉**97LODGING2**.

9. Save the file as **LODGING2**.

10. Copy the range A1:D10 to the Clipboard.

11. Switch back to the **HSOATRIP2** Web page in Word and link the worksheet object on the last line of the document.

12. Switch back to the **LODGING2** file in Excel.

13. Change the exchange rate in cells C5, C6, C7, and C8 to .85.

14. Select the range A1:D10 and apply the Colorful2 AutoFormat.

15. Increase the font size in the selected range to 12 points, and then adjust column widths as necessary.

16. Switch back to Word to see if the link is updated in **HSOATRIP2**.

    ✓ *If necessary, update the link manually.*

17. Center the object horizontally in the document.

18. Check the spelling and grammar.

19. Display the document in Web Page Preview. It should look similar to Illustration B.

20. Close Web Page Preview.

21. Save and close all open documents, and exit all open applications.

28-point
sans serif —# Tour Montreal's Botanical Gardens

*54 points of space*

↓

Join members of the Horticultural Shop Owners Association on an exciting four-day trip to beautiful

↓ *2x*

**Montreal, Canada**

↓ *2x*

Contact Ms. Knowlton at the association for more information.

↓ *2x*

Highlights include:

↓ *2x*

- Four days/three nights including transportation and lodging
- Knowledgeable tour guides
- Fine dining
- Magnificent gardens
- Optional sightseeing

↓ *2x*

Exchange rates are improving daily. The current cost of lodging is listed below:

*12-point
sans serif*

↓ *4x to leave three blank lines*

*Illustration B*

# Tour Montreal's Botanical Gardens

Join members of the Horticultural Shop Owners Association on an exciting four-day trip to beautiful

**Montreal, Canada**

Contact Ms. Knowlton at the association for more information.

Highlights include:

- Four days/three nights including transportation and lodging
- Knowledgeable tour guides
- Fine dining
- Magnificent gardens
- Optional sightseeing

Exchange rates are improving daily. The current cost of lodging is listed below:

| Lodging Packages; Four Days, Three Nights* Montreal, Canada | | | | |
|---|---|---|---|---|
| *Accommodations* | *Cost (CAD)* | | *Exchange Rate* | *Cost (USD)* |
| *Four Star* | $ | 575.00 | 0.85 | $ 676.47 |
| *Three Star* | $ | 515.00 | 0.85 | $ 605.88 |
| *Economy* | $ | 465.00 | 0.85 | $ 547.06 |
| *Budget* | $ | 350.00 | 0.85 | $ 411.76 |

**\*Rates Based on Double Occupancy**

# Exercise 98

## Skills Covered:

◆ **Use an Access Database as a Merge Data Source**
◆ **Change the Data Source for a Merge**

You are a store manager for Liberty Blooms. You want to send out mailings to your customers about upcoming sales and events, but you want to customize the mailings for customers you know are interested in cut flowers and for customers you know are interested in gardening. You have all of the mailing information stored in an Access database, with queries that filter out the two groups. In this exercise, you will create a form letter document that can be customized and then merge it first with one query and then again with the other query. You will then use all names in the database to generate envelopes.

## Exercise Directions

1. Use Windows to make a copy of the 💿**98BLOOMSDATA.mdb** Access database.

   ✓ *To copy an Access database, right-click the file in the Window's Explorer window, and select Copy. Then go to where you wish to copy the file. Right-click on the destination folder, and select Paste. Right-click on the copied file and select Rename to rename the file.*

2. Name the copied database file **BLOOMSDATA.mdb**.

3. Start Word, if necessary.

4. Create a new blank document and save it as **CUTTERS**.

5. Use Mail Merge to create a form letter that uses the *Cut Flowers* query in the **BLOOMSDATA** database as the data source.

6. Type the letter shown in Illustration A, inserting merge fields and merge blocks as necessary.

7. Merge all of the letters to a new document and save it as **CUTTERLETS**.

8. Check the spelling and grammar in the document.

9. Print just the first letter.

10. Close the document, saving all changes.

11. Save the **CUTTERS** document, and then save it as a new document with the name **GARDENERS**.

12. Go back through the steps of mail merge until the Select recipients step is displayed in the task pane.

13. Change the data source for the merge to the *Gardening* query in the **BLOOMSDATA** database.

14. Merge all of the letters to a new document and save it as **GARDENLETS**.

15. Check the spelling and grammar in the document.

16. Print just the first letter.

17. Close the document, saving all changes. Close the **GARDENERS** document, saving all changes.

18. Create a new blank document and save it as **MAILALL**.

19. Use Mail Merge to create envelopes for all of the letters, using the **Addresses** table in the **BLOOMSDATA** database as the data source.

    ✓ *You may type your own return address if you want.*

20. Merge the envelopes to a new document, and save it as **BLOOMSENV**.

21. Print the first page.

22. Close all open documents, saving all changes.

*Illustration A*

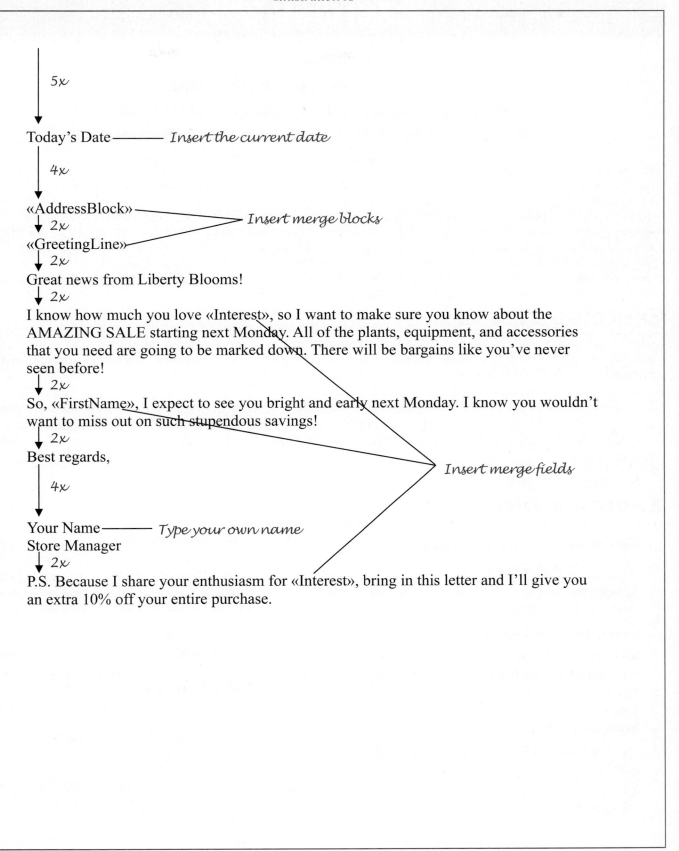

5x

Today's Date ———— *Insert the current date*

4x

«AddressBlock» ⟍
2x                    *Insert merge blocks*
«GreetingLine»

2x

Great news from Liberty Blooms!

2x

I know how much you love «Interest», so I want to make sure you know about the AMAZING SALE starting next Monday. All of the plants, equipment, and accessories that you need are going to be marked down. There will be bargains like you've never seen before!

2x

So, «FirstName», I expect to see you bright and early next Monday. I know you wouldn't want to miss out on such stupendous savings!

2x

Best regards,

4x

Your Name ———— *Type your own name*
Store Manager

2x

P.S. Because I share your enthusiasm for «Interest», bring in this letter and I'll give you an extra 10% off your entire purchase.

*Insert merge fields*

# Exercise 99

**Skills Covered:**

◆ **Locate Data on the Internet**
◆ **Make Web Data Available for use Offline**
◆ **Edit and Format a Table in a Word Document**
◆ **Send a Word Document via E-mail**

To promote the home delivery service for Blue Sky Dairy, the owners wants to take photos that can be used for publicity and marketing. They have asked you to research the features and prices of digital cameras, and then forward the information to them so they can review it and make a decision about which one to purchase. You will use the CNET Web site to locate information about digital camera devices. You will save the information in a Word document, edit the document, and then e-mail the document to the company owners for review.

If you are connected to the Internet, use the suggested site to gather the required information, or select other appropriate Web sites. If you are not connected to the Internet, locate the information in newspaper ads. If you use a live connection, you may have to modify the steps to achieve the desired result, as the content of the live Web pages changes frequently.

The e-mail address supplied in this exercise is fictitious. If you are connected to the Internet and have an account with a mail service provider, you may substitute your own, your instructor's, or a classmate's e-mail address. If you try to send the document to the fictitious address, you will receive a message that it is undeliverable.

## Exercise Directions

### Locate Data on the Internet

1. Start Word if necessary.
2. Create the document shown in Illustration A, or open 💿 **99CAMERAS**.
3. Save the file as **CAMERAS**.
4. Display the Web toolbar.

   ✓ *If you do not have Internet access, skip to step 2 under Make Web Data Available Offline.*

5. Log on to the Internet and go to the www.cnet.com Web site.
6. On the CNET home page, click the <u>Electronics Reviews</u> link.

7. Next to Compare top-rated products:, click the <u>Cameras</u> link.

   ✓ *The links may have changed since the writing of this book. If you are unable to locate this information at this site, browse other sites for the information.*

### Make Web Data Available for Use Offline

1. Save the page in Web Archive format with the file name **COMPARE**.
2. Disconnect from the Internet.
3. Open the **COMPARE** file in Word.

   ✓ *Or, open 💿 **Compare.htm***.

4. Scroll down in the file and select the 14 table rows beginning with the row labeled **Color Support**.

5. Copy the table to the Windows Clipboard.

6. Paste the table from the Clipboard onto the last line of the **CAMERAS** document.

7. Close the **COMPARE** document. You do not have to save changes.

## Edit and Format a Table in a Word Document

1. Use the following steps to modify and format the table in the **CAMERAS** document as shown in Illustration B.

2. Select the entire table.

3. On the Table page of the Table Properties dialog box, set the Preferred Width of the table to 6".

4. In the Format Paragraph dialog box, set alignment to left, set left and right indents and before and after spacing to 0, set line spacing to single, and set special indents to (none).

5. Delete the blank row between **Battery type** and **Product Name**.

6. Delete the row labeled **Full Specifications**.

7. Remove all hyperlinks from the **Product Name** row.

8. Delete the hypertext **Check latest prices**, the soft line break, and the text **Price range**: from all cells in the **Where to Buy** row, so that only the price range remains.

9. Increase the font size of the pricing values to 10 points.

10. Move the **Product Name** and **Where to Buy** rows to the top of the table.

11. Replace the label **Where to Buy** with the label **Price Range**.

12. Use the Table 3D effects 2 AutoFormat to format the table. If necessary, apply bold to the first row.

13. Center the table on the page.

14. Check the spelling and grammar in the document.

15. Preview the **CAMERAS** document. It should look similar to the one in Illustration B. If necessary, adjust column widths and row heights.

## Send a Word document via E-Mail

1. Send the document via e-mail for review to: mail@blueskydairy.net.

   ✓ *This is a fictitious e-mail address. Ask your instructor if you should substitute an actual address in this step.*

2. Disconnect from the Internet.

3. Close all open documents, saving all changes.

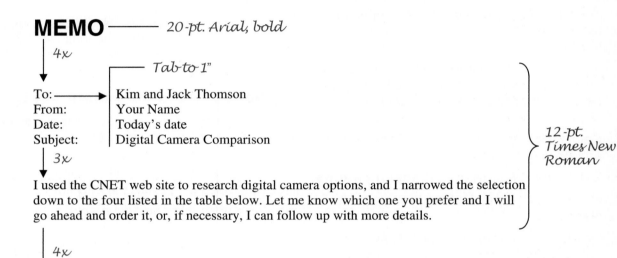

# Blue Sky **BLUE SKY DAIRY COMPANY**

### HIGHWAY 73 ❖ CAMBRIDGE, WISCONSIN 53523

TELEPHONE: (608) 555-2697 ❖ FACSIMILE: (608) 555-2698 ❖ E-MAIL: MAIL@BLUESKYDAIRY.NET

*Insert dairyhead AutoText entry created in Exercise 74.*

## MEMO —— *20-pt. Arial, bold*

*4x*

*Tab to 1"*

To: → Kim and Jack Thomson
From: Your Name
Date: Today's date
Subject: Digital Camera Comparison

*3x*

I used the CNET web site to research digital camera options, and I narrowed the selection down to the four listed in the table below. Let me know which one you prefer and I will go ahead and order it, or, if necessary, I can follow up with more details.

*12-pt. Times New Roman*

*4x*

*Illustration B*

# Blue Sky BLUE SKY DAIRY COMPANY

### HIGHWAY 73 ❖ CAMBRIDGE, WISCONSIN 53523
TELEPHONE: (608) 555-2697 ❖ FACSIMILE: (608) 555-2698 ❖ E-MAIL: MAIL@BLUESKYDAIRY.NET

## MEMO

To:          Kim and Jack Thomson
From:        Your Name
Date:        Today's date
Subject:     Digital Camera Comparison

I used the CNET web site to research digital camera options, and I narrowed the selection
down to the four listed in the table below. Let me know which one you prefer and I will
go ahead and order it, or, if necessary, I can follow up with more details.

| Product Name | Canon PowerShot A20 | Toshiba PDR-M61 | Kodak DC3800 Zoom | Fujifilm FinePix 1400 Zoom |
|---|---|---|---|---|
| Price Range | $305 to $399 | $256 to $369 | $309 to $460 | $222 to $259 |
| Color support | -- | Color ( 24-bit (16.7M colors) ) | -- | Color ( 24-bit (16.7M colors) ) |
| Audio input support | -- | -- | -- | Not available |
| Interface type | USB | -- | USB | USB |
| Focus range | 10.2 in - 1 infinity | -- | -- | 3.5 in - 1 infinity |
| Analog video format | -- | -- | -- | NTSC, PAL |
| Still image format | JPEG | JPEG | JPEG | JPEG |
| Still image capture resolution | 1600 X 1200 | 1792 x 1200 | 1792 x 1184 | 640 x 480, 1280 x 1024 |
| Memory / RAM installed (max) | -- | -- | -- | None |
| Memory / Flash installed (max) | 8 MB Flash CompactFlash Card | 8 MB ( 128 MB ) | 8MB CompactFlash Card | 4 MB ( 64 MB ) - Flash SmartMedia card |
| Battery type | -- | 4 x Alkaline AA type | 2 x Alkaline AA type | alkaline |

# Exercise 100

**Skills Covered:**

◆ **Create an Outline in Word**

◆ **Create a PowerPoint Presentation From a Word Outline**

◆ **Generate Presentation Handouts with Word**

◆ **Send the Handouts via E-mail for Review**

The Horticultural Shop Owners Association wants you to create a presentation to use at an informational meeting about the trip to the botanical gardens in Montreal. You will start with a Word outline. You will also use Word to create handouts for the meeting, which you will first send to the association's president for review.

The e-mail address supplied in this exercise is fictitious. If you are connected to the Internet and have an account with a mail service provider, you may substitute your own, your instructor's, or a classmate's e-mail address. If you try to send the document to the fictitious address, you will receive a message that it is undeliverable.

## Exercise Directions

1. Start Word, if necessary, and create the document shown in Illustration A, or open the file 💿 **100TOUROUT**.

   ✓ *Use the Heading 1 and Heading 2 styles only.*

2. Save the document as **TOUROUT**.

3. Check the spelling and grammar in the document.

4. Send the outline to Microsoft Office PowerPoint.

5. Save the new presentation file as **TOURPRES**.

6. Apply the Title Slide layout to slide 1.

   ✓ *If necessary, ask your instructor for information on working in PowerPoint.*

7. Apply the Maple Slide Design to the presentation.

8. Apply the Split Horizontal In slide transition at slow speed to all slides in the presentation, set to advance on a mouse click or automatically after 10 seconds.

9. Preview the slide show from the beginning.

10. Save all changes.

11. Send the presentation to Word. Select options to paste the slides into the document, and use the layout that displays blank lines to the right of the slides.

12. Save the new Word document as **TOURHAND**.

13. Move the insertion point to the beginning of the document and insert a page break.

14. On the new first page, type the following lines of text in 20-point Arial, centered, with 12 points of space between each line (substitute your own name for the sample text **Your Name**):
    **Horticultural Shop Owners Association**
    **Annual Garden Tour Presentation Handout**
    **Draft 1**
    **Prepared by**
    **Your Name**

15. Create a footer on each page in the document with the page number flush left and today's date flush right.

16. Check the spelling and grammar in the document.

17. Preview the document, it should look similar to Illustration B.

18. Save the changes.

19. Send the document via e-mail for review to: mail@hsoa.net.

    ✓ *This is a fictitious e-mail address. Ask your instructor if you should substitute an actual address in this step.*

20. Disconnect from the Internet.

21. Close all open documents, saving all changes.

*Illustration A*

✪ **Tour the Montreal Botanical Gardens**
  - *Presented by*
  - *The Horticultural Shop Owners Association*

✪ **Join HSOA's Annual Garden Tour**
  - *Visit the world-renowned Montreal Botanical Gardens.*
  - *Spend four days and three nights in exciting Montreal, Canada.*
  - *See the early summer plants in bloom.*
  - *Enjoy free time to explore the city and its environs.*
  - *Travel in the company of fellow HSOA members.*

✪ **Tour Highlights**
  - *Travel by luxury coach*
  - *Experienced tour guides*
  - *Customized tour plans*
  - *Fine dining*
  - *Magnificent gardens*
  - *Exciting city*

✪ **Itinerary**
  - *June 15 a.m.: Depart Baltimore, Maryland*
  - *June 15 p.m.: Arrive Montreal, Canada*
  - *June 16 a.m.: Garden tour*
  - *June 16 p.m.: Free*
  - *June 17 a.m.: Garden tour and lecture*
  - *June 17 p.m.: Optional city tour*
  - *June 18 a.m.: Depart Montreal, Canada*
  - *June 18 p.m.: Arrive Baltimore, Maryland*

✪ **Registration and Pricing Information**
  - *Members: $1,195.00, inclusive*
  - *Non-members: $1,350, inclusive*
  - *Early bird rates available prior to May 15.*

# Horticultural Shop Owners Association

# Annual Garden Tour Presentation Handout

# Draft 1

# Prepared by

# Your Name

Page 1                                                    Today's Date

526

*Illustration B (Page 2 of 3)*

Slide 1

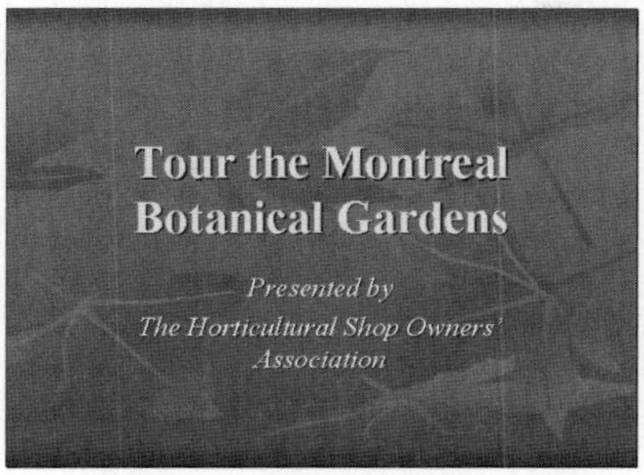

Slide 2

Slide 3

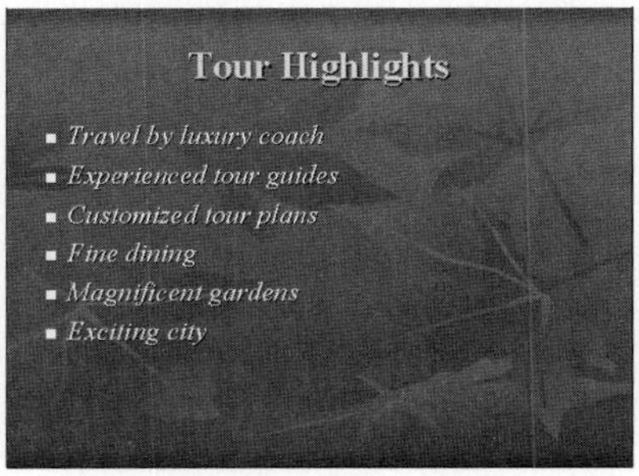

Today's Date

Slide 4

**Itinerary**

- June 15 a.m.: Depart Baltimore, Maryland
- June 15 p.m.: Arrive Montreal, Canada
- June 16 a.m.: Garden tour
- June 16 p.m.: Free
- June 17 a.m.: Garden tour and lecture
- June 17 p.m.: Optional city tour
- June 18 a.m.: Depart Montreal, Canada
- June 18 p.m.: Arrive Baltimore, Maryland

Slide 5

**Registration and Pricing Information**

- Members: $1,195.00, inclusive
- Non-members: $1,350, inclusive
- Early bird rates available prior to May 15.

Page 3

Today's Date

# Exercise 101

## Skills Covered:

◆ **Create a Home Page Using a Table**
◆ **Link the Home Page to a Presentation Web Site**
◆ **Link the Home Page to an Internet Site**
◆ **Add a Web Page to Your Favorites Folder**
◆ **Print a Web Page**

The Horticultural Shop Owners' Association has hired you to improve its Web site. It already has a presentation Web site created from a PowerPoint presentation about a trip to the botanical gardens in Montreal, as well as a single Web page providing information about regional meetings, but you must design a Home page and set up necessary links. In this exercise, you will create two Web pages in Word using tables. You will link the pages to each other and to the existing presentation Web site. You will provide links from the Home page to a site on the Internet about the botanical gardens. You will also save a Web page to your favorites folder and print a Web page.

If you do not have a live connection to the Internet you may use the Web page files provided with this book.

## Exercise Directions

1. Start Word, if necessary, and create the document shown in Illustration A.

   a. Create a table with ten rows and two columns.

   b. Set row heights as follows:

      • Row 1: at least 1.75"

      • Rows 3 and 4: at least .5"

      • Rows 6 and 8: at least 1.5"

      • Rows 2, 5, 7, 9, and 10: at least .25"

   c. Set the width of column 1 to approximately 5" wide.

   d. Set the width of column 2 to approximately 2.5" wide.

   e. Merge the cells across row 3, and then merge the cells across row 4.

   f. Type all text in a sans serif font, using the font formatting and alignments specified in Illustration A.

   g. Use the Clip Art task pane to locate the three clip art pictures shown in Illustration A and insert them in the appropriate cells.

   ✓ *If you cannot locate the same pictures, select others, or use the* 💿 **GARDEN2.jpg**, 💿 **SUNFLOWER1.jpg**, *and* 💿 **CONFERENCE1.wmf** *files supplied with this book.*

   h. Set the height of each clip art picture to 1.5". Leave the aspect ratio locked so the width will adjust automatically.

   i. Center each picture horizontally and vertically within its cell.

   j. Apply borders as shown in Illustration A.

2. Save the document as a Web Page with the name **SITE** and the Web page title **HSOA Home Page**.

3. Apply the Sumi Painting theme to the page.

4. Save the changes to the document.

5. Create a new document in Word and create the document shown in Illustration B.

   a. Create a table with ten rows and two columns.

   b. Merge the cells in row 1, merge the cells in row 2, and then merge the cells in row 10.

c. In column 1, merge the cells in rows 3 and 4, then merge the cells in rows 5 and 6, then merge the cells in rows 7 and 8.

d. The rows in column 2 should not be merged.

e. Set row height for rows 1 and 2 to at least 1" and for rows 3 through 10 to at least .5".

f. Type the 14-point sans serif font except where indicated, using the formatting and alignment shown on Illustration B.

g. Apply a 15% gray shade for the darker cells and a 5% gray shade for the lighter cells.

h. Use a 1½ pt. double border as shown, or a ½ pt. single border, as shown.

6. Save the document as a Web Page with the name **MEETINGS** and the Web page title **Regional Meetings.**

7. Apply the Newsprint background to the document.

8. Insert a hyperlink from the text **HOME** to the **SITE** Web page file.

9. Check the spelling and grammar in the document.

10. Save the file and close it.

11. In the **SITE** Web page file in Word, select the text **Tour the Gardens** and insert a hyperlink to the PowerPoint Web presentation file 💿**101TOUR.mht**.

12. Select the clip art picture of the garden and insert another hyperlink to 💿**101TOUR.mht**.

13. Link the text **Schedule** with the **MEETINGS** Web page file.

14. Link the clip art picture of the meeting to the **MEETINGS** file, as well.

15. Use the text **Montreal Botanical Gardens** to create a hyperlink to the official Web site, at the URL address: www2.ville.montreal.qc.ca/jardin

16. Check the spelling and grammar in the document.

17. Use Web Page Preview to check the **SITE** Home page.

18. Test the links to the presentation site and to the schedule page.

   ✓ *While in Web Page Preview, browse the presentation sites using the Outline on the left side of the screen or the Forward and Back buttons. Use the Back button on the Web toolbar to return to the Home page.*

   ✓ *If you are using a browser that does not support frames, you may have a problem accessing the PowerPoint Web presentation. Ask your instructor for more information.*

19. If you have a live connection to the Internet, test the link to the Montreal Botanical Gardens Web site and browse the site.

   a. Add a page from the site to your Favorites folder.

   b. Print a page from the site.

20. If you do not have a live connection to the Internet, add the **MEETINGS** page to your Favorites folder, and print it from Internet Explorer.

21. Disconnect from the Internet, if necessary. Close Web Page Preview.

22. Save and close all open documents, and exit Word.

*Illustration A*

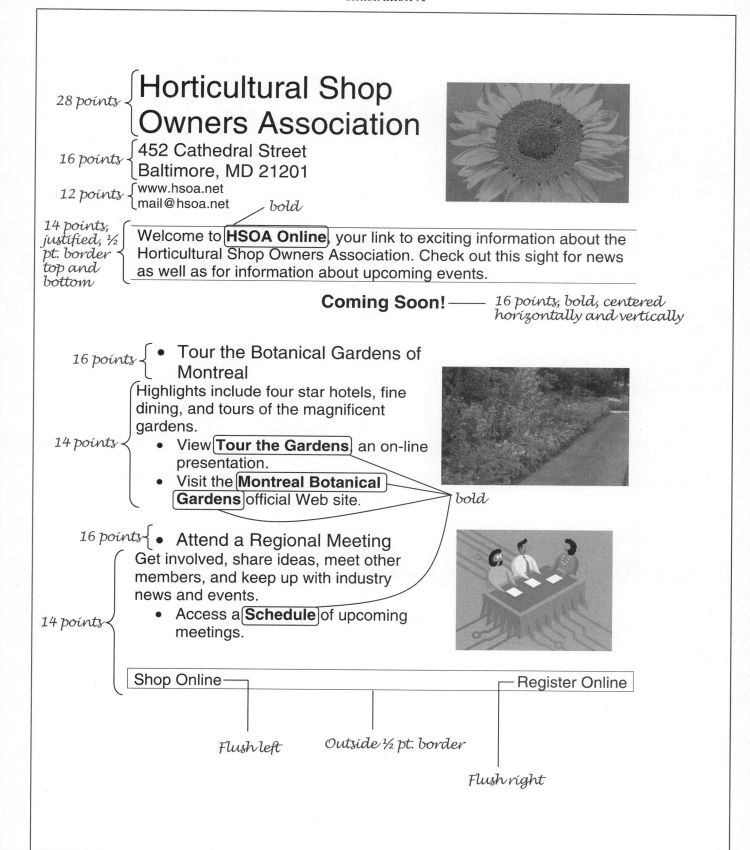

28 points {
# Horticultural Shop Owners Association

16 points {
452 Cathedral Street
Baltimore, MD 21201

12 points {
www.hsoa.net
mail@hsoa.net

*bold*

14 points, justified, ½ pt. border top and bottom {
Welcome to **HSOA Online**, your link to exciting information about the Horticultural Shop Owners Association. Check out this sight for news as well as for information about upcoming events.

**Coming Soon!** —— *16 points, bold, centered horizontally and vertically*

16 points {
- Tour the Botanical Gardens of Montreal

14 points {
Highlights include four star hotels, fine dining, and tours of the magnificent gardens.
- View **Tour the Gardens**, an on-line presentation.
- Visit the **Montreal Botanical Gardens** official Web site.

*bold*

16 points {
- Attend a Regional Meeting

14 points {
Get involved, share ideas, meet other members, and keep up with industry news and events.
- Access a **Schedule** of upcoming meetings.

Shop Online —— —— Register Online

*Flush left*        *Outside ½ pt. border*

*Flush right*

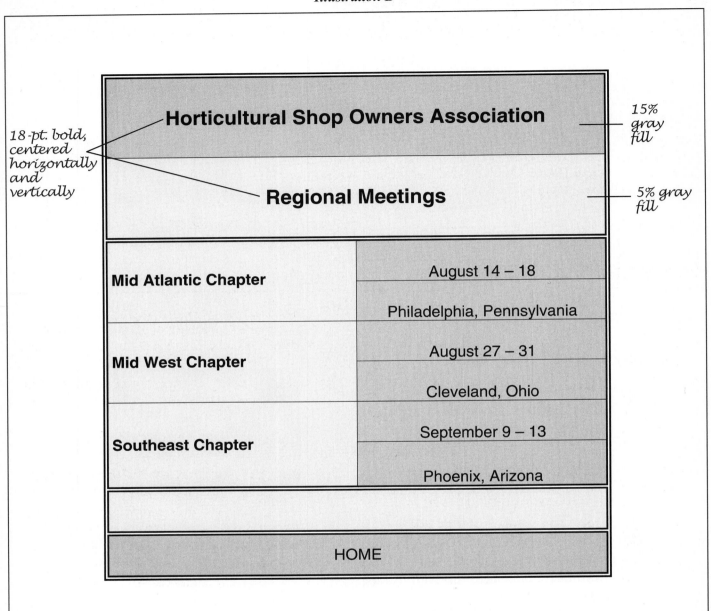

18-pt. bold, centered horizontally and vertically

15% gray fill

**Horticultural Shop Owners Association**

**Regional Meetings**

5% gray fill

| | |
|---|---|
| **Mid Atlantic Chapter** | August 14 – 18<br><br>Philadelphia, Pennsylvania |
| **Mid West Chapter** | August 27 – 31<br><br>Cleveland, Ohio |
| **Southeast Chapter** | September 9 – 13<br><br>Phoenix, Arizona |

HOME

# Exercise 102

## ◆ Plan a Team Project ◆ Complete a Research report

Liberty Blooms Flower Shop has asked you to be part of a team that is researching ways that the shop could use the Internet. In this exercise, you will work in a group to learn about how retail stores, such as flower shops, can benefit from using the World Wide Web. You will also learn about potential pitfalls. Finally, you will type up and present a one-page report that details your findings.

There is no sample solution file for this project, as each team will end up with a different result.

## Exercise Directions

1. Meet as a group to discuss the project and decide the approach you want to take.
2. Agree on a main thesis. Some ideas to consider include:
   - What makes an effective Web site?
   - Should online shopping be used in place of or in addition to in store shopping?
   - How can a retailer advertise on the Web?
3. Decide what sources you will use to gather the information you need. You might use the Internet, a library, or you might contact retailers directly to ask them about their experiences.
4. Set goals for the team as a whole.
5. Set individual goals so each team member understands his or her responsibility. You must decide how the work will be divided. For example, will all team members be involved in research? If so, one member might be responsible for research on the Internet, and another might be responsible for research at the library. Or, one might look for information about benefits of the Internet, and another might look for pitfalls. Another approach is to have each team member responsible for a different aspect of the project. For example, one might be responsible for managing and organizing the project, two might handle the research, and someone else might type the report.
6. Create a schedule, including deadlines for each important milestone, such as when all research must be complete and when a draft of the typed report must be complete.
7. Agree on the way to record source information so you have it available to include in the one-page report.
8. When the planning and organization are complete, begin the project.
9. Work together to complete the research, and meet regularly to discuss your results.
10. Use your research to organize and create the one-page report. Format the report correctly, including margins, headings, headers or footers, and footnotes or endnotes.
11. When the report is complete, check the spelling and grammar.
12. Correct errors as necessary.
13. Display the document in Print Preview.
14. Print the document and have someone proofread it.
15. Make changes and corrections as necessary.
16. Display the document in Print Preview again, and then print the document.
17. Close the file, saving all changes.
18. Present your report to the other teams.

# Exercise 103

## Skills Covered:

◆ **Use Smart Tags to Locate Financial Data on the Internet**

◆ **Copy Data from the Internet into an Excel Worksheet**

◆ **Use Excel Worksheet Data to Create a Word Table**

◆ **Attach a Word Document to an E-mail Message**

A group of employees at Long Shot, Inc. has formed an investment club. As the Club Treasurer you have been tracking the portfolio. You believe it is time to sell some stock in order to spread the investments into other market segments. In this exercise, you will use smart tags to access the Internet to look up the current trading prices of the stocks. You will copy the information into an Excel worksheet you have already prepared, then copy the entire worksheet into a Word document. Finally, you will attach the Word document to an e-mail message and send it to the club president.

You will need Internet Access to complete all the steps in the exercise. The e-mail address supplied in this exercise is fictitious. If you try to send the message it will come back as undeliverable. If you have an Internet connection and a mail service provider, your instructor may want you to substitute a real email address.

## Exercise Directions

1. Start Word if necessary and create the memo document shown in Illustration A, or open the document ⊙ **103INVEST.doc**.

2. Save the file as **INVEST.doc**.

3. Start Microsoft Excel and open the workbook ⊙ **103STOCKS.xls**.

4. Save the file as **STOCKS.xls**.

5. Replace the sample text **Today's Date** with the current date.

6. Move the mouse pointer over the ticker symbol for Amazon.com.

   ✓ *The Smart Tag Actions button is displayed. If smart tags are not displayed in the worksheet, make sure the Label Data with Smart Tags option is selected on the Smart Tags tab of the AutoCorrect Options dialog box, and that all recognizers are selected. (Using smart tags in Excel is similar to using them in Word).*

7. Click the Smart Tag Actions button.

   ✓ *If you don't have Internet access, locate the stock prices in a newspaper.*

8. On the Actions menu, click Stock Quote on MSN Money Central.

9. Sign in to your Internet Service Provider as prompted.

10. On the Money Central stock quote page that is displayed, select the stock price in the Last row and copy it to the Clipboard.

    ✓ *The last price is the price at which the stock last traded. It is usually listed in the first row in bold under the company name. Be careful to copy only the stock price with no additional spaces before it or after it. If you copy additional spaces you may see an error in the Excel worksheet when you paste the data. If so, delete the data from the cell and try again.*

11. Switch to the Excel worksheet and past it into cell F6. If necessary, adjust column widths to display all data.

    ✓ *The worksheet is set up to calculate the current value and the return on investment.*

12. If you have an Internet connection, repeat steps 6 through 10 to gather the last trade information for the other four companies in the Excel worksheet.

    ✓ *Use the smart tag for each ticker symbol to get a stock quote, and then copy and paste the last trade data into the appropriate cells in column F.*

13. When you have gathered all of the data you need to complete the Excel worksheet, disconnect from the Internet.

14. In the **STOCKS.xls** worksheet, copy the range A1:H10 to the clipboard.

15. Close the Excel file, saving all changes, and exit Excel.

16. Switch to the **INVEST.doc** Word document, and paste the worksheet on the last line of the memo.

17. Apply the Table Contemporary AutoFormat to the table in the Word document.

18. Delete the space(s) after the dollar signs in the **Original Investment**, **Value**, and **Return** columns, and adjust column widths so the numbers don't wrap.

19. Center the entire table horizontally on the page.

20. Check the spelling and grammar in the document.

21. Preview the Word document. It should look similar to Illustration B.

    ✓ *The current market prices will vary.*

22. Create a new e-mail message.

23. Enter the following header information (leave the CC: field blank):

    To: **mail@longshotinc.net**

    Subject: **Stock Prices**

24. Type the message: **Here's the information I promised. Get back to me ASAP – these stocks are volatile and we have to act fast**.

25. Attach the **INVEST.doc** document to the message and send it.

    ✓ *Log on to the Internet as necessary.*

26. Close the **INVEST.doc** file, saving all changes.

*Illustration A*

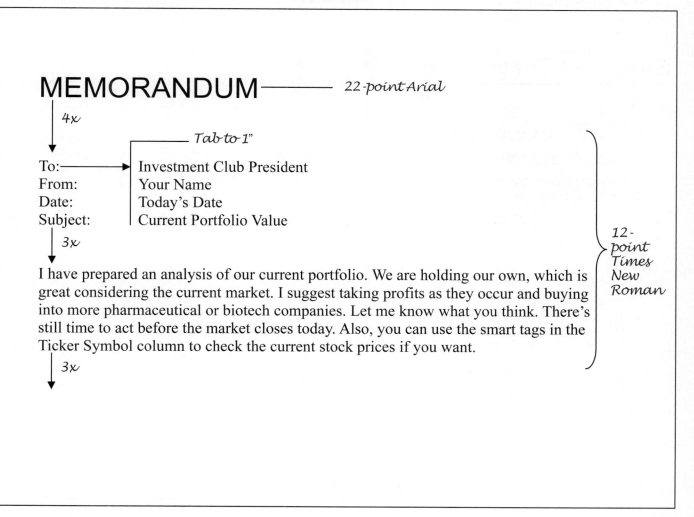

MEMORANDUM ——————— 22-point Arial

↓ 4x

———— Tab to 1"

To: ———→ Investment Club President
From:        Your Name
Date:        Today's Date
Subject:     Current Portfolio Value

↓ 3x

I have prepared an analysis of our current portfolio. We are holding our own, which is great considering the current market. I suggest taking profits as they occur and buying into more pharmaceutical or biotech companies. Let me know what you think. There's still time to act before the market closes today. Also, you can use the smart tags in the Ticker Symbol column to check the current stock prices if you want.

↓ 3x

12-point Times New Roman

# MEMORANDUM

To:         Investment Club President
From:       Your Name
Date:       Today's Date
Subject:    Current Portfolio Value

I have prepared an analysis of our current portfolio. We are holding our own, which is great considering the current market. I suggest taking profits as they occur and buying into more pharmaceutical or biotech companies. Let me know what you think. There's still time to act before the market closes today. Also, you can use the smart tags in the Ticker Symbol column to check the current stock prices if you want.

| Long Shot, Inc. | | | | | | |
|---|---|---|---|---|---|---|
| Investment Club | | | | | | |
| Date: | Today's Date | | | | | |
| | | | | | | |
| Company | Ticker Symbol | Shares Owned | Purchase Price | Original Investment | Last Trade | Value | Return |
| Amazon.com | AMZN | 100 | 31.45 | $3,145.00 | 47.49 | $4,749.00 | $1,604.00 |
| Biogen, Inc. | BGEN | 125 | 46.25 | $5,781.25 | 43.18 | $5,397.50 | $(383.75) |
| Cisco Systems, Inc. | CSCO | 100 | 22.33 | $2,233.00 | 21.11 | $2,111.00 | $(122.00) |
| Eli Lilly and Company | LLY | 125 | 61.48 | $7,685.00 | 60.67 | $7,583.75 | $(101.25) |
| Intel Corp | INTC | 100 | 44.48 | $4,448.00 | 29.07 | $2,907.00 | $(1,541.00) |

# Exercise 104

Skills Covered:

◆ **Import Data from Excel into Word**
◆ **Import Data from Access into Word**

As the Director of Training at Long Shot, Inc., you want to send a memo to the Director of Human Resources with information about three new instructors you would like to hire. You already have their names and addresses stored in an Access database file, and you have information about the courses they will teach in an Excel worksheet file. In this exercise, you import the information from the Excel file and the Access file into a Word memo document.

## Exercise Directions

✓ *Before starting this exercise, copy the Access database* 💿 **104HIRES.mdb**. *Rename the copy* **HIRES**.

1. Start Word and Access, if necessary.

2. Open the Access database file **HIRES**.

3. Open the New Hires table.

4. Select the three records in the table and copy them to the Clipboard.

5. Open the Word document 💿 **104LSIHIRES**.

6. Save the document as **LSIHIRES**.

7. Replace the sample text **Your Name** with your own name, and the sample date **Today's date** with the current date.

8. Position the insertion point on the last line of the document.

9. Paste the Access data from the Clipboard into the Word memo.

10. Close the **HIRES** database file.

11. In the **LSIHIRES** document, delete the first row in the table (New Hires).

12. Delete the three blank columns from the table (Company Name, Address 2, and Country).

13. Move the insertion point to the end of the document and insert a blank line.

14. Save the changes to the **LSIHIRES** document.

15. Open the Excel worksheet file 💿 **104COURSES.xls**.

16. Save the file as **COURSES**.

17. Select the range A2:C8 and copy the selection to the Clipboard.

18. Switch to the **LSIHIRES** document.

19. Paste the Excel data from the Clipboard on to the last line of the **LSIHIRES** document.

20. Display the document in Print Preview. It should look similar to Illustration A.

21. Print the document.

22. Close all open programs and documents, saving all changes.

# Long Shot, Inc.

## INTERDEPARTMENT MEMORANDUM

To:         Director of Human Resources
From:       Your Name
Date:       Today's date
Re:         Training Department Expenses

I have made a decision regarding the hiring of three new instructors for the training department. Below you will find their contact information as well as a schedule detailing the courses I would like them to teach. Please tender their offers as soon as possible. Please give me a call if you have any questions. Thanks.

| Title | First Name | Last Name | Address Line 1 | City | State | ZIP Code | Home Phone | Work Phone | E-mail Address |
|-------|-----------|-----------|----------------|------|-------|----------|-----------|-----------|----------------|
| Mr. | George | Kaplan | 980 Main Street | Ithaca | NY | 14850 | 607-555-1234 | 607-555-4321 | gkaplan@mail.com |
| Ms. | Patricia | Boyd | 65 Blueberry Lane | Ithaca | NY | 14850 | 607-555-5678 | 607-555-8765 | pboyd@mail.com |
| Mrs. | Hannah | Thompson | 3232 Chestnut Street | Ithaca | NY | 14850 | 607-555-9012 | 607-555-2109 | hthomspon@mail.com |

| COURSE NAME | SESSIONS OFFERED | INSTRUCTOR |
|-------------|------------------|------------|
| Word Processing 1 | Fall | H. Thompson |
| Word Processing 2 | Fall | G. Kaplan |
| Word Processing 3 | Winter | G. Kaplan |
| Using the Internet | Spring | P. Boyd |
| Database Management | Winter | P. Boyd |
| Spreadsheet Basics | Spring | H. Thompson |

# Exercise 105

## Skills Covered:

◆ **Use Graphics Objects to Create a Double-Sided Flyer**
◆ **Insert a File** ◆ **Apply Newsletter Formatting**
◆ **Use Mail Merge to Generate Mailing Labels**

Blue Sky Dairy has asked you to create a flyer suitable for mailing to let customers know about the essay contest and the home delivery service. In this exercise, you will create a two-page document that can be printed as a double-sided flyer, folded in half, sealed, and mailed. To set up the document you will use columns, sections, text boxes, and clip art. When the flyer is complete, you will use a mail merge to create mailing labels to use to send the flyer to customers.

## Exercise Directions

✓ *Before starting this exercise, copy the Access database* 💿 **105DAIRYDATA.mdb**. *Rename the copy* **DAIRYDATA**.

1. Start Word, if necessary, and create a new blank document.

2. Save the document as **2SIDES**.

3. Insert a blank line, and then insert a page break. This creates a document with two pages with a blank line on each page.

4. Position the insertion point at the top of the document and create the page shown in Illustration A. This will be the outside of the flyer when it is folded for mailing.

   a. Insert a text box for entering the return address.

   b. Size the text box to .75" high and 2.5" wide.

   c. Make sure there is no border around the box.

   d. Position the text box in the upper-left corner of the page, .5" to the right of the page and .25" below the page.

   e. Enter the text shown in Illustration A. Use a sans serif font. Type the company name in 14 points and the address in 12 points.

   f. Insert another text box to mark where the mailing label will go.

   g. Size the second text box to accommodate your mailing labels. For the default label (Avery Standard 2160 Mini-Address) make the box 1.25" high by 2.75" wide, and apply a dotted border.

   h. Center the text box horizontally on the page, and set the vertical absolute position to 2.31" below the paragraph.

   i. Enter the text shown in Illustration A. Use a 12-point serif font, centered.

   j. Insert a clip art picture of a cow below the return address box.

   ✓ *If necessary, use the file* 💿 **COW1.wmf** *supplied with this book.*

   k. Size the picture to 1.5" high (the width should adjust automatically).

   l. Set text wrapping to Tight.

   m. Position the picture -.5" to the right of the margin and 0" below the paragraph.

   n. Insert the Explosion 2 AutoShape. This shape will be printed on the back of the outside of the flyer when it is folded for mailing.

   o. Format the AutoShape in the 3-D Style 2, with a Light Turquoise fill.

   p. Size the AutoShape to 4.25" high by 6.5" wide.

   q. Position the AutoShape horizontally centered on the page and vertically 6" below the page.

   r. Add the text shown in Illustration A to the shape, using a 26-point bold, sans serif font, centered.

5. Save the document.

6. Preview the document. Page 1 should look similar to Illustration A.

7. Position the insertion point on the second page of the document.

8. Insert the file ⊙ **105SIDEB**. This is the text for the inside of the flyer.

   ✓ *Alternatively, type the text as shown in Illustration B.*

9. Format the page as shown in Illustration B:

   a. Use 14-point Arial unless otherwise marked.

   b. Center the first three lines, the two headlines, and the last paragraph, and leave all other paragraphs flush left.

   c. Apply a border under the second line, as shown in the illustration.

   d. Leave 6 points of space after the second line, then 3 points of space after all other paragraphs.

   e. Insert a continuous section break at the beginning of the fourth line.

   f. Insert a continuous section break at the beginning of the last paragraph on the page.

   g. Leave 12 points of space before the last paragraph on the page.

   h. Format Section 2 into two columns of equal width.

   i. Apply bullet lists as shown in Illustration B.

   j. Apply dropped capitals as shown in Illustration B.

   k. If necessary, insert a column break after the first bulleted list.

   l. Insert clip art pictures as shown in Illustration B.

      ✓ *If necessary, use the ⊙ DELIVERY.wmf and ⊙ PEN.wmf files supplied with this book.*

   m. Set text wrap for the clip art to Square.

   n. Size both pictures to 1.5" high, and leave the aspect ratio locked so the width will adjust automatically.

   o. Position the clip art pictures as shown in Illustration B.

10. Check the spelling and grammar in the document.

11. Preview page 2. It should look similar to the one in Illustration B.

12. Print page 1 of the document.

13. Reload the printed document in the printer so that you can print on the other side.

    ✓ *Ask your instructor for information on loading paper into the printer for double-sided copying. Often, the side that has already been printed is inserted printed side up, with the top pointing in.*

14. Print page 2 of the document.

15. Create a new blank document and save it as **DAIRYLABELS**.

16. Use Mail Merge to generate mailing labels, using the **DAIRYDATA** database as the data source.

17. Use the default mailing label format.

18. Merge the labels to a new document and save it as **ALLLABELS**.

19. Close all open documents, saving all changes.

*Illustration A*

Blue Sky Dairy Co.
Highway 73
Cambridge, WI 53523

Attach mailing label here

# EXCITING NEWS FROM BLUE SKY DAIRY!

*36 pts.* ——

# Blue Sky Dairy Co.

*Paragraph border — underline*

"Where Quality is Our Middle Name" —— *16 pts.*

## Don't Miss Out on All the Fun —— *20 pts.*

*18 pts.* —— ### Essay Contest

**P**articipate in the first ever Blue Sky Dairy Essay Contest! We are thrilled to sponsor an essay contest specifically for teens. The topic for the first contest is Break Away from the Herd. There will be four divisions for four age groups: Junior Division includes students in grades 1 through 4; Middle Division includes students in grades 5 through 9; and Senior Division includes students in grades 10 through 12.

Prizes include:

- Scholarships
- Computer equipment
- Gift certificates
- Travel vouchers

### Home Delivery Service —— *18 pts.*

**B**lue Sky Dairy is pleased to announce that it is starting a home delivery service. At first, Blue Sky trucks will provide delivery to subscribers in the local area, but we hope to expand the program soon to all areas. Home delivery insures that you receive the best quality products when you need them, without having to make a trip to the store.

Products that can be ordered for home delivery include:

- Milk
- Butter
- Cream
- Half and Half
- Ice Cream

For more information about the essay contest, the home delivery service, or any of the other exciting happenings at Blue Sky, call: 608-555-2697. Or visit our website at: www.blueskydairy.net.

# Exercise 106

You want to convince the President of Long Shot, Inc. that the next board meeting should take place offsite at a destination somewhere outside the United States. You have decided that the best way to make your point is to create a report that you can present visually and orally to the president and the board of directors.

In this exercise, you will select and research a destination and create a report. The report should include information about the location, how to get there, the types of accommodations available, and why it is a suitable destination for a Long Shot, Inc. board meeting. You should plan on an oral presentation lasting between three and five minutes and you should prepare text documents to use as support materials. For example, you can create handouts and visual aids that you can use on a poster. The presentation materials should include graphics as well as text. For example, you should create graphs to show financial information, or to illustrate something about the destination itself. You should use WordArt objects, clip art, or pictures to enhance your handouts and visual aids. You may complete the exercise individually or in teams.

There is no sample solution file for this project, as the results will vary.

## Exercise Directions

1. Begin this exercise by creating a schedule for completing the report.

2. The schedule should include time for planning, research, writing and document creation, review, editing, and presentation.

3. Once you have a schedule, begin planning the report.

4. First, select a destination.

5. Decide how you want to conduct your research. You may use the Internet, your library, or ask a travel agent to send you brochures or other information.

6. Think about the types of documents you want to create to support your presentation. For example, you may want to create an outline to use for notes while you talk, a one-page report to hand out to the agents, and lists of important facts that you can print on colored paper or using interesting font formatting and then display on a poster.

   ✓ *Keep in mind that all visual aids should be large enough for the audience to see from six feet away.*

7. Once you have a plan, begin the research. Use Word to compile and store information about the destination, such as where it is, the climate, a brief history, and attractions that make it a desirable tourist destination. Don't forget to keep a list of sources to use in a bibliography or footnotes.

8. You should also include information about travel and costs. For example, how can you get to your selected destination? Do you need any special type of documentation or vaccinations? What types of accommodations are available? How much does it cost for food and lodging? Are there modern conveniences such as Internet access in the hotels?

9. When you complete your research, use Word to create the documents you will need for your presentation. In addition to handouts and a visual display, you must write the notes you will use for the oral presentation. Remember that you are trying to convince them to hold a meeting at your selected site.

10. Practice presenting the report orally. It should be between three and five minutes long.

11. Ask your peers to review your documents, and to listen to you practice your report. Incorporate their suggestions into your work to improve the presentation.

12. Finalize the documents and polish your oral presentation.

13. Print the documents to use as handouts and the notes you will need to use during your presentation.

14. Print the documents to use as visual aids, and mount them on a poster.

15. Present your report.

16. Save and close all open files, and exit all applications.

# Index

# Notes

# Notes

# Notes

# Notes

# Notes

# Notes